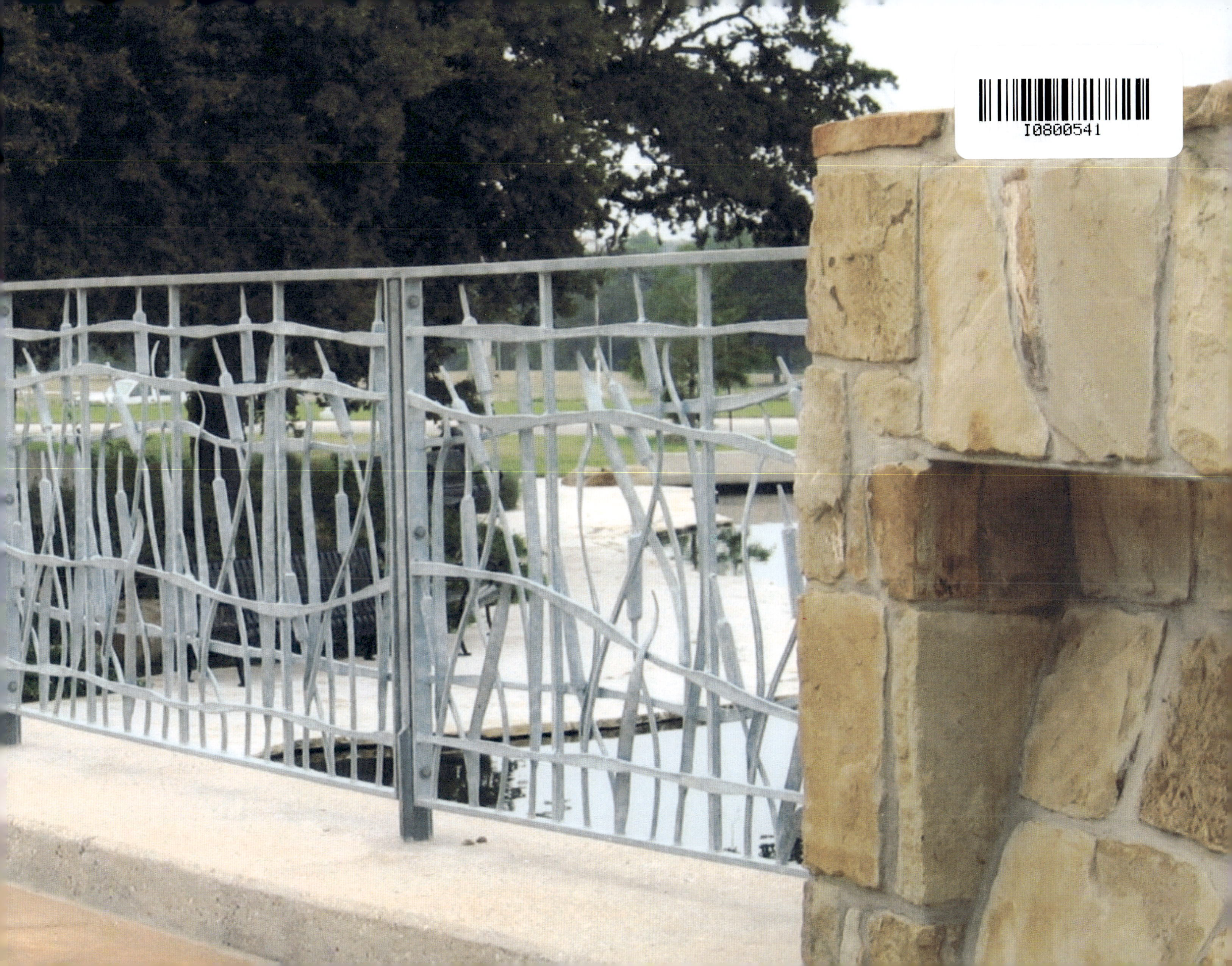

I0800541

IRONWORK TODAY
INSIDE & OUT

IRONWORK TODAY INSIDE & OUT

Dona Z. Meilach

Schiffer Publishing Ltd

4880 Lower Valley Road, Atglen, PA 19310 USA

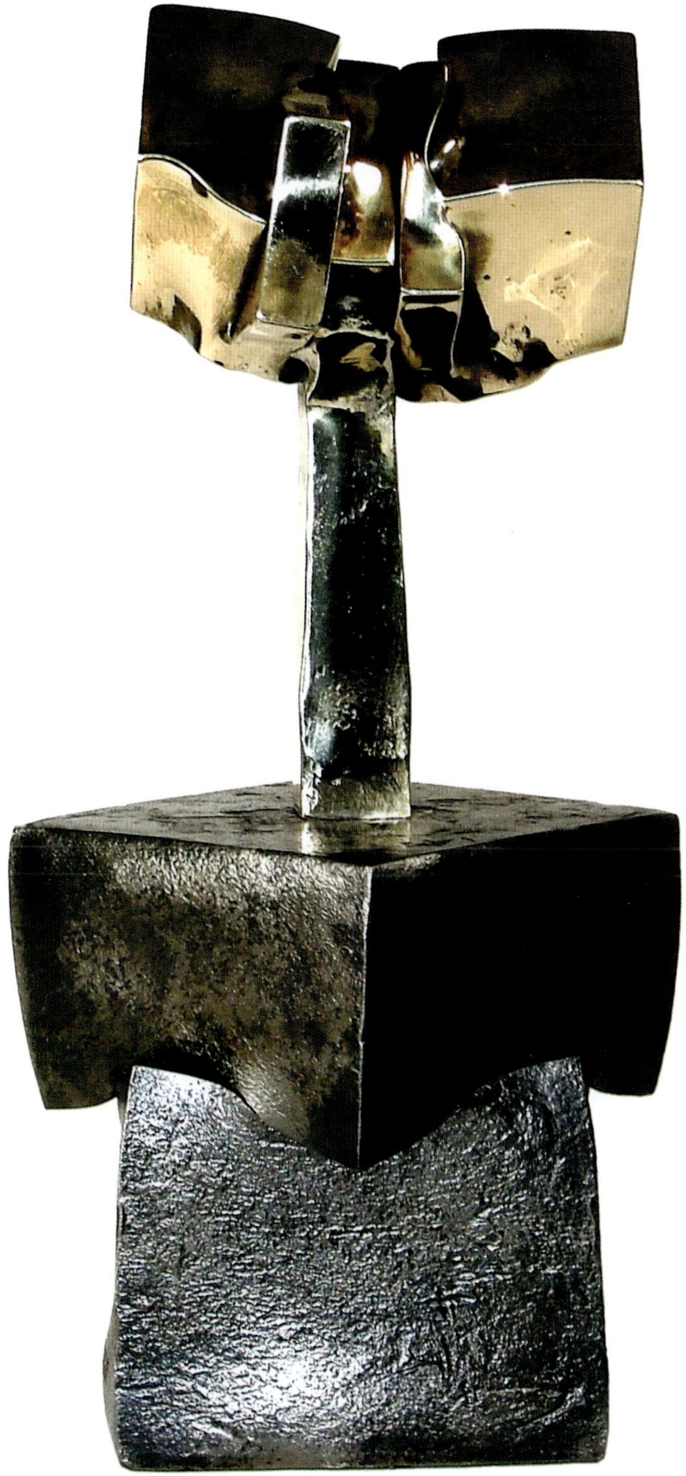

OTHER ART-CRAFT BOOKS
by DONA Z. MEILACH

Blacksmithing:
Architectural Ironwork
The Contemporary Blacksmith
Decorative & Sculptural Ironwork
Direct Metal Sculpture
Fireplace Accessories

Also:
Wood Art Today
Art Jewelry Today
Teapots: Makers and Collectors
Contemporary Stone Sculpture
Sculpture Casting, *with Dennis Kowal*
Creating Small Wood Objects as Functional Sculpture
How to Create Your Own Designs, *with Jay & Bill Hinz*
Collage and Assemblage, *with Elvie TenHoor*
Macrame: Creative Design in Knotting
Woodworking: The New Wave
Contemporary Art with Wood
Creating Modern Furniture
Batik and Tie Die
Ethnic Jewelry
Printmaking
Box Art
and others

Library of Congress Cataloging-in-Publication Data

Meilach, Dona Z.
Ironwork today : inside & out / Dona Z. Meilach.
p. cm.
Includes bibliographical references and index.
ISBN 0-7643-2390-3 (hard cover)
1. Ironwork—United States—History—20th century. I. Title.

NK8212.M45 2006
739.40973'0904—dc22
2005028431

Cover design and layout, Dona Z. Meilach
Type set in Benguiat BT/Souvenir Lt BT
Title Page: *Horizontal Pillar* by Frederic A. Crist
ISBN: 0-7643-2390-3
Printed in China

Published by Schiffer Publishing Ltd.
4880 Lower Valley Road
Atglen, PA 19310
Phone: (610) 593-1777; Fax: (610) 593-2002
E-mail: Info@schifferbooks.com

For the largest selection of fine reference books on this and related subjects, please visit our web site at **www.schifferbooks.com**
We are always looking for people to write books on new and related subjects. If you have an idea for a book please contact us at the above address.

This book may be purchased from the publisher.
Include $3.95 for shipping.
Please try your bookstore first.
You may write for a free catalog.

In Europe, Schiffer books are distributed by
Bushwood Books
6 Marksbury Ave.
Kew Gardens
Surrey TW9 4JF England
Phone: 44 (0) 20 8392-8585; Fax: 44 (0) 20 8392-9876
E-mail: info@bushwoodbooks.co.uk
Free postage in the U.K., Europe; air mail at cost.

This book is dedicated to
Stephen Bondi
whose powerful legacy of ironwork objects,
designs, research, and attitude
are sorely missed.

Acknowledgments

I work alone for hours, days, and months organizing pictures and setting forth words, but I am never lonely. A book like this involves interaction with many artists who submitted photos and then answered my myriad questions as I tried to describe everything correctly. I am grateful to everyone who sent photos, CDs, and e-mails, and to the photographers whose special talents help make the book beautiful.

I am particularly indebted to the artists who suggested which photos to use from the hundreds of slides, prints, and images on cd's too numerous to tally. Thank you Richard Schrader, Kenneth Capps, and Sue Kaye for sharing your trained artistic viewpoints.

The physical and virtual problems associated with assembling, viewing, and selecting this material require computer skills that go far beyond writing. My ultimate thanks should go to Google's software, Picasa, that lets me put the contents of every CD on the computer for quick viewing and retrieval.

Robert C. Bentley and his team earn a gold star for providing the rich cache of examples so brilliantly photographed by Bruce Woodworth. If I needed one more photo to round out a premise, Bruce shot it and forwarded it quickly.

Helmet Hillenkamp was an invaluable source of material, not only for his own work, but also for steering me to others and for critiquing the copy. I was delighted that Robb Gunter, and his sons, Brad and Chad, were able to release photos of a project they had worked on for nearly two years, but were unable to allow to be published until now.

Jock Dempsy, guru of www.anvilfire.com, was willing, and anxious as always, to announce my request for photos. His popular web site is a favorite among blacksmiths, and many other metalworkers. The response was gratifying. My thanks, too, to the ABANA Chapters and to the editors of *The Anvil's Ring* for their help in reaching contributors. Rob Edwards and Mimi Clark seem to anticipate what and when I will be involved in another project.

Thanks to my brother, Seymour Zweigoron, whose technical and literary background was invaluable for pinpointing errors that pop-up in a manuscript draft. My husband, Dr. Melvin Meilach, continues to tolerate my book-writing compulsion despite the hours it keeps me at the computer…or maybe because of them. Meeting so many people in the arts has enriched both of our lives.

Working with Nancy and Peter Schiffer and the staff at Schiffer Publishing, as they move the project from manuscript through galleys and proofs to the final book, is their miracle of publishing. I enjoy being a part of it.

Preface

Among the joys of writing these books is the fallout that results. People whose work has been represented in earlier books have reported invitations to exhibit in galleries, enter shows, make sales, become part of museum and private collections, and participate in overseas exhibitions.

As I finalize the manuscript of this, my sixth book on metalworking, I delight at the reports that the earlier books have helped create a renaissance in artist-blacksmithing. I revel in letters that tell me they have helped create a person's career, put someone in touch with others, and discovered resources they didn't know existed.

While the physical act of writing is a lonely profession, contacts with artists by letter, email, phone, and at blacksmith conferences cancel out the tedium of the thousands of hours spent at the computer. I am warmed by correspondents from far-off corners of the earth: Russia, Germany, England, Ireland, Taiwan, Australia, Canada, China, and other countries. These people are anxious to show what they are creating, and they underscore the international reach of the information.

This book represents a continuing investigation and modern history of the vitality of contemporary ironwork— the blacksmiths who create it, and the artistic climate that fosters it. When I wrote *Decorative & Sculptural Ironwork* in 1977, I had no idea it would help spark the interest that was smoldering in the embers of small forges across the country. Nearly thirty years later, that spark has grown to a hot fire and artistic ironwork has become a viable and expressive art form. There is much being wrought, many people are excited about the medium, and schools are offering blacksmithing workshops. There are casual and organized "hammer fests" where novices and experienced smiths meet to share experiences, see, and hear who is doing what.

Initially, I wondered if there was enough new work to justify another book. I didn't have to wonder long. As word was out, photos poured in. The bigger problem was finding space in the pages for all the exciting examples and doing justice to the artists and the variety. It wasn't easy to select only 482 photos from the 3000 plus submitted by more than 250 artists.

Organizing such a bounty of material is a daunting challenge; that done, it's a question of how many photos can be used in any one chapter. Forty-four are in the sculpture chapter, for example, but 538 photos of sculpture were submitted.

So, once again, as in 1995 when *The Contemporary Blacksmith* generated almost enough photos to justify four more books, I can't let the surplus not see the light of day. Stay tuned for another book of wonderful surprises for the artist-blacksmith, the collector, the museum curator…everyone interested in this versatile material for functional and non-functional art.

Dona Z. Meilach
Carlsbad, CA 92209
February 2006

Contents

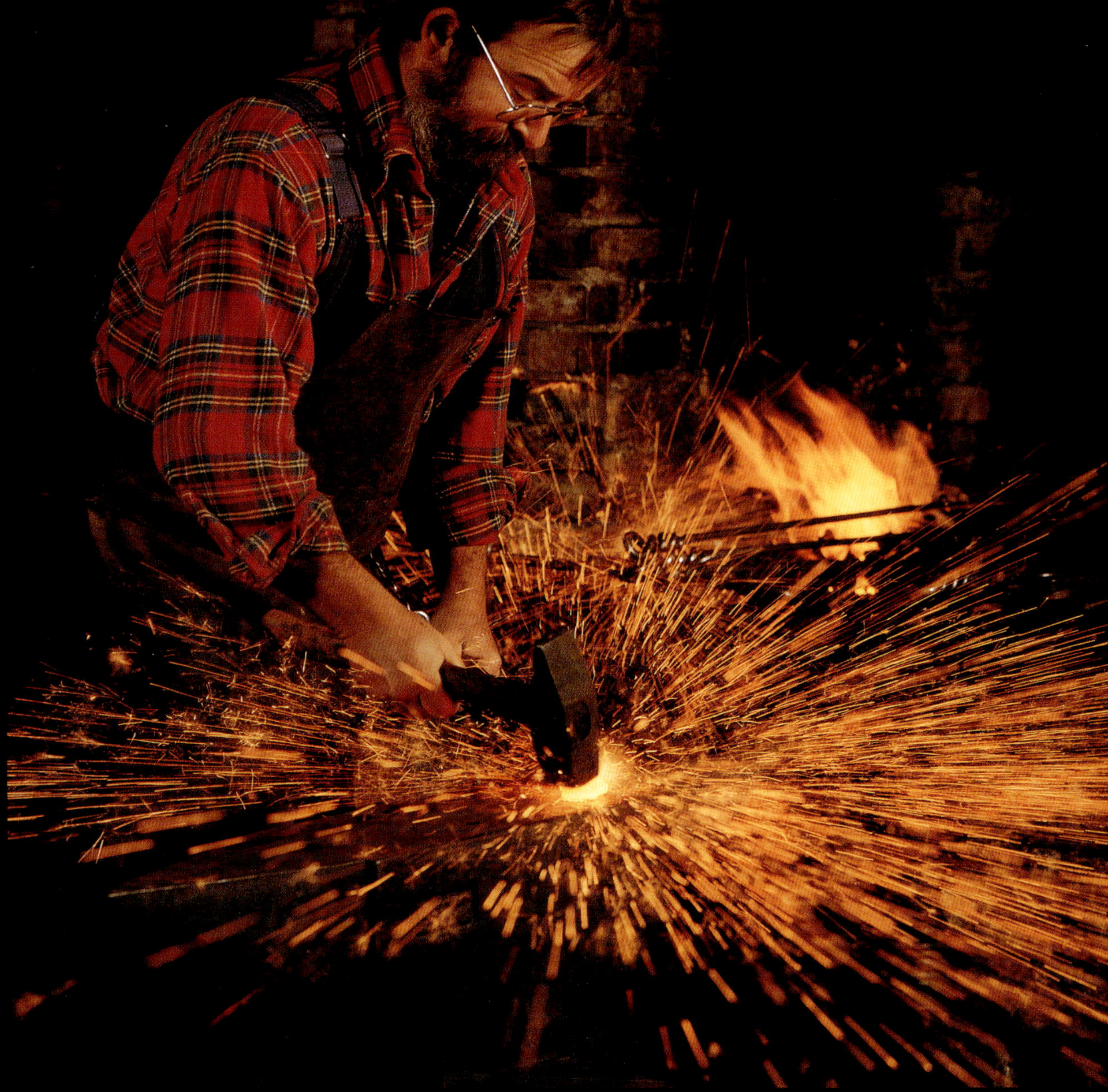

John Little. Sparks fly as the hammer strikes the hot metal ...one of the dramas of blacksmithing procedures. This typical activity is repeated infinitely in a blacksmith's shop. *Photo, Kerry Doubleday*

Chapter 1. Ironwork Today Inside and Out

Ironwork is all around us. It is inside our homes as kitchen utensils, locks on our doors, and as railings and banisters. It is outside in staircases, bridges, fences, benches, signage, and sculptures. Most people take ironwork for granted. Those who work in iron and understand its pervasiveness know how it permeates almost every aspect of our lives.

Hopefully, the examples in this book will increase people's awareness of the infinite ways iron is used. They will begin to "see" ironwork, and may begin to think about who creates with it and question how it is done. Artist-blacksmiths have accomplished all the ironwork examples in these pages. Blacksmiths you ask? Don't they shoe horses? Yes, some do. They are termed "farriers," an activity that is only one aspect of working iron.

Blacksmiths ply their art form, and it is an art form, to create functional and non-functional items that are as essential to today's lifestyle as paper, mortar, bricks, and plaster. The image of the blacksmith at his anvil repairing farm tools is part of our early lore. But he also made the grand staircases, the elegant fences and gates, the grilles and railings, the church dividers, shoe scrapers, fireplace tools, and so much more.

The blacksmith was an important figure in mythology. To the ancient Greeks, Hephaestus, the son of Zeus and Hera, was the god of fire, especially the blacksmith's fire. As the patron of all craftsmen, principally metalworkers, he manufactured awesome articles from metals and various materials. He made weapons and armor for other gods and for heroes. The Cyclopes were his workmen and assistants, and together, they fashioned Zeus's scepter and the thunderbolts he used to tame an unruly rebellious peoples.

Among the Romans, the god was named Vulcan. References to his name in products refer to heat-processed items with super abundant strength. In Norse mythology, he was the god Thor, and in Egypt he was Osiris.

The human blacksmiths of old were essential; they equipped warriors with swords, daggers, and spearheads. They gave the farmer the first efficient axe and ploughshare, and provided craftsmen with better tools than those fashioned from stone or bronze.

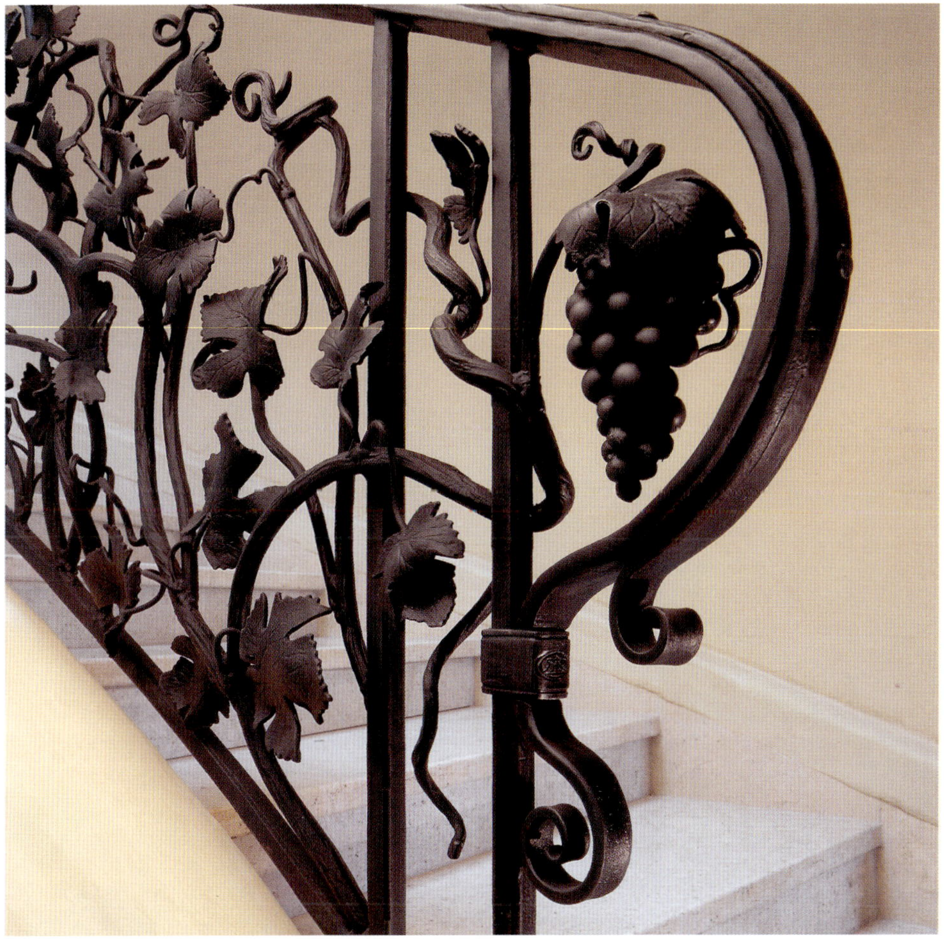

Butch Lee. Grape leaf cluster and vines (detail of a staircase ending). Railings are a major part of a blacksmith's work. Three-dimensional details like these attest to the artist's ability as a sculptor. *Photo, David Harris*

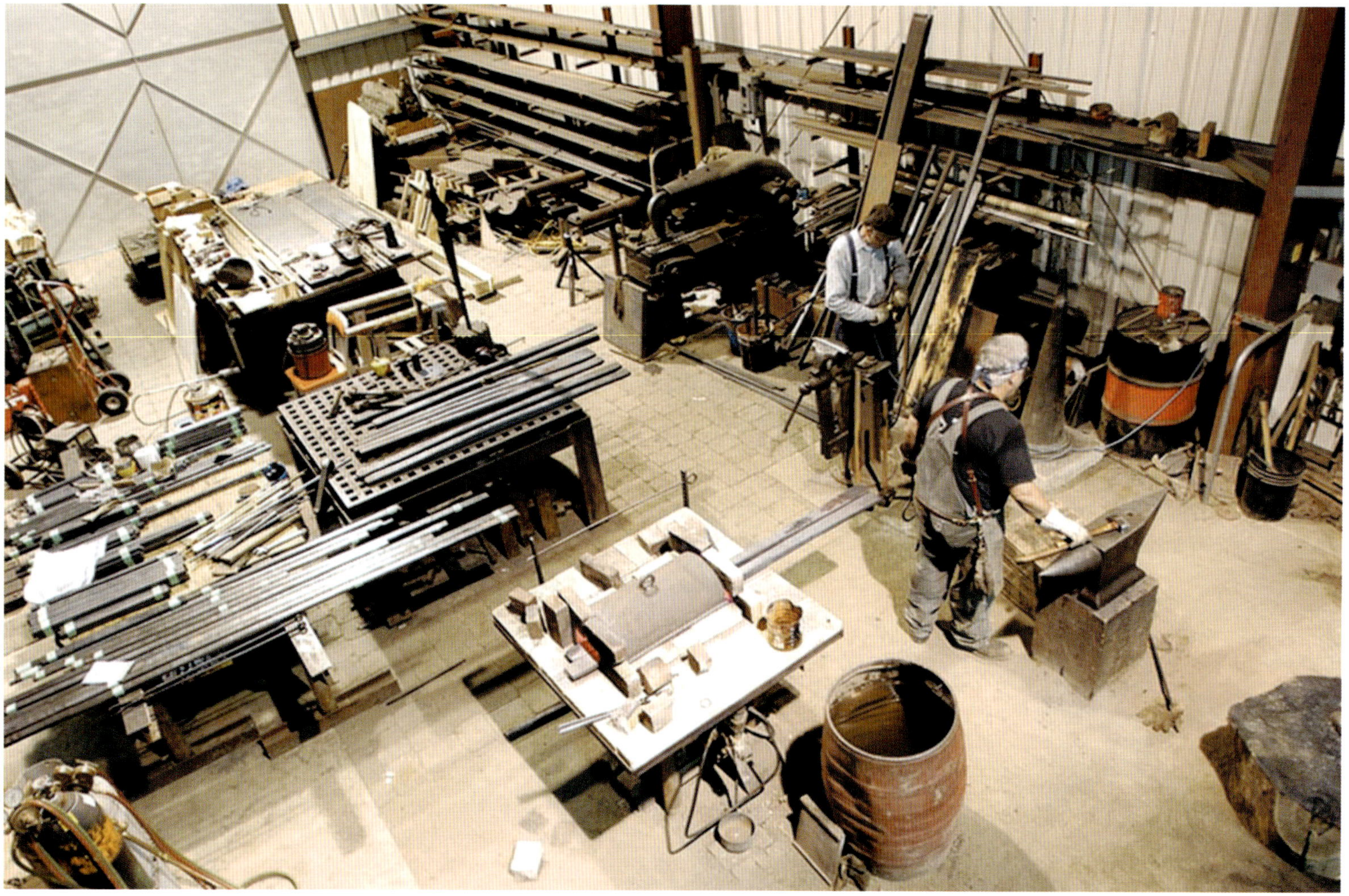

The blacksmith's shop. The ends of two bars are being heated in a gas forge (foreground) while Ken Williams, right, and Russell Jaqua, prepare tools for working with the hot steel. *Photo, Peter Kuhnlein*

Blacksmiths created the magnificent ironwork in Europe that heralded the Art Nouveau period in the late 1900s and well into the 1920s. They were mostly anonymous artisans and did not sign their work. The designs were more likely created by an architect and then made by the artisan. That changed as Art Nouveau spread from Belgium into France, Italy, and Spain. Victor Horta, Gustave Strauven, Ernest Blérot, and George's Peerboom are associated with this Art Nouveau movement in Brussels, Belgium. It was further developed by Antonio Gaudí in Spain, Victor Horta in France, and Allessandro Mazzucotelli of Italy.

The blacksmith emerged as an "artist" about the 1930s with the development of efficient and portable tools for welding. Only a few sculptors had tackled iron as an art form but it was enough to light a fire. During the late 1960s and early 1970s there was an unprecedented creative climate and recognition of crafts as art, thanks to the interest of Jacqueline Kennedy and her legacy. She brought crafts into the White House and deemed them as valuable and as highly collectable as paintings and sculpture. She acknowledged and celebrated the people who made them.

She recognized that clay, fibers, silver, gold, wood, and yes, iron, and many materials relegated to "crafts" were indeed, "art media". There were heated discussions about what is art and what is craft. Many arguments denouncing crafts as art were challenged. Such positions were eventually laid to rest as more people became involved in making and collecting crafts. By the 1980s the demand for classes swelled, and schools incorporated curricula in many media, and mostly they were oversubscribed.

Twenty-five years ago, only a handful of schools taught blacksmithing, or "hot metal," classes. Today, there are many. In 1973, fifty artist-blacksmiths met at Lumpkin, Georgia at the invitation of Alex W. Bealer, an amateur blacksmith and author of *The Art of Blacksmithing* (1969). That meeting was the beginning of the Artist-Blacksmith's Association of North America (ABANA) that, today, boasts over 5000 members.

Professor L. Brent Kington had already introduced hot iron classes at Southern Illinois University at Carbondale, Illinois. Kington was familiar with the work of artists David Smith, Julio Gonzales, Alberto Giacometti, and Eduardo Chillida, as inspiration for artist-blacksmithing as sculpture. Many practicing artist-blacksmiths today took their first blacksmithing classes under Kington's aegis. James Wallace, a student at Carbondale in the 1970s, eventually founded *The National Ornamental Metal Museum*, in Memphis, Tennessee, in 1978. It is the only museum devoted to ironwork.

As interest in crafts burgeoned, The American Craft Museum emerged, magazines such as *Craft Horizons (now American Crafts)* and *The Anvil's Ring* began publishing for a growing membership. The activity was duplicated in England, Germany, and other countries. The rest is history. Much of it can be found in my earlier books and in other books that deal with the subject.

Since those early days, ABANA chapters exist in almost every state in America. The British Art Blacksmithing Association (BABA) was formed. Blacksmithing meets and "hammer fests" are held frequently and tours are organized to visit and share information with smiths in other countries.

Today, talented artists are exploring the infinite potential of this malleable material. The designs and shapes that are evolving have sparked unprecedented activity among people for whom working with hot metal is a career, a hobby, and a passion.

The Blacksmith's Tools and Studio

Recently, I was amazed to discover that the proprietor of a large, local fireplace accessory shop had no idea how her merchandise was made. She had never been in a blacksmith shop and didn't know what an anvil was. What a shame, I thought; part of appreciating what emerges from the hand of the smith is an understanding of how it happens. Watching the iron glow in the fire, then soften so it can be manipulated, is almost a magical experience. And, when two or

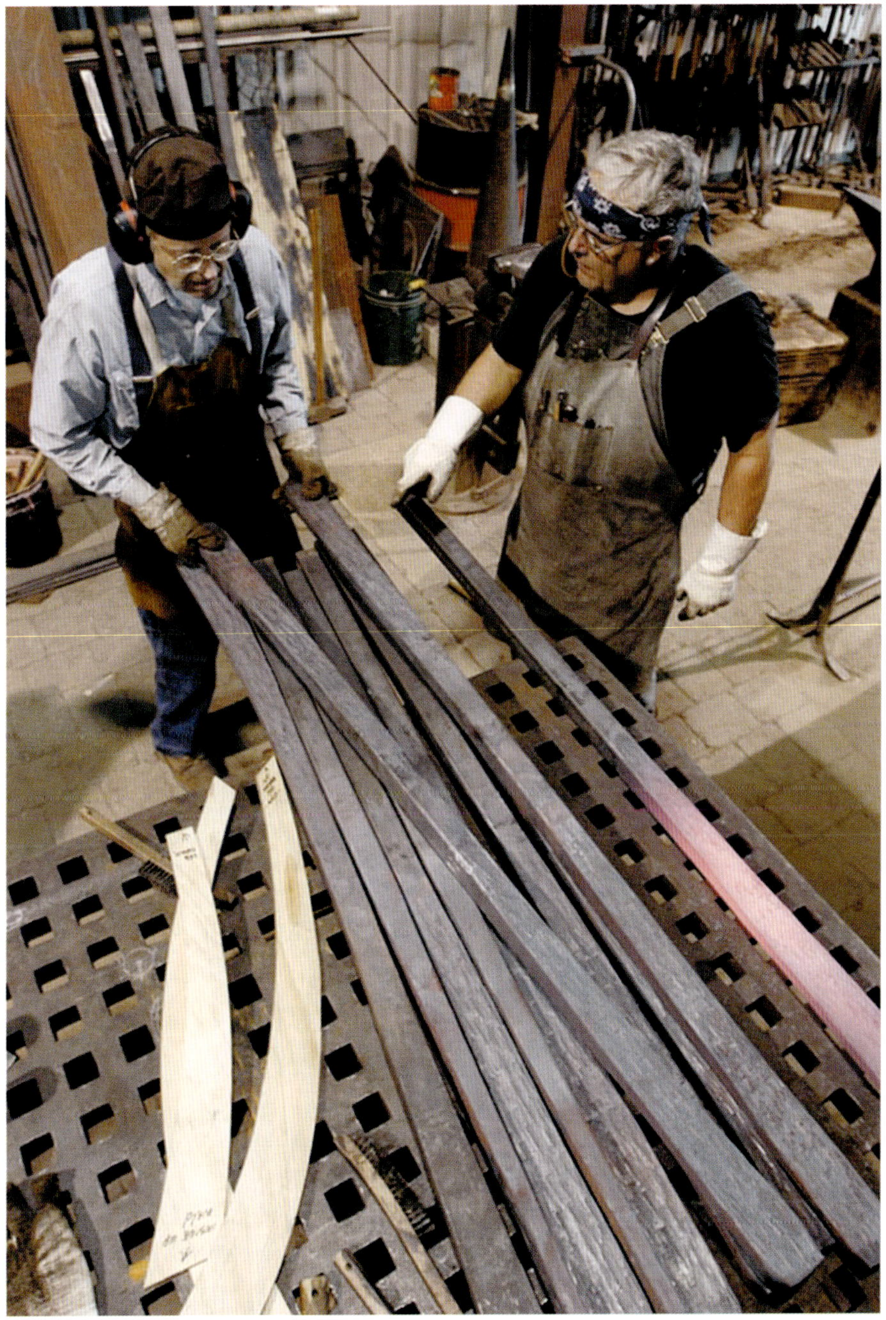

The artist-blacksmith's materials can be bars, sheet metal, and scrap metal. Ken Williams' workshop. Russell Jaqua, left; Ken Williams, right. *Photo, Peter Kuhnlein*

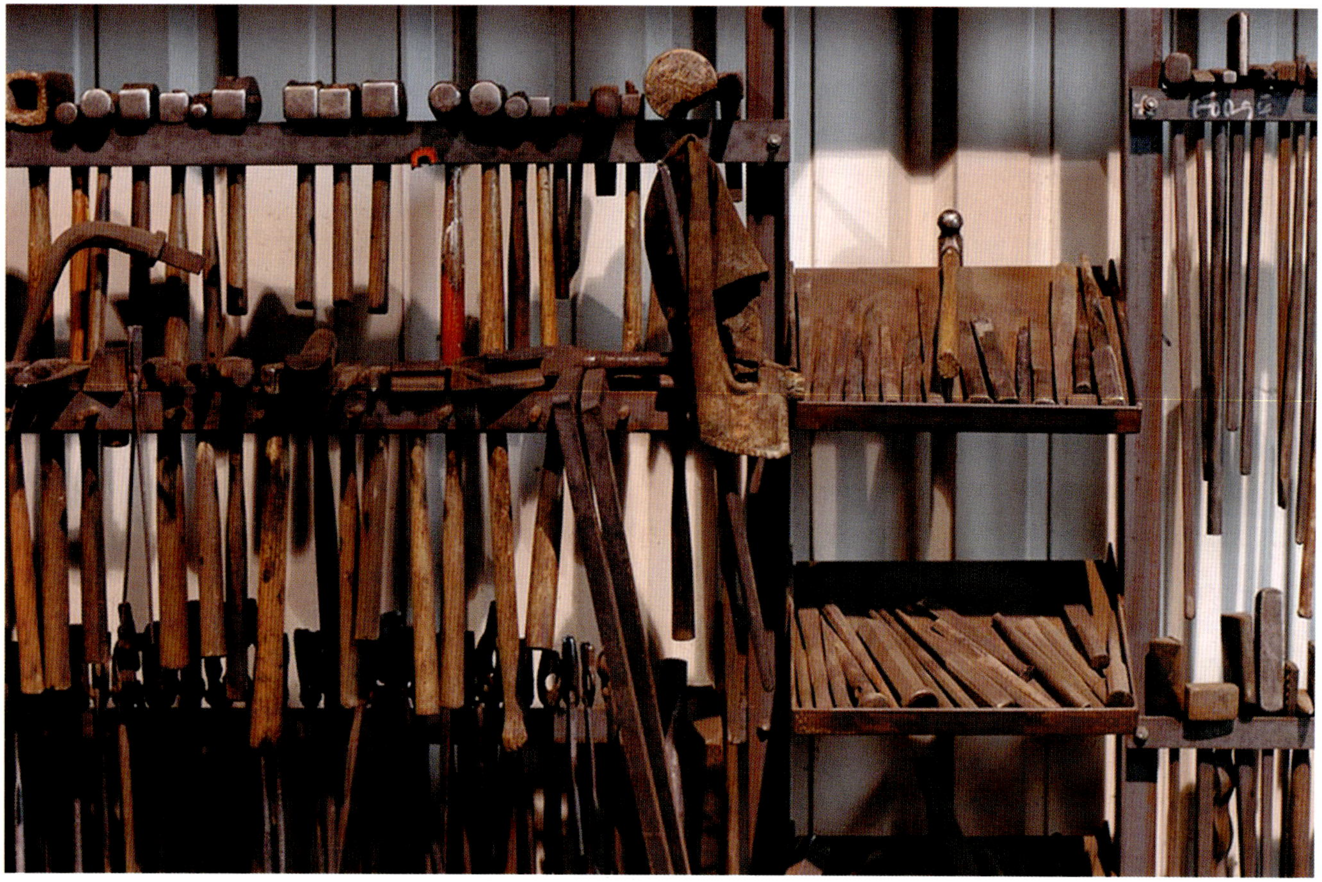

A variety of hand tools hang ready for use in Ken William's workshop. They include the ubiquitous hammers in different weights, tongs, and specialty tools. Smiths often fashion their own tools to meet specific needs. *Photo, Peter Kuhnlein*

more smiths work in a rhythm, it's like watching a beautifully choreographed dance. These are miraculous moments that everyone should experience.

A blacksmith shop may be as complete and sophisticated as the one shown, but it could also consist of a small portable gas or coal forge in a back yard outfitted with an anvil, basic tools, and a bucket of water.

The *forge*, the unit that produces the fire, may be set up to use coal or gas. John Little's forge in the photo on page 8 is coal fired and you can see the flames behind the smith. As the smith hammered the hot iron, the camera caught the drama of the flying sparks. The forge in the photo on page 10 is gas powered (on the square base at the front of the picture) and large enough for the rods to be placed within it a section at a time. When the metal is heated to the proper heat color, it is twisted or hammered until it cools and is no longer malleable. The procedure is repeated until the desired form is reached.

The *anvil* is the next essential blacksmith's tool; it is the blacksmith's workbench. It has a solid base with a smooth top and a round or square horn extending horizontally from the base. An anvil can weigh from 100 to about 600 pounds. The weight is based on the size of the work for which it will be used. It has two holes on its face. One hole is square and called the "hardie hole" that accommodates a "hardie" tool used for shaping the hot metal. The other anvil hole is called a "pritchel hole." It is round and mostly used for punching holes.

Hammers, tongs, chisels, fullers, and a variety of other tools may be used. Often the smith will fashion his own tools for a particular job. Tongs, particularly, have to be adapted to, or made anew, for each job, so that they can hold the hot iron piece firmly and securely when hammering it with heavy blows. Vises are used for securing the material.

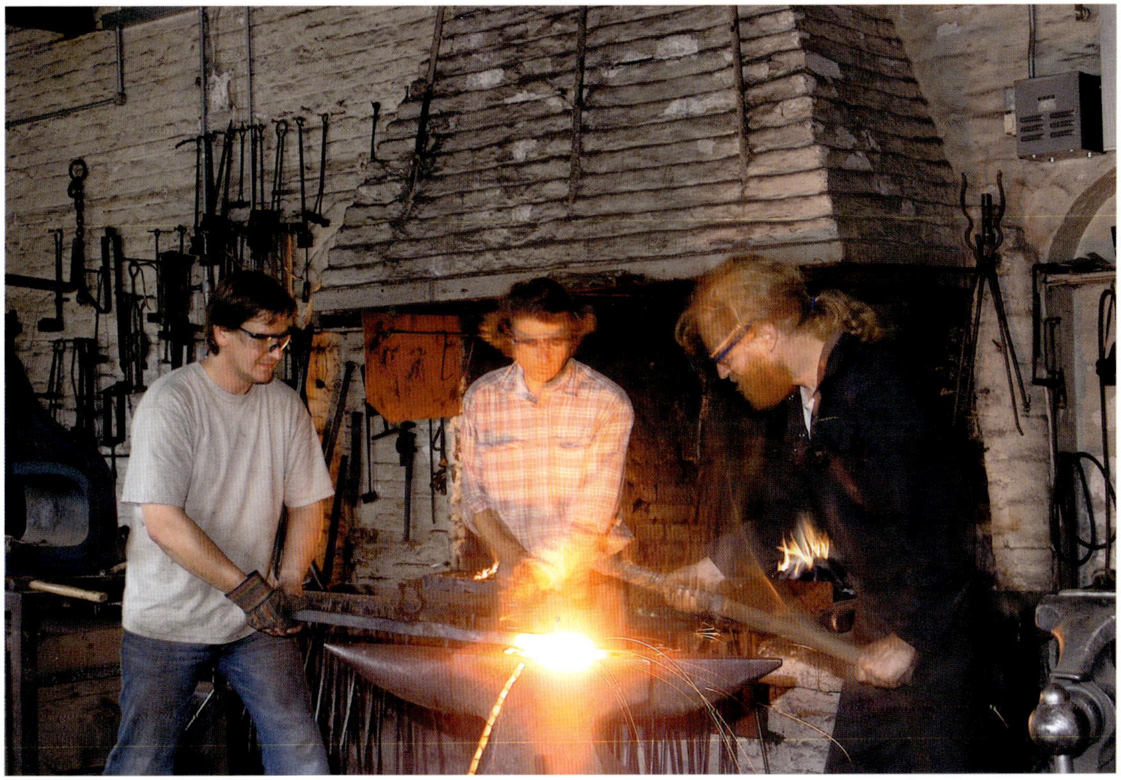

Coal forges are used in some shops. Forming the hot iron may require "strikers" to help hammer the shapes while the piece is in a malleable stage. Paul Elliott, center, works with two helpers as strikers. Each takes a turn hitting the hot metal using timed rhythmic movements. Nick Morn on the left and Brian Davis on the right. *Photo, Jackie Phillips*

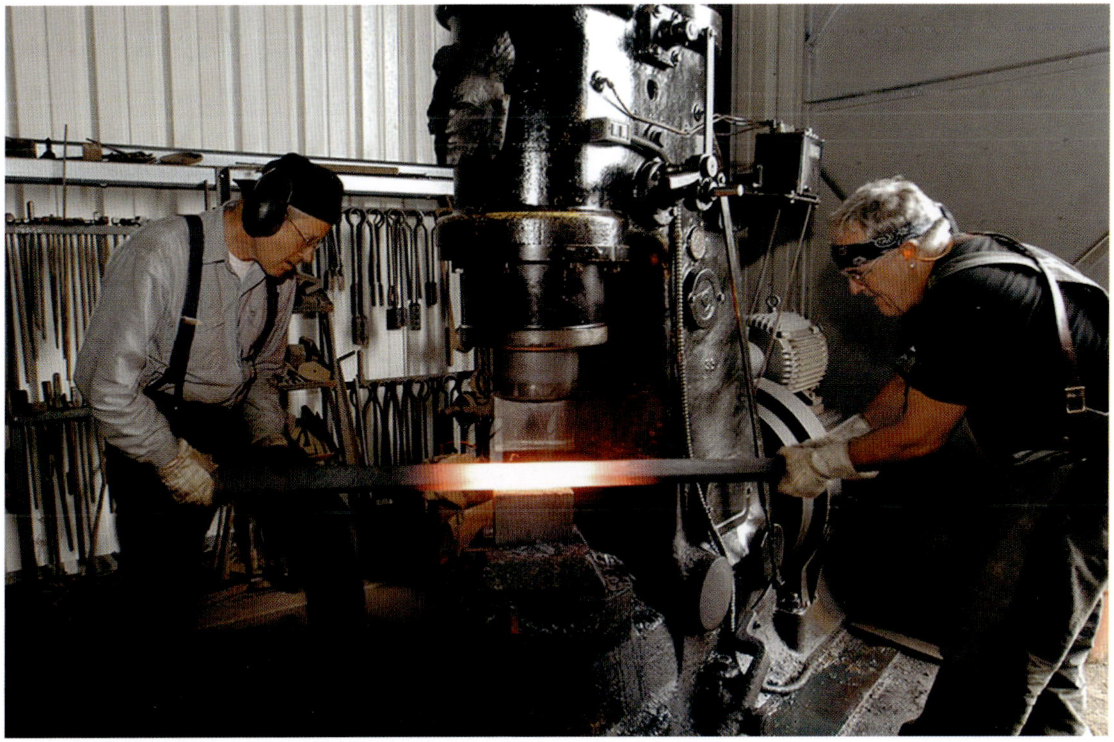

Power hammers are often used to work the hot metal for small and large jobs. Ken Williams, right, and Russell Jaqua hold the bars on each end preparing to make a twist in the heated part of the rod. *Photo, Peter Kuhnlein*

Jim Gallucci drills holes for the base of the sculpture.

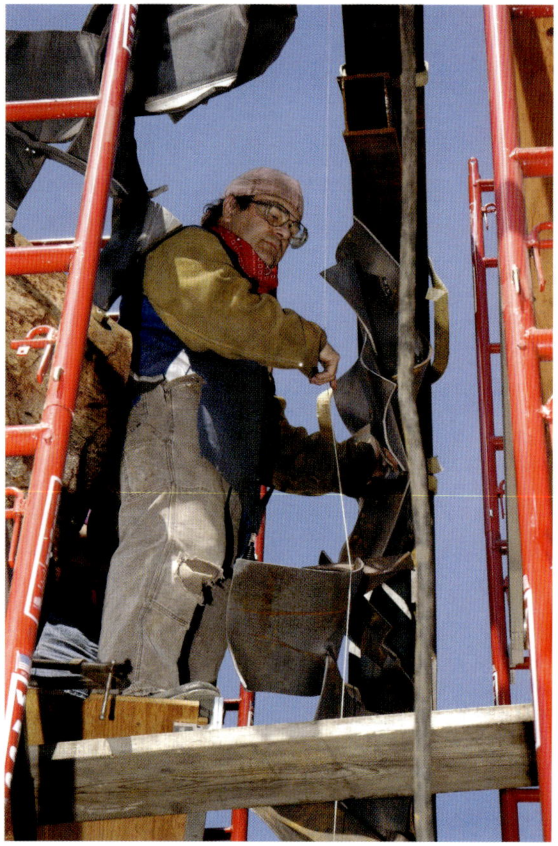

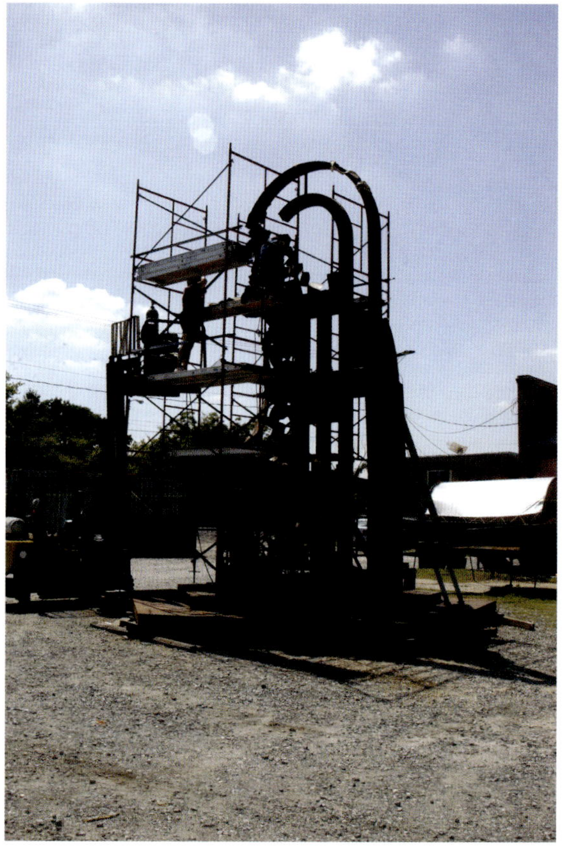

Jim Gallucci. *9-11 Sculpture Project* during installation. A scaffold was built for the assembly process. *Photo, David Brown*

Power hammers are indispensable for large jobs and working heavy pieces of iron. The increased productivity they bring makes the blacksmith's profession competitive in today's metalworking world. The materials may be rods, flat metals, found, and recycled metals. The smith soon learns the types of metals he likes to work with and may combine iron with other materials. Most shops also have welding units and a variety of machine tools such as drills, sanders, and grinders for polishing and finishing the final pieces.

Metal sculptures are frequently made for public art and placed outdoors because the materials hold up over time in different weather conditions. A variety of such projects are shown in this chapter. Also shown is the potential for complex, very large pieces that may be purely public sculpture, pieces for amusement parks, and fountains.

John Little Sums Up His Thoughts About Working Iron

"Cold, hard iron seems an unlikely medium with which to create organic form. Its nature is strong and stubborn. The methods used to manipulate this material seem so antithetical to a natural process. It is, after all, a process of intense heat and violent force that allows the blacksmith to change the shape of the material and create form and line to suit some preconceived design. But the irony is that the hot metal cannot simply be beaten into obedience. The work must reflect an intimate understanding of the nature of the material and the processes of blacksmithing. The work, to be good, must be a cooperative effort between brain, eye, hand, heat, hammer, and anvil.

"A novice smith's work usually appears forced and beaten up. With time and understanding comes increased grace of form with less effort. In many ways the popular image of the blacksmith being master by brute strength over a difficult medium is simply wrong. The best work comes from the hands of a smith comfortable enough to dance and play with the hot metal. At this point, it seems a very natural process indeed. The iron withdrawn from a coal fire at yellow heat is placed on the anvil with respect, like a living thing, and is forged into a new alignment. The rhythmic hammer adds energy with each blow— energy direct from the smith's body. During that brief time of forgeable heat, it's as though the smith's energy and the energy of the hot metal conspire to allow the new form to emerge."

John Little

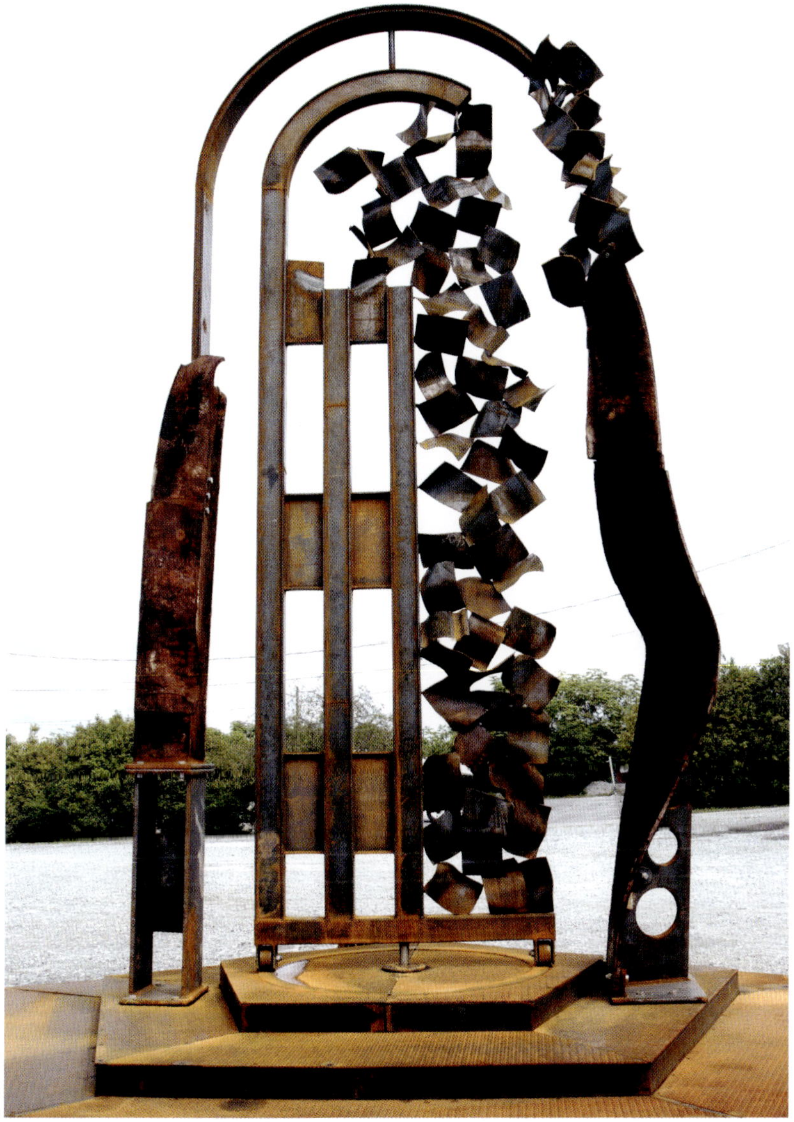

Jim Gallucci and assistants. *9-11 Sculpture Project* was started in December, 2001 with 16 tons of steel from the World Trade Center debris. The objective was to have the sculpture travel around the country as a reminder of that day that changed the world. 23' high. *Photo, David Brown*

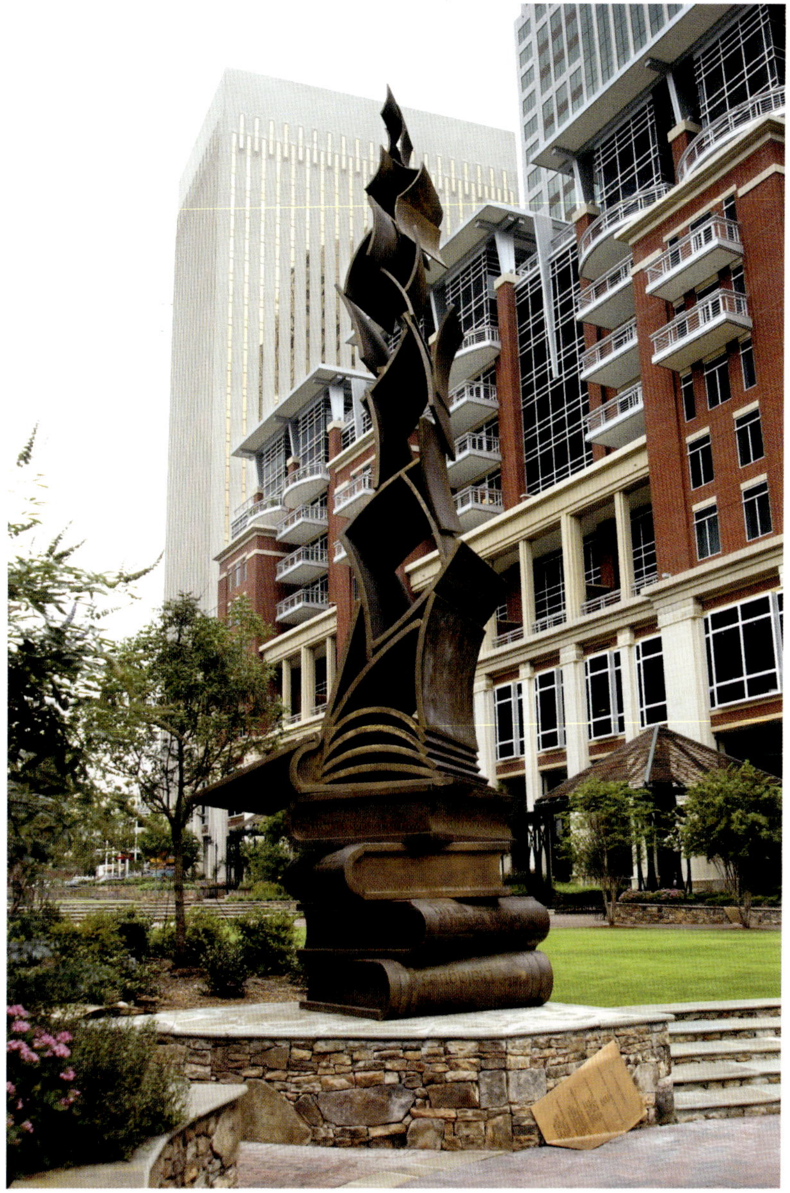

Jim Gallucci. *Book and Pages*. Bronze. *Book and Pages* is situated in the Grand entry to "The Green", a park built over an 800-car underground parking garage in Charlotte, North Carolina. Each book has a title on its spine and together, they represent the essences of western literature. 33' high, 5' wide, 5' deep. *Photo, David Brown*

A main difference between forged iron (left) and bronze sculpture (right) is that forged iron work is a "direct" process. The artist works directly on the materials as he forms the object. A bronze sculpture requires that an original model be fashioned in clay or wax. A mold is made. Molten metal is poured into the mold and it displaces or "burns out" the clay or wax. When the molten metal solidifies, the mold is removed to reveal the object in the metal. It is considered an "indirect" method.

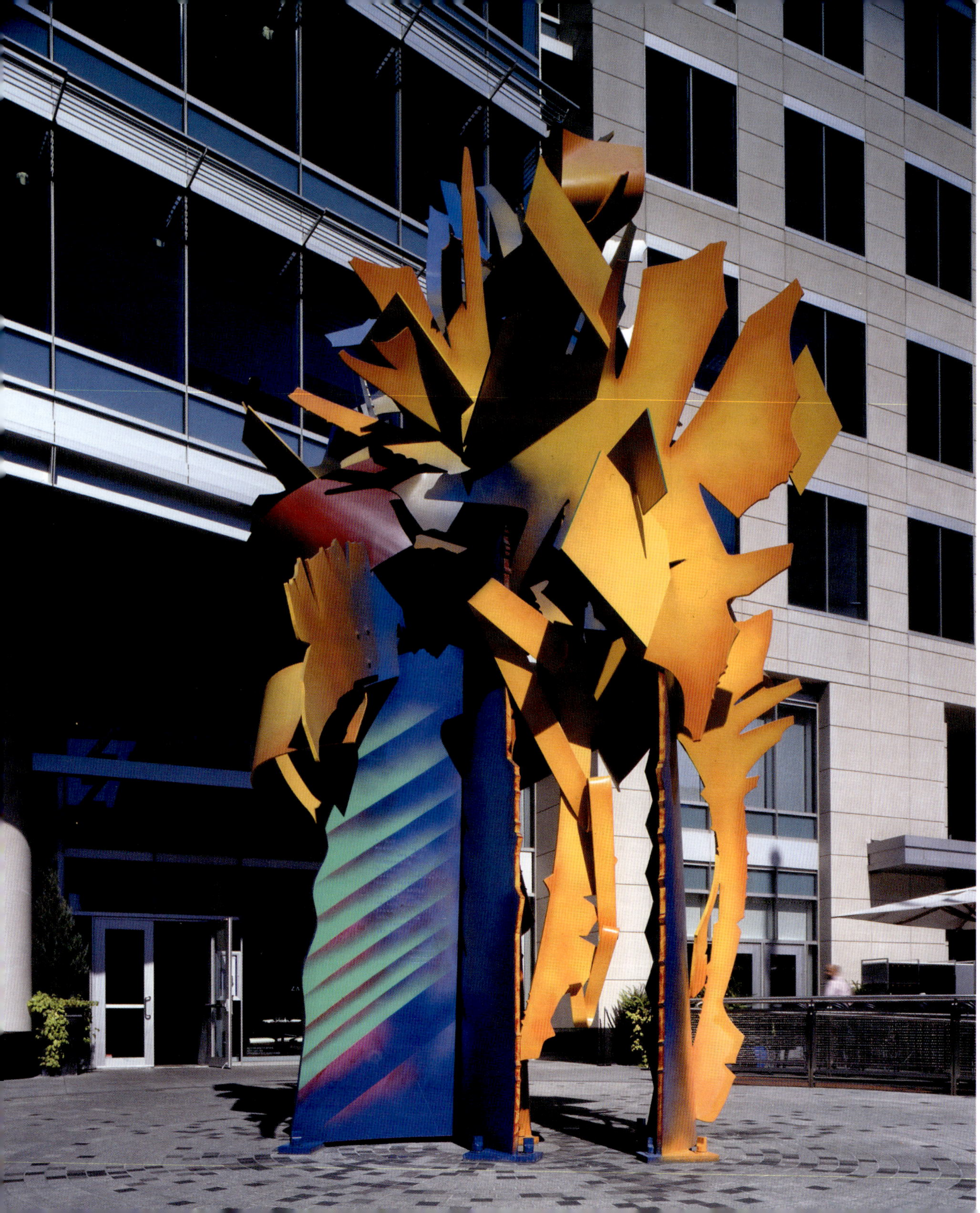

Albert Paley. *Epoch, 2004.* Formed and fabricated steel, polychrome. Washington D.C. Commission of the Arts and Humanities DC Creates Public Art Program. 24' high, 12' wide, 11' deep. *Photo, Dan Cunningham*

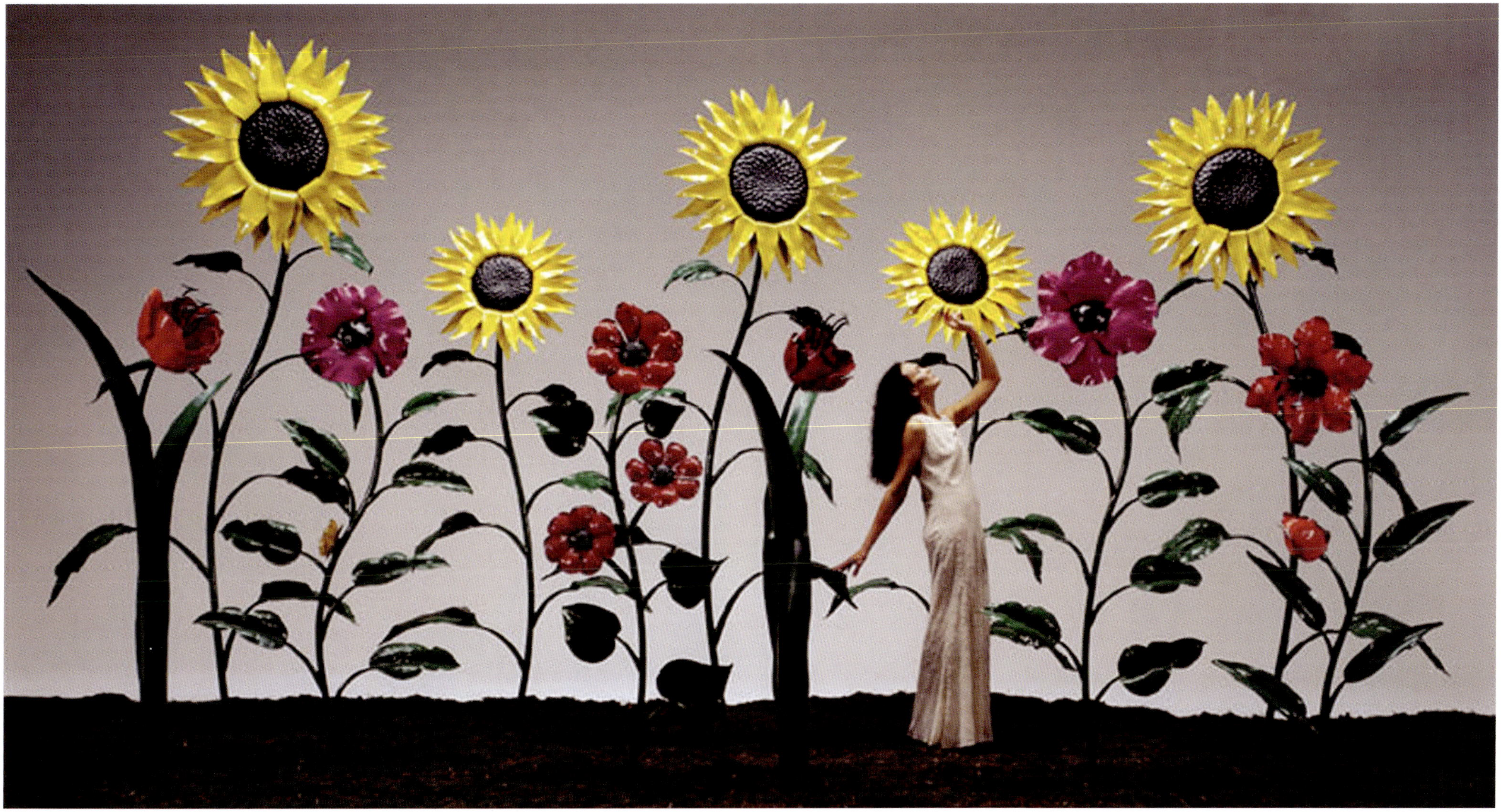

Jeff Fetty. *Trace Fork Sculpture Garden*. Forged steel and paint. Studio photo before outdoor installation. 10' high, 23' wide. *Photo, artist*

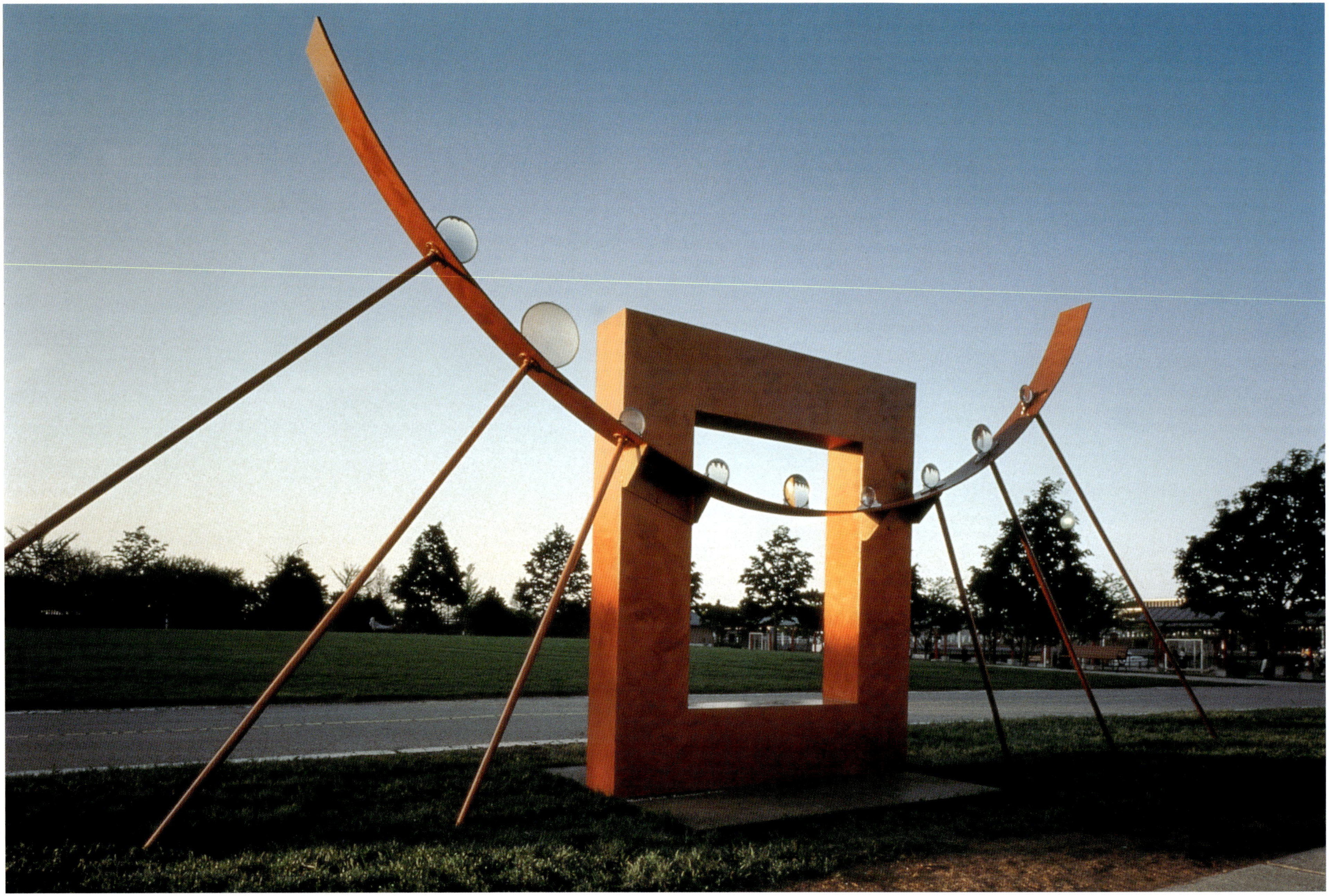

Nicole Beck. *Quasarc 2001*. Rolled, welded, painted steel with magnifying lenses. Installed at Pier Walk, Chicago, Illinois. 10' high, 25' wide, 5' deep. *Photo, artist*

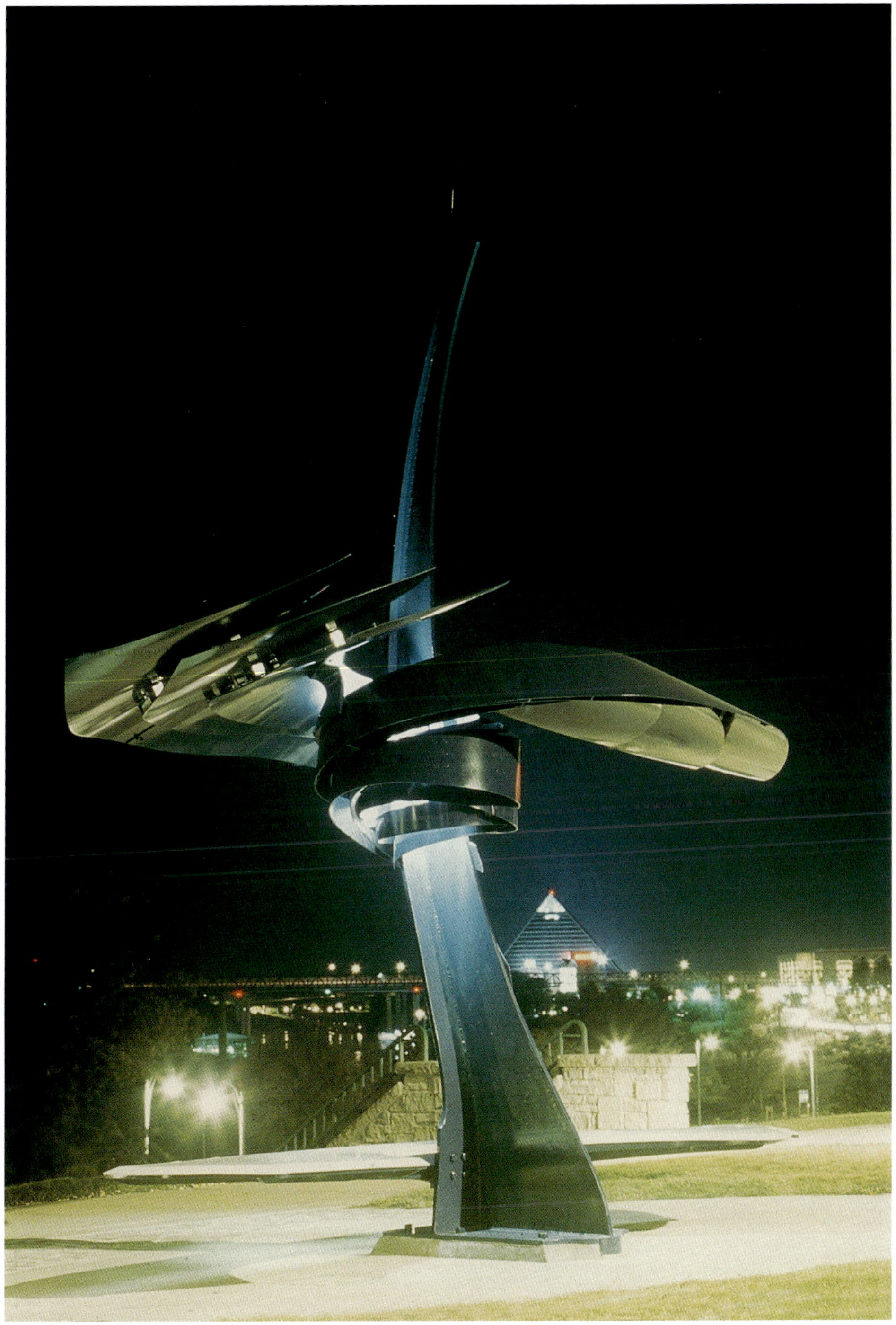

John Medwedeff. *Whirl.* Forged and fabricated steel and aluminum. 18' high, 21' wide, 8' deep. *Photo, Jeff Bruce*

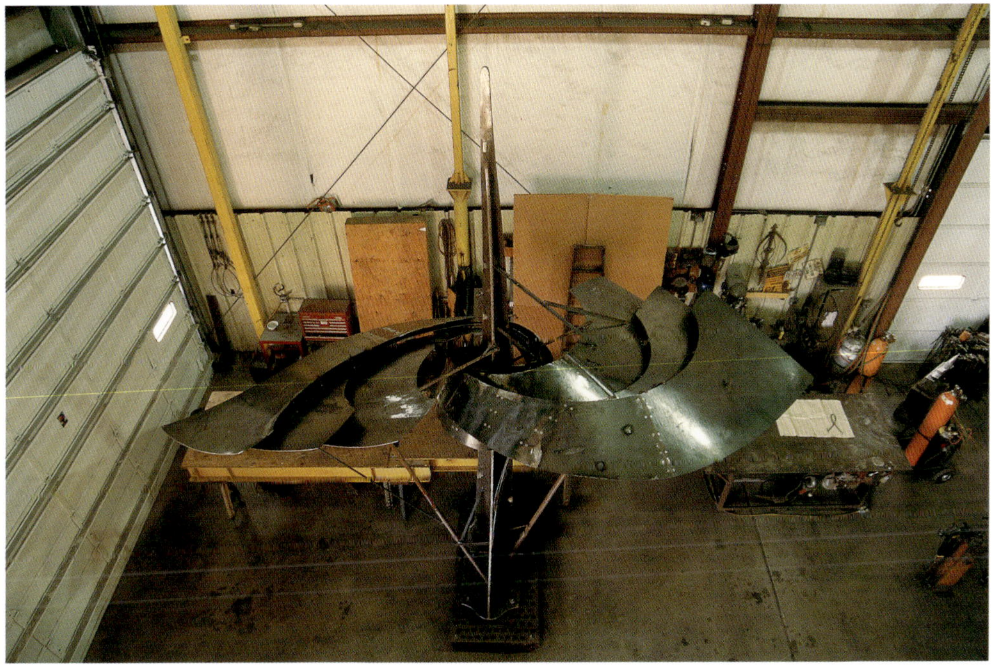

John Medwedeff. *Whirl* in progress. *Photo, Jeff Bruce*

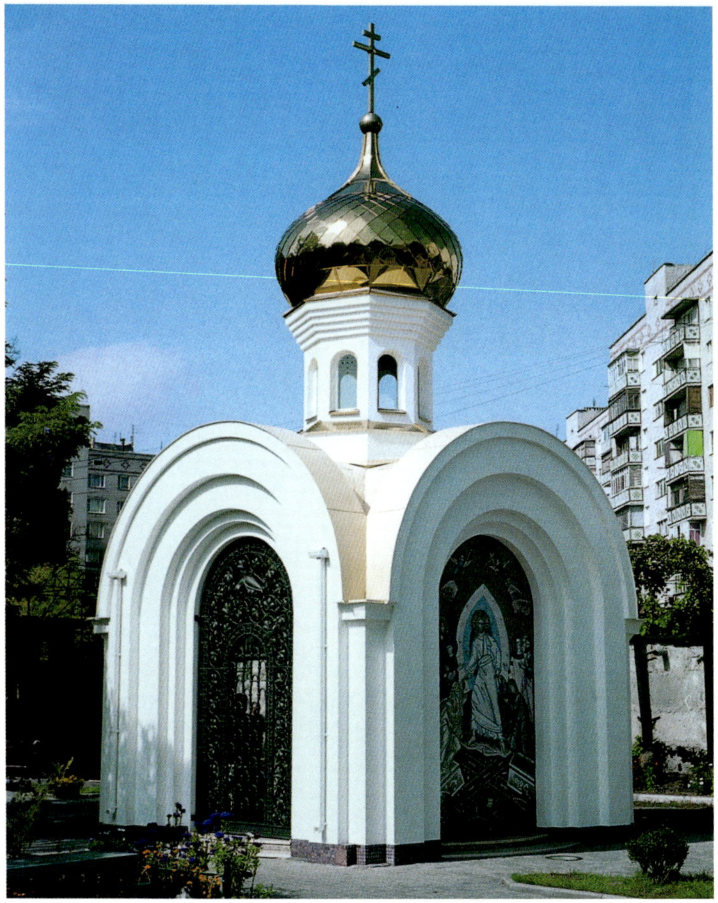

Nikolay Semenov and Egor Bavykin. Design by Nikolay Semenov. St. Nikolay Chapel. Odessa, 2003. When gates and grilles are such an integral design of a building, they fall into the category of public art. *Photo, Semenov*

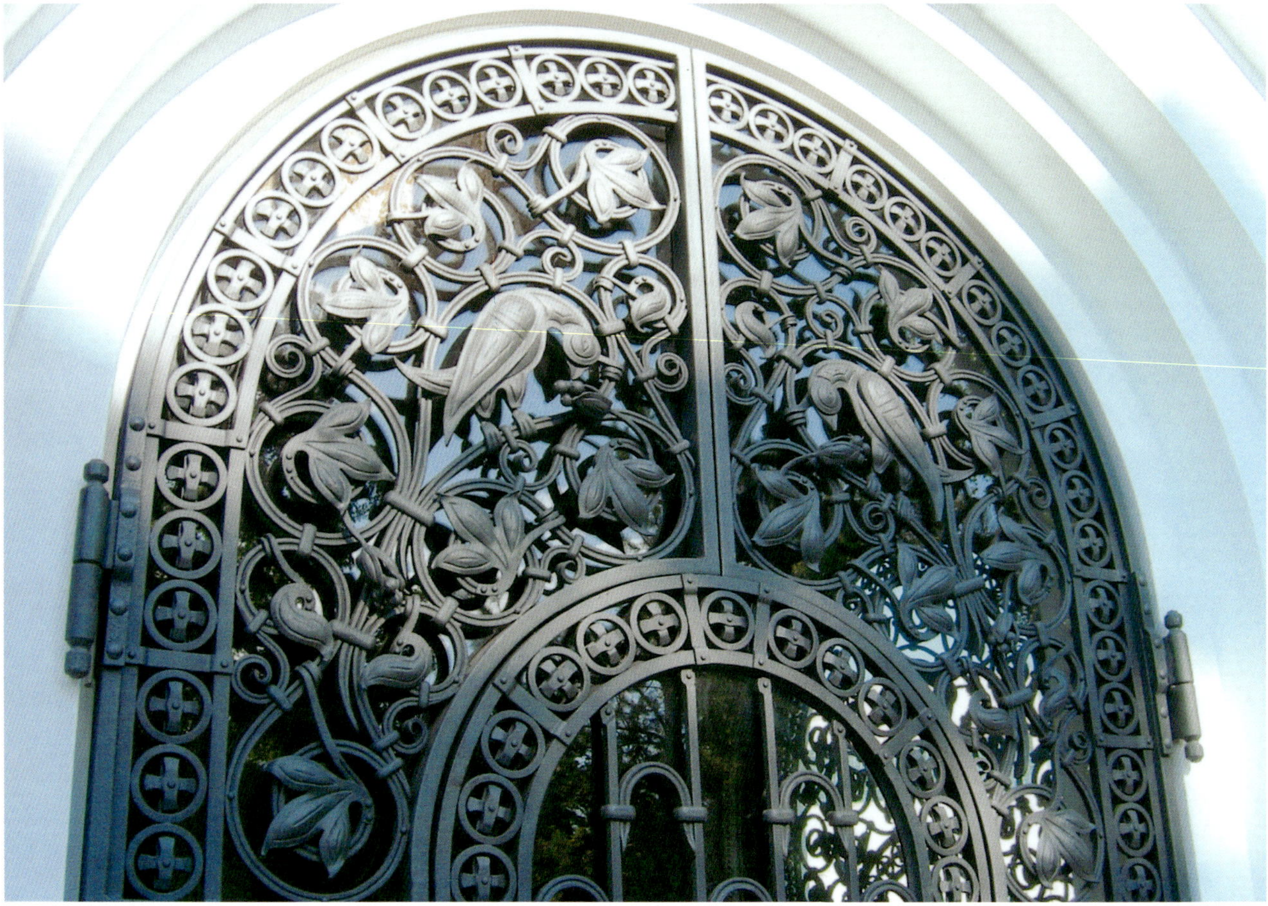

Nikolay Semenov and Egor Bavykin. Design by Nikolay Semenov. Detail of gate in the St. Nikolay Chapel. Odessa, 2003. *Photo, Semenov*

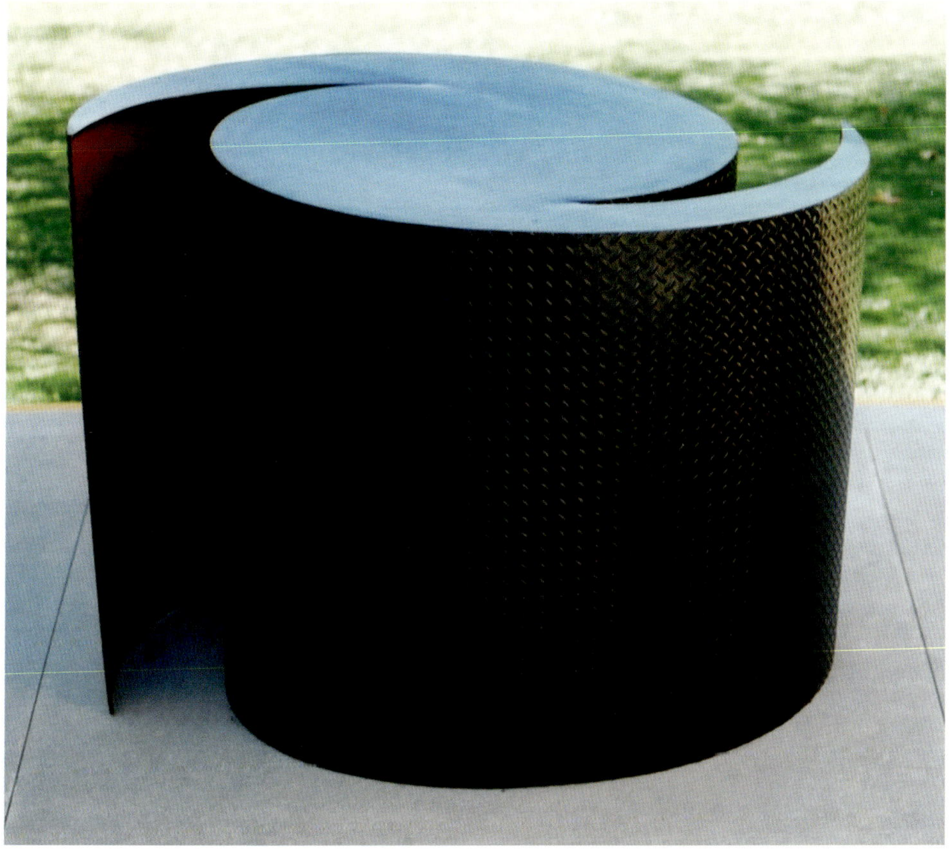

Kenneth Capps. *Amazon*. Painted Steel. 49" high, 64" wide, 46" deep. *Photo, artist*

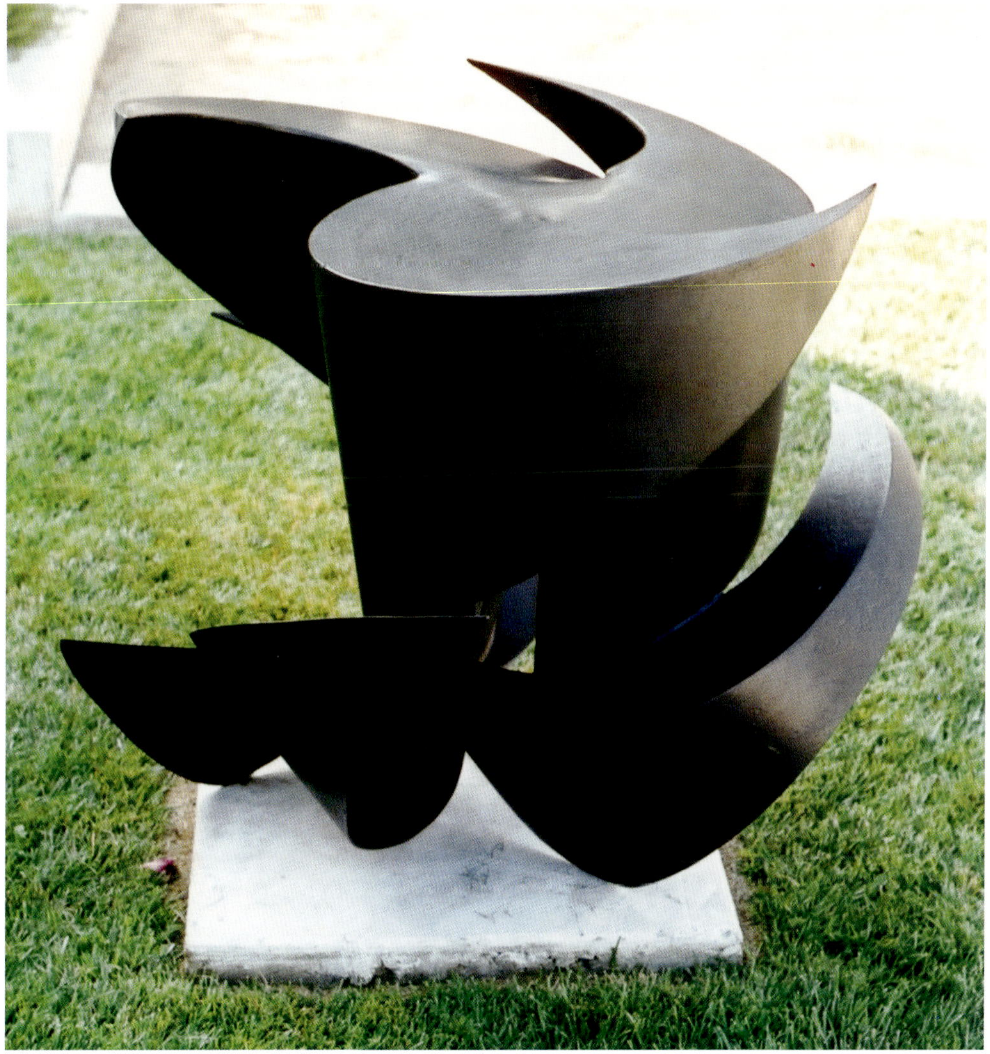

Kenneth Capps. *PULZ.B.* Zinc and steel. 43" high, 44" wide, 44" deep. *Photo, artist*

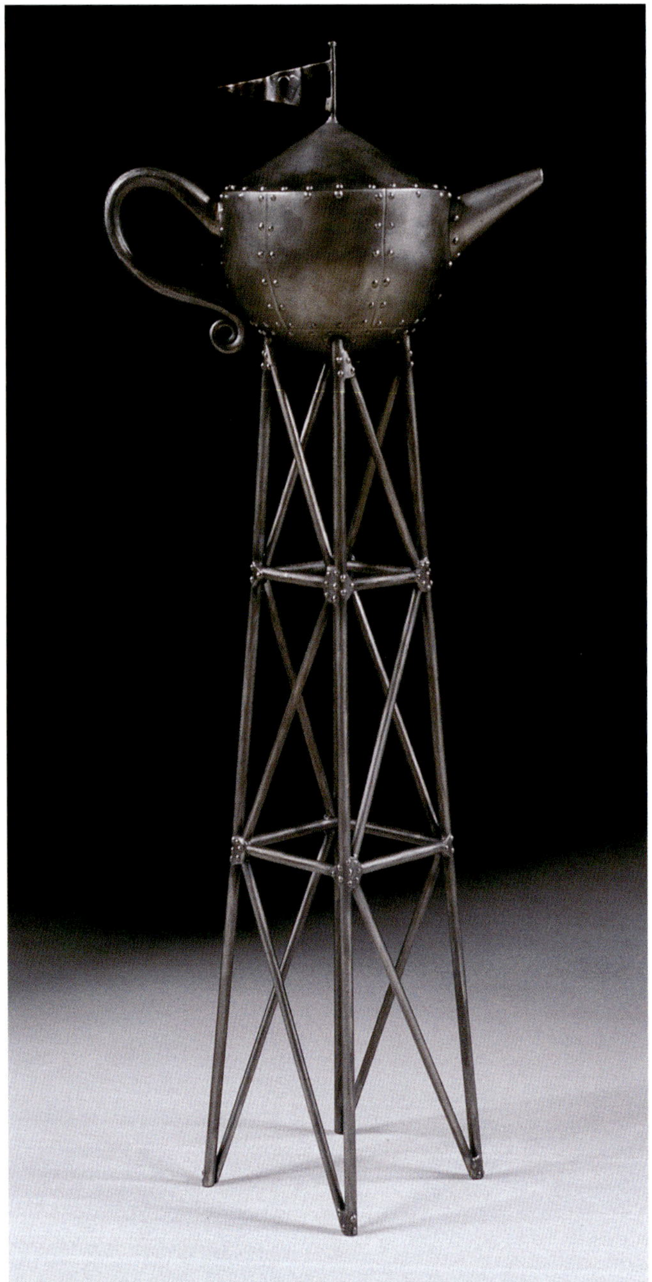

David Gignac. *Love's Water Tower Teapot.* Forged and fabricated steel with a wax finish. 32" high, 12" wide, 6" deep. *Photo, artist*

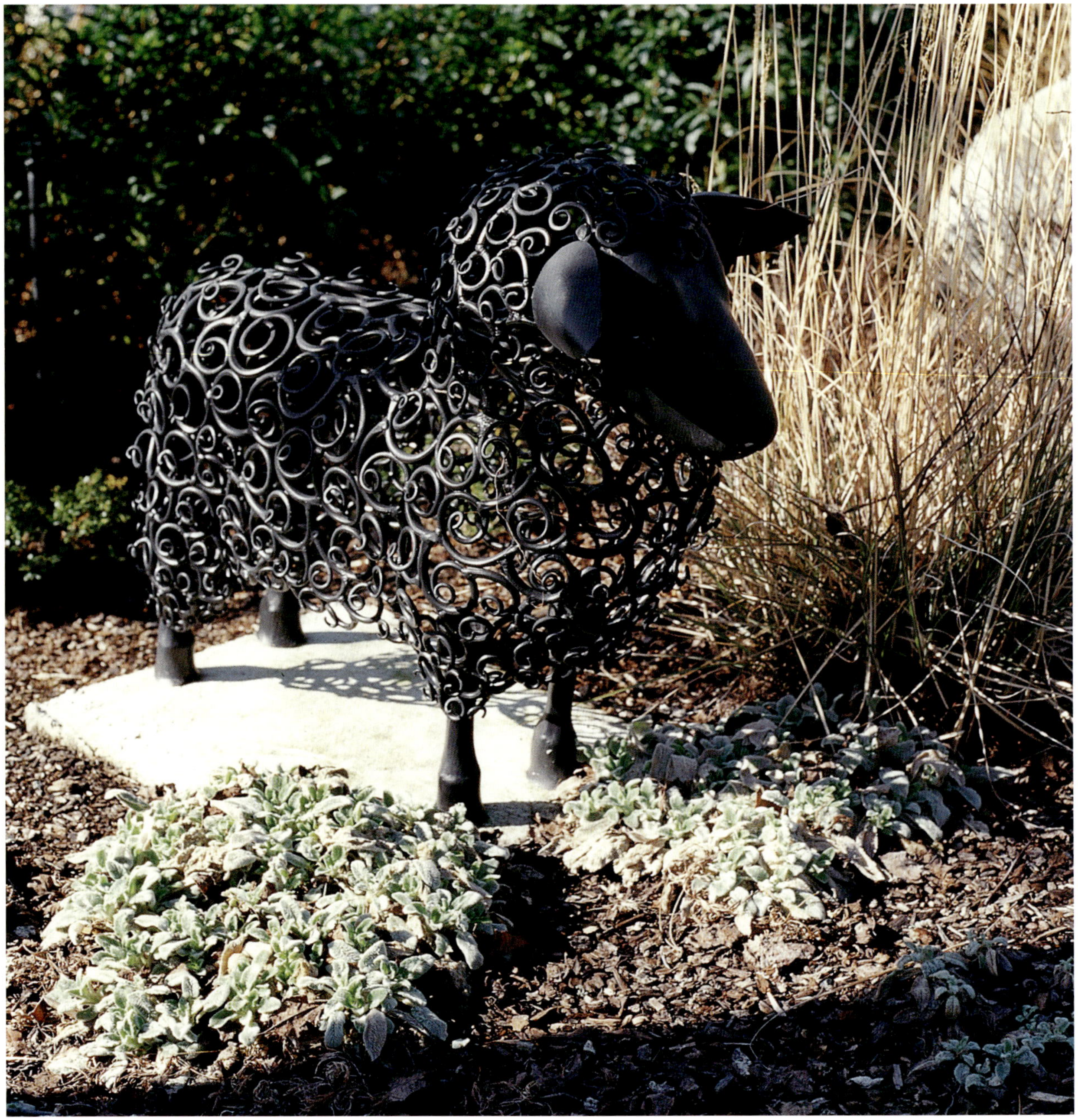

Scott Szloch. *Wooly Sheep.* 20" high, 40" wide, 15" deep. *Photo, artist*

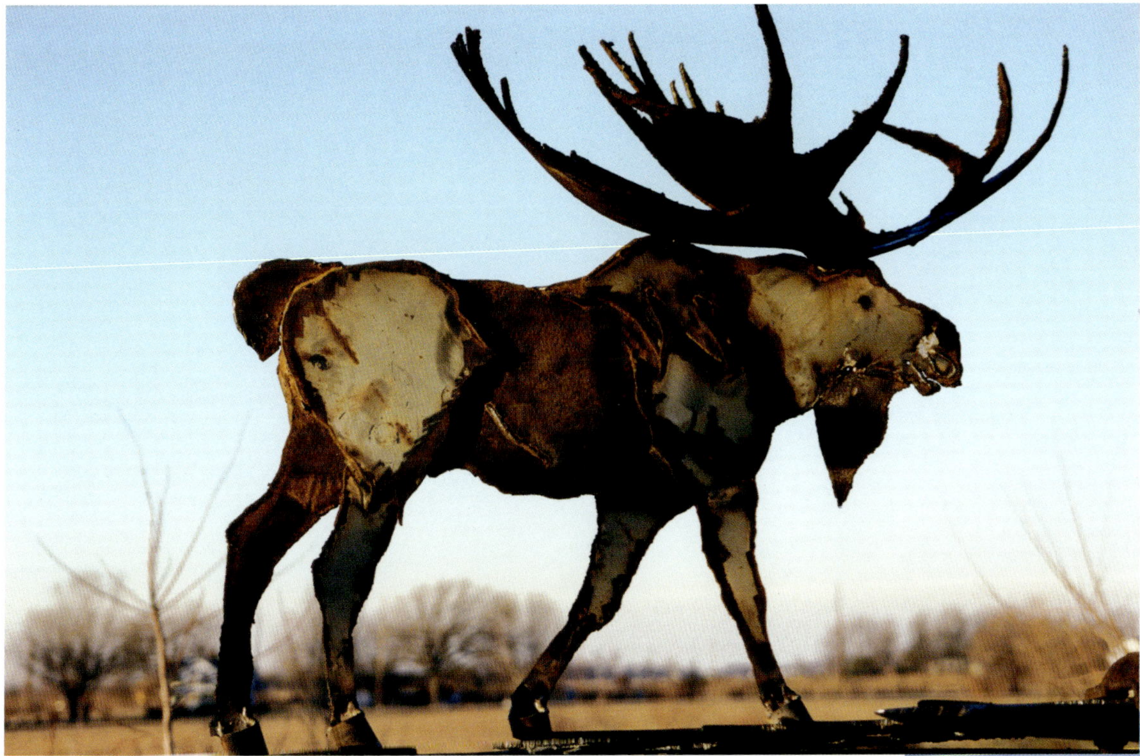

Mike Sohikian. *Moose.* Forged and fabricated steel. 35' high, 2.5' wide 2' deep. *Collection, Cecil and Connie Barker, Swanton, Ohio. Photo, artist*

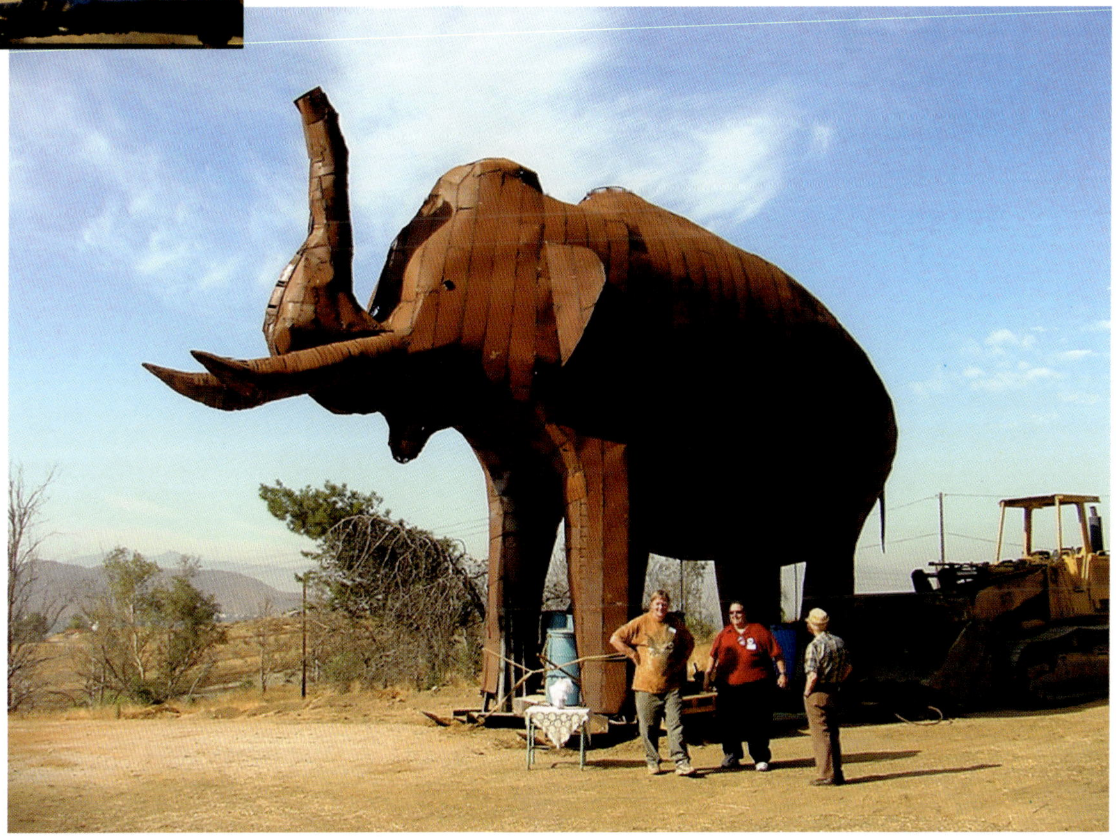

Klaus Duebbert. *Wooly Mammoth*. Bar steel and 16-gauge metal strips. Installed at the Jurupa Mountains Cultural Center, Riverside, California. 40' high, 27' wide. *Photo, artist*

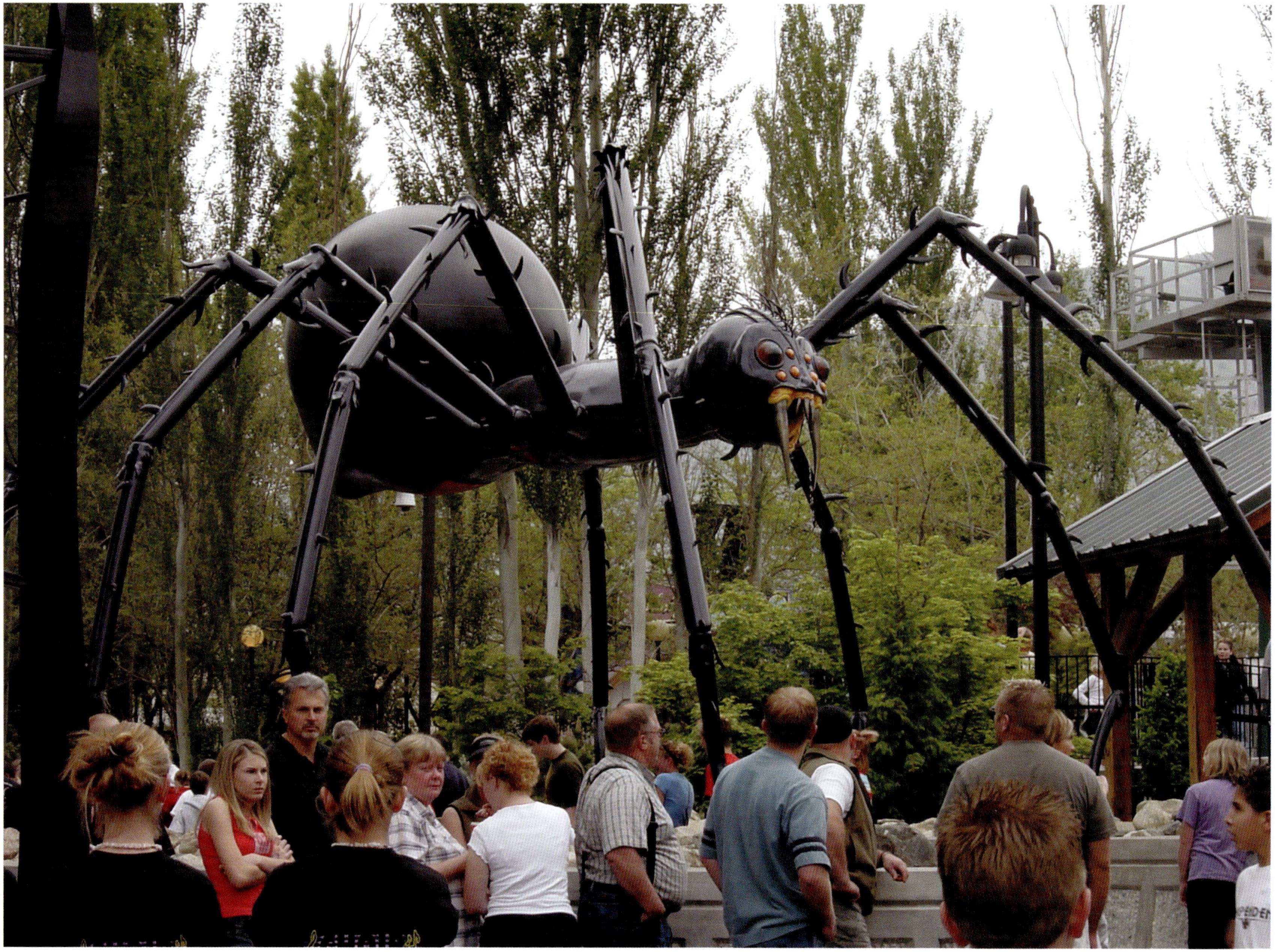

Richard Prazen. *Black Widow Spider* for the entrance to a theme park ride. Riders walk through the legs of this unlikely drooling, hissing, giant steel Black Widow spider. It was created with the artistry, brain, and brawn of the dedicated team of blacksmiths at Pioneer Manufacturing and Blacksmithing, Inc. West Valley City, Utah. 14' high, 27' diam. *Photo, artist*

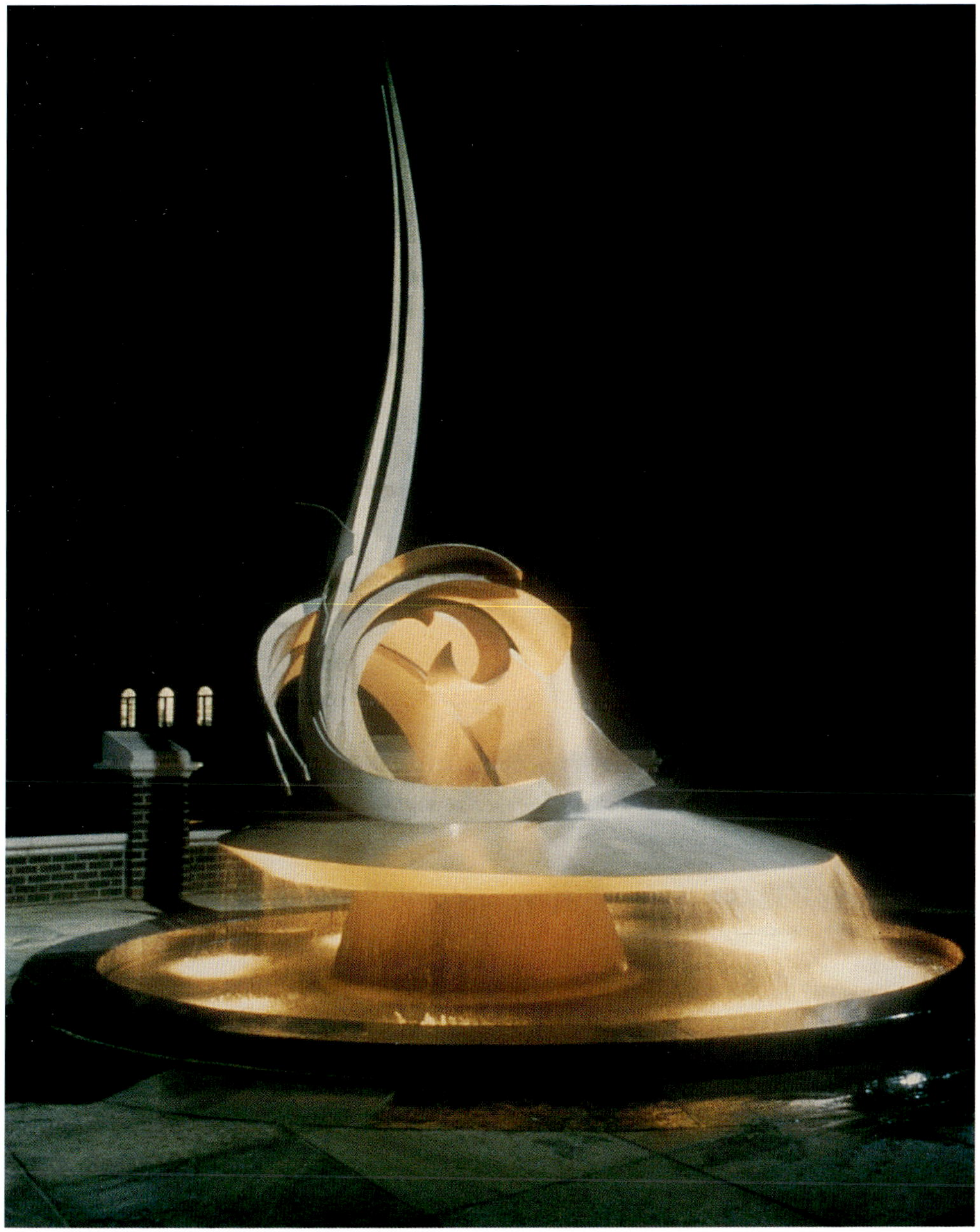

John Medwedeff. *Millennium Plaza Fountain*. Forged and fabricated bronze. Clarksville, Tennessee. 16' high, 8' wide, 9' deep. *Photo, artist*

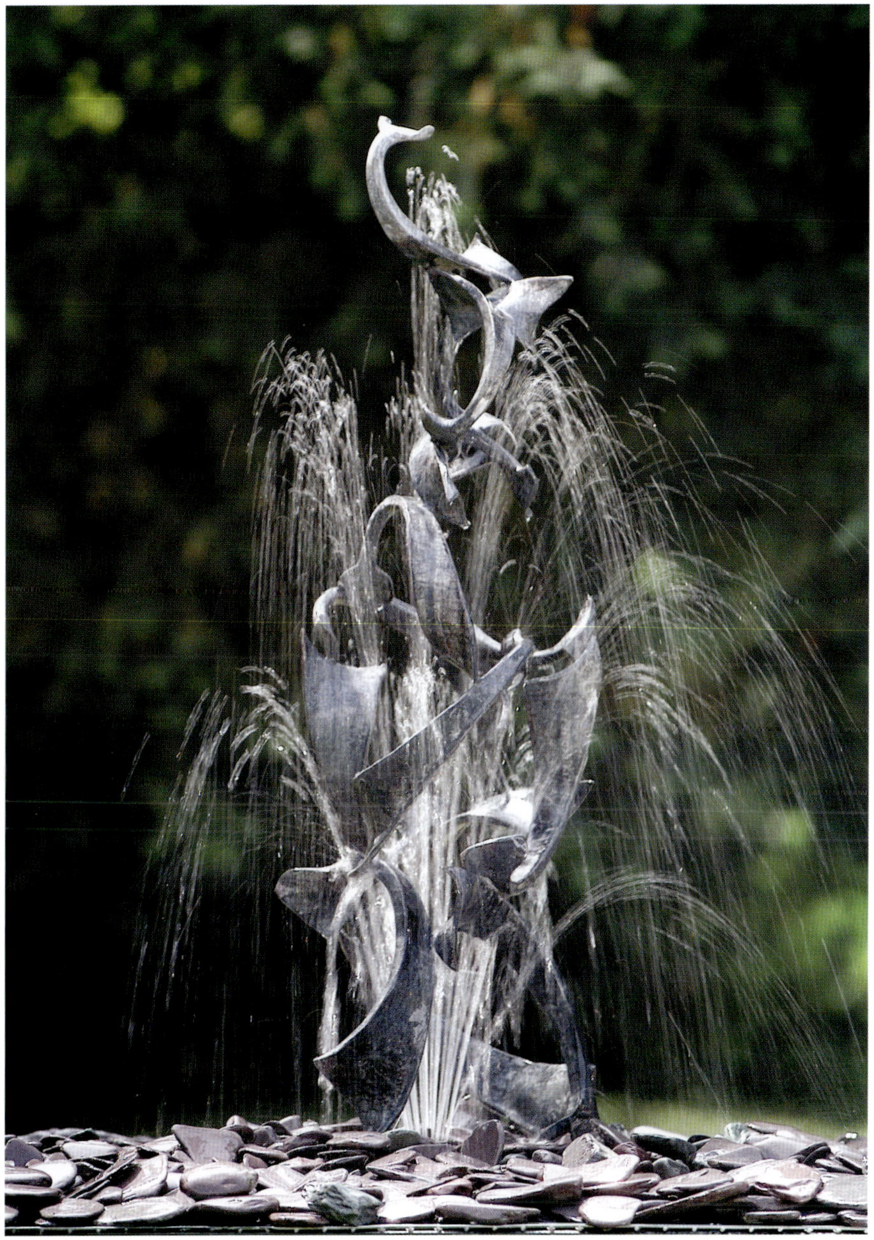

Paul Elliott. *Fish Fountain.* Mild steel galvanised and acid etched. For this small water sculpture for a private garden, the object was to create movement and sound. A built-in movement is designed to fling water droplets from various points of the fountain to create a glistening, sparkling ornament suggesting fish leaping up a waterfall. 37" high. *Photo, Jackie Phillips*

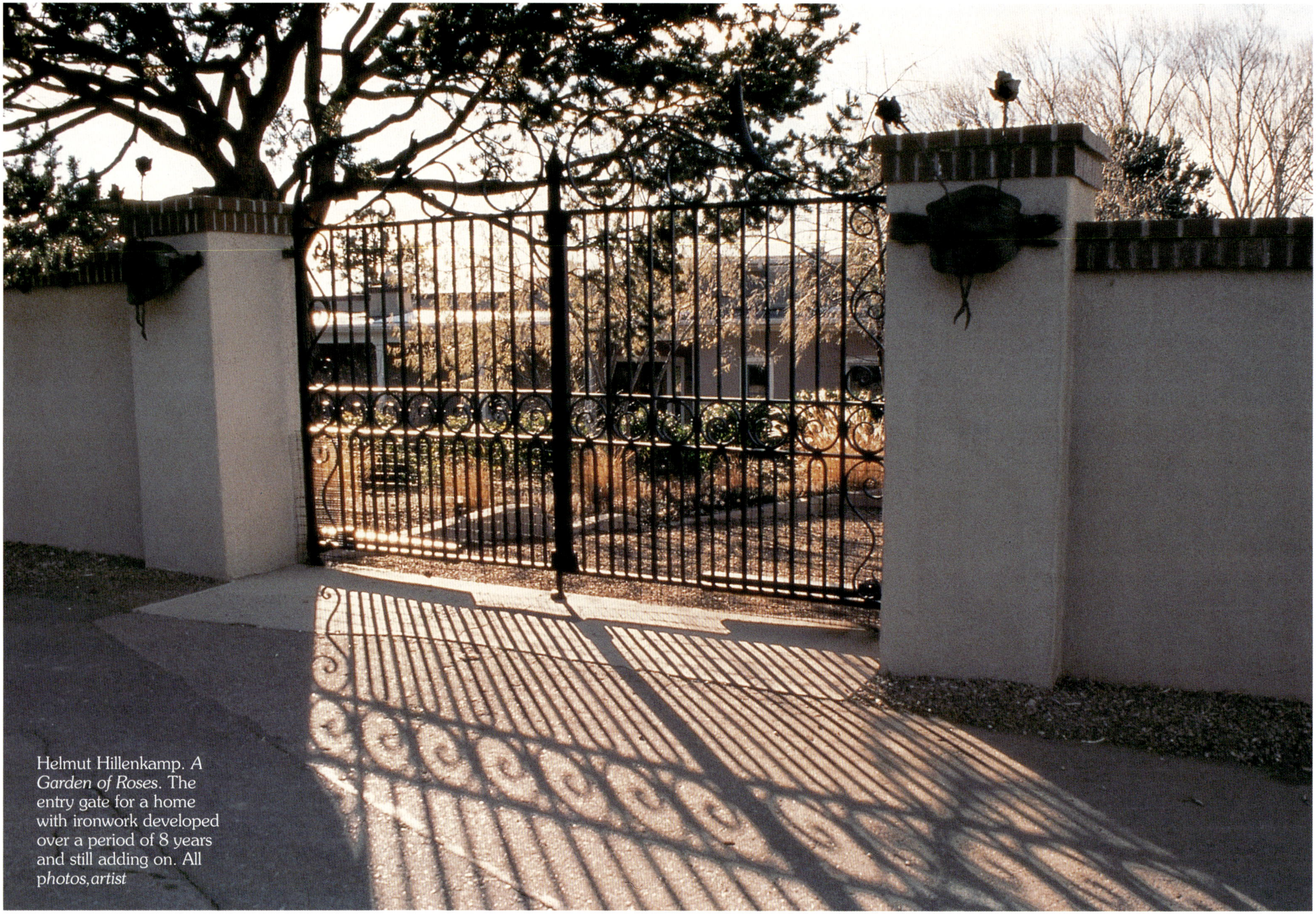

Helmut Hillenkamp. *A Garden of Roses*. The entry gate for a home with ironwork developed over a period of 8 years and still adding on. All *photos,artist*

Chapter 2. All-encompassing Projects

Sometimes commissions come along that require total immersion on the part of the artist-blacksmith. In the following examples, homeowners, designers, builders, and architects have engaged the artist-blacksmith to be totally involved in creating an environment around a theme. Such a commission can test the talents of those involved, and often the challenge is too good to pass up. The smiths and their helpers have devoted thousands of hours to the commissions shown in this chapter. Their decisions and experiences can serve as examples to other smiths and to anyone who may commission ironwork. Fortunately, each artist has photographed the processes and final pieces. Helmut Hillenkamp has developed a DVD showing his work. Robb Gunter and Robert C. Bentley both have CD's showing their projects as they developed. These make excellent chronicles of the work and serve as promotions for future jobs.

Helmut Hillenkamp of Santa Fe, New Mexico, worked with a homeowner whose passion for roses was expressed in ironwork décor. These iron roses have been blooming for over 8 years and show no sign of diminishing. Robb Gunter of Tijeras, New Mexico, and his two sons, Brad and Chad, devoted nearly two years to creating interior and exterior ironwork for a home in Arizona. It meant refusing, or delaying, projects for other clients while they devoted all their time, energies, and resources to the needs for this one stately residence.

Robert C. Bentley gave up his 26-year-old ironwork establishment to work full time for one client, the Martin & Weyrich Winery. In a short time he brought in four other smiths to create all the ironwork for a new resort, The Villa Toscana, in Paso Robles, California.

Restoration of an old hotel in Miami, Florida's, South Beach area proved an all-consuming project for several months for John Boyd Smith, of Savannah, Georgia. And Nick Such tackled the conversion of a garage into an artist's studio in Sierra Madre, California.

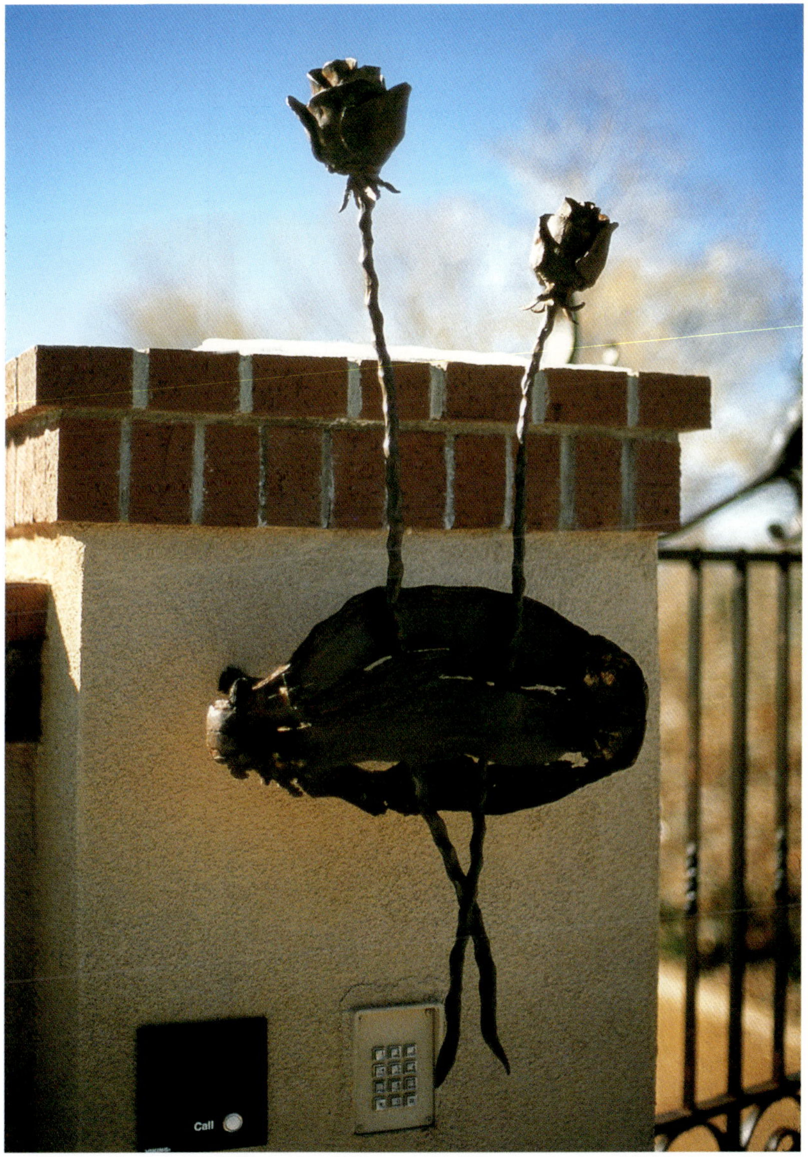

Helmut Hillenkamp. Sconce with roses on posts at each side of the entry gate.

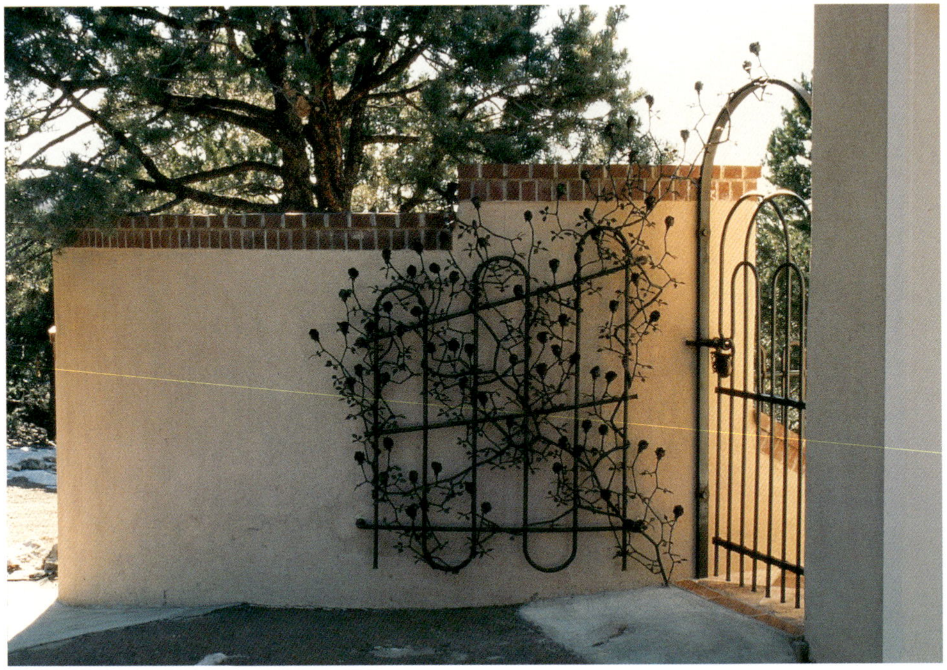

Helmut Hillenkamp. Trellis and gate with roses. *Photo, artist*

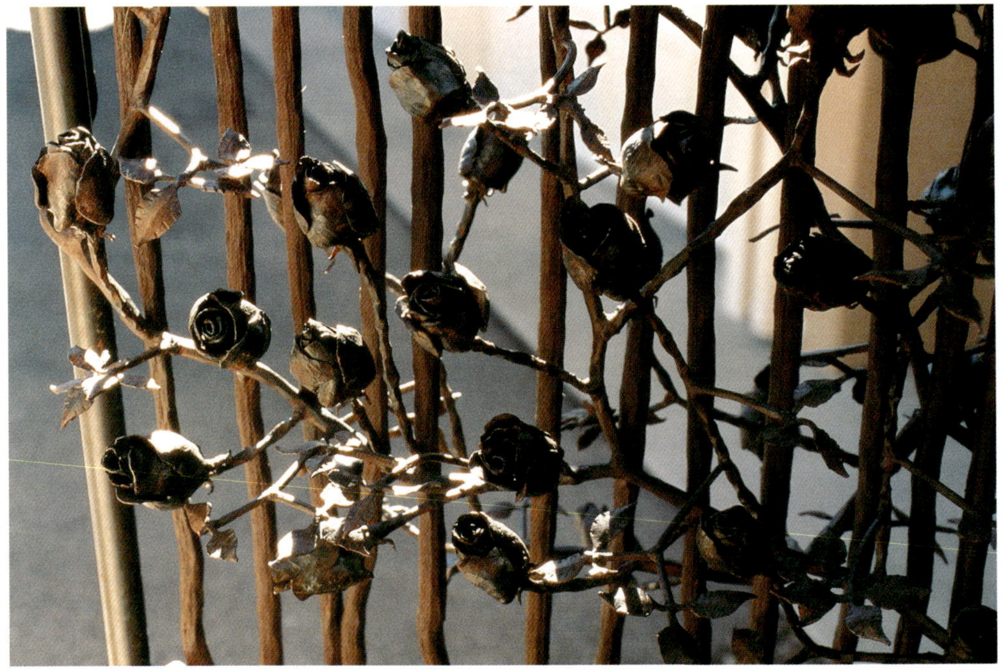

Helmut Hillenkamp. Detail of roses on the trellis…each rose is formed from one piece of round steel.

Helmet Hillenkamp's Garden of Roses

Helmut Hillenkamp recalls that his work on the house incorporating the Sleeping Beauty motif began in 1996 after he had just won his Green Card and was able to work legally in the United States. His ad in the yellow pages saying he would work with "German reliability and excellence", brought a phone call from a handyman in Santa Fe, New Mexico, who needed someone to build an iron gate to replace a wooden one that often blew down. He says, "Little did I know that this job would eventually turn into the most exciting and longest lasting relationship with a customer so far."

Over the next eight years, about 2500 hours were required for creating gates, railings, light fixtures, and hundreds of hand-forged roses growing in a Sleeping Beauty motif over an iron bench, a trellis, and several gates.

The house, originally built in the forties by John Gaw Meem, a famous local architect, had been dropped from the historic register because of the owner's creative additions. Notes Hillenkamp, "It is no longer historically correct, but it is more beautiful than before and filled with a sprit of aliveness and freedom, retaining a sense of tradition and integrity that develops with the times."

Hillenkamp's first gate was modern with a minimal design using some structural interweaving and a fancy lock by Manuel Guerra of Ecuador.

A year later, the owner added a driveway and hired Hillenkamp to create two large driveway gates for which he used mortise and tenon joinery and no electrical or oxyacetylene welding. He says, "It took 1000 hours and, fortunately, I had a number of journeymen students from Germany and England who helped." Unfortunately he had underbid the job, but the owner sent him a Christmas letter with a $5000 tip which was a happy surprise and put things into balance again.

Shortly later came another commission for outside lighting. Hillenkamp evolved rough Damascus steel, worked it with inventive techniques and muriatic acid to achieve the desired finish. The owner requested roses as part of the design. The large size required Hillenkamp to develop a way to forge roses differently from any he had ever seen. Each rose is made from one piece of a length of 1" round metal stock (the method can be found on his Web site). There were thirteen fixtures on outside walls. Later, additional roses were used on a small outside bench where real roses in season mingle with the iron roses.

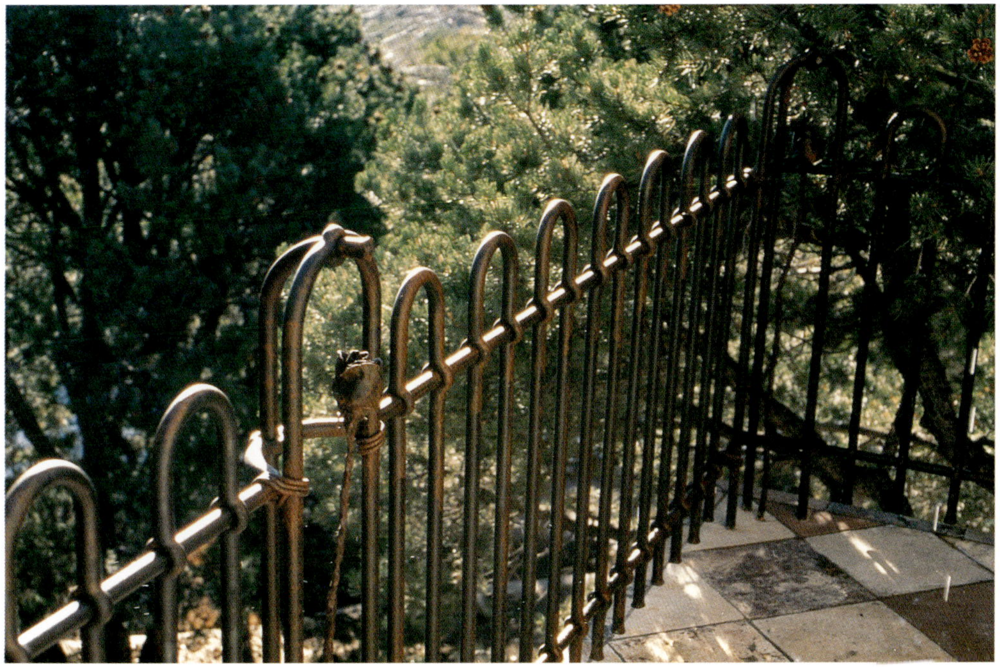

Helmut Hillenkamp. Fence. *Photo, artist*

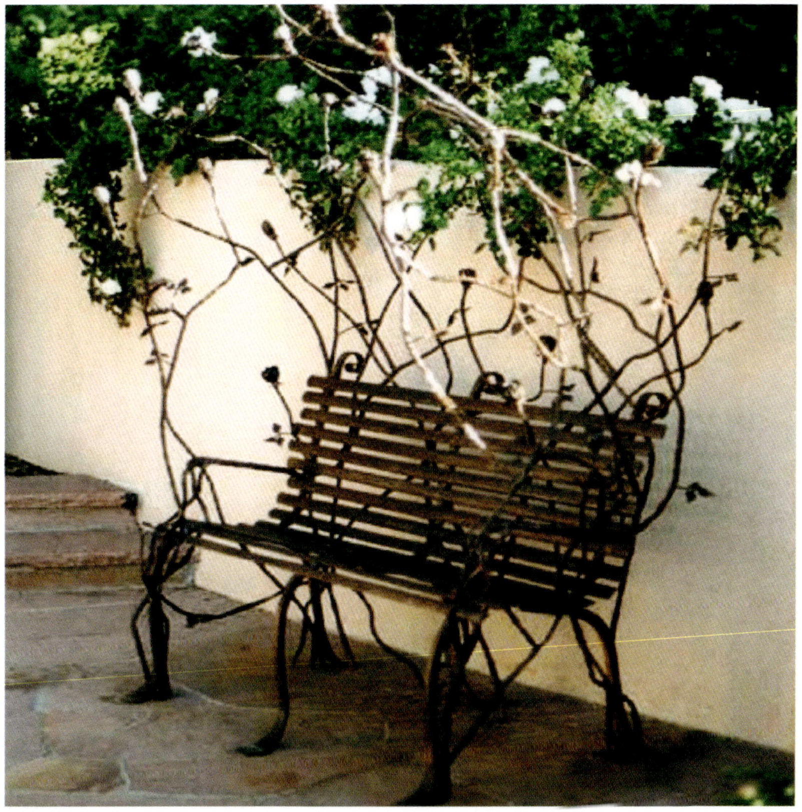

Helmut Hillenkamp. Bench with roses. *Photo, artist*

These projects were followed with a commission for 150 feet of banister railing. Every post has a small niche in which a lonely rose grows. A back entry gate using the same theme was his next project commission.

The entrance to the guesthouse courtyard has a forged iron gate emulating weathered wood. It looks like an "overgrown wild head of hair of roses". It too, has an intricate lock by Manuel Guerra. An ironwork rose covered trellis is next to the first gate, on the other side of the driveway.

There are also the beginnings of a small forged greenhouse, and at this writing he is working on a hand made, forge welded driveway chain hanging from a large post. Of course, iron roses will be growing up this post, too.

Hillenkamp says that working on this house has been a fruitful, challenging, and rewarding time. Creating an entire environment over a decade is unusual, as is using true traditional techniques in innovative ways. He is grateful for his many helpers and students. He especially wants to acknowledge the work of Christen Boyd and Adam Frank who have shared the labor and excitement of this opportunity.

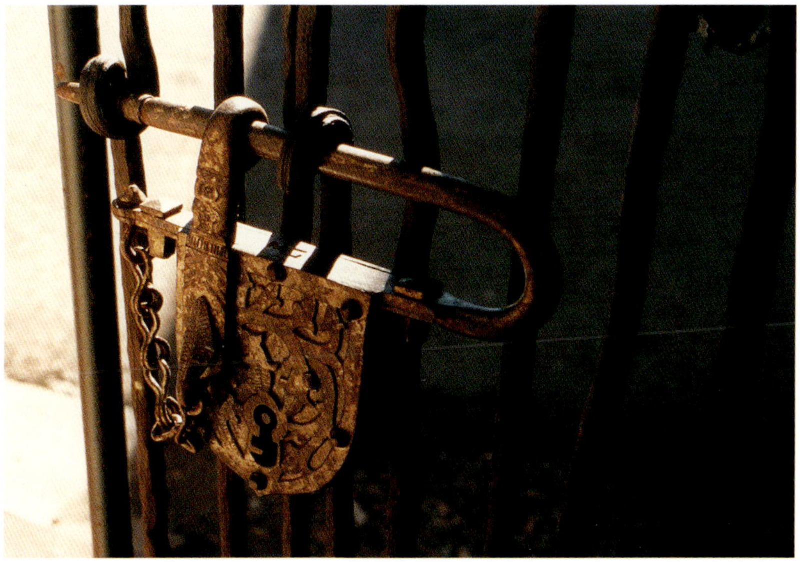

Manuel Guerra, Hand made lock. *Courtesy and photo, Helmut Hillenkamp*

Robb Gunter's Gamble

When Robb Gunter of Tijeras, New Mexico was contacted to create everything for a new home in Arizona, it offered a lifetime opportunity. It was also a job that would require him, his two sons, and a few other helpers, to devote nearly two years to the job and tell their other good customers they would have to wait.

The project designer, Morrelli, provided concept sketches of each piece with the understanding that the Gunters would have artistic freedom to make changes where needed and add details as long he maintained the overall design esthetics. All technical aspects of making everything work, fit, and function were Gunter's responsibility. That included wiring chandeliers to comply with UL Code, and the support structures for lifting and hanging the heavy chandeliers. All this was to be hidden above the carved ceilings...problems that required engineering, experience, problem solving, and a lot of common sense.

Gunter explains that the two great room chandeliers each had 24 arms with 2 wires each. The Grand staircase chandelier required 50 wires inside the hollow of a black walnut center. The dining room fixture had two separate circuits in the one chandelier. One problem was locating a manufacturer who could produce the alabaster bowls and globes needed for the chandeliers and sconces. They had to be made in Spain.

Morelli provided clay models of the front entry door hardware, and paper models of the two sitting room chandeliers based on an Art Deco theme that was repeated in the entry door hardware and elsewhere in the ironwork for the residence. These were built with the help of Stephen Lee, a student of Gunter's. The curved glasswork was done by Denise Taylor. Other pieces were left to the Gunter's to design.

Robb and his sons, Brad and Chad, worked on the project for 22 months straight, usually about 60 hours a week. Each tackled the objects that they liked to do. They made only 9 trips to the job site to take measurements, make patterns and templates, and do installation. Only the hardware installation for the 53 doors was assigned to a door specialist.

Gunter smiles when he recalls that the initial contract was for only about one-third of the final project. "It just to continued to grow in scope and size."

The bottom line is that this once-in-a-lifetime gamble paid off and the results are stunning. His waiting clients were lined up when he was ready to return to work with them.

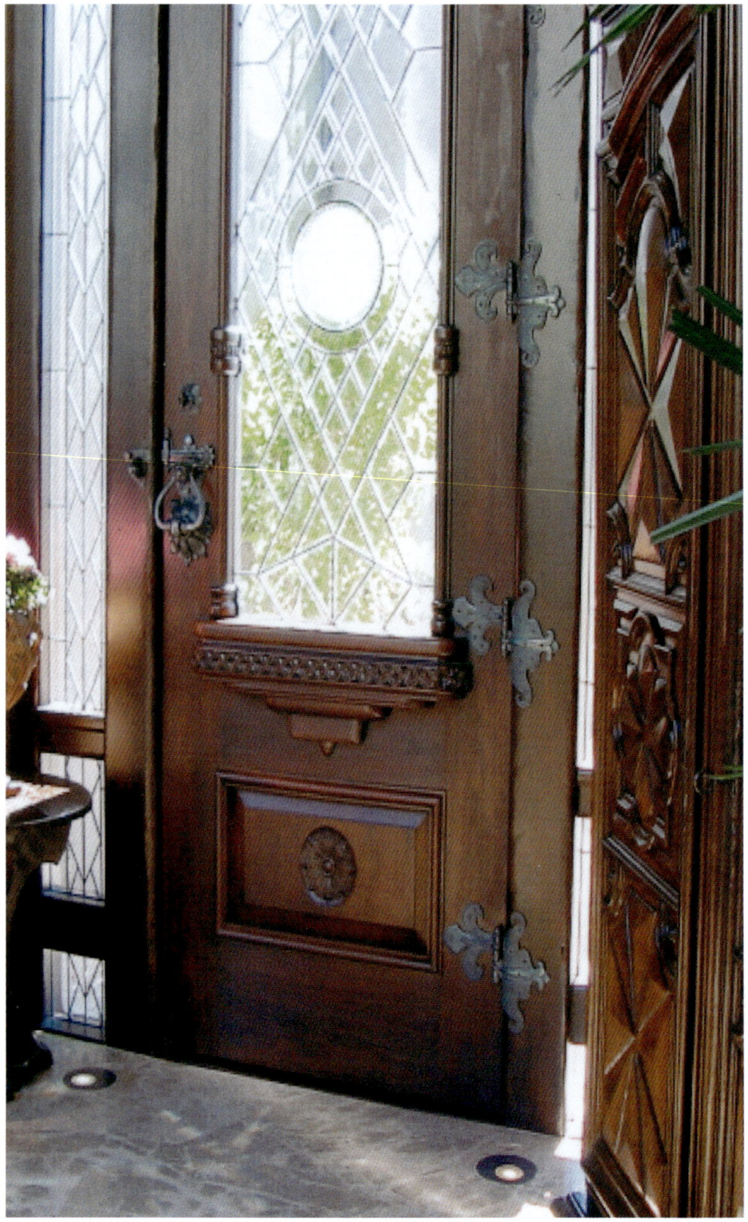

Robb Gunter. Doorknobs with decorative plates were produced for 52 doors. Knockers and hinges were hand made for the front entry door and pool gate. *All photos, Robb Gunter*

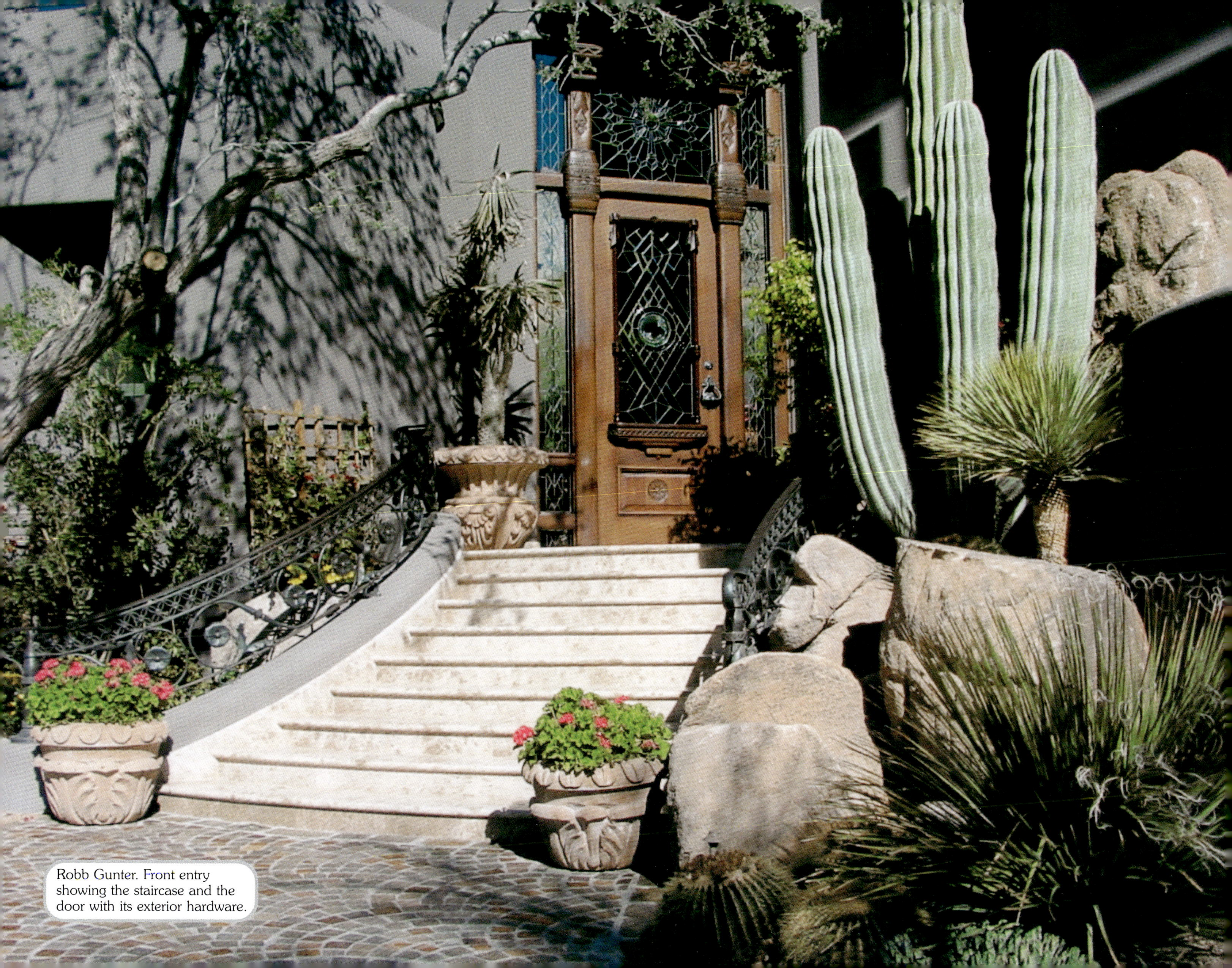

Robb Gunter. Front entry showing the staircase and the door with its exterior hardware.

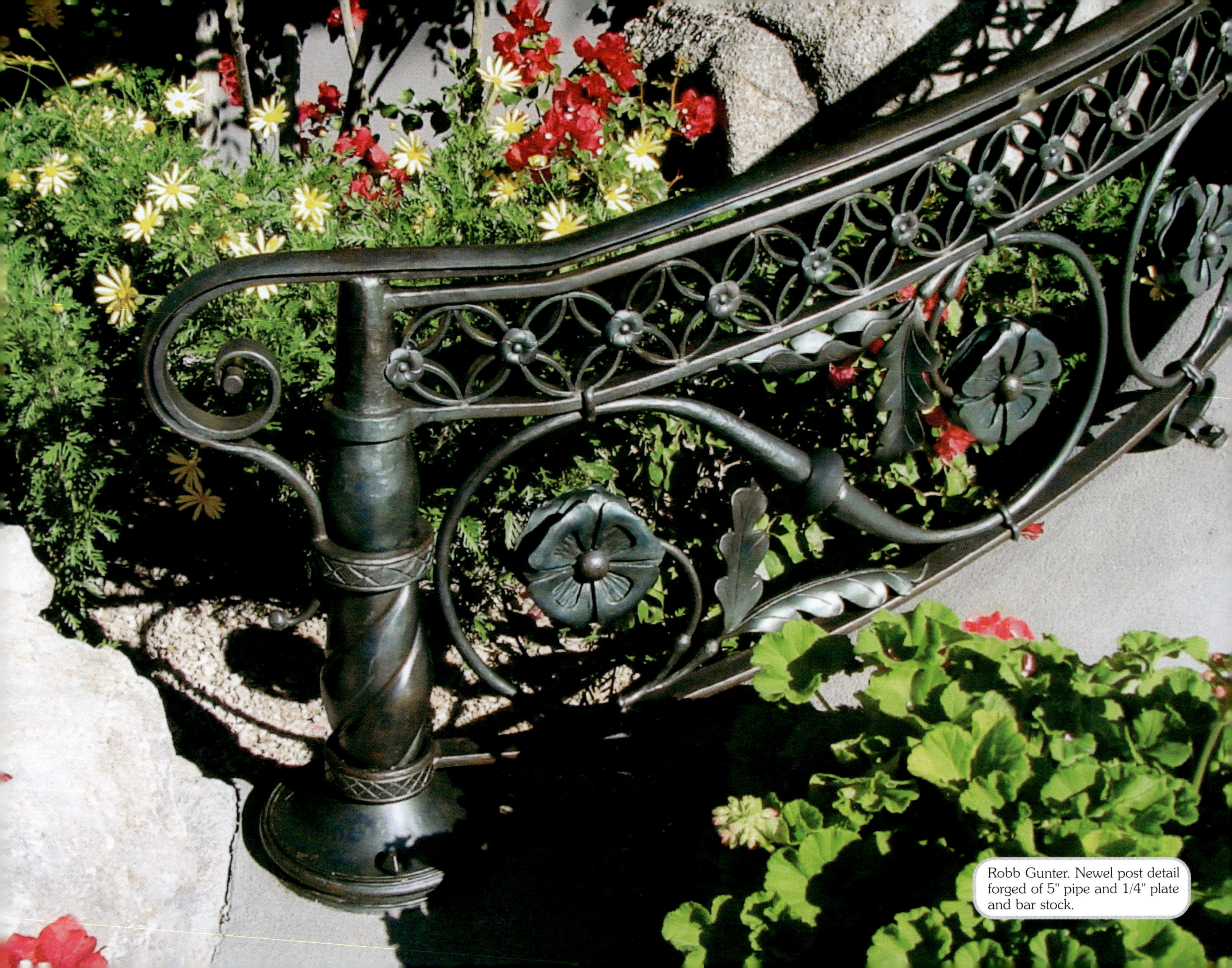

Robb Gunter. Newel post detail forged of 5" pipe and 1/4" plate and bar stock.

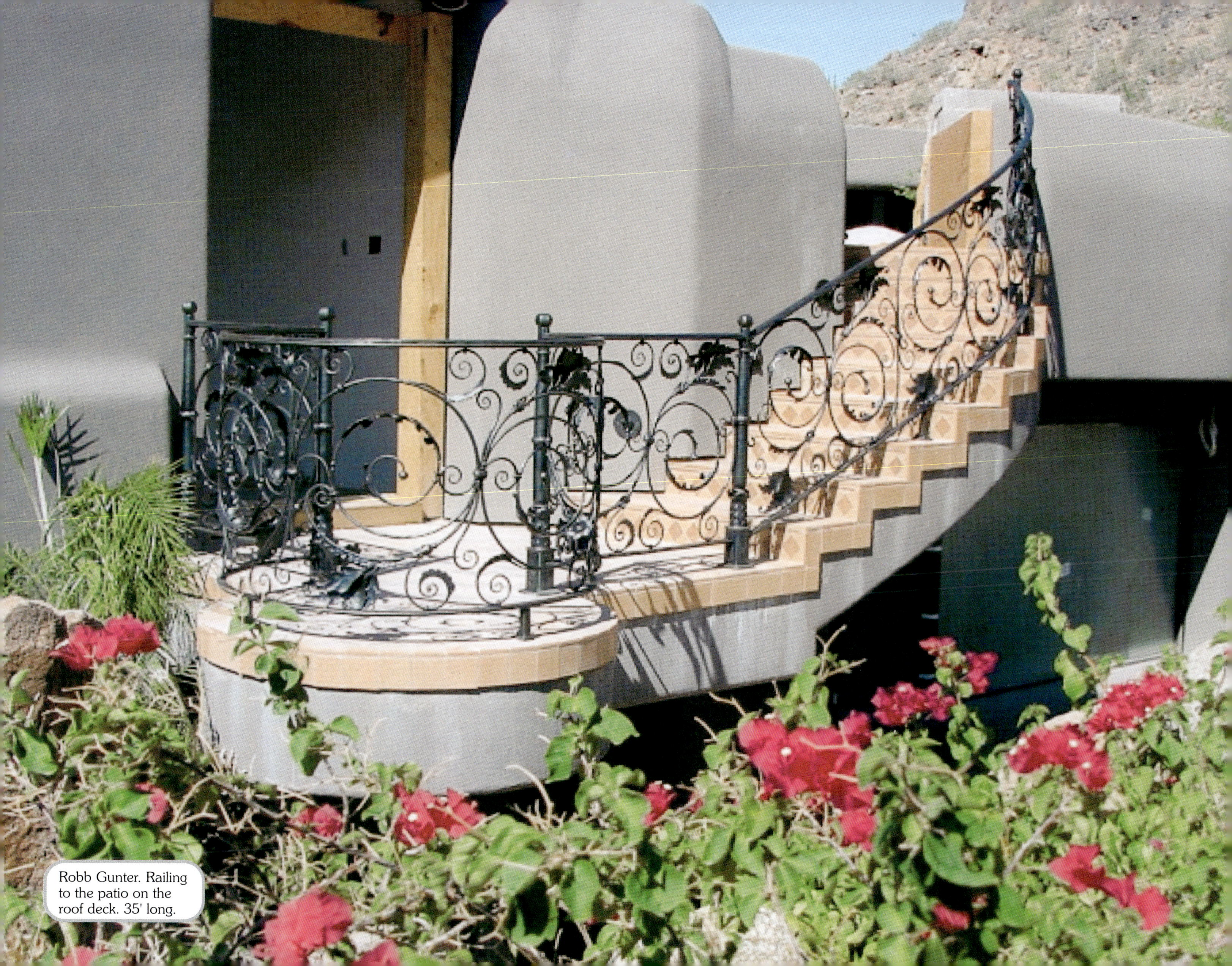

Robb Gunter. Railing to the patio on the roof deck. 35' long.

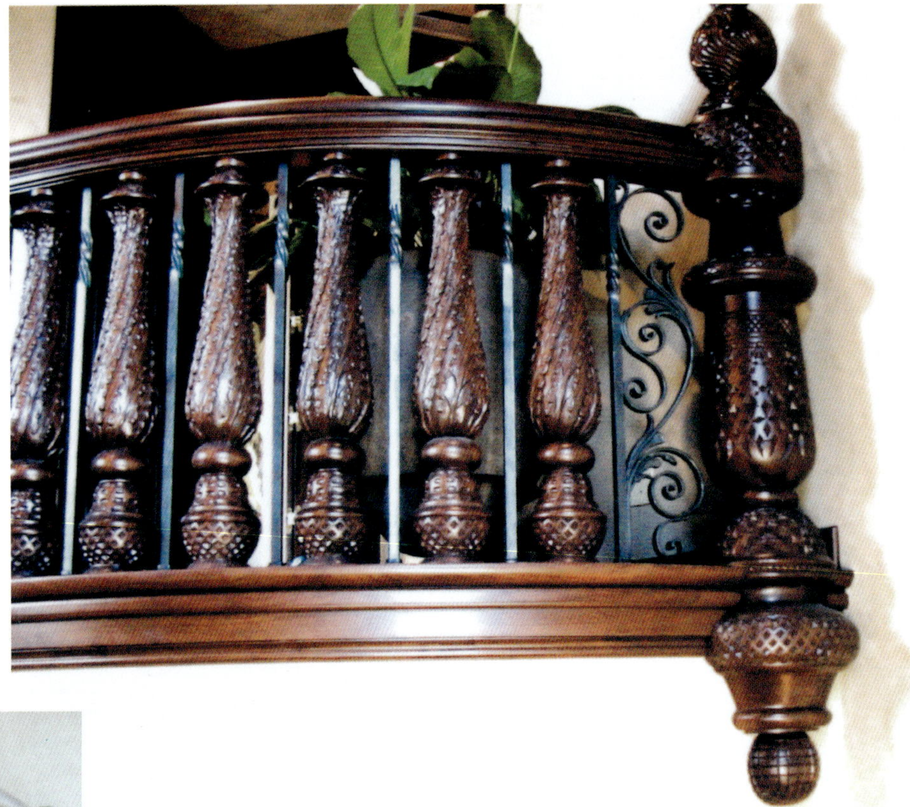

Robb Gunter. Upper newel and termination of the 360° circular grand staircase.

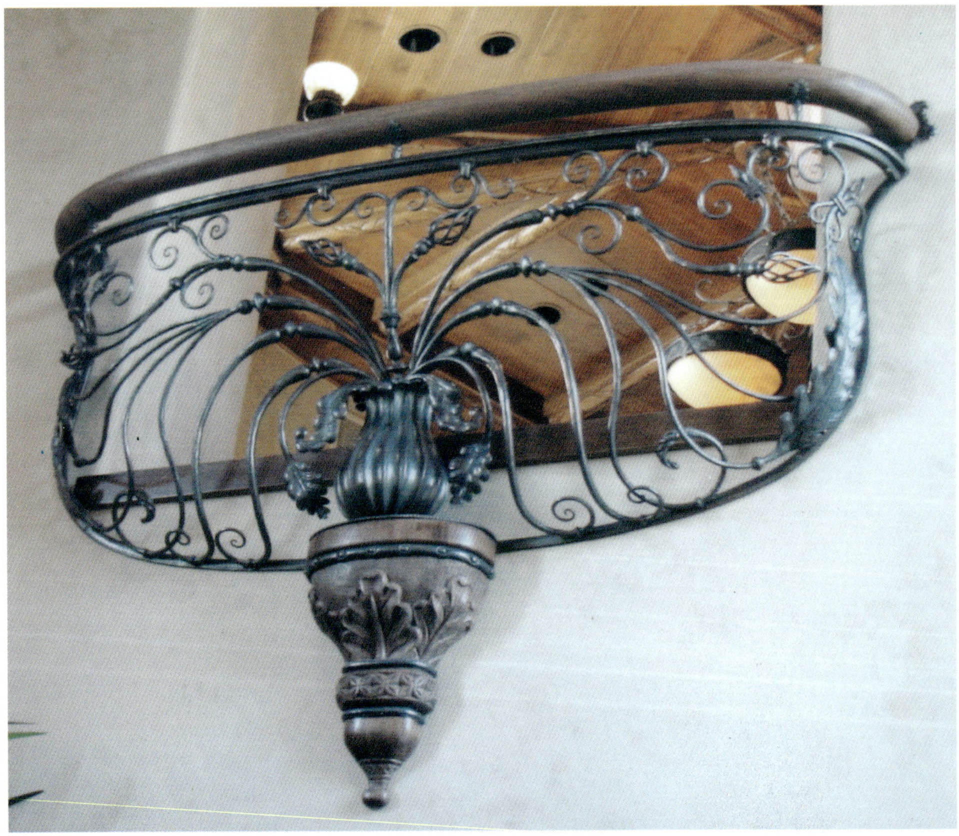

Robb Gunter. Romeo and Juliet balcony in the entry foyer.

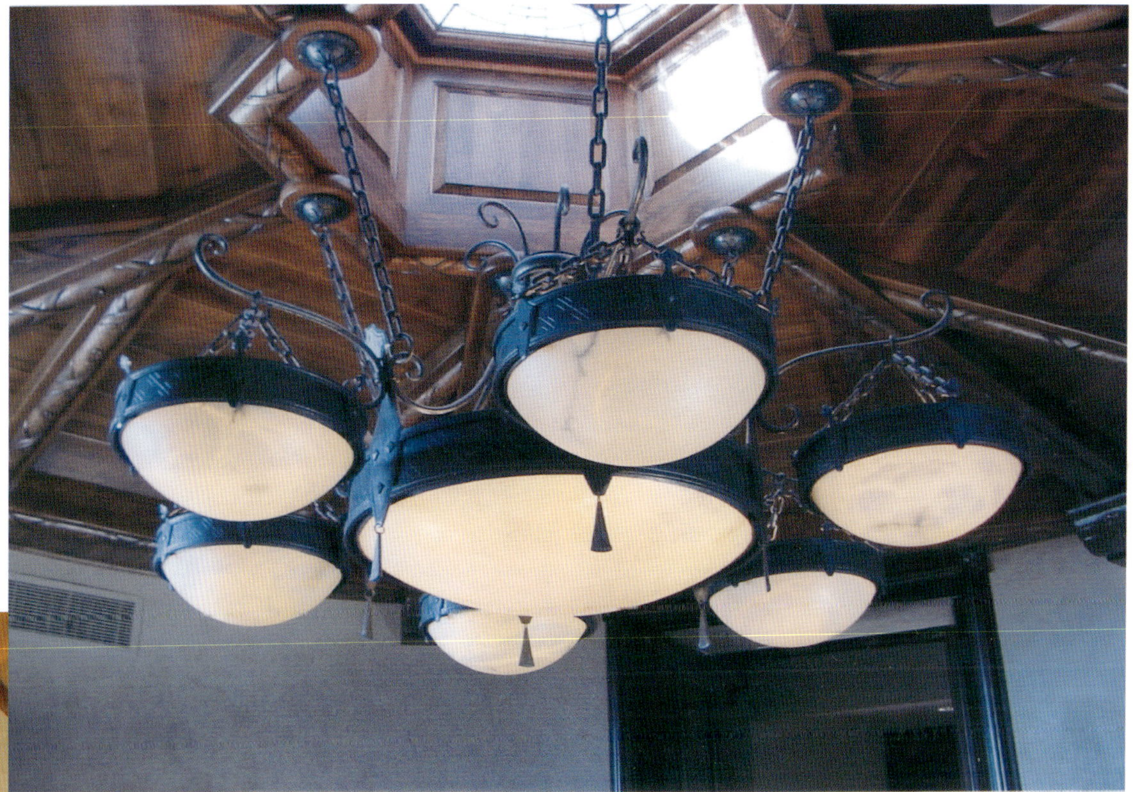

Chad Gunter. Grand staircase chandelier with alabaster bowls made in Spain. It represents a flower with the blooms opened up. 8' diam.

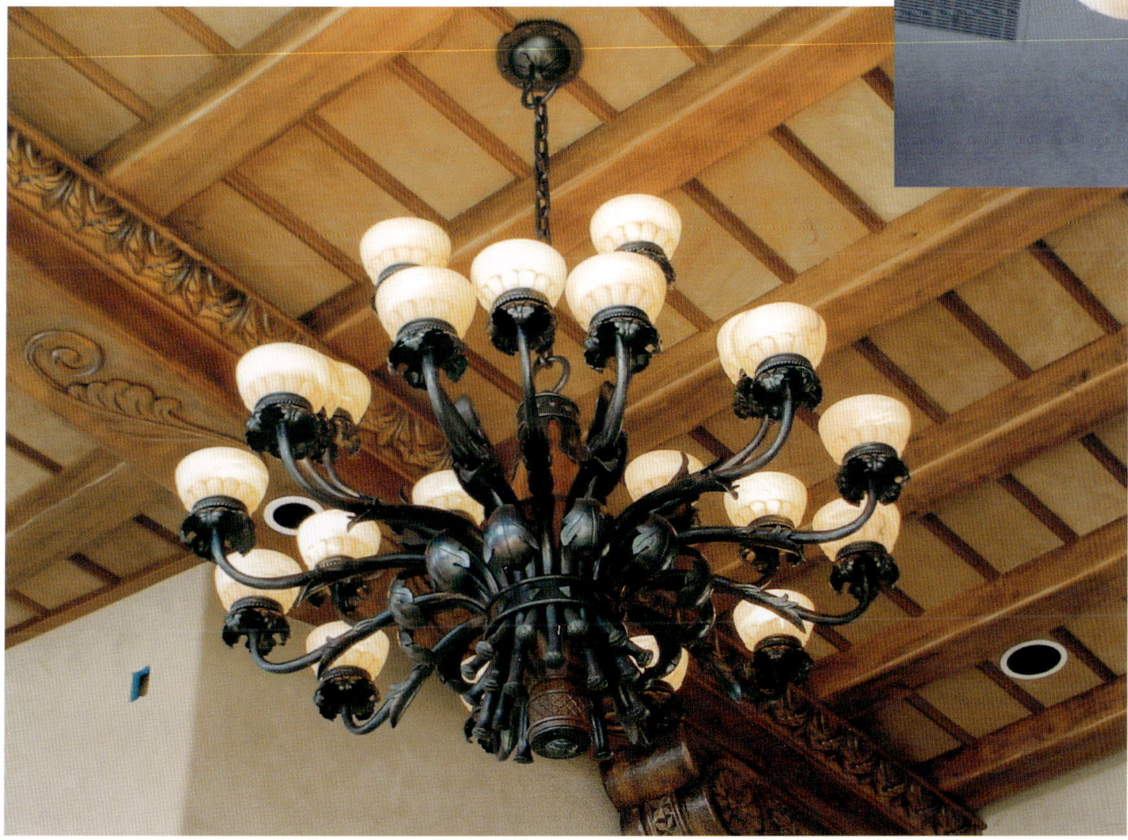

Brad and Chad Gunter. One of two great room chandeliers seen from below. Each has 24 arms and globes.

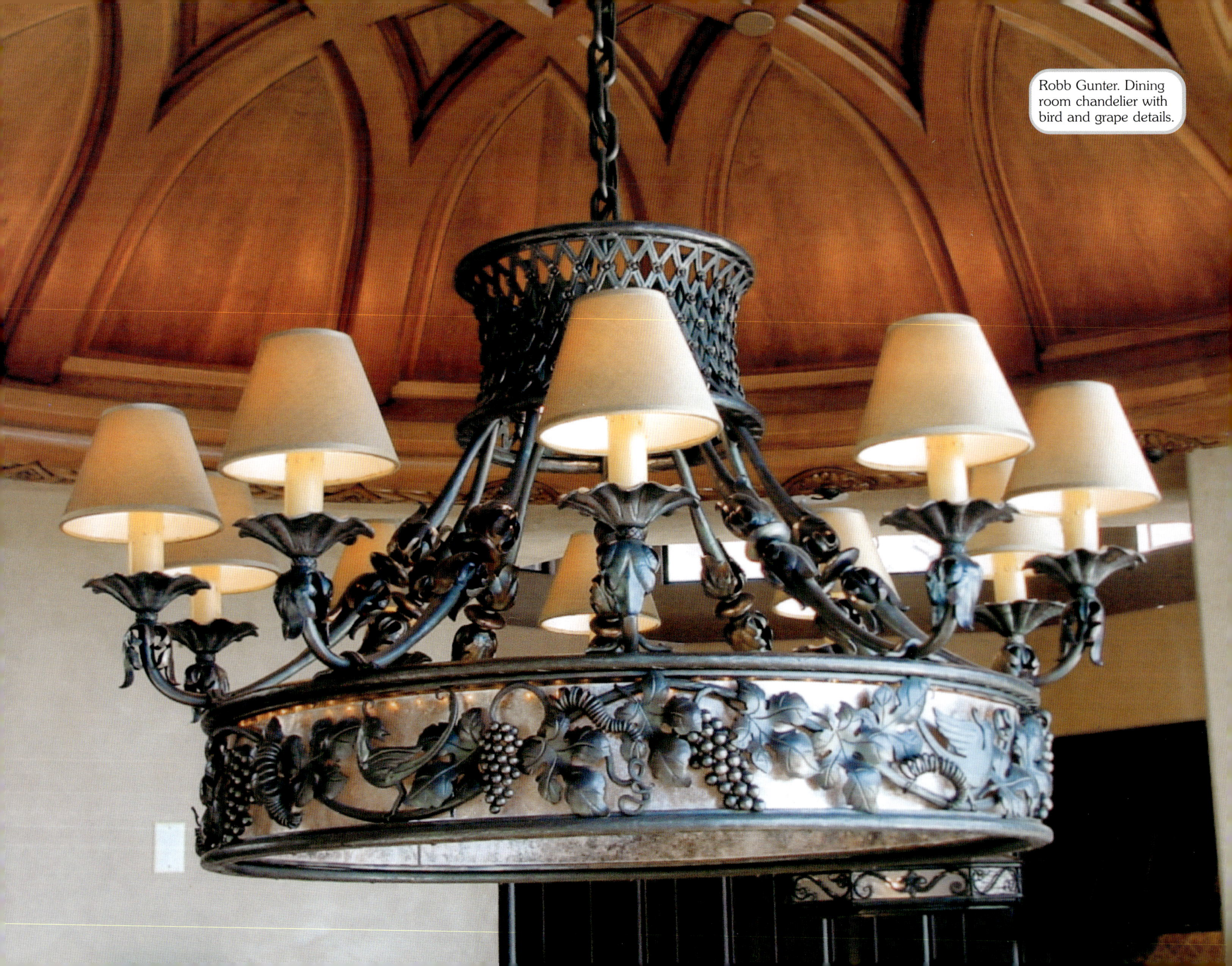

Robb Gunter. Dining room chandelier with bird and grape details.

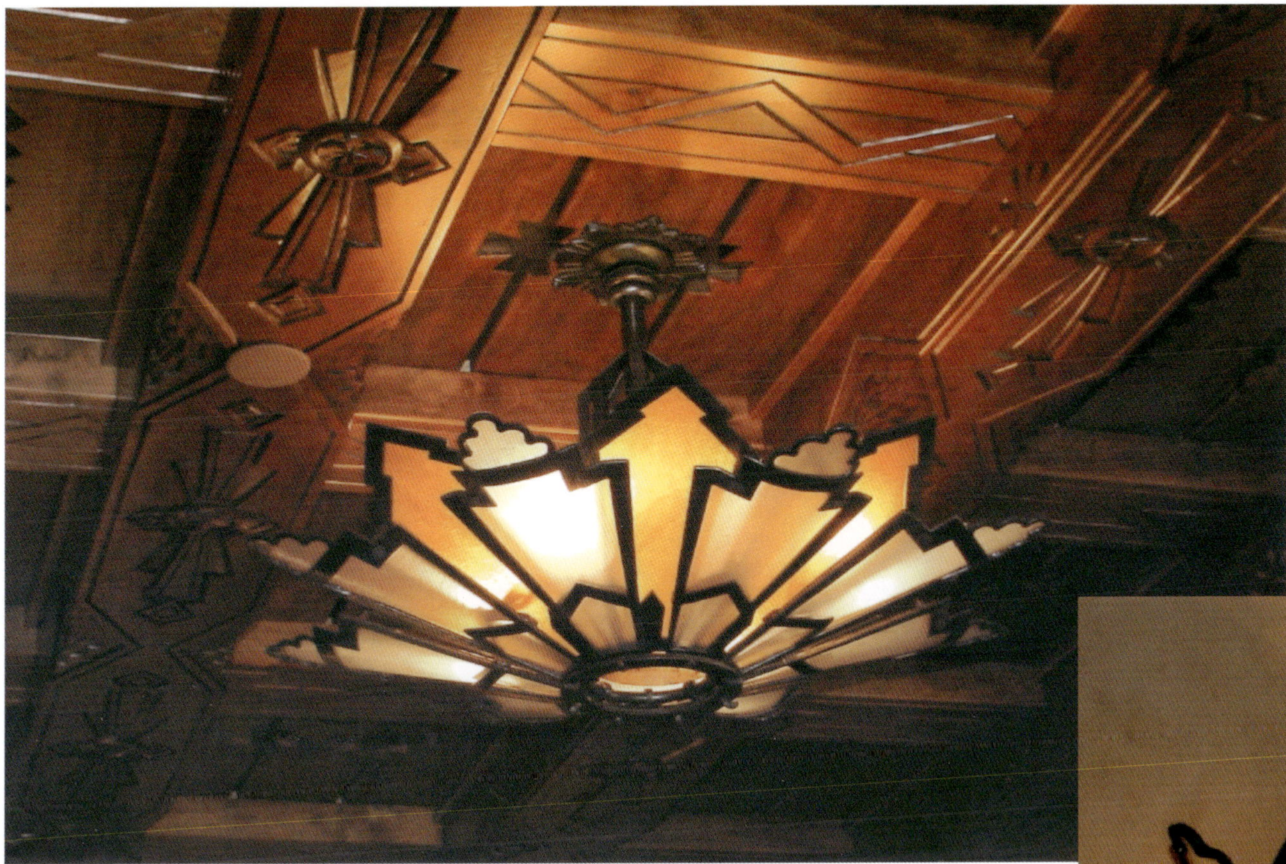

Robb Gunter. Slumped bowl fixture for galley ceiling.

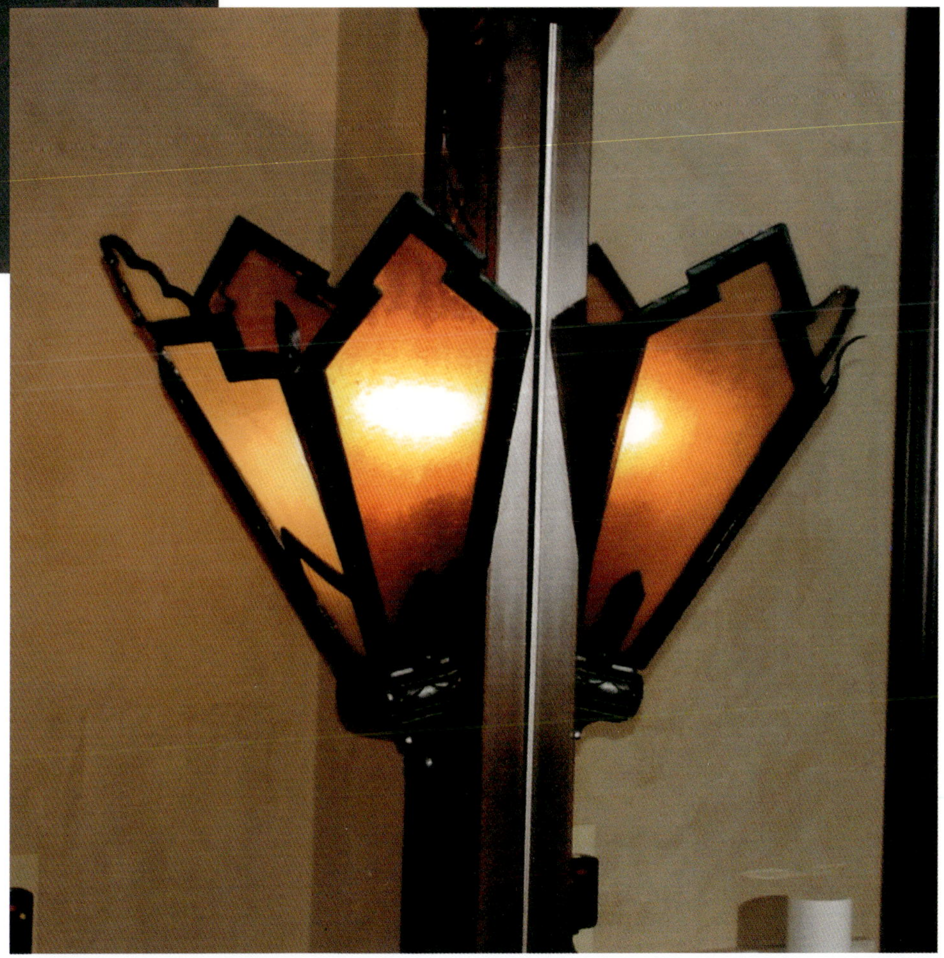

Robb Gunter. Wall sconce for guest bath.

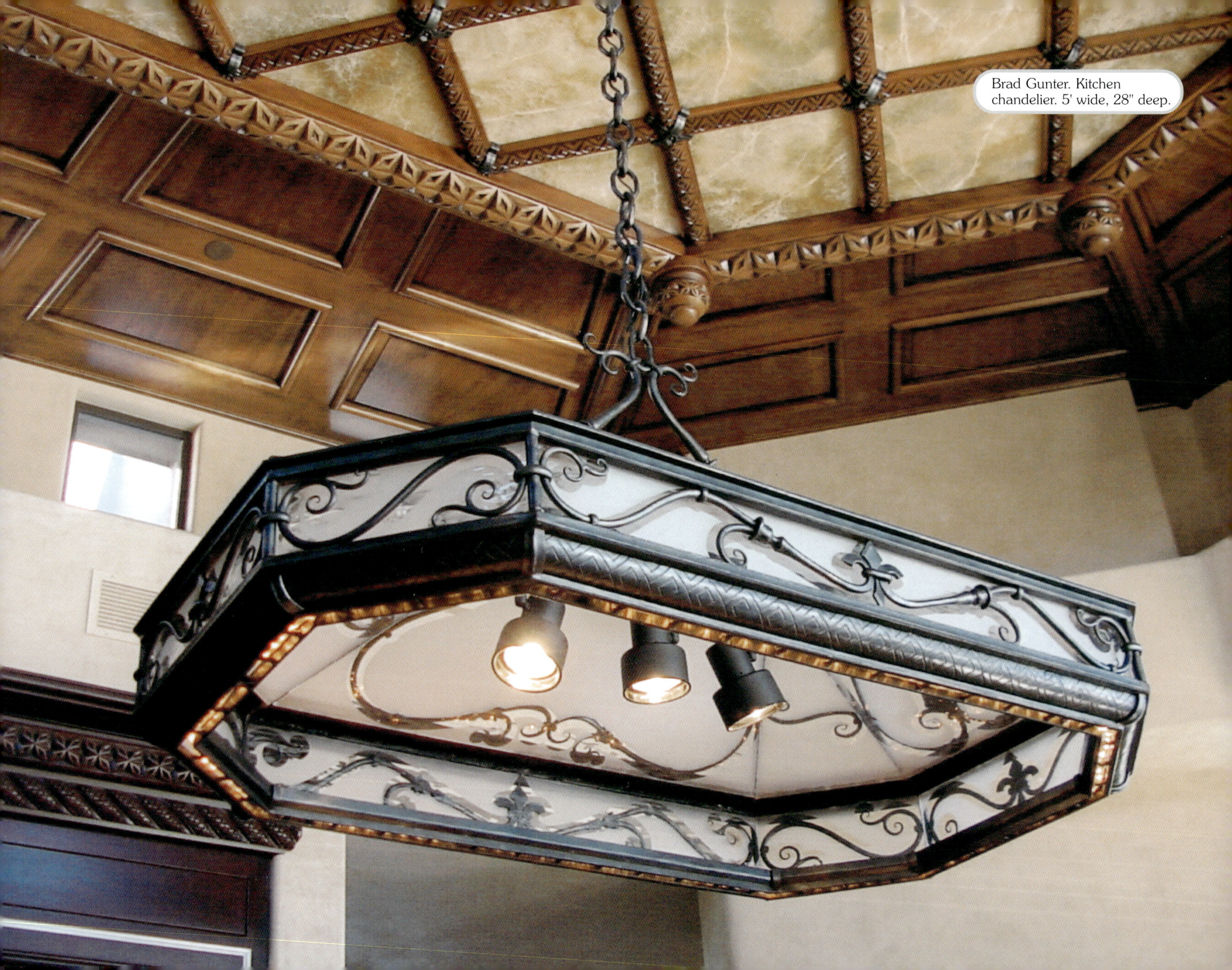

Brad Gunter. Kitchen chandelier. 5' wide, 28" deep.

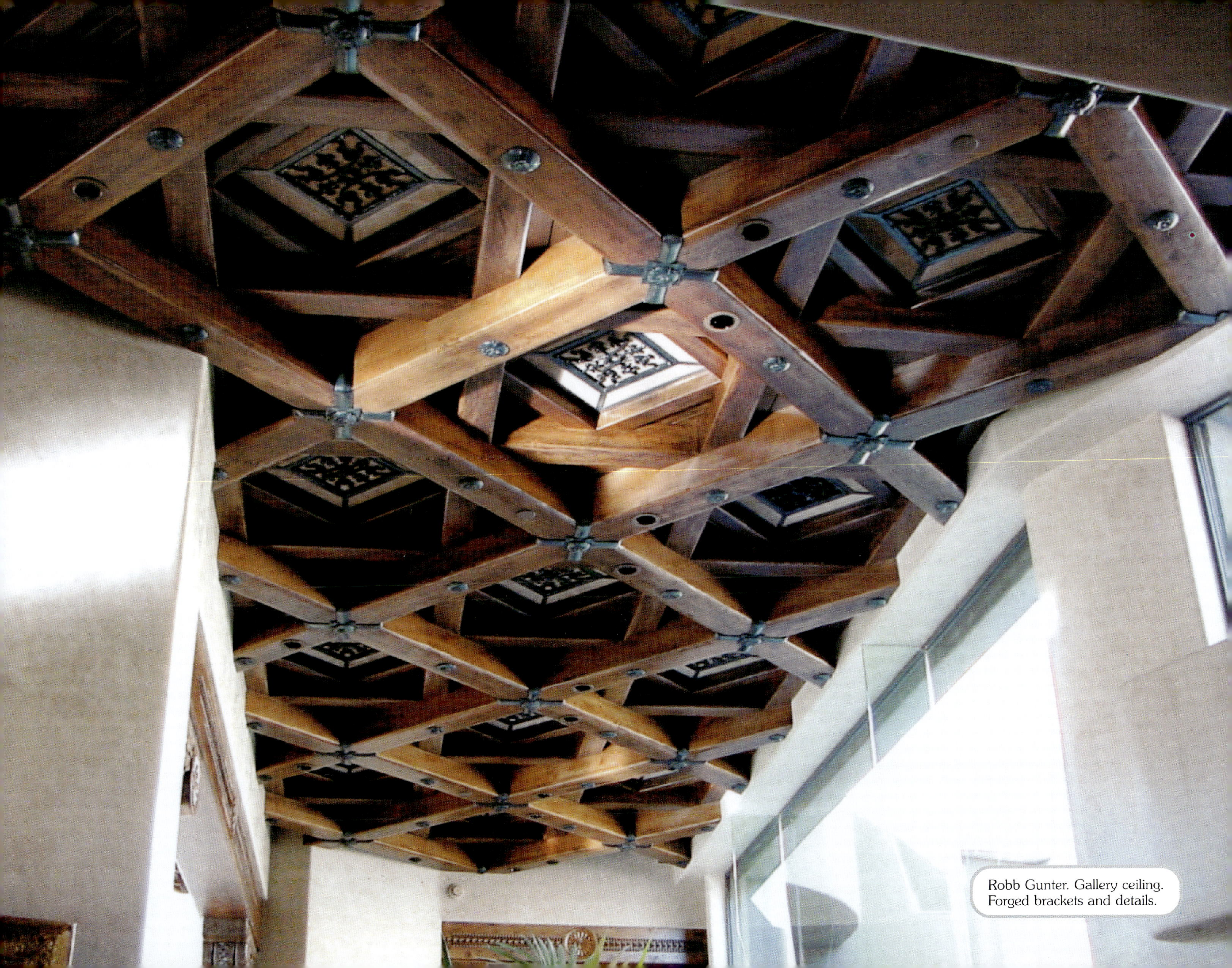

Robb Gunter. Gallery ceiling. Forged brackets and details.

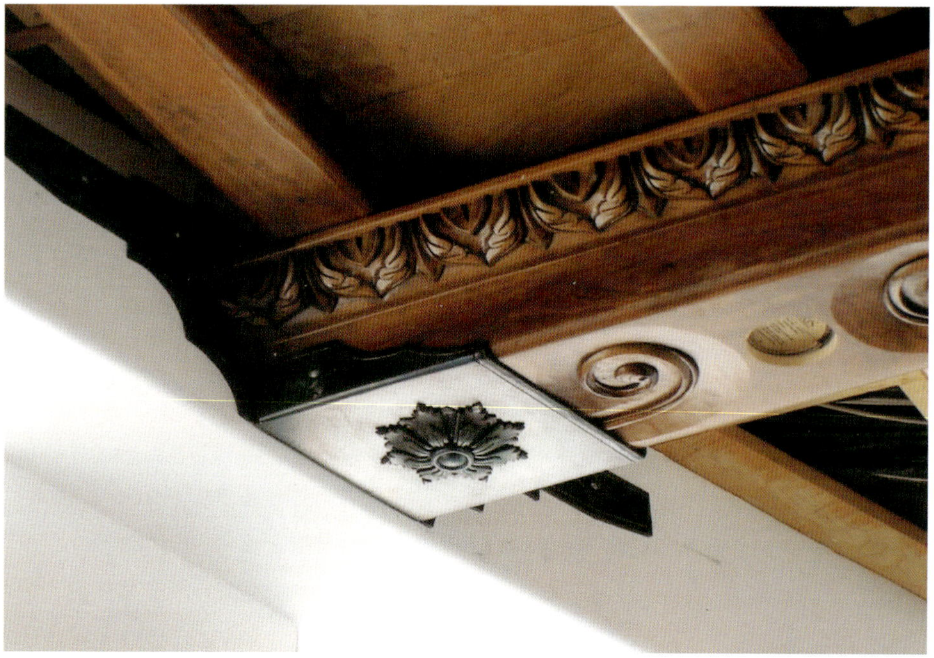

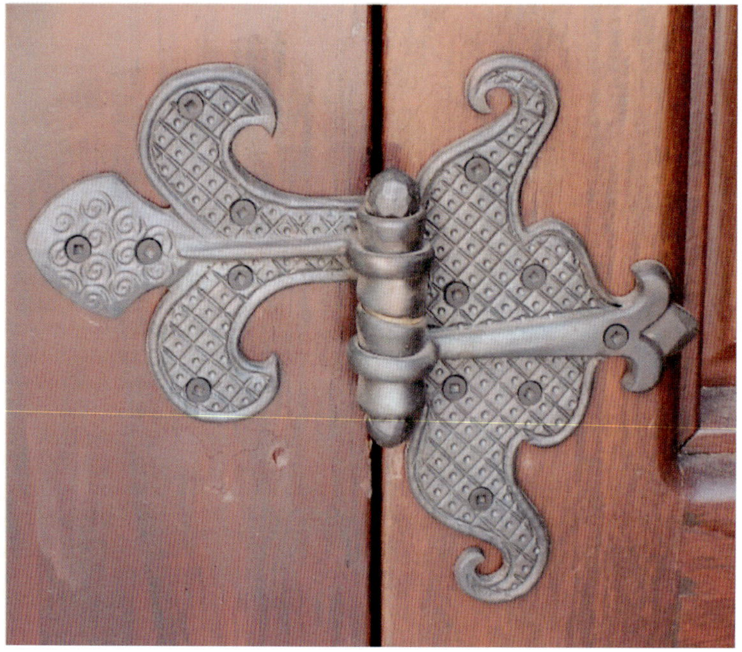

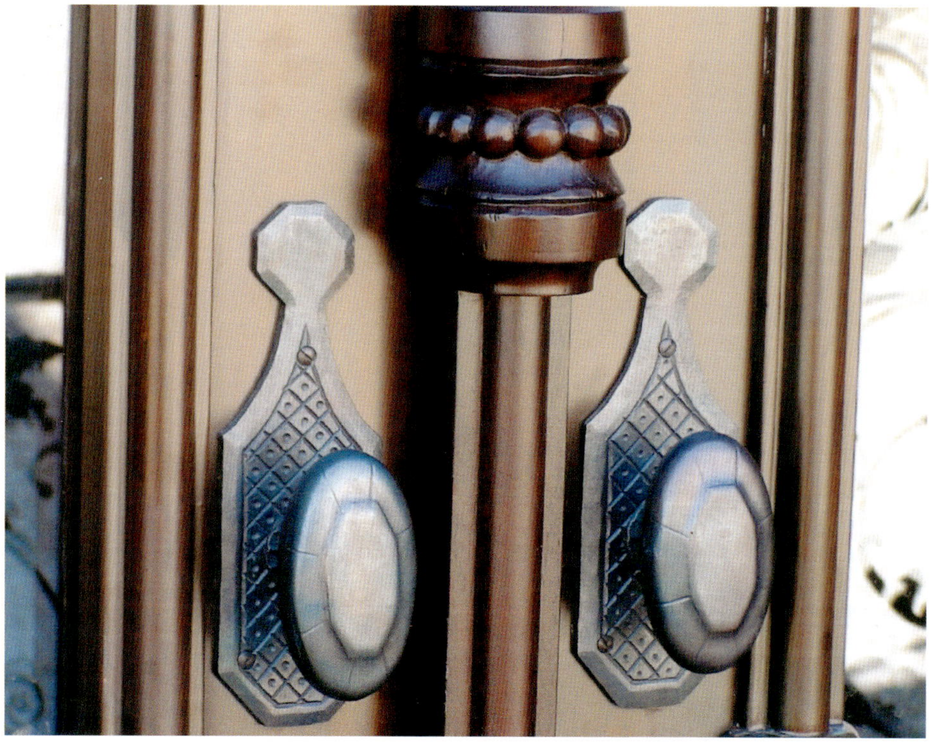

Above, left:
Robb Gunter. One of 6 beam brackets forged from 3/8" plate. 5' long.

Above:
Robb Gunter. Pool gate hinge, one half the size of the entry door hinges.

Left:
Brad and Chad Gunter. Doorknobs and plates were built for 52 doors.

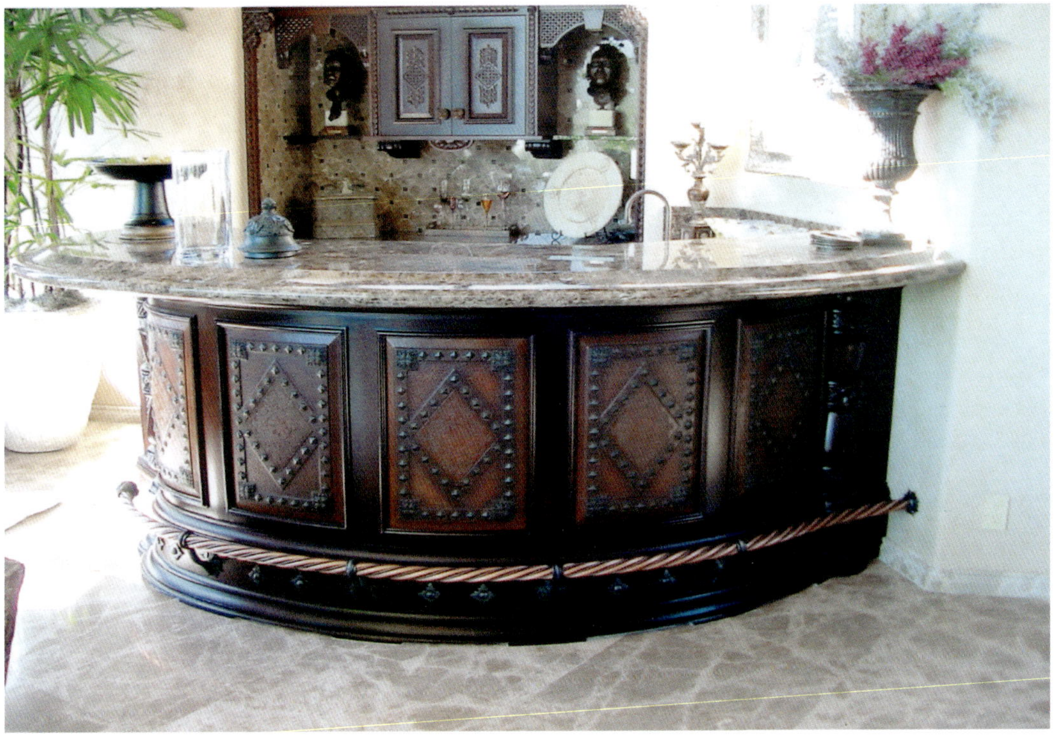

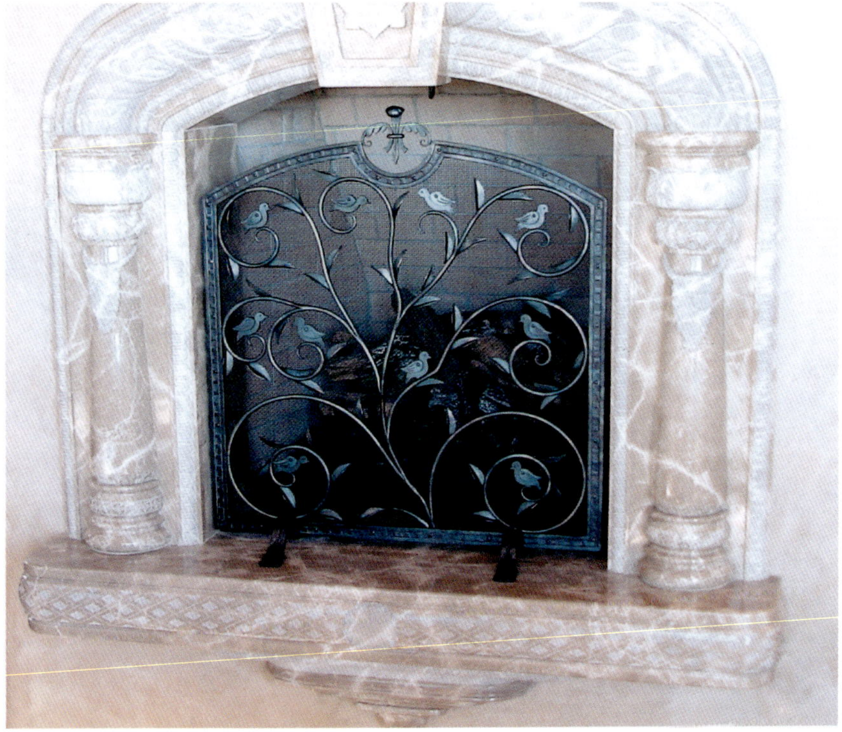

Above:
Robb Gunter. Great room bar.

Above, right:
Chad Gunter. Dining room fireplace screen with birds.

Right:
Chad Gunter. Master bedroom fireplace screen.

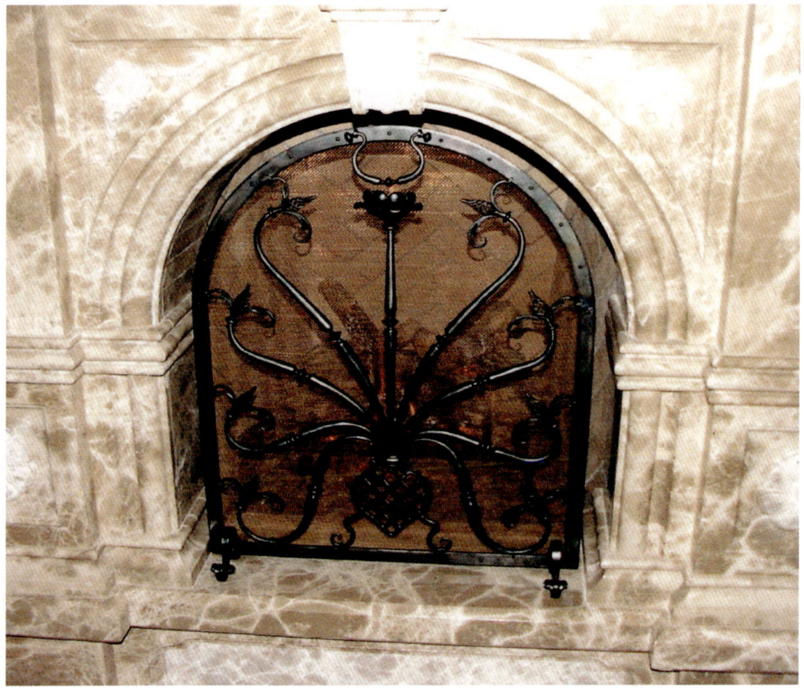

Robert C. Bentley's Lucky Life Change

Robert C. Bentley had run his own metalwork shop for twenty-six years when he was asked to bid on a job that entailed building a new resort based on the vision of a well-known designer in the area. That was the turning point in Bentley's career. The project demanded unconventional construction that would represent major challenges. Bentley advised the designer, Wendy Lawless, that typical iron subcontractors would compromise details and, therefore, he recommended an in-house iron contractor.

Property owner David Weyrich agreed and Bentley was hired. His first task was to assemble a qualified crew. Luck continued to hover around Bentley when Russ Windbiel, who had just closed his own business, entered the picture. Three more men were added with different skills and, within a few months, work progressed on the up-scale bed and breakfast that would eventually be named The Villa Toscana.

Bentley brought more than ironwork skills to the job; he is a renaissance man who will settle for nothing less that 125% perfection. When the design called for unique procedures, Bentley solved problems and developed methods that were so innovative that the city's planning board appreciated his attention to details and they co-operated with the unique concepts of working with energy efficient attachments. For example, Lawless insisted that the iron appear to "grow" out of the stucco with the absence of visual fasteners or obvious connections.

The final tally of the ironwork at The Villa Toscana includes 647-lineal feet of hand-forged wrought iron, 138 feet of winding double staircase railing and fencing, over 100 hand wrought "old gas lamp"-style exterior wall mounts, 16 chandeliers each of a different size, shape and style, 11 interior fireplace screens for The Villa Toscana suites, 3 larger, hand wrought forged elegant screens for the public areas, 23 window grilles, 167 shutter straps, 11 exterior trash enclosures, hand-forged Villa Toscana logo crests installed on exterior members, two sliding gate entries with forged wreaths and flowers, two sculpted lion heads on fountains, fountain grating, woven lattice work for 35 chimney vents, numerous attachment brackets, a stand for a 400-gallon aquarium (in David Weyrich's private office), and a bronze interior handrail and cap.

And, oh yes, nearly everything has a stylized tulip which became The Villa Toscana logo. The designer had fallen in love with the flowers on a visit to Europe; they had inspired the idea and design concepts for The Villa Toscana.

But The Villa Toscana is not the end of Bentley's journey. He and his team have created an entry arch and gates for a Weyrich housing development, (page 86) and the restoration of a hotel of the early 1900s. Then there is the ironwork for the winery and, who knows what all is waiting on the drawing board for the talented team? They do know that every project will be a challenge that will fill their days doing what they love to do.

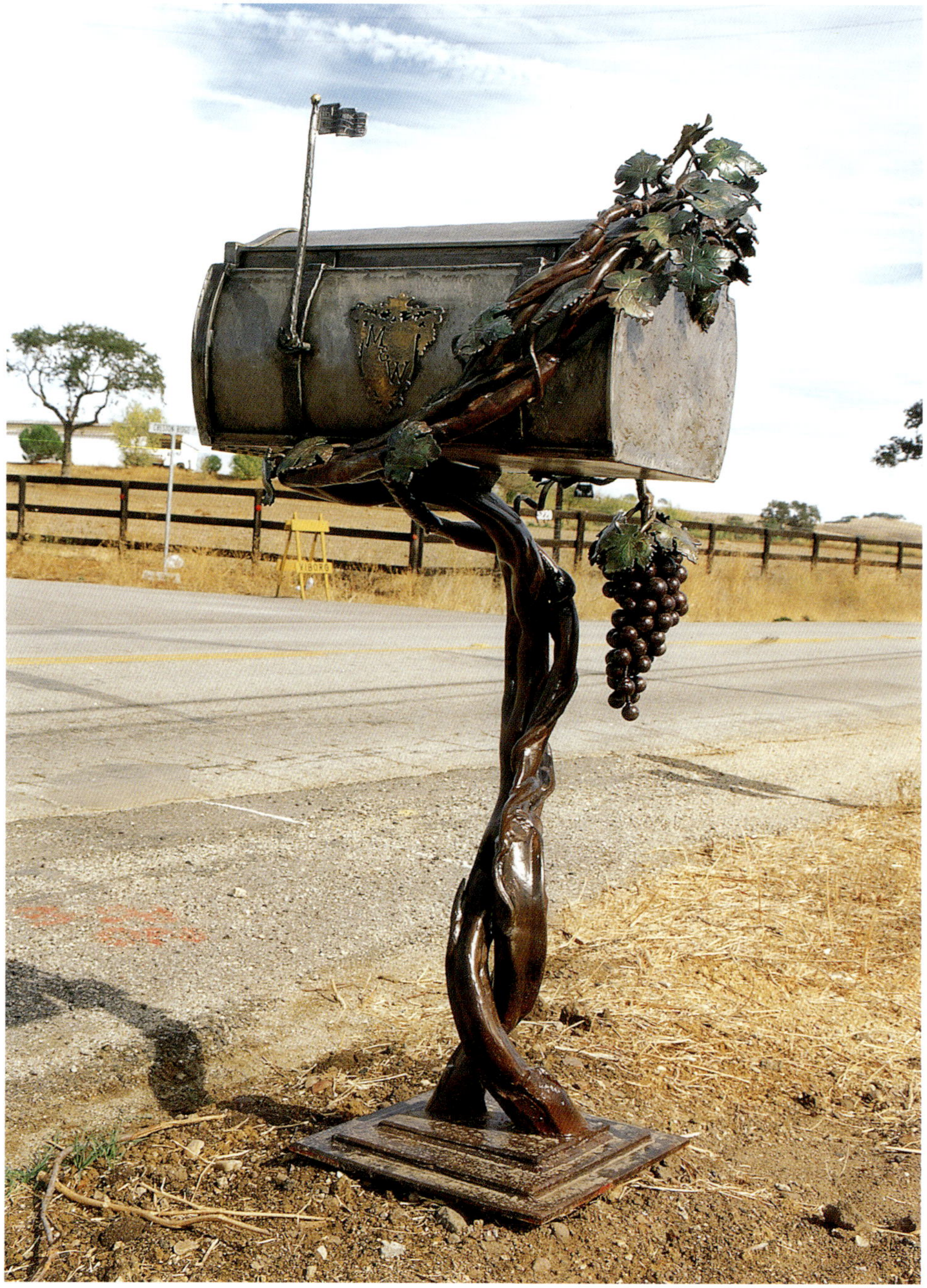

Robert C. Bentley. Mailbox with grapes, leaves, and Weyrich Winery logo. *Photo, Bruce Woodworth*

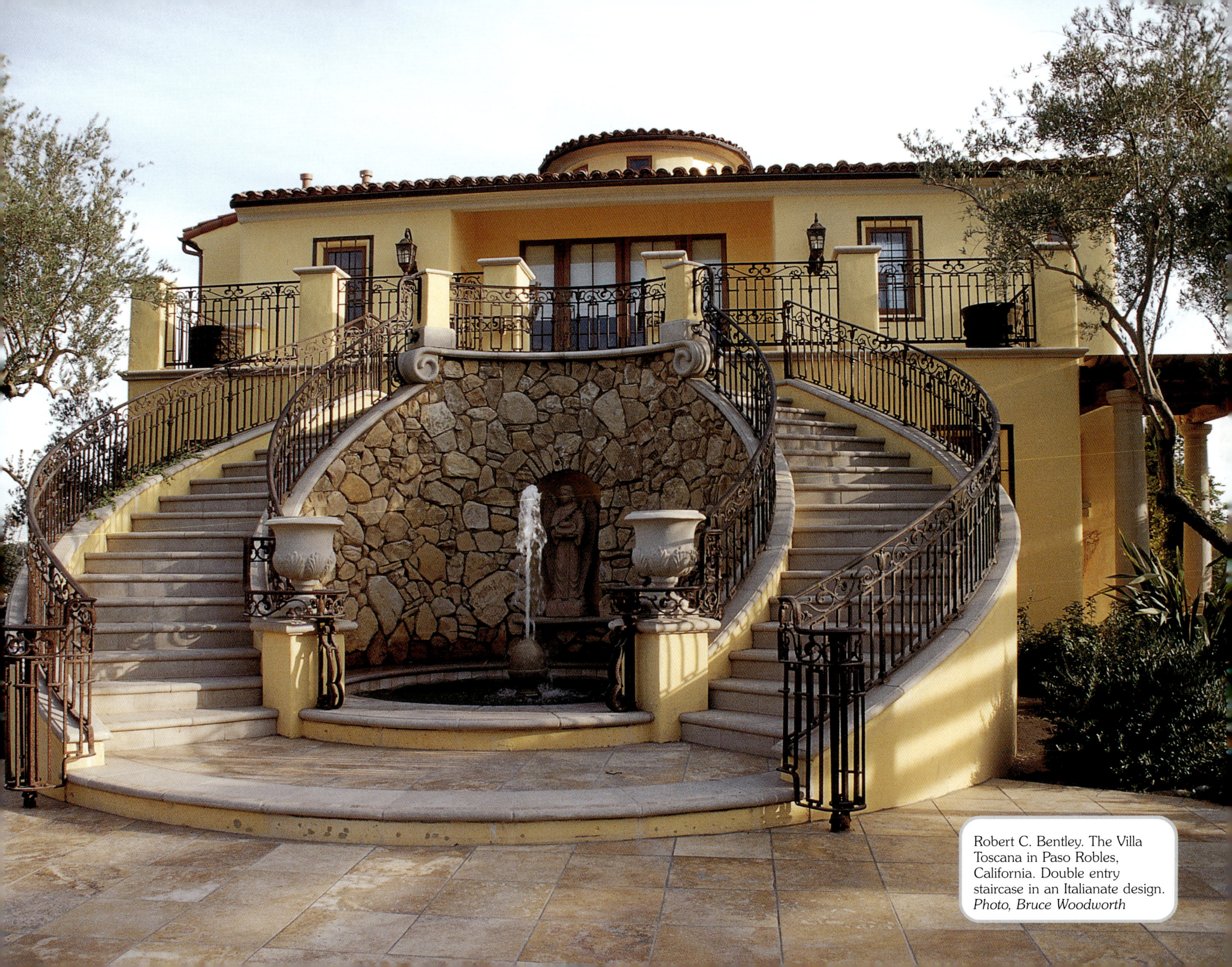

Robert C. Bentley. The Villa Toscana in Paso Robles, California. Double entry staircase in an Italianate design. *Photo, Bruce Woodworth*

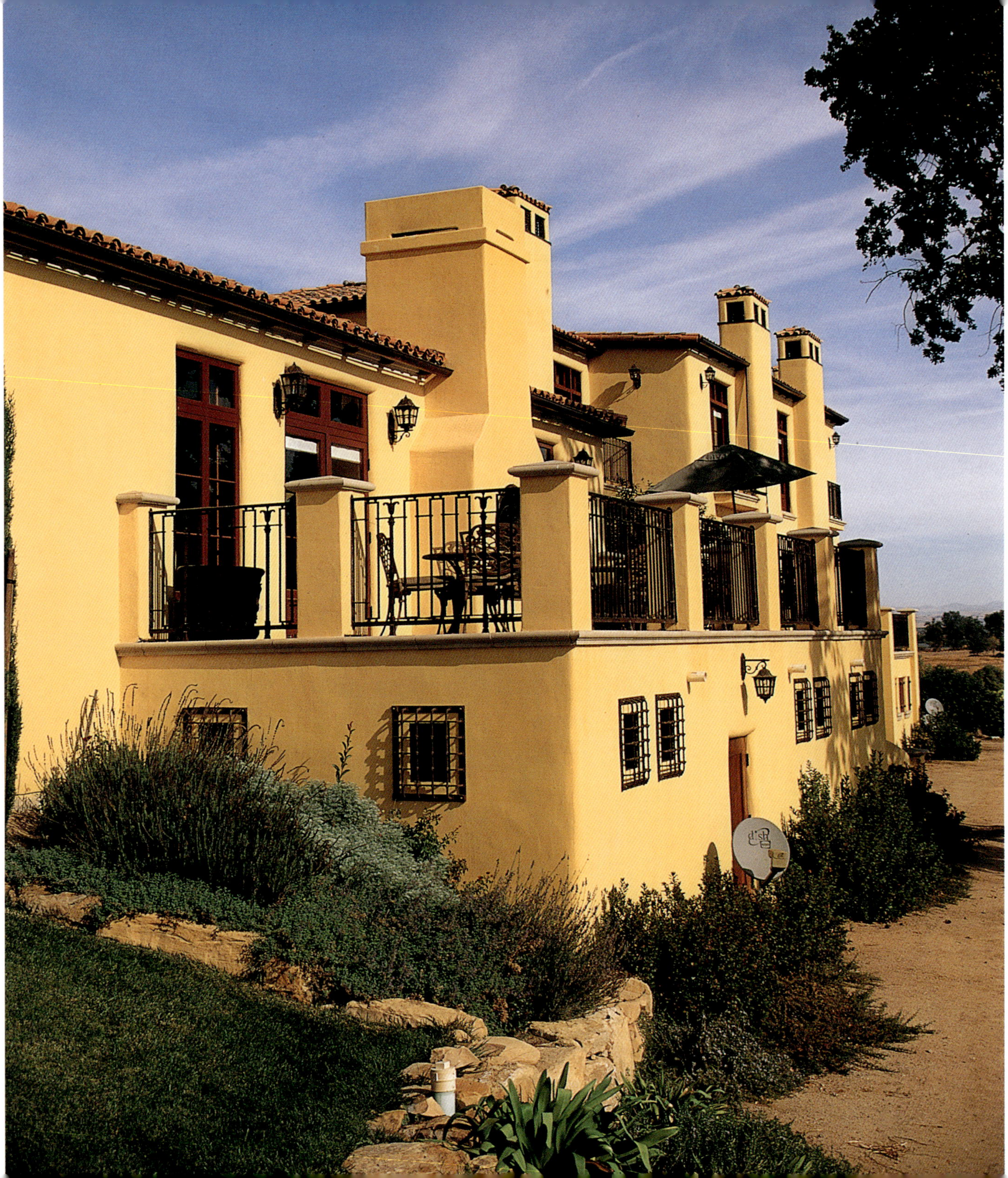

Robert C. Bentley. Railings, window grilles, sconces, and light fixtures were all custom designed for The Villa Toscana main building and guest rooms. *Photo, Bruce Woodworth*

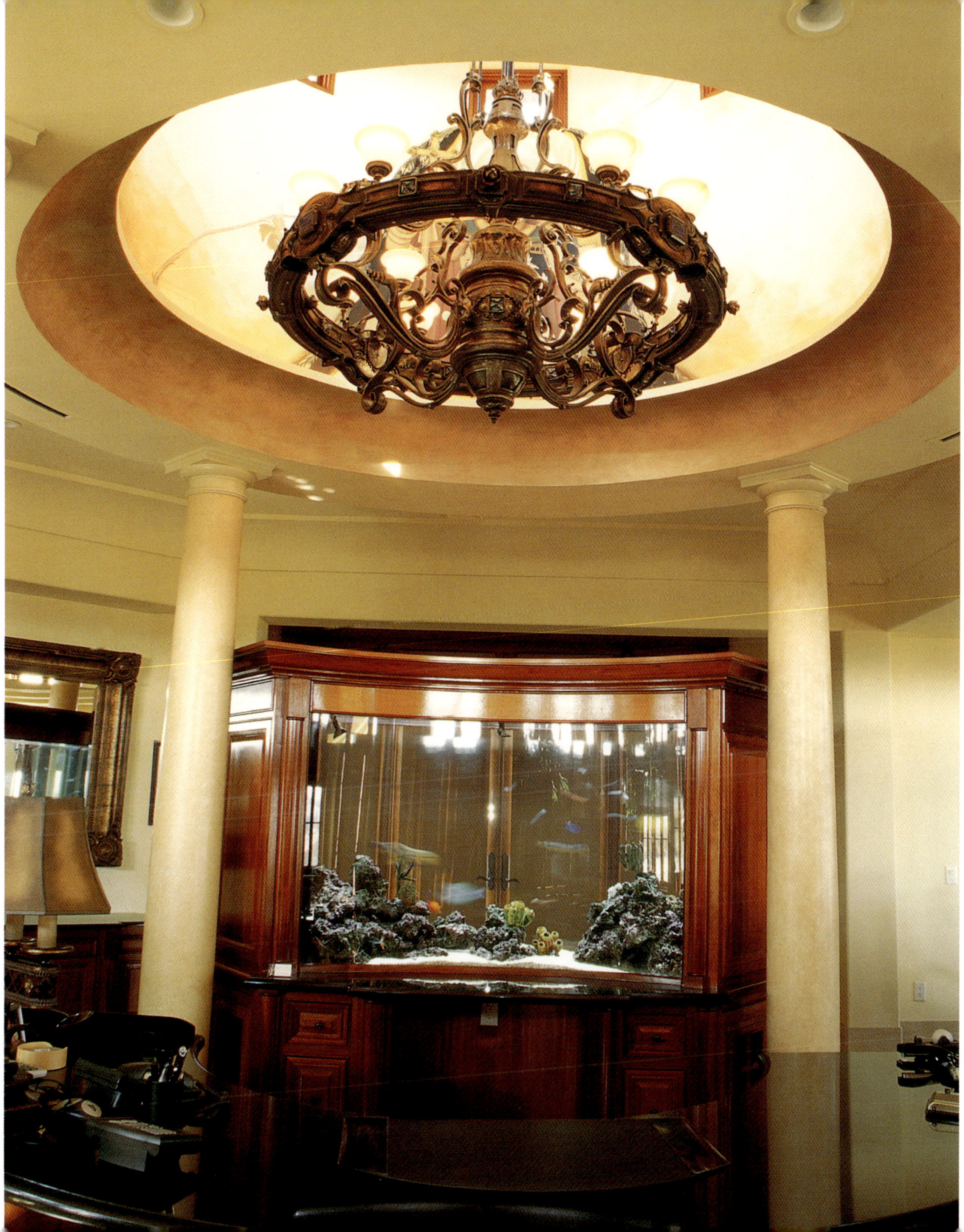

Robert C. Bentley. Light fixture over an aquarium in Mr. Weyrich's main office. *Photo, Bruce Woodworth*

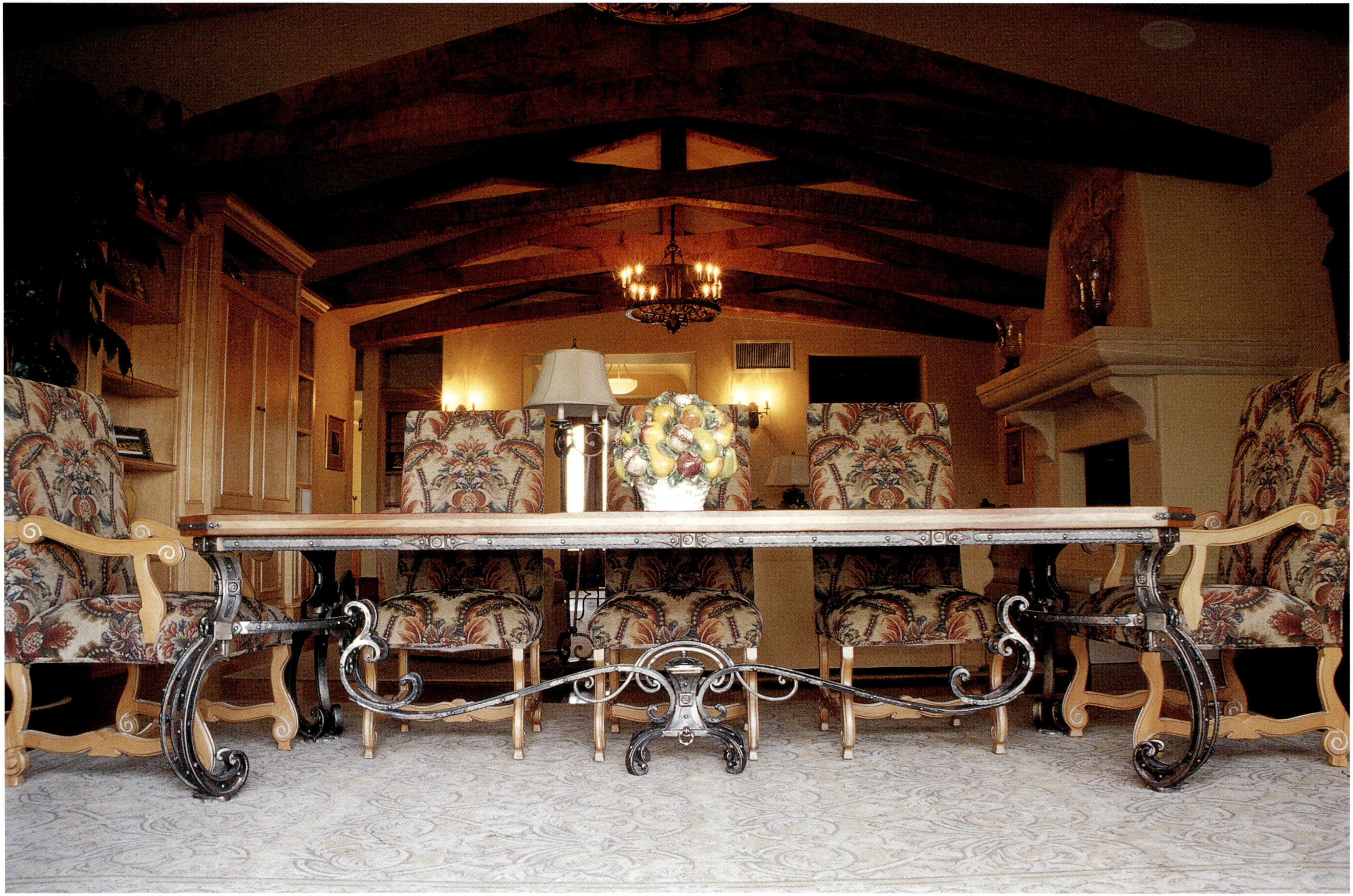

Robert C. Bentley. Table base, light fixture, lamps, and sconces were all included in the accessories designed for the Villa Toscana. *Photo, Bruce Woodworth*

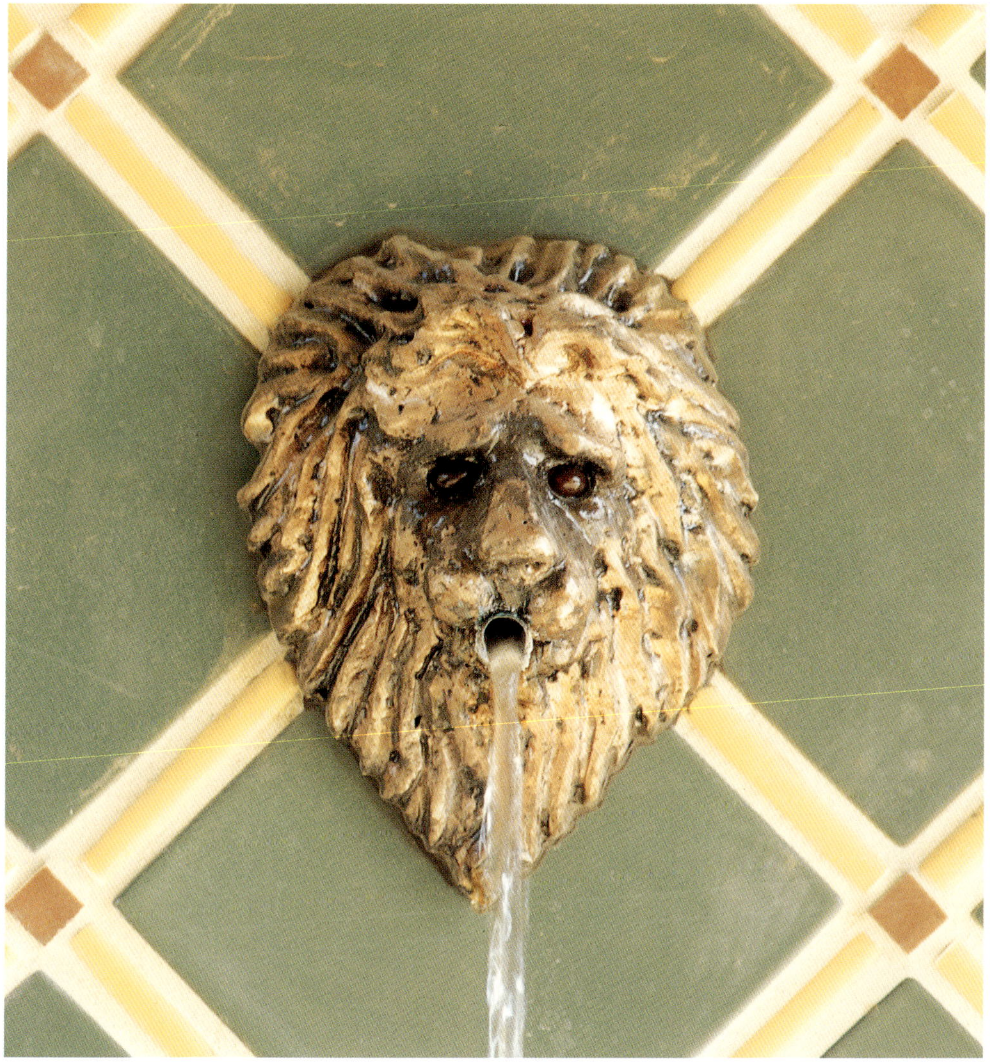

Robert C. Bentley. Lion head detail forged and then cast. *Photo, Bruce Woodworth*

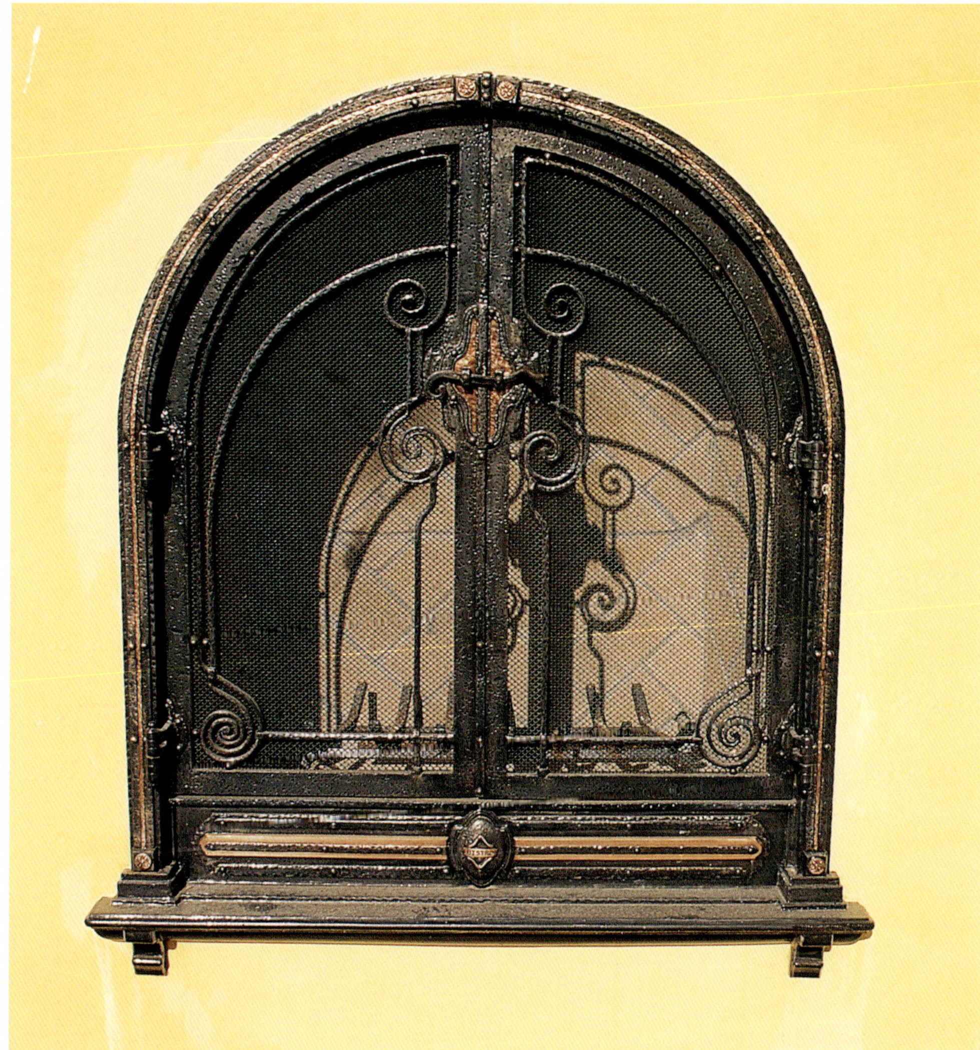

Robert C. Bentley. One of several outdoor fireplace screens. *Photo, Bruce Woodworth*

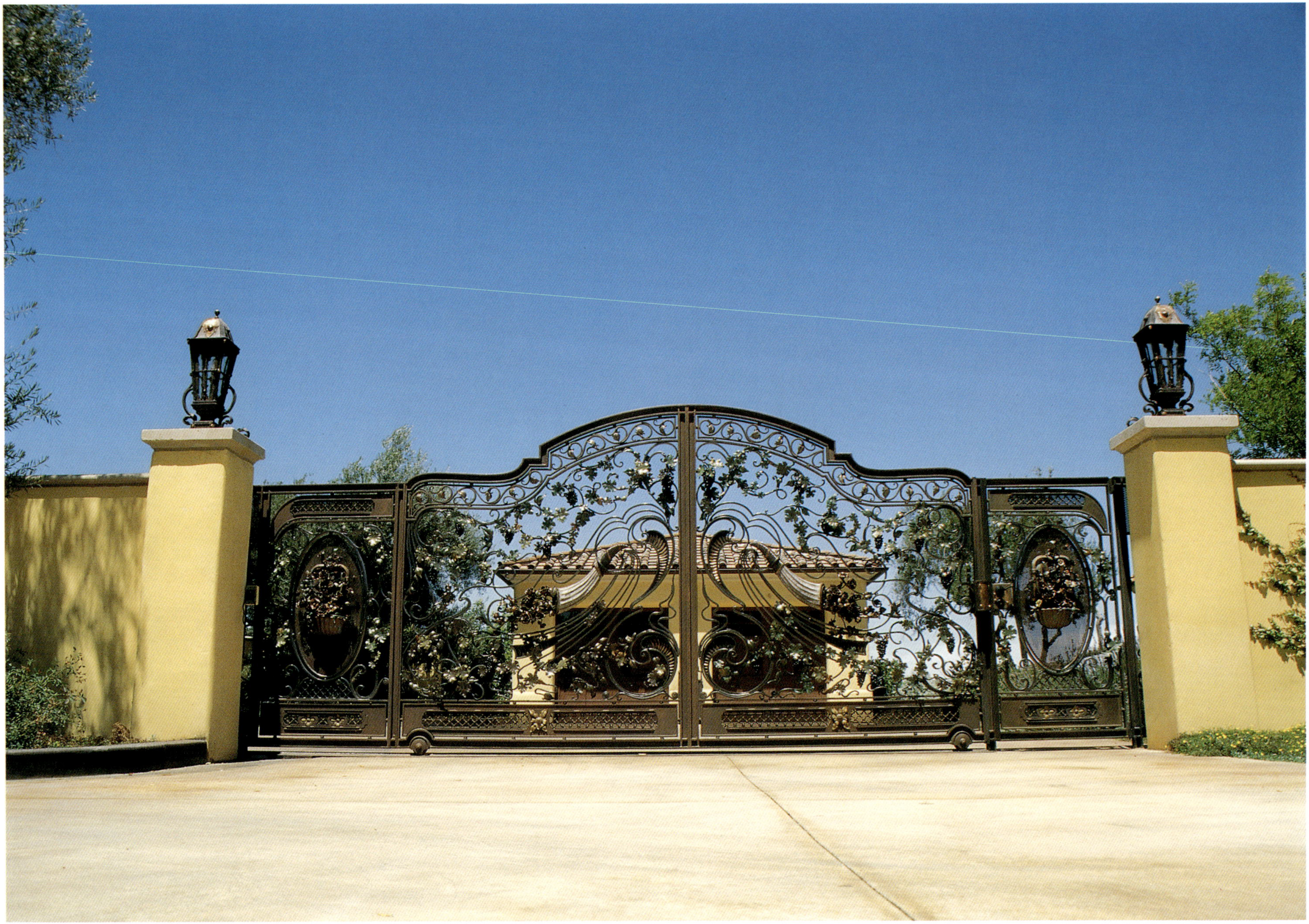

Robert C. Bentley. Gates to one of the villas. *Photo, Bruce Woodworth*

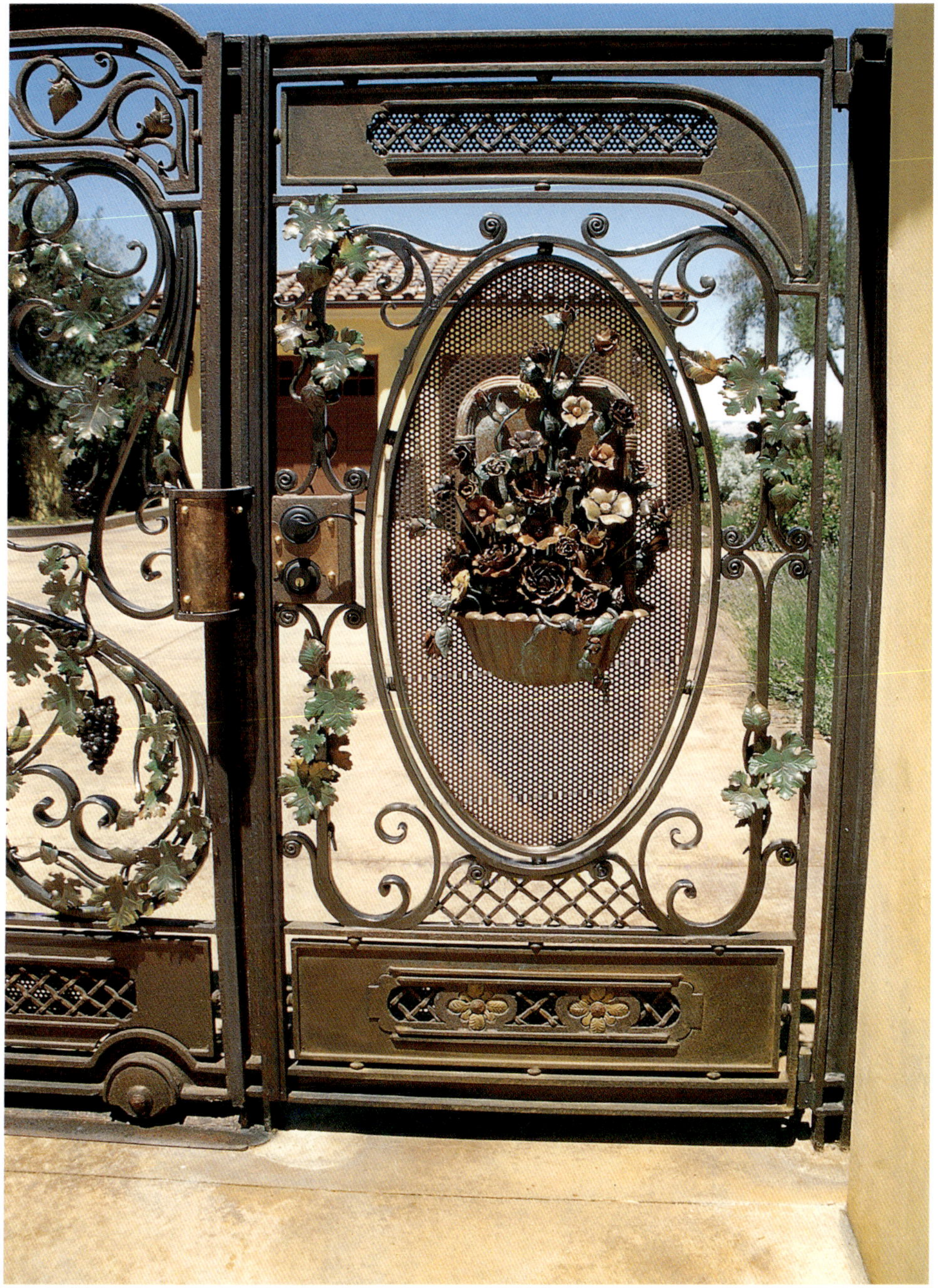

Robert C. Bentley. Floral bouquet on the entry gates. *Photo, Bruce Woodworth*

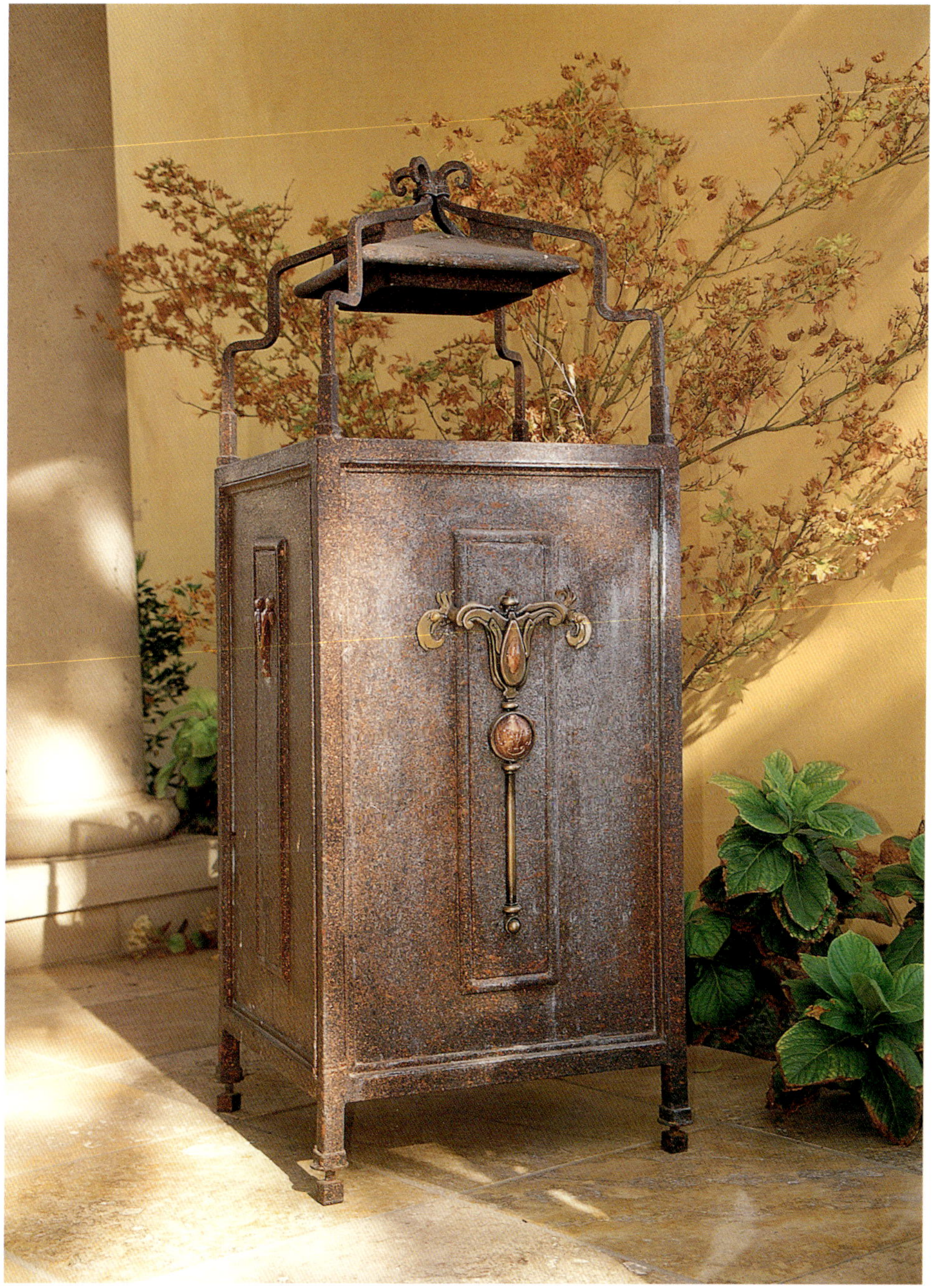

Robert C. Bentley. Refuse container with The Villa Toscana tulip logo. *Photo, Bruce Woodworth*

Restorations and Conversions

Many projects throughout the book are for new construction or renewing older work. They may be for a fence, a railing, a bridge. But it's not often that a smith is called in to redo the major portions of a building and is allowed to use much of his own design. Both John Boyd Smith and Nick Such brought their talents into the picture and the clients gave them almost total carte blanc to create the look they described, and hoped to get. And they did.

John Boyd Smith's reputation won him the contract for redoing a major hotel in Miami Beach Florida's south beach area. The railings, tables, and panel dividers represent lush tropical growth. They are based on drawings of underwater plant life created by his wife, Rhonda Neil Fleming, who snorkels and dives. The tropical flora of the area inspired the leaves and trees.

Nick Such's experience is quite different. The photos shown are from a job that called for converting a garage into a painting studio/ workspace. The owner, Kelly Adachi, a graphic artist, made small sketches for a screen door and a stair railing. Such selected the ones he liked, scaled them up, and interpreted them in metal. Another conversion, (not shown) involved creating a residence from an old Los Angeles Baptist church.

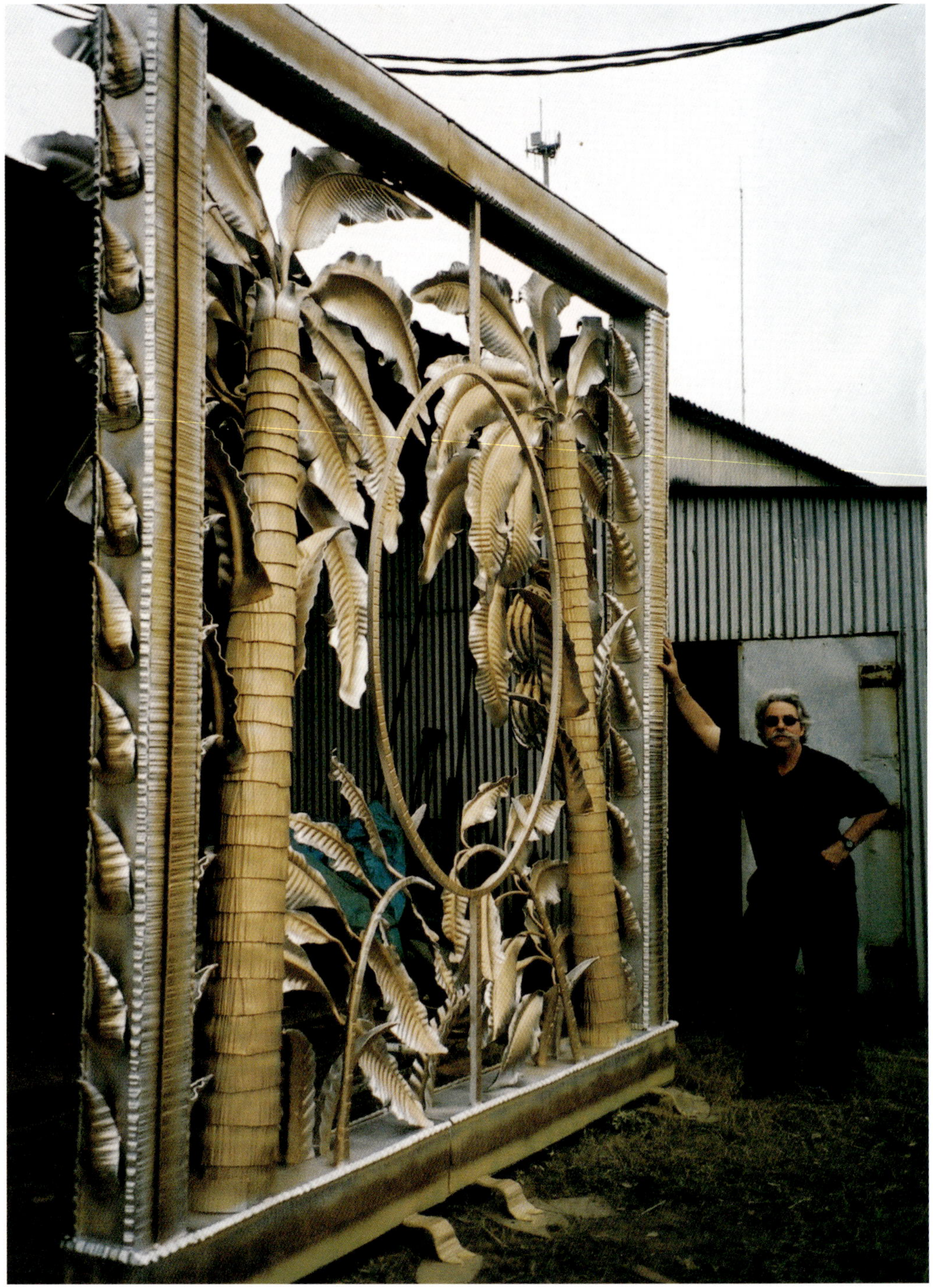

John Boyd Smith. Restoration of a hotel lobby in south Miami Beach, Florida, included railings, decorative screens, lobby tables, and other items. One of two life-size, three-dimensional, banana leaf screens ready for installation in the hotel's lobby. John appears to be holding up one of the 12' x 12' and 6,000-pound screens. A large glass oval in "sunset" color bronzed glass was centered in the finished screens. *Photo, Rhonda Neil Fleming*

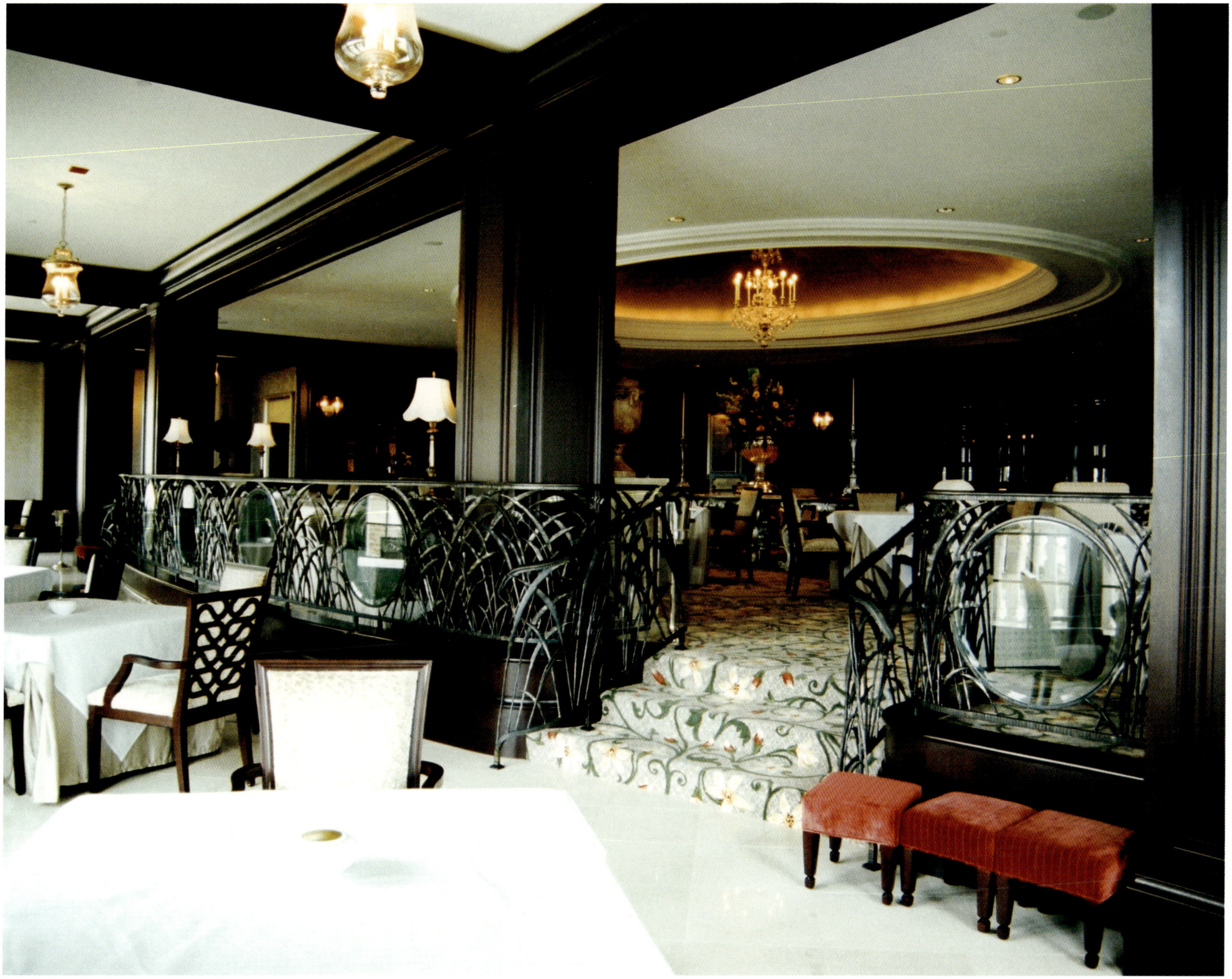

John Boyd Smith. Hand railing for the hotel's dining area.

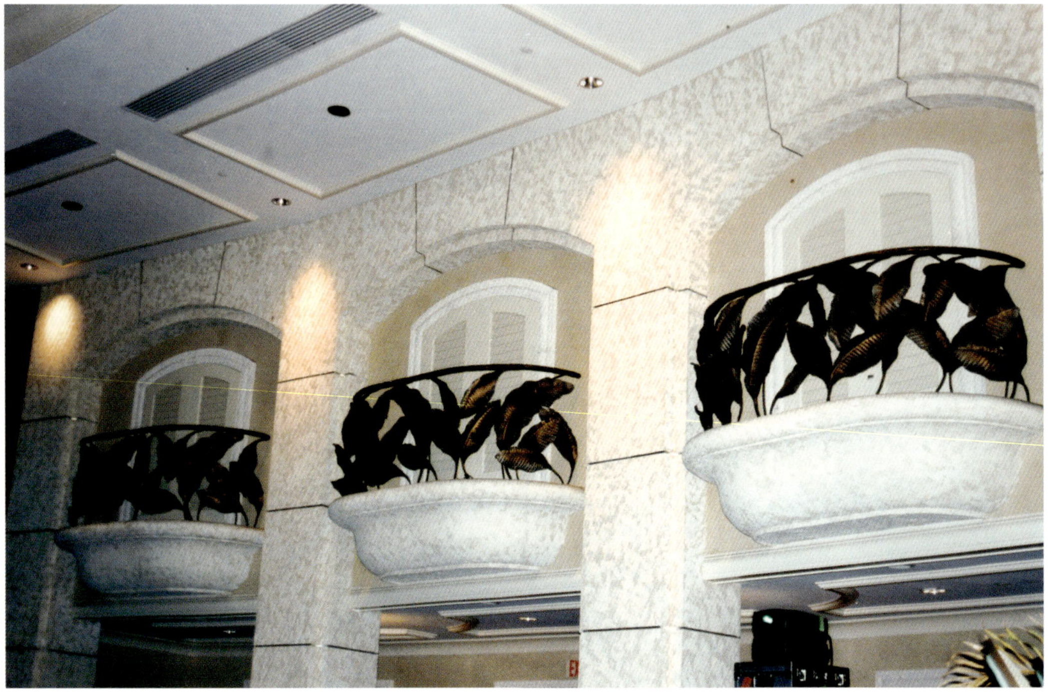

John Boyd Smith. Balconies with banana leaf railings.

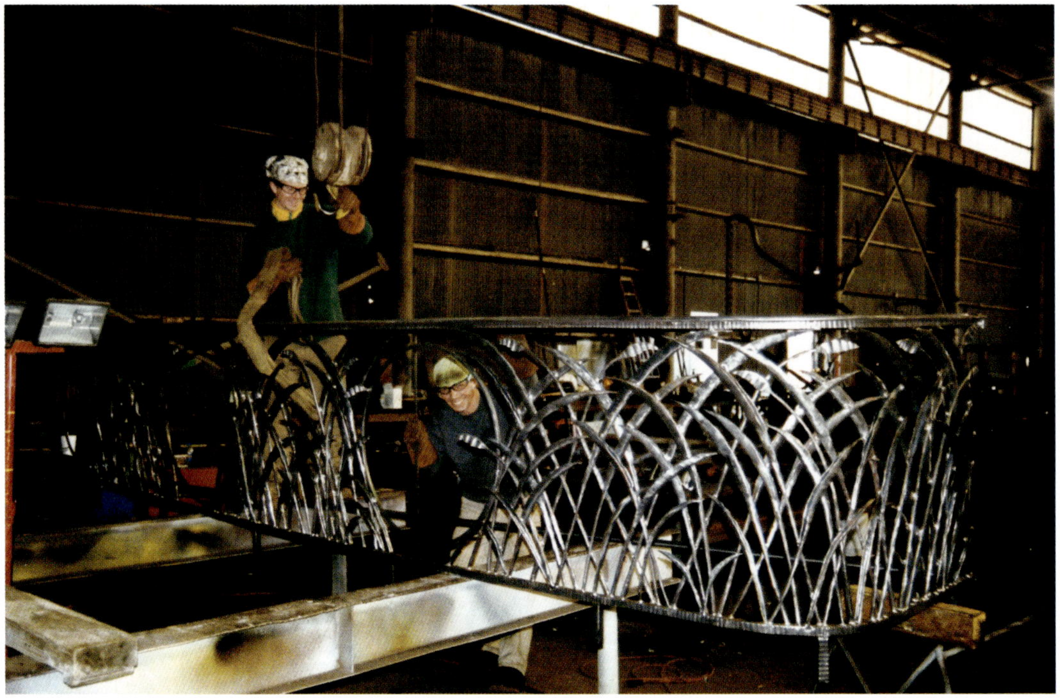

John Boyd Smith. Preparing for installation of the dining room railing.

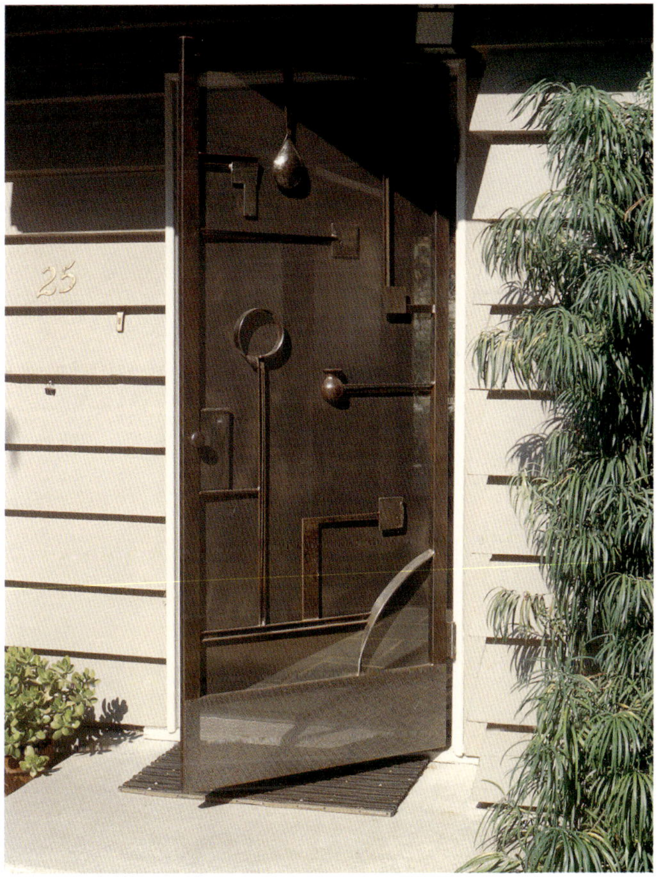

Nick Such. Adachi House restoration, Los Angeles, California. Screen door from a drawing by Kelly Adachi. Forged and welded stainless steel and cast iron. 7' high, 3' wide *Photo, artist*

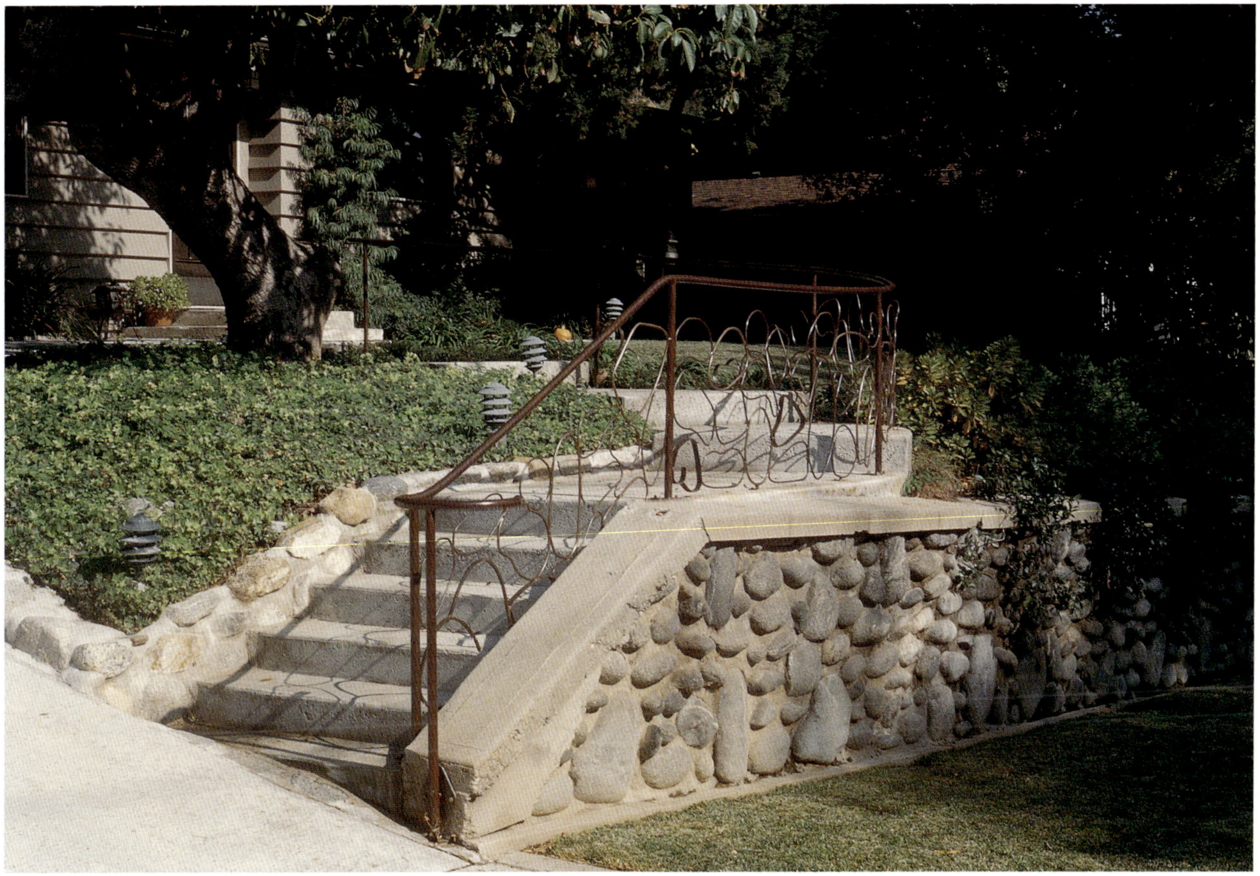

Nick Such. Adachi House handrail that mirrors the stonework design on the wall below. Forged and welded steel rusted and sealed. *Photo, artist*

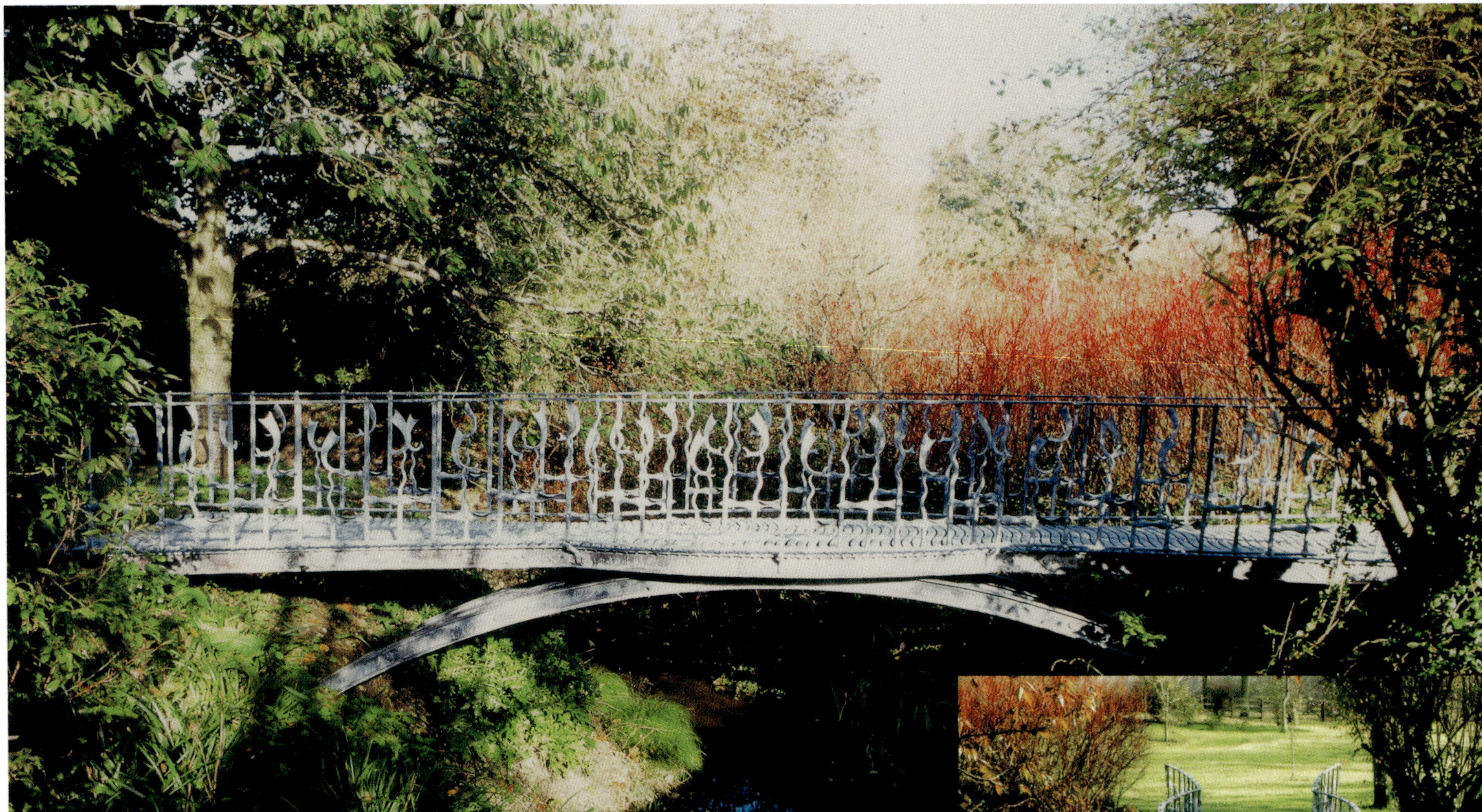

Paul Elliott. Avon Tributary Bridge. Mild Steel with a galvanized and acid etched finish. Installed in the gardens of an old Priory in Wiltshire, England. The bridge spans a tributary of the river Avon and weighs almost 4 tons. It was produced in 3 sections with over 1000 rivets in the floor alone. 32' long.

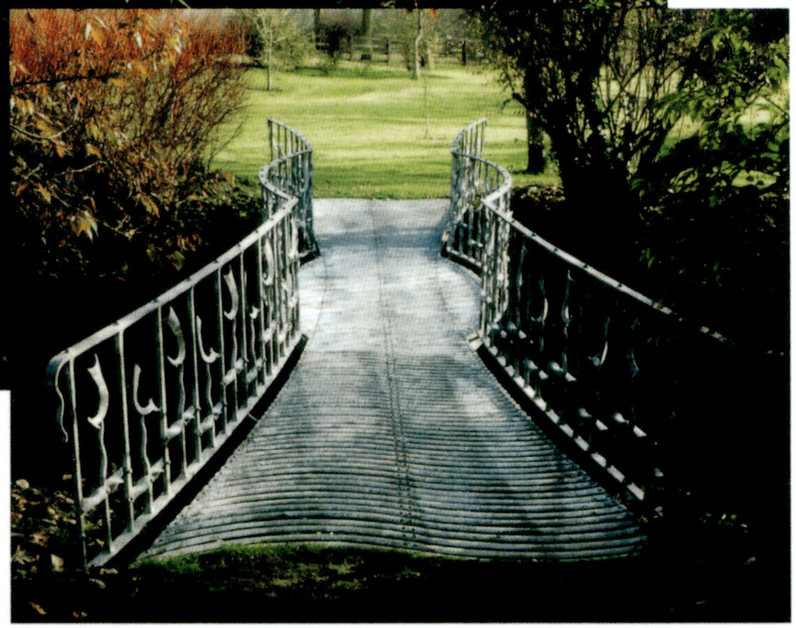

Right: Interior view of the Avon Tributary Bridge showing the curved slatted floor. *Photos, Paul Elliott*

Chapter 3. Railings and Grilles

Railings installed on bridges and staircases enhance our environments. Grilles for windows and doors also fall into this category, plus they provide security. Many railings today are fabricated from pre-shaped pieces. They may be assembled in a cut and paste procedure. Select the kinds of bars you like from a catalog, arrange them to fit a space, weld them together and voila, instant staircase or railings are fabricated and some may consider these "customized".

Ironwork railings composed of pre-made forged and cast components save time and lower the cost of ironwork. Builders who develop projects put ironwork railings in upscale houses because people love them. But the same railings usually appear in all the houses in a housing complex, so they are not "customized" in the true sense of the word.

Conversely, the one-of-a kind railing can be infinitely customized. The examples shown will underscore the difference between a cut and paste railing, and one that is made to reflect the occupant's interests, or the special architectural requirements of a building.

It's easy to admire a finished, installed railing but an understanding of how the railing is designed and made will increase your appreciation of this unique art form. You will also begin to notice stair railings in hotels and public buildings, even in scenes of elegant homes used in movie settings.

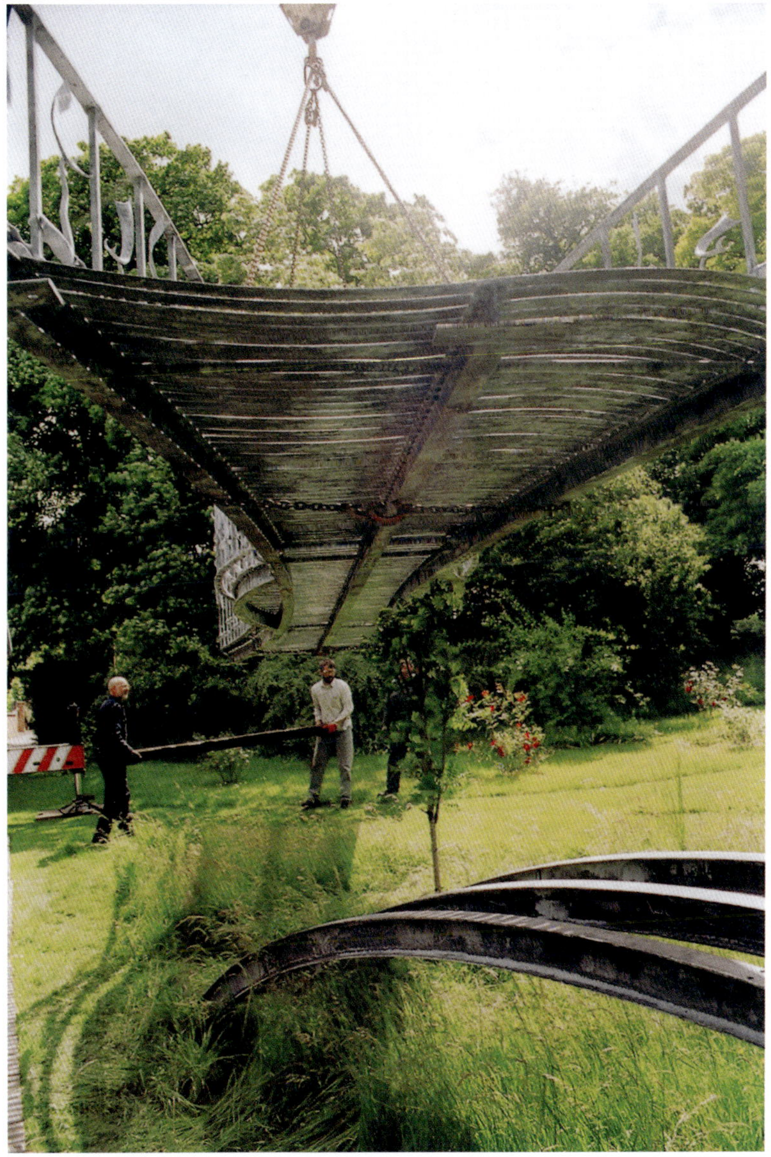

Paul Elliott. The installation of the Avon Tributary Bridge required cranes to move it from the shop area to the site. View from below in preparation for installation. *Photo, Paul Elliott*

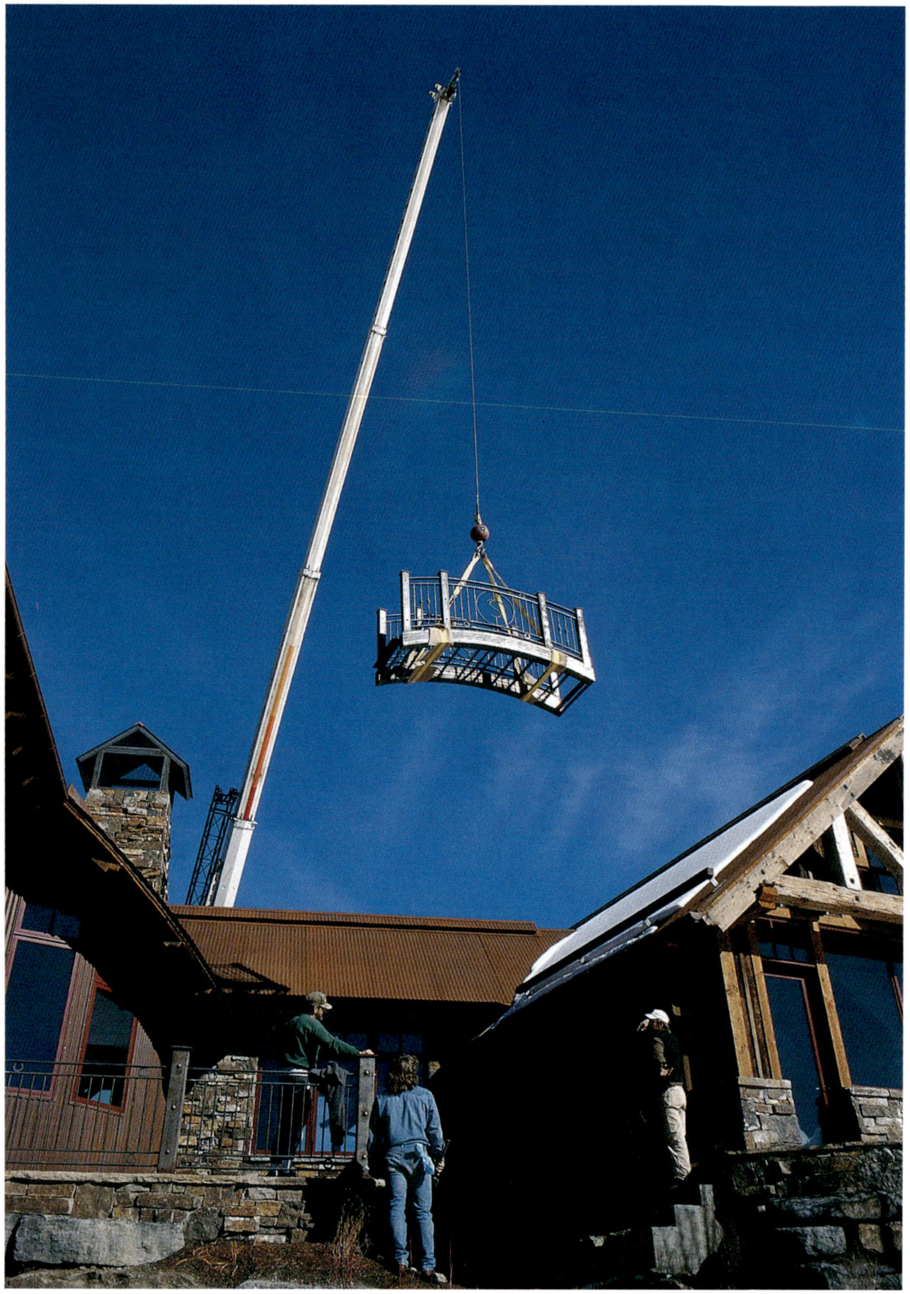

Stephen E. Lee. A small bridge requires huge engineering skills to transport it from the studio to the site. The bridge, to be placed in front of the house, must be lifted over the house with a crane. *Photo, Kate Hoover*

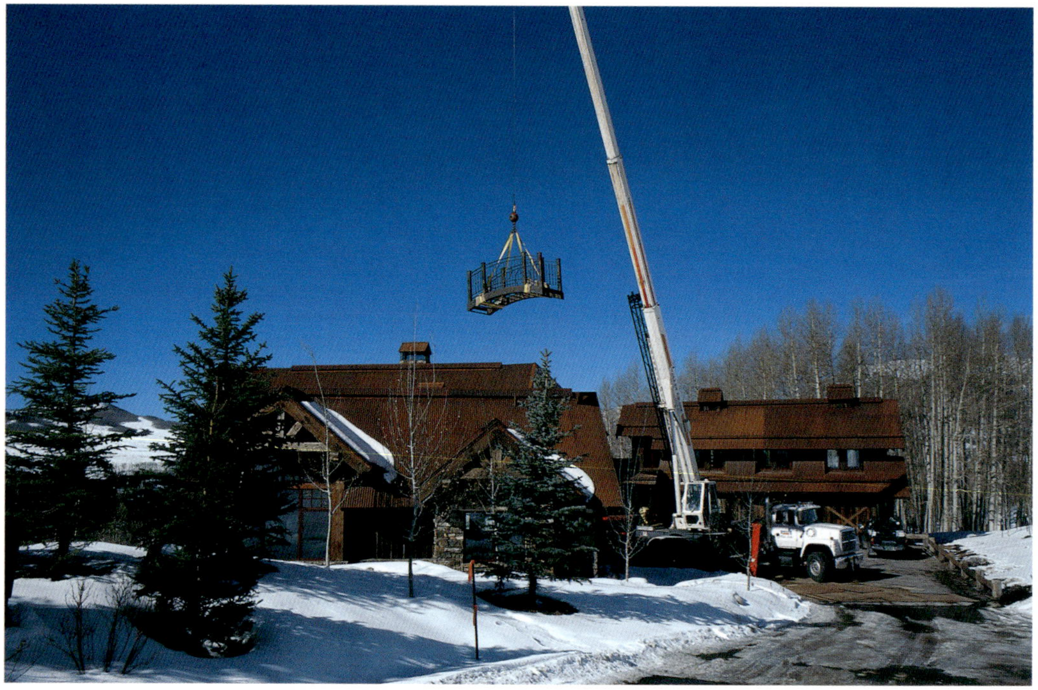

Stephen E. Lee. The crane lowers it to within feet of its placement. *Photo, Kate Hoover*

Many railings made in an artist-blacksmith's shop are the work of a team of metal workers with different skills. The floral railing on page 65 is the combined work of Robert Walsh, Keith Johnson, and Roger Loyson. Walsh explains that it began with the design that evolved with the client's input. Walsh prepared and developed the drawings and storyboards indicating the procedures and timelines. Keith Johnson took over production and, says, Walsh, "He somehow makes fabulous objects magically appear on the face of his anvil".

While scrolls and bars dominate railing design, other forms may be incorporated based on a client's interests. Reuel Darling's *Kokopelli* railing is obviously for someone whose interests are in American Indian design. Dimitri Gerakaris's challenge was forming huge dragons for the balcony railing of a home. Butch Lee's porch railing is composed of tulips, and Craig Kaviar's railing has a pumpkin vine with pumpkins in the railing end.

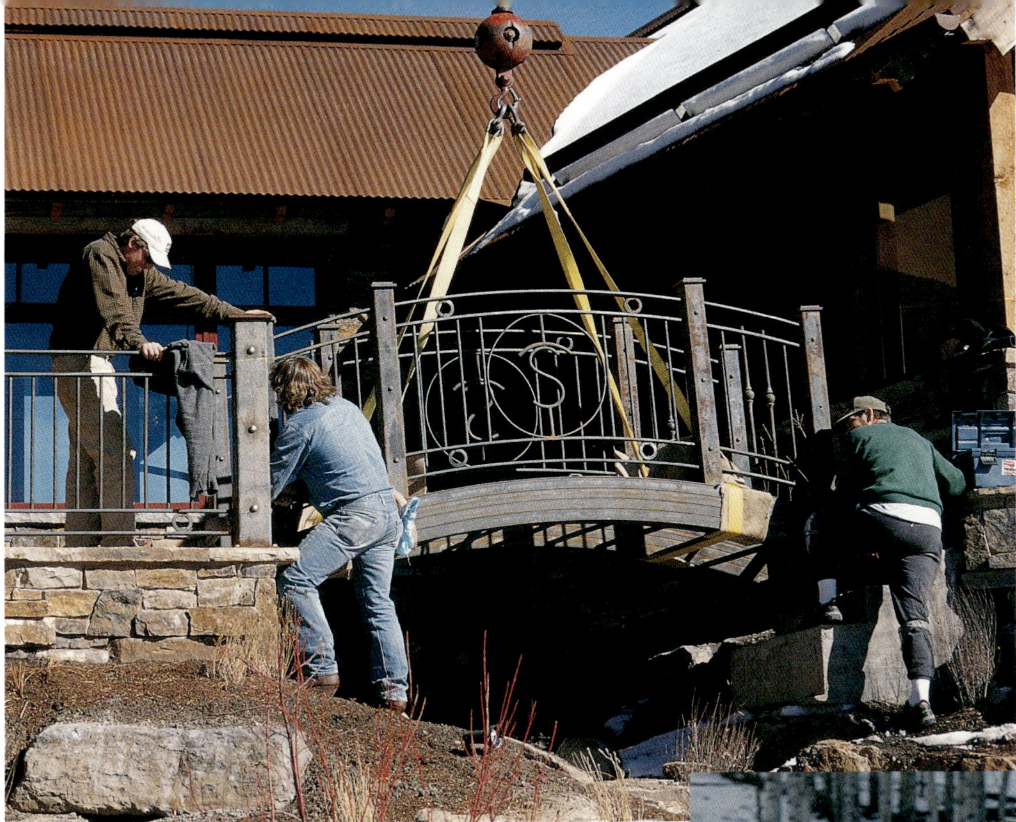

Stephen E. Lee. The workmen take over and bolt it into place. Left to right: Mike Osborne, Stephen Lee, and Mike Courtney. *Photo, Kate Hoover*

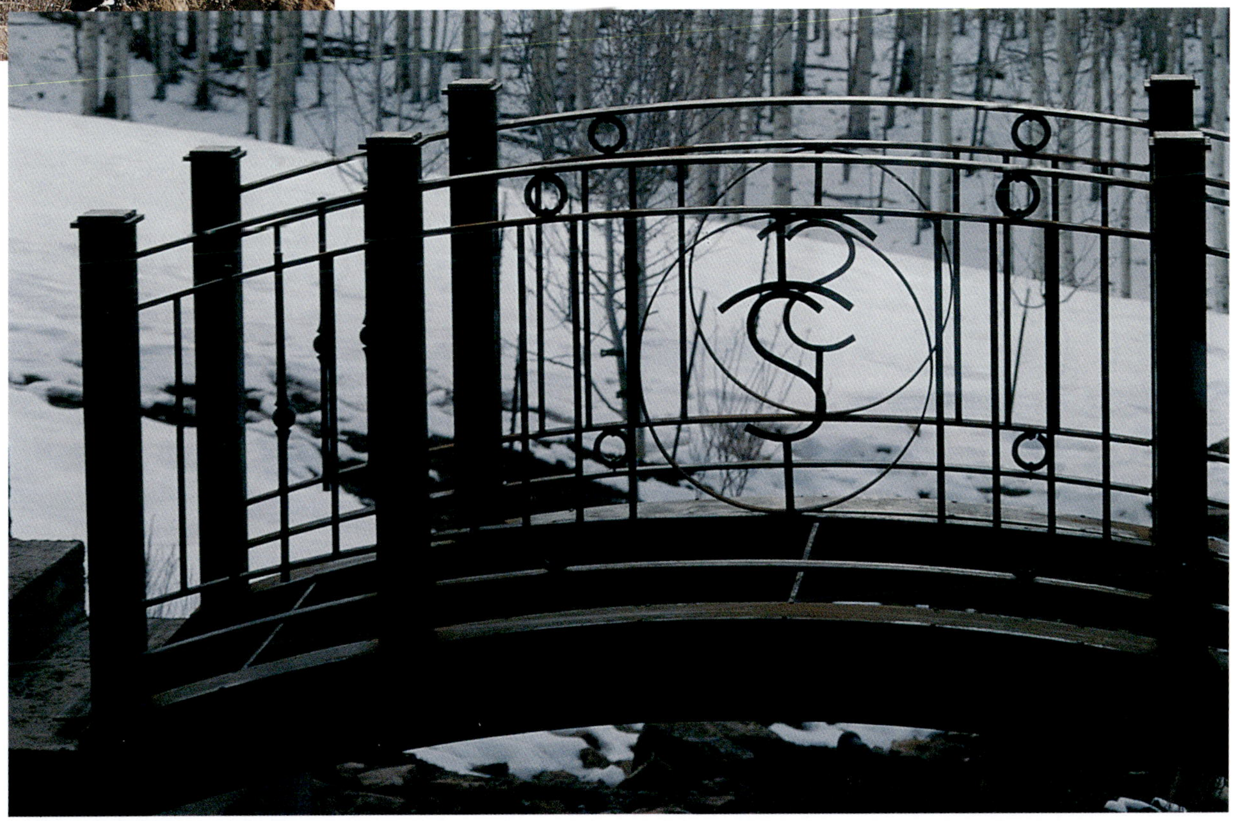

Stephen E. Lee. The bridge spans two parts of the house. *Photo, Kate Hoover*

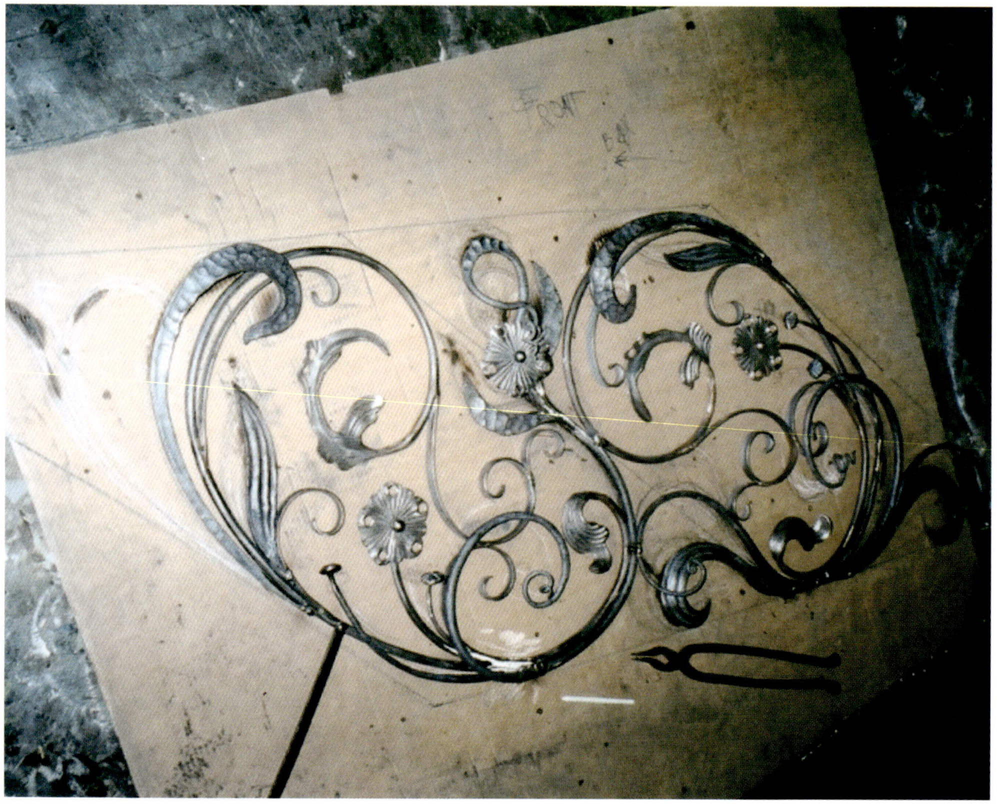

Sergey Sakirkin. Every staircase and railing project begins with a drawing that is blown up to size. Pieces are then forged according to the drawing and the ironwork is fabricated following the paper drawing. *Photo, Richard Prazen*

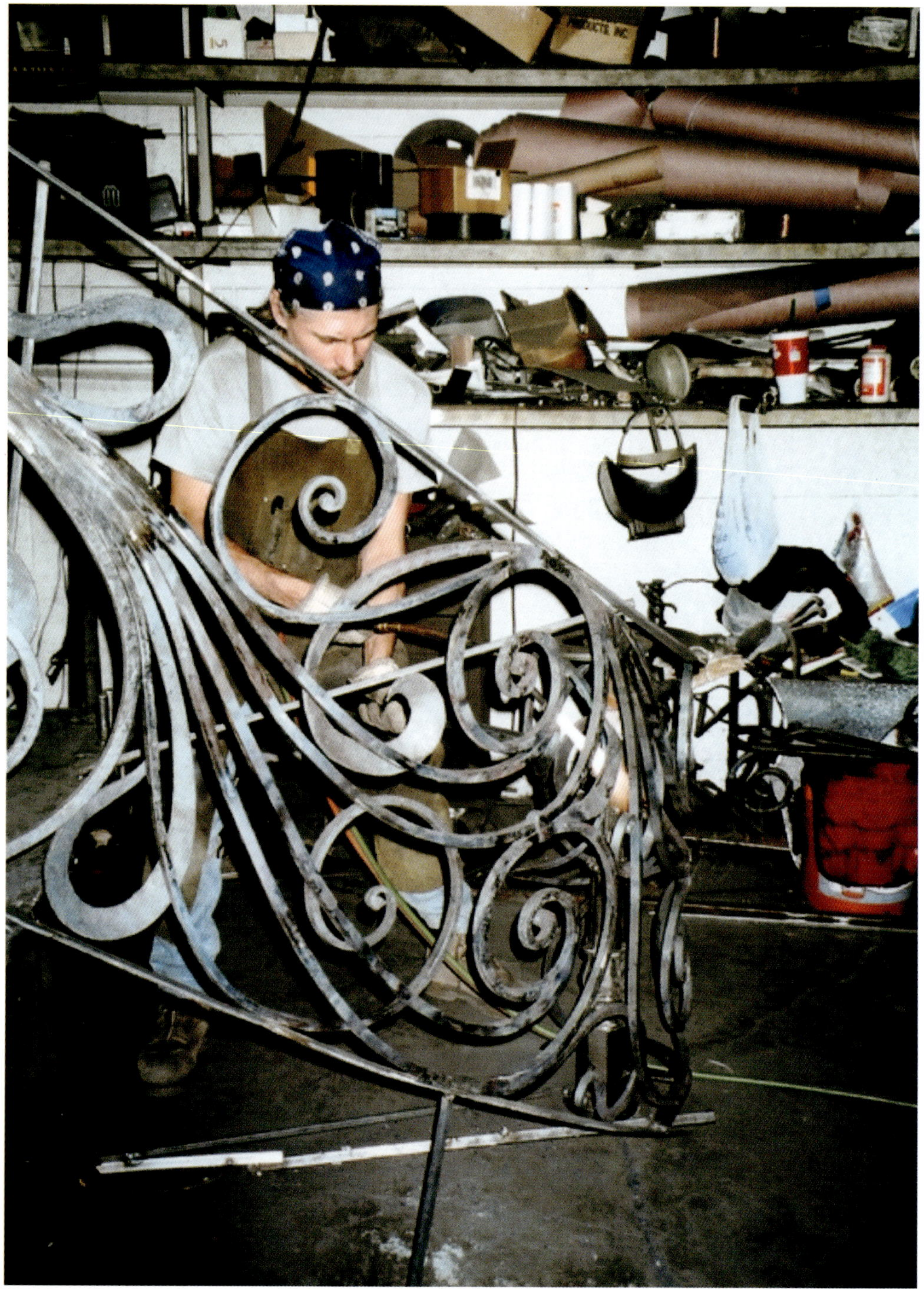

Sergey Sakirkin. The ironwork grows as forged parts are added. It is set up on props angled exactly as the staircase will be after it is installed. *Photo, Courtesy, artist*

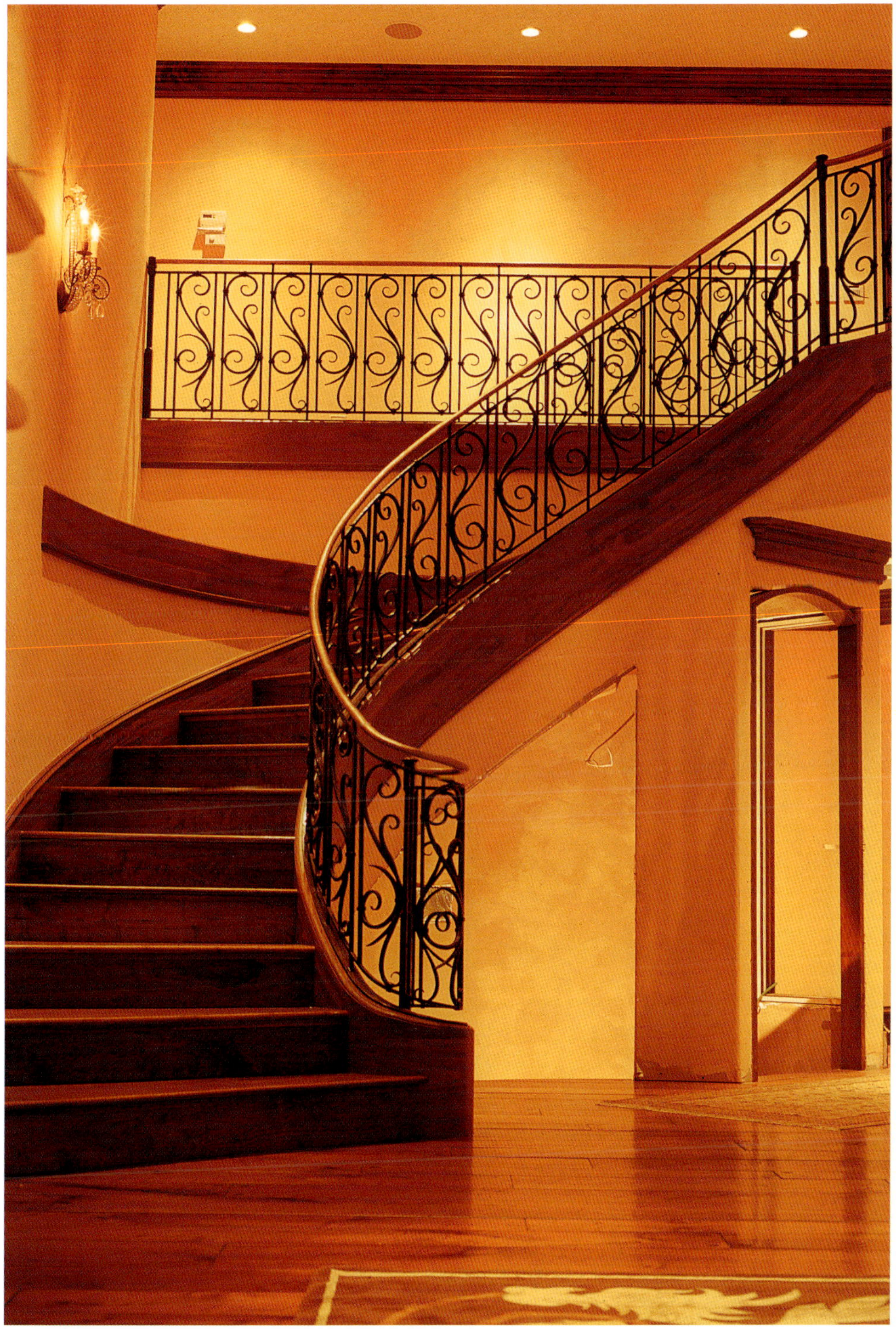

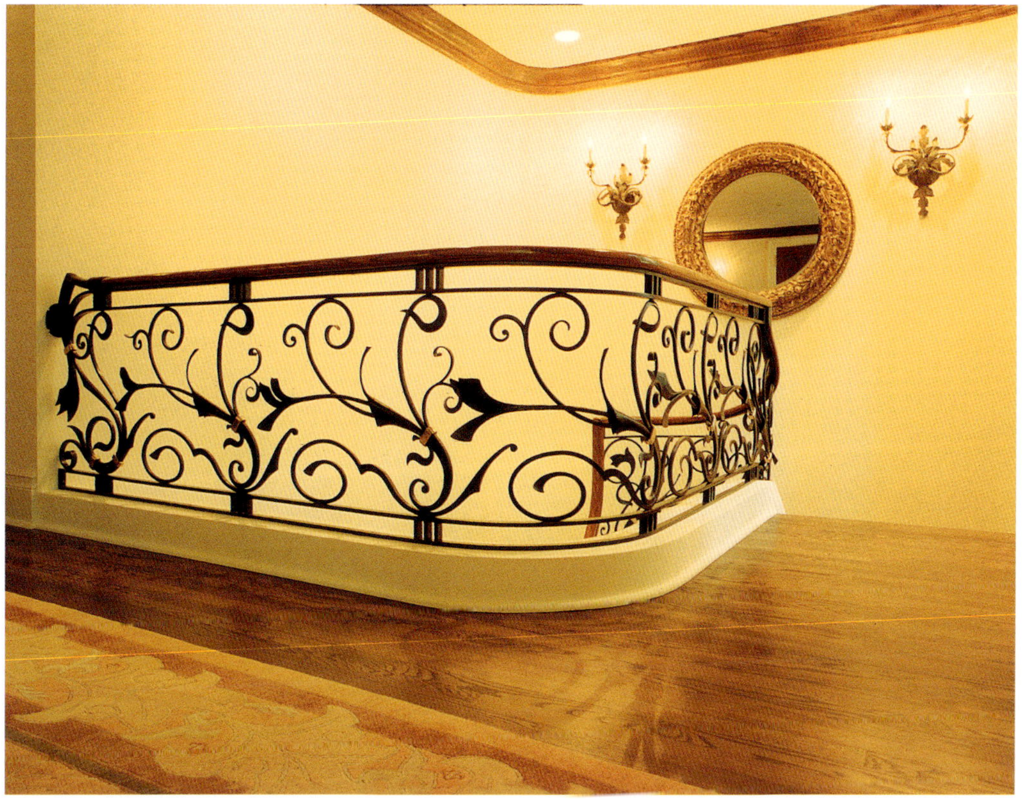

John Medwedeff. Grand staircase, landing view. Forged wrought iron, steel, bronze, and laminated oak. 34" high, 32' long. *Photo, courtesy, artist*

Shawn Lovell. Curved staircase. Forged steel. Traditional forged elements. 3' high, 42' long. *Photo, artist*

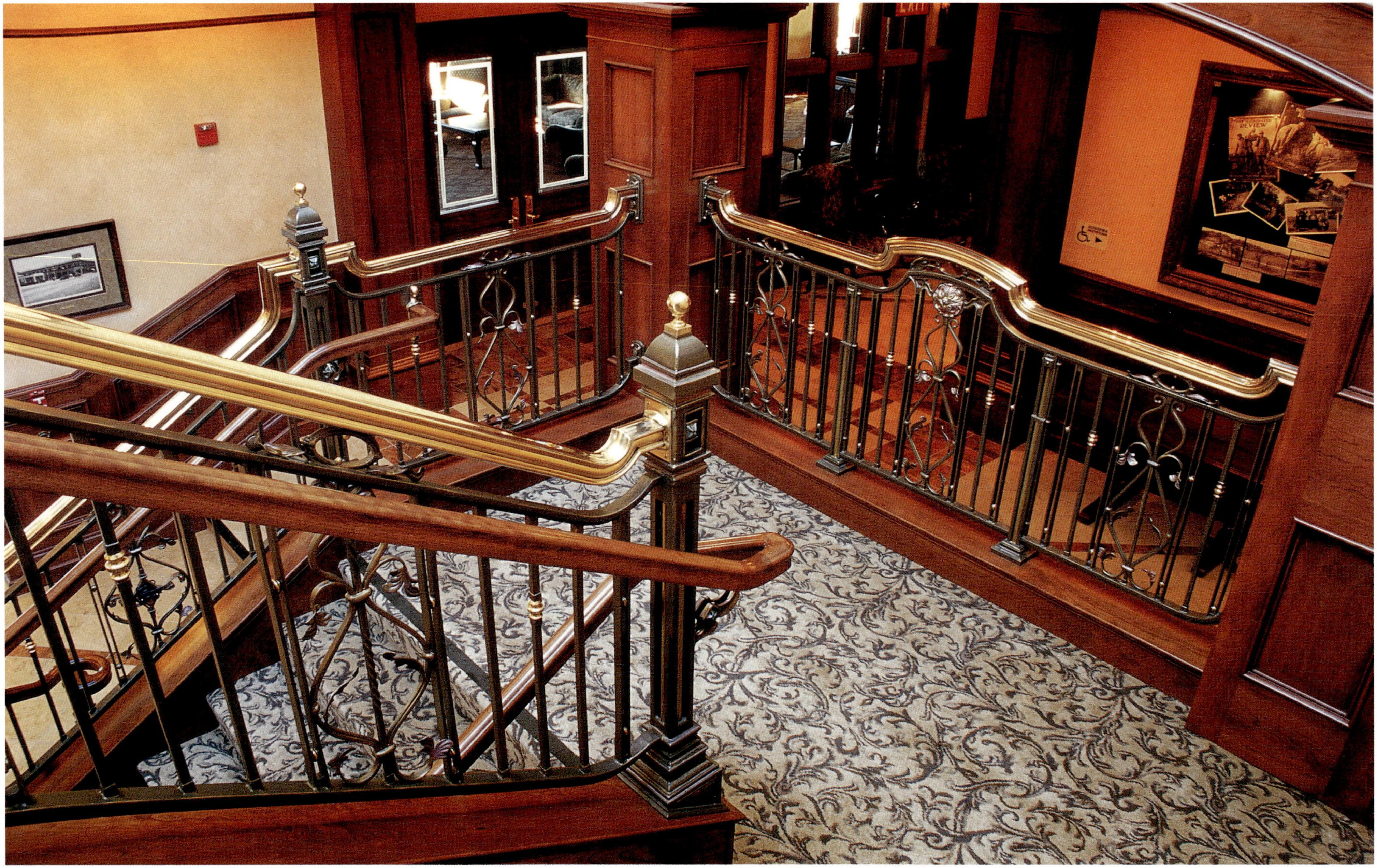

Robert C. Bentley. The new grand staircase for the refurbished early 1900s Hotel Carlton, Paso Robles, California. Iron, bronze, and wood. An early restoration lacked the integrity of the building. Bentley's research led him to use new materials to replicate the original staircase, yet retain the romance, liveliness, and shapes of the original. *Photo, Bruce Woodworth*

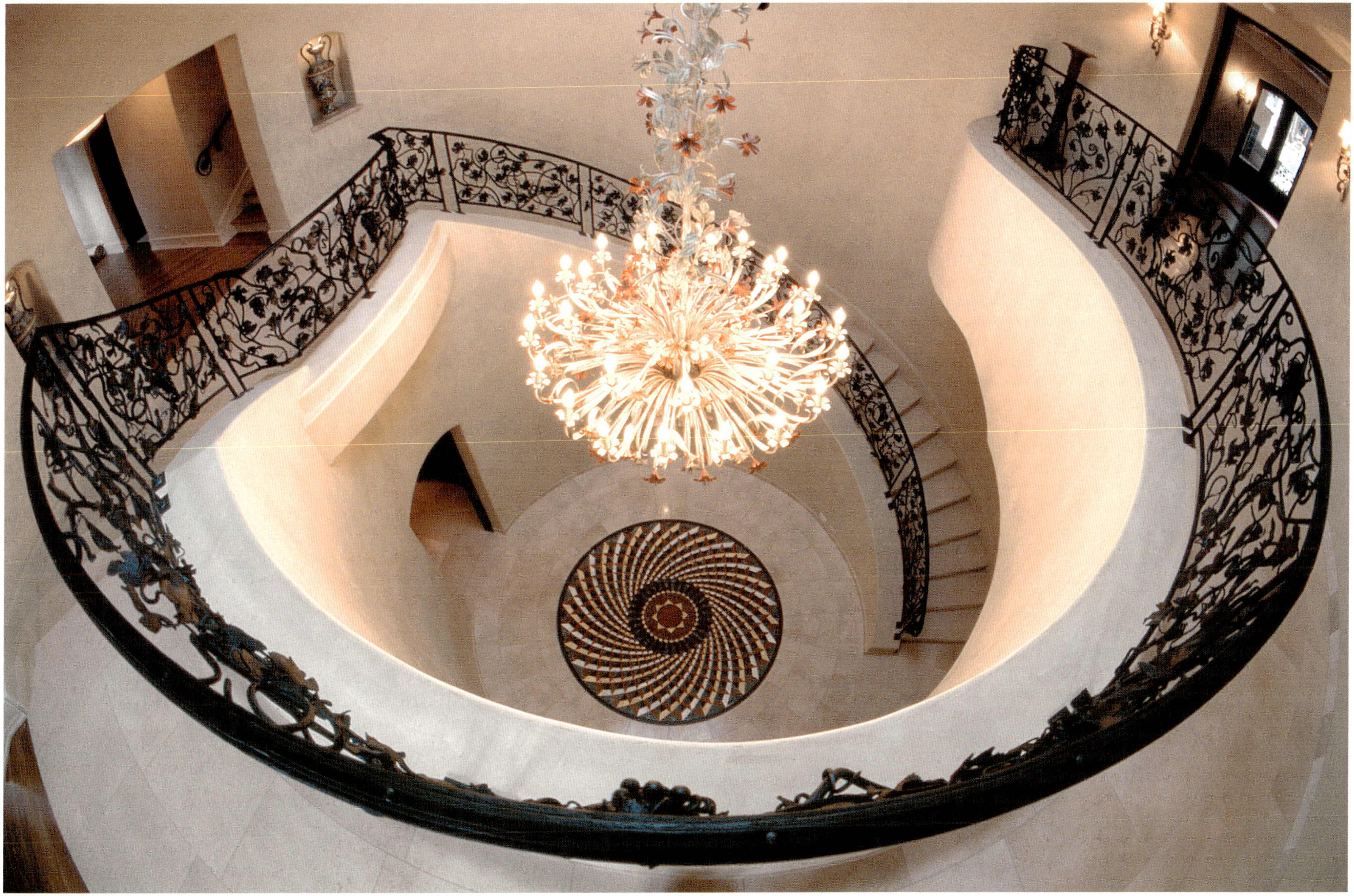

Butch Lee. Grape vine railing is a double laminate. It contains 450 leaves, 32 grape clusters and 2300' of vine leaves. 67' long. *Photo, David Harres*

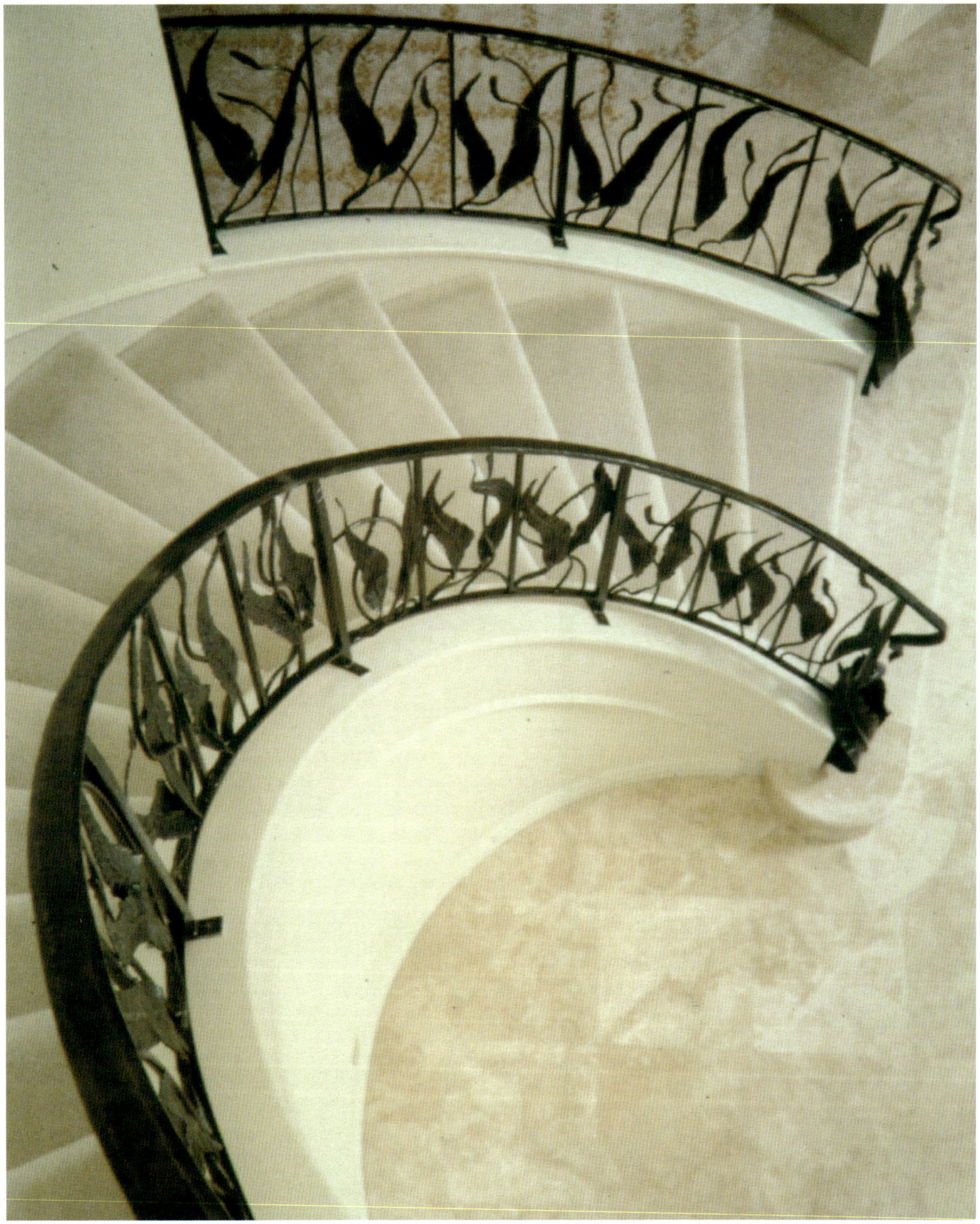

Lars Stanley, assisted by Larry Crawford and Robert Abdallah. *The Shelburne Staircase.* Forged and fabricated of steel components with large leaves forged from steel angle iron. Each panel was treated as a canvas on which to devise an aesthetic pattern with leaves and grass forms. Each one is different but still complements the whole and complies with code requirements at the time. 30' long. *Photo, artist*

Lars Stanley. Detail of rail ending.

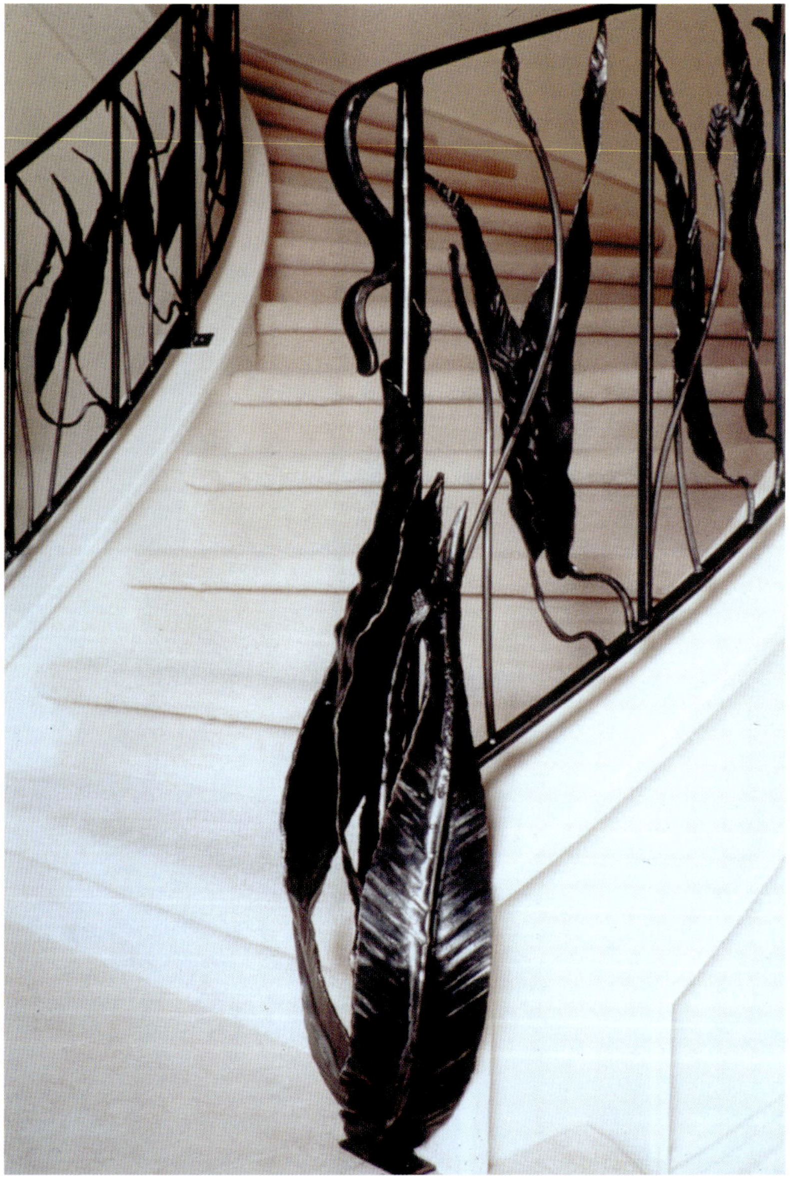

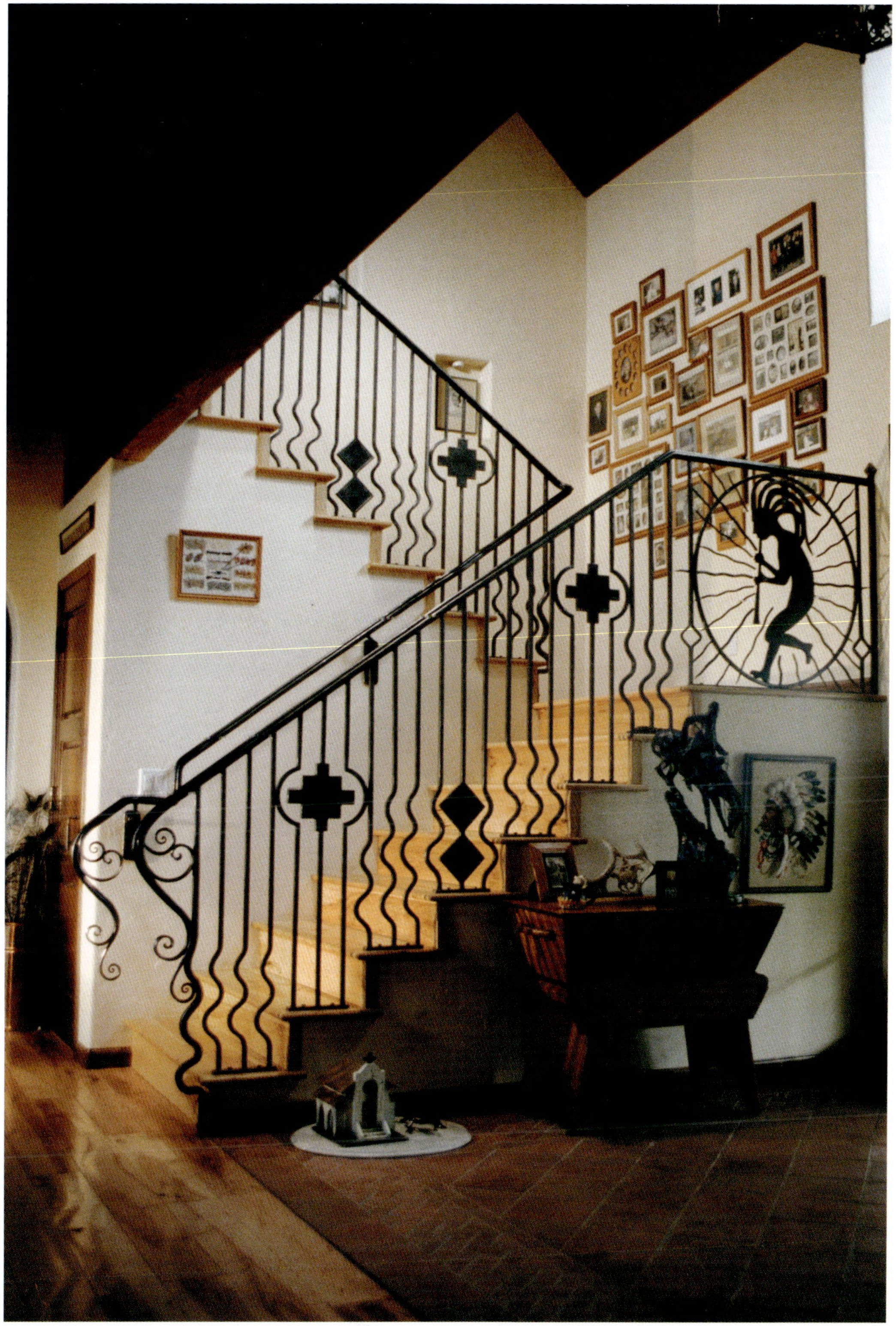

Reuel Darling. Kokopelli staircase for a private home owned by American Indian art collectors. Various symbols incorporated in the staircase represent specific tribes. *Photo, Jodi Darling*

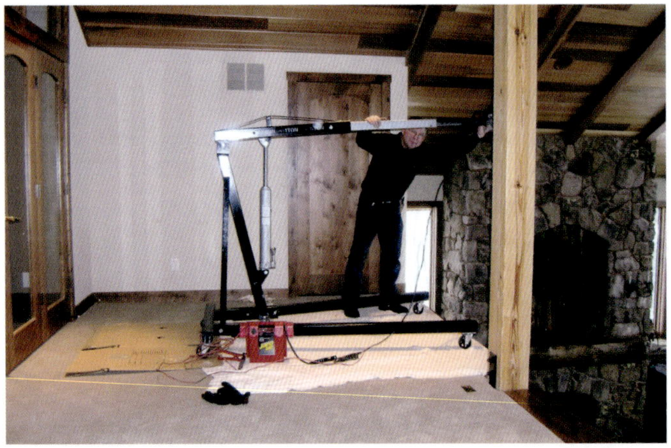

Robert Walsh, Keith Johnson, and Robert Loyson. To install the railing on the following page, Roger Loyson modified an engine hoist to serve as an electric winch powered by a portable battery pack.

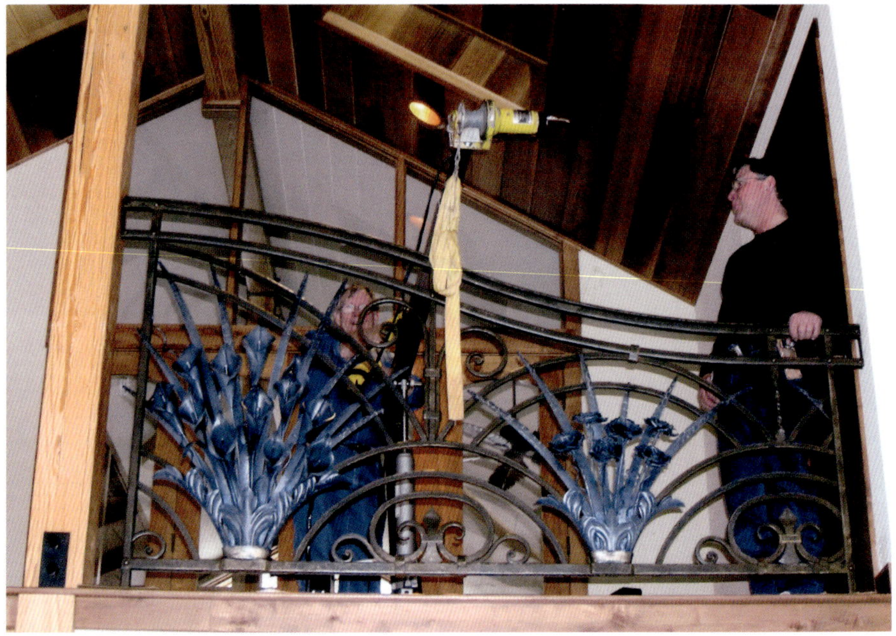

Robert Walsh, Keith Johnson, and Robert Loyson. The railing was lifted to the proper height and the hoist was rolled backwards to position the railing on the landing. *Photos, Robert Walsh*

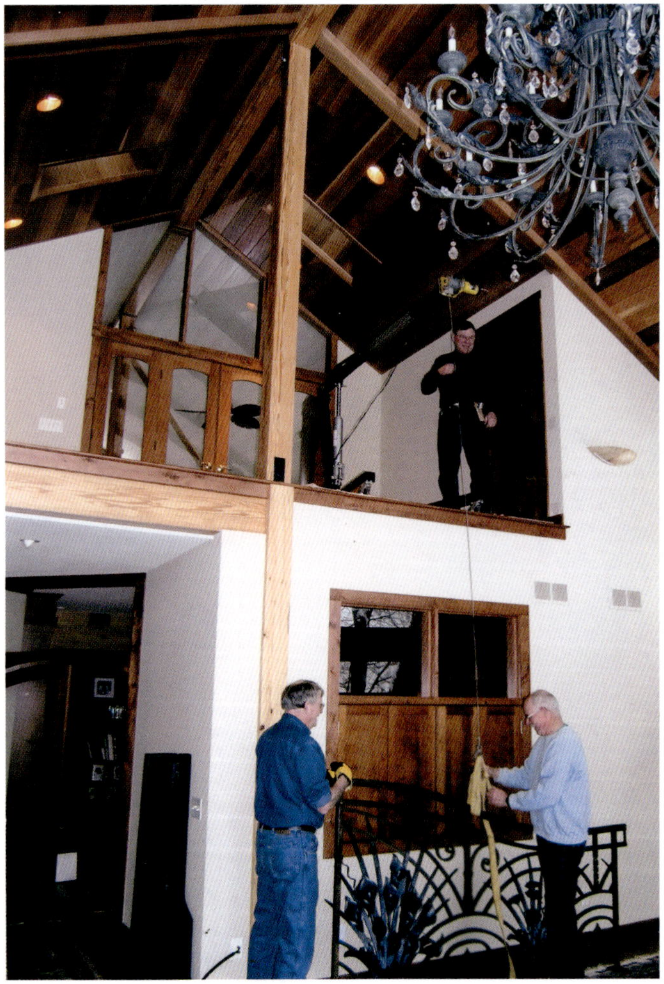

Robert Walsh, Keith Johnson, and Robert Loyson. With the winch in place, cables were dropped. Peter Stanaitis and Keith Johnson attach them to the railing. *Photo, Robert Walsh*

After the metalwork was accomplished, Roger Loyson, a master painter/finisher added the final patinas and coatings. Installation often requires anticipating and improvising solutions to perceived problems. To raise each half of the heavy railing to the second floor position, Loyson attached a battery-powered winch on the end of a cherry picker used for removing motors from cars. The picker is easily disassembled so its parts could be taken to the second floor and reassembled. The picker was then wheeled to the balcony edge allowing a welded extension to protrude over the edge. Cables and hooks were lowered and attached to the railing so it could be easily raised to the correct height. Then the picker was rolled backwards and the first half of the railing was in place. The process was repeated for the second half. *Photos, Robert Walsh*

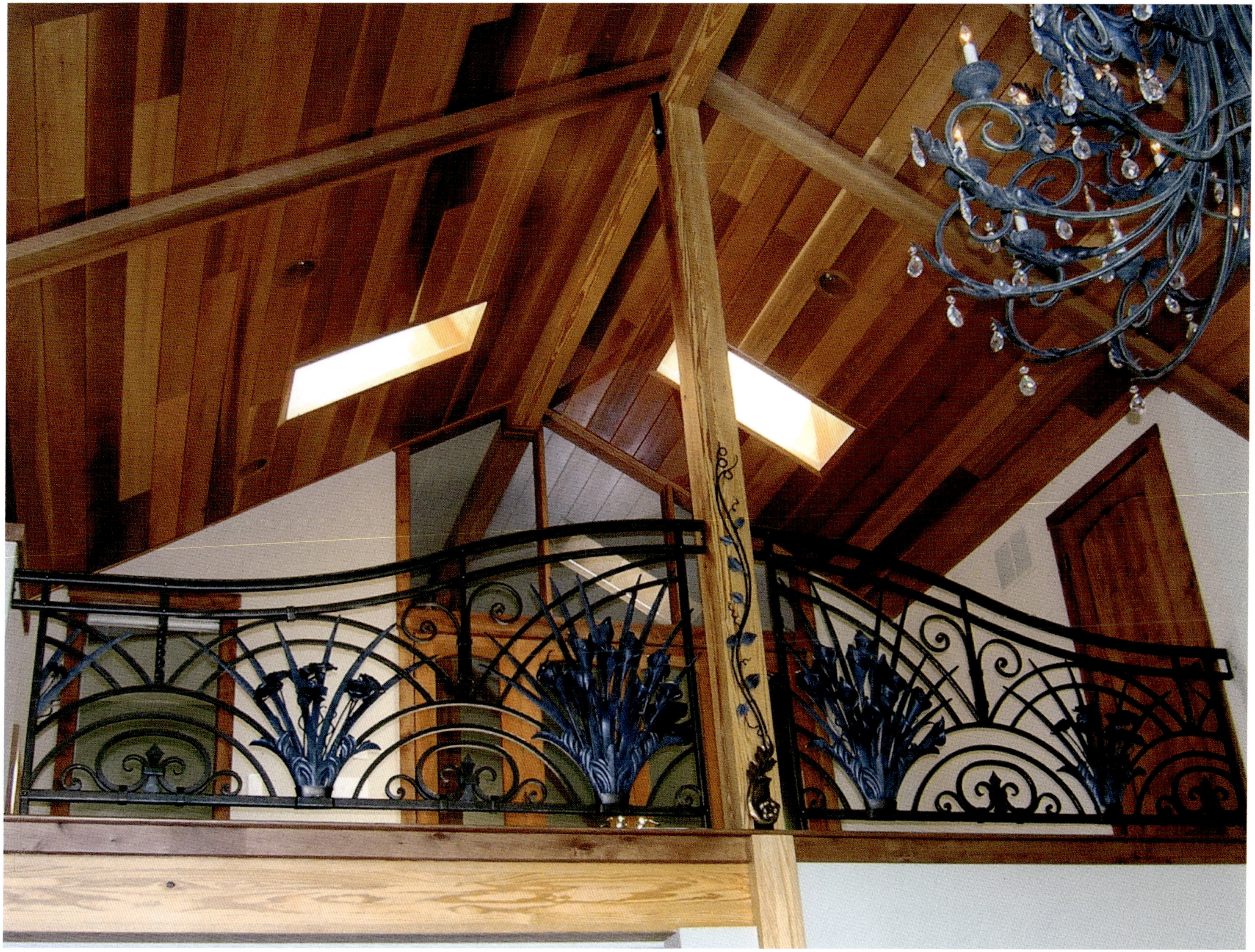

Robert Walsh, Keith Johnson, and Robert Loyson. The finished railing. The second half of the railing was hoisted as the first. Innovative use of equipment is normal for many blacksmiths where specific jobs pose new problems that require brilliant solutions. *Photo, Robert Walsh*

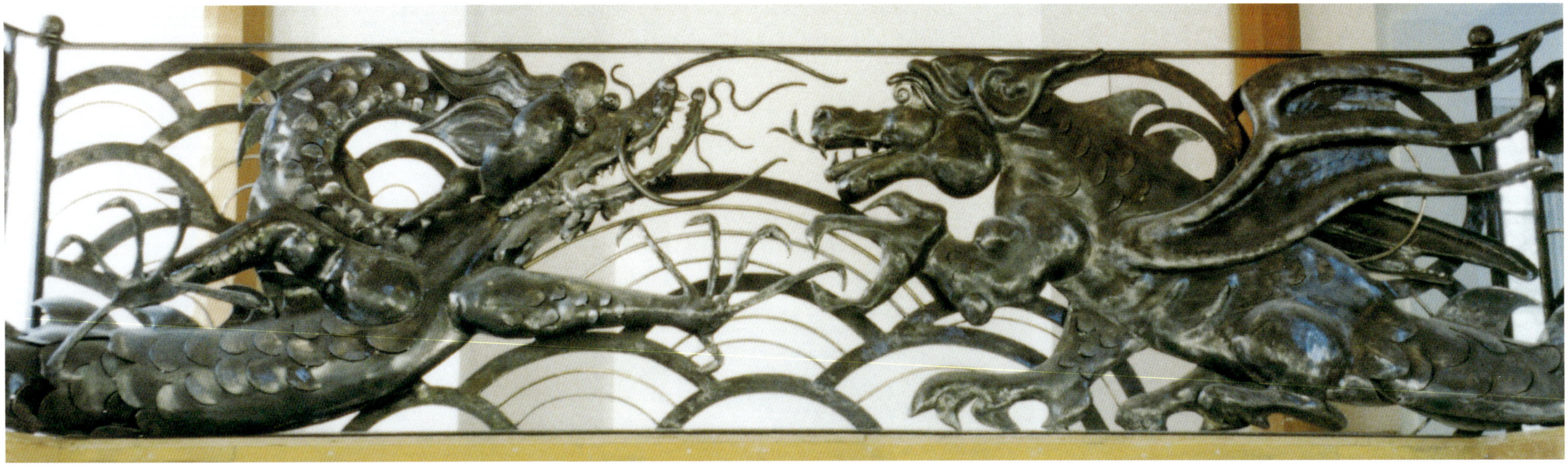

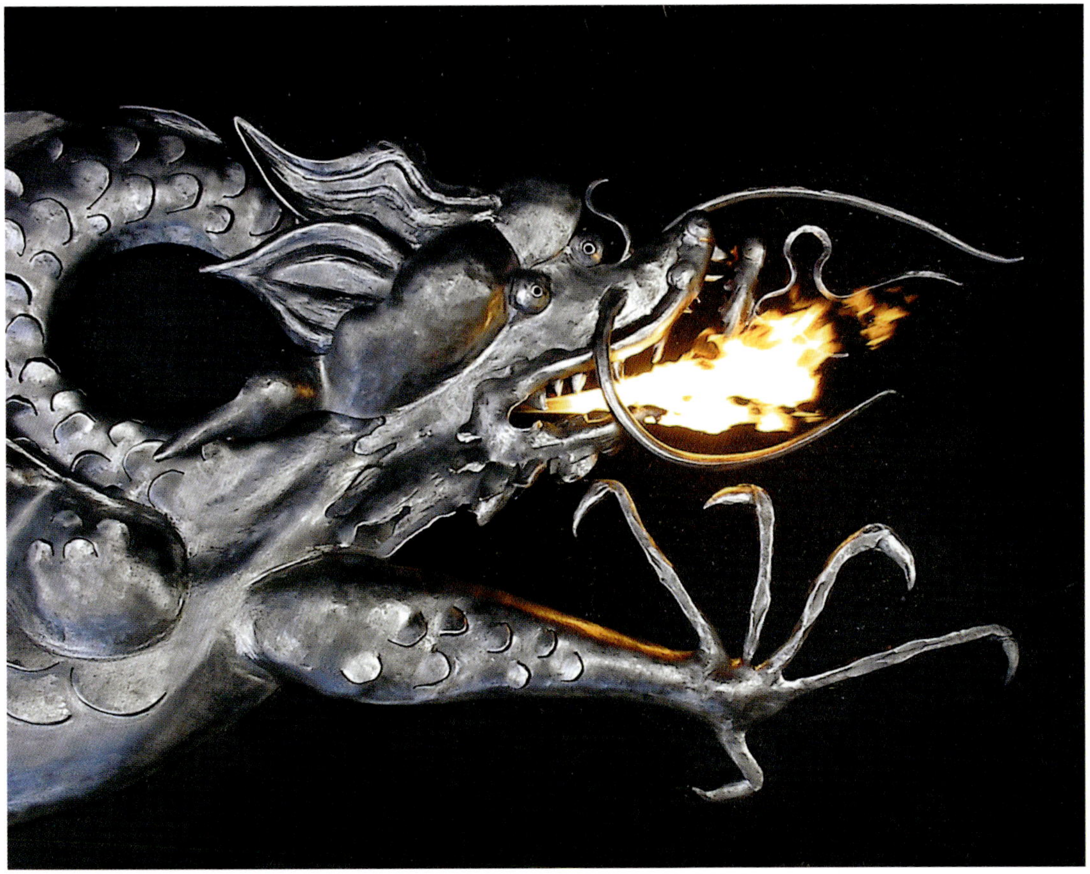

Dimitri Gerakaris. Balcony Rail (detail). Forged and fabricated steel. For the "Great Room" of a Connecticut residence. The railing portrays dragons associated with the culture of the owners. 35' long. *Photo, J.D. Messick, © D.Gerakaris*

Dimitri Gerakaris. Detail of the dragon shaped with forging and repoussé techniques. *Photo, J.D. Messick, ©D.Gerakaris*

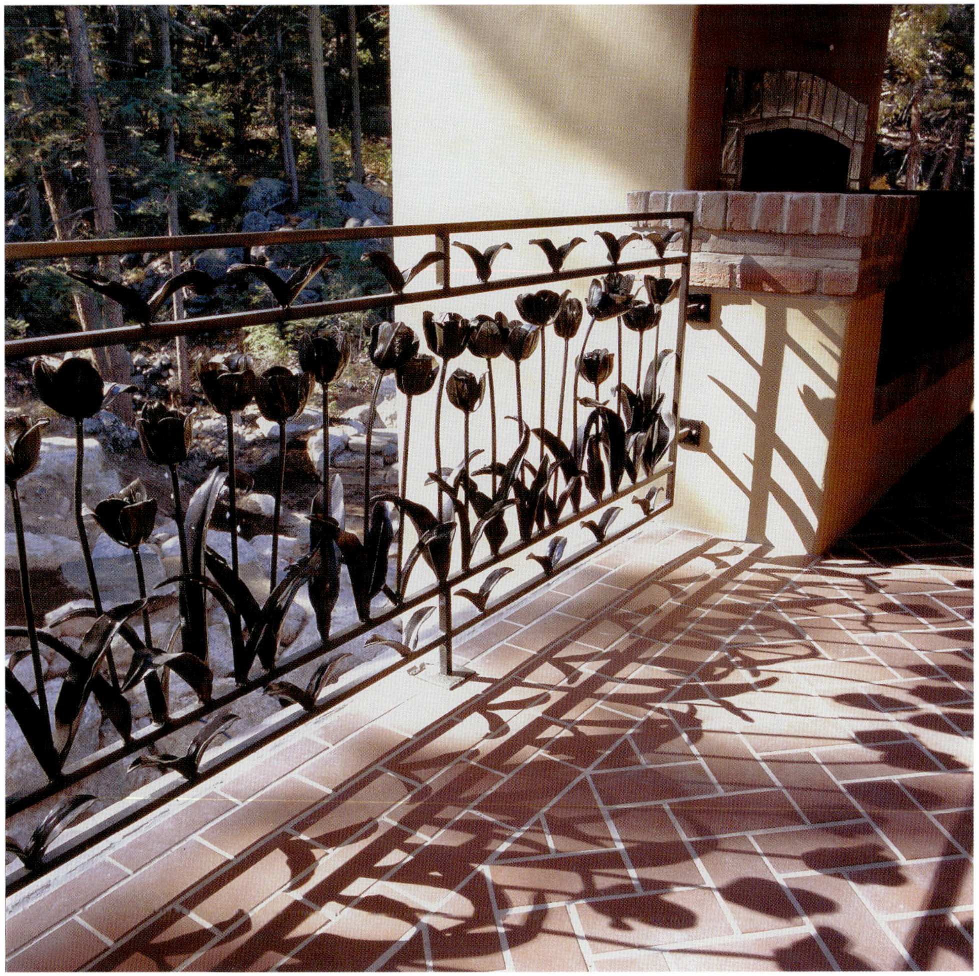

Butch Lee. Tulip railing for an outdoor terrace. Made with 56 tulips, each with a pistil within. 23' long. *Photo, David Harres*

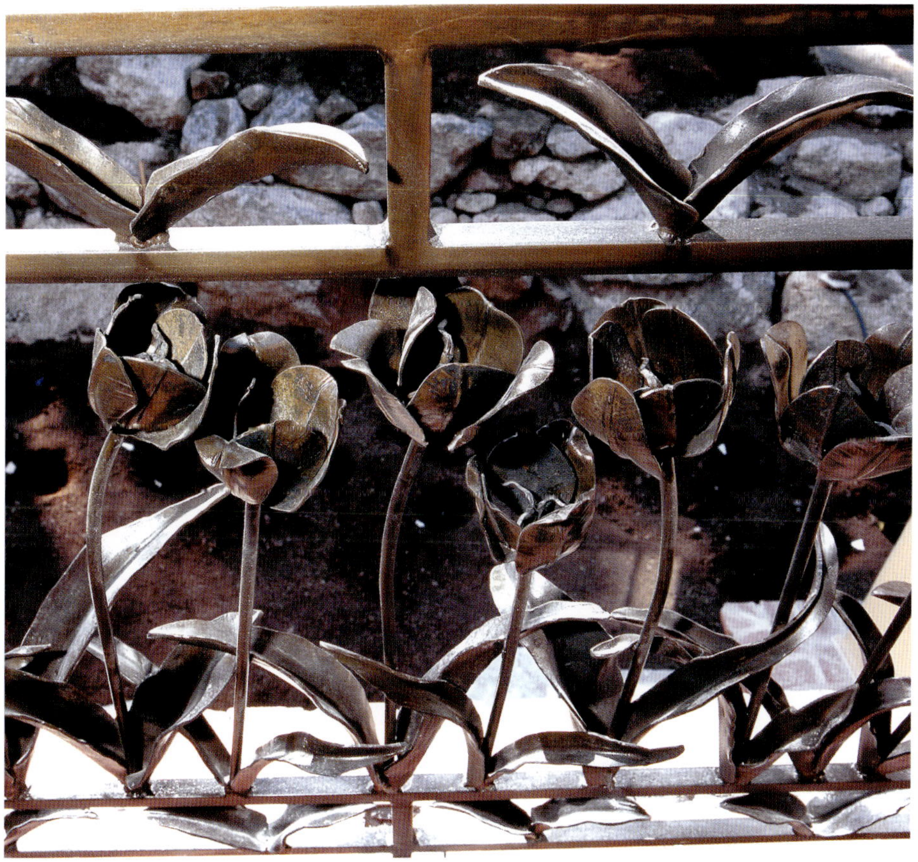

Butch Lee. Tulip detail. *Photo, David Harres*

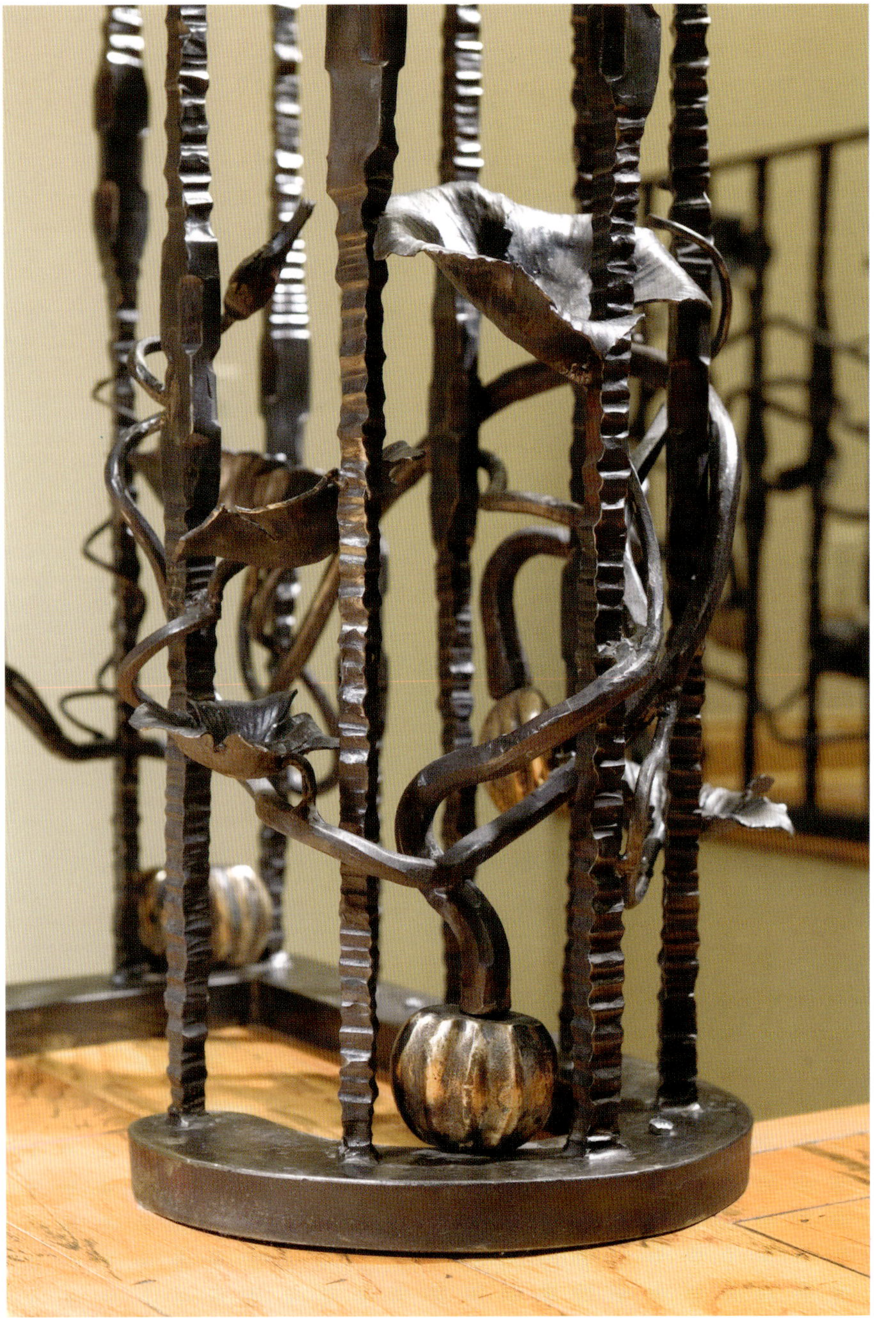

Craig Kaviar. End detail of a "pumpkin" handrail. Forged iron and bronze. *Photo, James Moses*

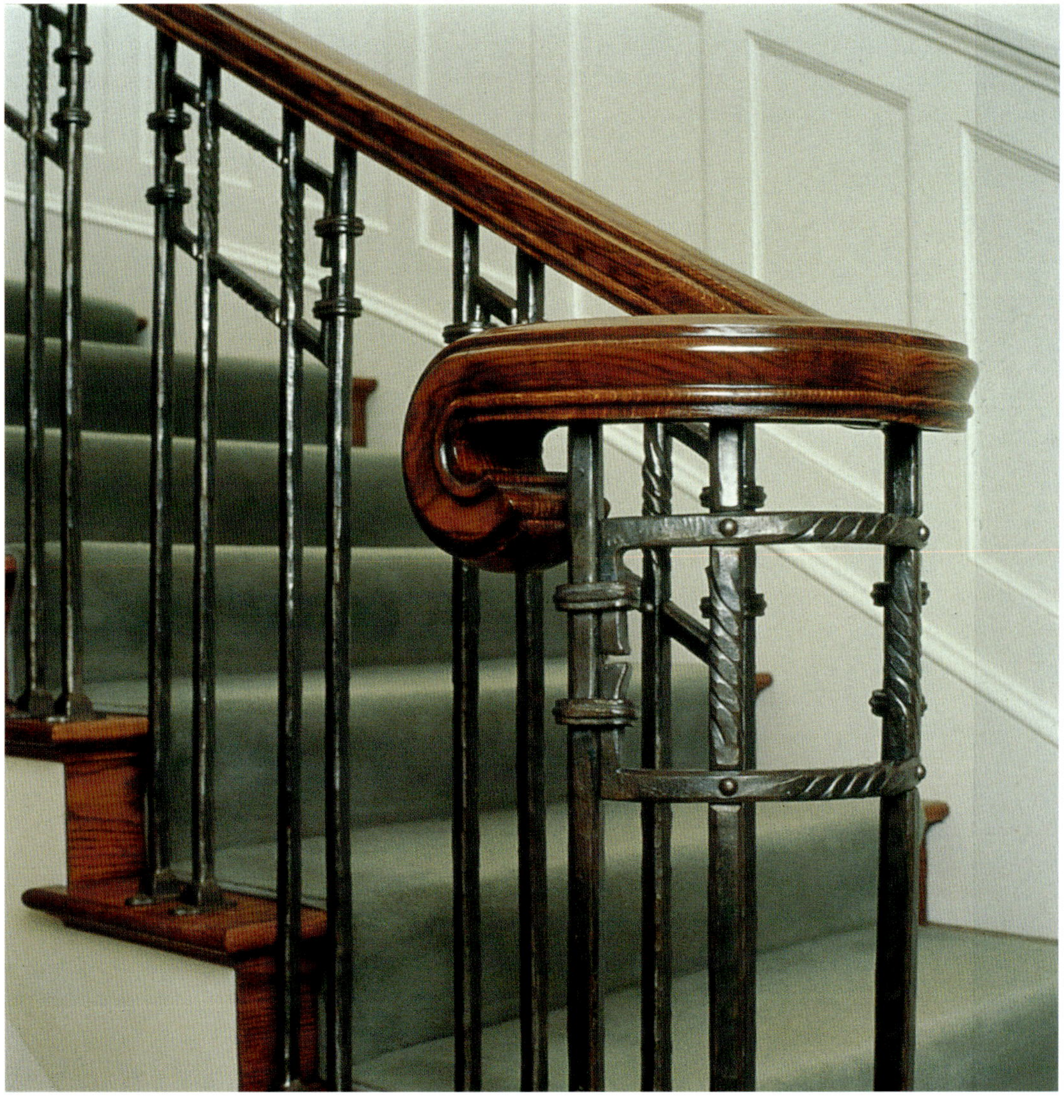

John-Pierre Masbanji. Railing detail showing the newel end with twisted and half-notched detail. Waxed pewter highlighted finish. *Photo, James Chen*

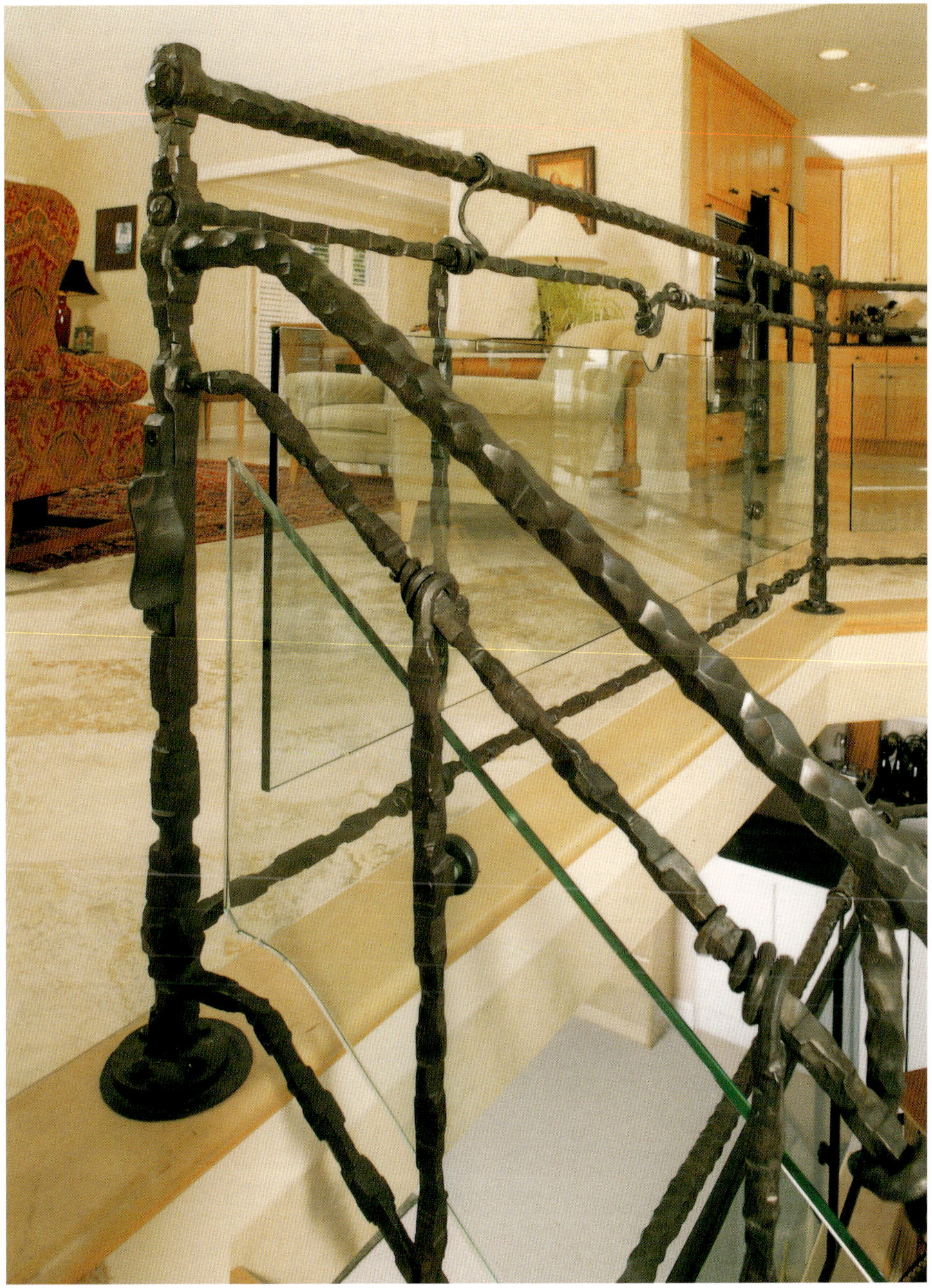

Craig Kaviar. Waggner hand rails. Forged iron and glass handrail for three floors of a contemporary house. 55' of railing. *Photo, artist*

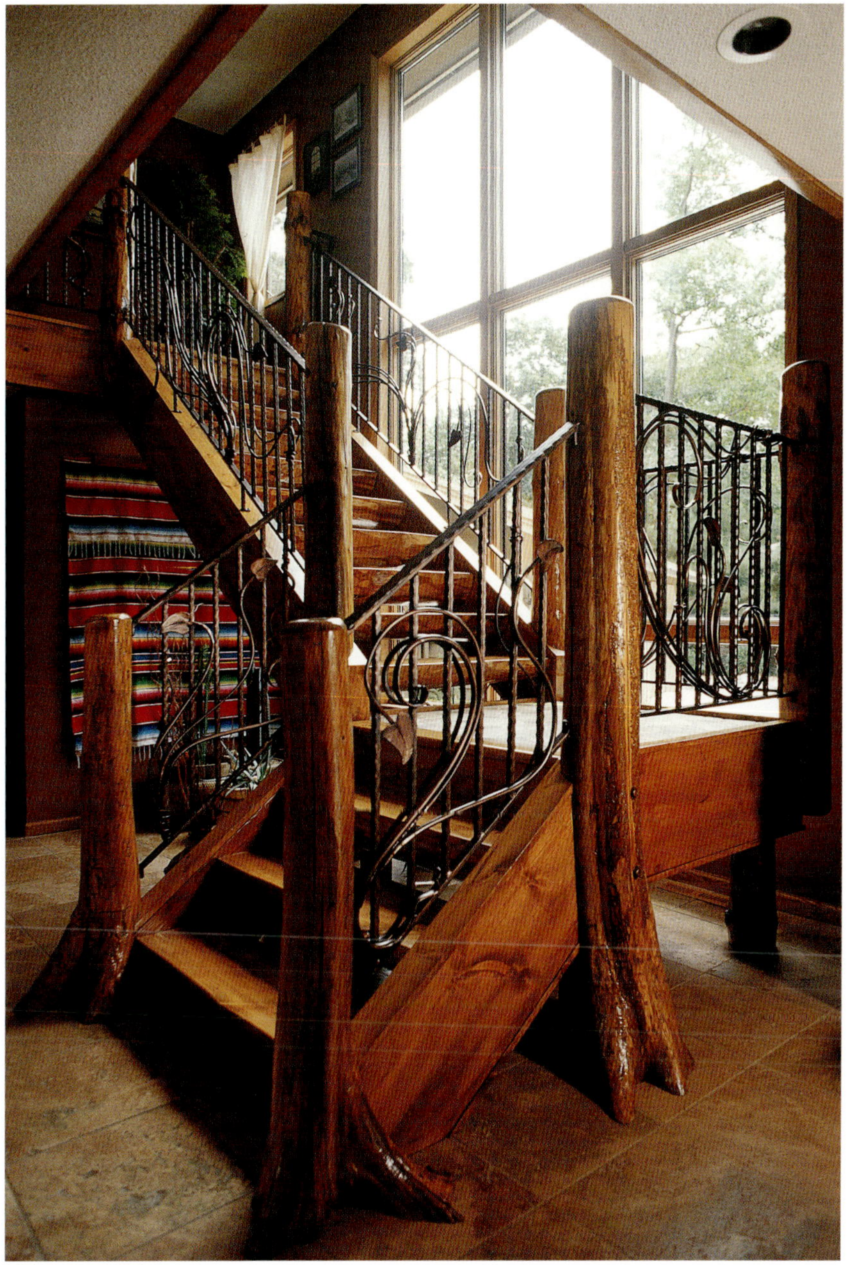

Lisa Elias. *Nature railing.* Mild steel, powder coated matte black, hand painted with a copper wash. The wood posts are simulated to look like tree trunks with roots. The commission for a private residence included 80-feet of railing and two small interior gates. *Photo, artist*

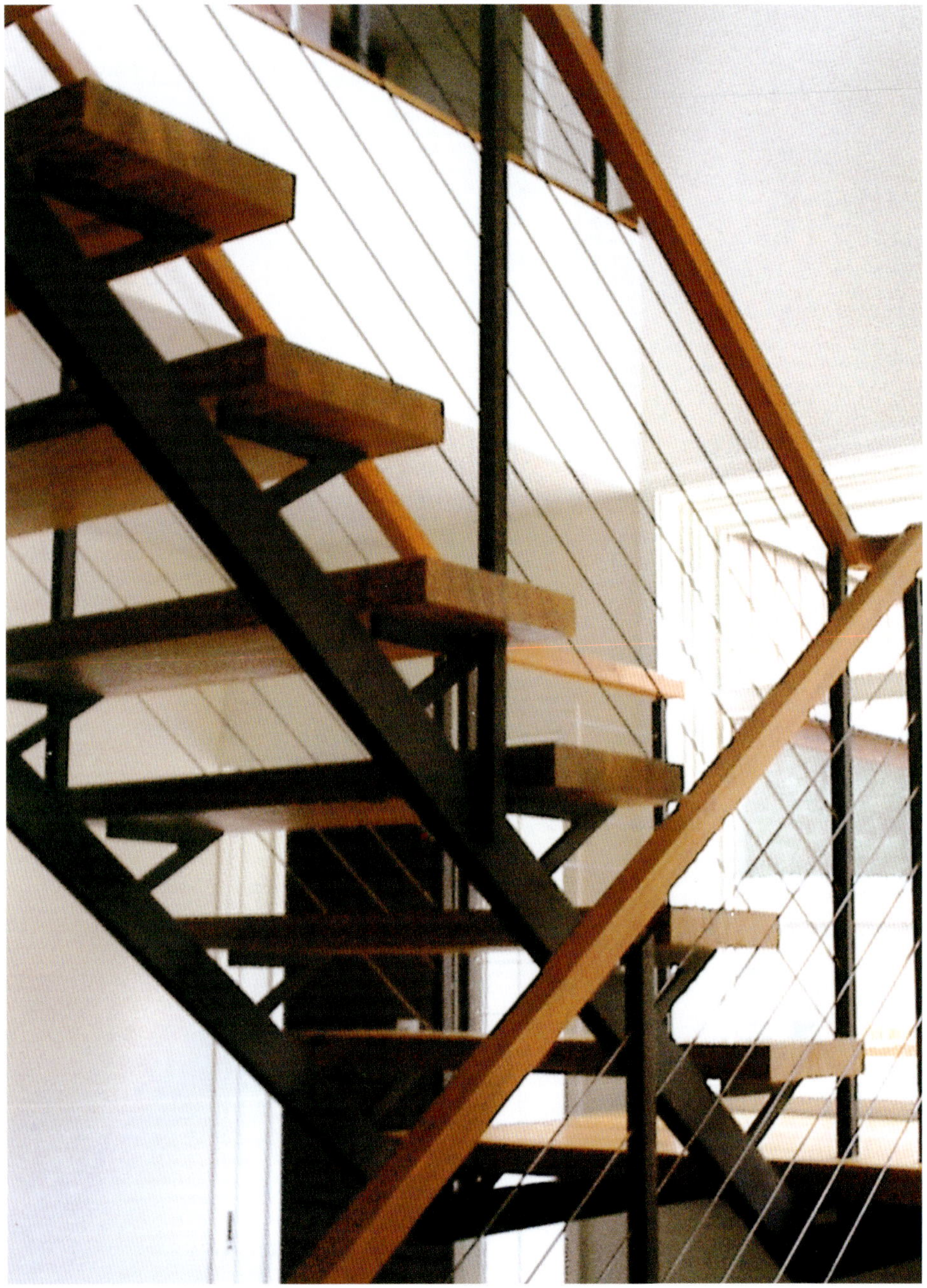

Cape Cod Fabrications. Monumental stair and rail system. Close-up of the mid-stair transition. Sandblasted and gun blued carbon steel with clear coat finish. Stainless steel cables with an acid patina. *Photo, CCF Architectural Metals*

Elmer Roush and Lynda Metcalfe. *Laurel and Willow Railing*. Private residence, Jamestown, Tennessee. *Photo, artists*

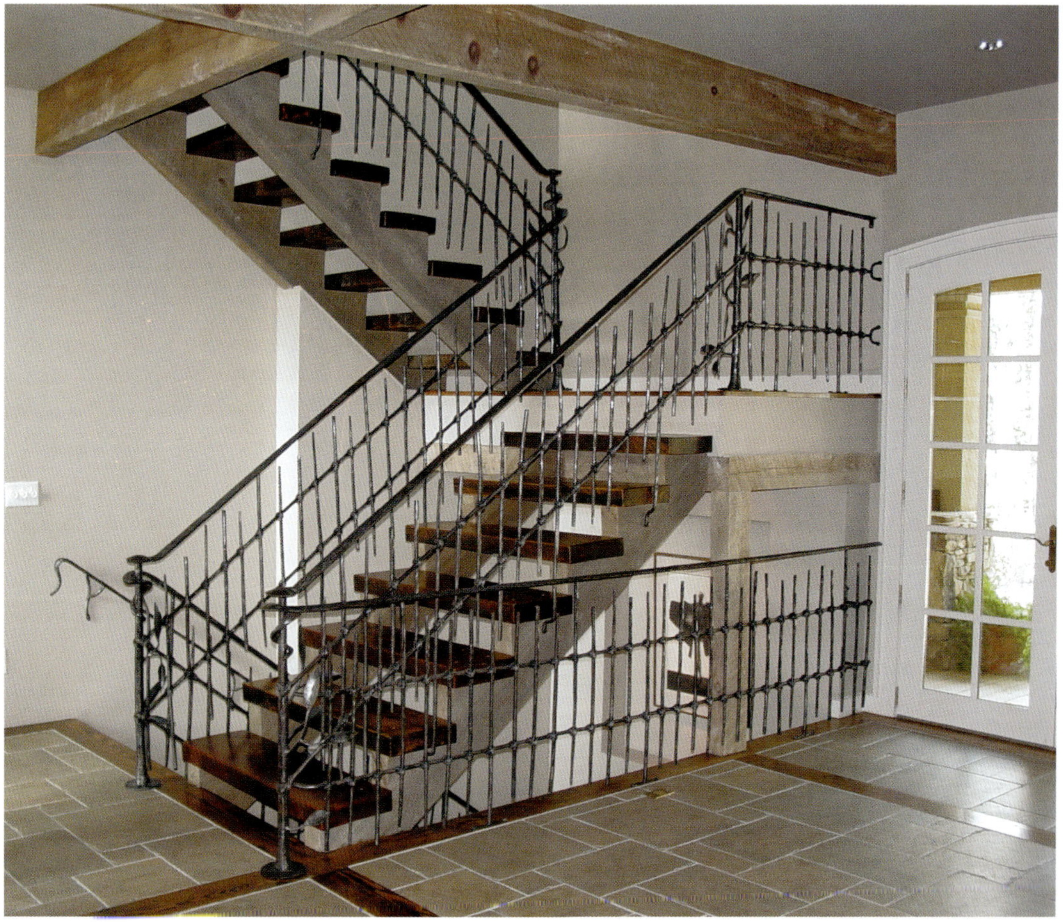

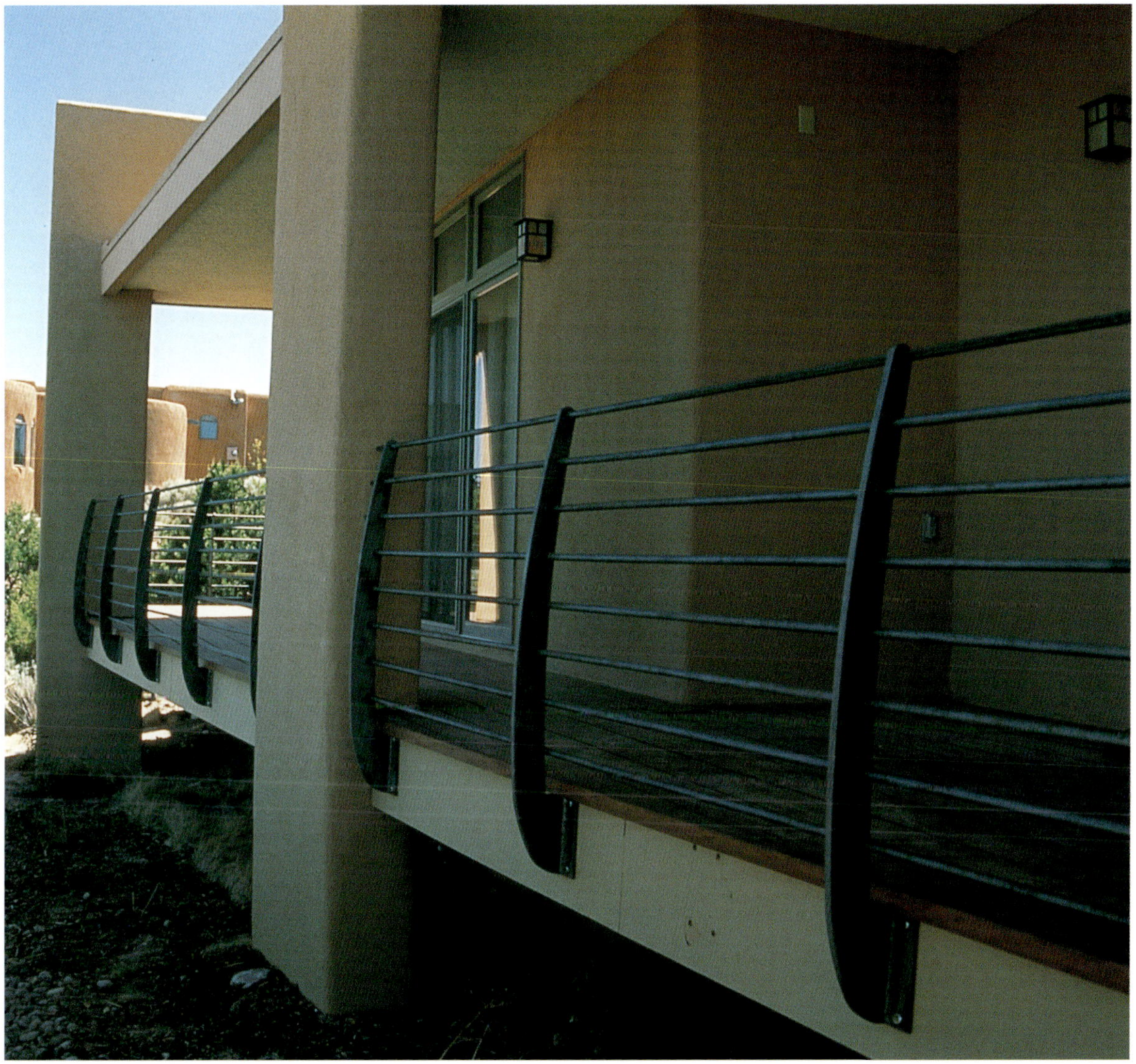

Helmut Hillenkamp. Railing for a private residence in Santa Fe, New Mexico. The railing was designed so that it would interfere only minimally with the views of the landscape. The posts are water jet cut and the round bars are pinned into them. The design concept was to evoke a nautical feeling as if one were on board a ship looking out over the desert. *Photos, artist*

Detail of the corner. *Photo, artist*

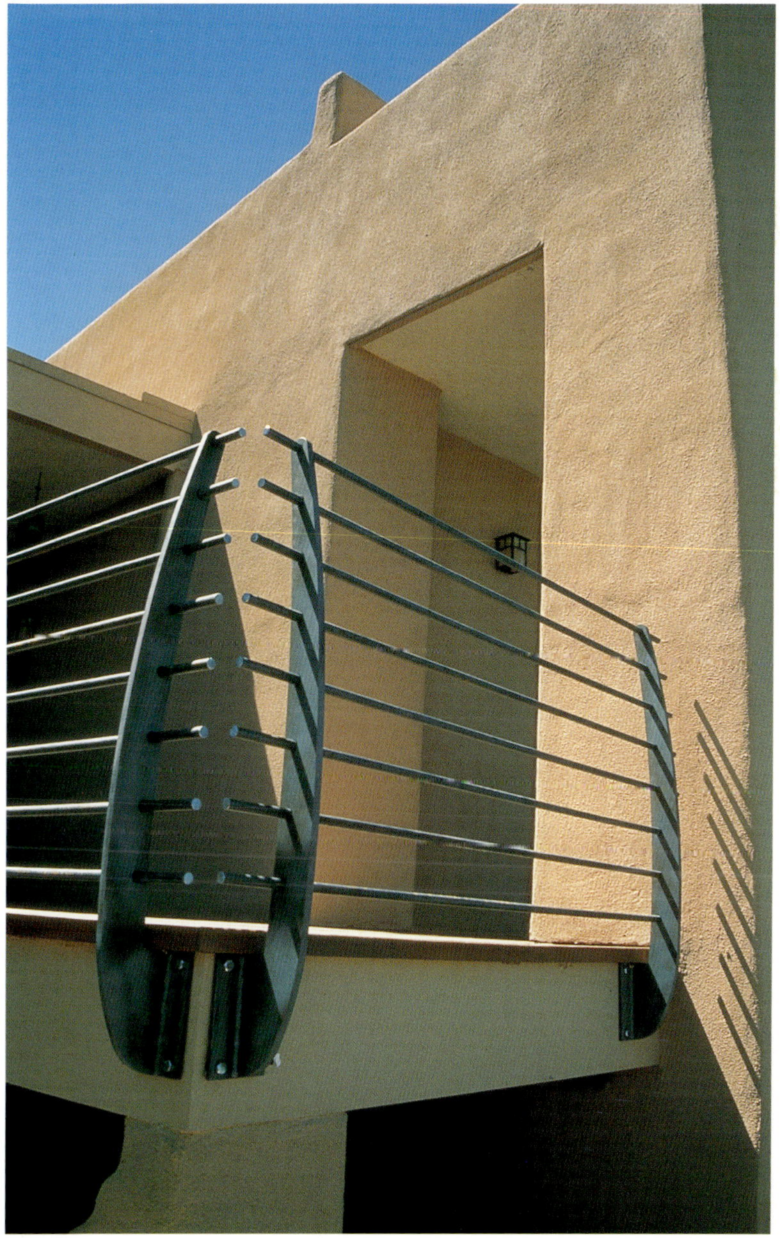

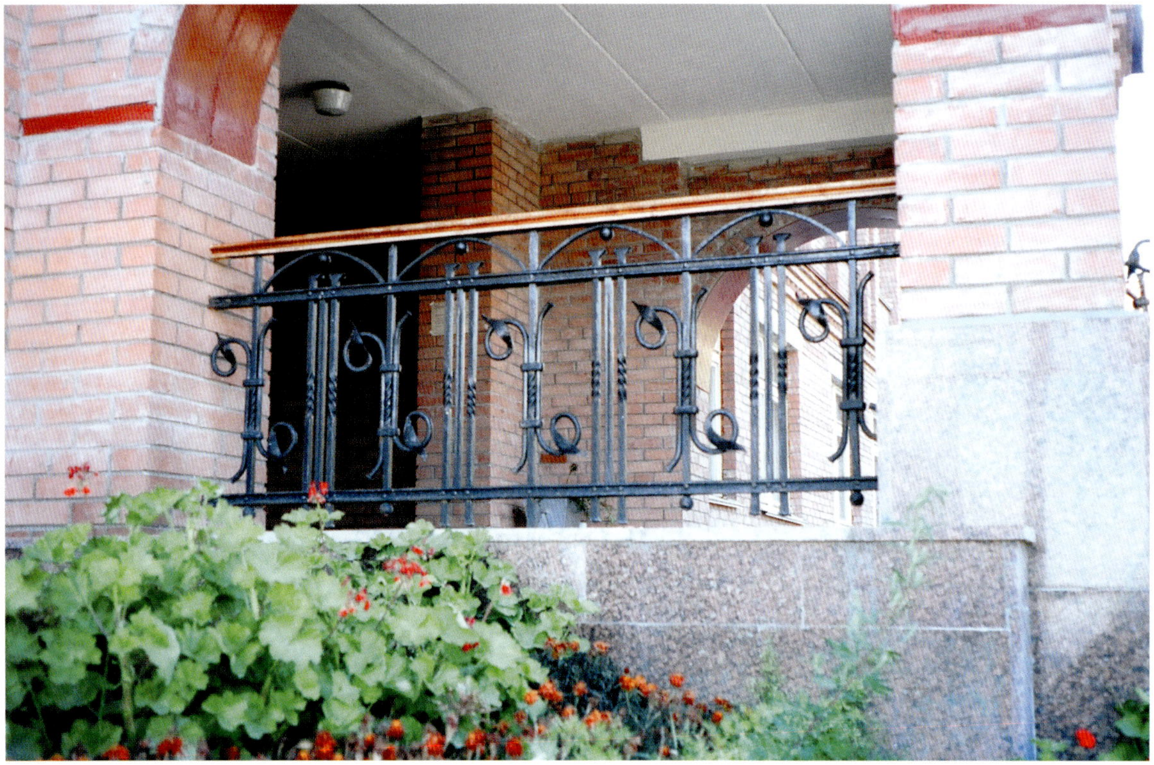

Sergey Sakirkin with Schram. Railing. Forged steel, for a hospital in Russia. *Photo, artist*

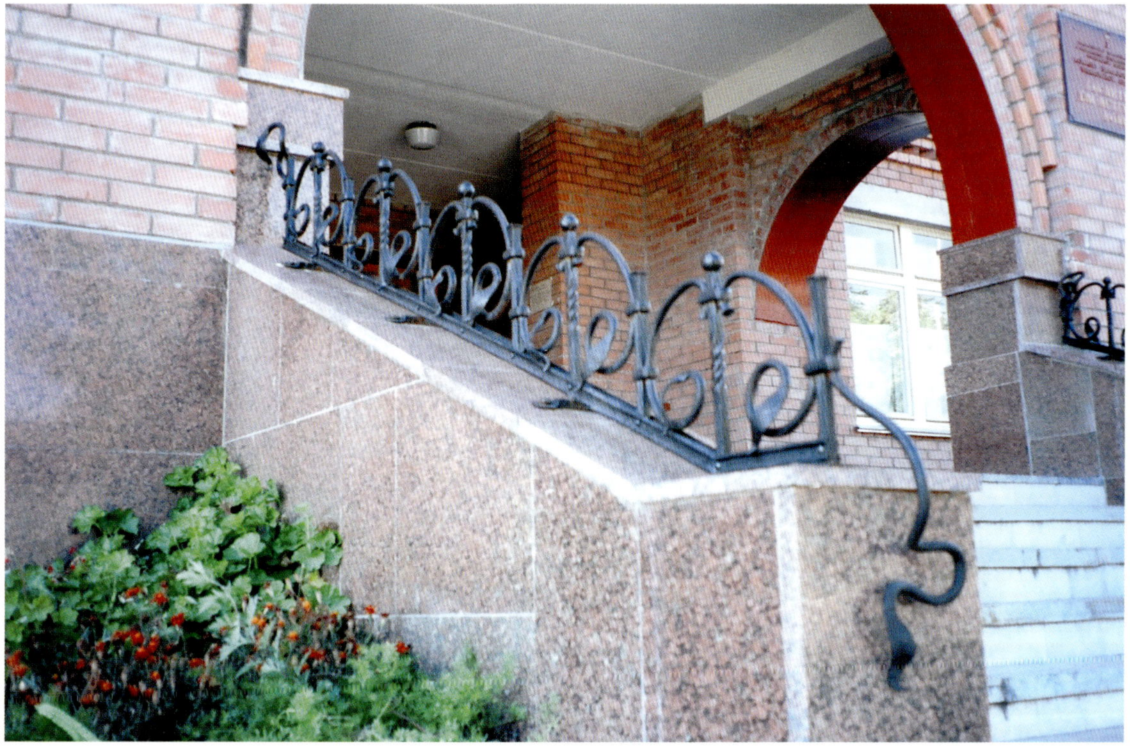

Sergey Sakirkin. Forged steel hand railing. 17" high, 10' long. *Photo, artist*

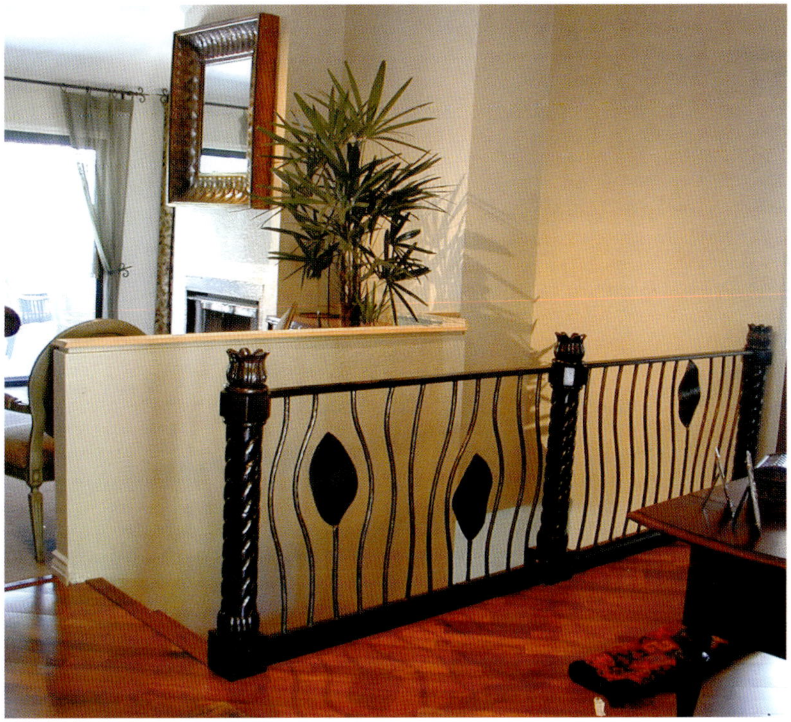

Andy Leritz/Deform. Banana Leaf railing. Forged iron and mahogany. The design was a collaboration between the client and the artist. The client wanted something tropical. 3' high, 12' long. *Photo, artist*

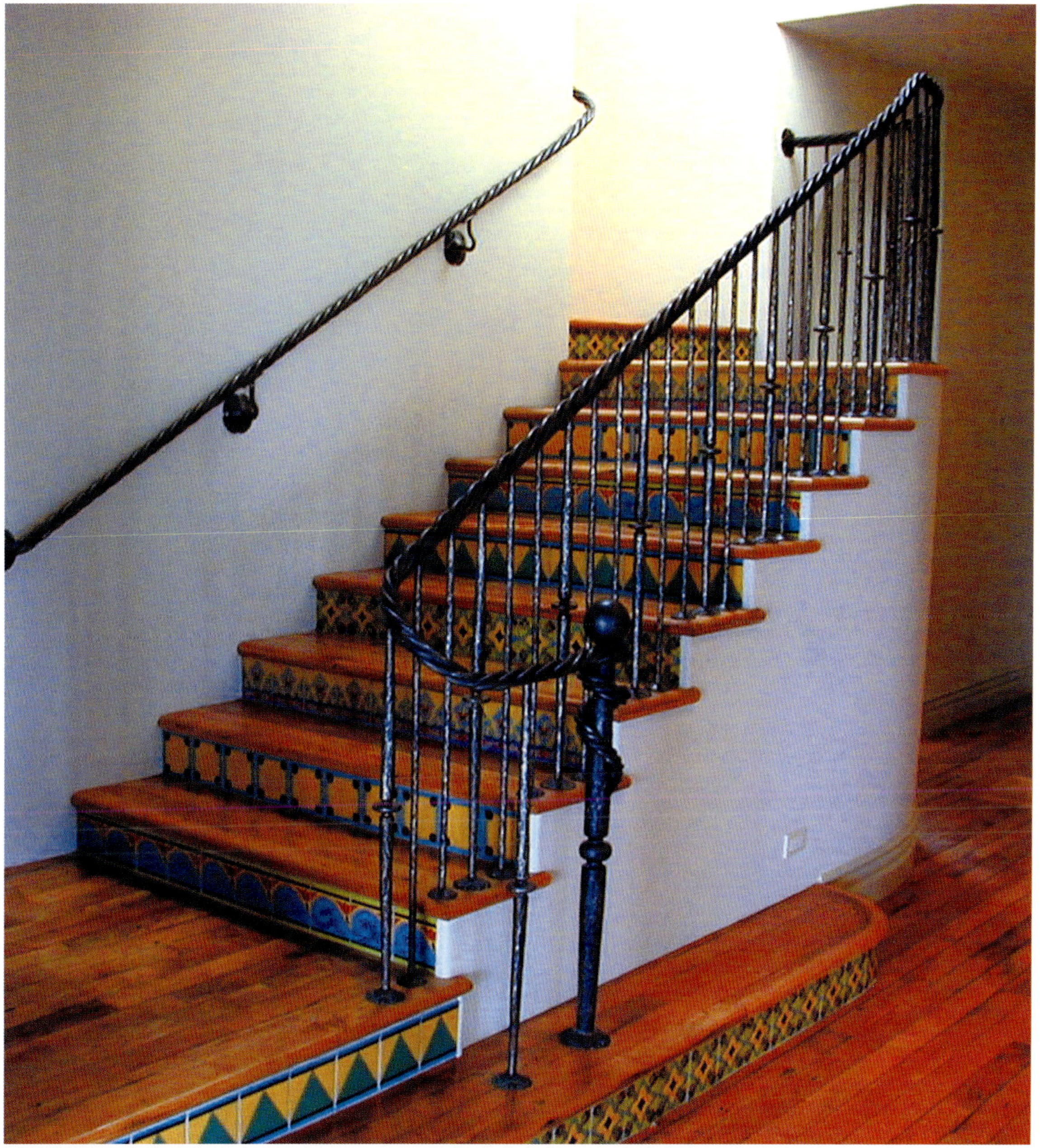

Greg Eng. Rope handrail and stair railing. Solid forged steel rope along the top wraps around a 2.5" forged pipe newel post. Mounted on Spanish picket floor plates with forged nails. The side handrail is 32' long and the railing is18' long. *Photo, Brenda Eng*

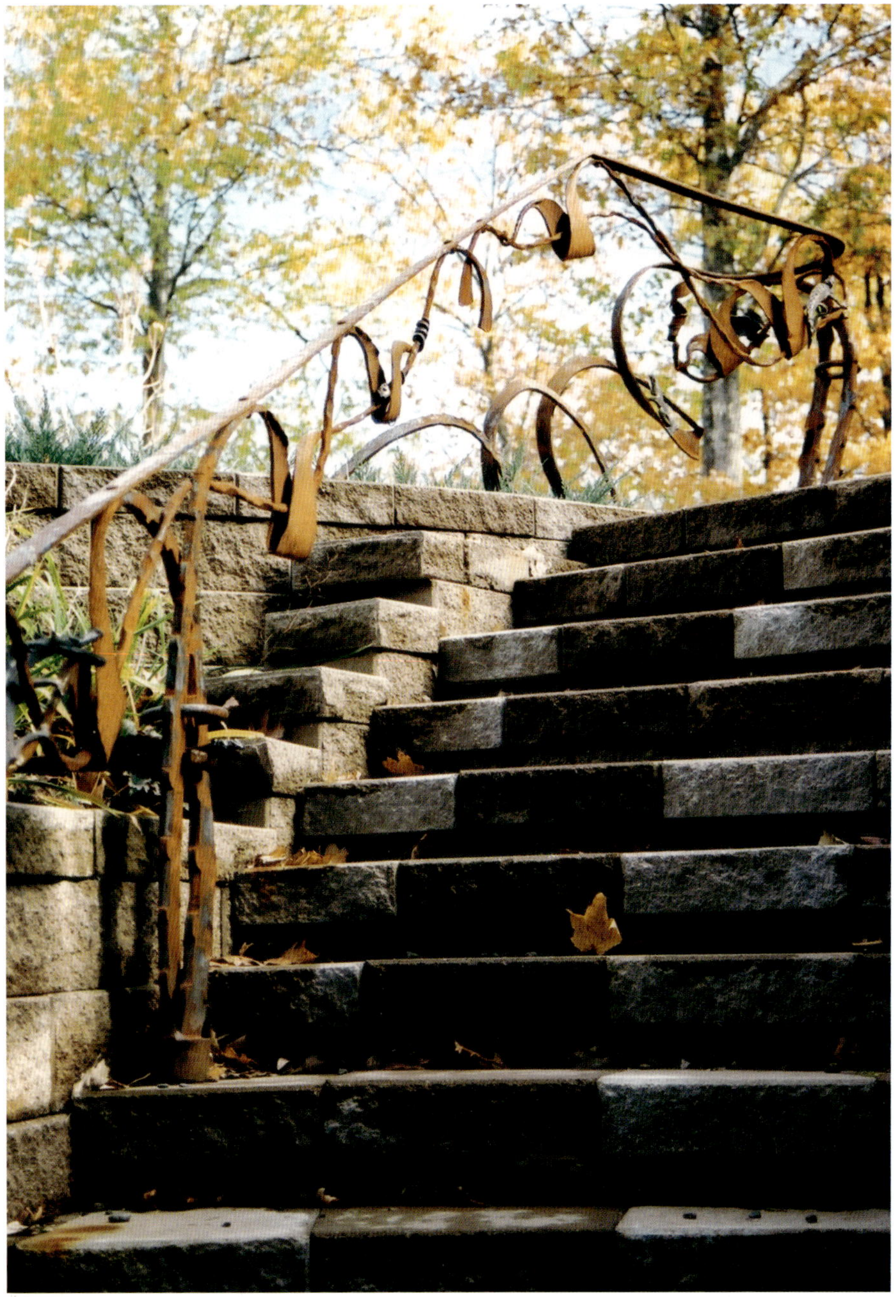

Bernard Heer. Railing No. 1. Free form iron with rust finish for an outdoor park. A forged mouse and other small park creatures peek out from the loops. *Photo, Sara Haugen*

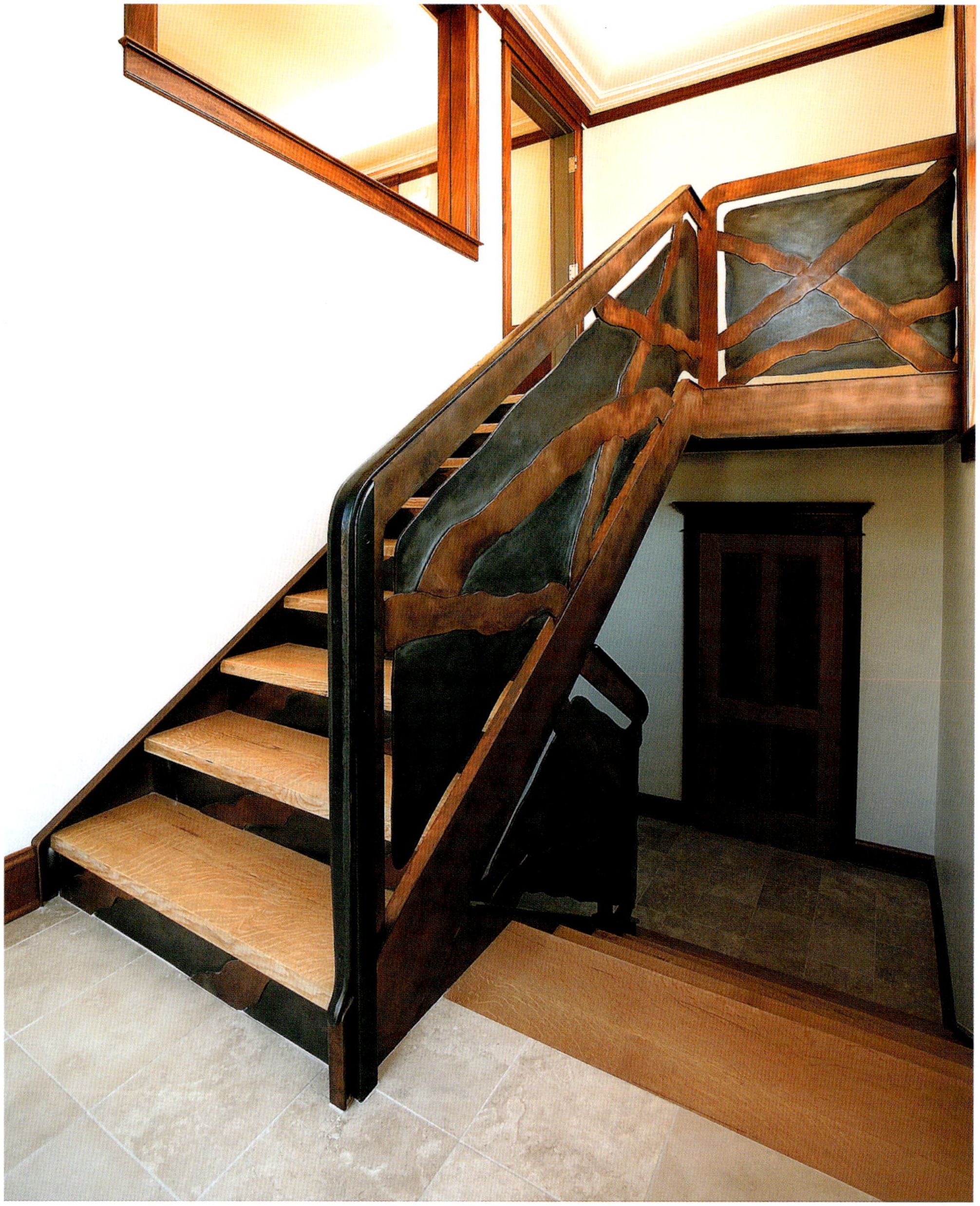

Jeff Fetty. Reed staircase. Heavy gauge box tubing with a copper patina. Part of a renovation of an oil and gas exploration company building in Charleston, West Virginia. The client's company deals with the geology, so the design and materials are symbolic. The act of traveling the staircase gives the impression of moving through the earth's strata. White oak was used as it was the wood of choice in the early days of the oil and gas industry. 34" high. *Photo, Jurgen*

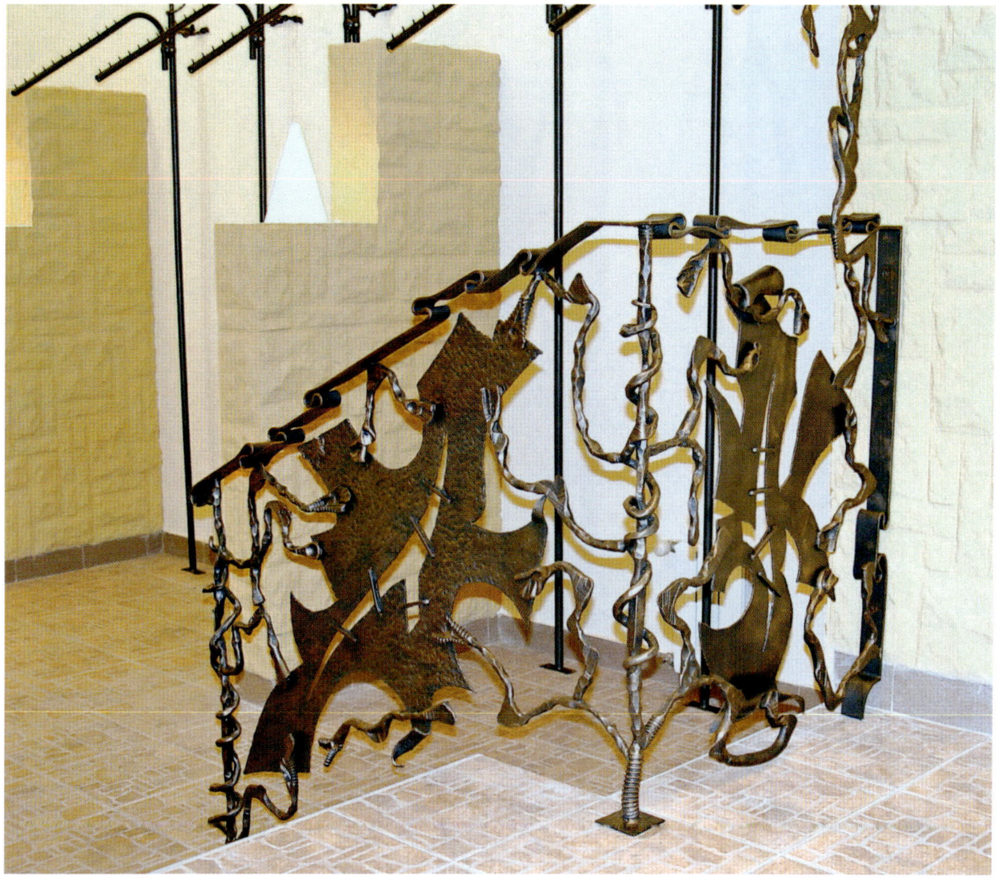

Vadim Filatov and Alexander Chumakov, Gvozd Studios. Boutique shop railings. One of two railings for a shop where the hanging devices and light fixtures have the same free form design scheme. Each railing is 14' long. *Photo, artists*

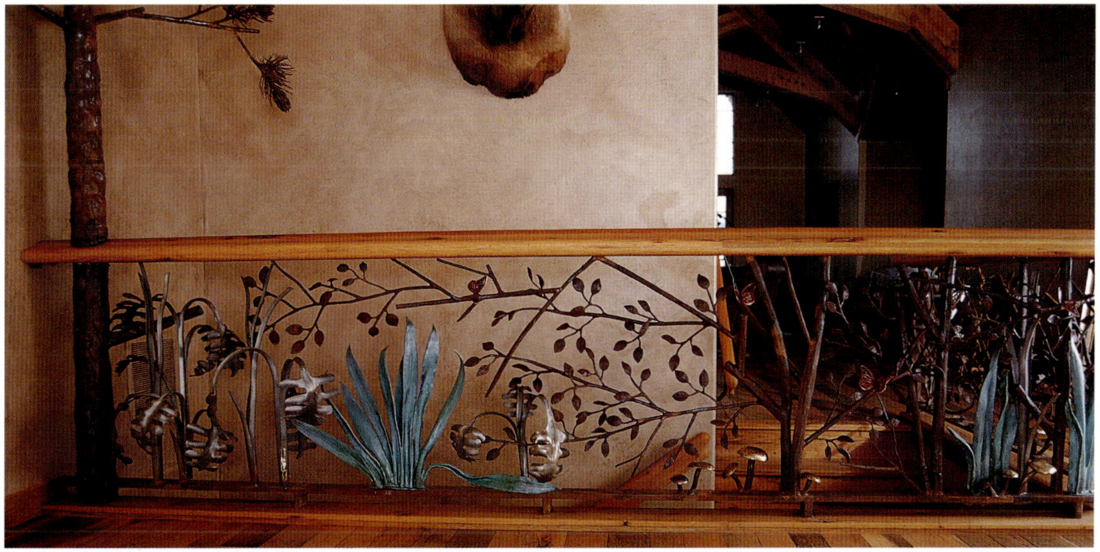

Doug Adelmann. *Organic Railing*. Steel vines and leaves, copper and acrylic butterflies, patinated copper leaves, bronze mushroom, stainless steel ferns. The railing is re-cycled wood scraps from an office floor. An 8' high forged tree is at the wall end. 3' high, 24' long. *Photo, Patsi Peterson*

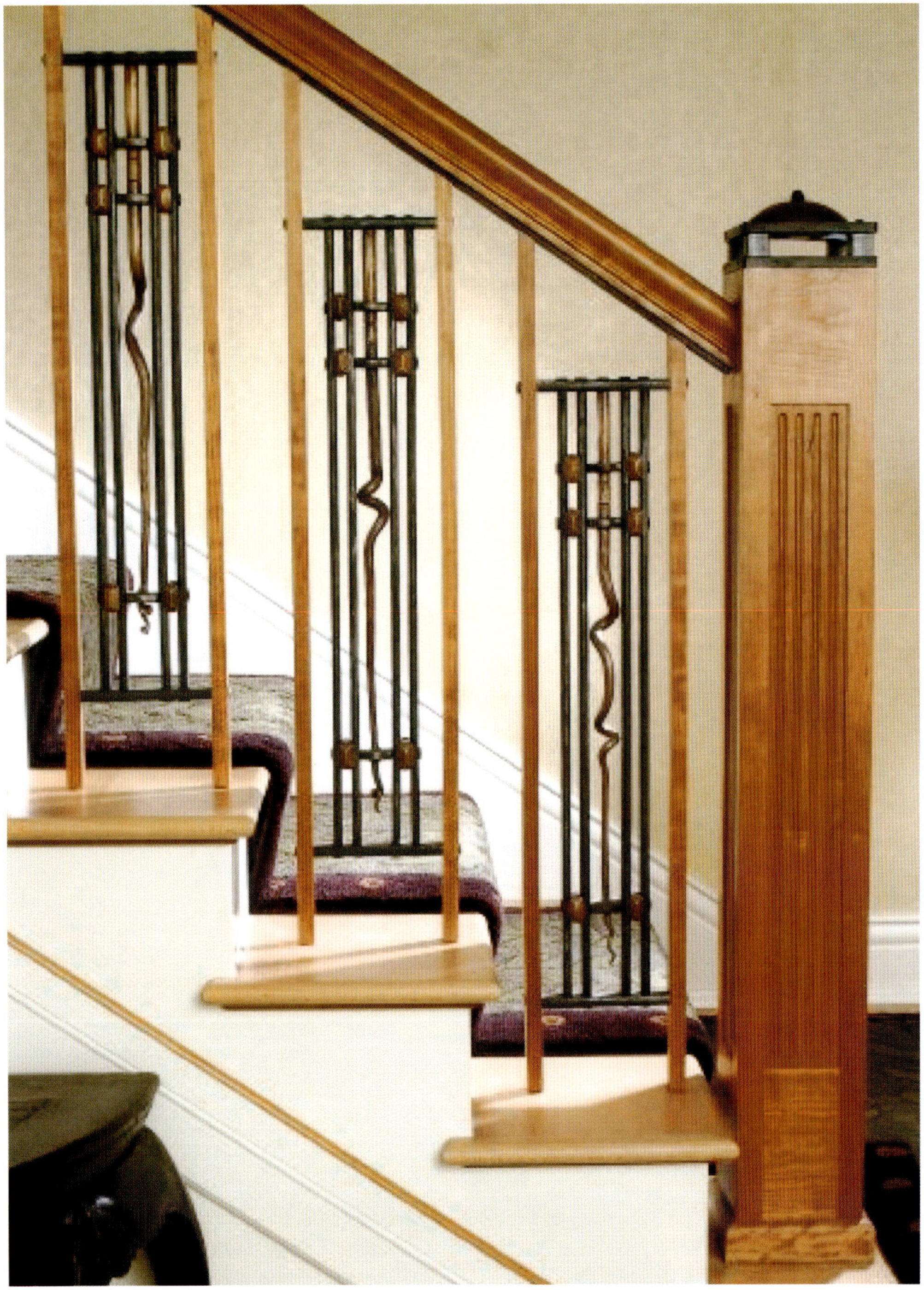

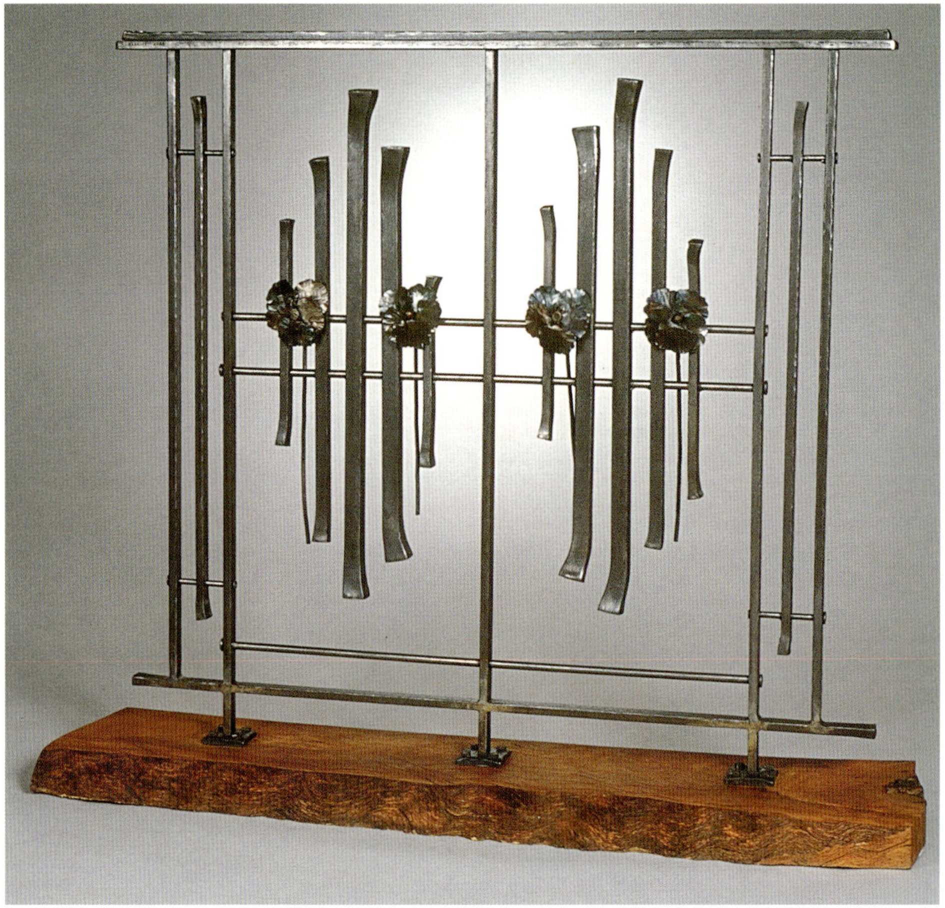

Susan Madacsi. Maquette of a handrail with pansies. Forged and fabricated steel. 48" high, 40" wide. *Photo, R. J. Phil*

Steve Lopes and staff. Stair rail inserts. Steel and copper panels set into wood uprights. A top for the newel post carries out the metal look. *Photo, Steve Lopes*

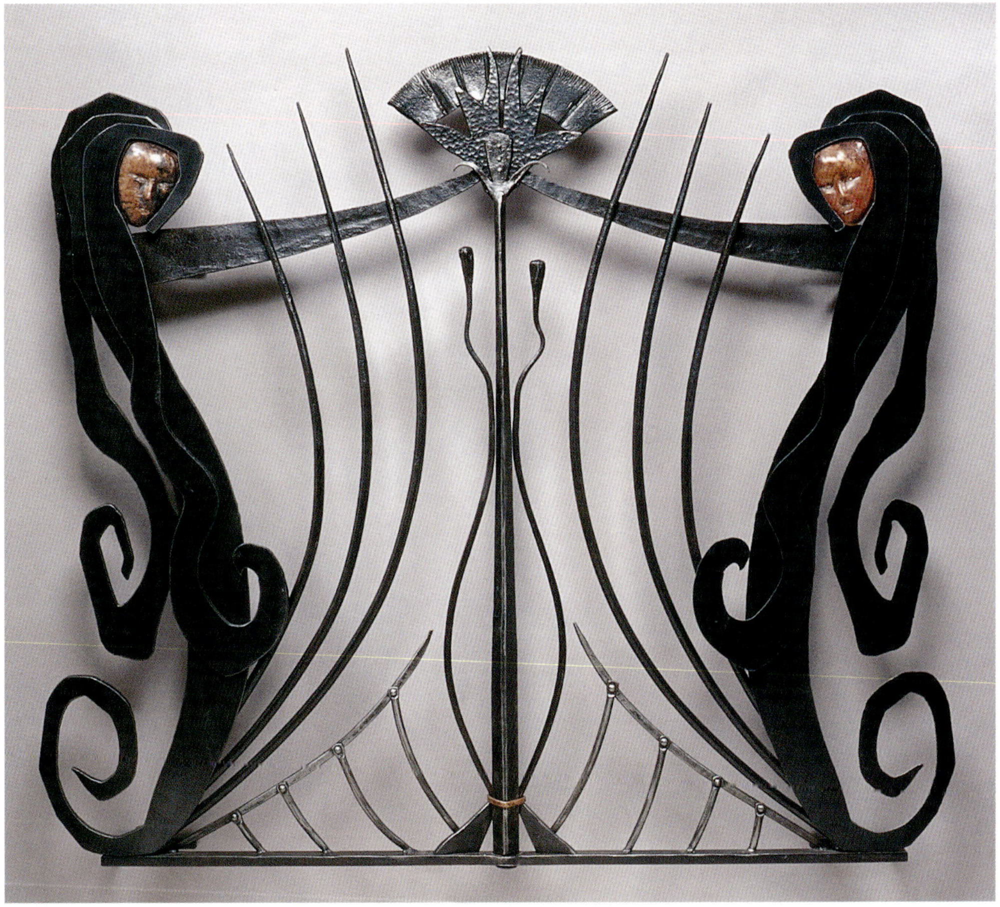

Lauren Osmolski. Grille. Forged iron with repoussé copper faces inserted at the top on each side. 46" square, 4" deep. *Photo, Doug Yaple*

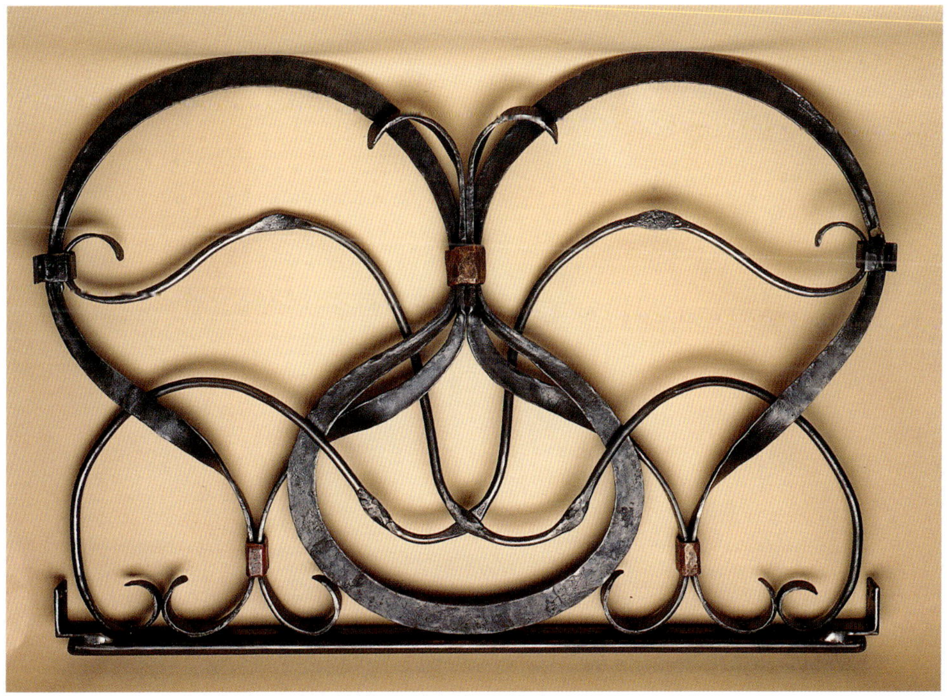

George Parker. *Mustache Grille*. Steel and copper. 36" high, 40" wide. Architect, Bill Taylor. *Photo, Ansen Seale*

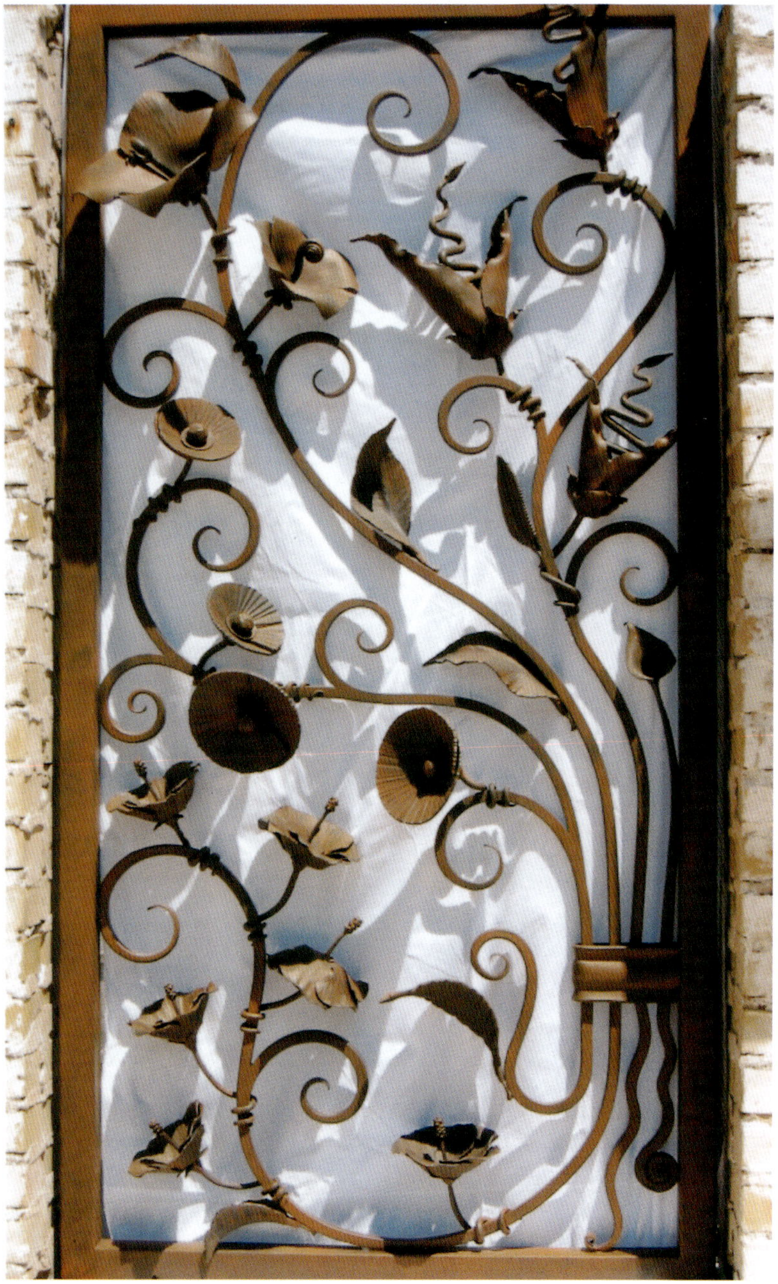

Katherine Kagler. One of two panels for the courtyard of the Design Center of Austin, Texas. Frame is made of 2" square tubing and the flowers are from junkyard sheet metal. One panel also functions as a passage gate with the locking mechanism integrated into the frame. The other panel is stationary. The "daisies" have ball bearings in the pistils allowing them to spin. The faux rust finish was purposely created so that the gate would not appear to rust over time. Each panel is 6' high, 3' wide. *Photo, artist*

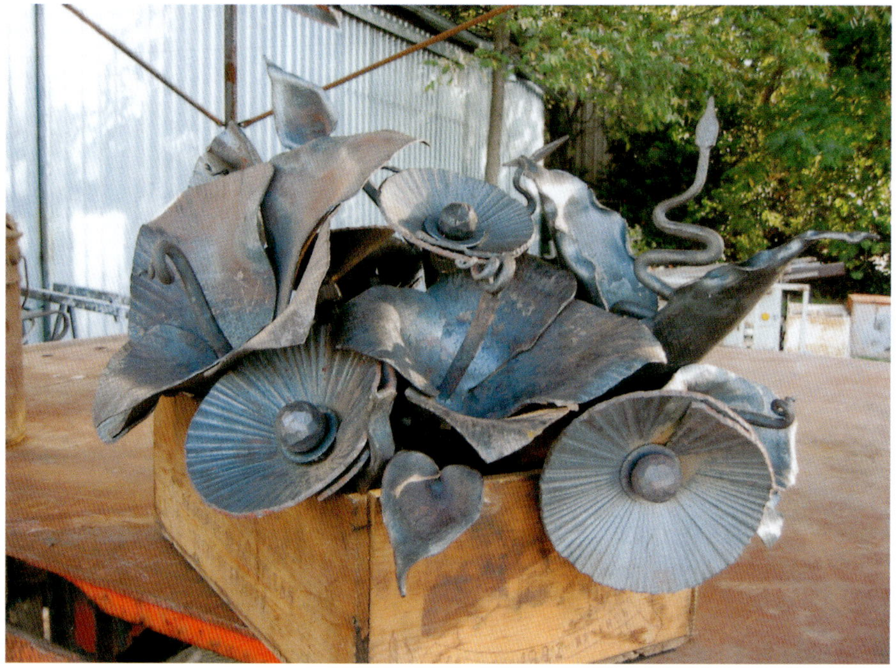

Katherine Kagler. Detail of the forged flowers fashioned from junkyard sheet metal. *Photo, artist*

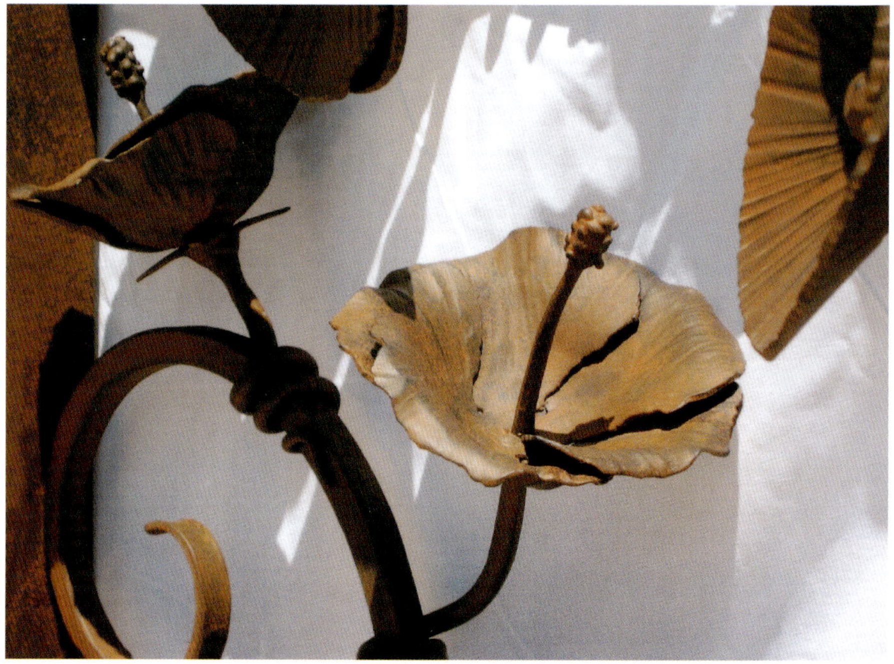

Katherine Kagler. Detail.

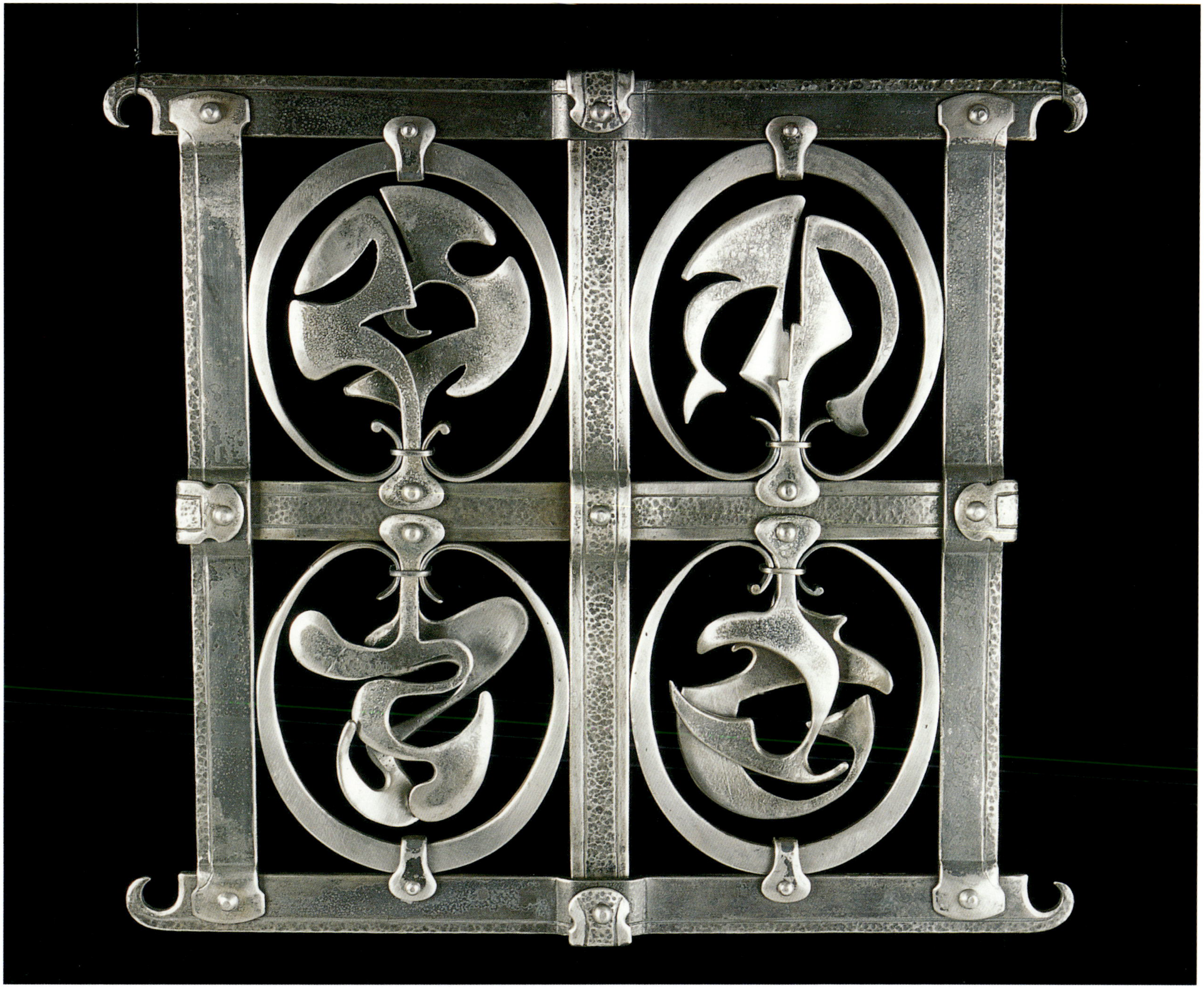

Matt Haugh. Square Dance. Forged iron architectural grille. 17" high 18" wide. *Photo, artist*

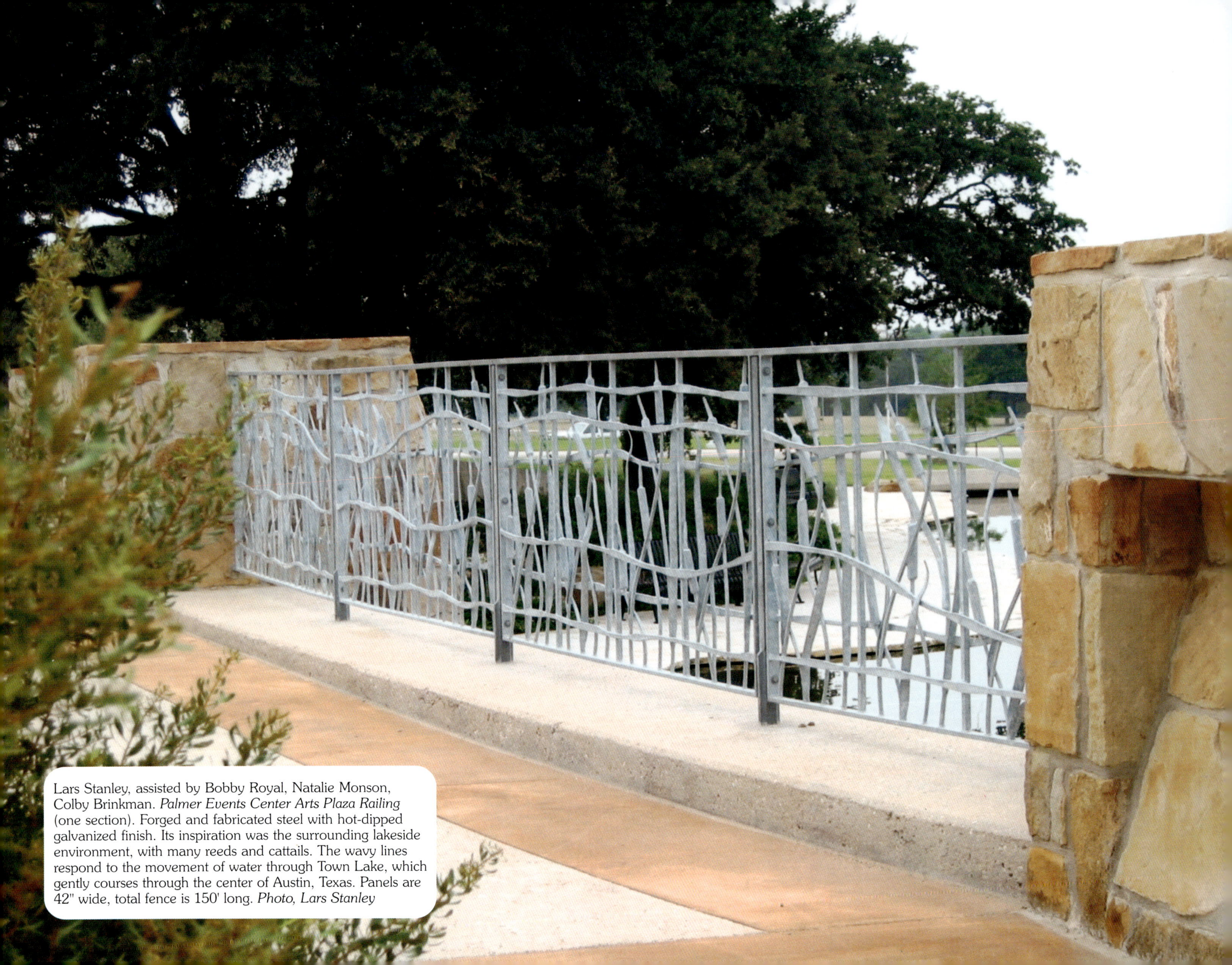

Lars Stanley, assisted by Bobby Royal, Natalie Monson, Colby Brinkman. *Palmer Events Center Arts Plaza Railing* (one section). Forged and fabricated steel with hot-dipped galvanized finish. Its inspiration was the surrounding lakeside environment, with many reeds and cattails. The wavy lines respond to the movement of water through Town Lake, which gently courses through the center of Austin, Texas. Panels are 42" wide, total fence is 150' long. *Photo, Lars Stanley*

Chapter 4. Fences, Gates, & Doors

Most everyone walks or drives by ironwork gates and fences everyday. We may frequently push gates and doors open and closed and lift ironwork latches. We hardly ever give their design a passing thought. Very often, they represent a unique art form that is overlooked. But once a person is aware of ironwork fences, gates, and doors, they notice them and no longer take them for granted. It's an "oh wow!" experience that enriches their life.

True, there are many mundane units made of horizontal and vertical bars row on row. Hopefully, those who are responsible for commissioning ironwork fences, gates, and doors will think many times and appreciate the beauty and uniqueness that a one-of-a kind, well designed unit can bring to their property.

Those who design and create ironwork should consider function, design, and practicality. Does the design of the gate and door complement the building or background? Adding a Gothic style gate to a modern house would strike a visually unharmonious note. An art deco design would also be out of character for a house in a Victorian style.

Fences, gates, and doors have the preconceived, obvious functions of in/out and security but they can have additional purposes. Lars Stanley's University of Texas fence creates a friendly border between the landscaped grounds of the Alumni Center and the main campus of the university. More important is that it funnels crowds that exit the huge stadium next door after football games around the delicate plants and sculptures on the campus grounds.

Design should also harmonize with the structure, the climate, and the surroundings. The Turtle fence, (page 91) for example, in front of a Hawaii beach house is perfectly in keeping with the environment. An Arts & Crafts Style gate and fence are appropriate for a building that exhibits these early 20th century characteristics. In addition to a building's historical style its accompanying ironwork gates and fences may incorporate animals, plants, water, fire, and, perhaps, tell a story.

Peter Fishbein's *Octopus* gate, greets those who enter a ground floor apartment in a brownstone building in Brooklyn, New York. It peeks out from its subterranean lair and brings a smile to the face of those who spot it

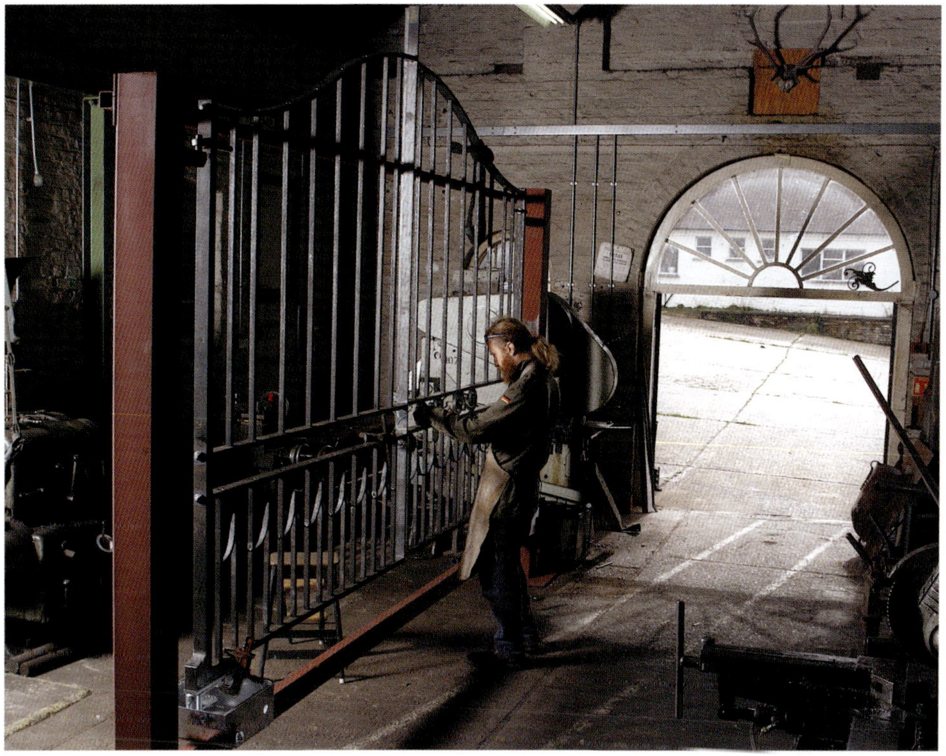

Paul Elliott. Gate in progress. A large project requires a large workspace. A finished gate this size can weigh up to about 1000 pounds. It requires engineering and heavy-duty equipment during construction as well as during installations. *14.5' high, 12.2' wide. Photo, Jackie Phillips*

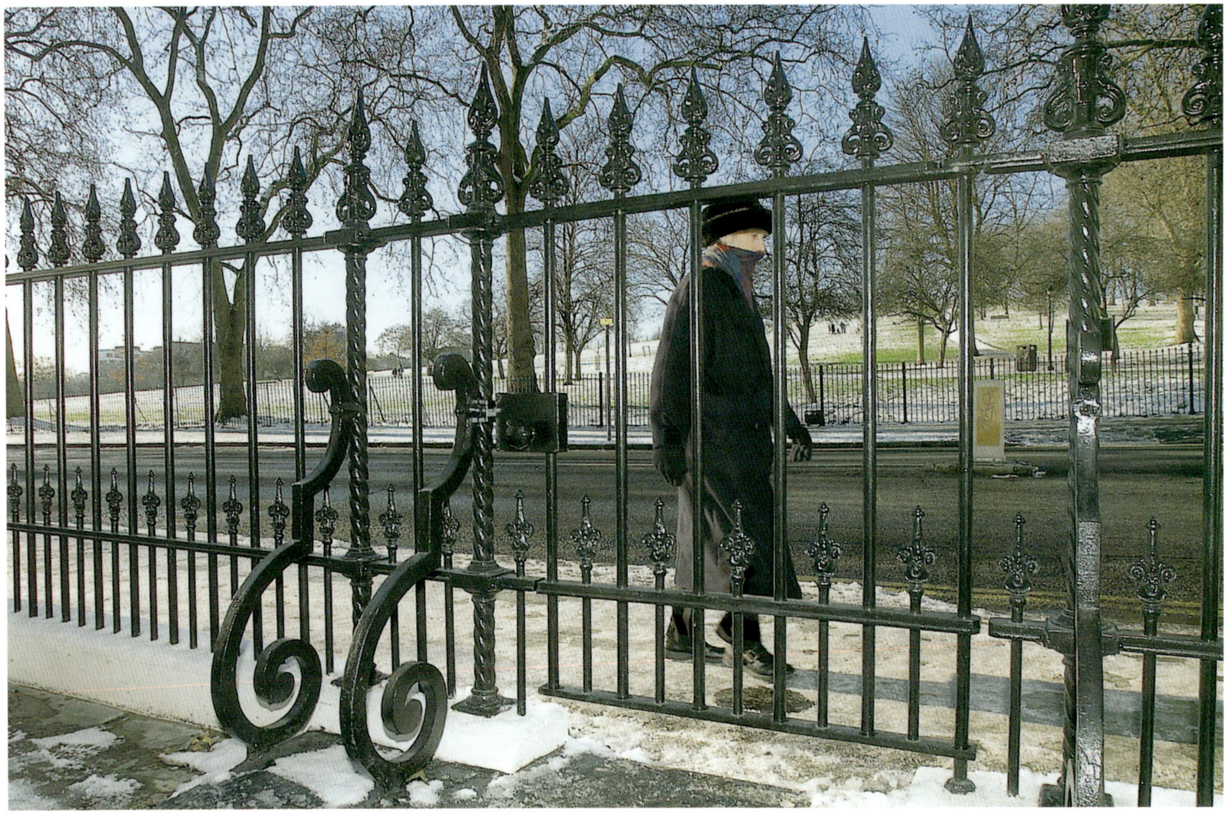

Paul Elliott. Traditional style fence and gate for a London park. *Photo, Jackie Phillips*

as they pass by. But it is meant to be a security gate and, as such, required substantial strength. A structural seaweed piece is attached to the wall, not part of the gate, but it ties in with the overall design.

Says Fishbein, "The challenge was fitting such an odd shaped space with a smoothly functional, and still artistic gate. The gate is not flat, but swells outward on top because the bottom had to clear the stair when opened." The finish was a challenge, too, said Fishbein. It was sandblasted, primed, and the octopus was painted with a rich bronze and rust powder. While still wet, a patina chemical that reacted with the metal powder was sprayed on. The result was a pattern of green verdigris and brown rust. The problem was that results were never consistent during testing. Others factors, such as temperature, humidity, how long the wet paints sit before a patina chemical is applied, also entered into the problems. The seaweed, too, needed much testing to achieve the desired result.

David King was teaching a welding class at a local community college, when a client requested a gate that included the flora, fauna and "feel" of the area's landscape. King presented his idea based on conversations with the clients. With the help of a few of his students, the final gate incorporated the rocky Salinas Valley in California's rolling hills and mountain ranges in the background. Amazingly, depending on where you stand, the mountain shape in the gate appears to be the background mountains.

Paul Elliott's commissions are infinitely varied. He says, "For me the real pleasure is in the look of the finished piece. This starts at the design stage because I visit a site, and have a strong sense of the visualized final piece *in situ*. Designs are produced as drawings, sample panels, or as a model (or maquette) to help clients visualize the piece."

Says Elliott, "Despite the absolute requirement that my work be pre-dominantly functional, such as a fence, gate, balcony, arbor, or seat; it is a design pre-requisite for me, that my work be appealing. I have been asked where I get inspiration for my designs, and I really don't know. All I can say is that Nature knows no straight lines, so shapes that flow, or have curves, are a feature of my favorite personal artistic work".

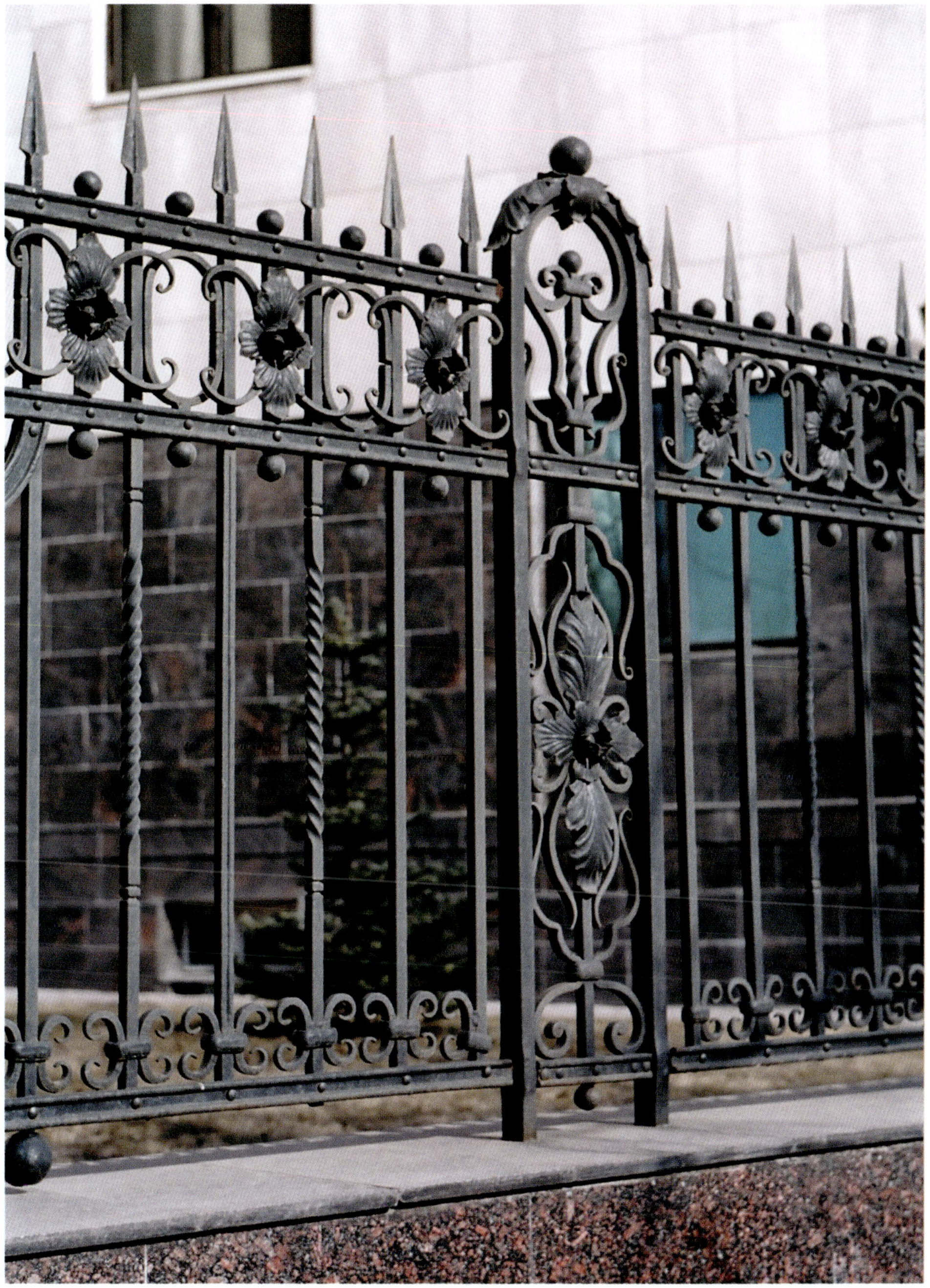

Sergey Sakirkin. Portion of a 500' fence and a large gate for the National Bank of Russia in Ulyanovsk, Russia. Created in the studios of Korch. *Photo, courtesy, artist*

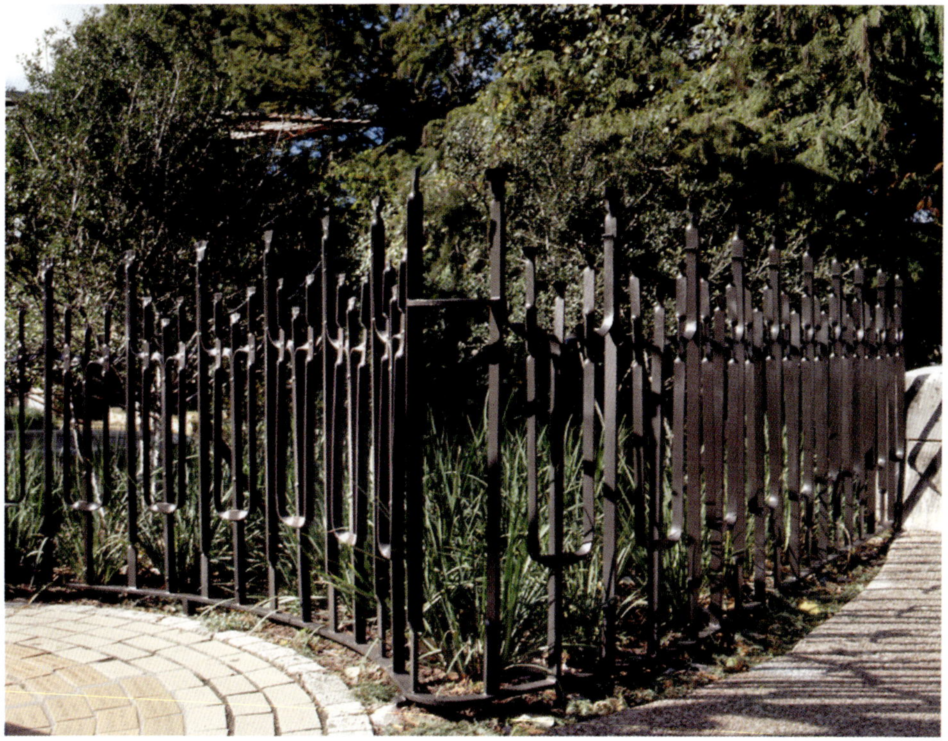

Lars Stanley, assisted by Bobby Royal, Troy DeFrates, Natalie Monson, Suzanne Baas. *University of Texas Alumni Center*. Fence, forged and fabricated steel with water-based, "low voc" painted finish. The pattern is derived from a subtly abstracted "UT" logo used as a symbol by the university. The forged ends of the uprights and their pattern within each fence panel respond to brick patterns of nearby large brick columns holding up an overhead trellis, designed by the Center's Architect, the late Charles Moore, FAIA. Panels are 48" high, total fence is 250' long. *Photo, Atelier Wong*

Mark Puigmarti recalls: "A stout, jovial man came to my shop one day. Holding a small sketch in his hand, he asked if I could reproduce a gate for his residence. I looked at the drawing, which consisted of straight vertical bars joined together with a horizontal bar at the bottom and an arced bar at the top. Hesitantly, I told him that I could if it's what he really wanted. He looked around the shop for a moment and anxiously declared, 'I want that instead' pointing to a piece under construction for the Caniron IV conference. I asked him why he changed his mind, and he said, 'I had no idea such a thing was possible'. We discussed a new design for his gate."

Almost every project in the pages that follow has a story, with problems and solutions that had to be tackled. Every artist-blacksmith agrees that it is satisfying to help people realize the possibilities in metal.

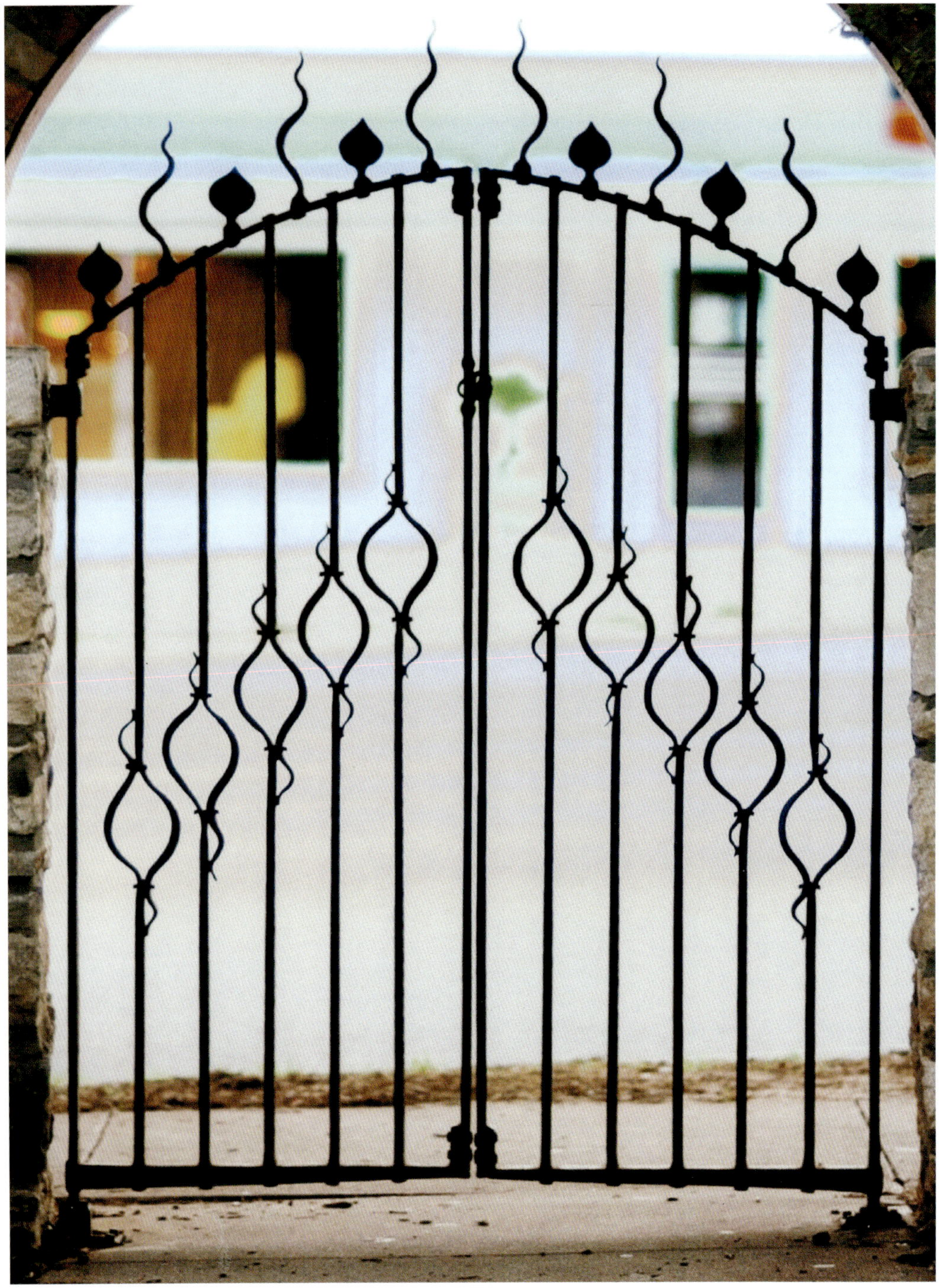

Katherine Kagler. Silhouette Gate. *Photo, artist*

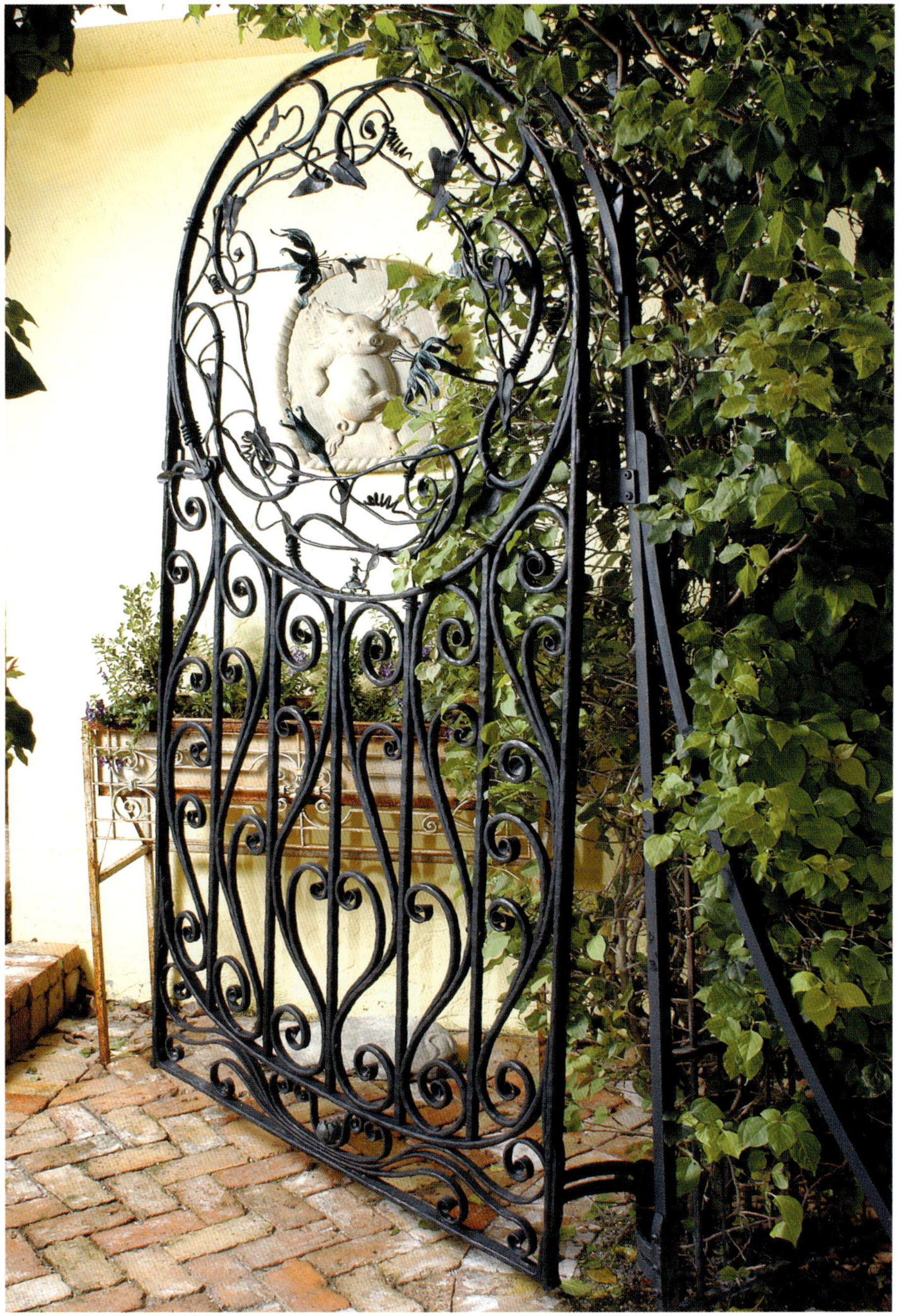

Robert Gardner and Eric Velleca. Steel forge welded and riveted bronze elements are assembled by TIG welding. The door self-closes using an offset hinge. 9' high, 3' wide. *Photo, artists*

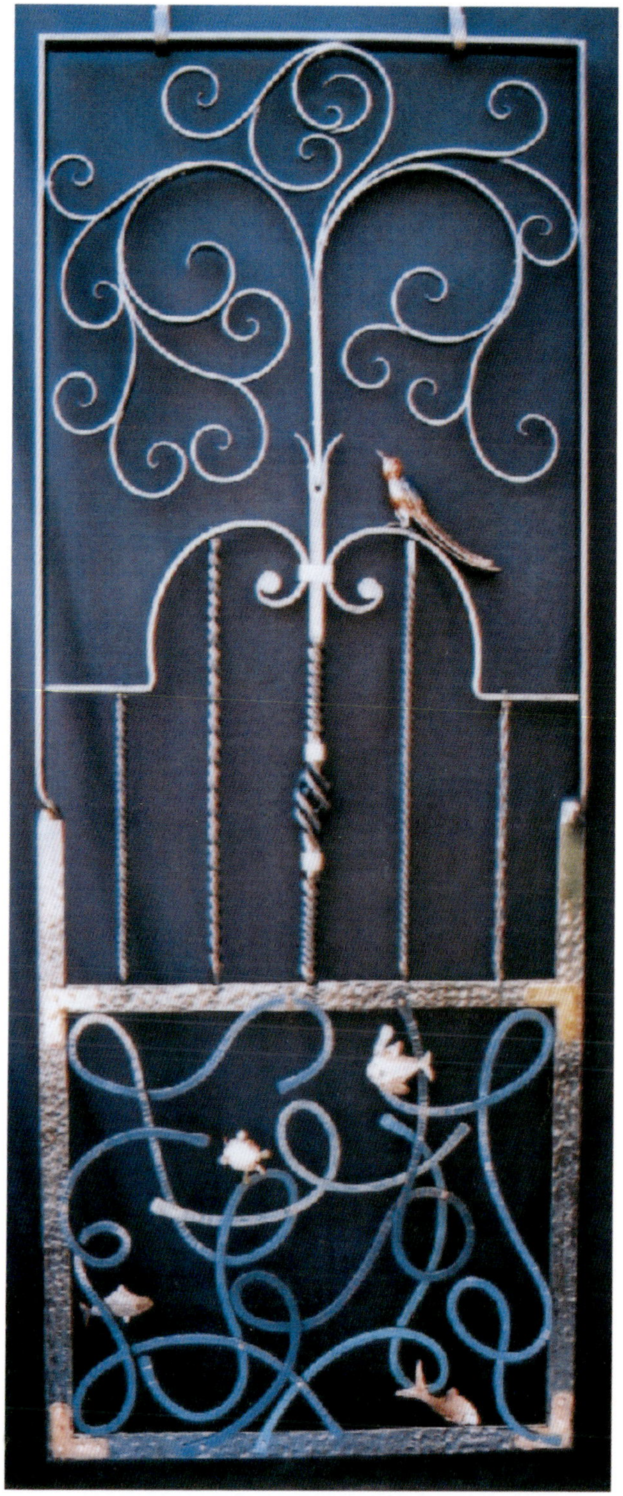

George Witzke and April Witzke. Fountain Gate. Mild steel, with copper rivets joining the fountain pieces. The bird and fish are also of forged mild steel with the exception of the copper turtle shell. The frame was darkened with gun bluing and sealed with a clear enamel sealer. Gilder's Paste was used for the color highlights. It is installed at the Mexidona store in Sedona, Arizona. 70" high, 32" wide. *Photo, April Witzke*

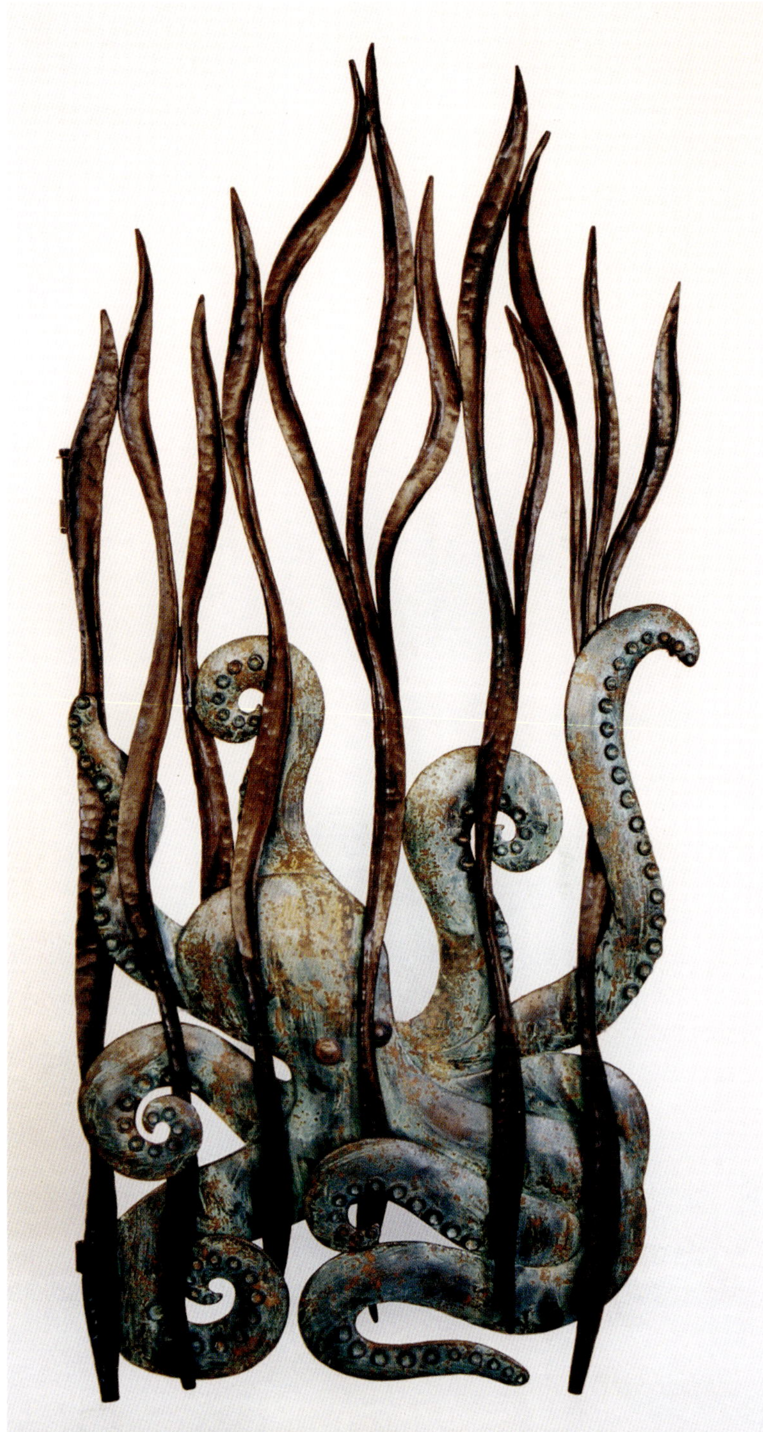

Peter Fishbein. *Octopus*. Security Gate. Wrought steel. The octopus "suction cups" are cut steel pipe brazed to the tentacles. 6.5' high, 3' wide. *Photo, artist*

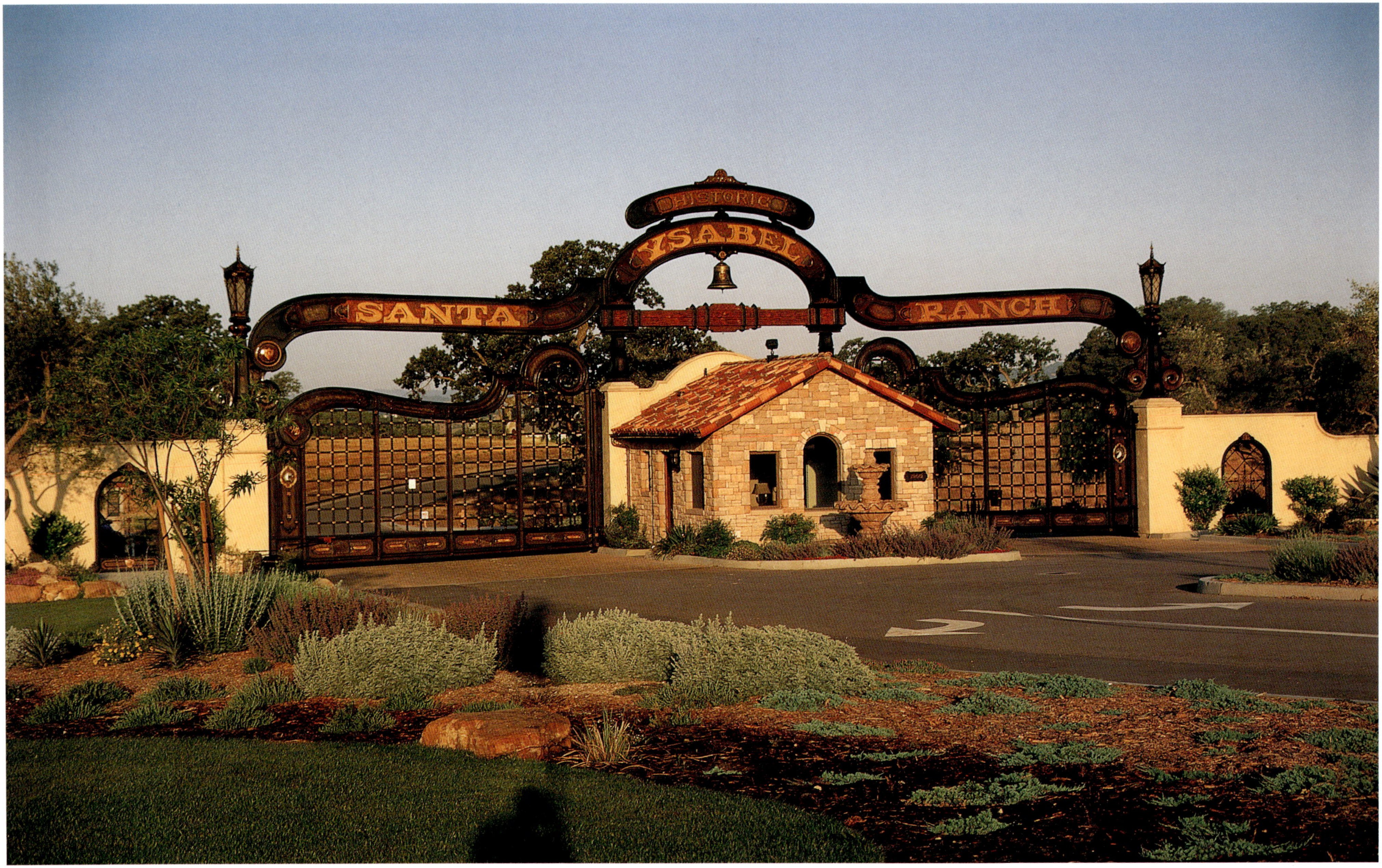

Robert C. Bentley with William Brown, Russell Windbiel, Doug Cook, and Matt Canaday. *Santa Ysabel Ranch Entry Gate and Arch*. A 7000 ton gate that combines esthetic and historical references of the mission that once occupied the land. It posed incredible engineering solutions for Bentley's team at the Weyrich Development Co. in Paso Robles, California. *Photo, Bruce Woodworth*

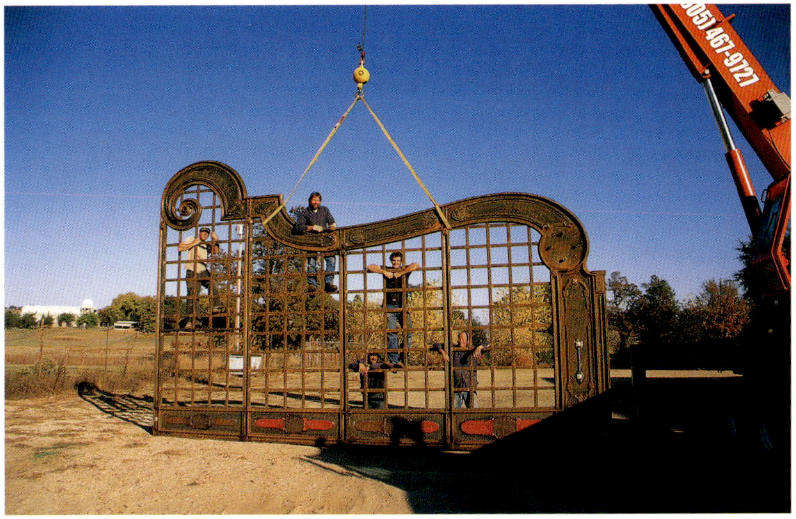

Robert C. Bentley The blacksmith team that helped create the gate supervised hoisting the parts into place. *Photo, Bruce Woodworth*

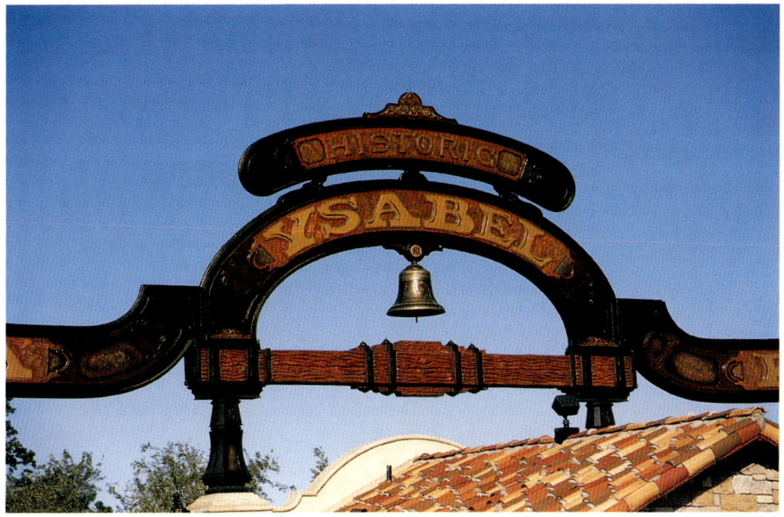

Robert C. Bentley. Arch with the bell that replicated the design and sound of the original mission bells. *Photo, Bruce Woodworth*

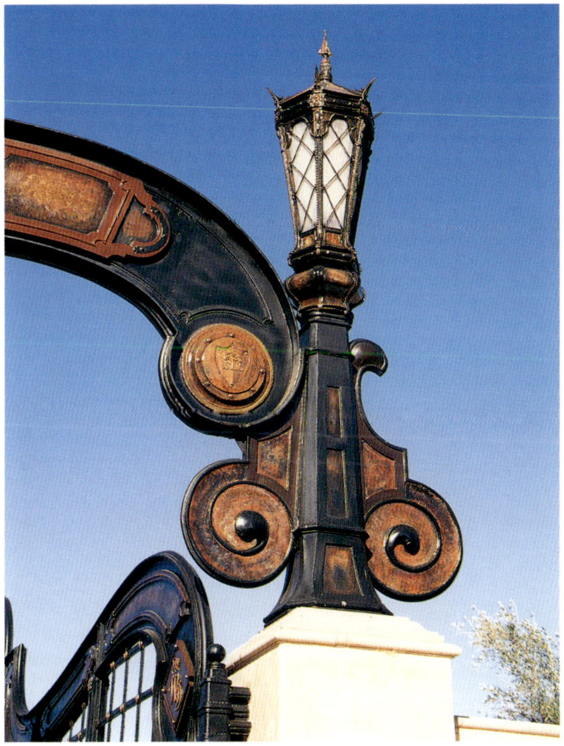

Robert C. Bentley. A 7' tall lamp tops each of the gate's columns. *Photo, Bruce Woodworth*

Robert C. Bentley and his four-man team of talented blacksmiths generate all the ironwork for the Weyrich Development Co., in Paso Robles, California. Studying their work is like digesting an encyclopedia of ironwork techniques. But there's much more because Bentley often has to invent engineering mechanisms. Creating these gates required that the blacksmiths become historians, archeologists, designers, and engineers.

Said Bentley, "Before we could proceed, we had to immerse ourselves in the history of the Chumash Indians, the early California missions and, specifically of the Santa Ysabel Ranch Property. This property would include a 150-home, gated community with recreational facilities and a 274-acre vineyard. Bentley's team also fashioned all the ironwork inside and outside for each home.

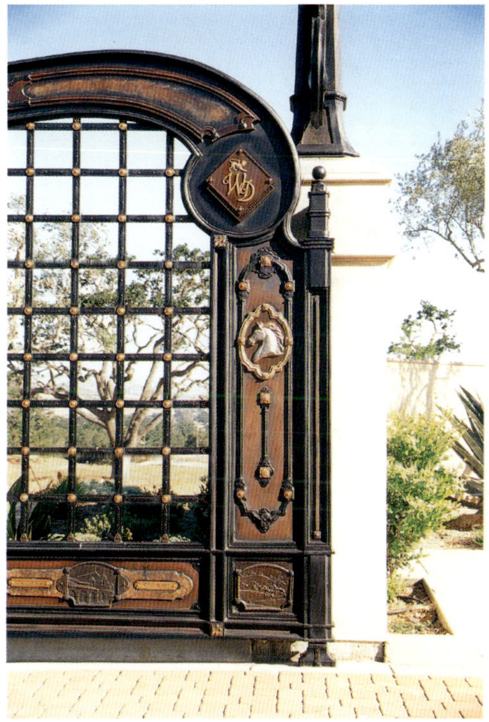

Robert C. Bentley. There is a casting of one of the original California Missions in each bottom panel of the gates. *Photo, Bruce Woodworth*

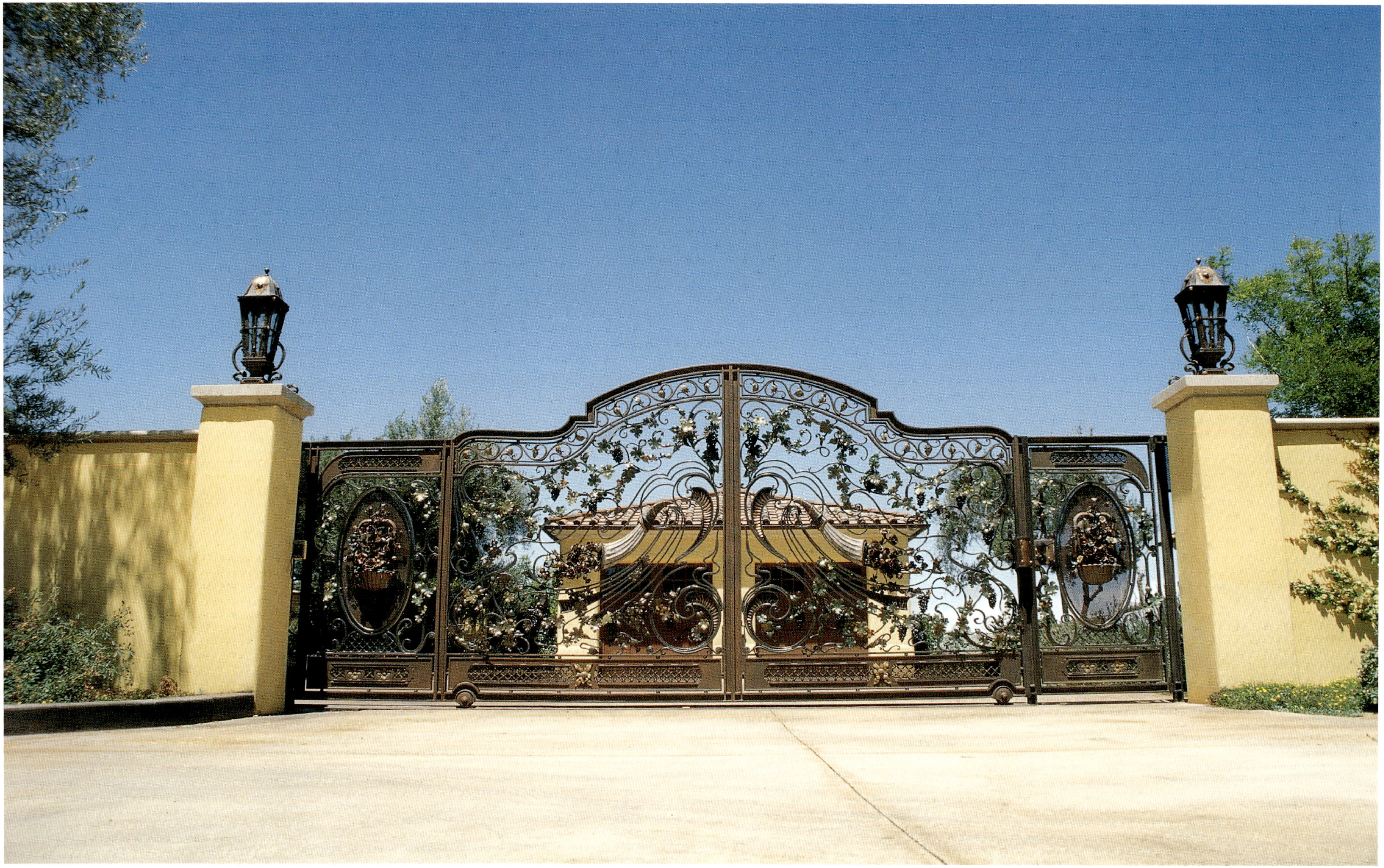

Robert C. Bentley and Russell Windbiel. *Gate at the Vintner's Cottage.* The Village Toscana. A grand floral arrangement bursting from concrete cornucopias, surrounded by a hand forged scroll motif done in a rich rust and gold finish. Each flower is hand painted. Two urns hold floral arrangements. There are two gates; a 16' wide sliding gate and a 3' wide passage gate. *Photo, Bruce Woodworth*

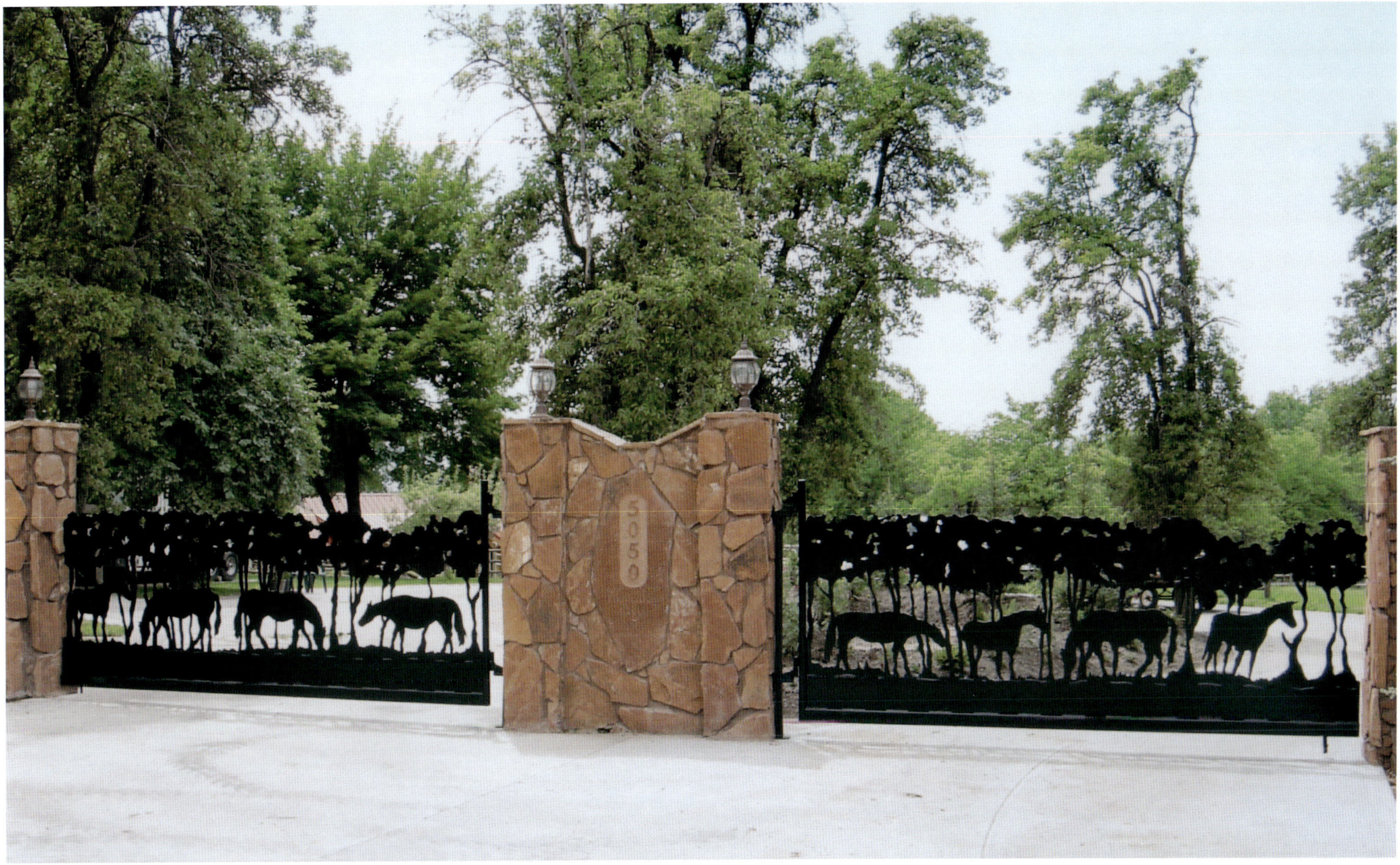

Richard Prazen. *Double gate with horses*. The object was to show horses quietly grazing in an orchard. An original drawing was enlarged and transferred to 1/4-inch sheet steel and plasma cut by hand. Says Prazen, "The client raises Paint horses to show, and it's nice to portray what the owners are about through the things that we create. I call it, 'functional sulpture'. It's a narrative about the clients' life." Each gate is 10' wide, one for entering and one for exiting the property. *Photo, artist*

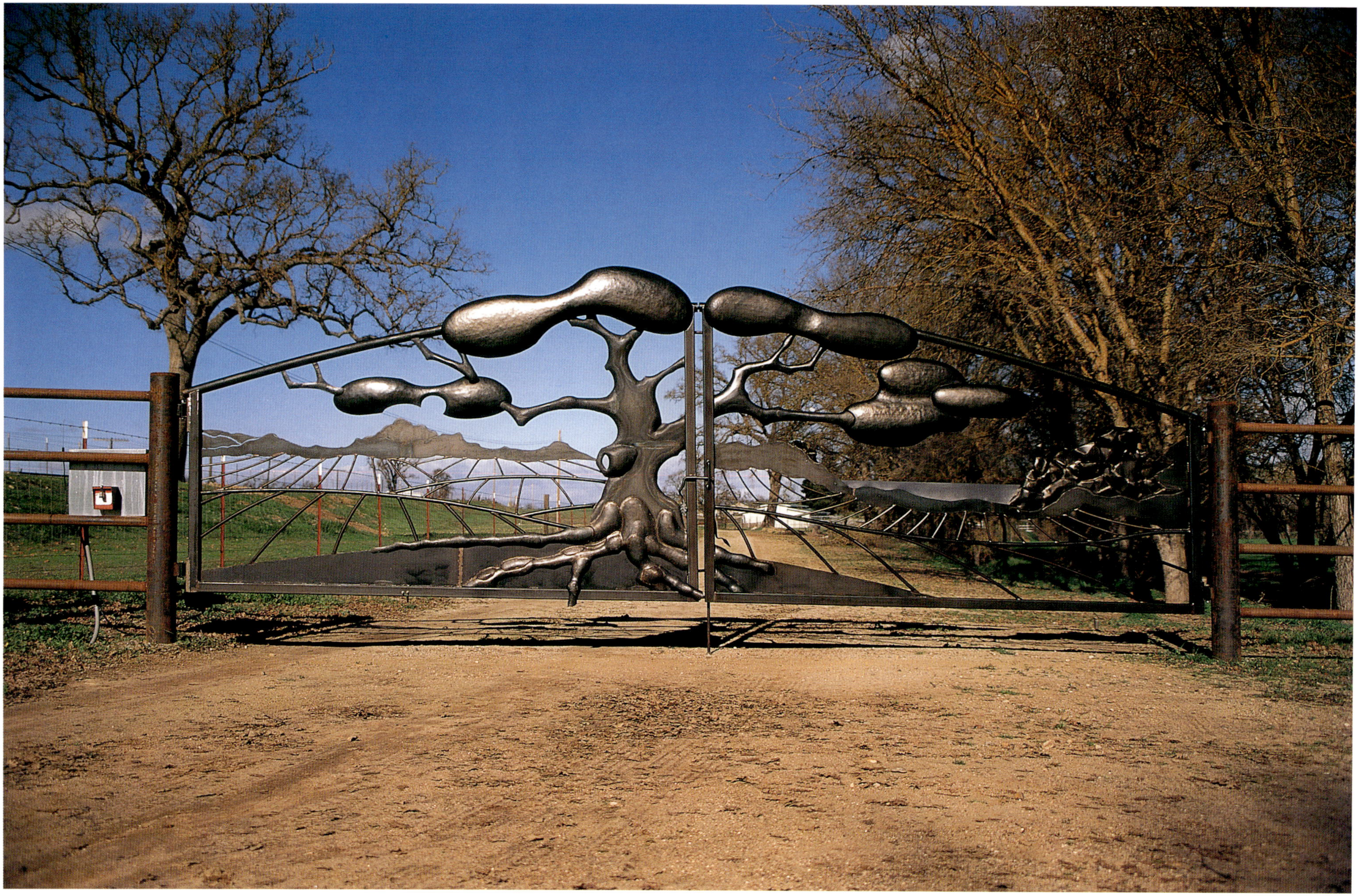

David S. King assisted by Aaron Elkins and other students. *Oak Tree gate*. Mild steel forged and fabricated. Installed at a private residence on the west coast. The challenge was to design the gate to tie in with the surrounding landscape. 6' high, 20' wide, and varies in depth from 3" to 6". *Photo, Bruce Woodworth*

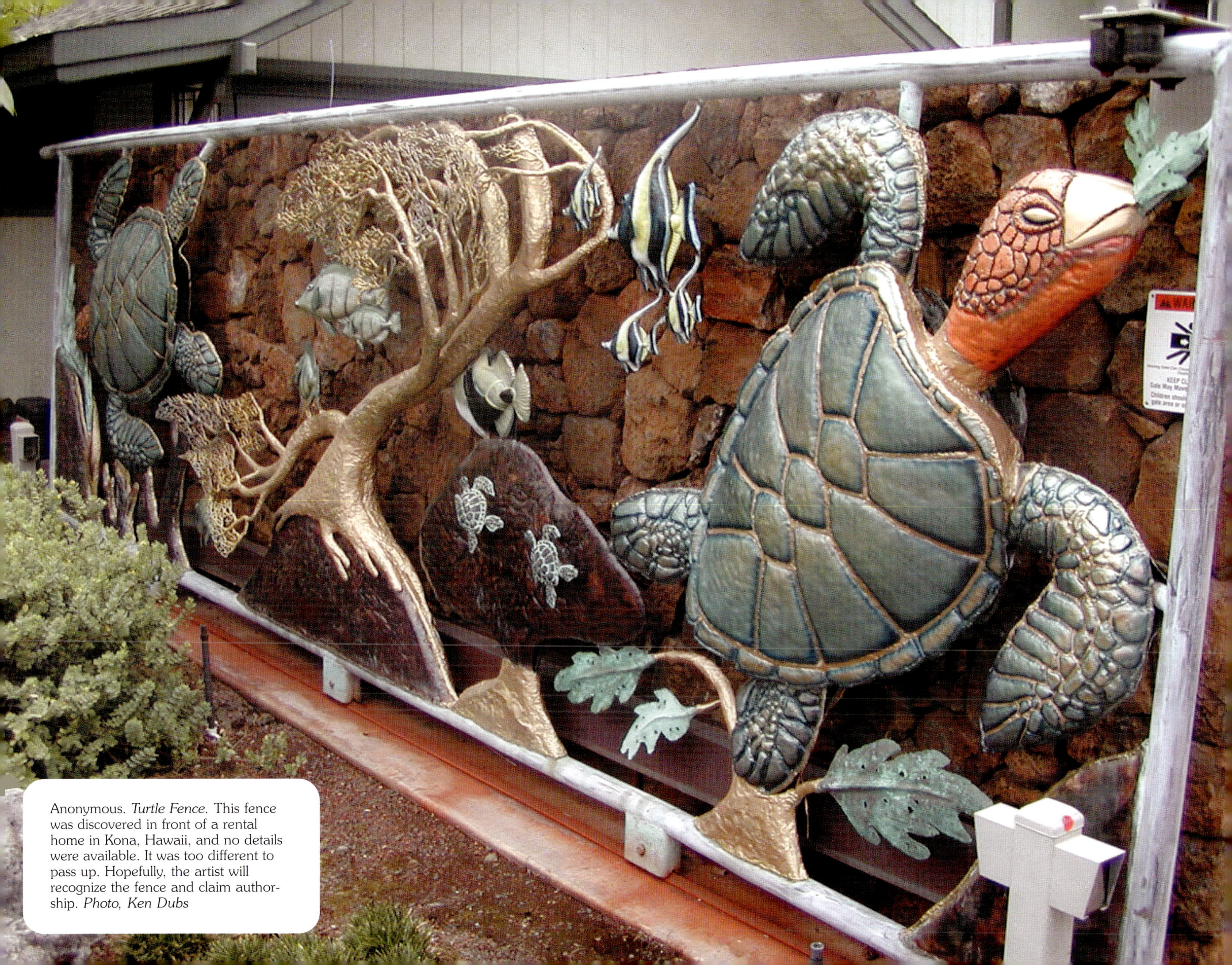

Anonymous. *Turtle Fence.* This fence was discovered in front of a rental home in Kona, Hawaii, and no details were available. It was too different to pass up. Hopefully, the artist will recognize the fence and claim authorship. *Photo, Ken Dubs*

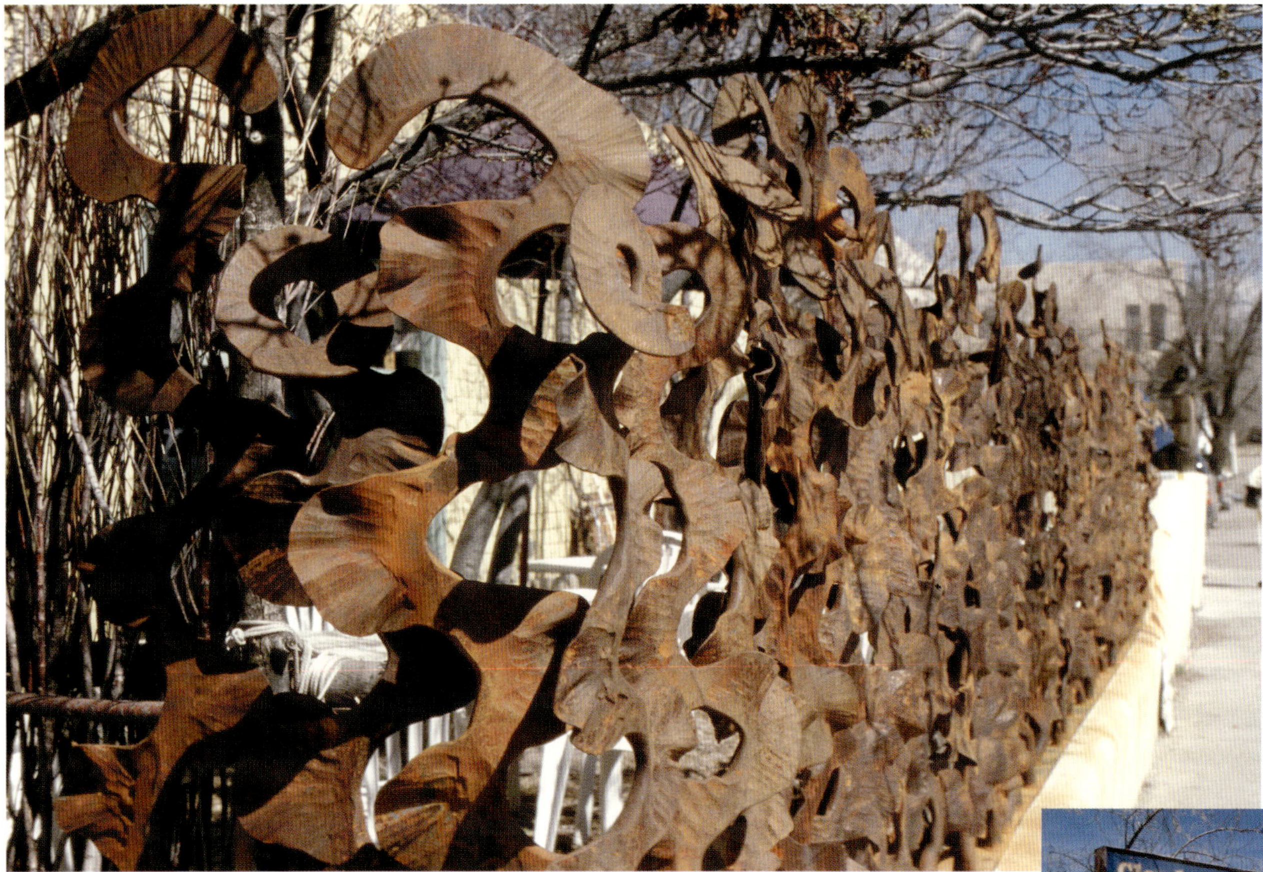

Helmut Hillenkamp. *Kelp Forest*. Installed at a restaurant in Santa Fe, New Mexico. Material 1-1/2" round bars, forged and welded onto a 3/4" x 3" solid bottom rail. The fence has an aquatic nature, which is strange in the desert. It serves as a kind of Feng Shuei wave breaker to separate the car energy in the street from the courtyard atmosphere within. The stiles were quenched in muriatic acid after forging, to yield a brown rusty runoff on the wall designed to resemble watery reflections or underwater roots. 5' high, plus 1.5' for the base height, 35' wide. *Photo, artist*

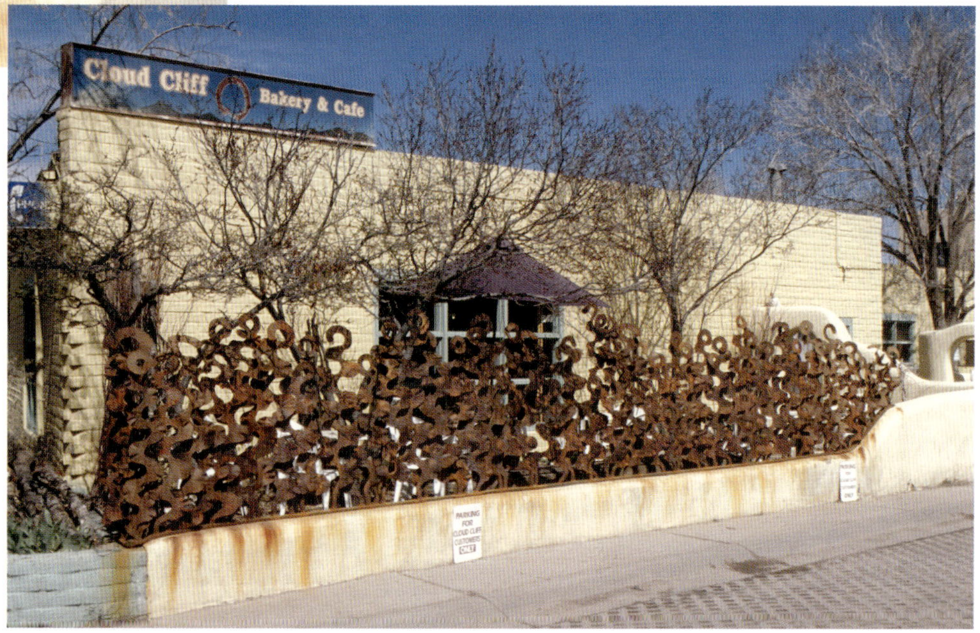

Helmut Hillenkamp. Whole fence. *Photo, artist*

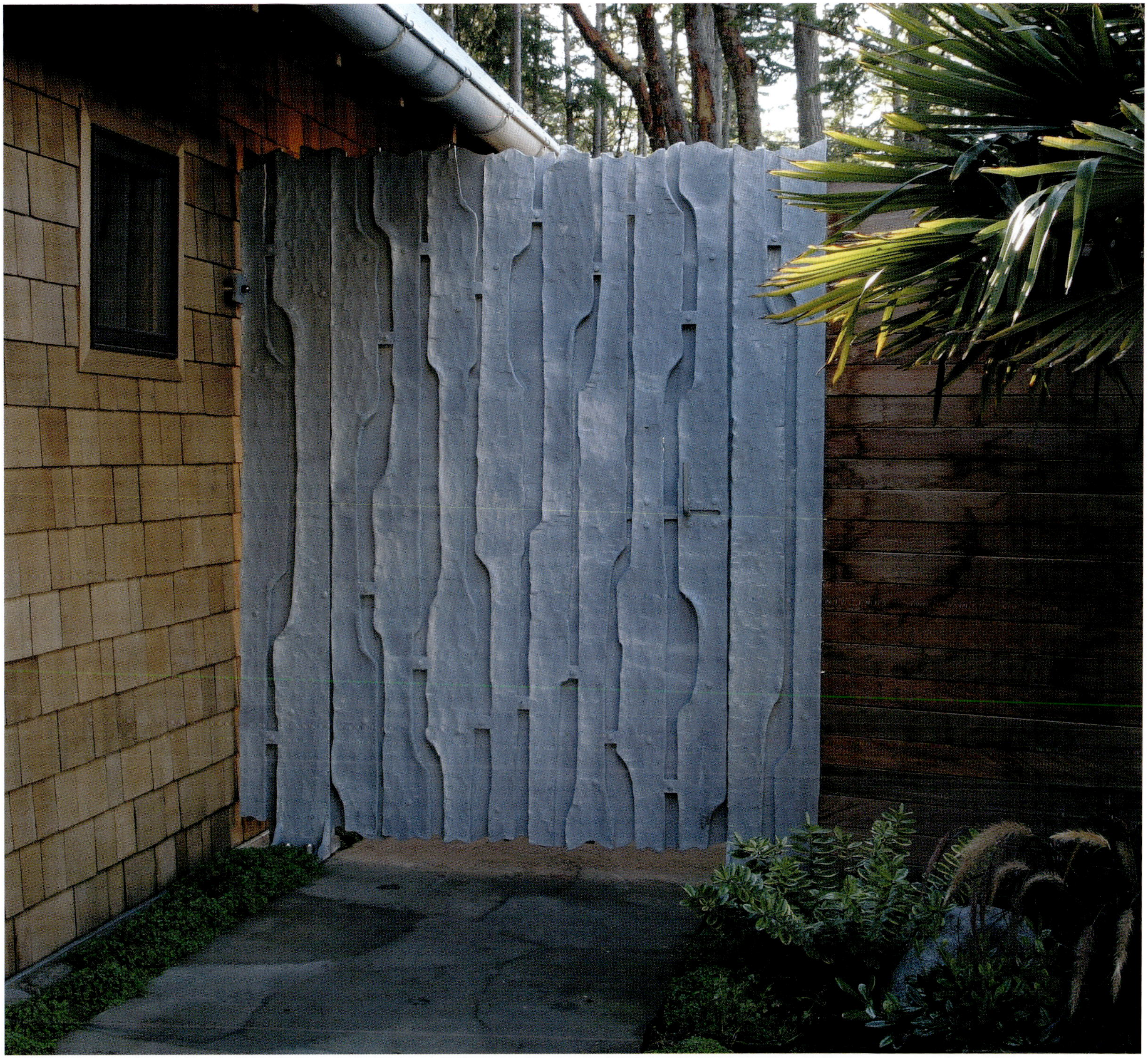

Russell Jaqua. *Privacy Gate.* Mild Steel with a galvanized finish. Says Jaqua, "I was asked to design a gate that featured an organic treatment and had to completely obscure vision into the inner courtyard. I was able to create a seemingly random texture and edge quality for each separate element using my Nazel 3B power hammer. Each piece was precisely planned to fit together almost like a puzzle, creating complete coverage tor the client." 84" high, 72" wide, 2" deep. *Photo, David Conklin*

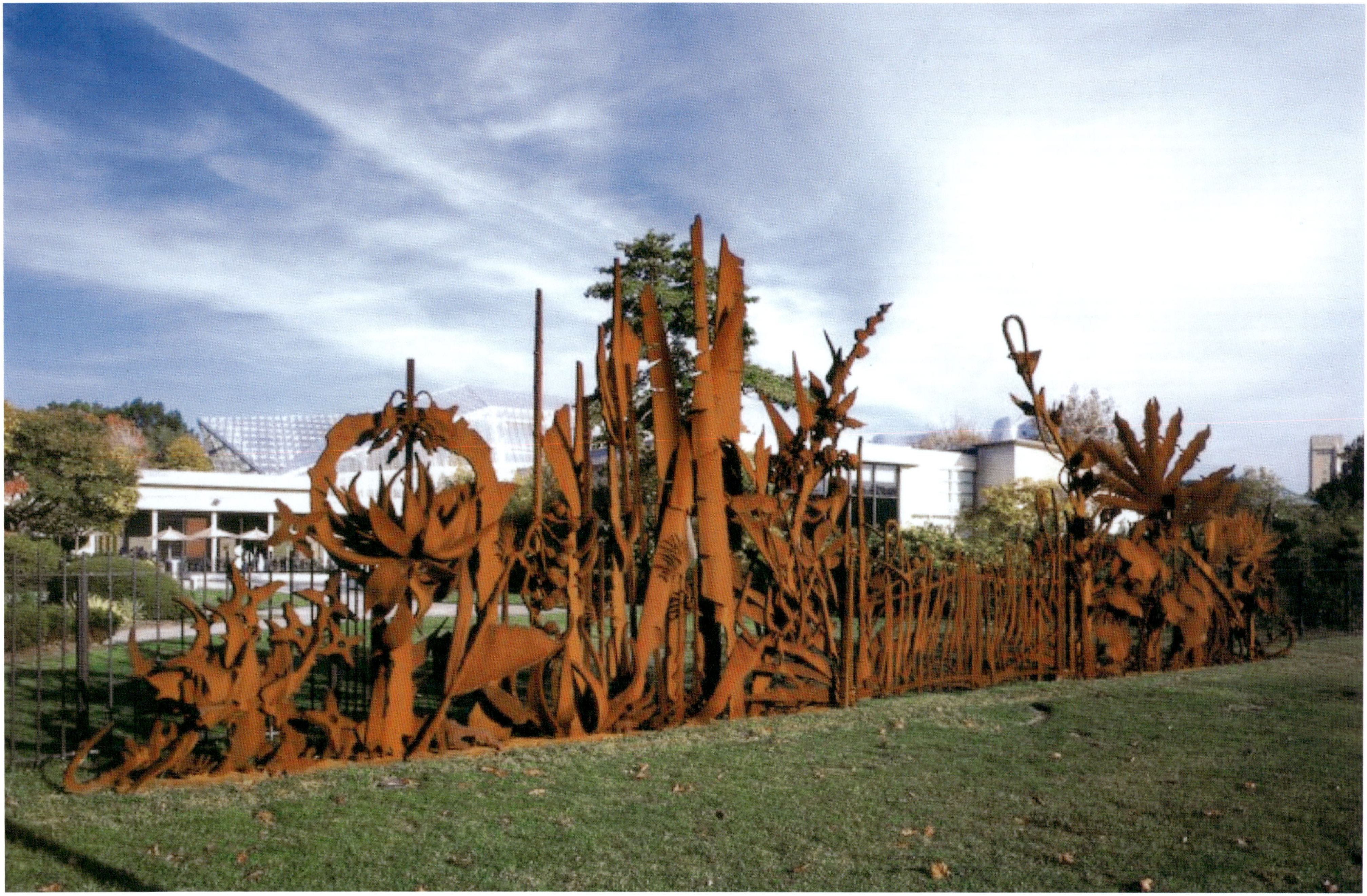

Albert Paley. *Kohl Gate for the Botanical Garden, Cleveland, Ohio*. Formed and fabricated steel with a weathered patina.15' high, 55' wide, 3' deep. *Photo, Dan Cunningham*

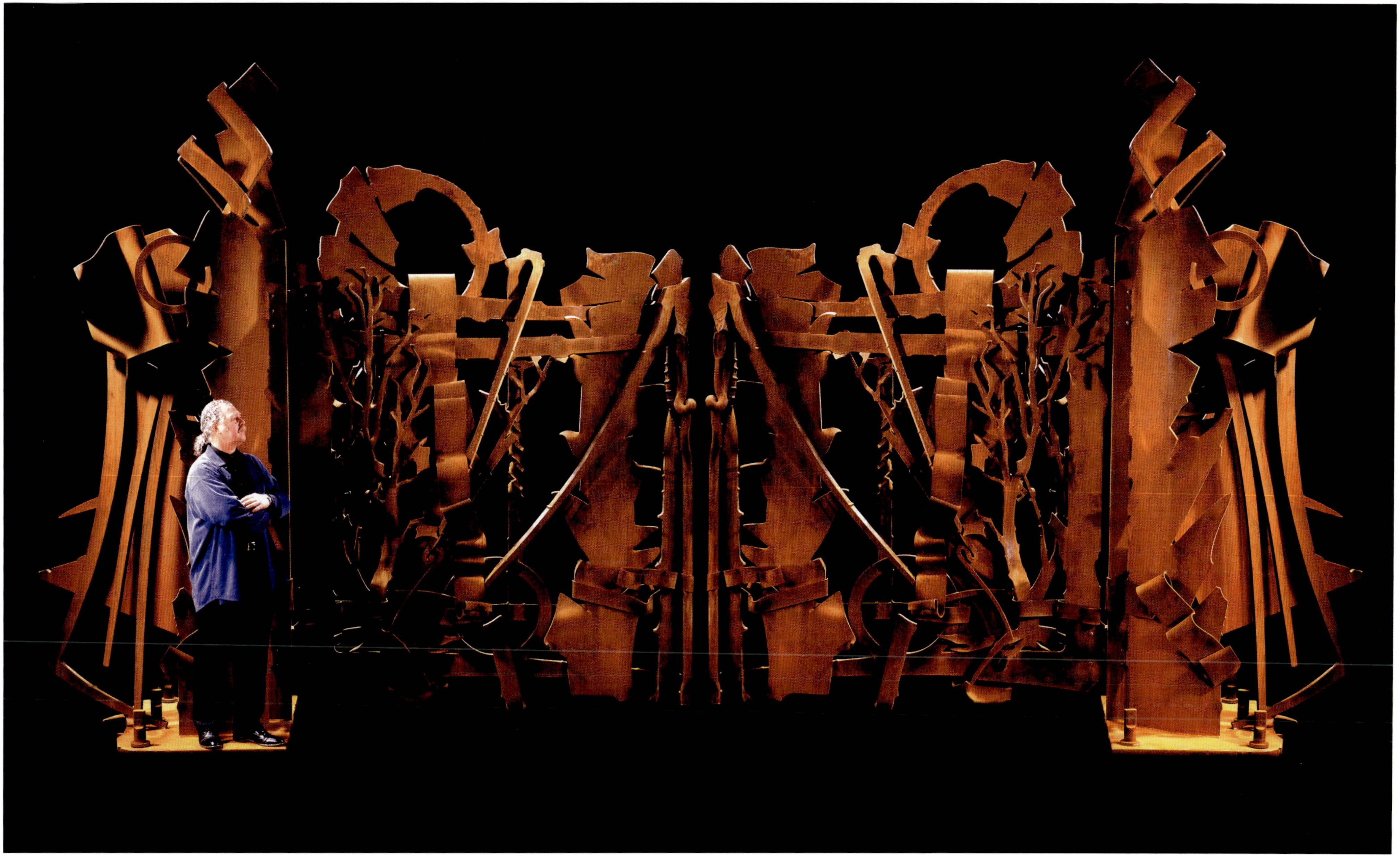

Albert Paley. Entrance Gate for a private New York residence. Formed and fabricated weathering steel.12' high, 24' wide, 4' deep. *Photo, Bruce Miller*

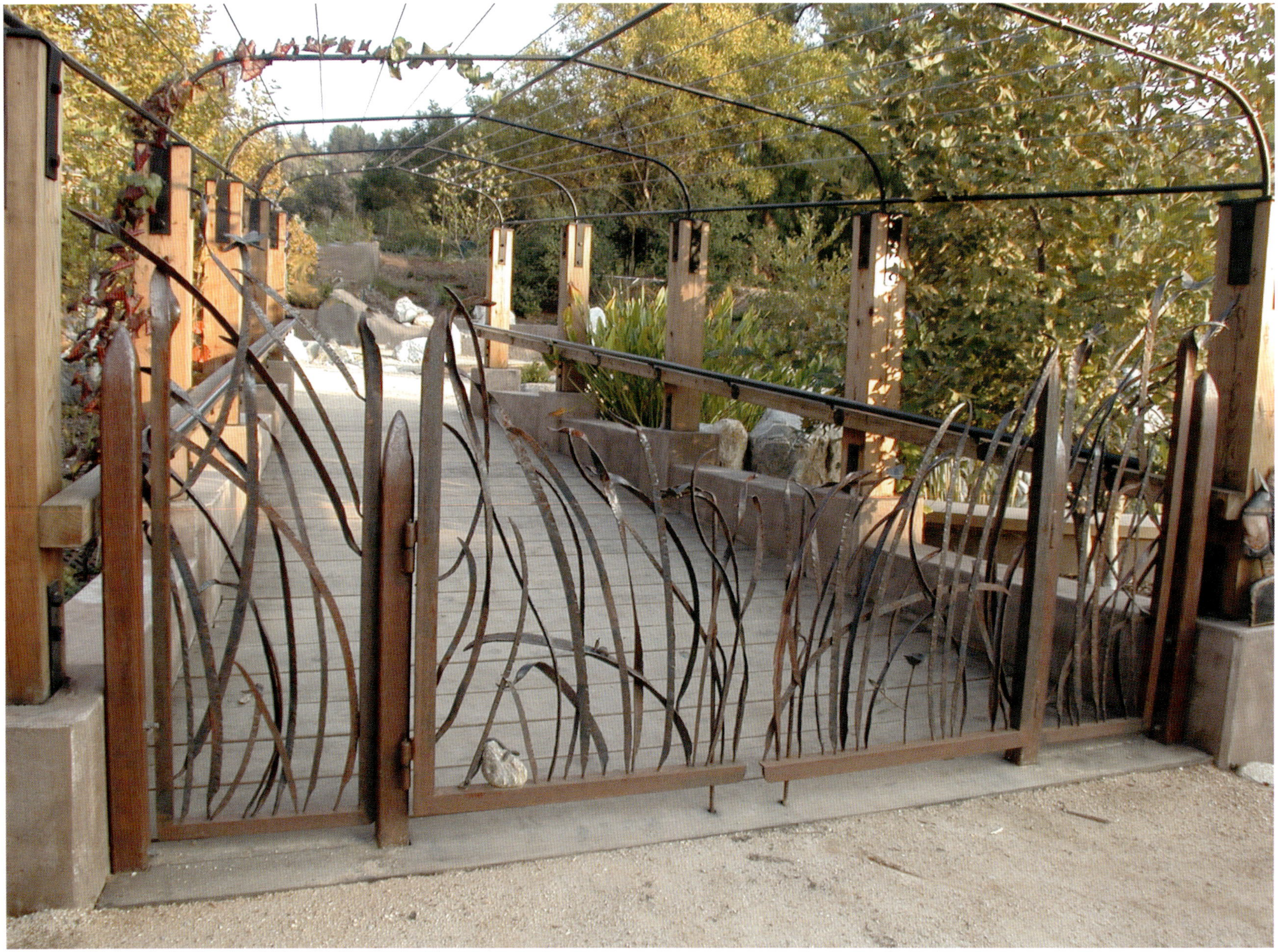

Heather McLarty. *Gate to Children's Woodland at the Audubon Center, Los Angeles, California*. Forged and fabricated steel with a rust finish. The "grass" theme is achieved using various hammer textured pieces of angle and flat bar. Assorted critters, including a snail, dragonflies, and butterflies made of silicon bronze or copper, are placed where observant children and adults may find them. A snake basks on a rock. 6' high, 11' wide. *Photo, Lisa Evans*

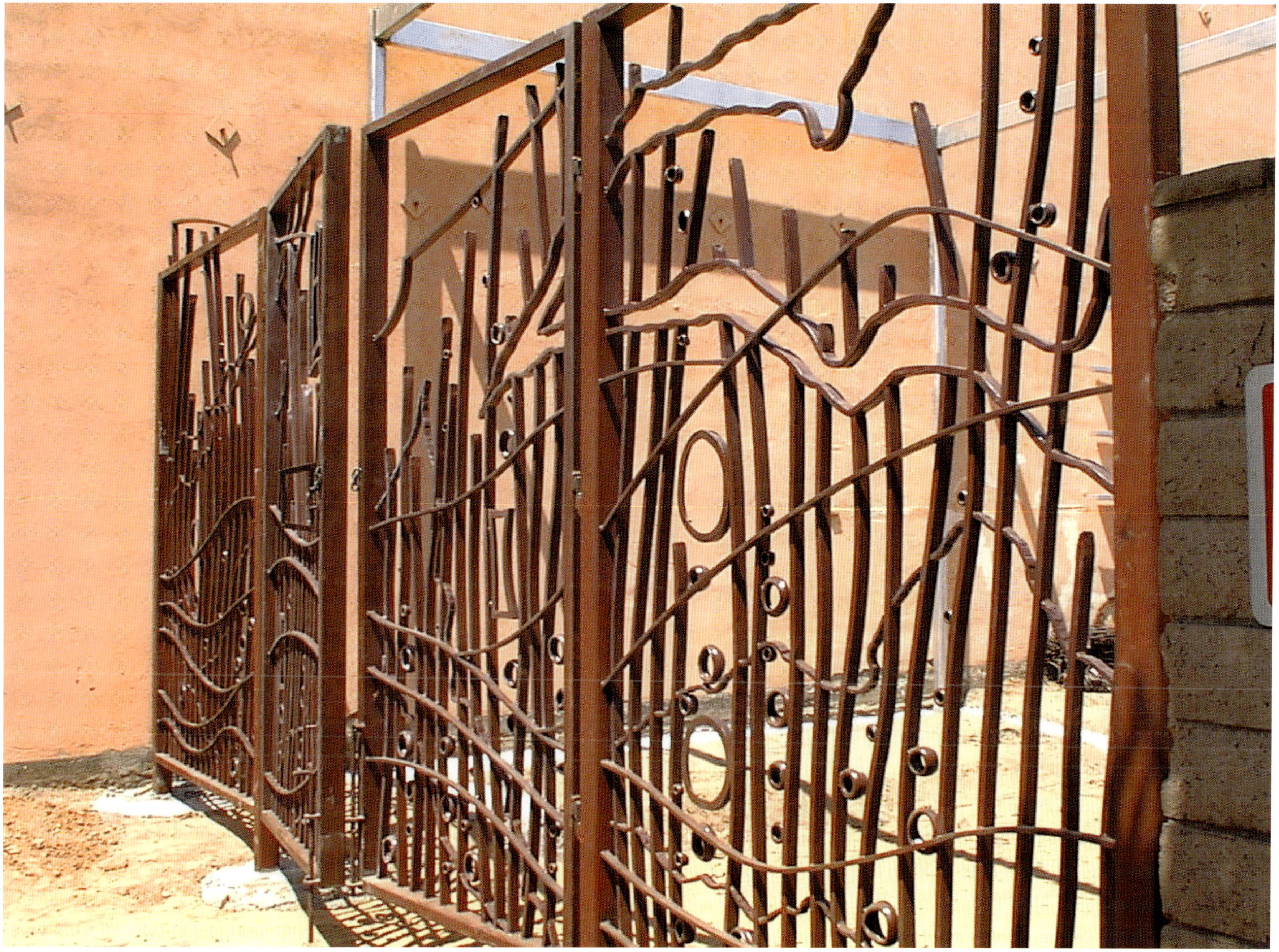

Lisa Jacobs. *Bubbles and Seaweed.* Steel with a rust finish. Forged and fabricated. Made for an Art Park Public Art Project in Long Beach, California. 14' high, 28' wide. *Photo, artist*

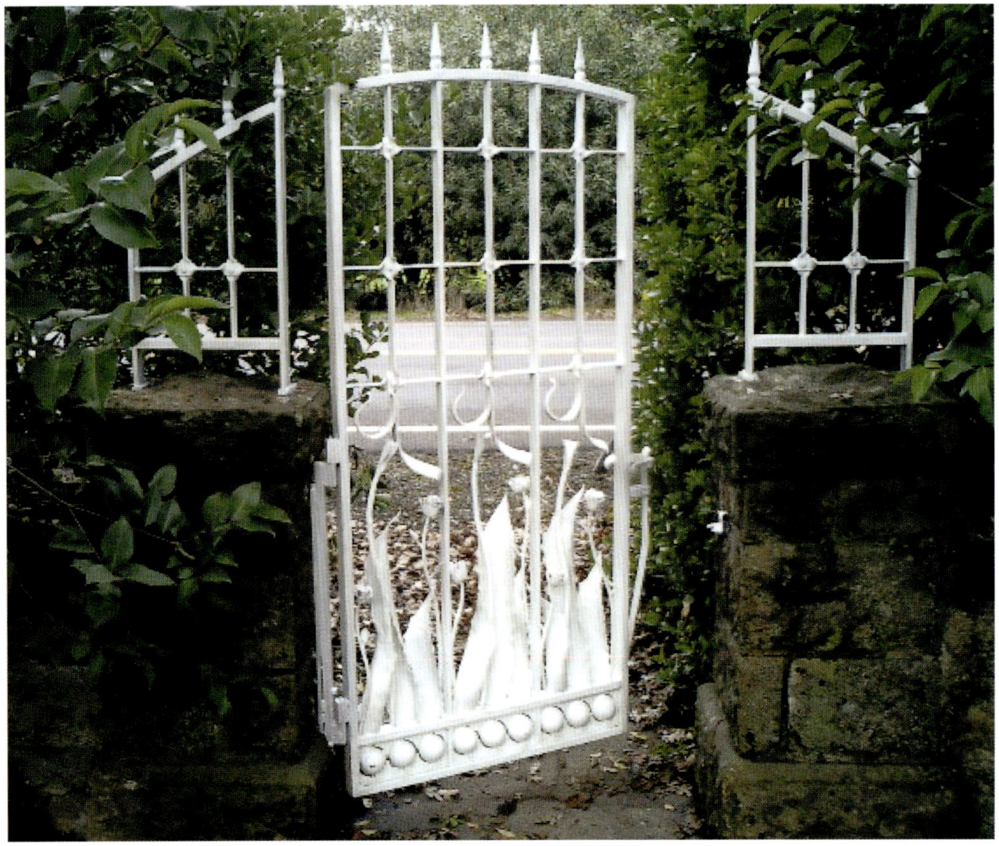

Lars Stanley, assisted by Suzanne Bass, Bobby Royal, Natalie Monson, Troy DeFrates, and Colby Brinkman. *Agave and Rose Vineyard Gates.* Forged and fabricated steel with painted finish. Inspired by the agaves and roses in the Napa Valley, California vineyard where it is installed. The biggest challenge was creating an agave leaf pattern that had movement and dynamic lines from all directions. The ball pattern and the scroll patterns at the gate bottoms reflect the Victorian detailing of the vineyard's 100-year old restored main building. This gate has side panels that help integrate it into the stone fence and make it appear larger than it is. Matching drive gates are 6' high, 16' wide with 8' panels. This pedestrian gate is about 7' high, 3' wide. *Photo, Lars Stanley*

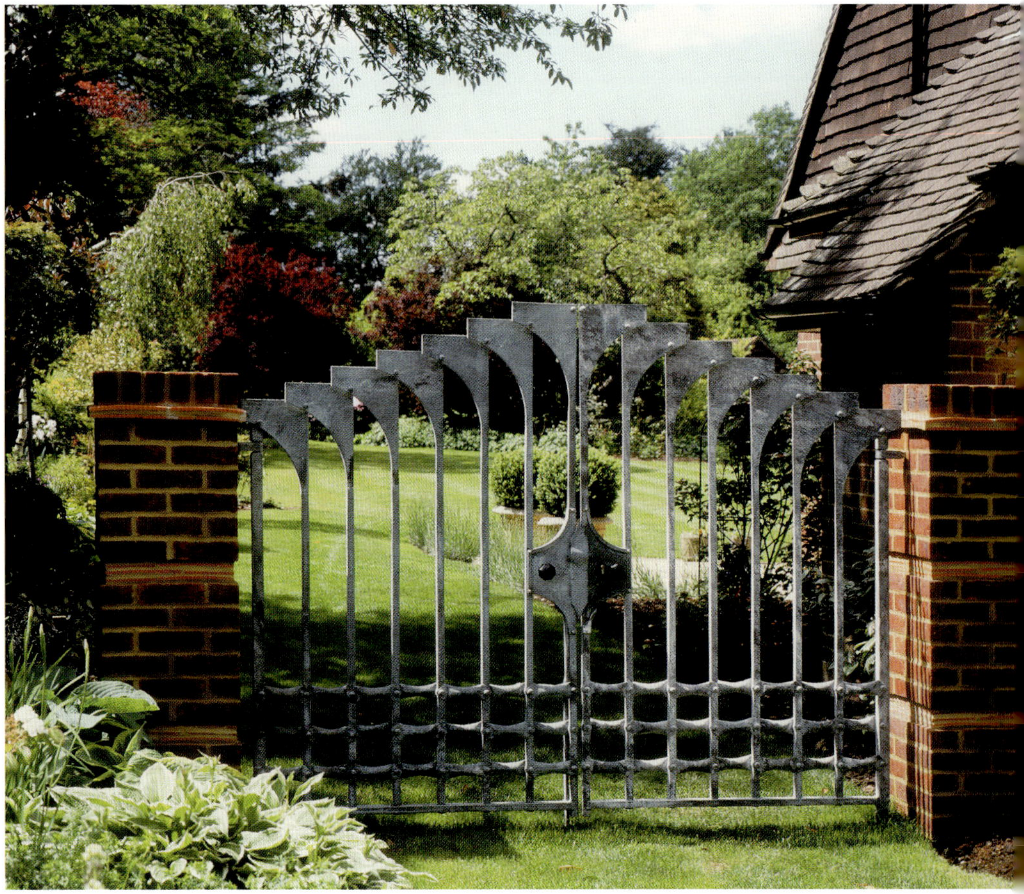

Paul Elliott. *Surrey Gate.* Art Deco style garden gate. Mild steel forged and riveted. The inspiration for the gate came from a beautifully textured weathered wooden pegged verandah surrounding the house and from the roof tiles. *Photo, Jackie Phillips*

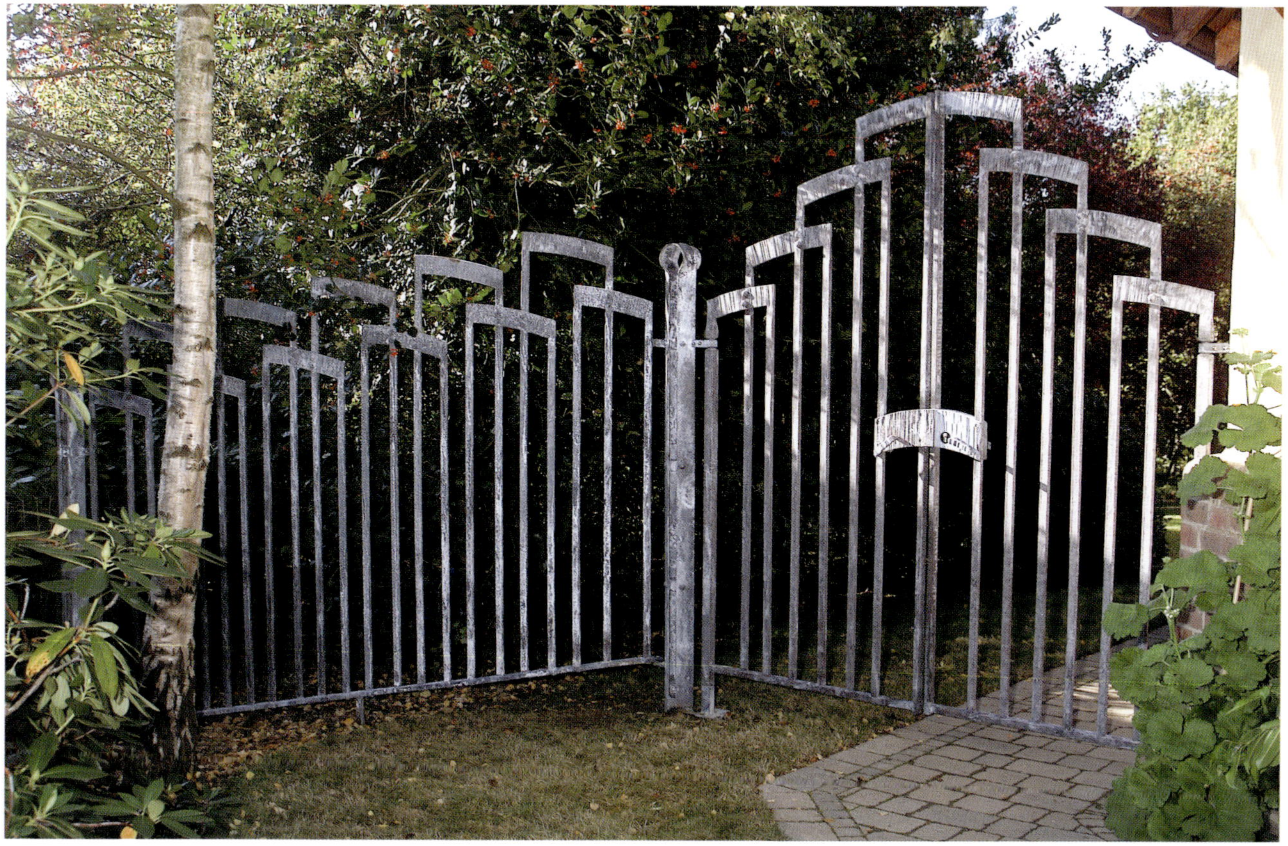

Paul Elliott. *Arts & Crafts Style Fencing and Gate.* Mild Steel galvanized and acid etched. The gates and railings were designed to frame and complement the view to the house. *Photo, Jackie Phillips*

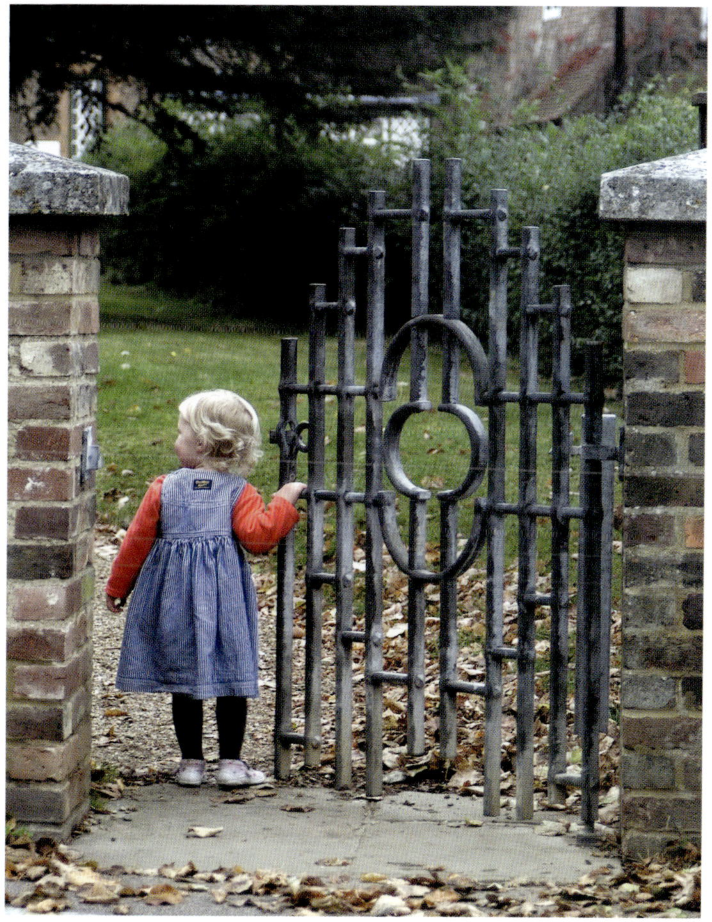

Paul Elliott. Aldbury Church memorial gate. *Photo, Jackie Phillips*

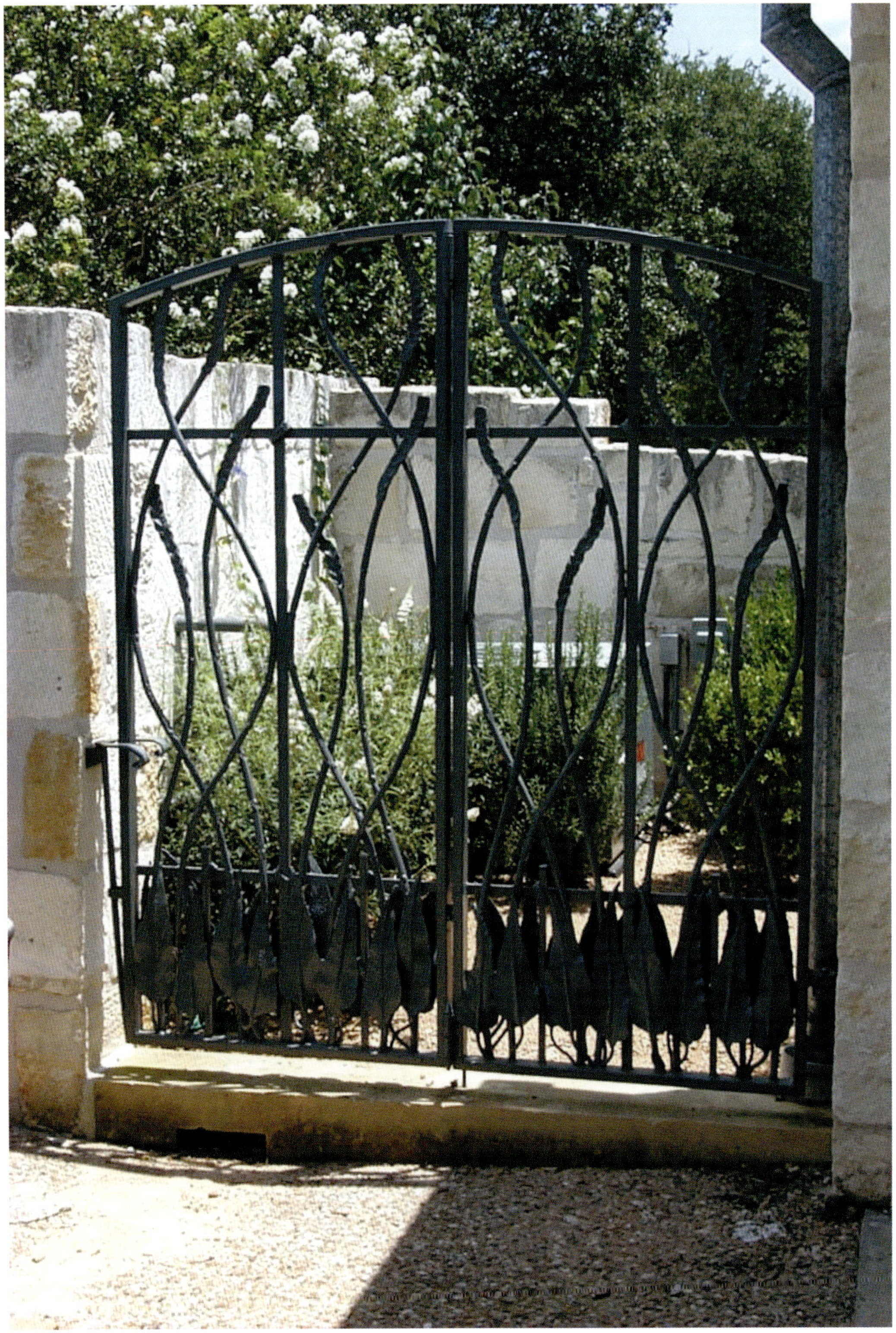

Lars Stanley. *Price Clark Gate 2*. Forged and fabricated steel with paint. Inspired by plants that the owner's felt were significant to them, such as the local grasses and leaves at the bottom. The leaves had to be close together to prevent the owner's small dogs from exiting. 6' high, 6' wide. *Photo,* artist

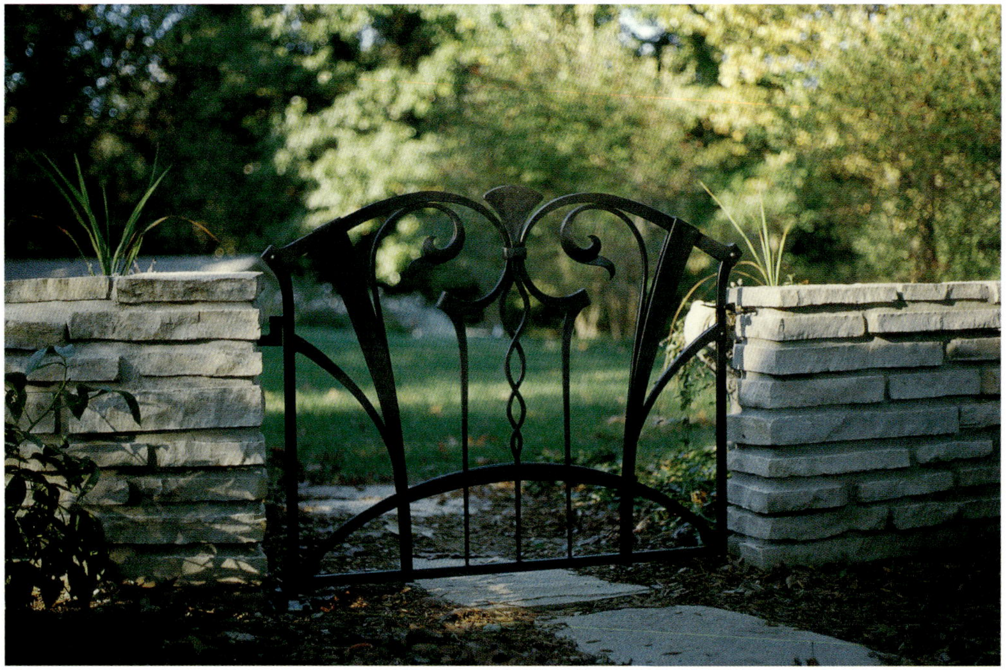

John Medwedeff. Garden gate. Forged steel. 36" high, 40" wide. *Photo, artist*

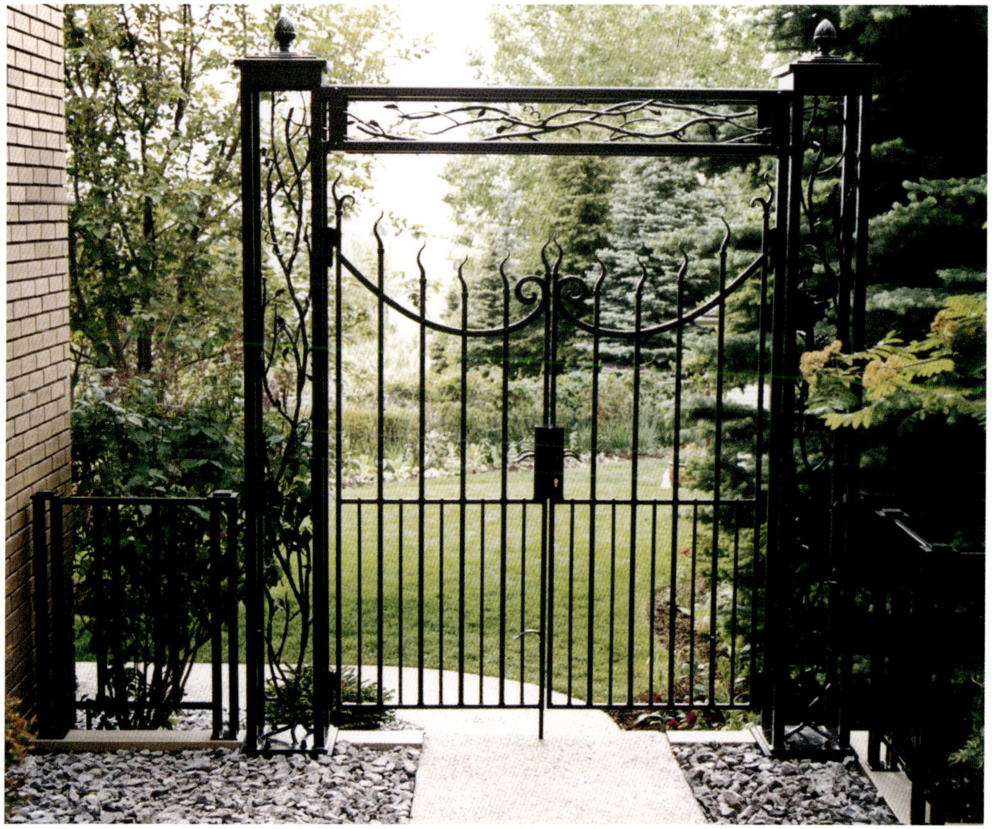

John Monteath and Brenda Field. Arbor gate and fence. Forged and fabricated mild steel with a black powder coat finish. 9' high, 7' wide with 1' square pillars. *Photo, artists*

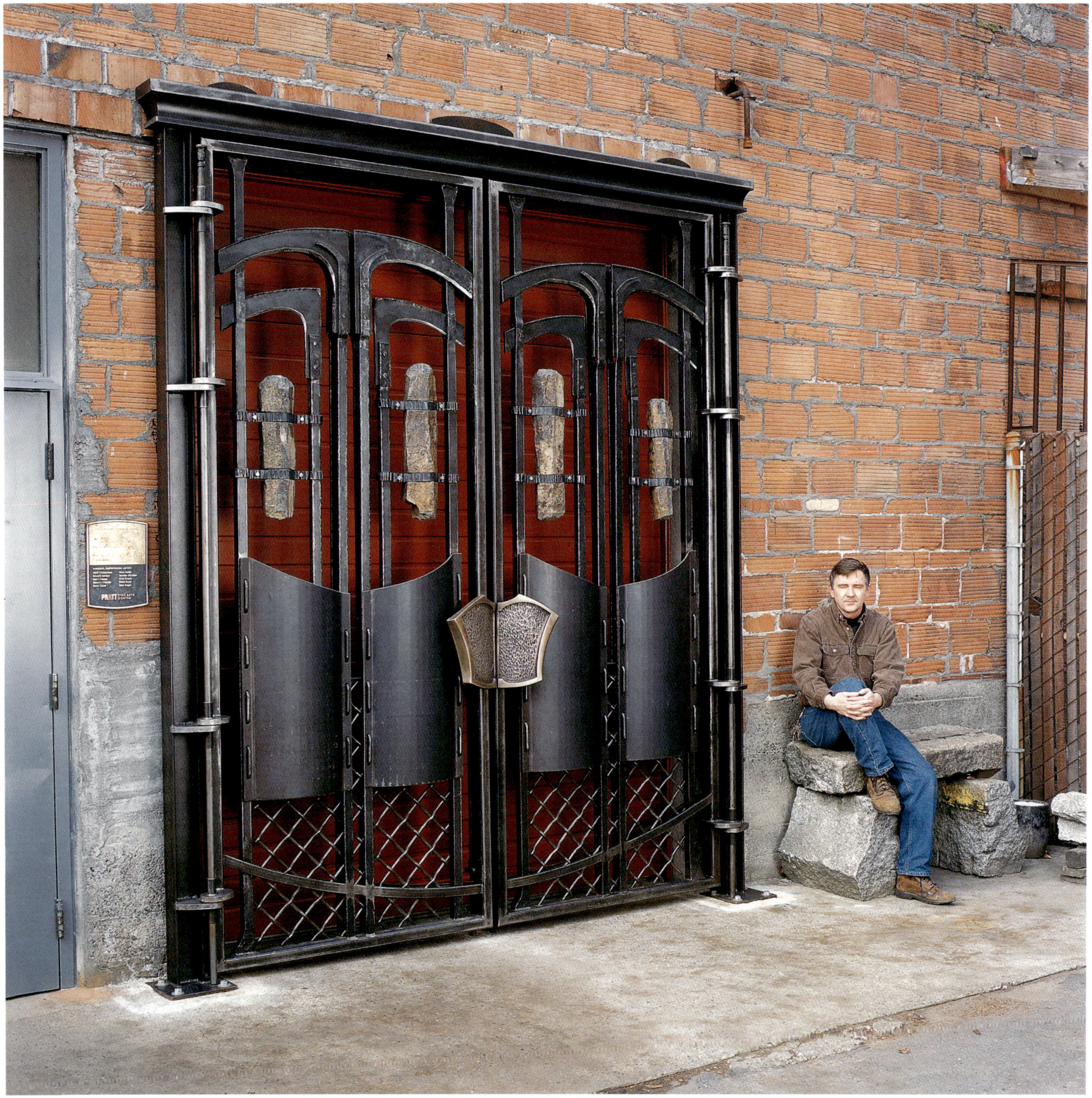

Sculpture Studio Gates, Pratt Fine Arts Center, Seattle, Washington. Forged and fabricated steel, basalt, sand-cast bronze. Built at Pratt Fine Arts Center as an advanced welding/forging class project. Stephen Marks, project designer and manager, instructor.
Michael Prendergast, project designer and bronze work; Scott Szloch, instructor; Sabah Al-Dhaher, stone work; students and participating artists: Mark Christiansen, Edward Benson, Sarah Fansler, Rebecca Hartzler, Frank Keyser, Marc Mullin, Jennifer Mundee, Chris Overly, Karen Rudd, and John Sager. 11' high, 9' wide. *Photo, William P. Wright*

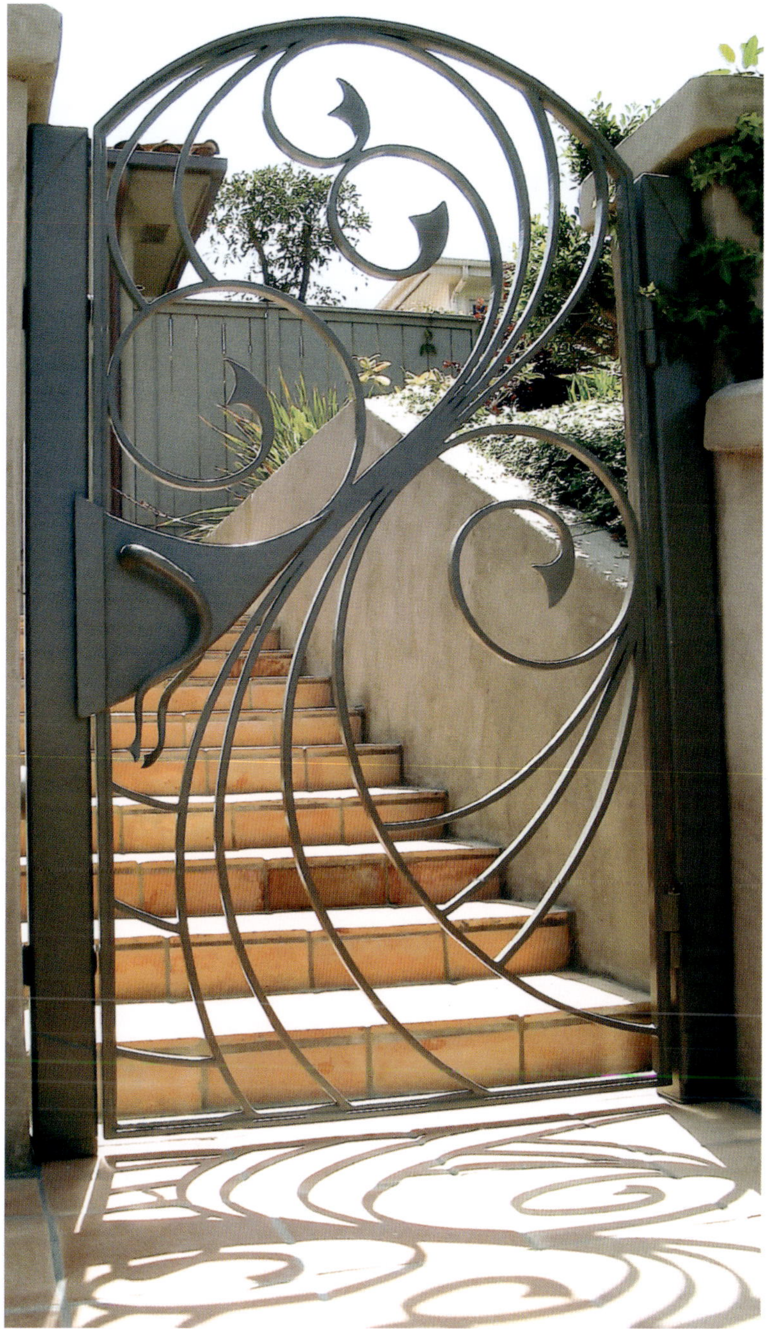

David Browne. *Swirling Water Entry Gate*. Forged and fabricated mild steel with epoxy paint. Installed in a private home in La Jolla, California. All electronic mechanisms are hidden within the left post and the gate is remotely controlled from inside.72" high, 40" wide. *Photo, JoAnne Palasi*

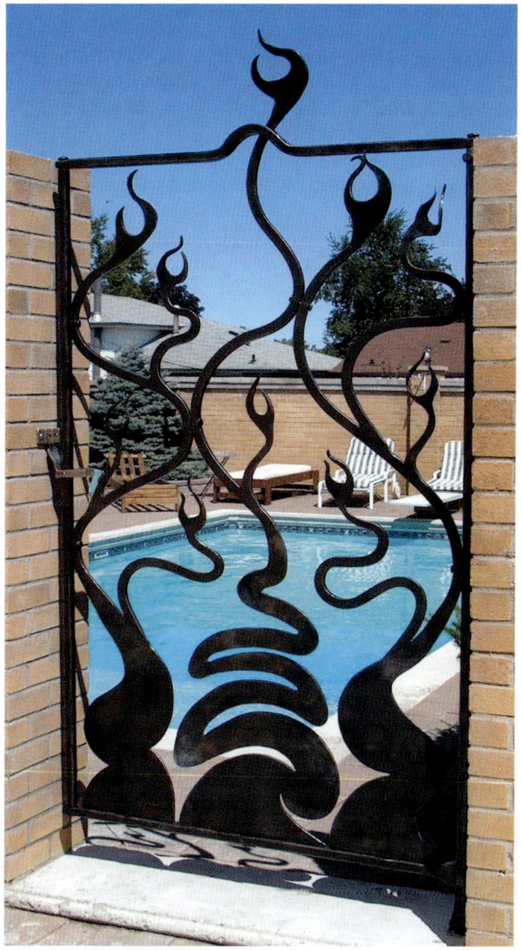

Mark Puigmarti. *Fire Dance Gate* and matching room divider. Forged and fabricated mild steel. 84" high, 40" wide. *Photo, artist*

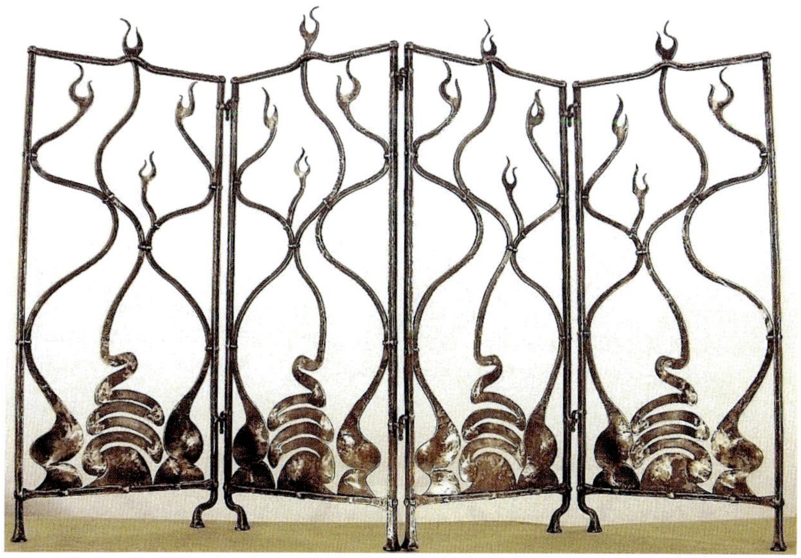

Mark Puigmarti. *Fire Dance Screen.* Room divider. Forged and fabricated mild steel. Four panels, each panel 32" wide, 72" high. 2003. *Fire Dance* was designed and executed as a stage backdrop for the Biannual Caniron Conference Number Four, in Hamilton, Ontario, Canada in 2003. The event theme was "share our fire", so a fire inspired design seemed fitting. The second criteria required that the object have a desirable function after the conference. *Photos, artist*

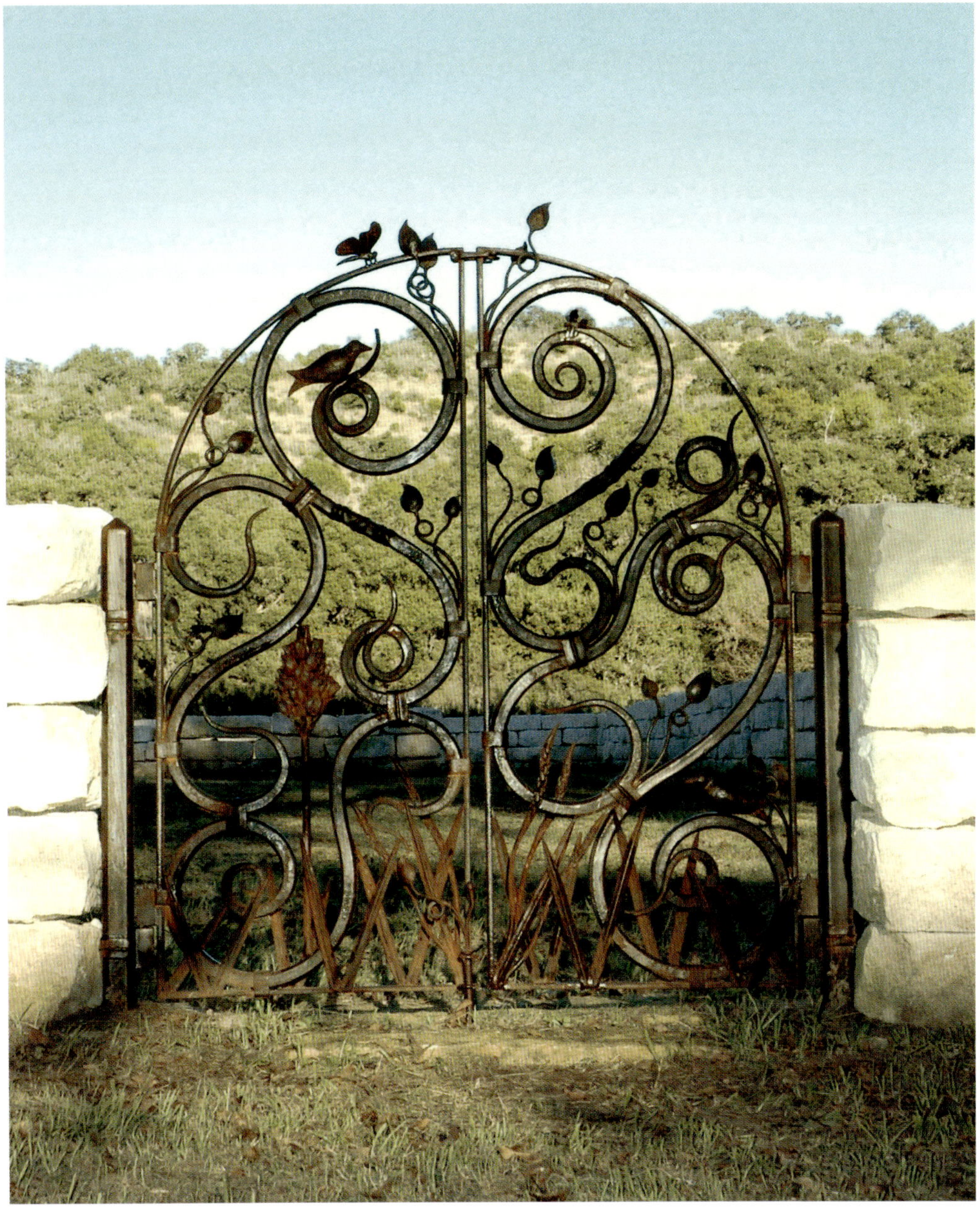

George Parker. Cemetery gate. The client wanted the gate to be all steel and include native Texas plants. There are yucca, bluebonnets, and indigenous grasses across the lower section to thwart armadillos from getting through and digging up the grounds. At the top, a pair of doves, a butterfly, and a dragonfly carry personal symbolism for the client. 5' high, 4' wide. *Photo, artist*

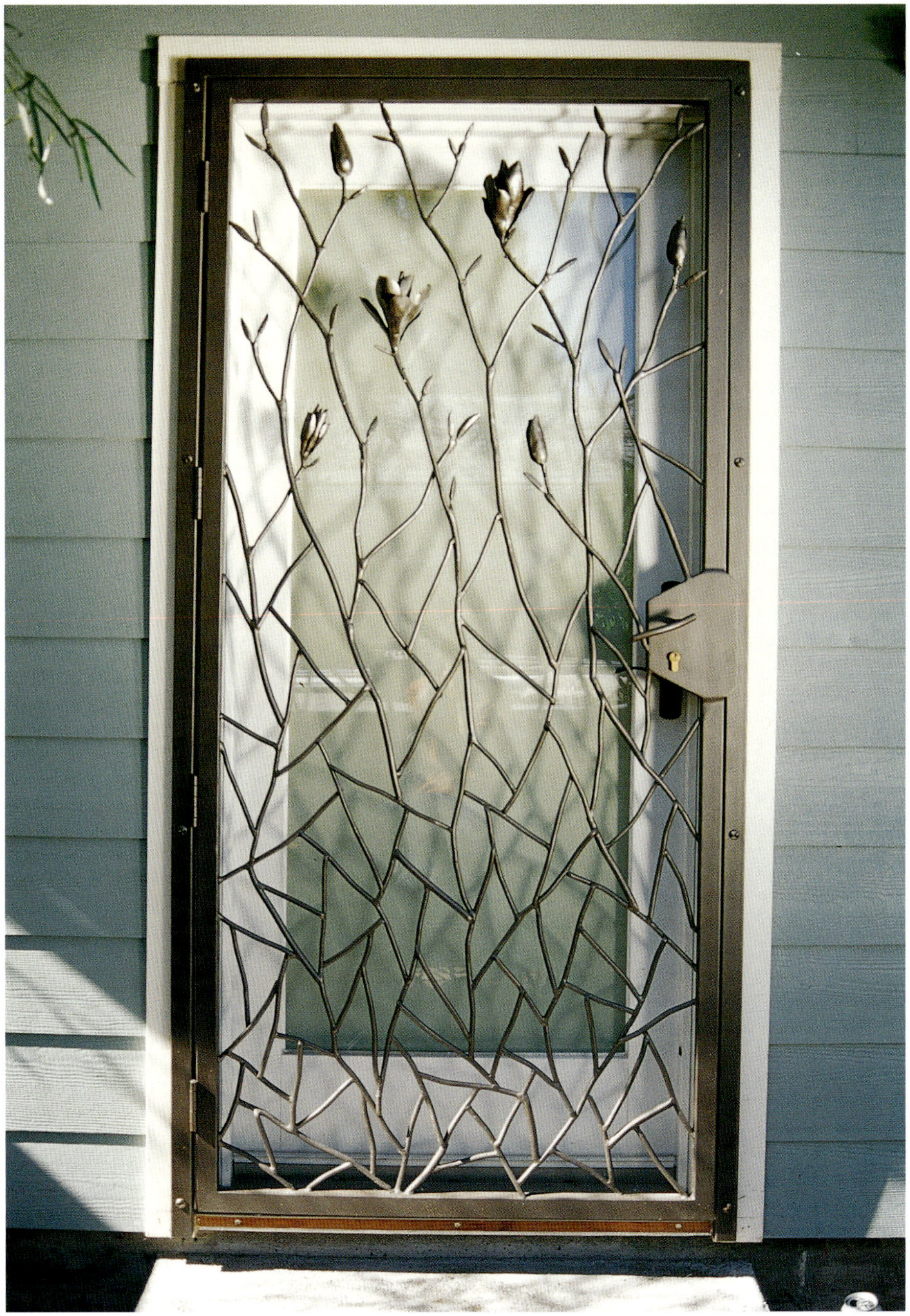

Shawn Lovell. *Magnolia Gate*. Forged and fabricated steel. 6.5' high, 3' wide. *Photo, artist*

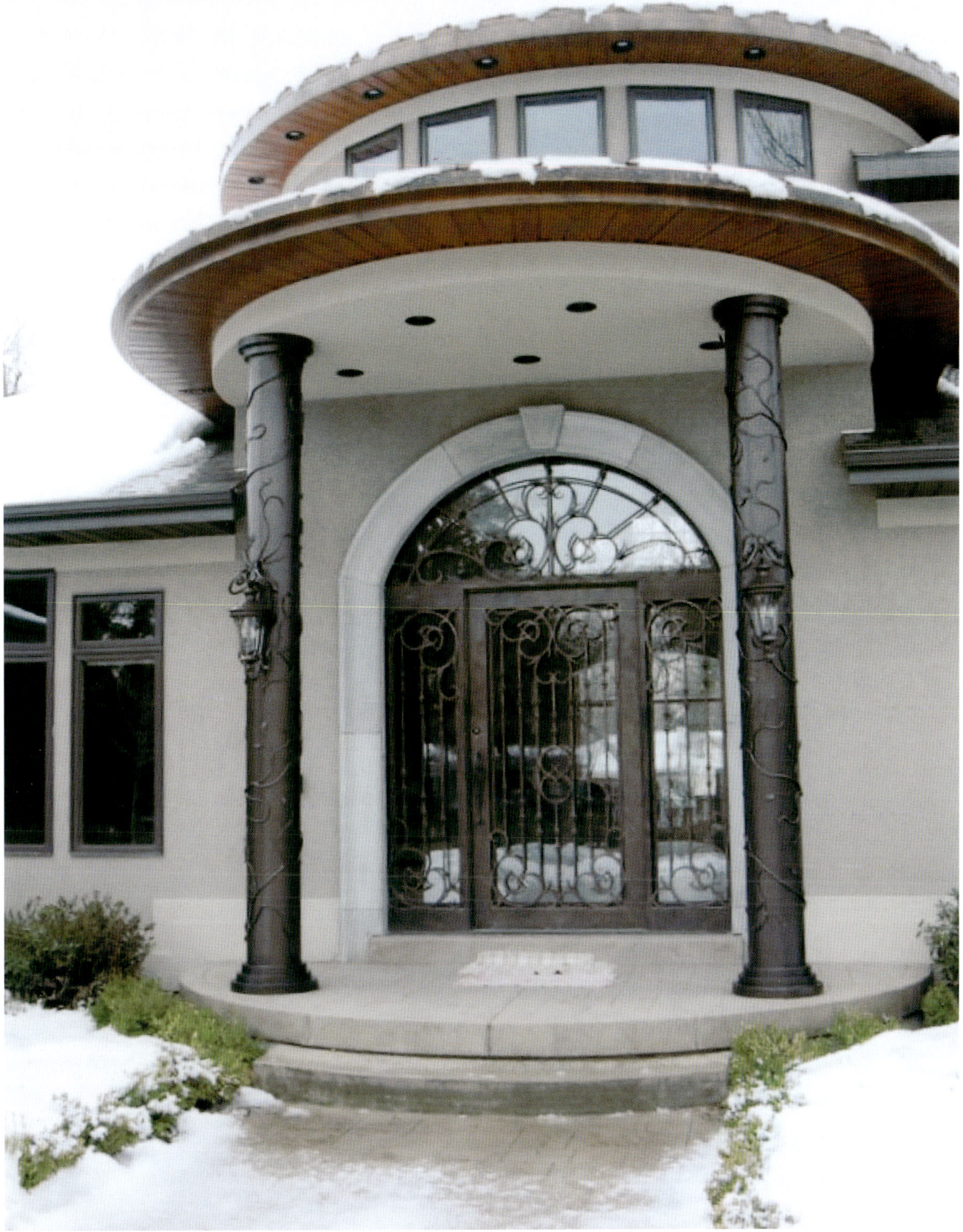

Richard Prazen. *Tachiki Residence*. The columns were added to the house front and wrapped in the iron vines with the sconce lighting added. The wrappings were made of 12-inch pipe split. The vines and leaves were made and assembled on site. They were powder coated and oil rubbed to a bronze finish. *Photo, artist*

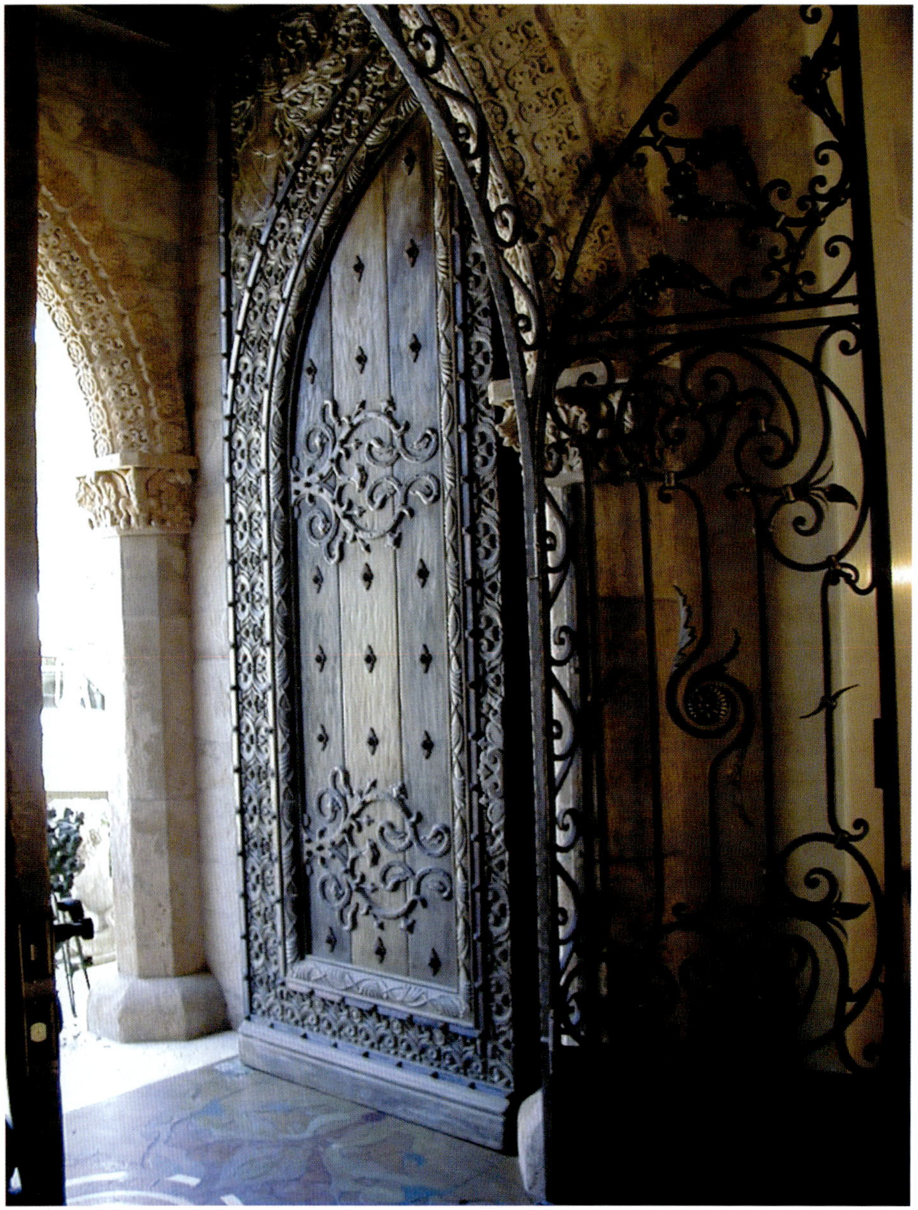

Greg Eng. Gothic door hardware. The pair of Gothic doorframes are hammered copper with the hinges riveted to forged steel. The copper was water jet cut and the steel was plasma cut. Elements were hammer grooved and beveled by forging then fabricated using MIG for steel and TIG for copper. The copper was given a brown patina and the forged steel was lightly rusted, and then buffed with pigmented wax burned in. Each door is 12' high and 4' wide. *Photo, Brenda Eng*

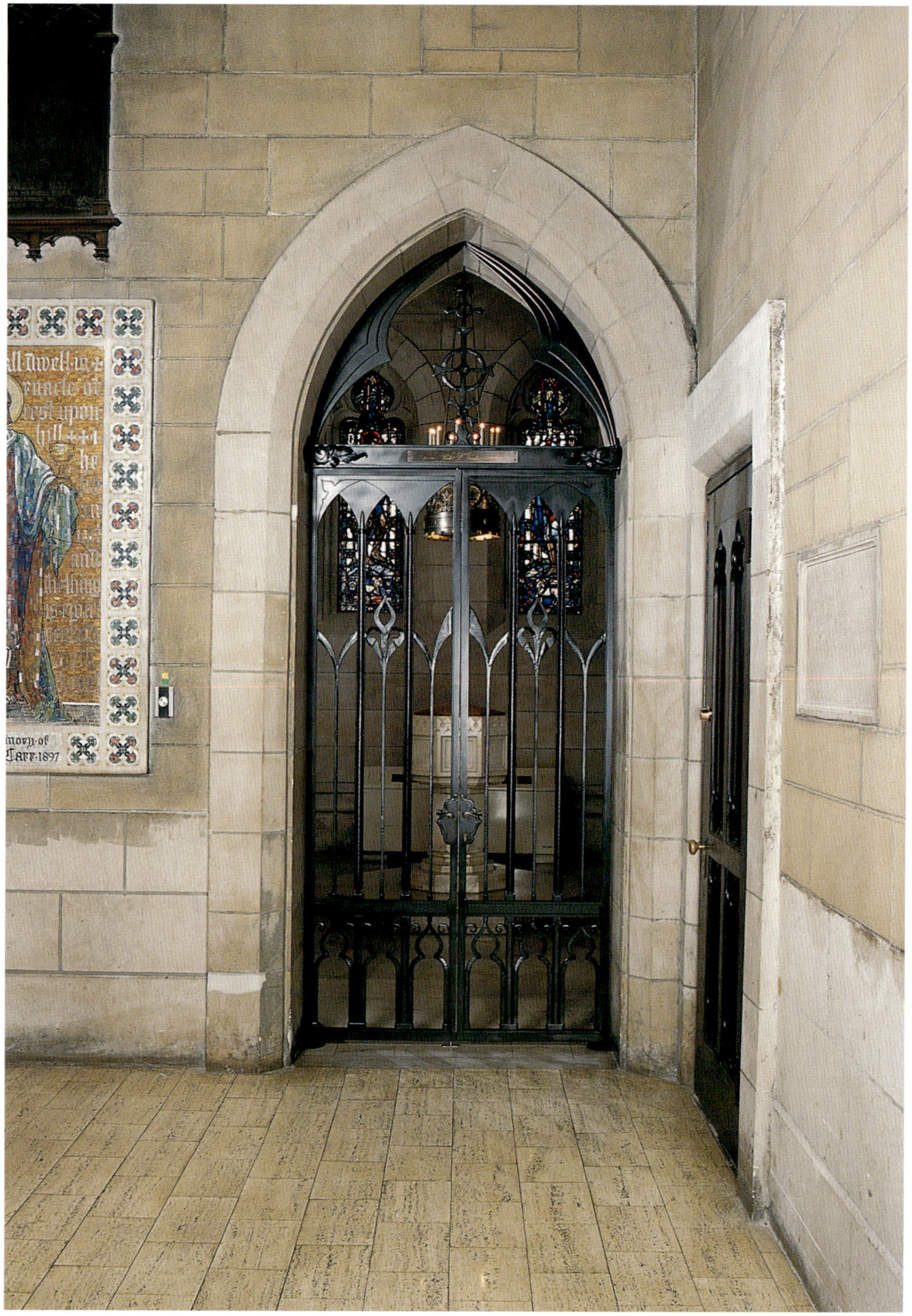

John Medwedeff. *Fricke Memorial Gate*. Forged and fabricated steel. Christ Church Cathedral, St. Louis, Missouri. 50" high, 11" wide, 1.5" deep. *Photo, Jeff Bruce*

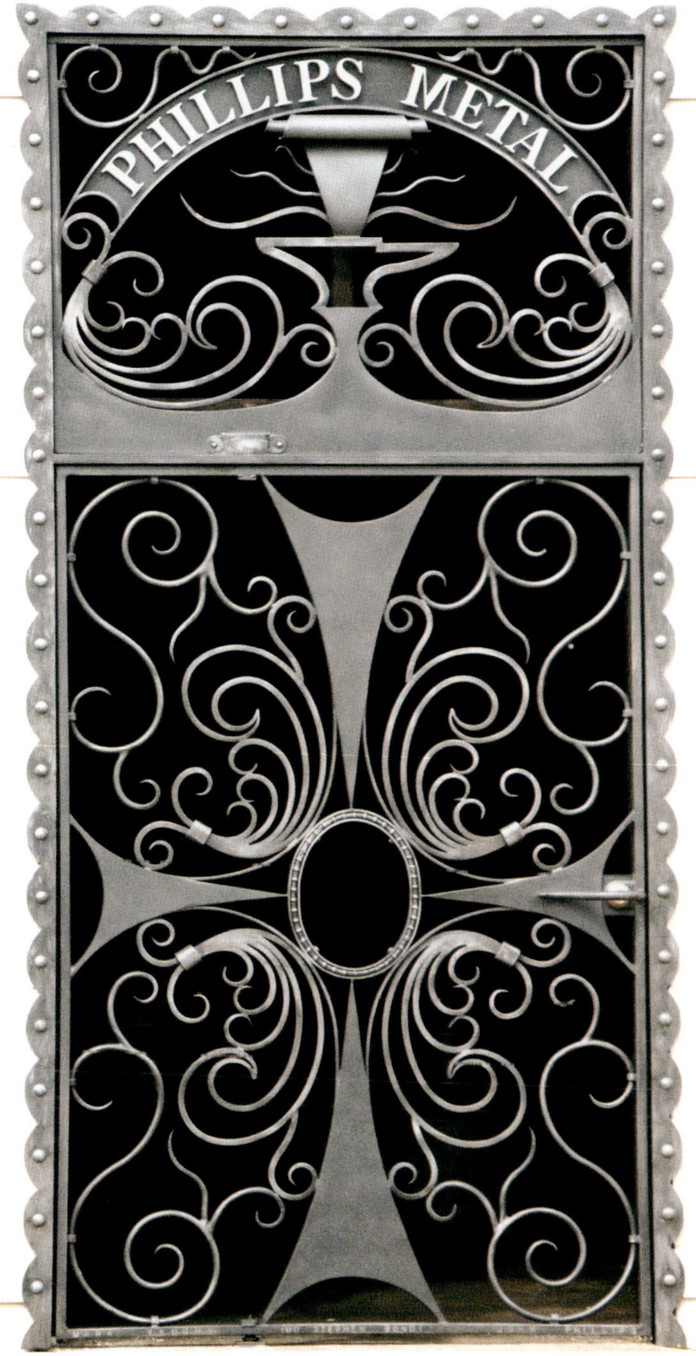

John Phillips and Mark Vaughn. Shop door. Forged and fabricated steel. One problem was how to maintain a fluid open/close motion for an 800-pound door. The artists also engineered a unique way of designing and aligning the hinges so that the shop cats could open the door. 11.5' high, 5.5' wide. *Photo, artist*

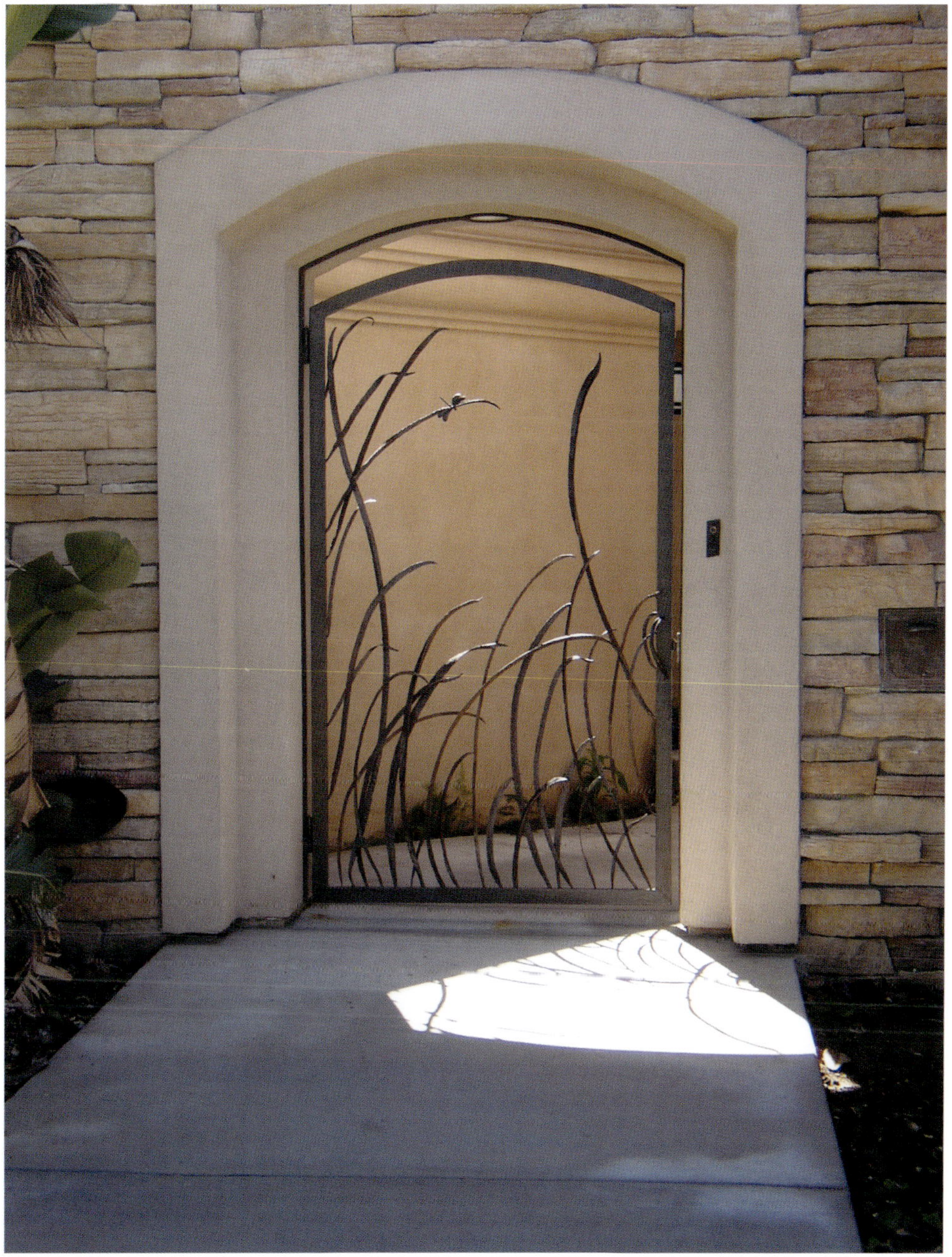

Heather McLarty. *Wind Gate*. Forged steel with rust finish. A bronze butterfly is perched on a blade of grass. The grasses appear to bend in the wind, a concept desired by the client. 7' high, 4' wide. *Photo, Troy Evans*

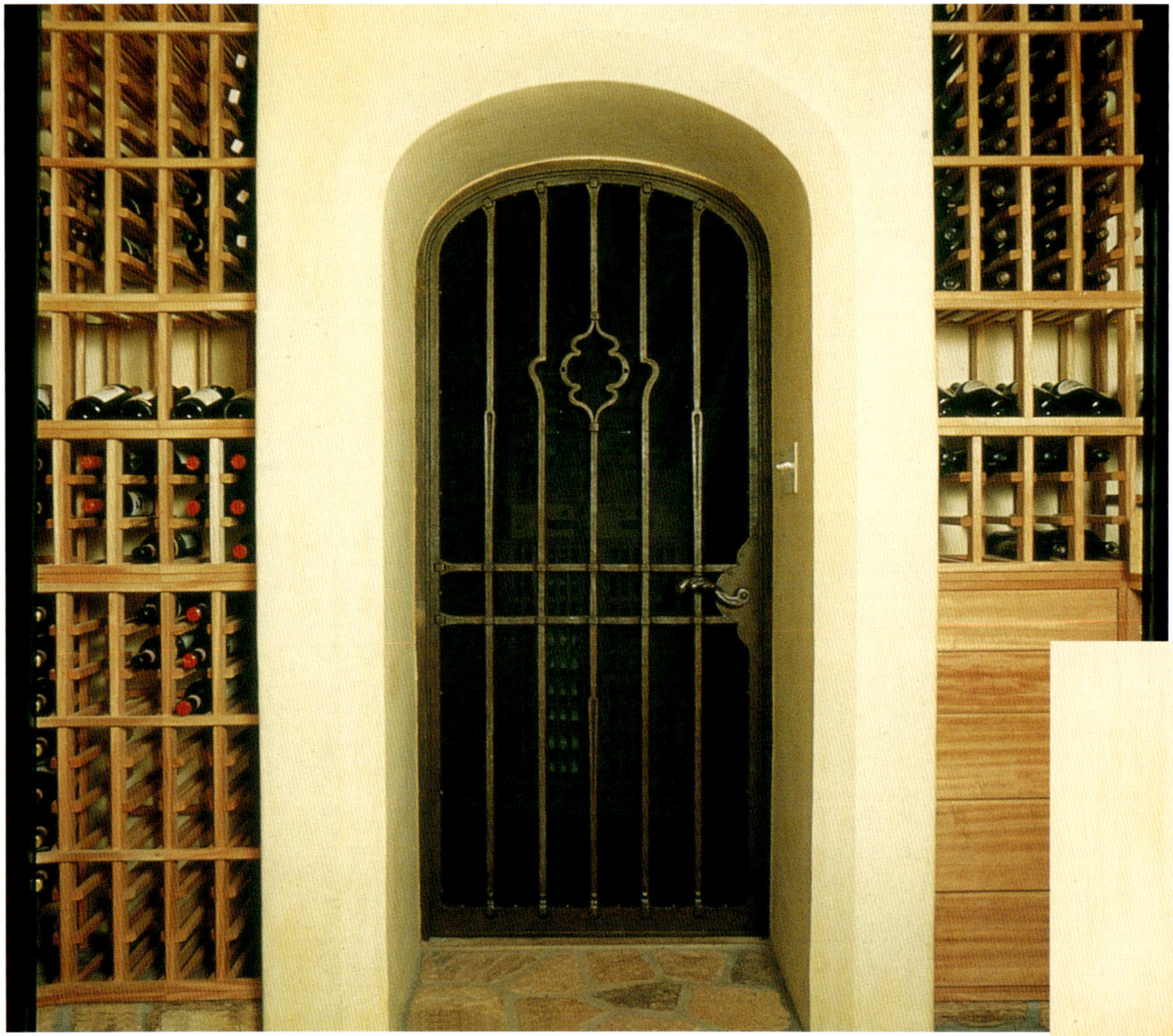

John-Pierre Masbanji. Wine cellar door. Hand forged pure iron with traditional joinery and a hand forged latch/lock plate. *Photo, James Chen*

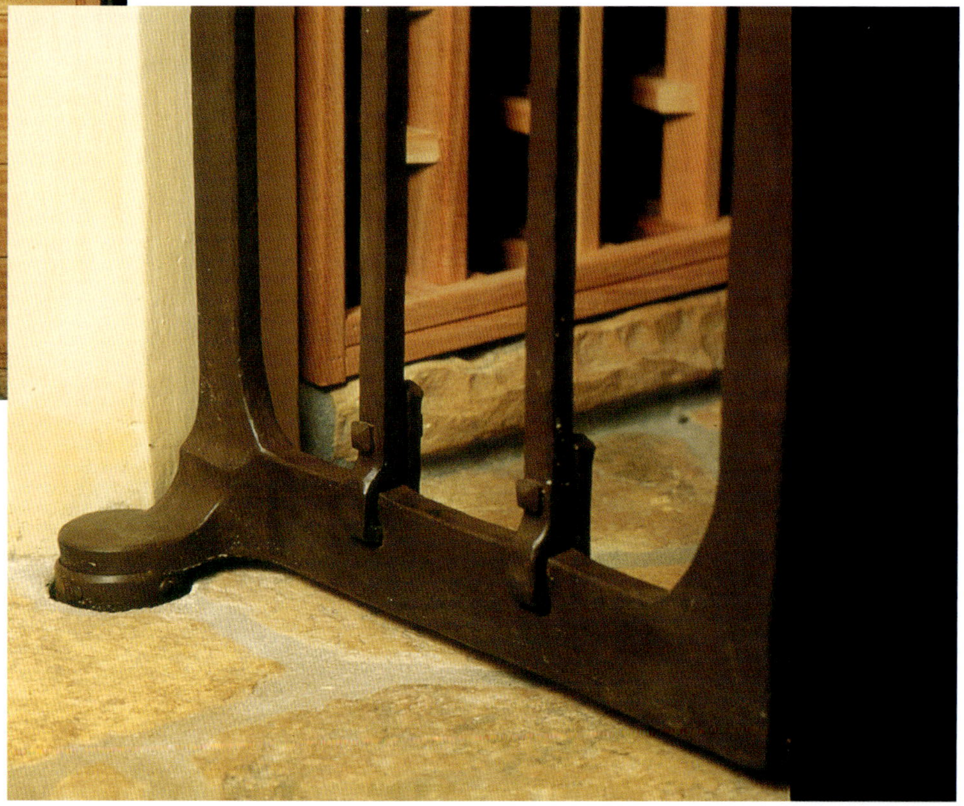

John-Pierre Masbanji. Detail shows the elegant joinery, shaping, and finish. *Photo, James Chen*

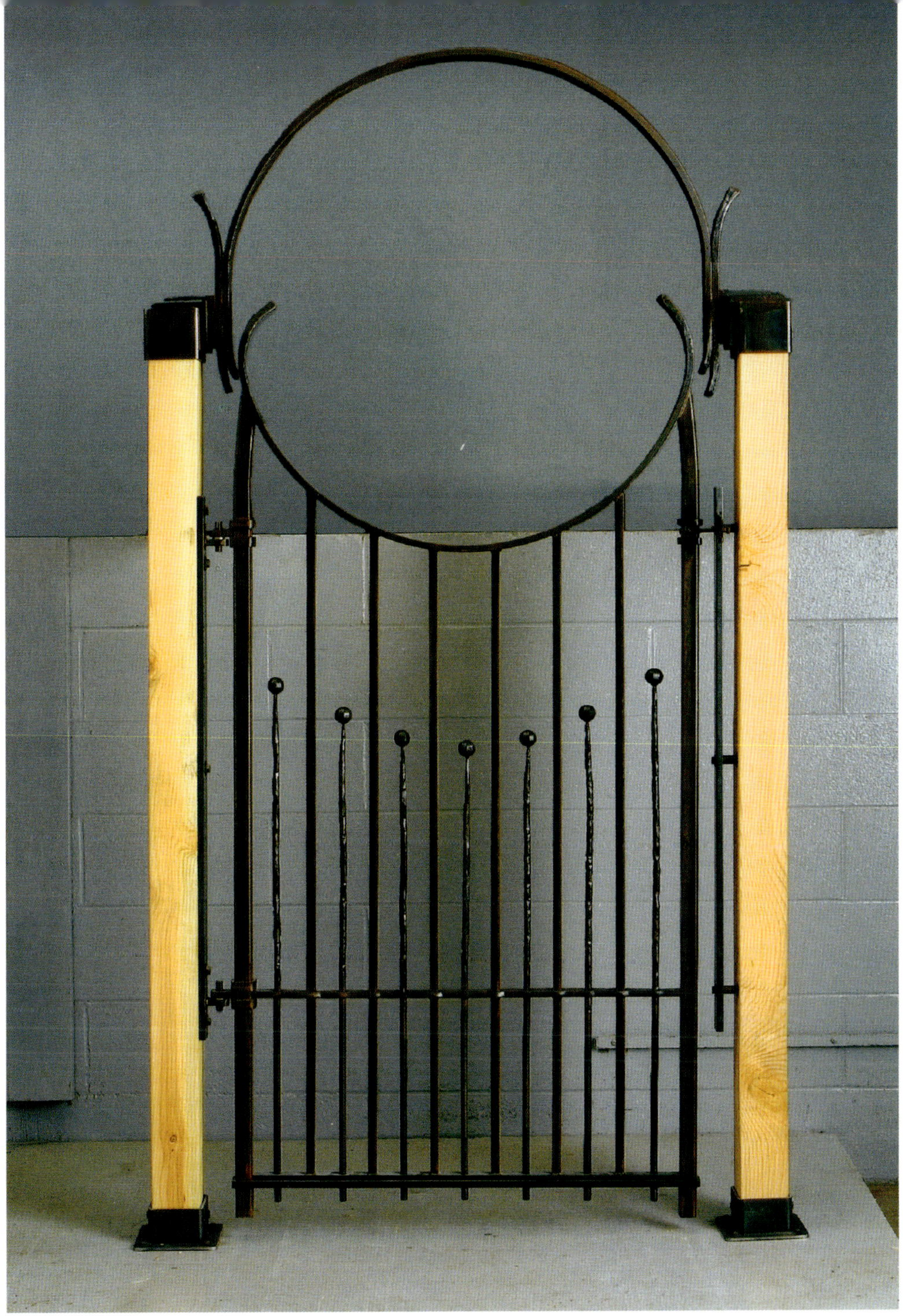

Stephen Marks. *Moon Gate*. Forged and fabricated steel. Garden gate for a private residence, Port Angeles, Washington. 86" high, 38" wide. *Photo, William P. Wright*

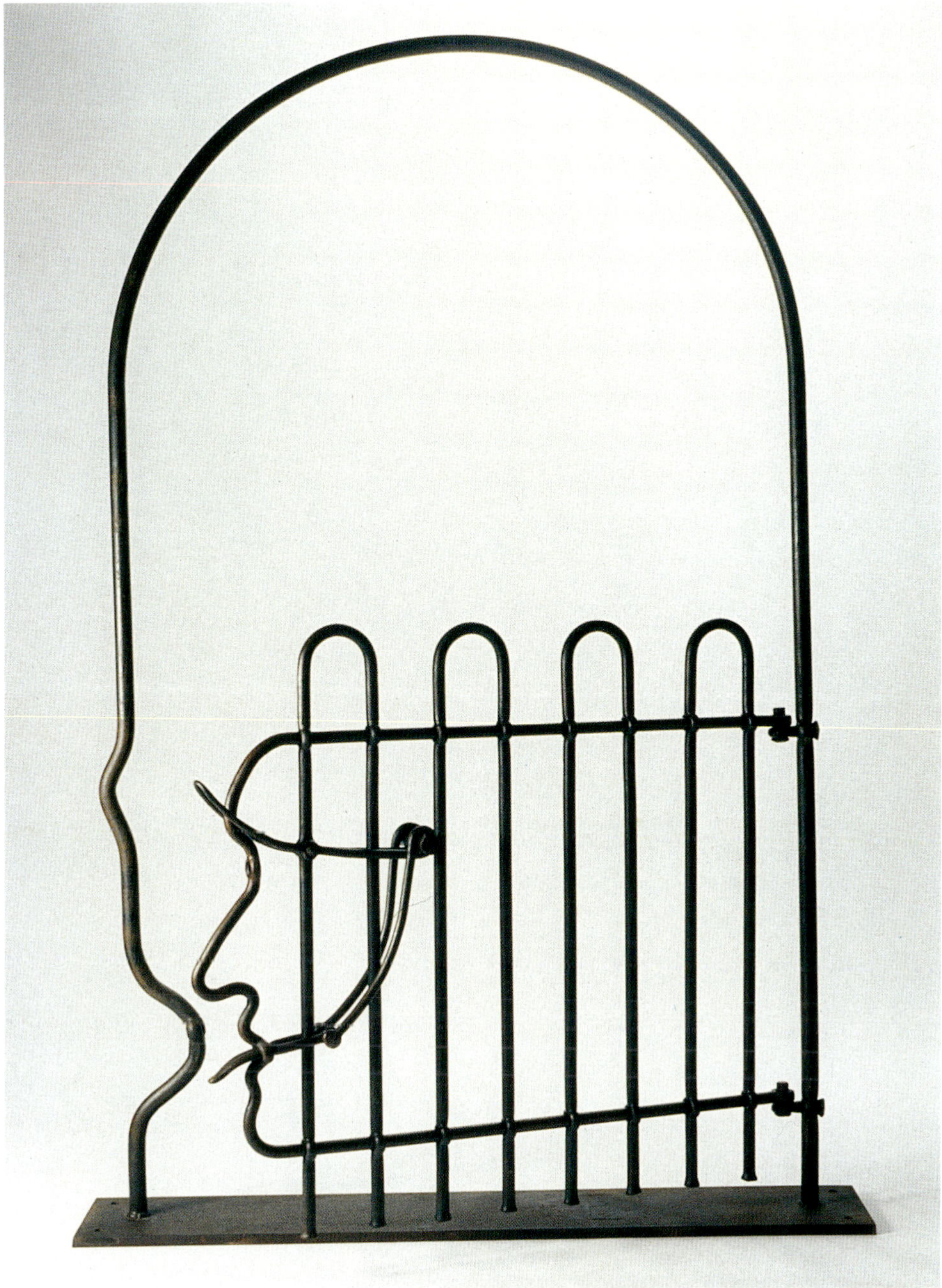

Helmut Hillenkamp, assisted by Christin Boyd. Locking Latch Gate. Grabbing the eyelash makes the eye blink and the tongue pull in from the hole in the arch, thus unlatching the gate. It is installed at the Esalen Institute in Big Sur, California. 90" high, 42" wide. *Photo, David Hoptman*

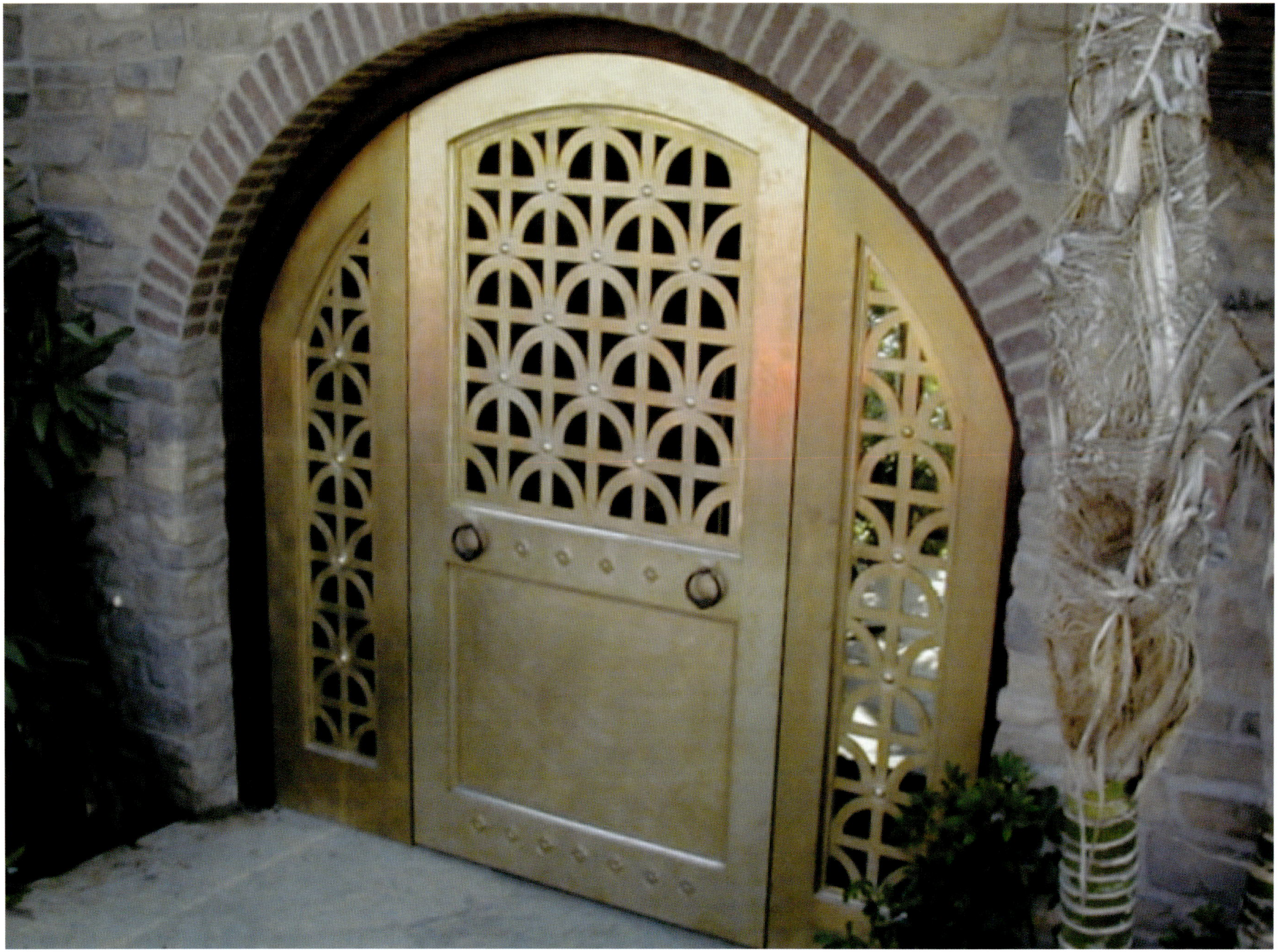

Greg Eng. Bronze doors. A sheet of mica sandwiched between two sheets of waterjet cut naval bronze for each of the inset panels. The frame is laminated bronze. Natural bronze finish. 93" high, 47" wide. *Photo, Brenda Eng*

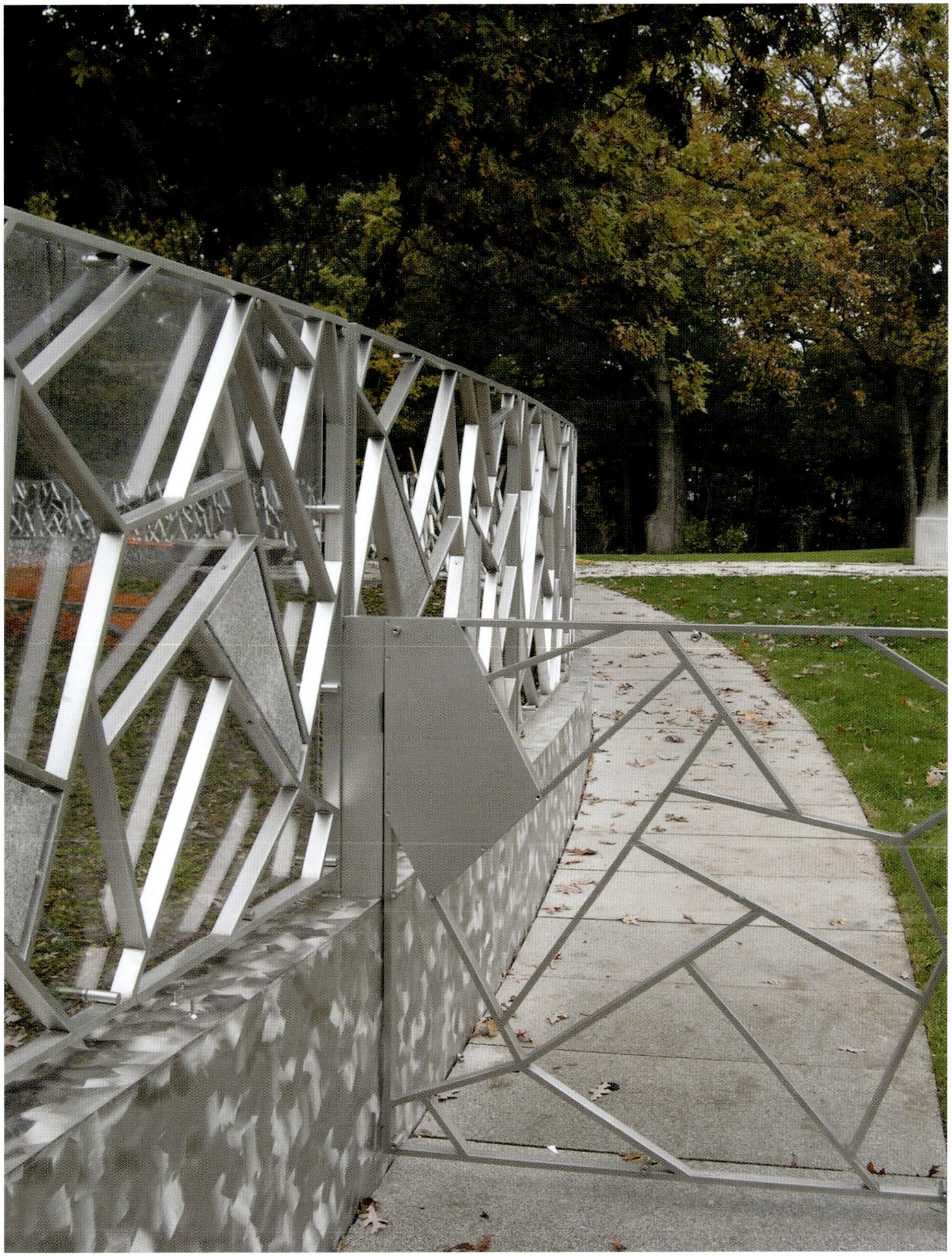

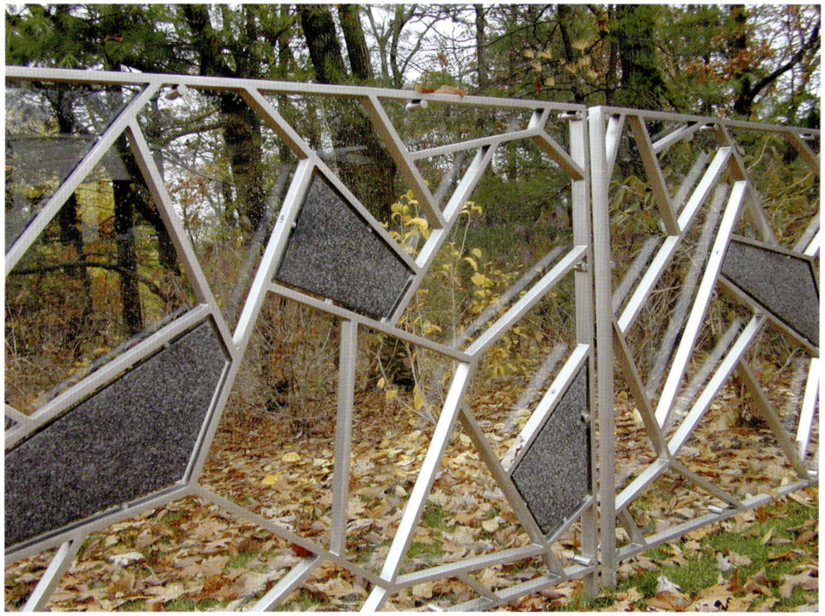

Detail

Cape Cod Fabrications Architectural Metalsmiths. Large pool fence and gate, with glass sections and other inserts. The entire substructure sits on a stainless steel bulkhead. All parts were laser cut and rolled to a consistent radius. Vandal finish. 1/2" x 5/8" true bar fabricated on a compound jig for accuracy. Polycarbonate panels were added to meet codes. *Photos, Cape Cod Fabrications*

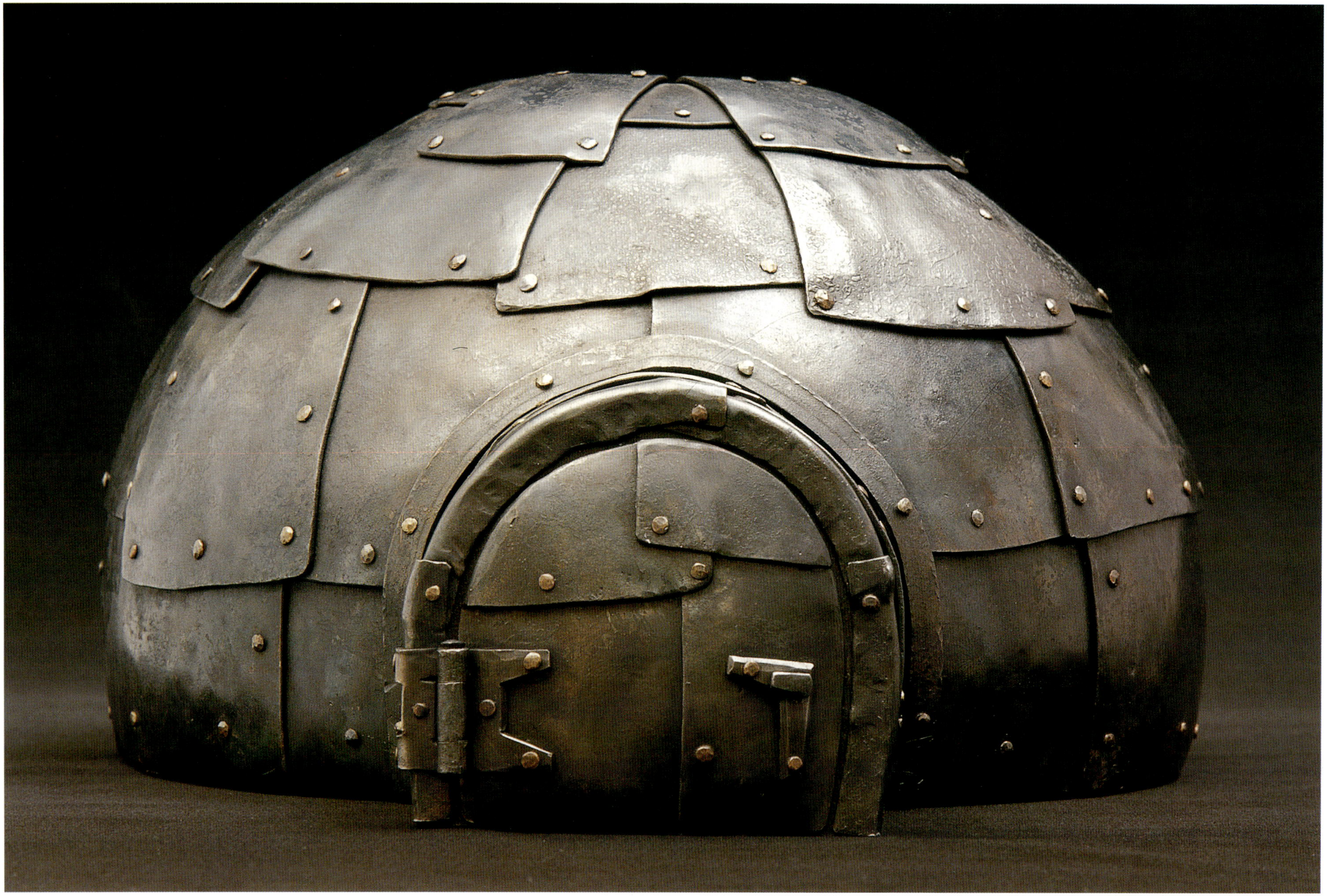

Patrick Maher. *Igloo.* Forged steel and steel plated with copper rivets. What began as a humorous piece evolved into a statement with deep metaphoric references related to current events.16" high, 18 wide, 10" deep. *Photo, artist*

Chapter 5. Sculpture

Looking at small pictures of sculptures is stimulating. It's an opportunity to peer briefly into the artistic results of many creative people. But one must look further than the flat image on the page; it's important to think about the processes, both physical and mental, that were required to result in the finished project.

The essence of a "good" sculpture can vary considerably and fall prey to clichés about sculpture, such as "Beauty is in the eye of the beholder." or "What does it mean?"

The pieces here are like the cream that rises to the top of a bottle of milk…in that the 40 or so sculptures selected were narrowed down from a compilation of 528 images submitted. It's a tough competition. The judging by no means resulted in consistent opinions as to what should be included.

Comments submitted by the artists helped shed light on their thinking and processes. Ultimately the pieces selected represent interesting subject matter from realism to abstract. They represent innovative ideas, exciting use of materials and techniques, and projects that will stimulate thinking. Possibly, they will kindle some latent idea to come to fruition and push the envelope further for combining metals in unique forms.

Marc Mullin's *Lilies* fooled me by their size. I did a double take when I saw him standing between them. They were unequivocally sculpture, not just another pretty flower.

Adam Clark, originally trained as a jewelry maker, sometimes has trouble defining why he works small items to a large scale. He says, "I don't fully connect to the way in which jewelry is presented, judged, and valued. It is an art form dominated heavily by its preciousness and commercial appeal. The artier work seems to center on proving its worth compared to accepted art forms. Perhaps all I am doing with this series of work is a cheap trick. Do I simply make jewelry larger and call it sculpture? Maybe I am defending the jewelers' position that they don't receive the respect they deserve due to the scale of their work."

David Gignac says, "My work is often driven by what I am thinking about while I am working. *Nomad*, for example, began as an idea on paper. Other pieces are often reactions to materials or ideas that emerge as I am working in the studio."

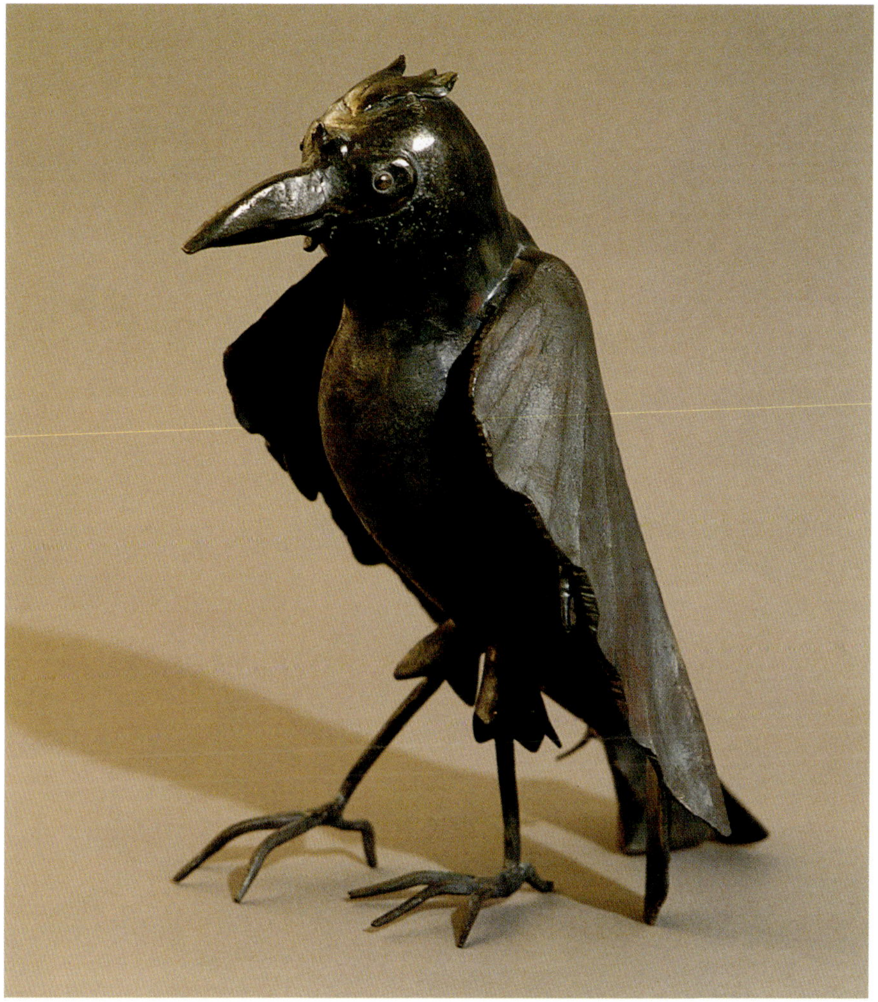

Patrick Maher. *Crow.* Forged and fabricated steel with a copper comb. One of 8 storybook images used atop pillars of a children's playground in a Seattle, Washington park. 14" high, 14" wide, 14" deep. *Photo, artist*

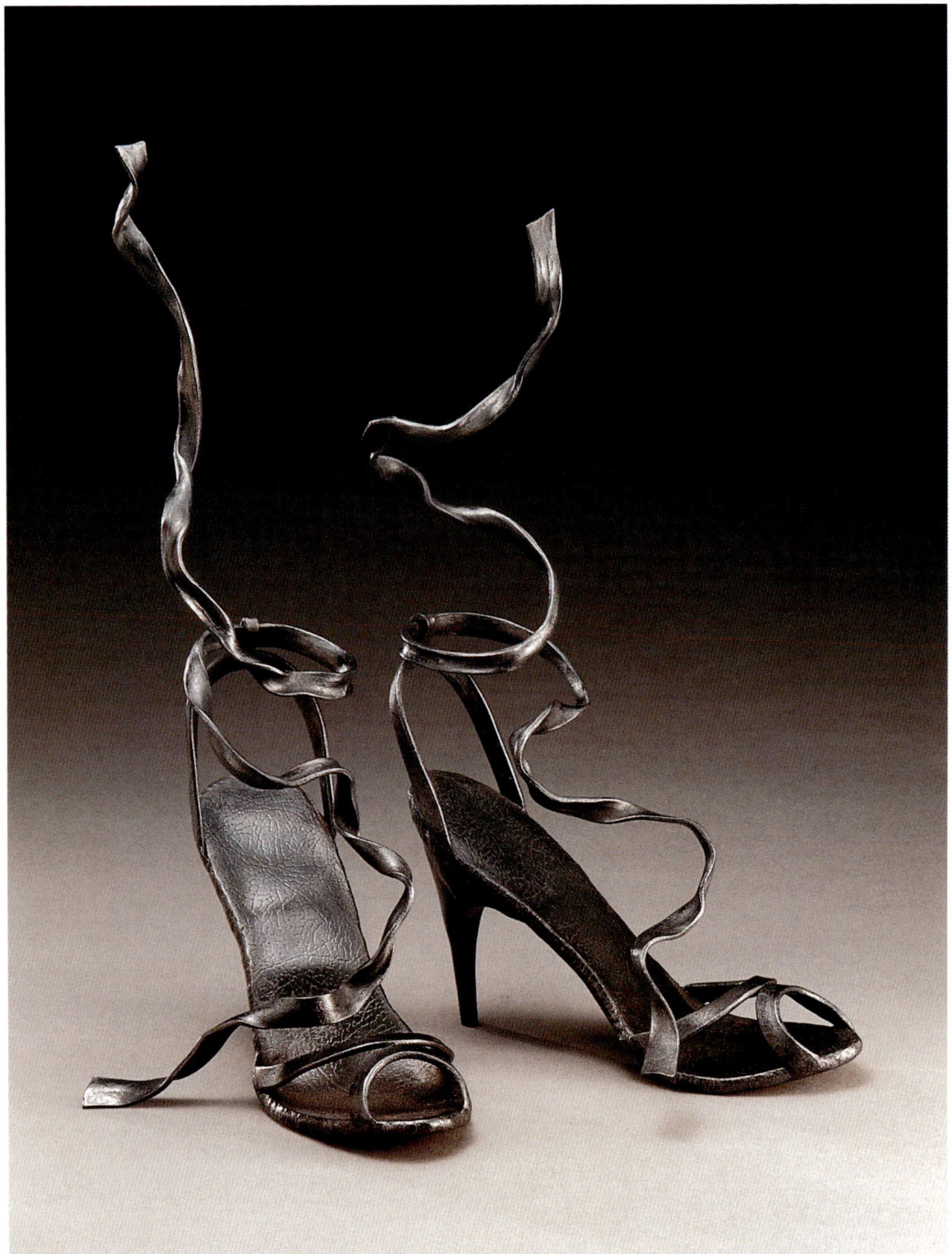

Elizabeth Brim. *Boogie*. Forged and fabricated steel dancing shoes. Brim's pieces always address something romantic and feminine. Size 7-1/2 shoe; 14" high. *Photo, Tom Mills*

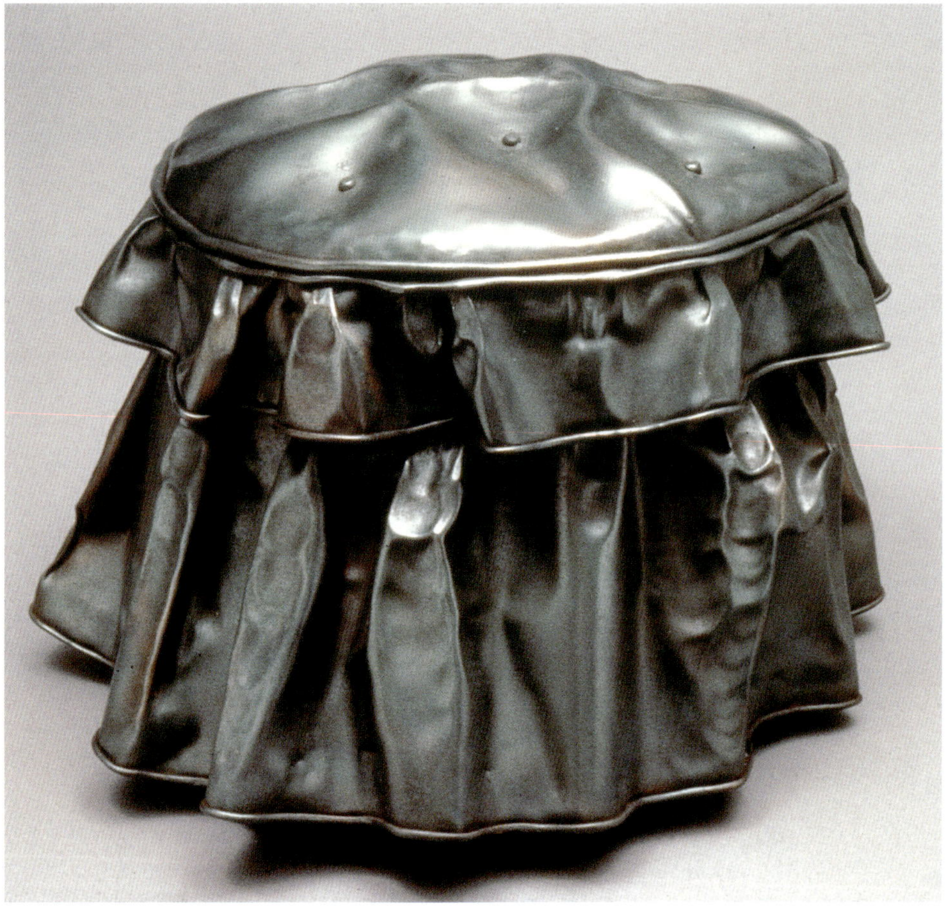

Elizabeth Brim. *Tuffet.* Inflated, forged, and fabricated steel. The footstool top was made of two pieces of metal welded at the edges and leaving small space for air to be pumped in so the surface would inflate. Additional forging and fabricating produced the shaped top and the side ruffles. 24" high, 24" diam. *Photo, Tom Mills*

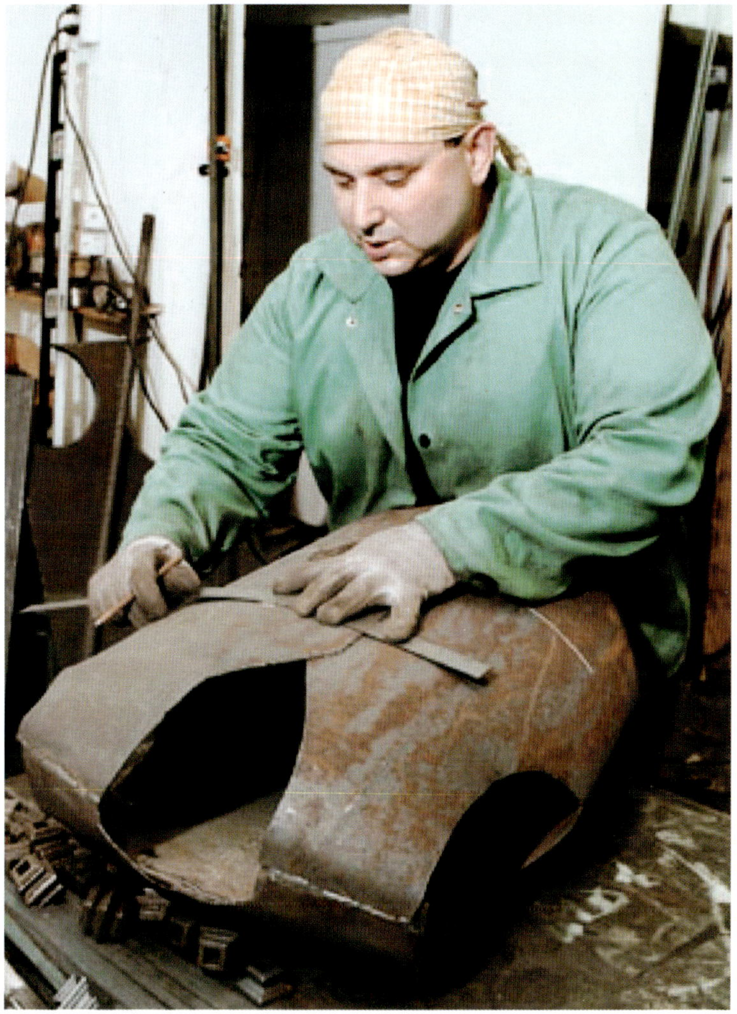

Raymond Miller works on a vest that will be mounted on a stand. It is his size. *Photo, artist*

Raymond Miller prides himself on making sculpture that challenges conventional wisdom, causing people to question that which they consider most ordinary and true, such as a tie made of fabric or a kite that is lightweight. Why would someone fashion a kite out of chains, or a vest of steel, or an iron necktie? For Raymond Miller, the answer is simple: in order to make you ask "why?"

"People think things are the way they are and can't be changed, and none of that is true. It's actually all made up. It lives in our language only, and language is a creation," says Miller, "[My work is] like tweaking someone's nose about it. It's like trying to knock the foundation out from underneath people's beliefs and have them question it for themselves."

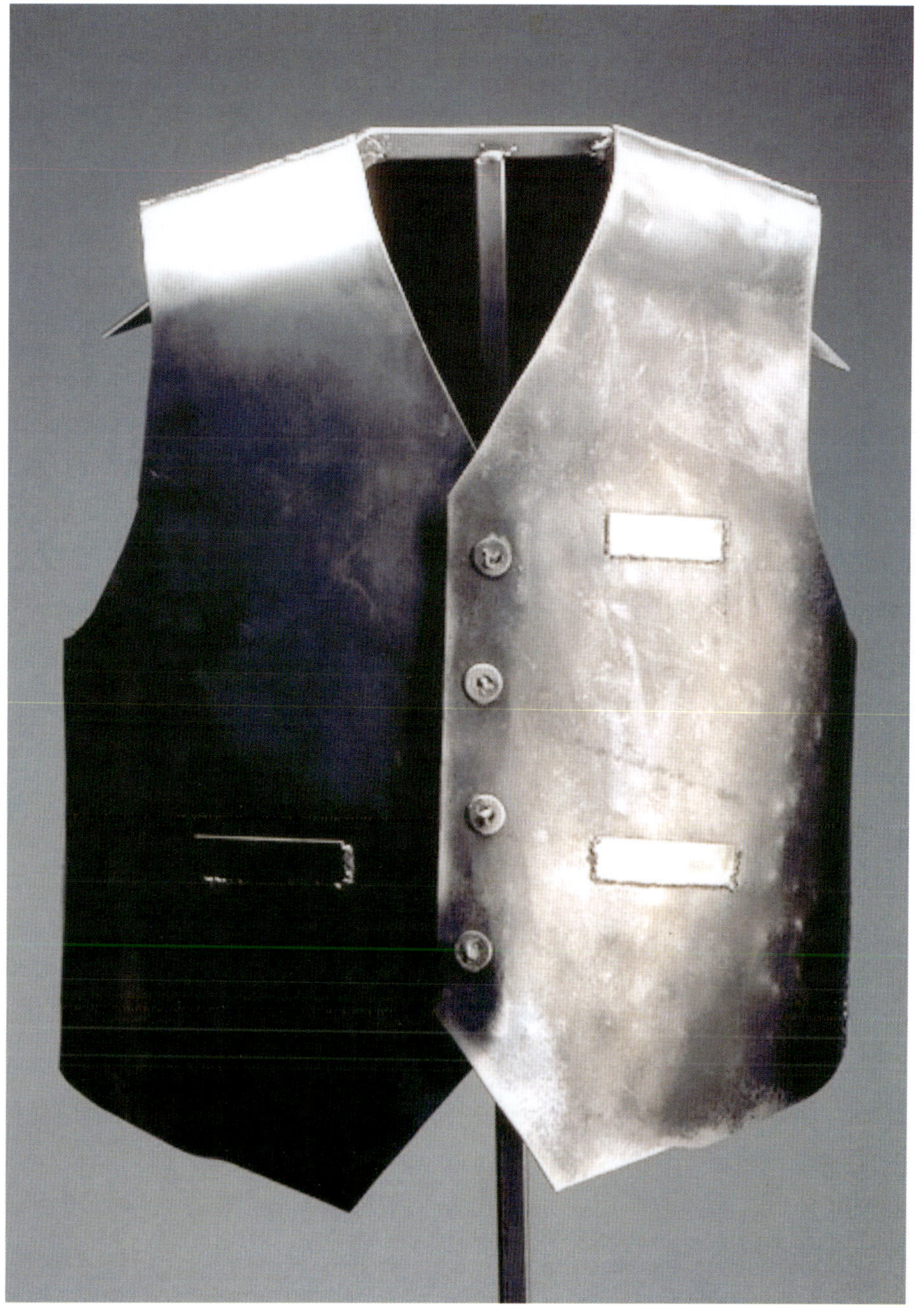

Raymond Miller. *Invest in Strength*. 60" high, 18" wide, 12" deep. *Photo, artist*

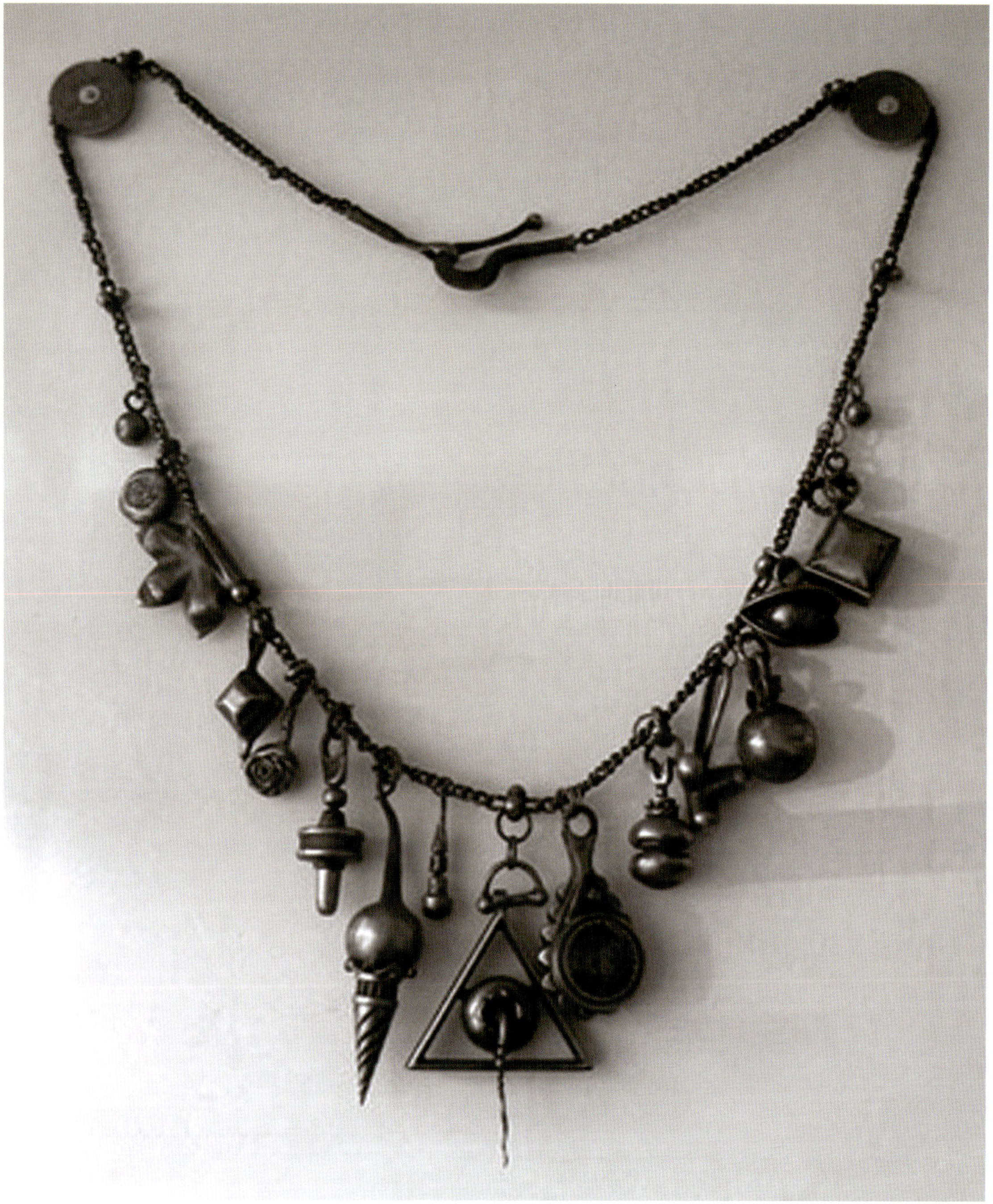

Adam Clark's iron "beads" are inventive elements in his 6-foot high sculptural necklace. *Photo, artist*

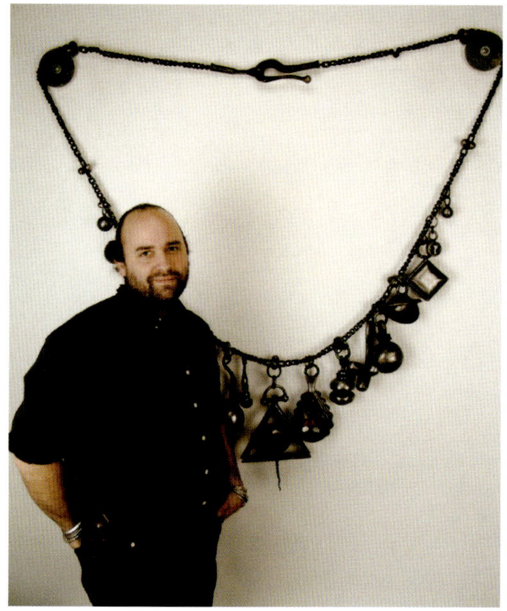

Adam Clark stands before his necklace to show a size relationship. *Photo, courtesy artist*

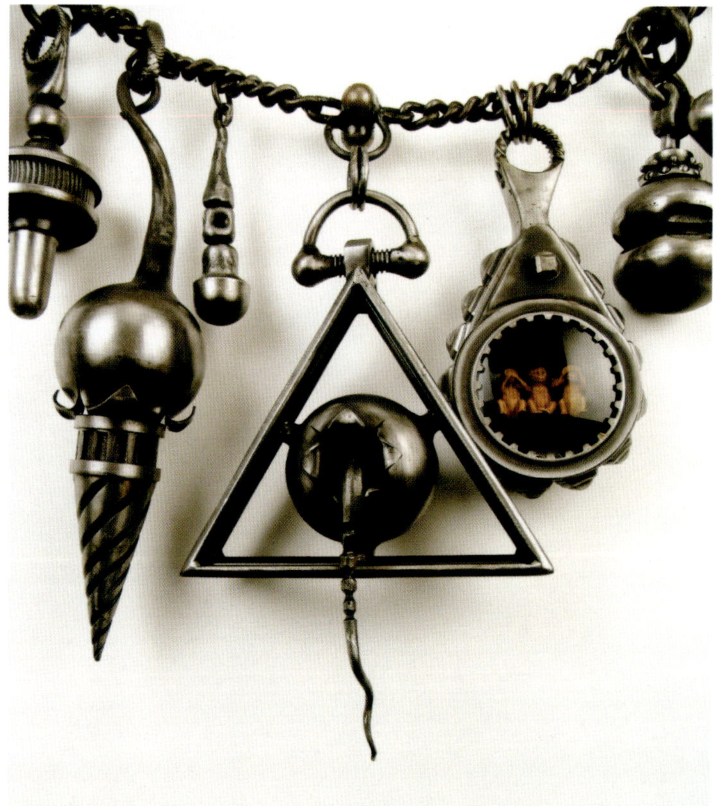

Adam Clark. Necklace's iron baubles (detail). *Photo, artist*

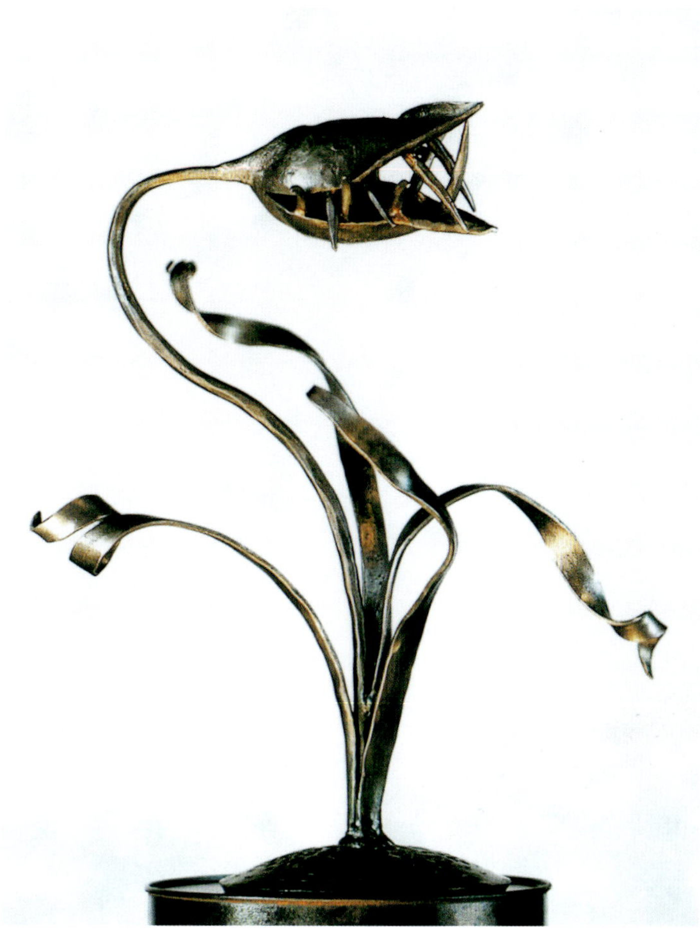

William A. Wojcik and Connie Badowski. *Bipartisan Flytrap*. Tabletop floral arrangement made for a show requiring some thing aromatic and funky. The carnivorous plant explores organic forms and the consuming nature of politics and power. 15" high, 12" diam. *Photo, Rafael Crisóstomo*

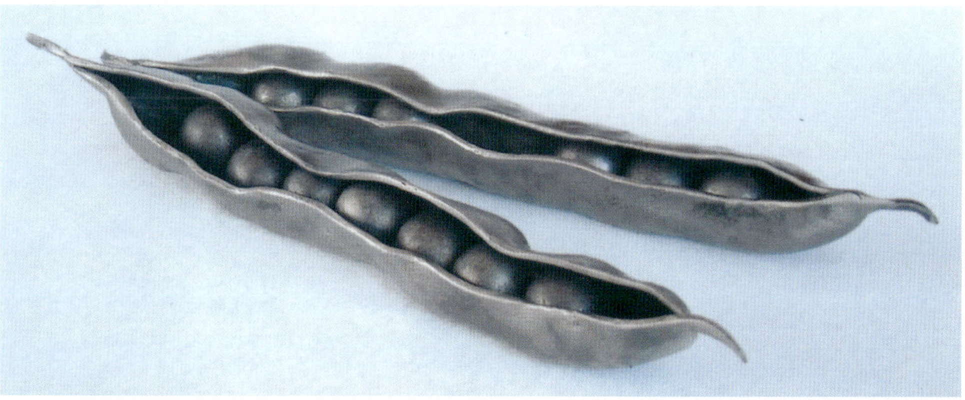

Karen Rudd. *Pea Pod*. Mild steel. 2" high, 10" long, 2" deep. *Photo, artist*

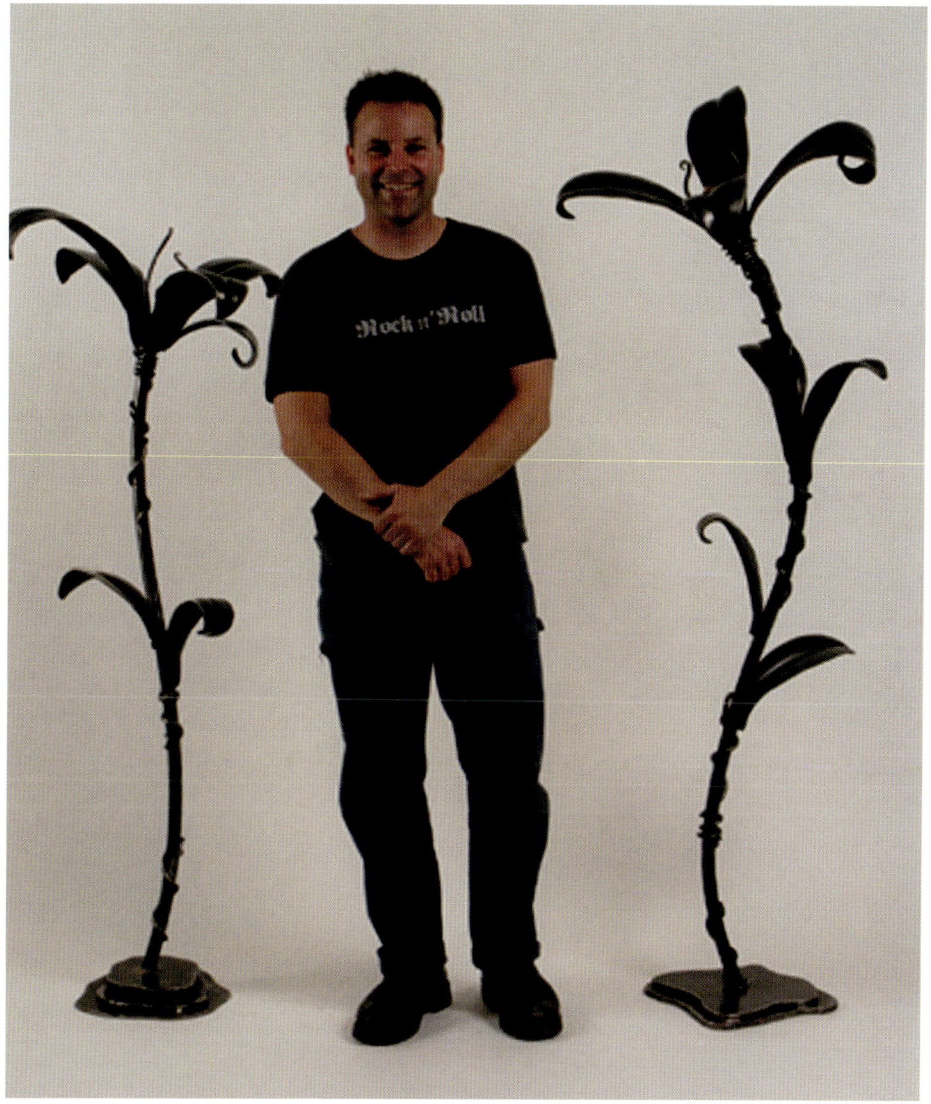

Marc Mullin. *Graceful Lily and Sultry Lilly*. 68" high, 28" wide. *Photo, Richard Nicol*

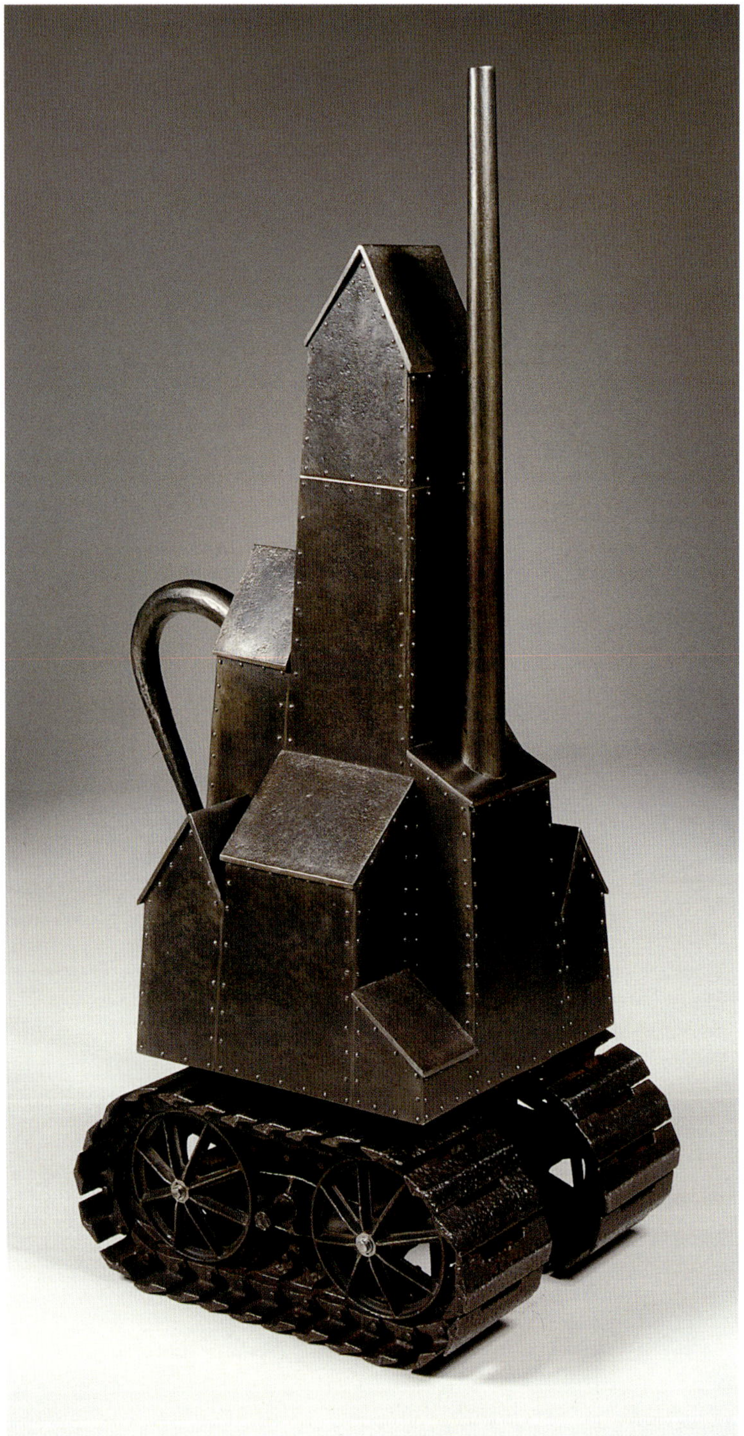

David Gignac. *Nomad*. Forged and fabricated recycled steel with a waxed finish. 54" high, 24" wide, 10" deep. *Photo, artist*

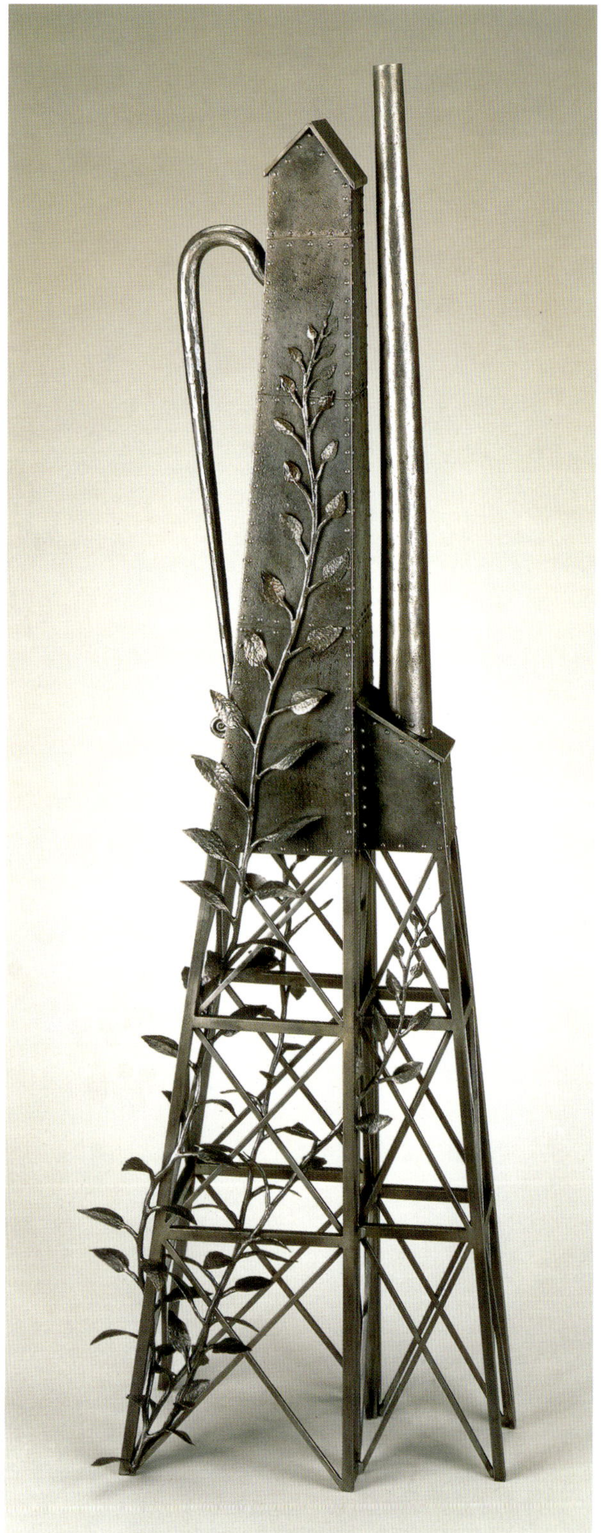

David Gignac. *Host*. Forged and fabricated using recycled steel and wax finish. 62" high, 17" wide, 12" deep. *Photo, Rob Vinedge*

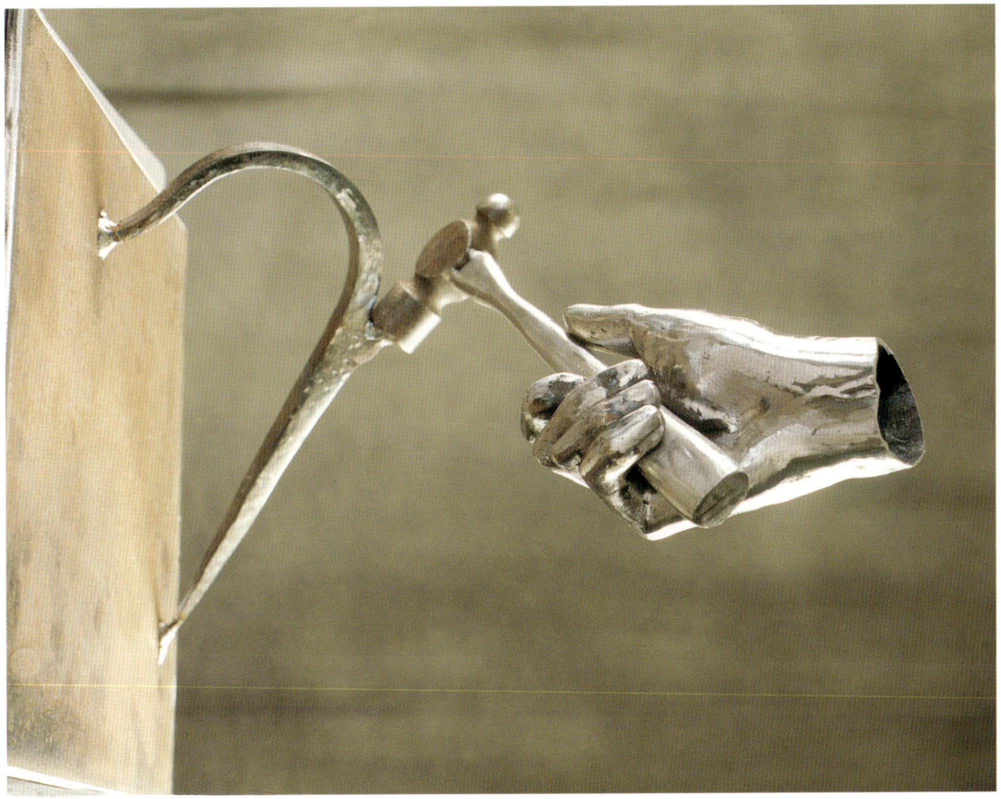

Nicole Beck. *Hand formed, 2003*. Forged and fabricated steel. Maquette for a large-scale sculpture. 14" high, 14" wide, 12" deep. Private collection. *Photo, Robert Bobber*

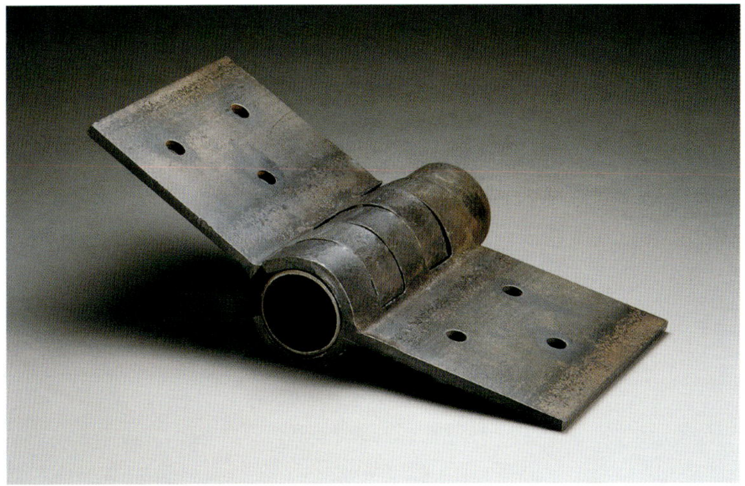

Jeff Wallin. *Turning Point*. Mild steel. 7" high, 29" wide, 17" deep. *Photo, artist*

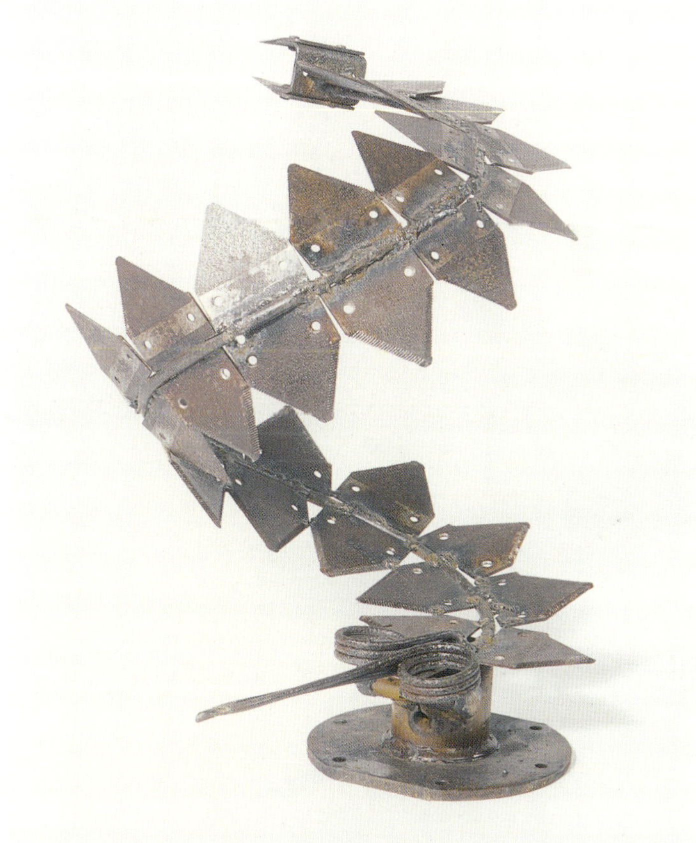

Ben Gatski. *Serpent*. Knives from an old hay mower and reclaimed rod. All work done by the artist using recycled farm machinery parts. 20" high, 10" wide, 10" deep. *Photo, Kate Gatski, The Wild Studio*

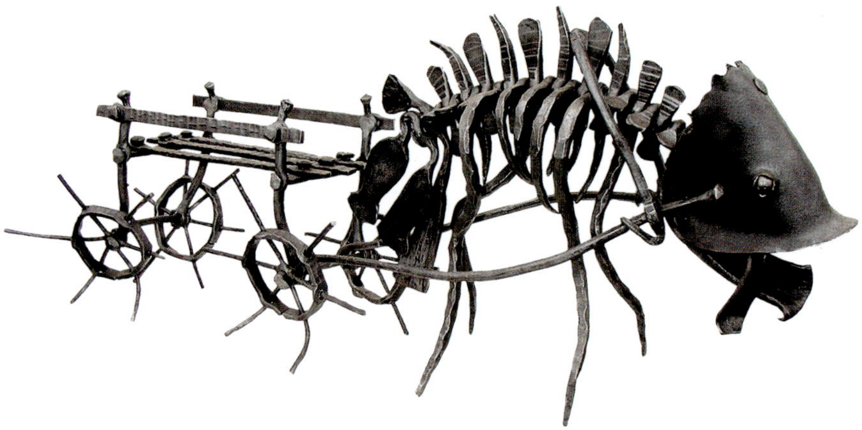

Vadim Filatov and Alexander Chumakov, Gvozd Studios. *Hard worker.* 12" high, 19" long. *Photo, artists*

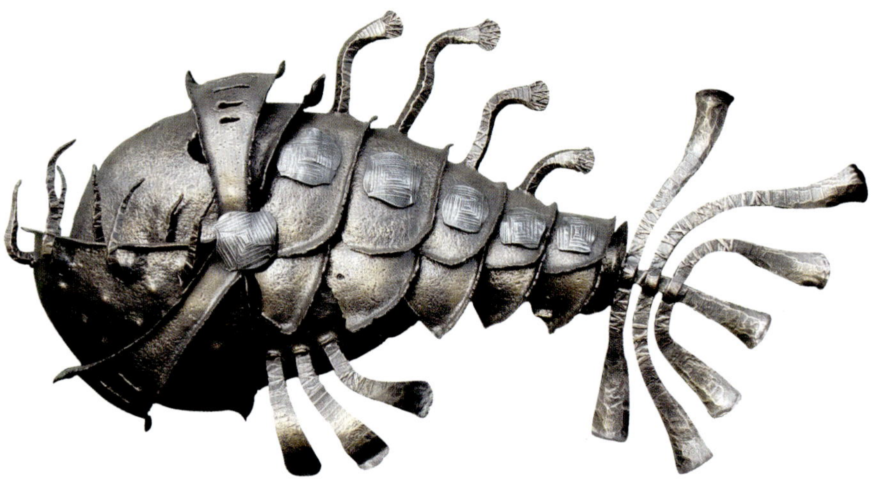

Vadim Filatov and Alexander Chumakov, Gvozd Studio. *Gladiator Fish.* Forged iron. 21" high, 40" long. *Photo, artists*

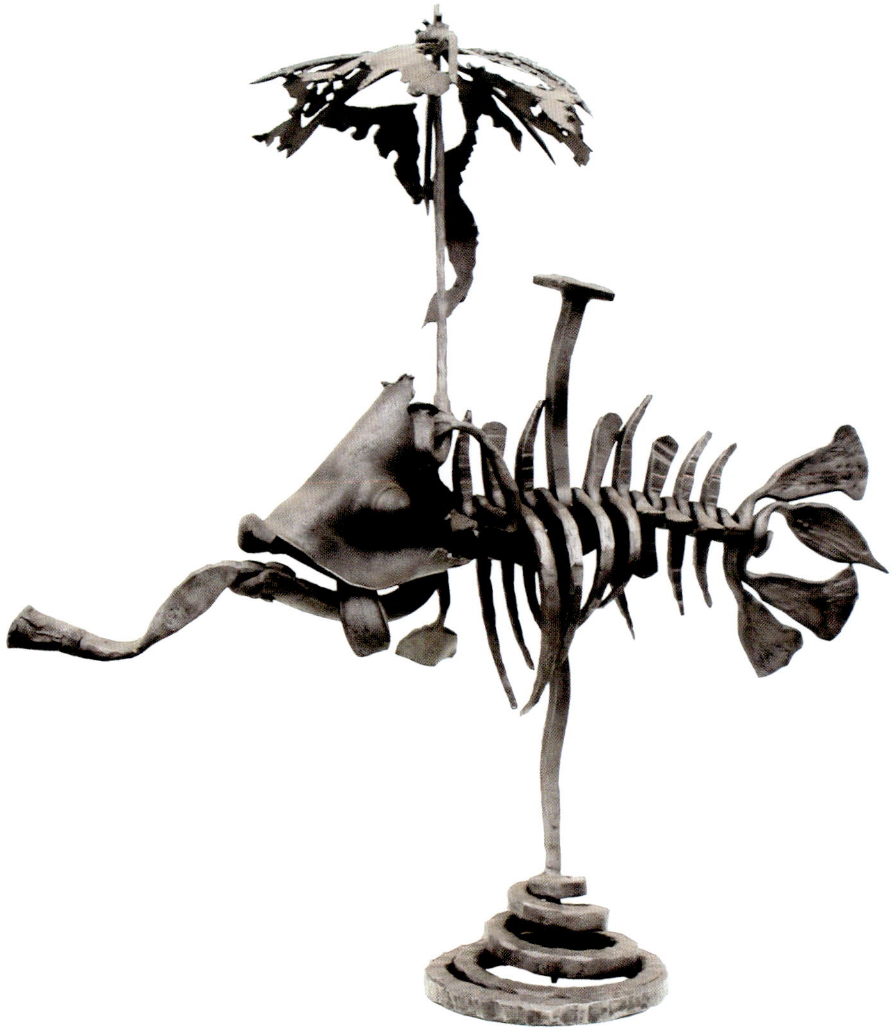

Vadim Filatov and Alexander Chumakov, Gvozd Studios. *Tramp*. Forged iron. 16" high, 14" wide *Photo, artists*

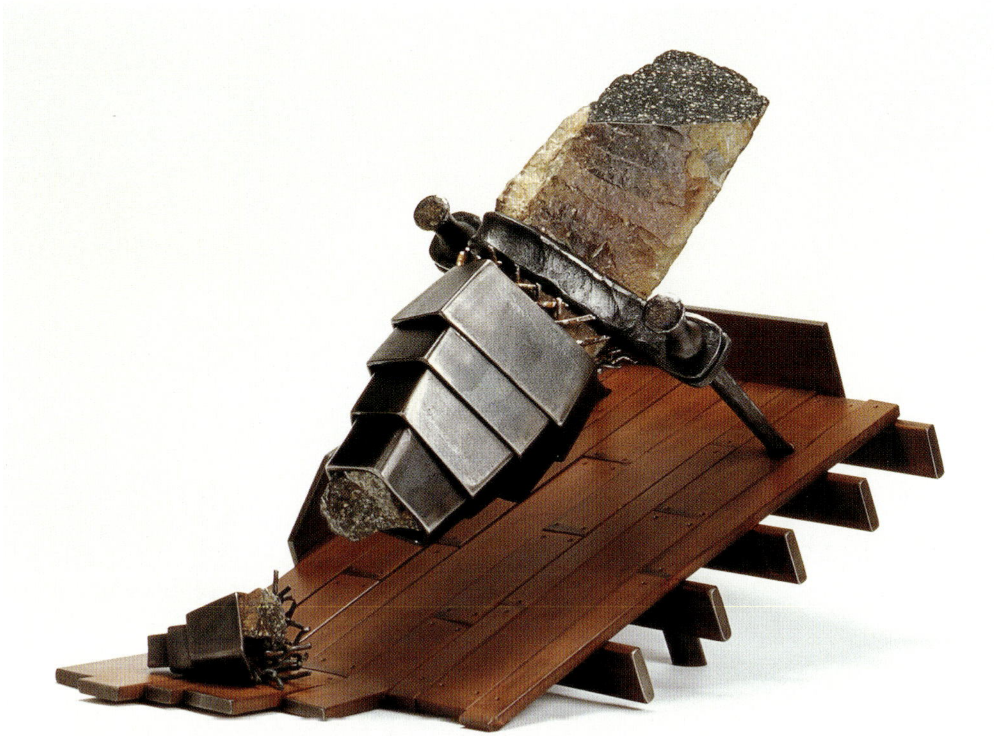

Stephen Marks. *Cracked and Pinned*. An abstract/realistic sculpture of a broken stone figure with a steel skin, pinned to a patinated floor. 16" high, 13" wide, 21" deep. *Photo, William Wright*

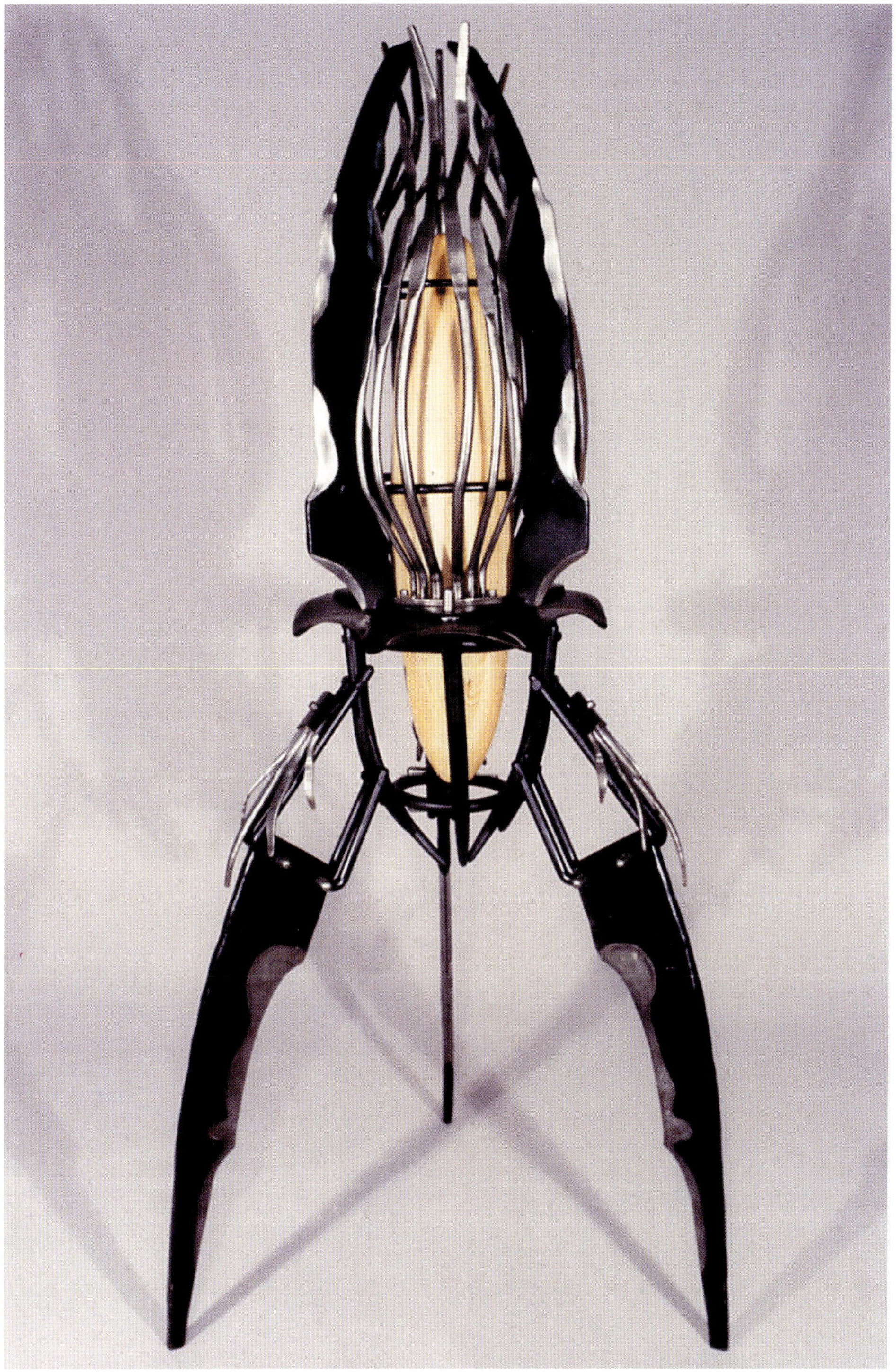

Donald Henson. *Proteus 2001*. Forged steel and red oak. 69" high, 31" wide, 28" deep. *Photo, artist*

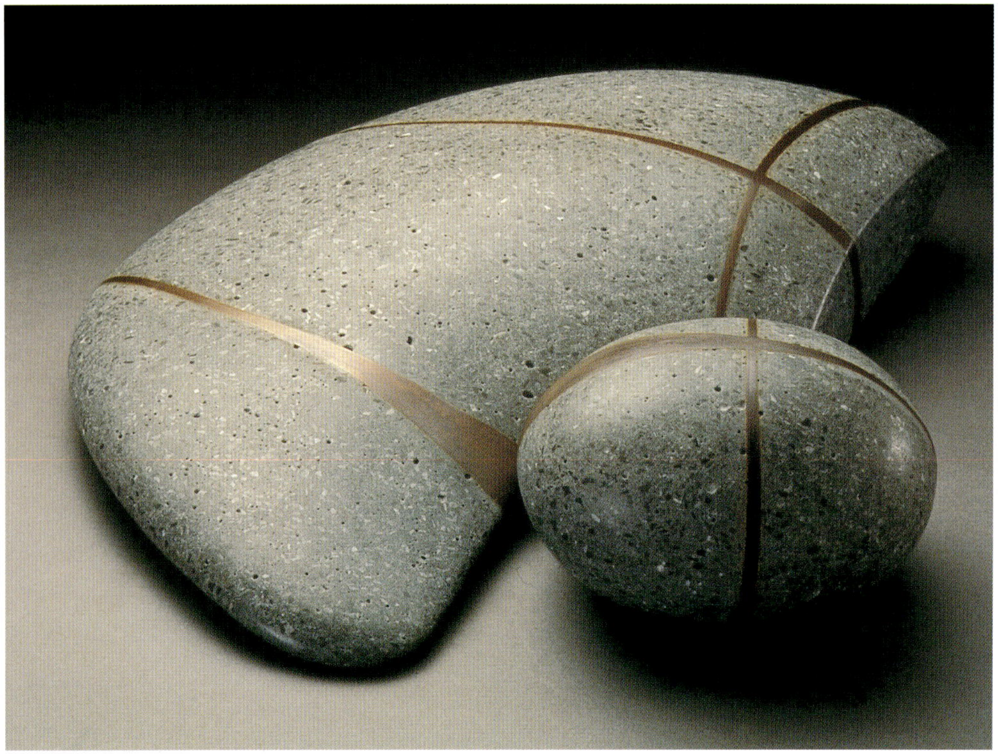

Rick Smith. *Untitled.* Steel and concrete. 8" high, 24" wide, 14" deep. *Photo, Tom Mills*

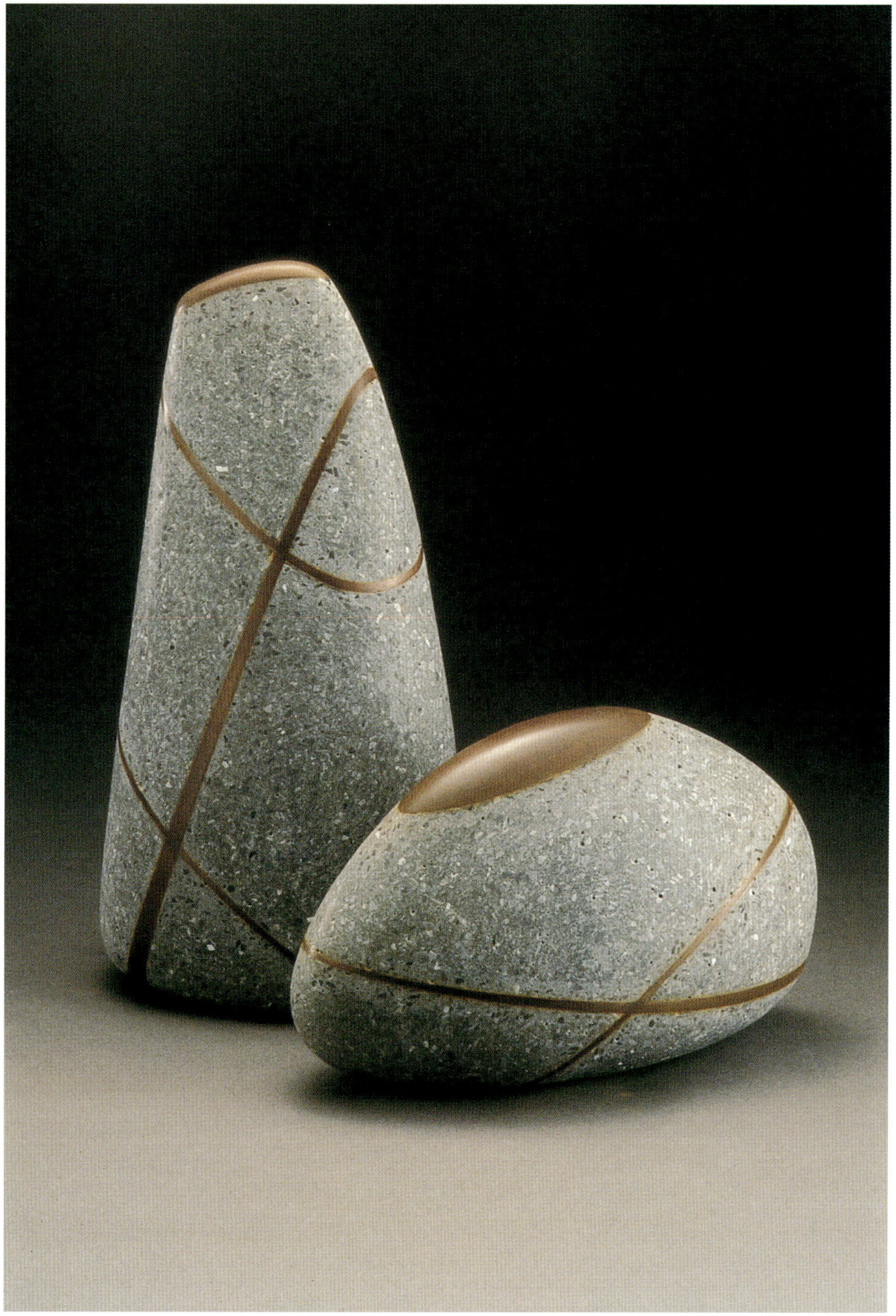

Rick Smith. *Grouping.* Steel and concrete. 16" high, 10" wide, 12" deep. *Photo, Tom Mills*

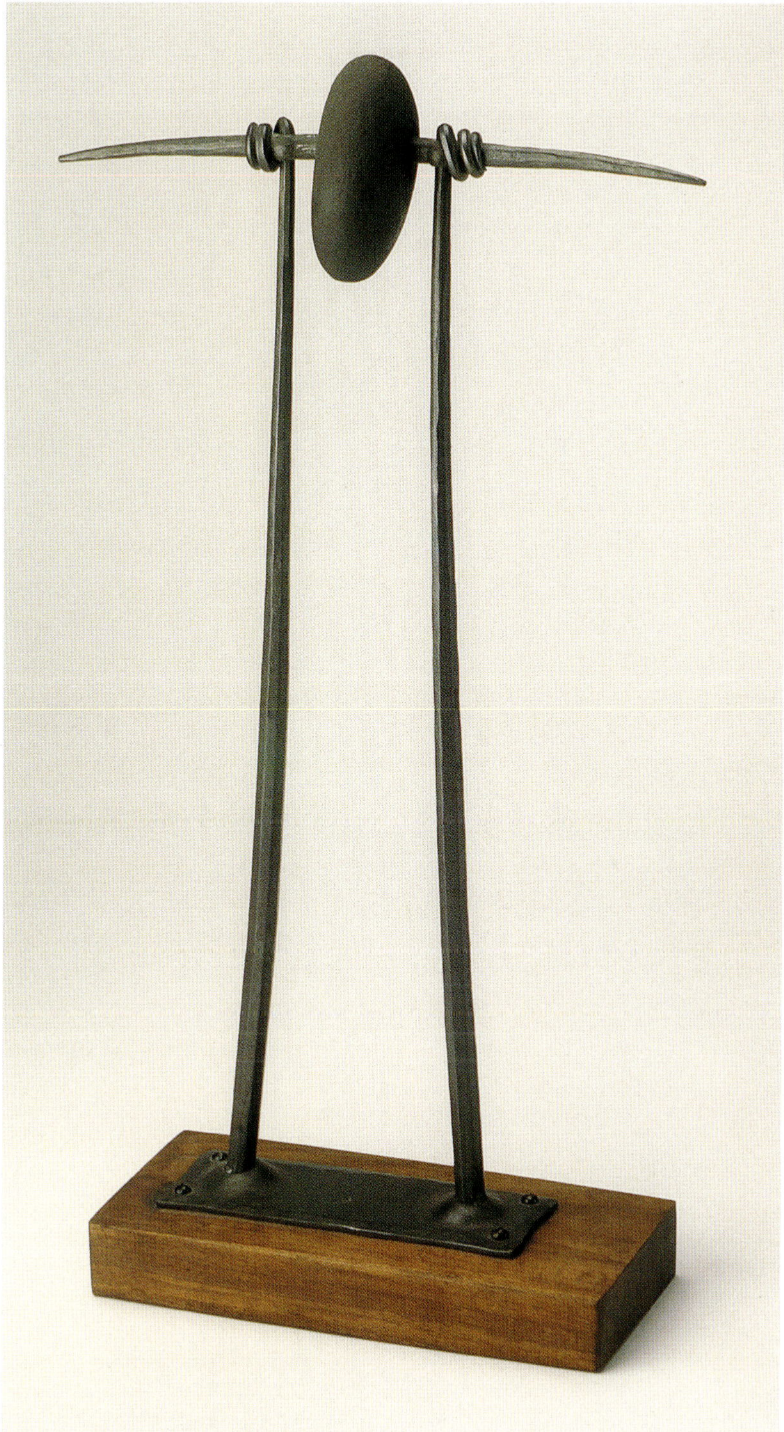

Doug Hendrickson. *Rock San.* 30" high, 16" wide, 6" deep. *Photo, artist*

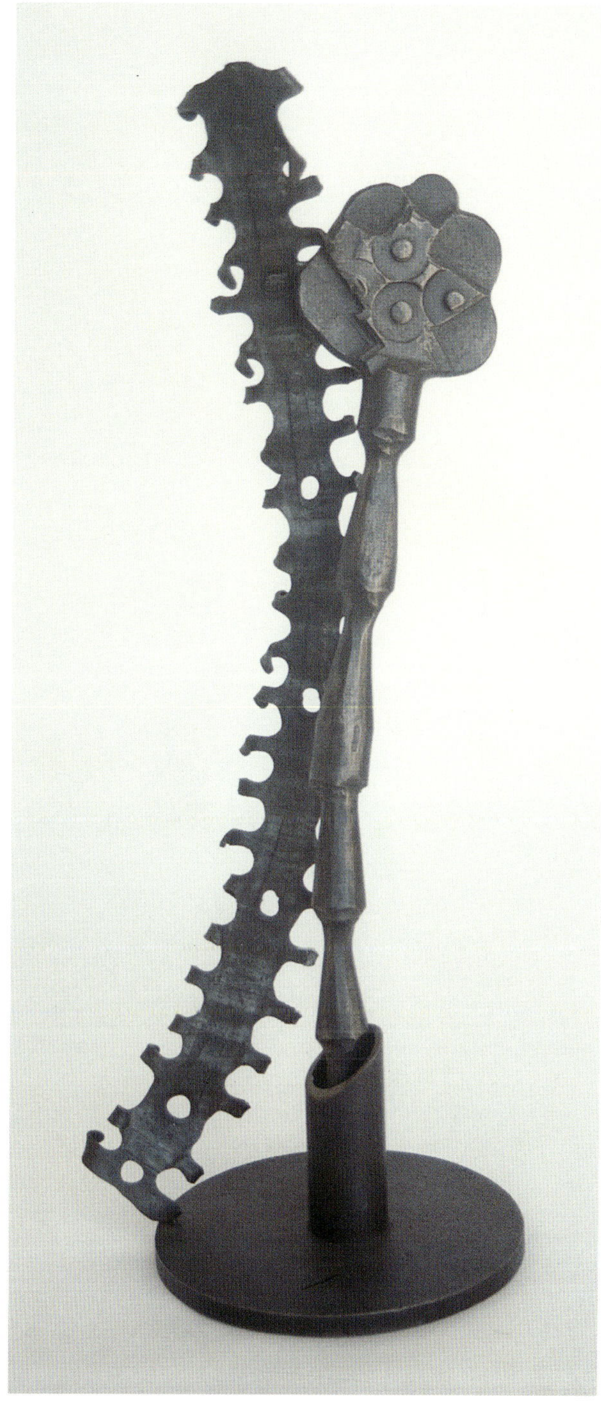

Theron Michael Ross. *Caterpillar.* Forged steel using a piece of cast-off farm equipment. 18" high. *Photo, artist*

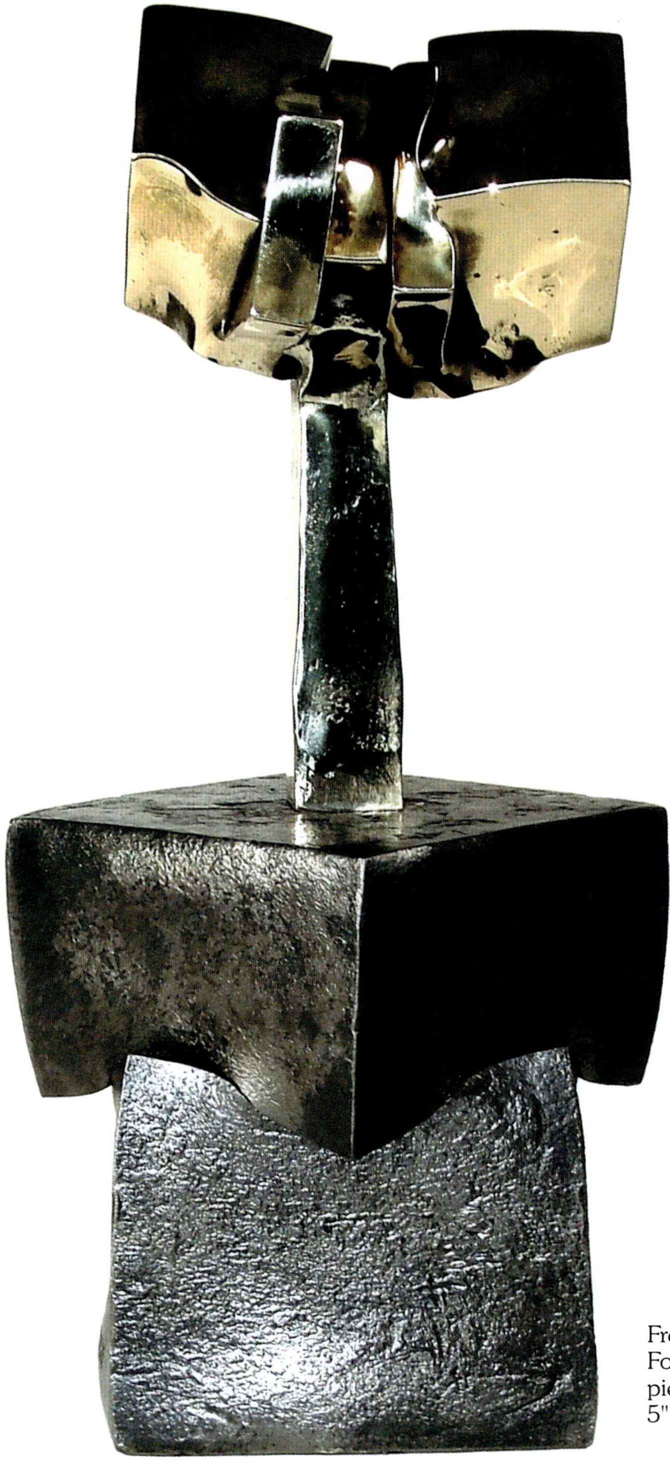

Frederic A. Crist. *Horizontal Pillar #8*. Forged steel and brass. Though small, this piece has a monumental feeling. 10" high, 5" wide, 5" deep. *Photo, artist*

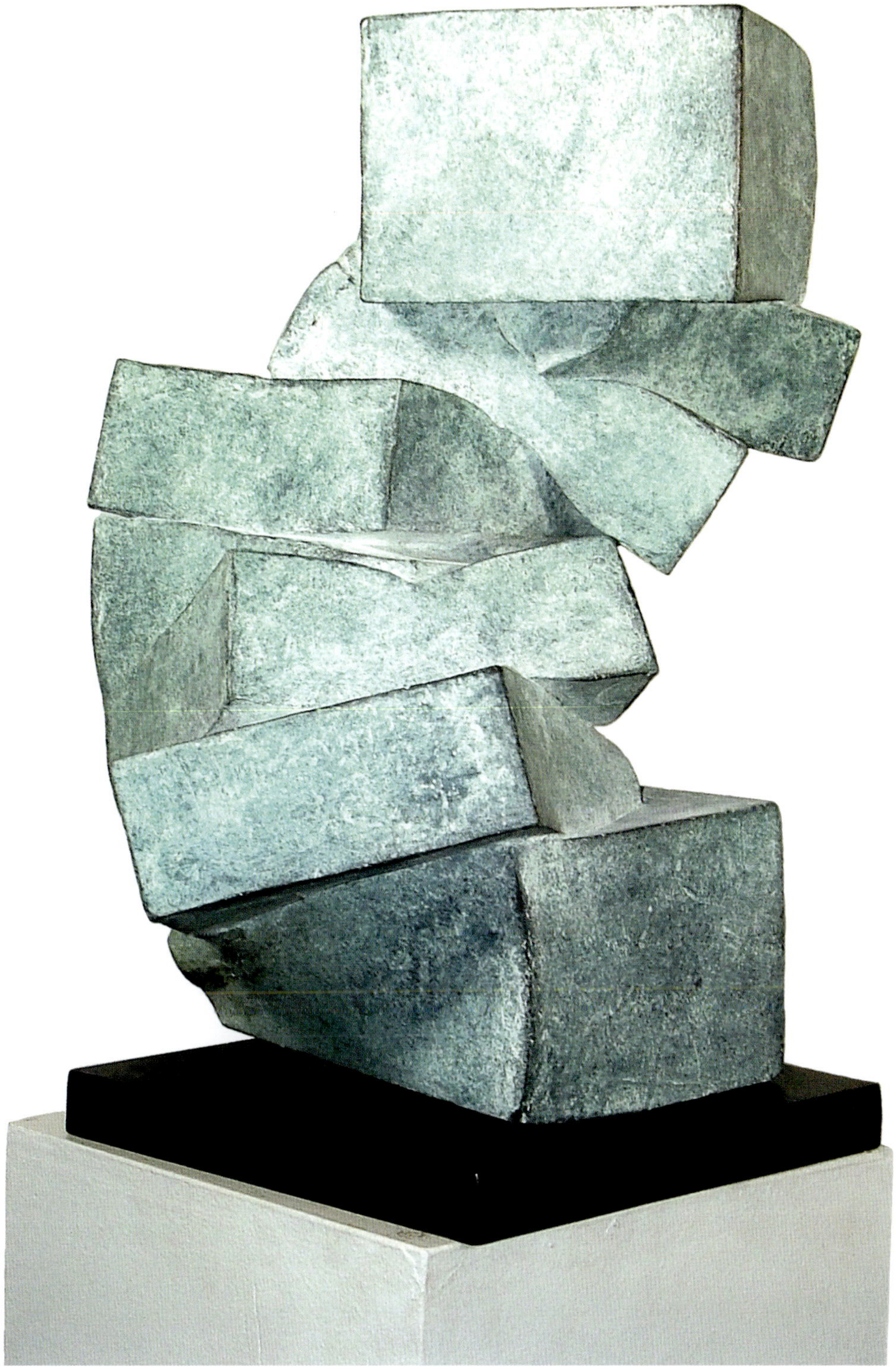

Frederic A. Crist. *Stacked Pillar #16*. Cast bronze. The mold was made from a forged sculpture titled Twisted Pillar. 23" high, 12" wide, 14" deep. *Photo, artist*

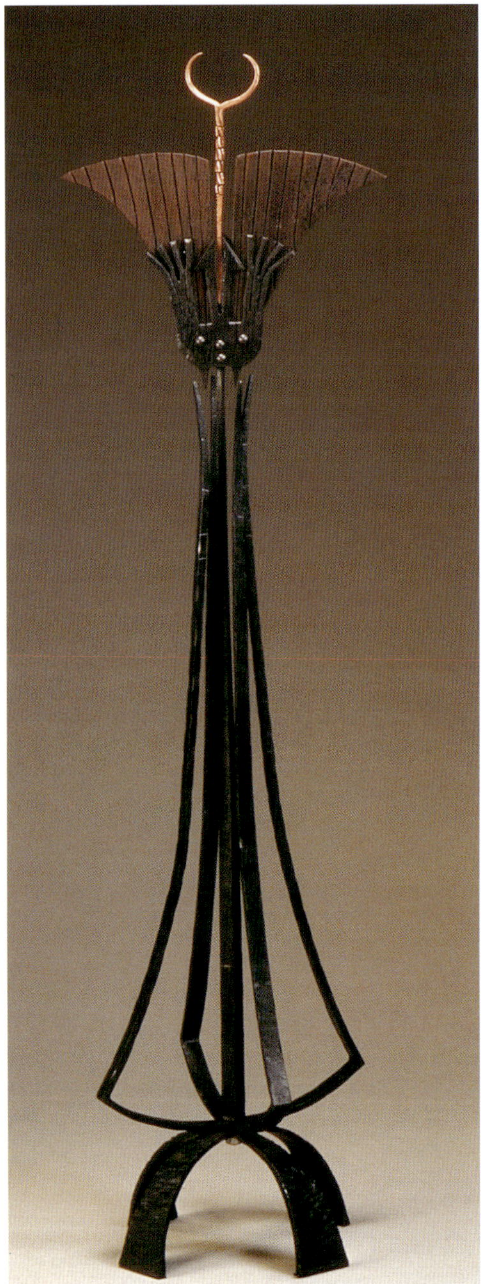

Lauren Osmolski. *Papyrus Study*. Steel and copper. 57" high, 12" wide, 12" deep. *Photo, Doug Yaple*

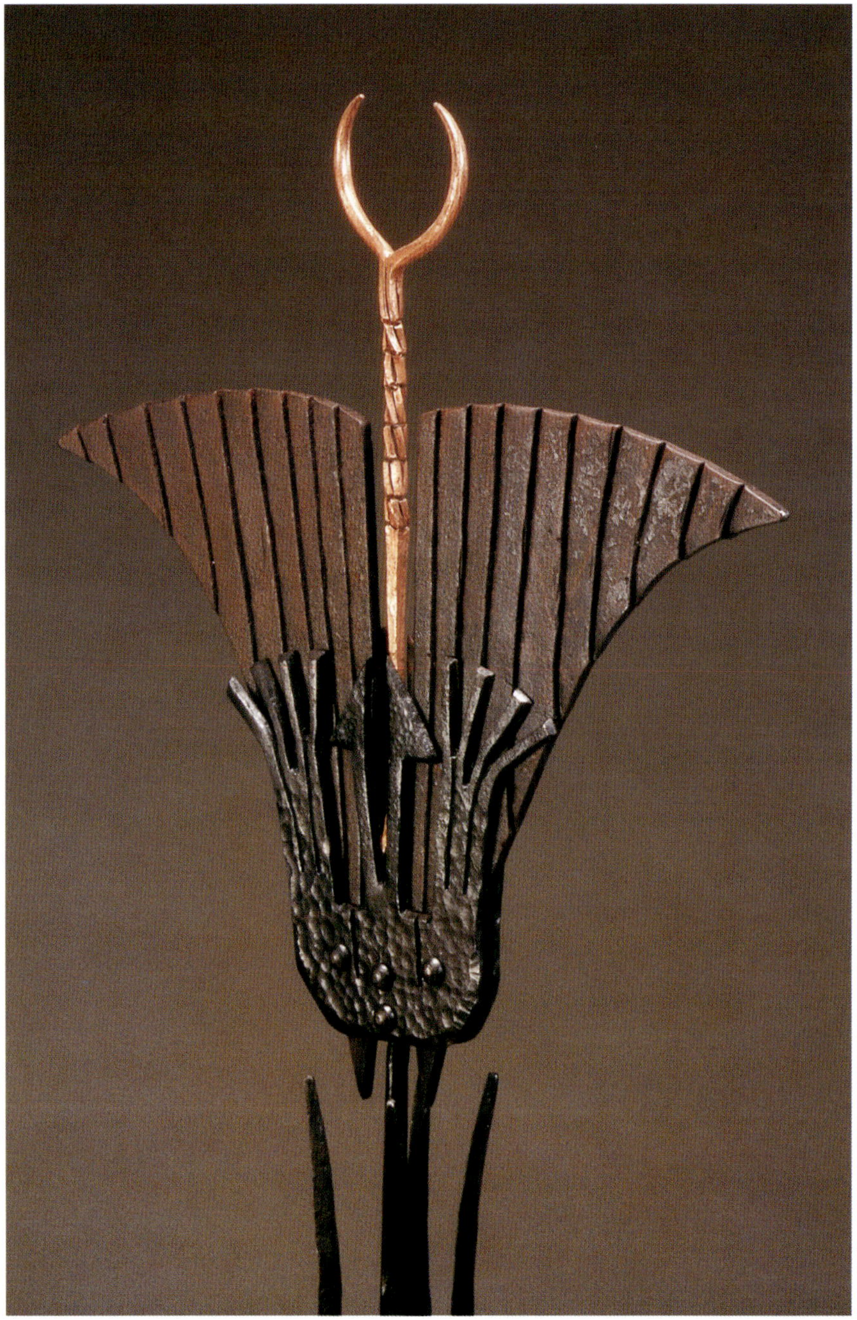

Lauren Osmolski. *Papyrus Study (top detail). Photo, Doug Yaple*

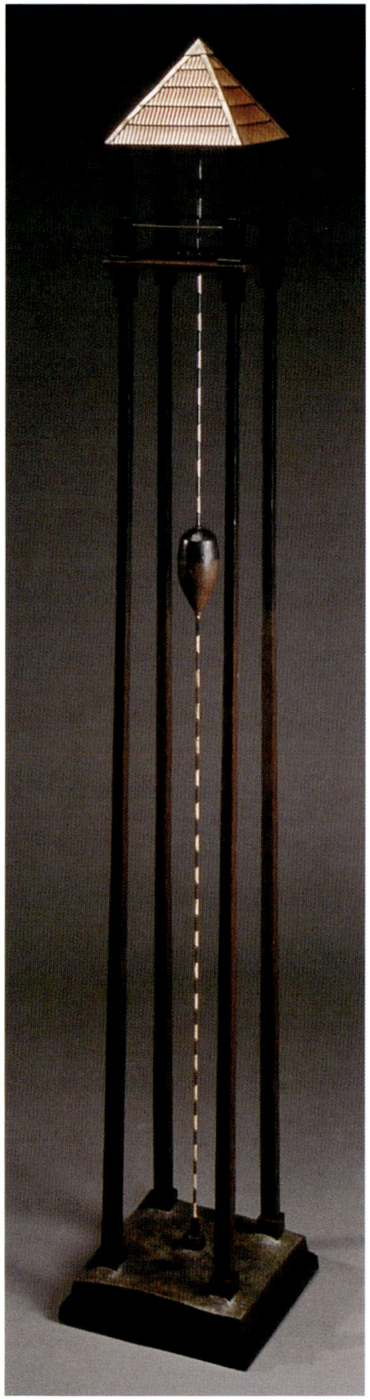

Eric Cuper. *Body Tower.* Forged and fabricated steel. 74" high, 12" wide, 12" deep. *Photo, Jeffrey Bruce*

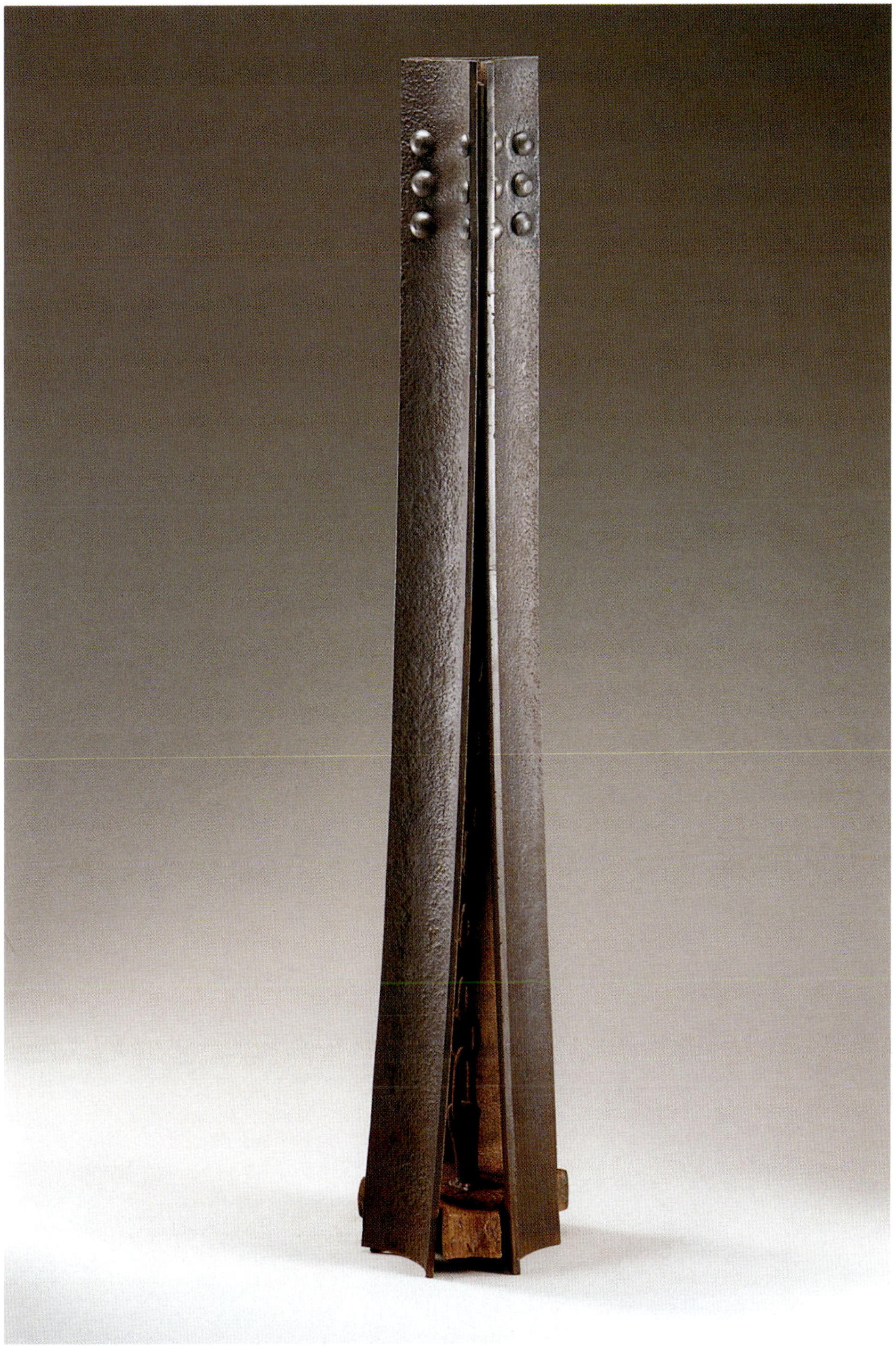

Jeff Wallin. *Uprising*. Mild steel. 60" high, 11" wide. *Photo, Tom Mills*

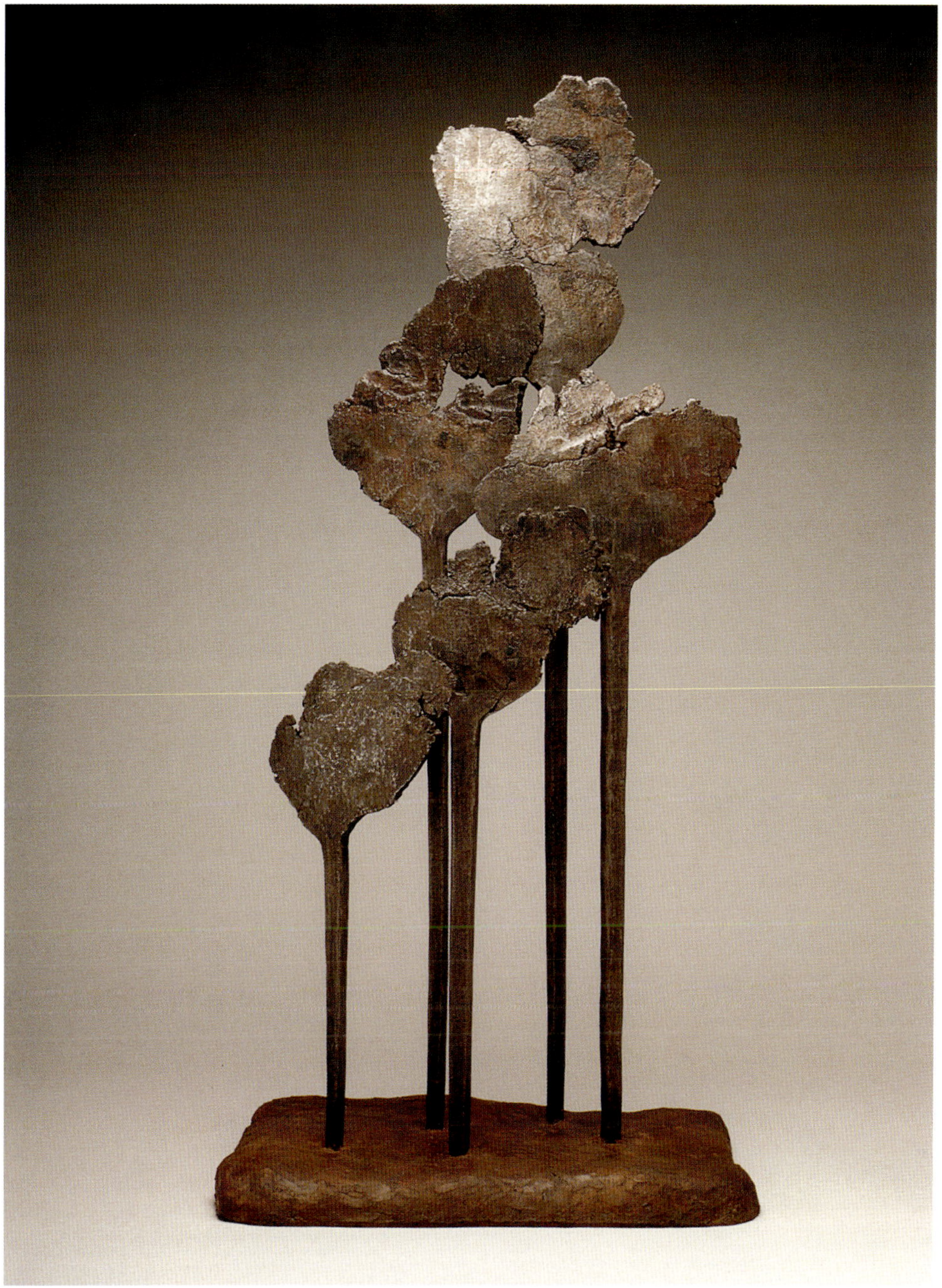

Lee Sauder. *Nyamakala 12*: *Alberto's Woodlot*. Bloomery iron on a concrete base. 26" high, 12" wide, 9" deep. *Photo, Ellen Martin*

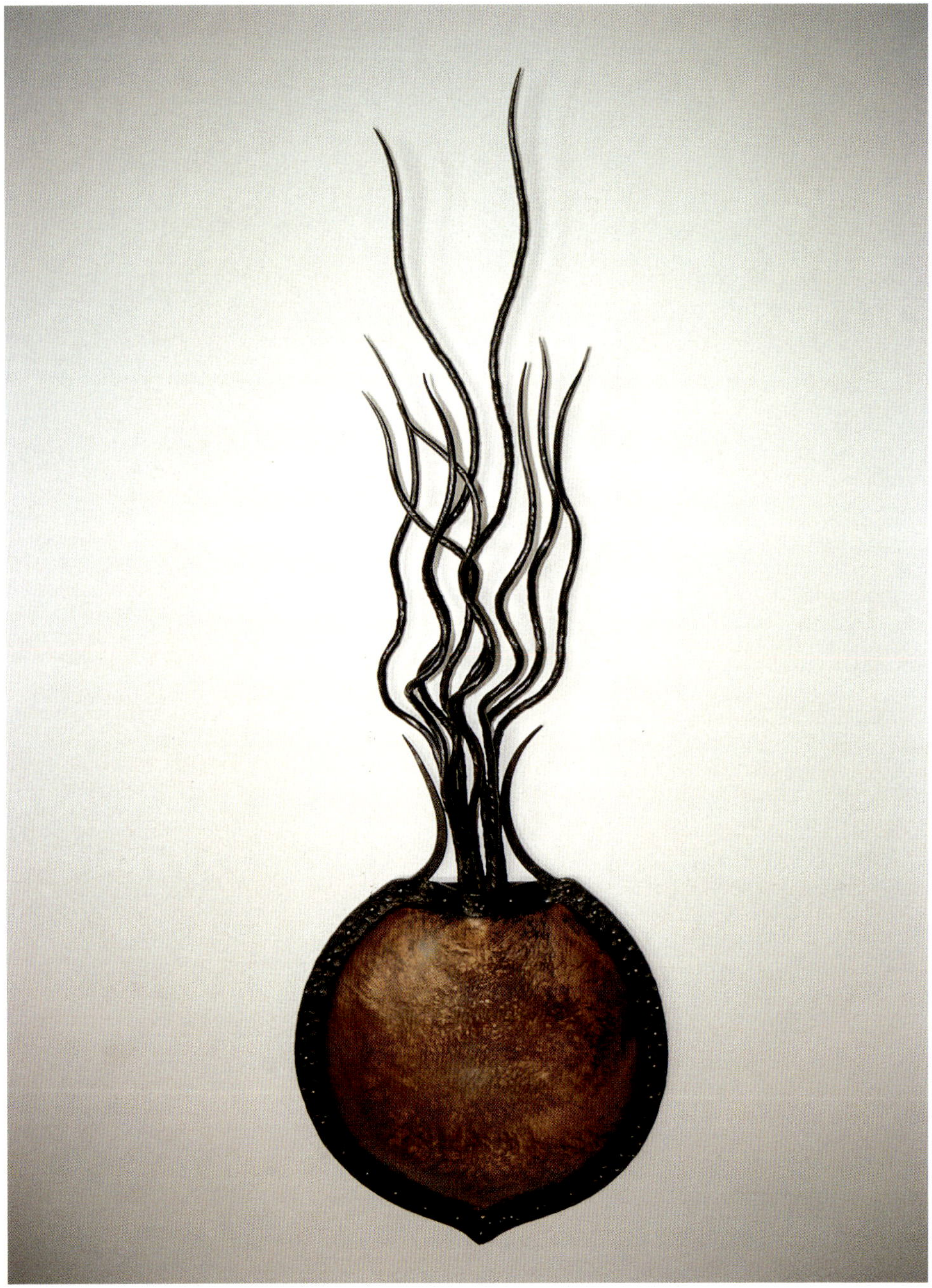

Jed Krieger. *Fishy.* Forged mild steel with a raised copper center riveted in place. Air currents within a building or home cause the ceiling suspended kinetic sculpture to move. 49" high, 16" wide. *Photo, Jane Ternary*

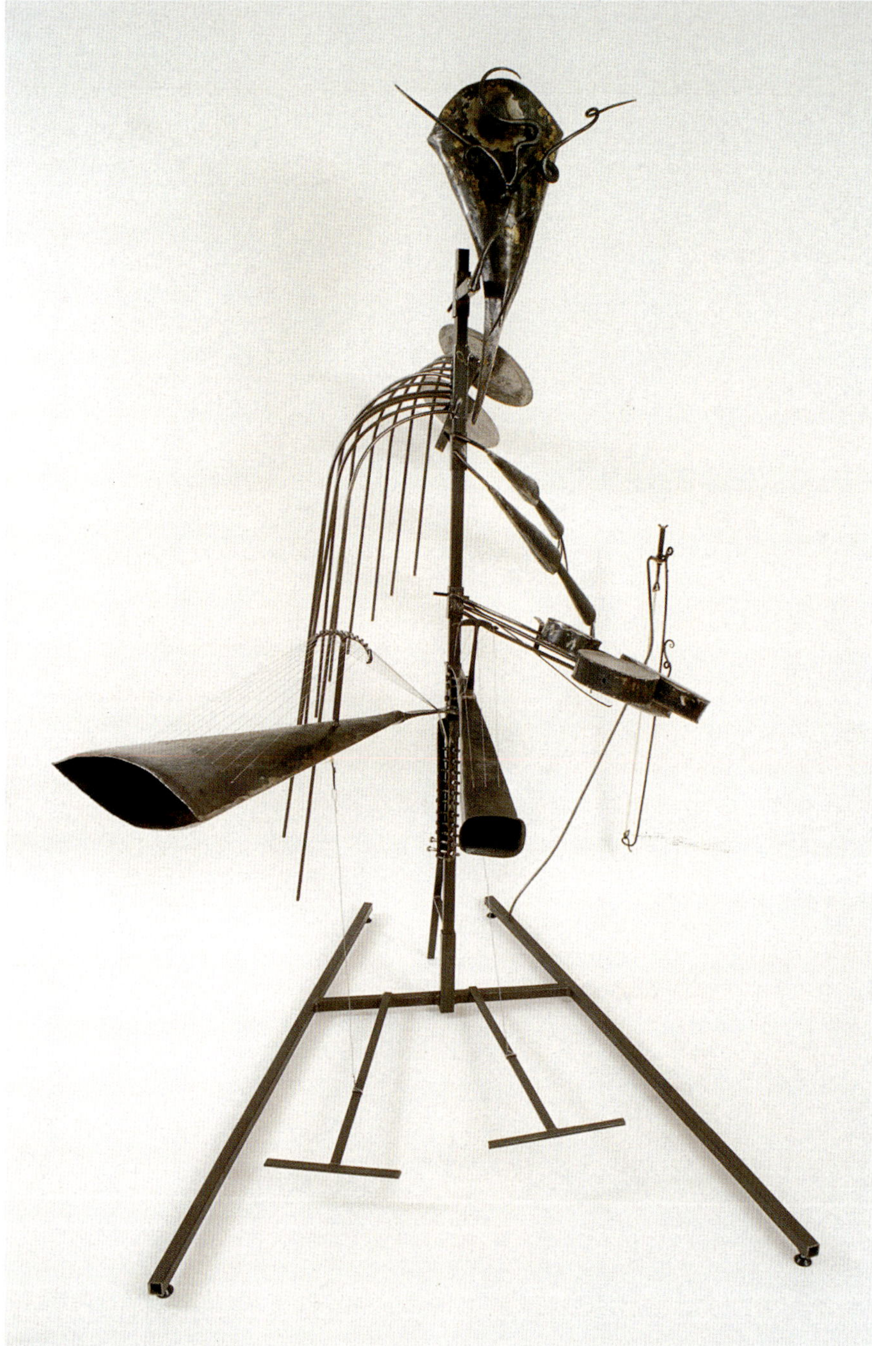

John Little. *Sagromides of Venus*. Sound sculpture incorporating hot and cold forged elements. Automobile coil springs, cowbells, and stainless steel welding wire. The 'cymbals' are forged from table-saw blades. The instrument has been used in jazz, classical and operatic venues. It can be disassembled for transporting. 6' tall. *Photo, Gary Castle*

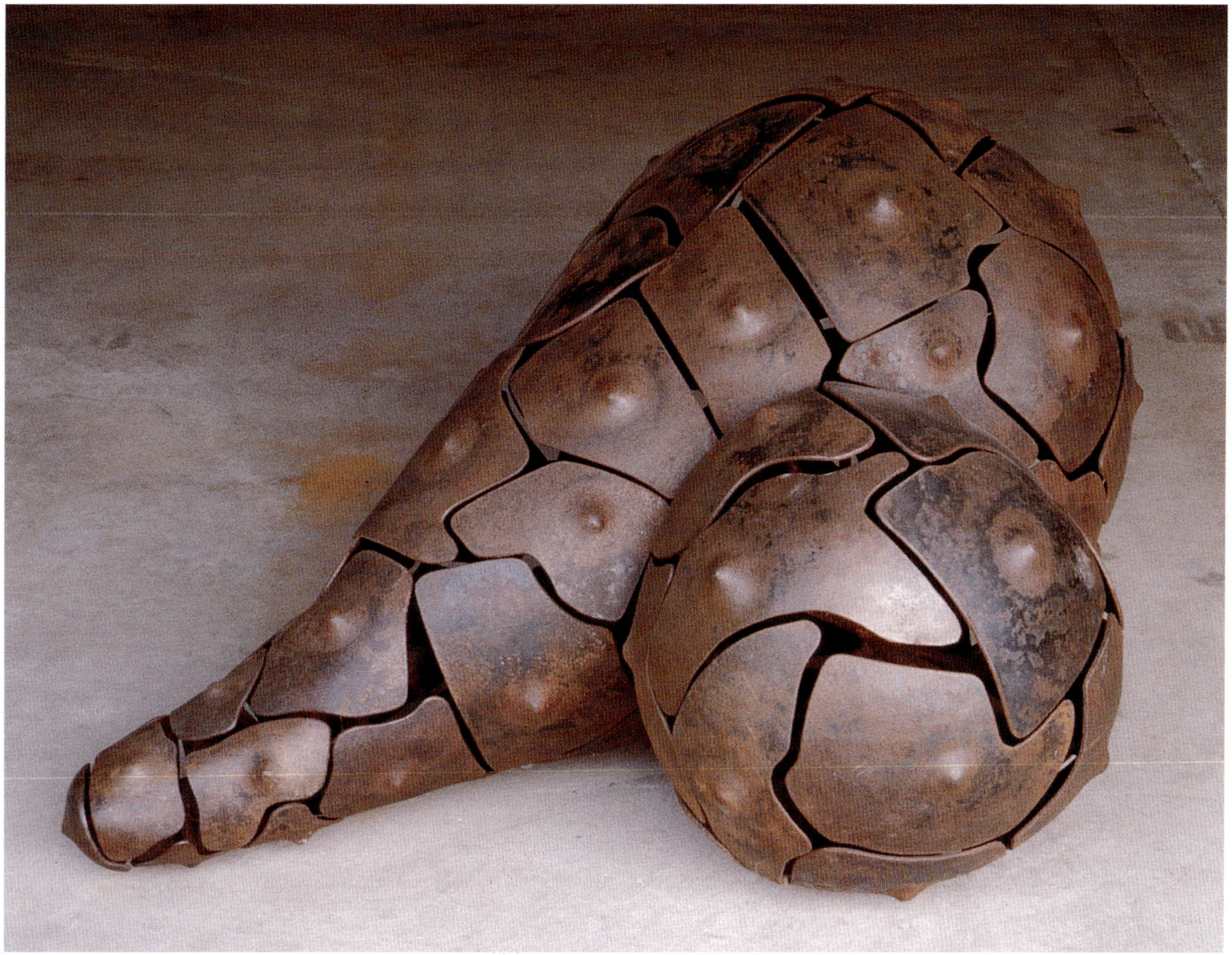

L. John Andrew. *Pokeweed*. Rusted steel. 20" high, 36" wide, 23" deep. *Photo, artist*

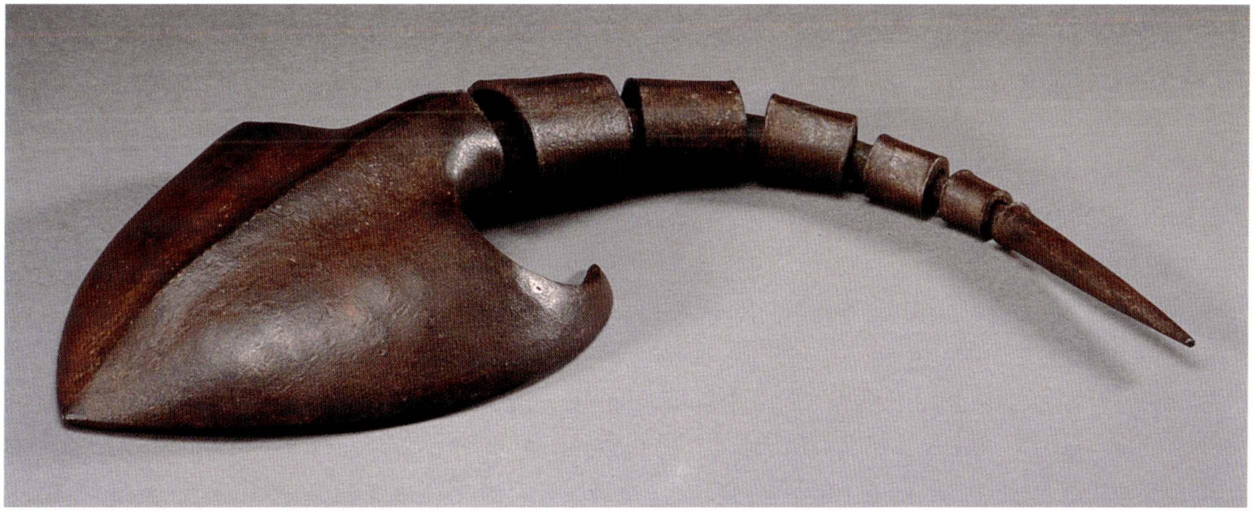

Eric Cuper. *Fossil Series #1*. Forged and fabricated steel. 3" high, 15" wide, 8" deep. *Photo, Jeffrey Bruce*

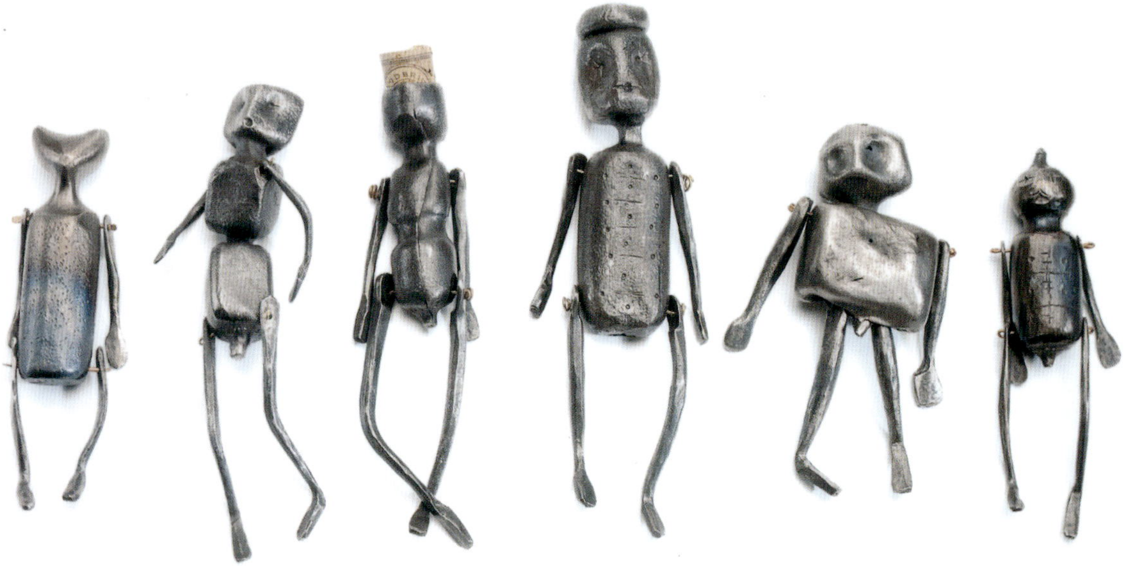

Connie Badowski. *Little Men.* Forged iron pipe and tubing. Sizes range from 6" to 9" tall. Each has a different head or body style. *Photo, Lea Christiano*

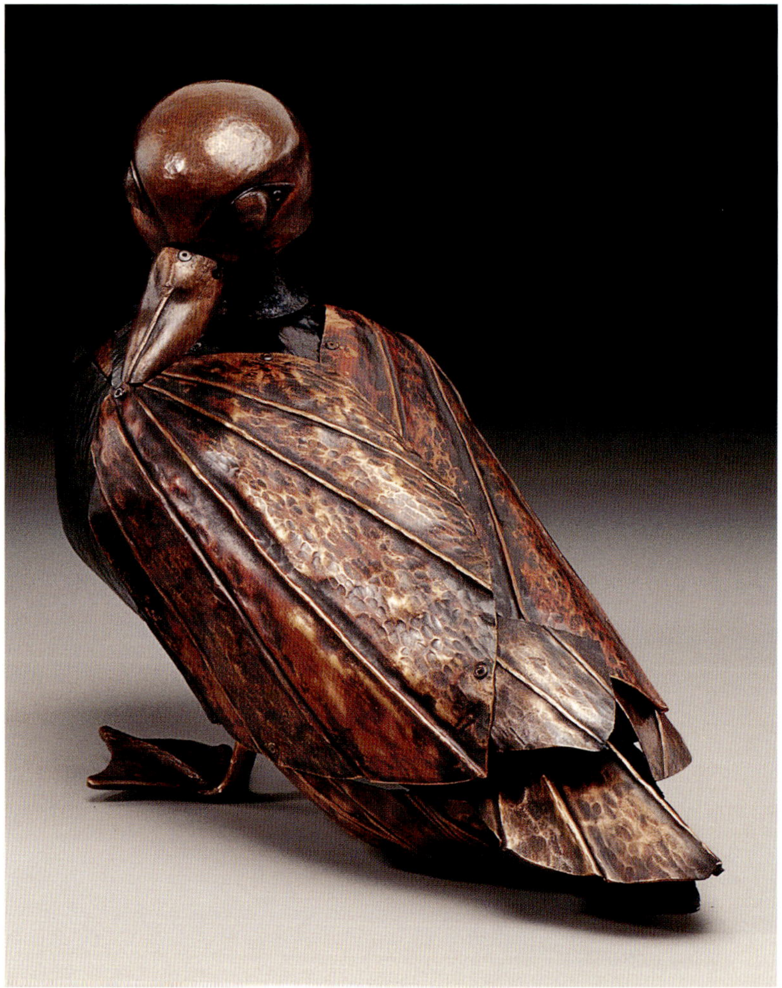

Erica Gordon. *Claire the Duck.* Forged and fabricated steel and copper animal sculpture using a variety of techniques. The copper has been raised, fold formed, and forged. 20" high, 12" wide, 6" diameter at widest point. *Photo, Rudy Hellman*

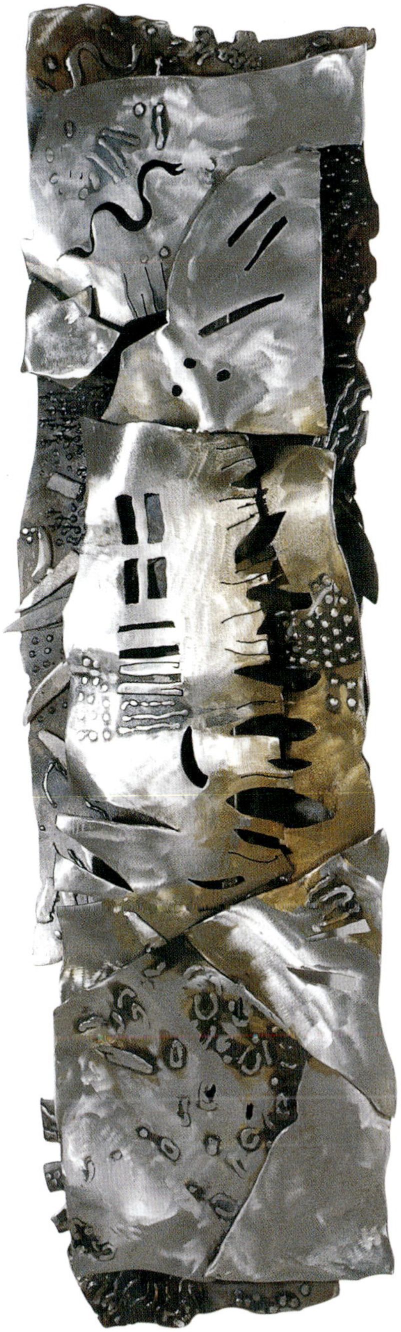

Joan Waters. *Window onto Night.* Hammered, welded steel with patinas. Wall sculpture. 42" high, 13" wide, 4" deep. *Photo, artist*

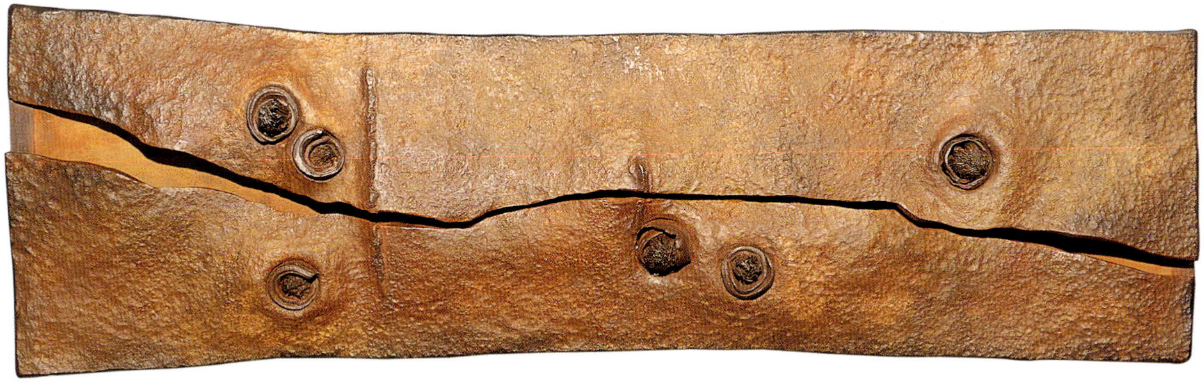

Nathan Blank. Untitled wall sculpture. Mild steel. 11" high, 35" wide, 1" deep. *Photo, artist*

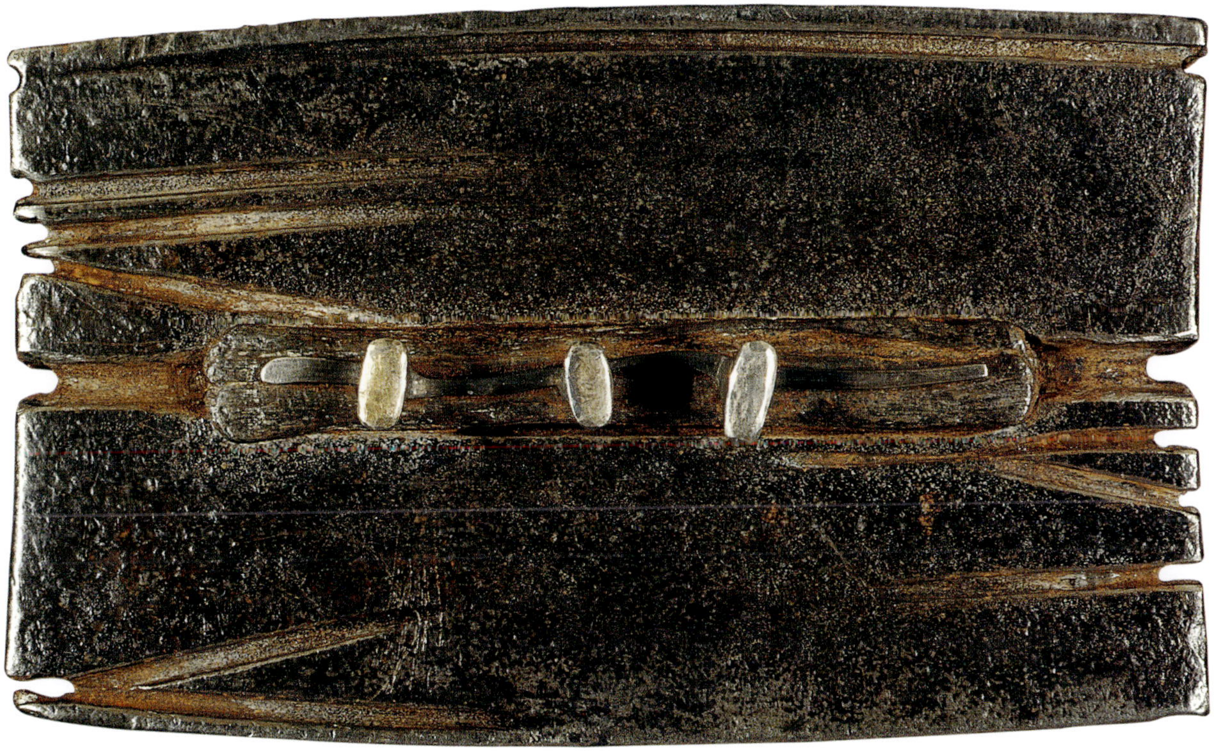

Amy Winkel. Untitled wall piece (Hammer series). Steel, wrought iron, and silver. 3" high, 5" wide, 1.25" deep. *Photo, Cheryl Brodie*

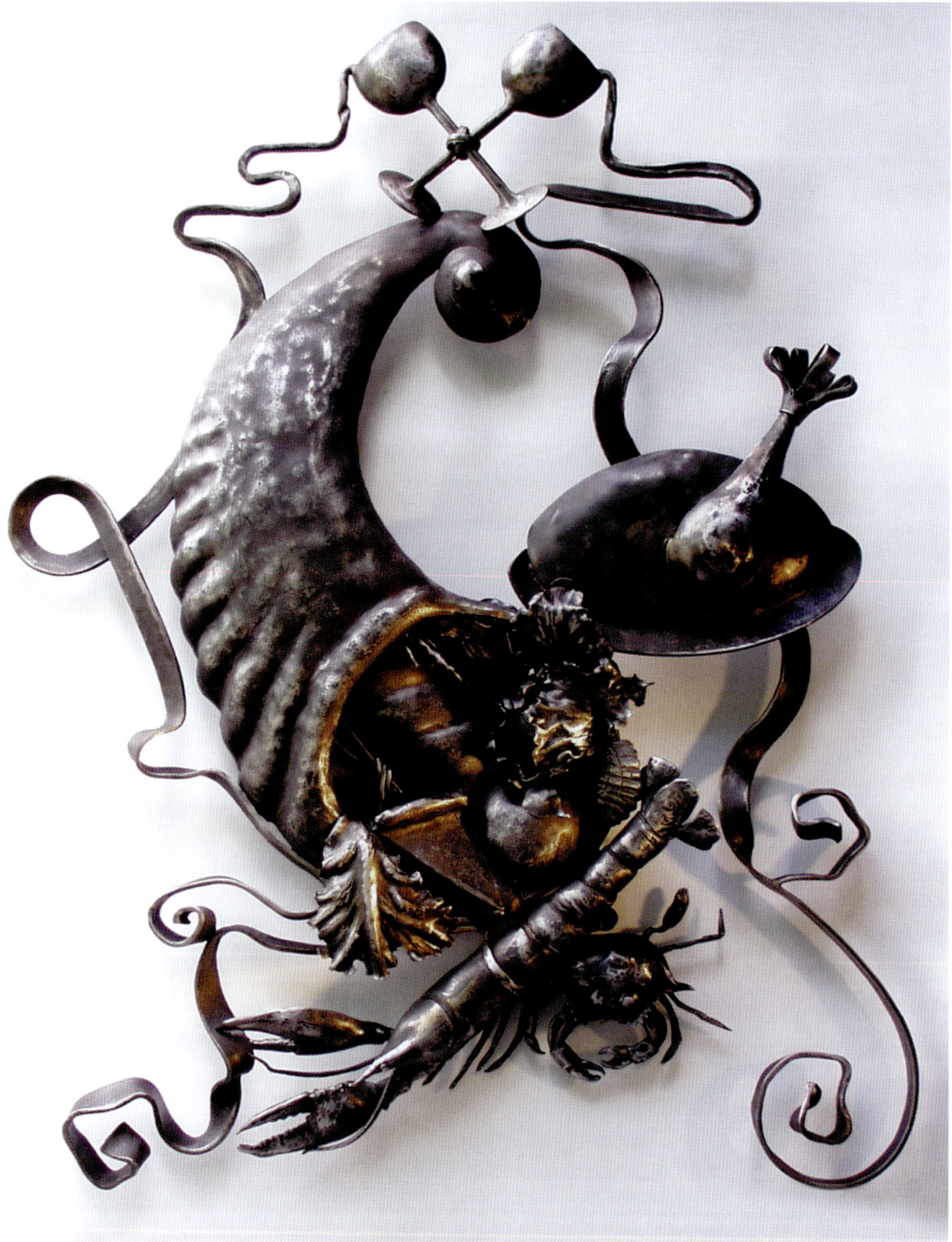

Dimitri Gerakaris. *Dining Room Relief Sculpture*. Forged and color-galvanized relief set into the exterior masonry of a Connecticut residence. It conveys the function of the room within and reflects the cuisine of the inhabitants' nationalities. 5.5' high, 4' wide. *Photo,©D.Gerakaris*

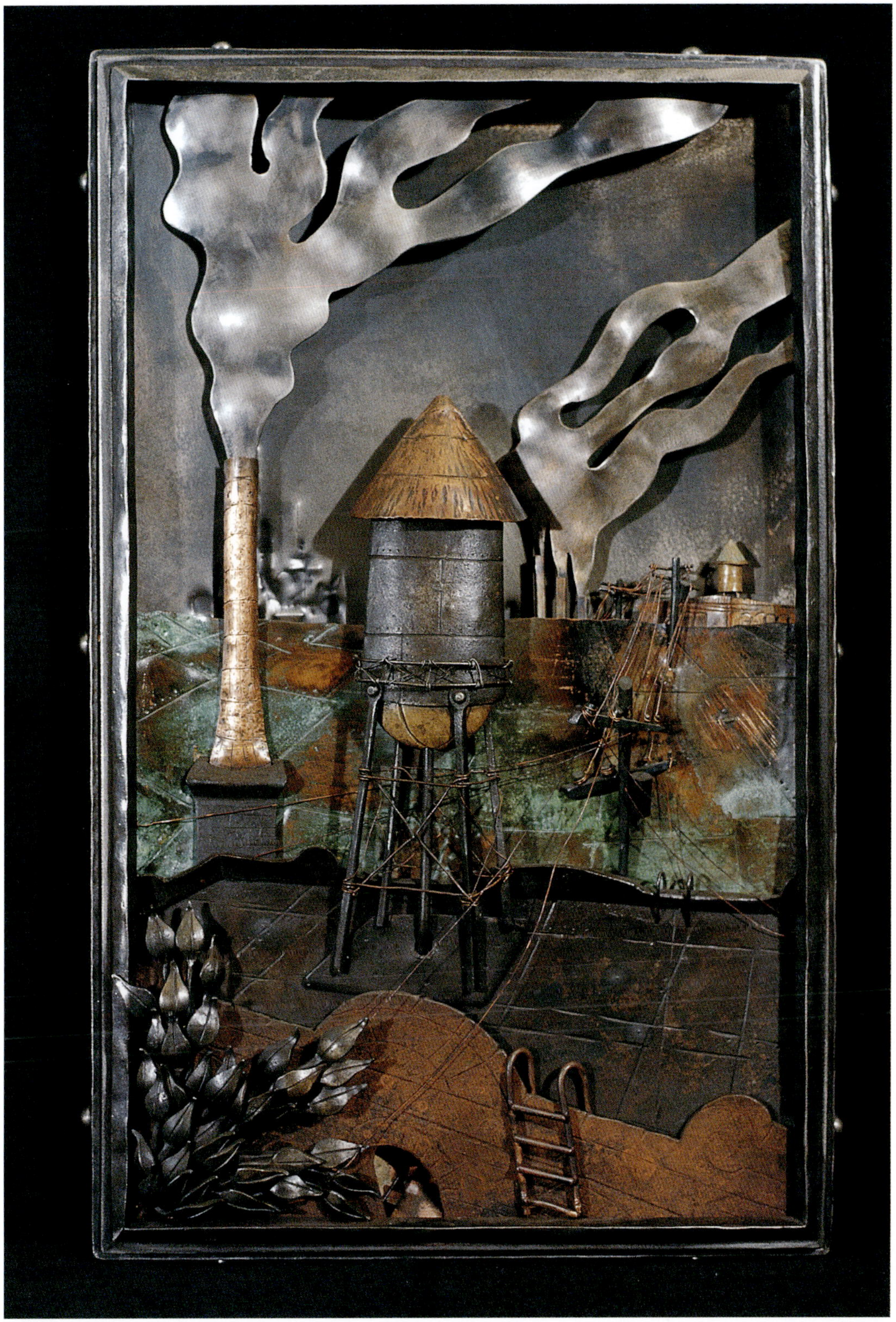

Patrick Maher. *Water Tower*. Forged steel, copper and brass. Perspective lines in metal create a sense of depth. The piece represents an industrial cityscape in a frame. 20" high, 14" wide. *Photo, artist*

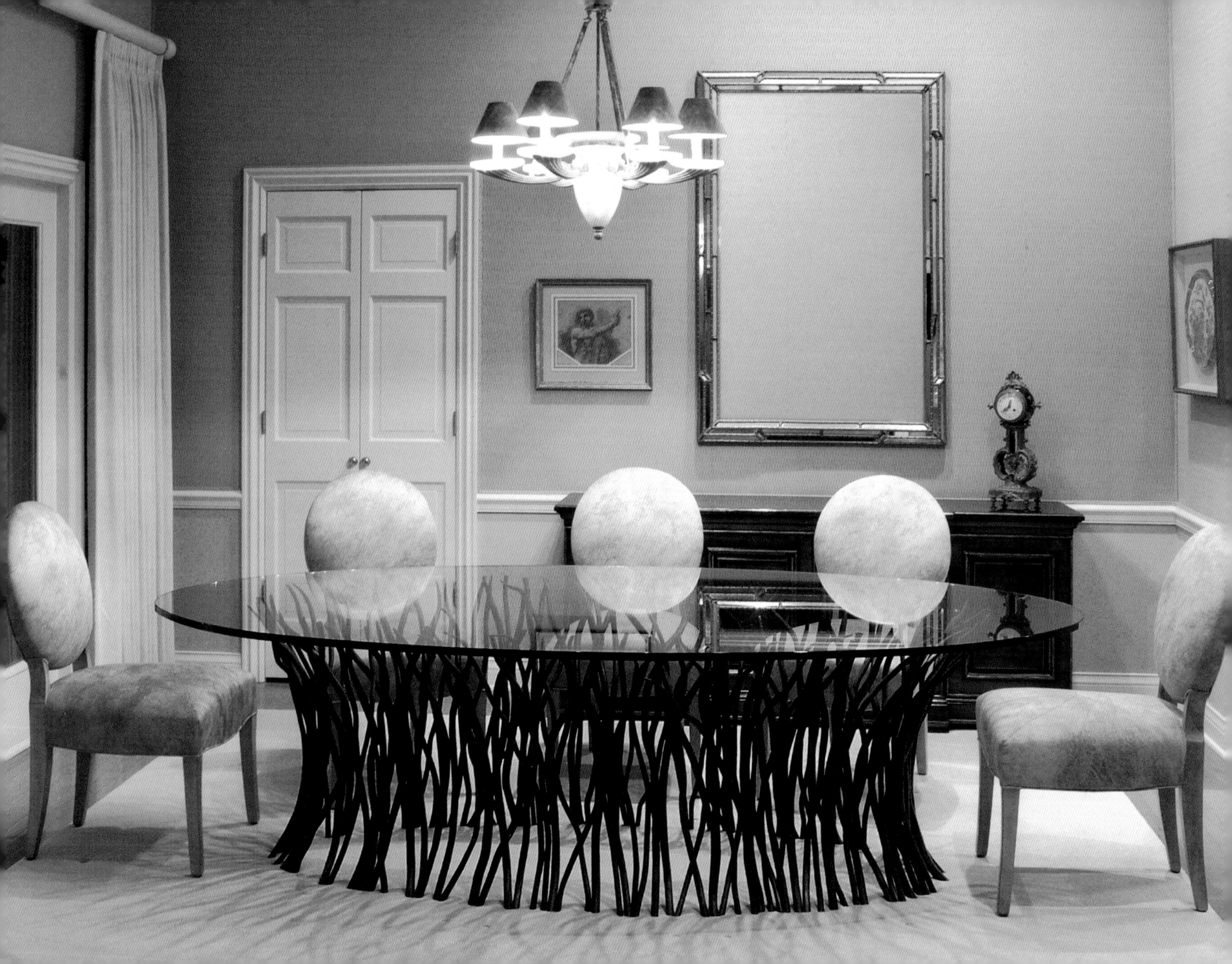

Chapter 6. Furniture

Never has iron been as popular and fashionable as it is today. Walk into any furniture store and you can observe an astonishing assortment of chairs, table bases, headboards, lighting fixtures, candelabra, fire screens, outdoor furniture, and accessories made of iron. Much of the mass produced pieces are imported from Mexico, China, and other countries where factories have been established to manufacture ironwork. A piece may be made in a shop that employs several smiths and each one works on parts at which he excels.

However, the artist-blacksmith who labors over a hot forge and shapes iron bars, and sheet metal produces unique one-of-a-kind furnishings for private clients. Occasionally, a blacksmith will create a "line" of products that are sold through furniture design companies, but even then, each piece is hand forged. Sometimes, small pieces are made, a mold is taken from them, and multiples are cast…resulting in cast iron objects that replicate the look of the hand-forged pieces.

The furniture examples that follow are made by the artist-blacksmith. Usually the artisan also designs the piece, but it can be formed to the specifications of an architect or interior designer.

Often, a piece of furniture is in the artist's minds eye and he or she produces a piece anxious to test techniques and methods. They may try piercing a tabletop to experiment with a design concept. They may see something that inspires a design and may draw the object first, and then determine how to produce it.

Opposite page:
Wiemann Iron Works. *Halpern table.* The title is based on the client's name. Solid bar steel rounds textured, then formed to a template to achieve consistent curves and height. Bars are between 1/4" and 1" round. The patinated color is finished with clear lacquer and wax. Top is 9' long and 4' wide. *Photos, Courtesy Wiemann*

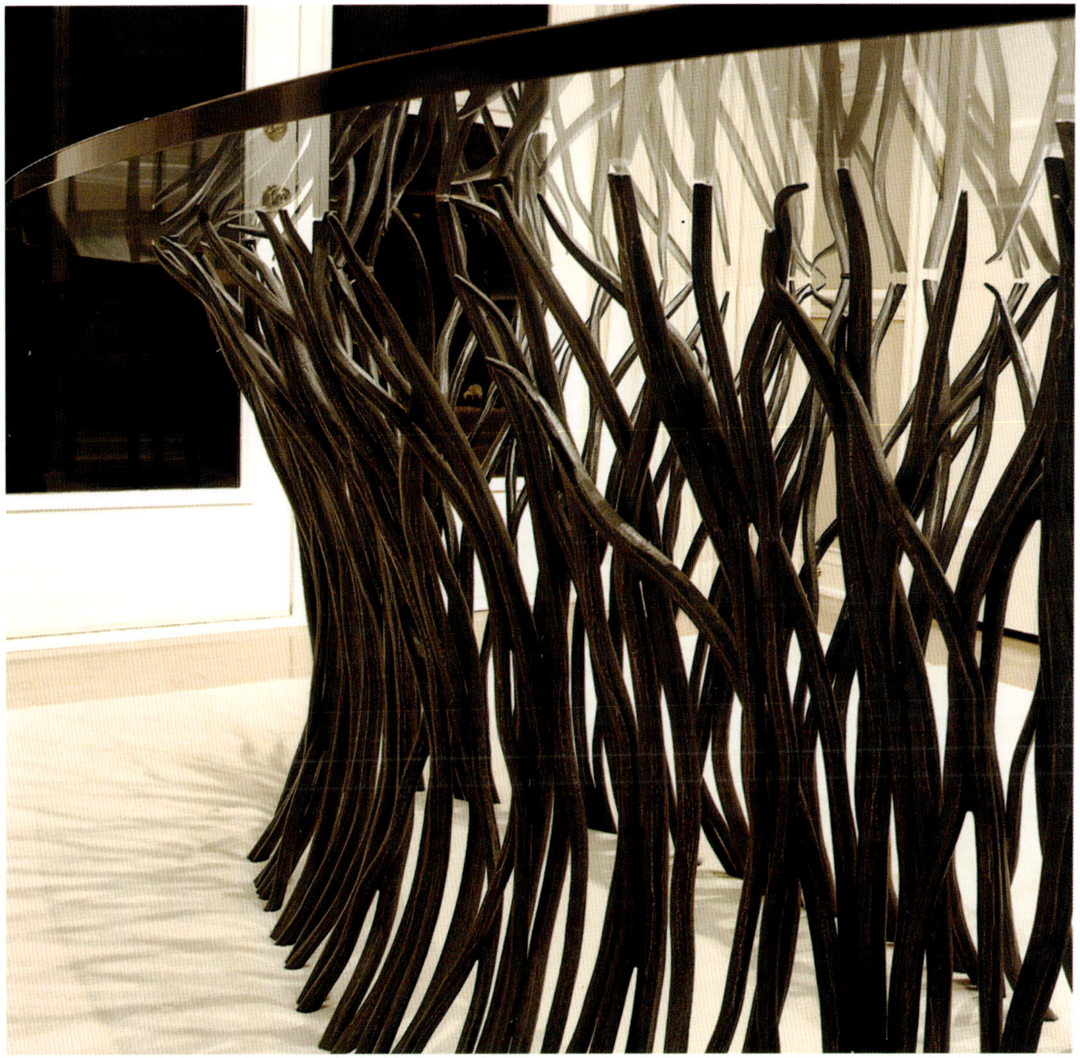

Wiemann. *Halpern table*, detail.

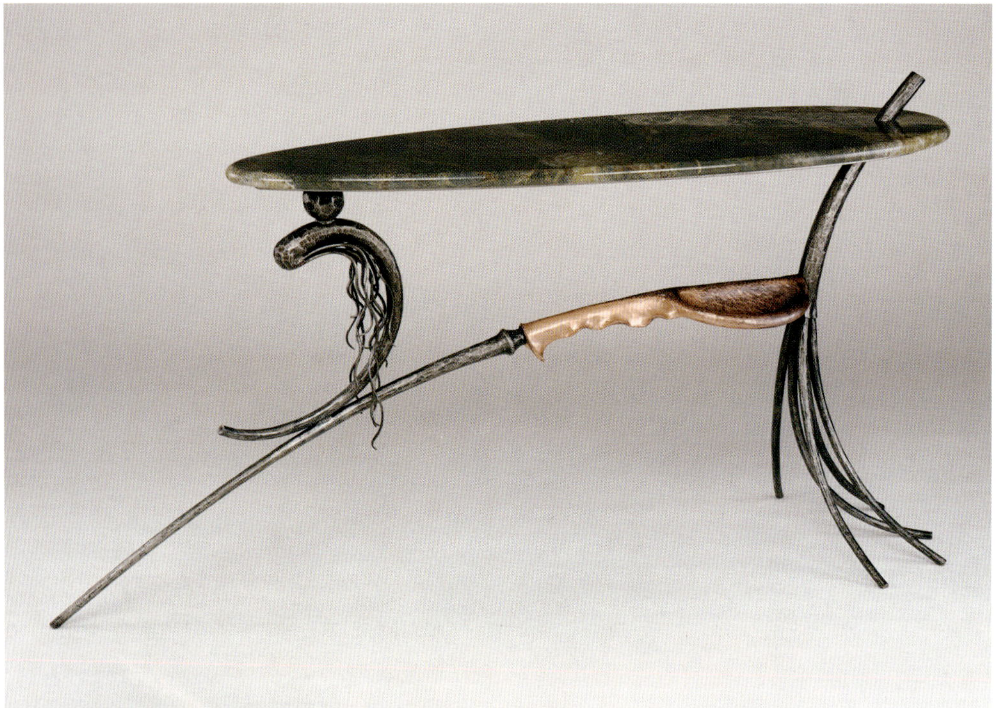

L. Joel Sanderson. *Subaqueous.* Iron copper and granite. 32" high, 69" wide, 20" deep. *Photo, Royal Images*

Inspiration for furniture pieces may be based on historic styles and objects. Art Nouveau and Art Deco often are interpreted in myriad ways for today's furniture. Traditional designs spark ideas for full pieces of furniture and, perhaps, only for details. Geometry plays an important role in making tables and cabinets practical. Shapes and details are inspired by nature as shown in table bases with leaves and flowers. Hugh Culley developed a technique for simulating pinecones in metal.

A table base might be completely free form. Jack Brubaker and Ira Wiesenfeld's tables are examples of this approach. Brubaker shapes a variety of pieces and then cuts them apart and reassembles the shapes into a table base. Wiesenfeld looks to the gnarled and bent cactus detritus found in his desert environment.

Whatever the inspiration, whatever techniques are involved, the ironworker must always find solutions for the problems posed by the materials and the designs. That's what keeps the art form so exciting.

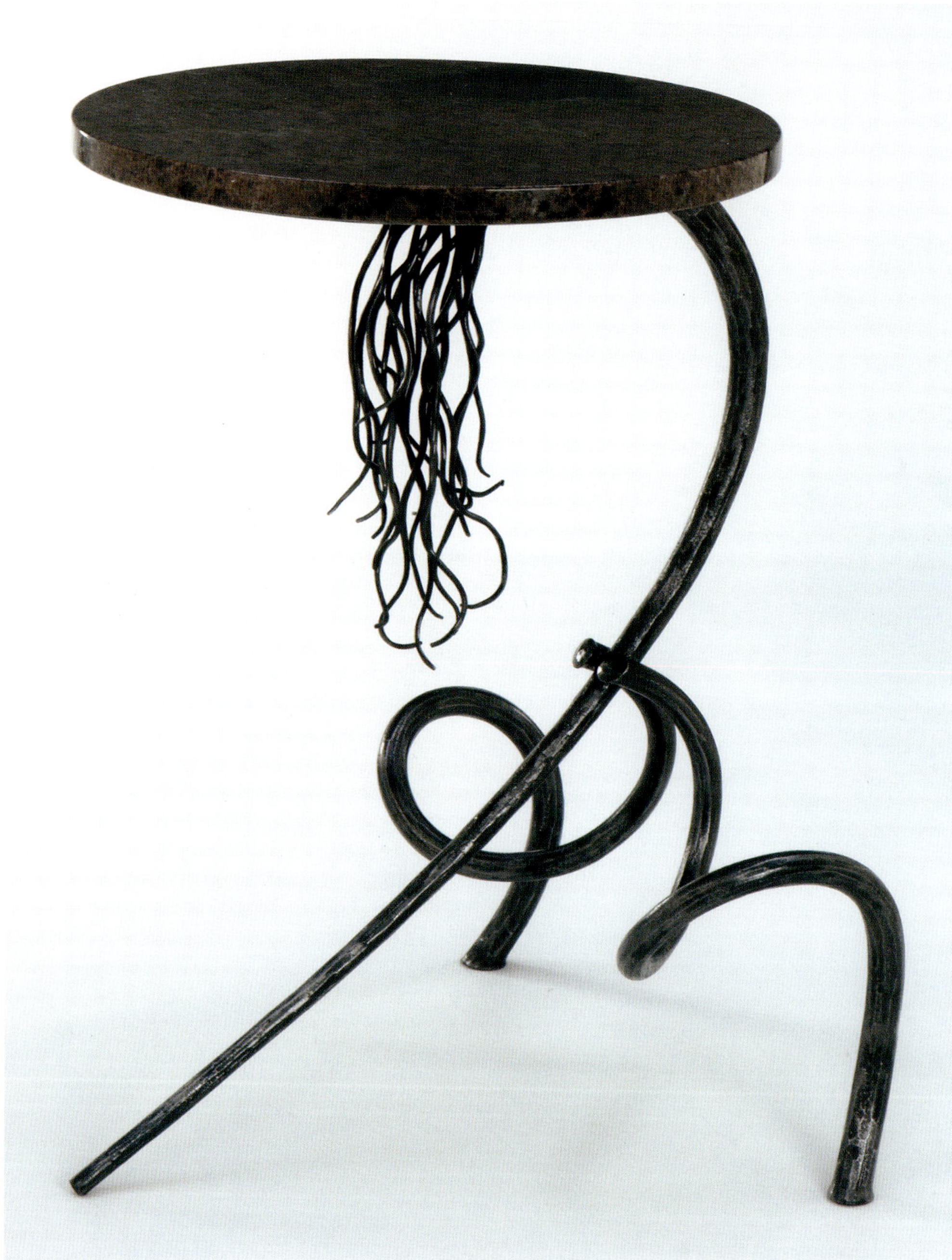

L. Joel Sanderson. *Old Man with a Hat.* Iron and granite. 32" high, 21" diam. *Photo, Royal Images*

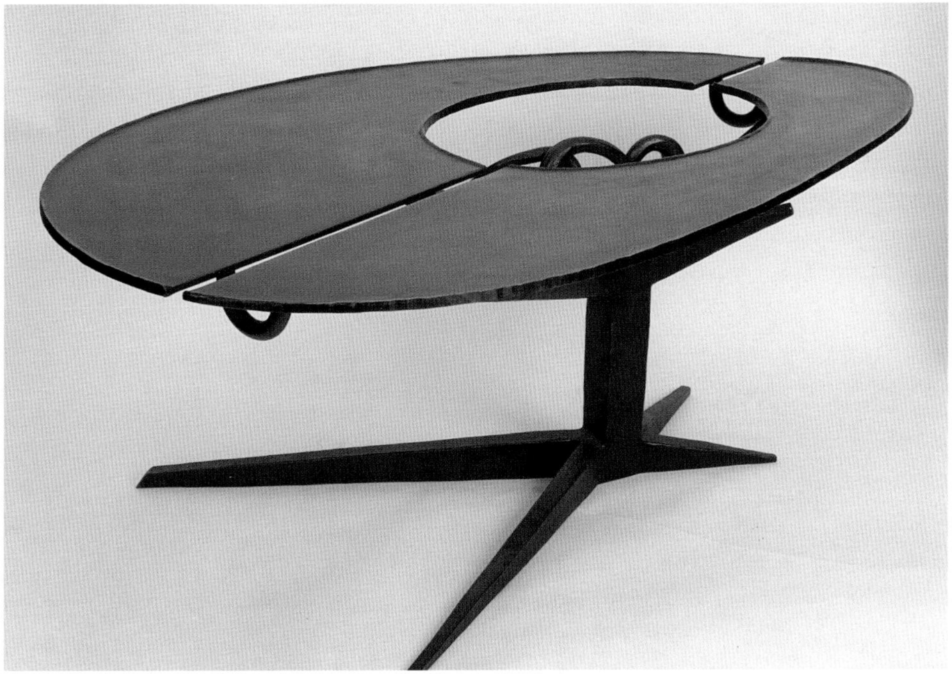

John Little. *Coffee Table*. Forged steel. Decorative details below the top are "discovered" through the egg-shaped top opening. 18" high, 38" wide. *Photo, Gary Castle*

Jeff Wallin. *Ellipse Table*. Mild steel and stainless steel. Ideas are based on industrial imagery combined with contemporary design and innovative joinery. 22" high, 25" wide, 16" deep. *Photo, Tom Mills*

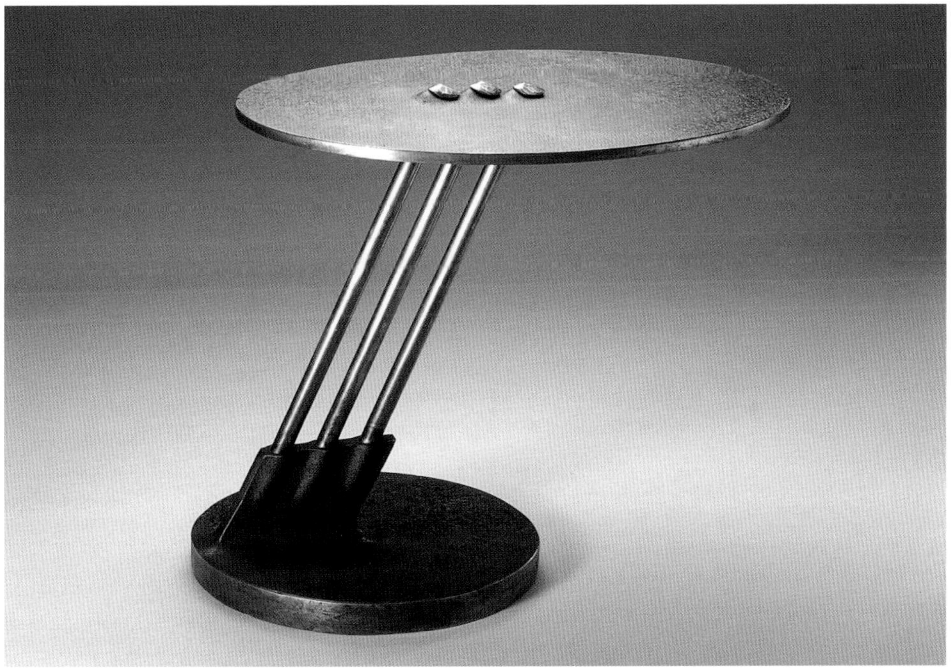

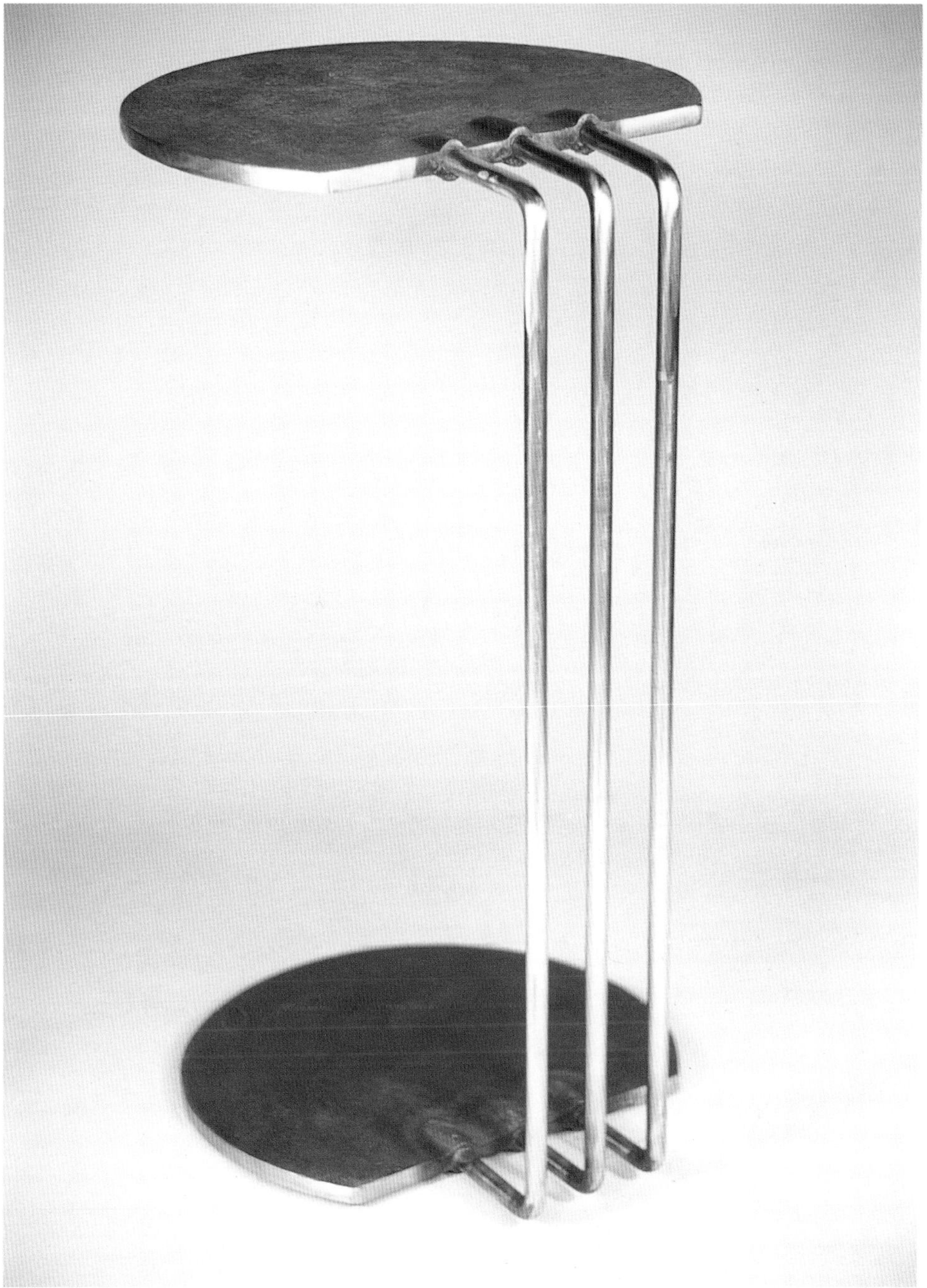

Jeff Wallin. *Macrochip Table*. Mild steel and stainless steel. 24" high, 13" wide. *Photo, Melissa Van Den Berg*

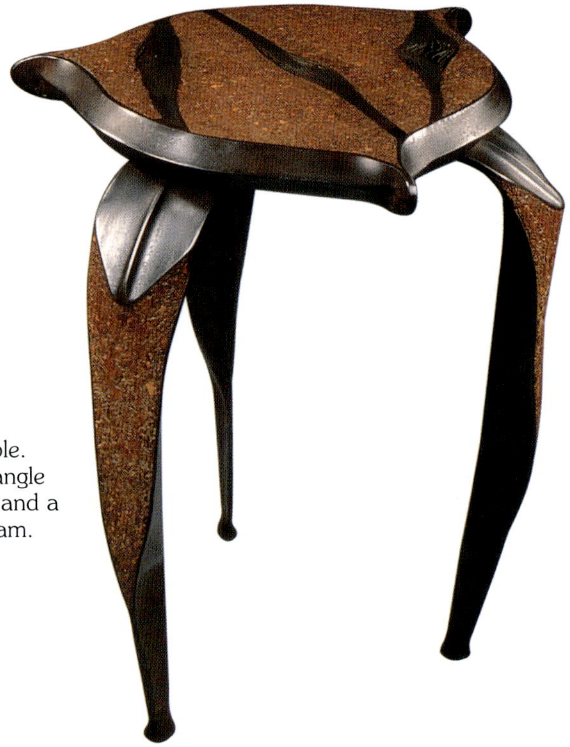

Nathan Blank. Side Table. Forged and fabricated angle iron with cast concrete, and a patina. 29" high, 14" diam. *Courtesy, artist*

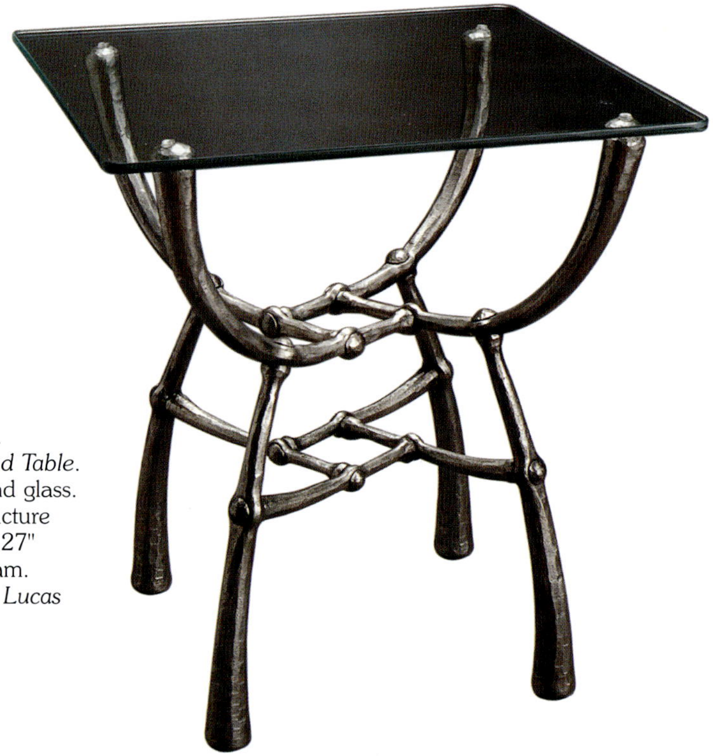

Benjamin O. Cowden. *End Table*. Mild steel and glass. Unusual structure and joinery. 27" high, 24" diam. *Photo, John Lucas*

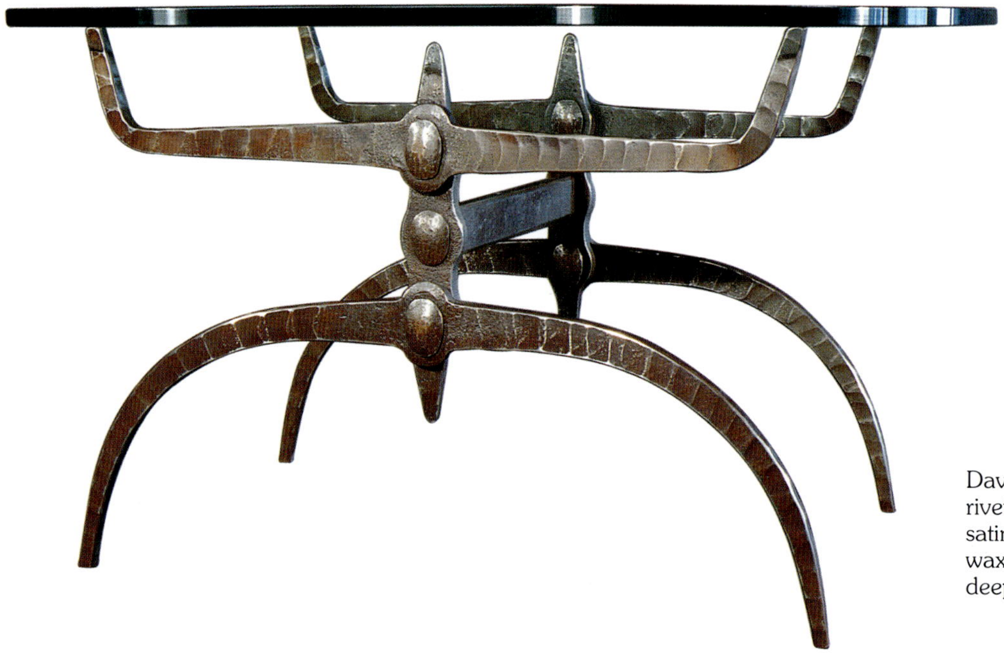

David Zatz. *Iron Horse Table.* Forged steel with riveted mortise and tenon construction. Sandblasted satin finish, with a hot ferric nitrate patina and a paste wax. An elliptical glass top. 19" high, 24" wide, 17" deep. *Photo, Ron Prager*

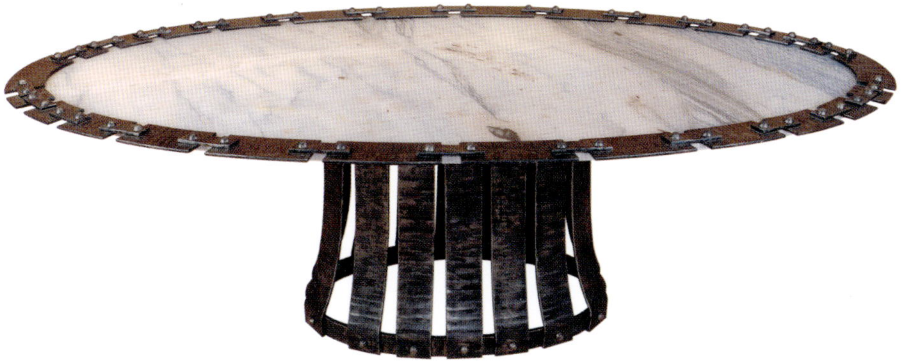

Paul Elliot. *Oval marble topped table*. 34" high, 9' wide, 4' deep. *Photo, Jackie Phillips*

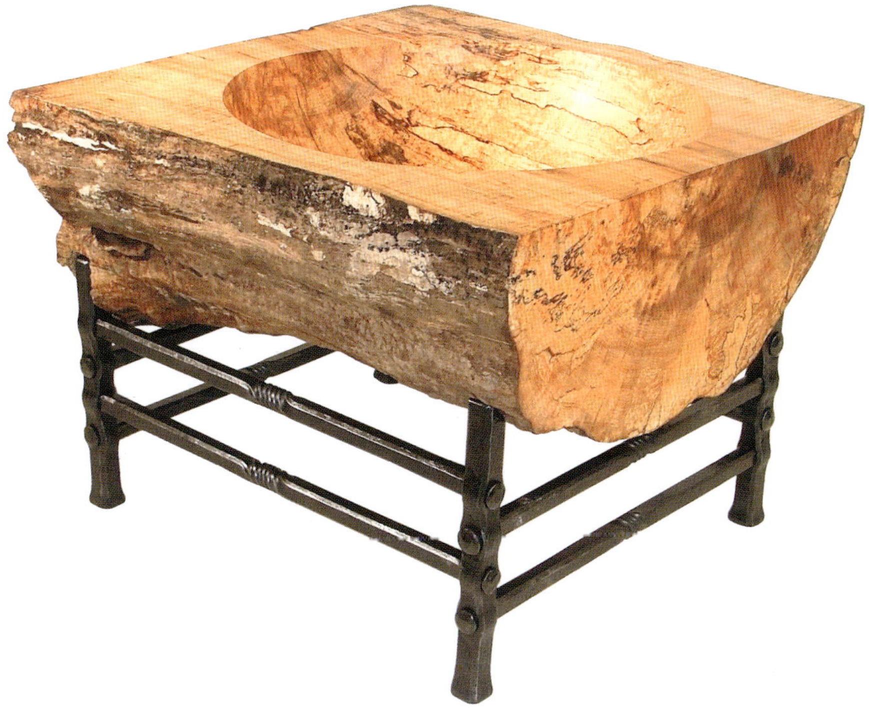

Frederic A. Crist and David W. Munn. *Spalded maple block table*. Forged steel base with maple top. Spalded maple has varying shades in the grain. 18" high, 24" wide, 16" deep. *Photo, Frederic Crist*

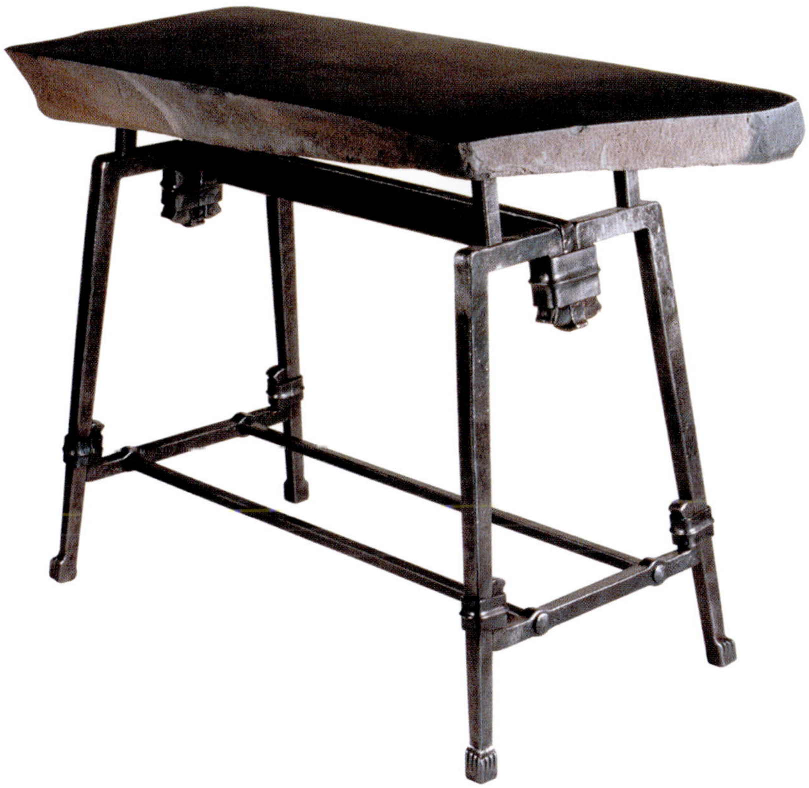

Jeff Holtby. *Table*. Iron legs with a basalt top by stonemason, Lloyd Whannel. 33" high, 48" wide. *Photo, David Gignac*

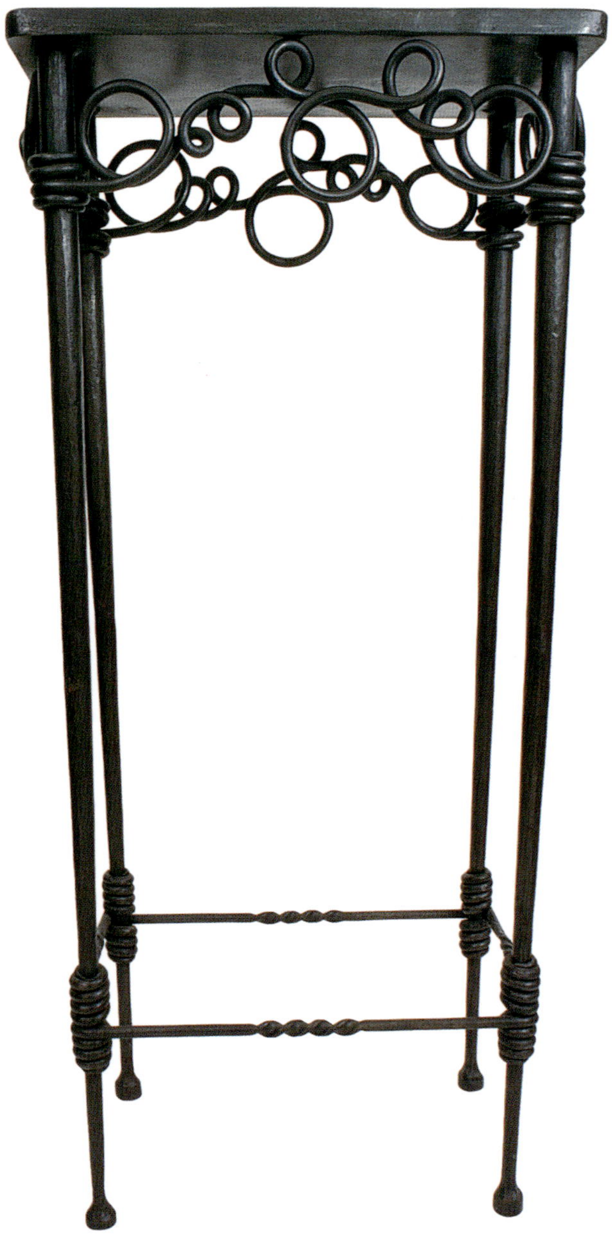

John Little. *Plinth*. Designed as a pottery display table. 36" high. *Photo, Gary Castle*

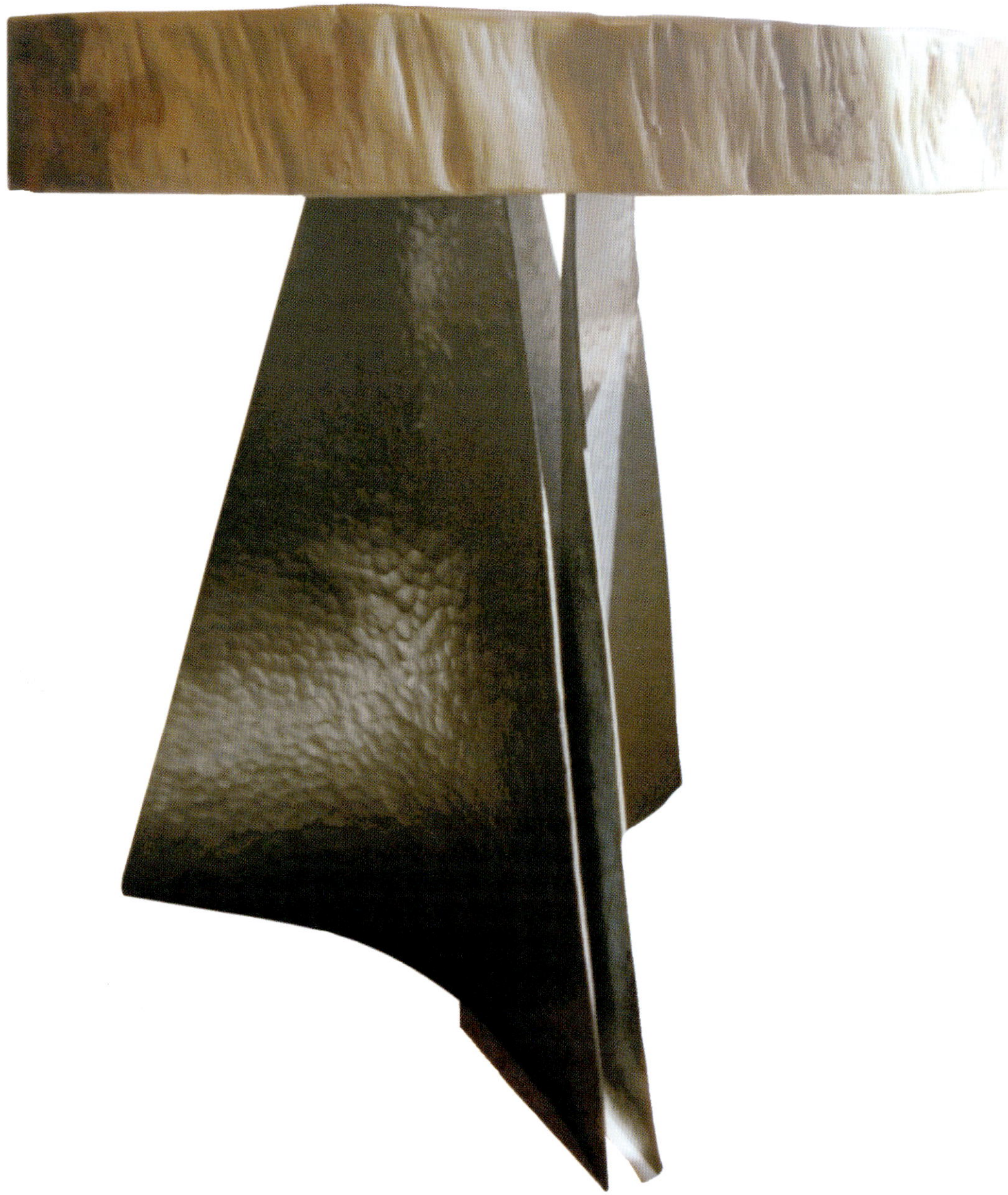

Aaron Craig. *Triangle Table*. Mild steel textured panels and juniper wood top. The texturing and curve of the table base sides are created with a 1.5" radius ball die under a power hammer. This creates a texture resembling one made by a ball pein hammer, only larger, and it makes the curve at the same time. Table base is 16" high and 16" wide at the base. The juniper slab adds another 3" in height and ranges from 18" to 24" wide. *Photo, Alexandra Pratt*

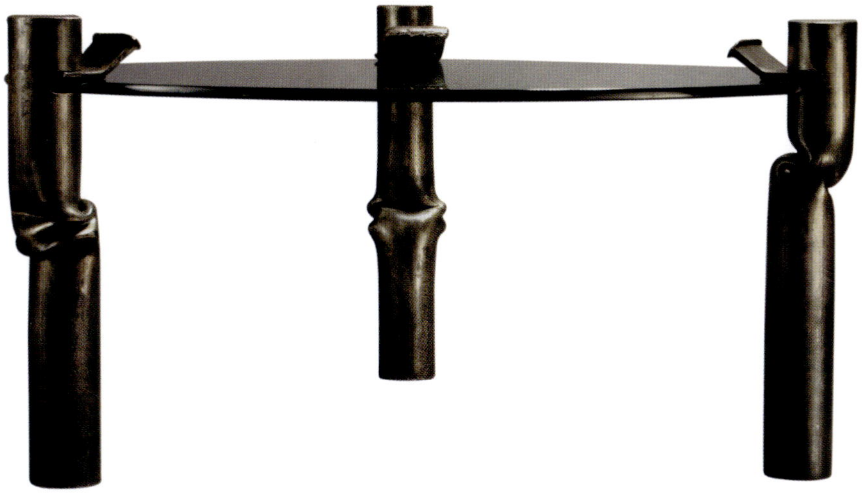

Jeff Fetty. *Round Wedge Table*. Hand forged steel and steel pipe with interior finish. It was the result of experimenting with vertical compression on another commission and, as is often the case, he began looking for other applications and possible products. The use of the wedge was something he had wanted to try for a number of years and finally found the place to do it. 17" high, 40" diam. with 36" diam. x 3/4" thick glass. *Photo, Gefeti*

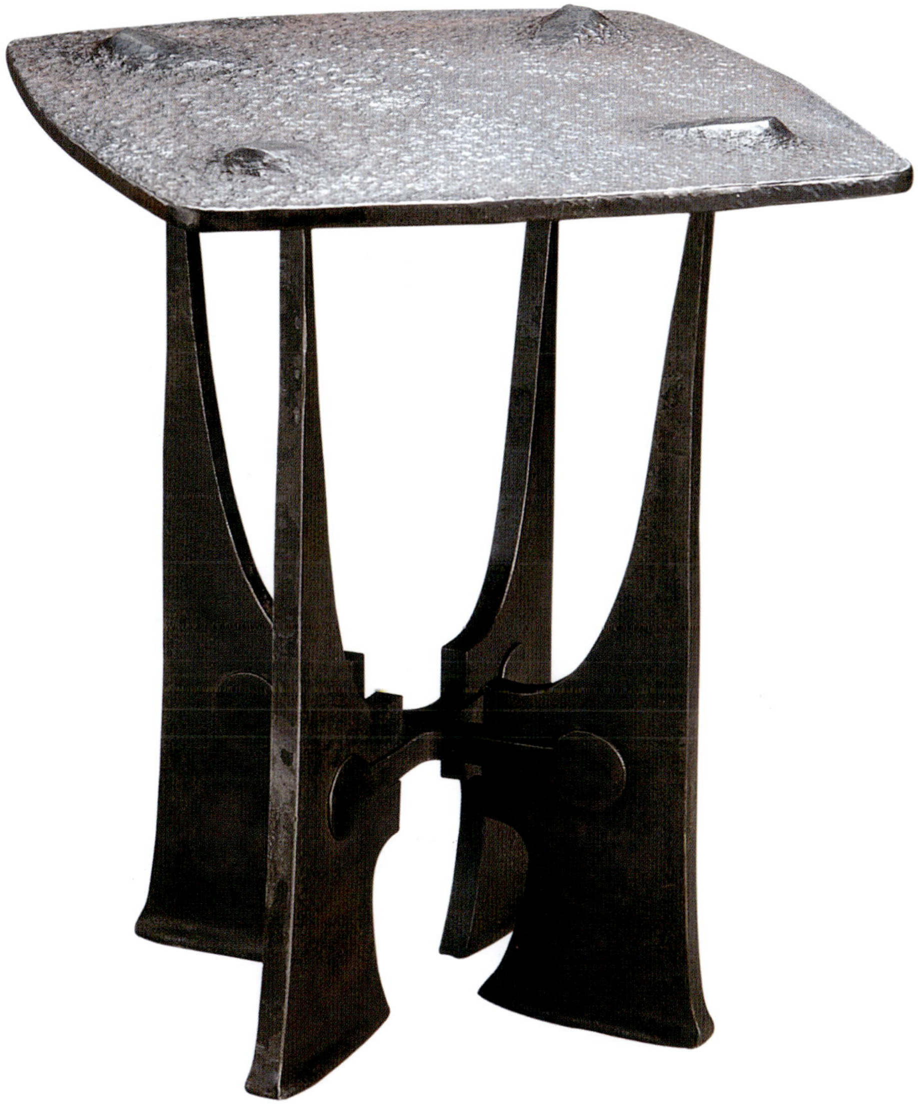

Jeff Wallin. *Hub Table*. Mild steel. 24" high, 19" wide. *Photo, Tom Mills*

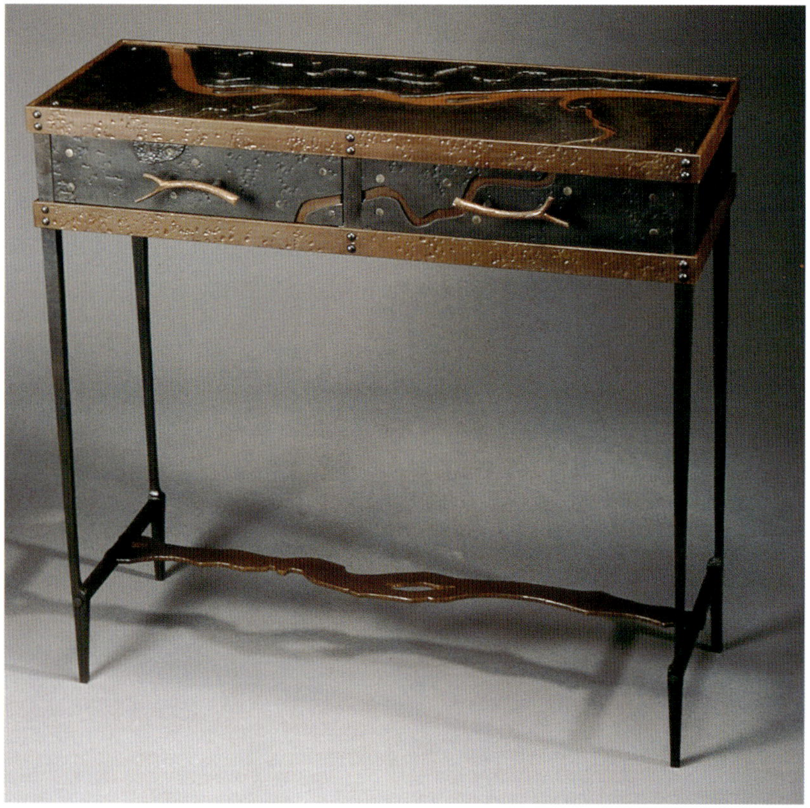

Eric Cuper. *Grand Tower Reliquary.* Forged and fabricated steel. 36" high, 36" wide, 15" deep. *Photo, Jeffrey Bruce*

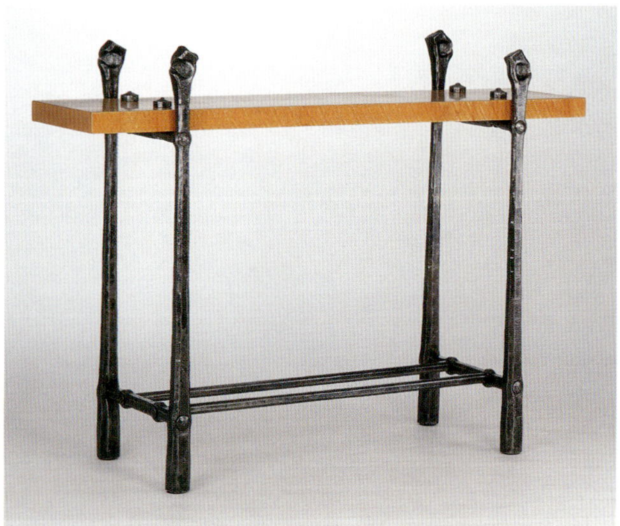

Michael Bendele. *Hall Table.* Mild steel frame with maple top. 38" high, 48" wide, 15" deep. *Photo, Jim King*

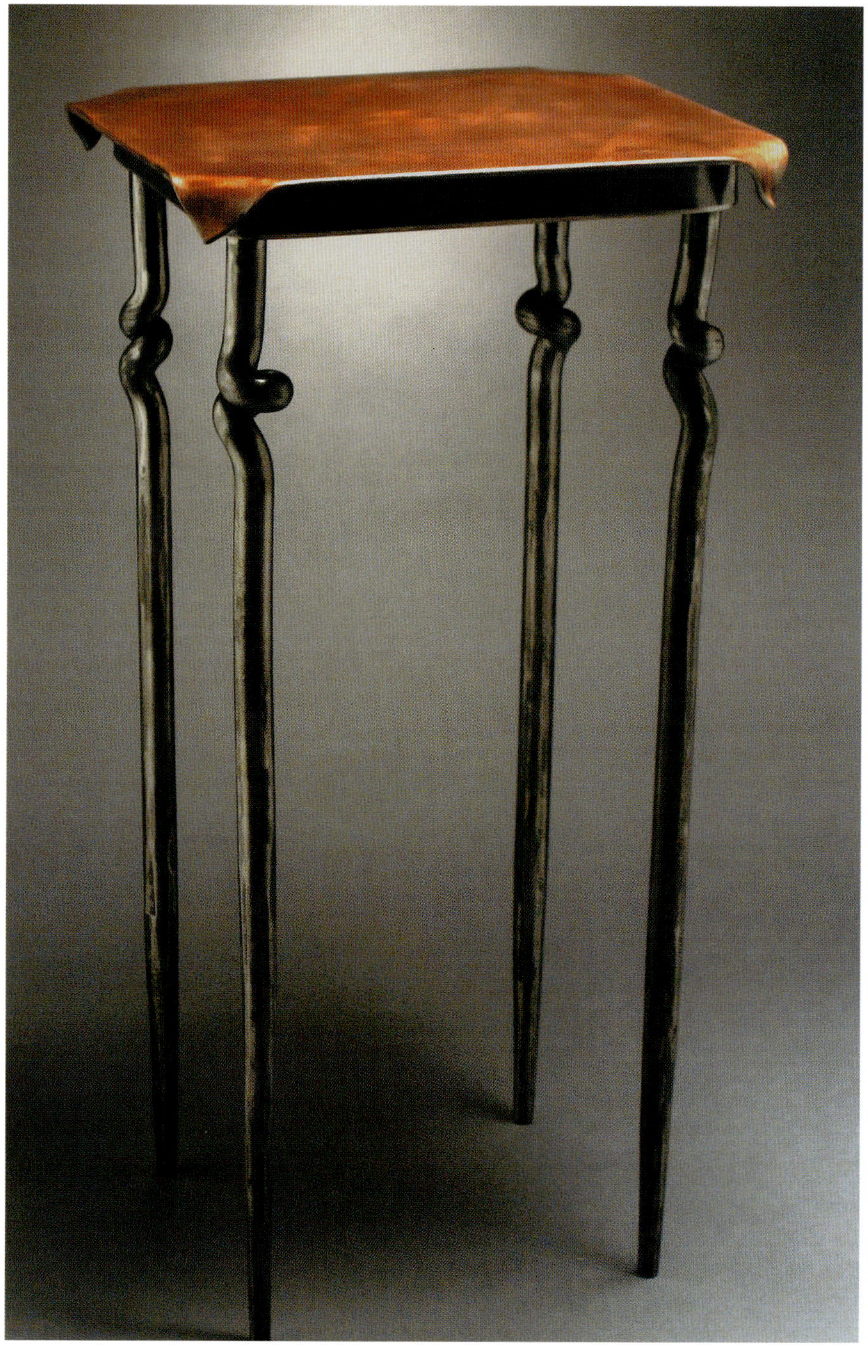

Jeff Fetty. *Occasional Table. Photo, Gefeti*

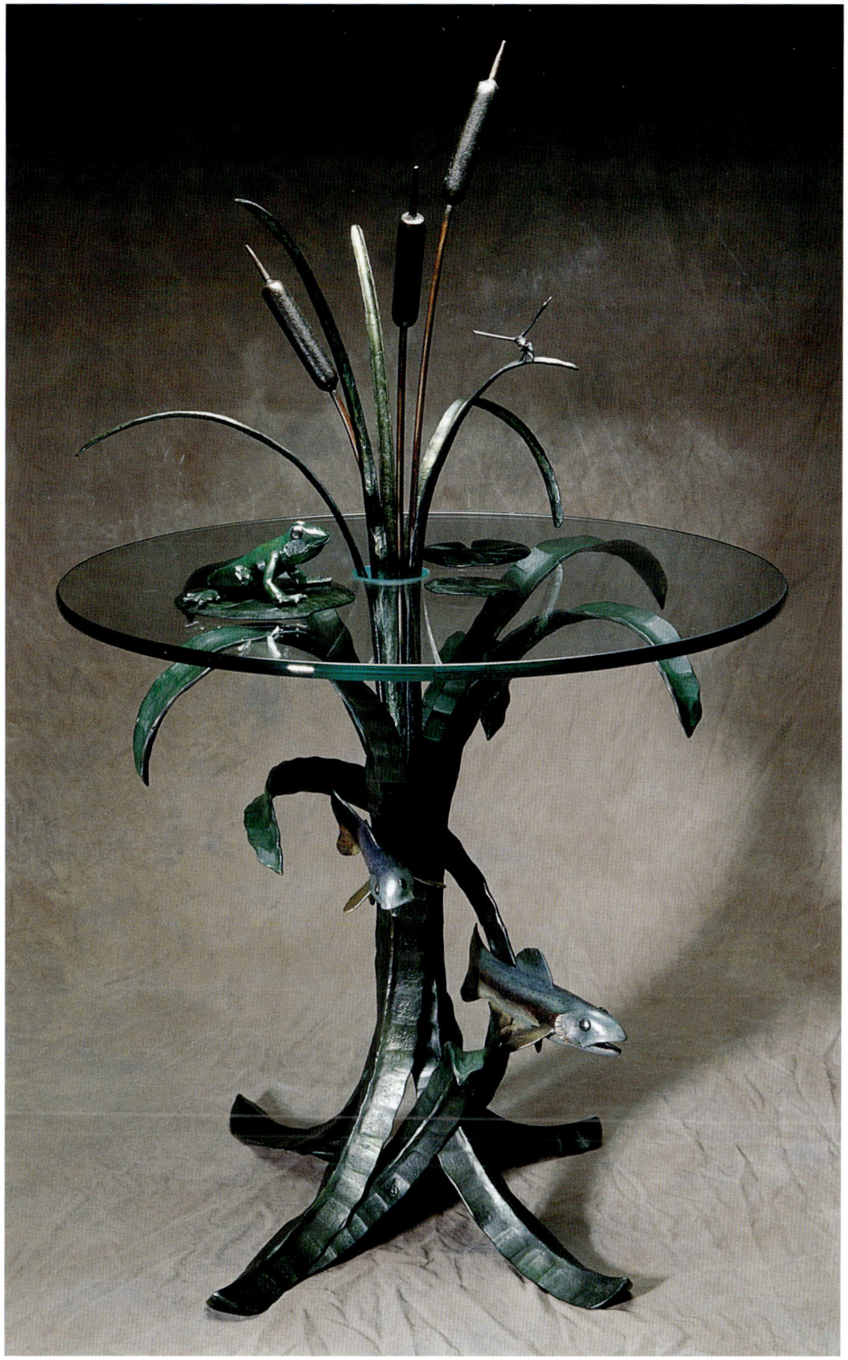

John Barron. *Pond Table*. Forged and fabricated mild steel, glass, and polychrome dye. The glass represents the water's surface. It is pierced by the cattails and supports the "floating" lily pads and frog perched on one of them. 36" high, 24" diam. *Photo, Keith Sutter*

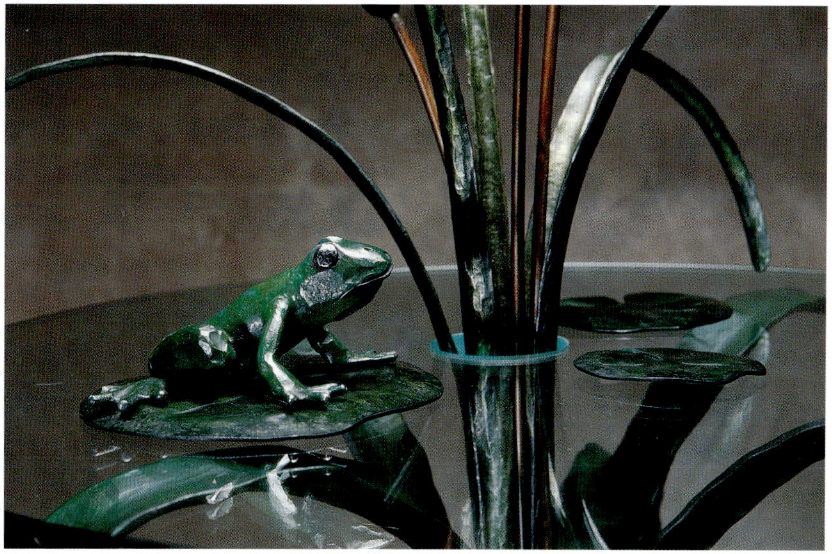

John Barron. Details of the frog, lily pads, and cattails piercing the glass tabletop. Below, fish swim around the base. *Photo, Keith Sutter*

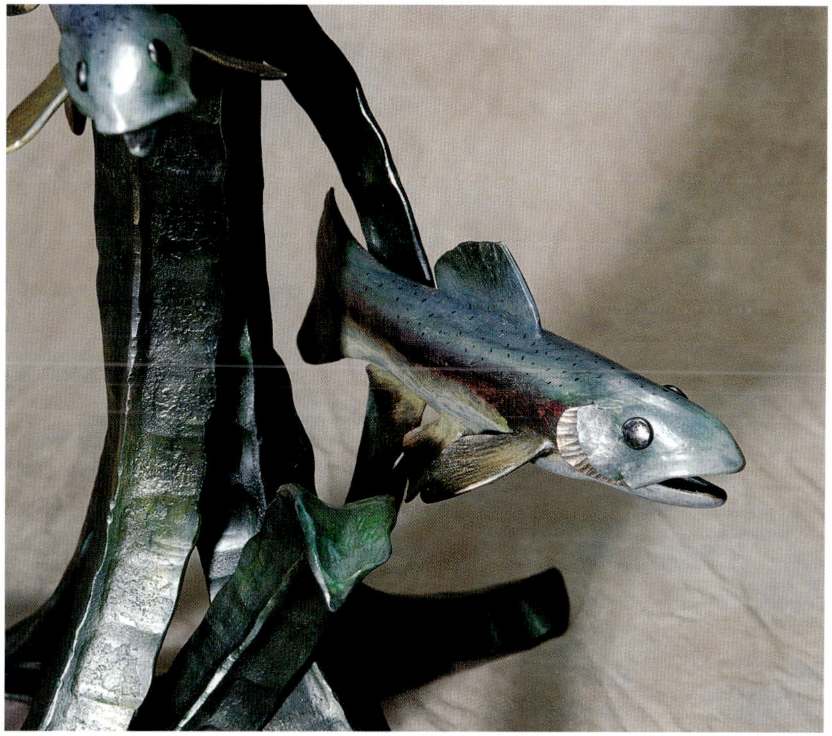

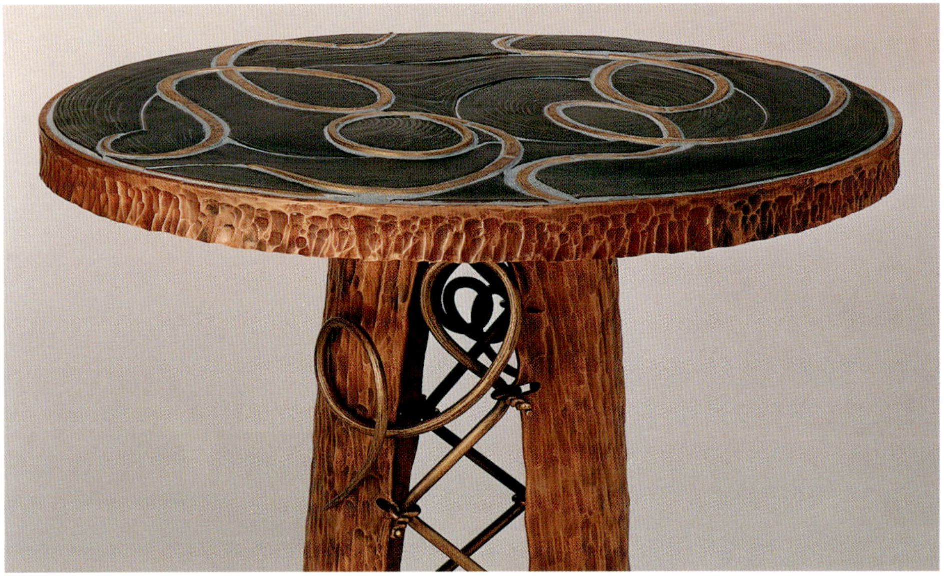

Michael Bendele. Table, detail of top showing bronze inlay in the stoneware. *Photo, Jim King*

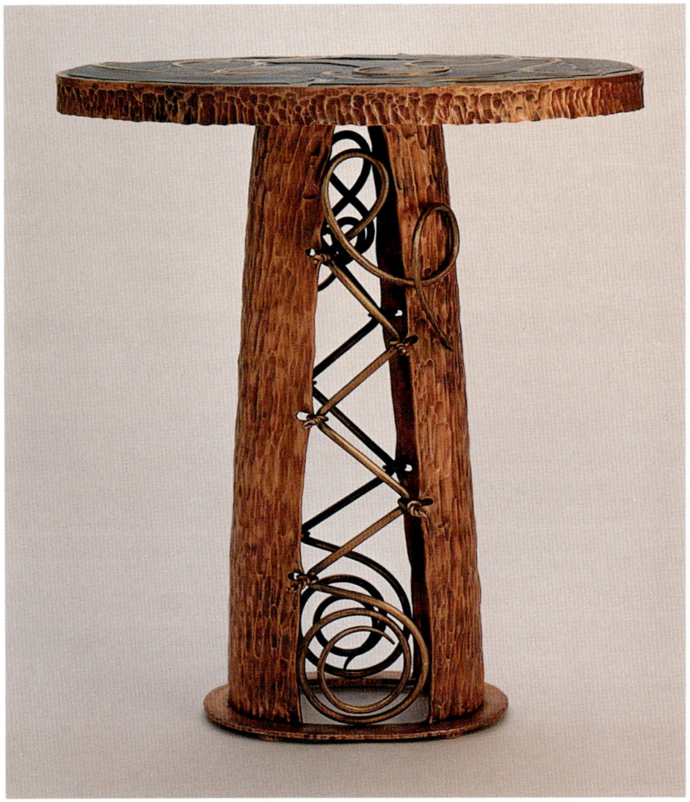

Michael Bendele. Table. Copper, silicon bronze, and stoneware. Stoneware by Mark Nafziger. 28" high, 24" wide, 17" deep. *Photo, Jim King*

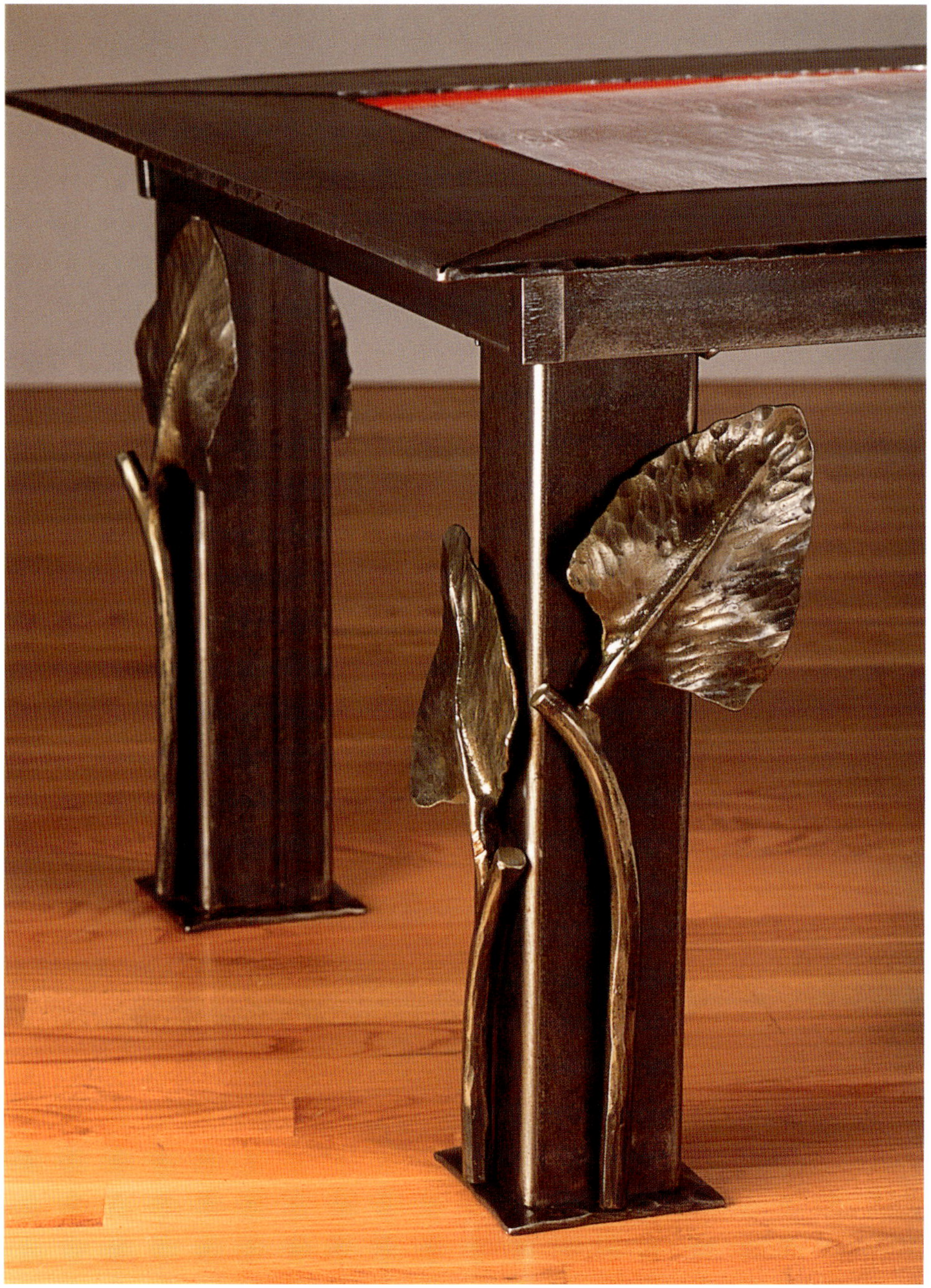

Susan Madacsi. *Table.* (Detail.) Steel, glass, and leather. 16" high, 62" wide, 30" deep. *Photo, R. J. Phil*

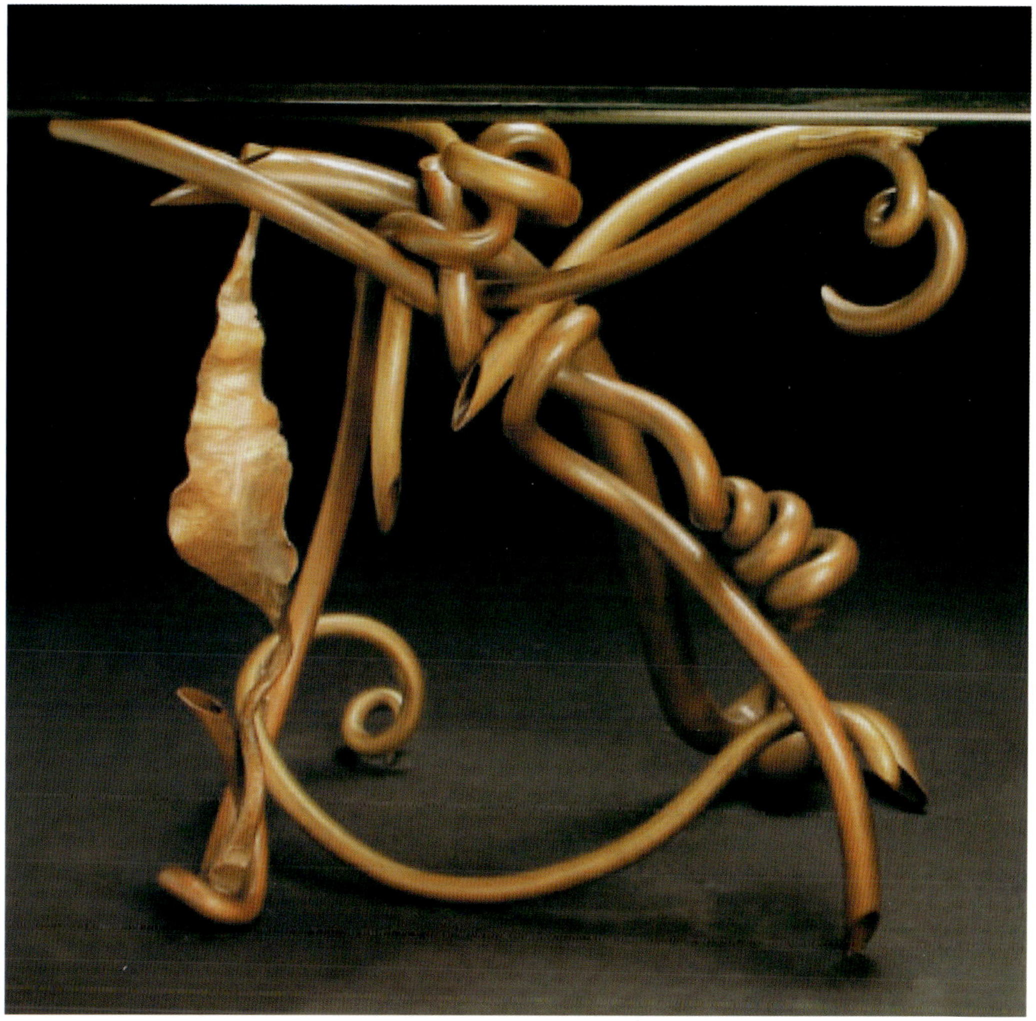

Jack Brubaker. *Gilt End Table*. Hot bent pipe and forged shapes assembled and finished with gilt metallic powders. The pipe is filled with sand, then heated and bent. While hot, one end is clamped in a vise and the other is walked around the vise to create the twisted pipe. Each pipe is bent into flowing shapes, and then cut into nicely shaped parts. These parts are assembled using them as if they were "found parts" rather than starting with a design and trying to bend the parts to preconceived shapes. *Photo, Dylan Long*

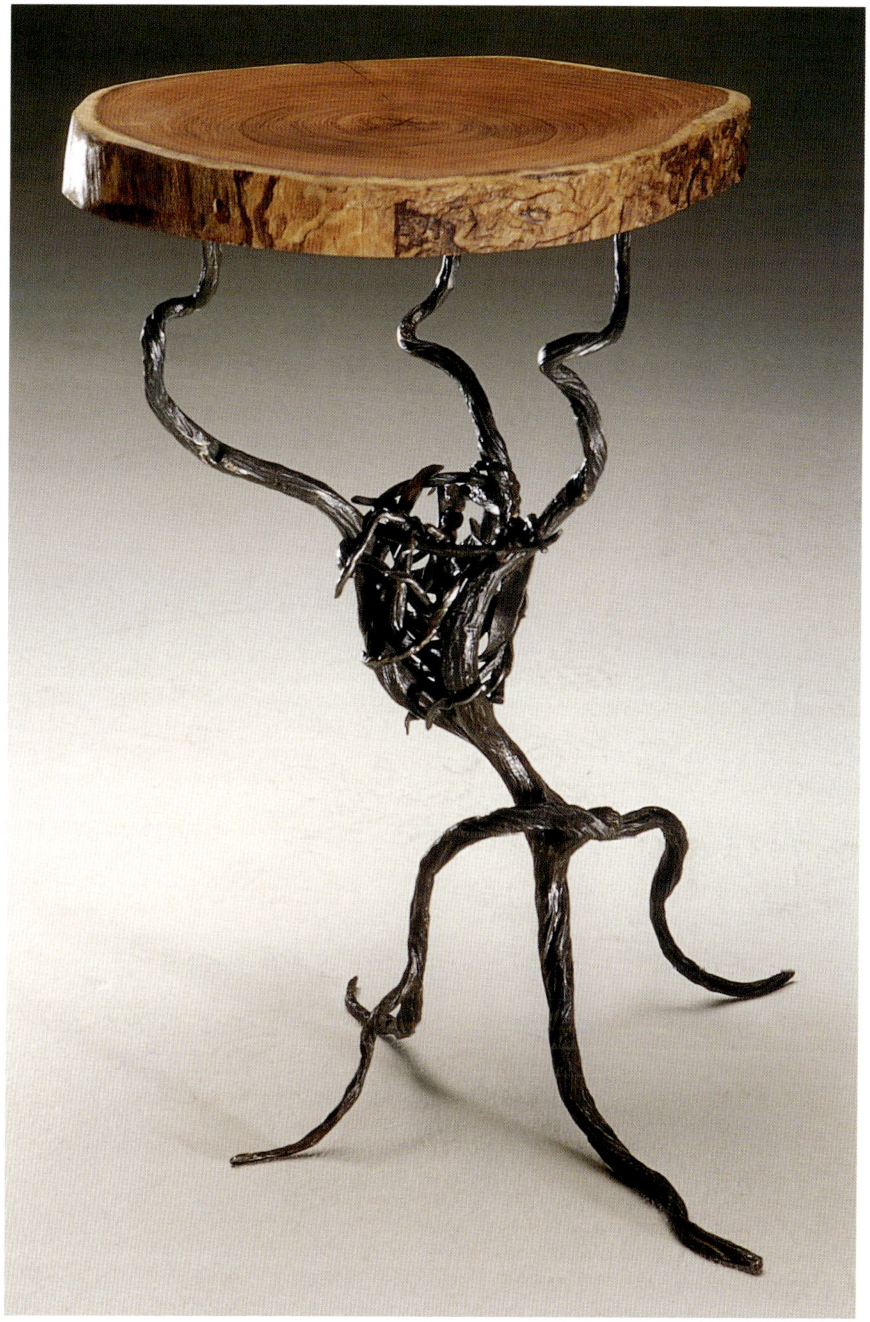

Ira Wiesenfeld. *End table*. Iron with mesquite and ash. 27" high, top varies from 13" to 17" wide and 2" thick. *Photo, Balfour Walker*

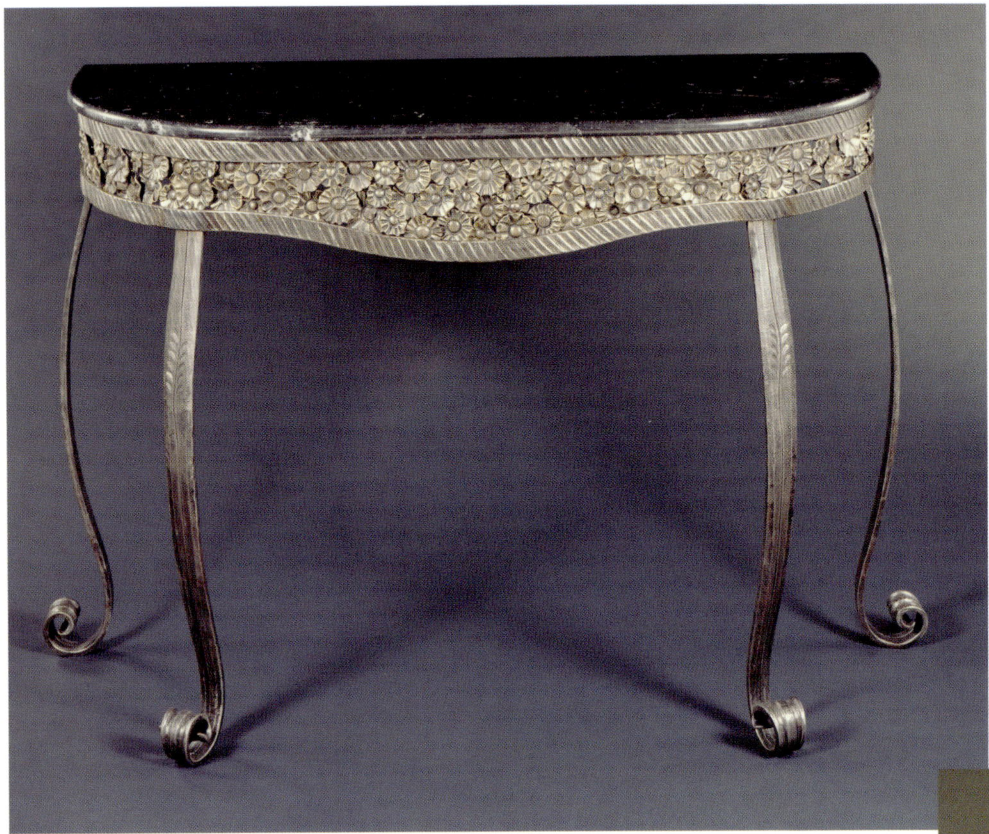

Jeff Fetty. *Console Table.* Forged steel with marble top. 30" high, 36" wide, 16" deep. *Photo. Artist*

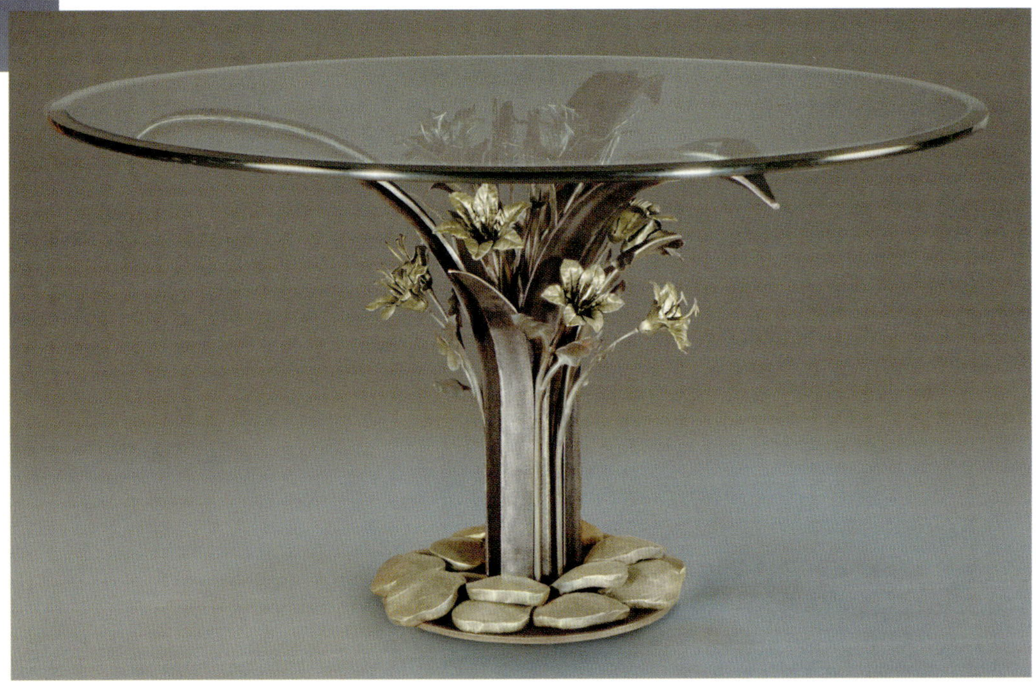

Jeff Fetty. *Lily Table.* Forged steel with glass top. 30" glass top. 30" high, 53" diam. *Photo, artist*

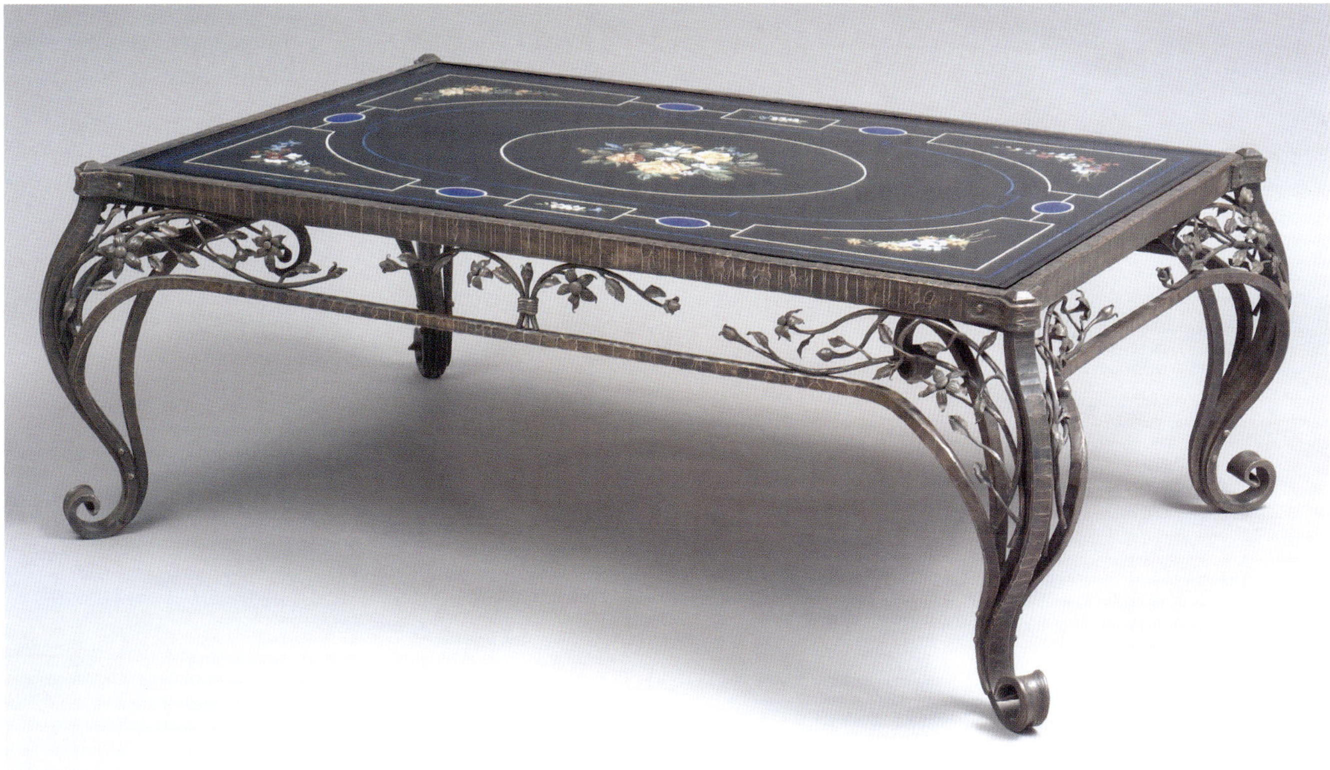

Robert Gardner and Eric Velleca. Bronze table base with hand forged leaves, buds and flowers. The mosaic marble top is by Tacconi Mauro of Florence, Italy. 18" high, 50" long, 34" wide. *Photo, Ken Nelson*

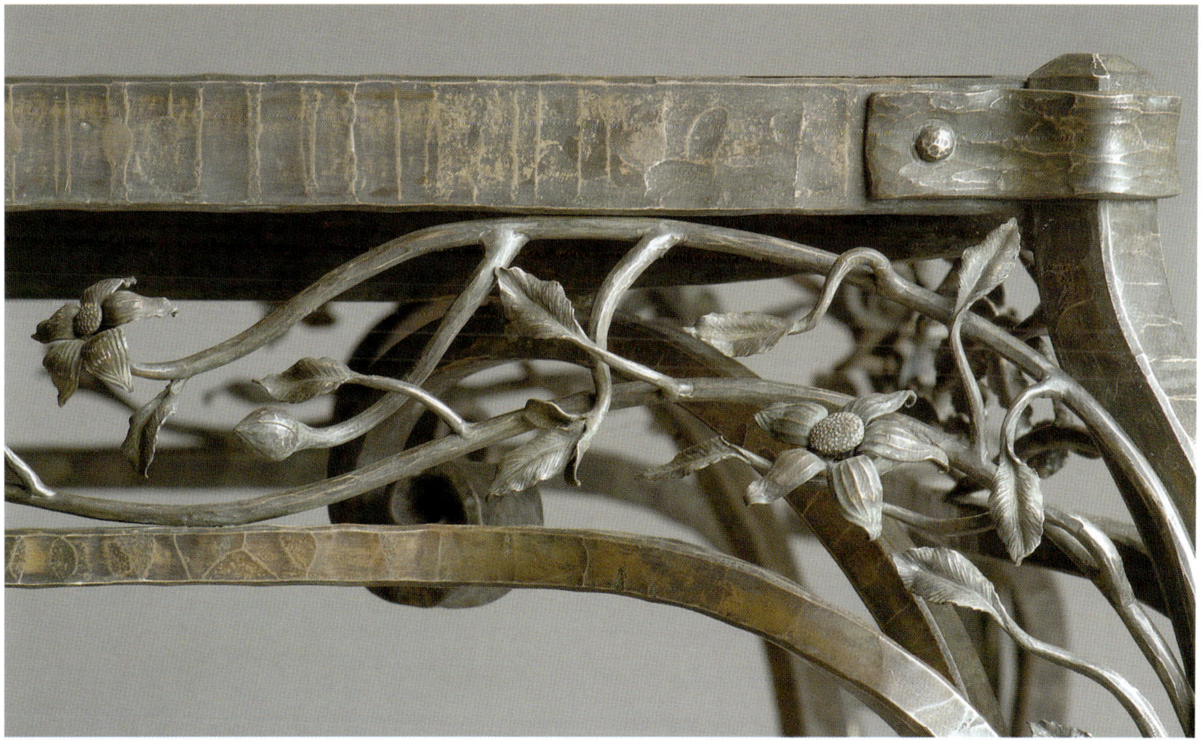

Robert Gardner and Eric Velleca. Detail of table showing the hand forged leaves, buds, tendrils, and vines assembled by TIG welding. *Photo, Ken Nelson*

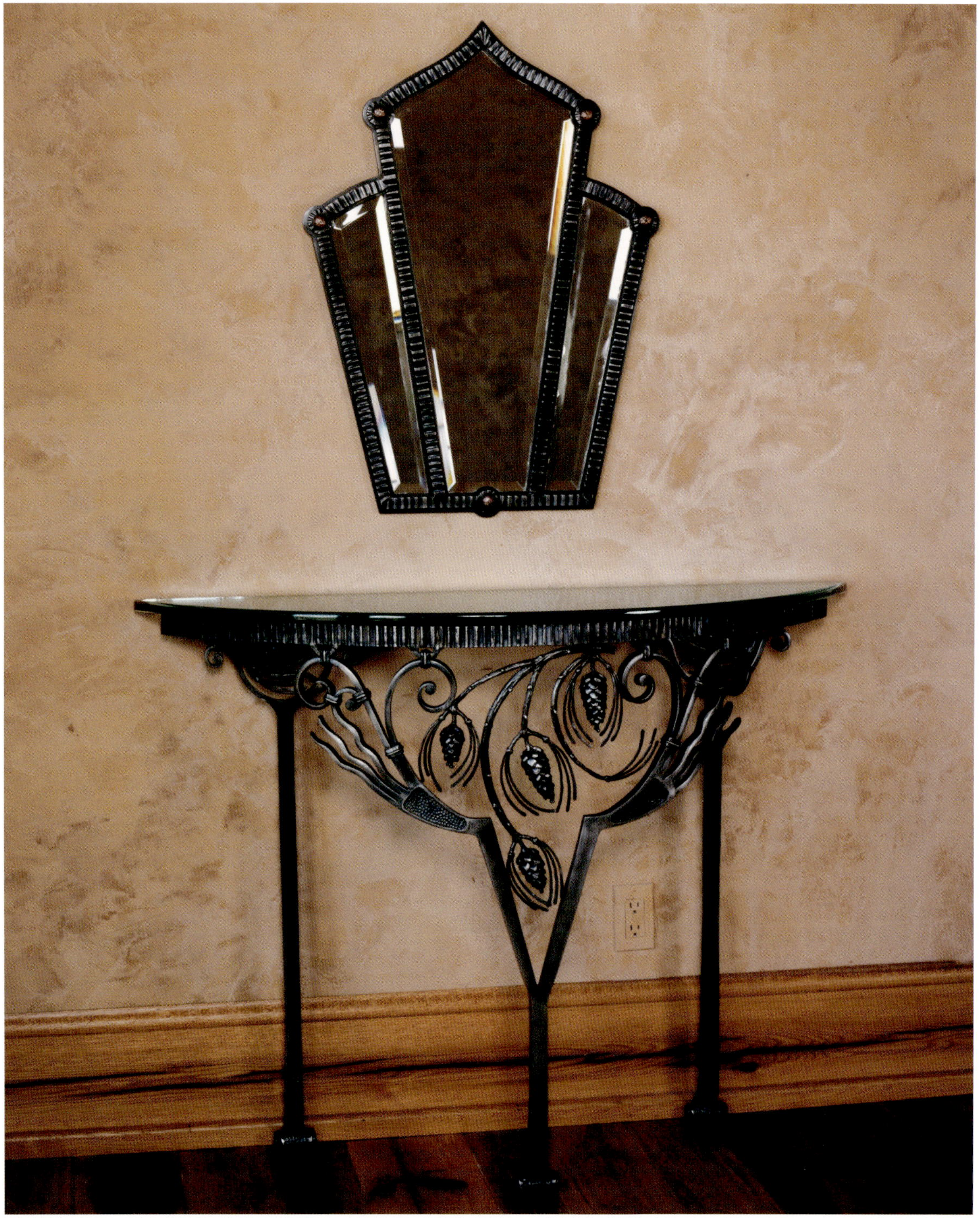

Hugh Culley. *Pine Console Table and Mirror*. Forged and fabricated steel and glass. Table 36" high, 13" deep, 46" wide. Mirror, 31" high, 23" wide. *Photo, Richard Prehn*

Hugh Culley writes: "I wanted this piece to be a unique shape by creating a curved and split front leg, and having three legs for support. I have worked on developing my own style of pinecones for about two years, and thought about incorporating them into a table even longer. I didn't try to create an Art Déco feel to the table but it evolved that way. The mirror, with copper accent buttons, was completed after the table. The two pieces complement one another in a grouping, yet each piece retains enough personality and strength to stand alone."

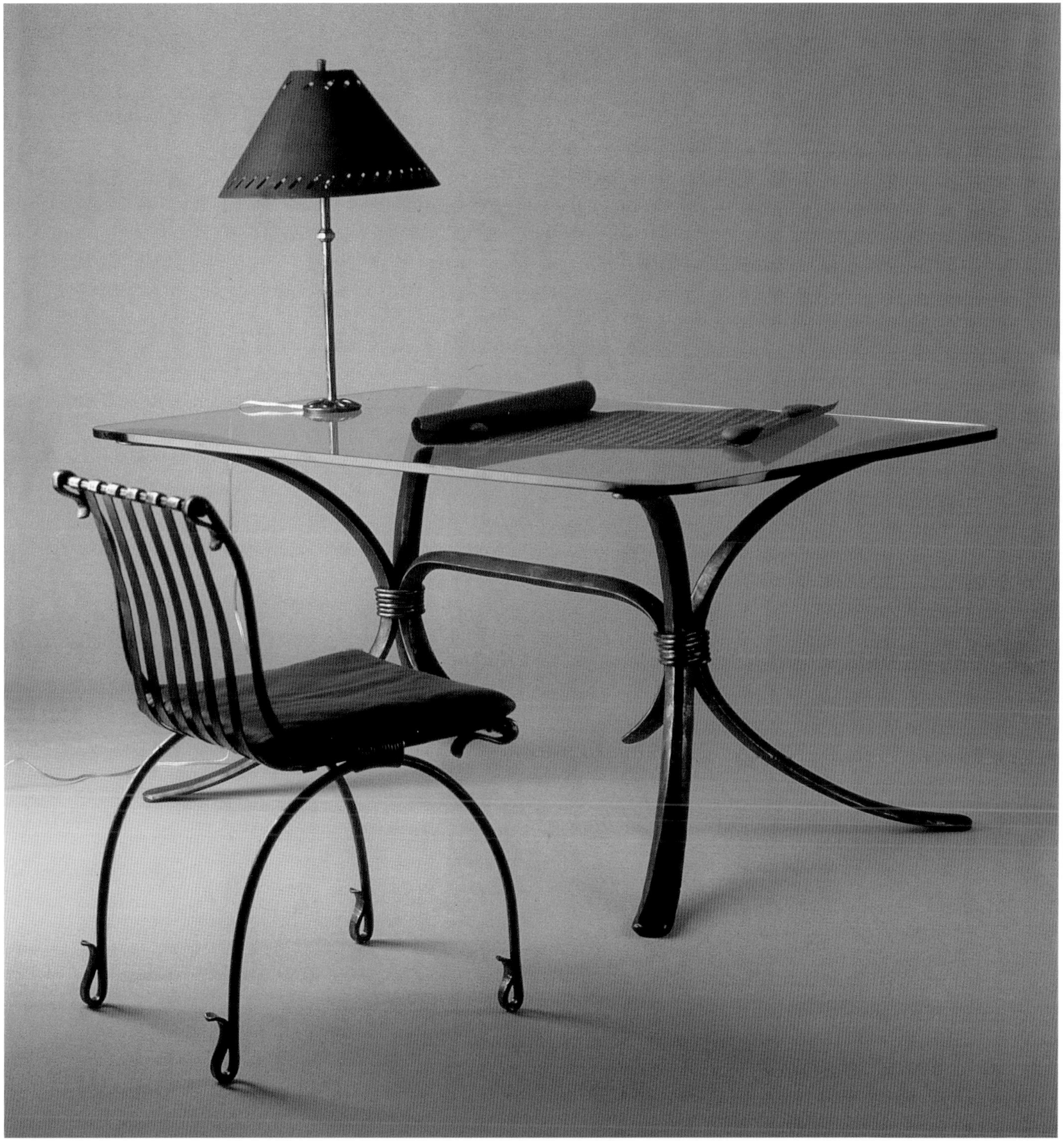

Christopher Thomson. *Office suite*. The glass-topped desk has an ironwork base. Ironwork chair and an Etruscan style desk lamp with a rust steel shade. *Photo, David Marlow*

Seating

Stools,benches, and chairs all have histories unique to their styles and times. Probably the earliest known seating, other than rocks, is the Egyptian folding stool that drew many variations on the simple structure. Benches are an extension of the stool. Next came the chair. In ancient times, it was probably the throne or the paladin that had the required elements, a seat, a back, and legs.

Since then, there have been Parsons chairs, Windsor chairs, Adirondack chairs, confession chairs, and rocking chairs—all made of wood. Somewhere along the historical line, someone made a chair of iron, and today iron chairs are ubiquitous for both indoor and outdoor use. Shown are only a few of the innovative bench and chair styles artist-blacksmiths are creating.

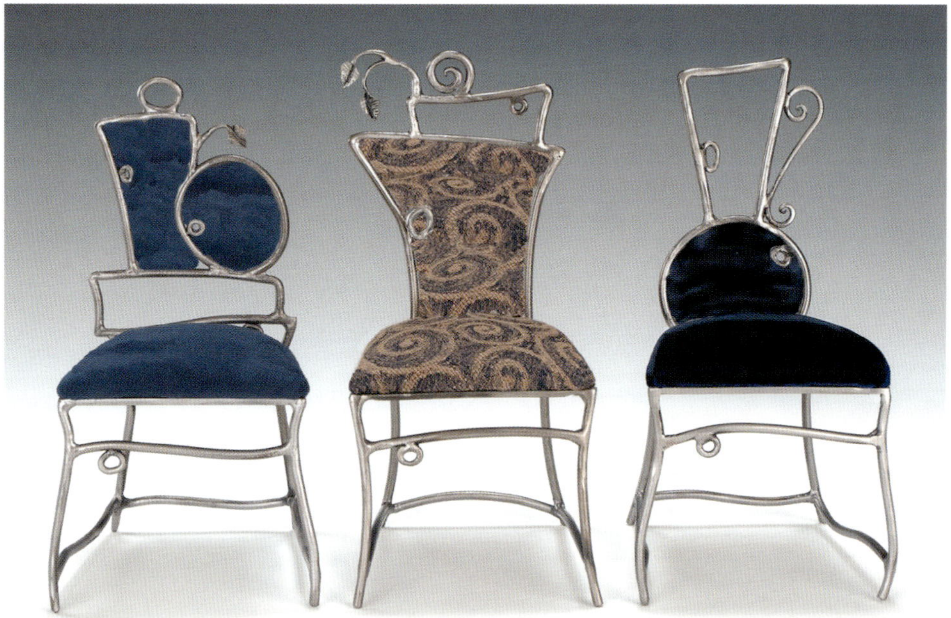

Lisa Jacobs. *Madhatter Chairs.* Fluid lines, interesting textures, with the joinery obvious and incorporated as a design element. *Photo, David Winterhaulter*

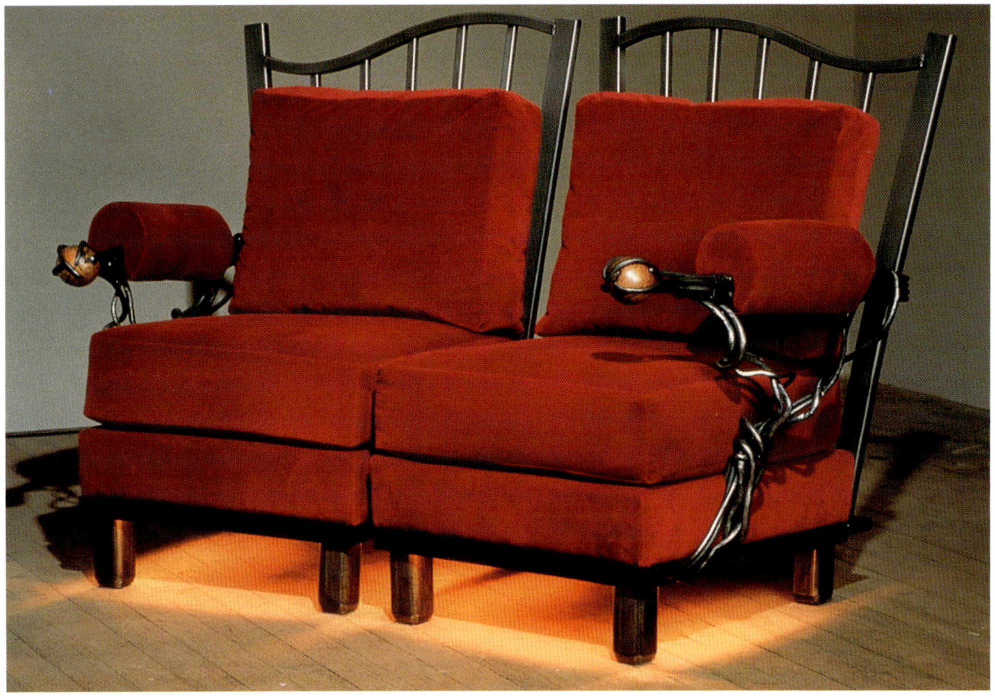

Stephen Marks. *Love Seat*. Steel, copper, and velvet with accent lights beneath the seat. 43" high, 64" wide, 32" deep. *Photo, William P. Wright*

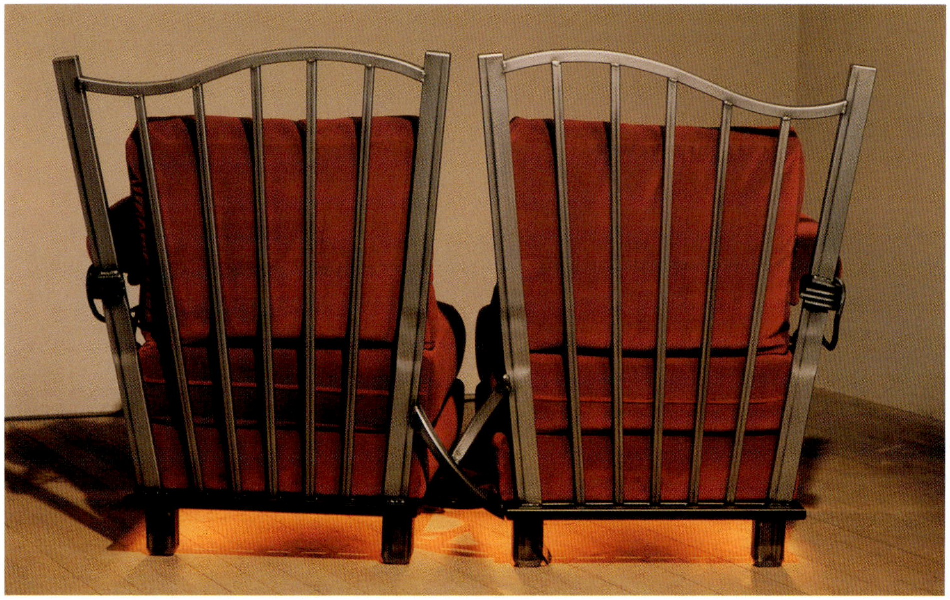

Stephen Marks. Back view of Love Seat.

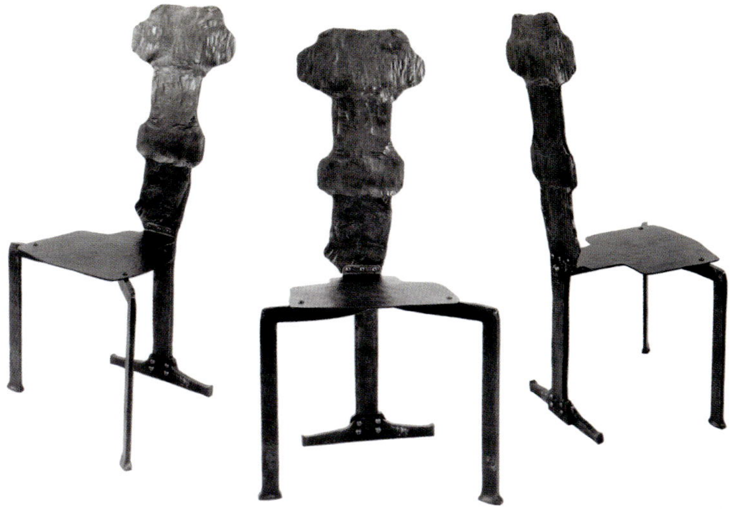

Frederic A. Crist and David W. Munn. Kirili Chair (3 views). Forged steel. 42" high, 20" wide, 16" deep.

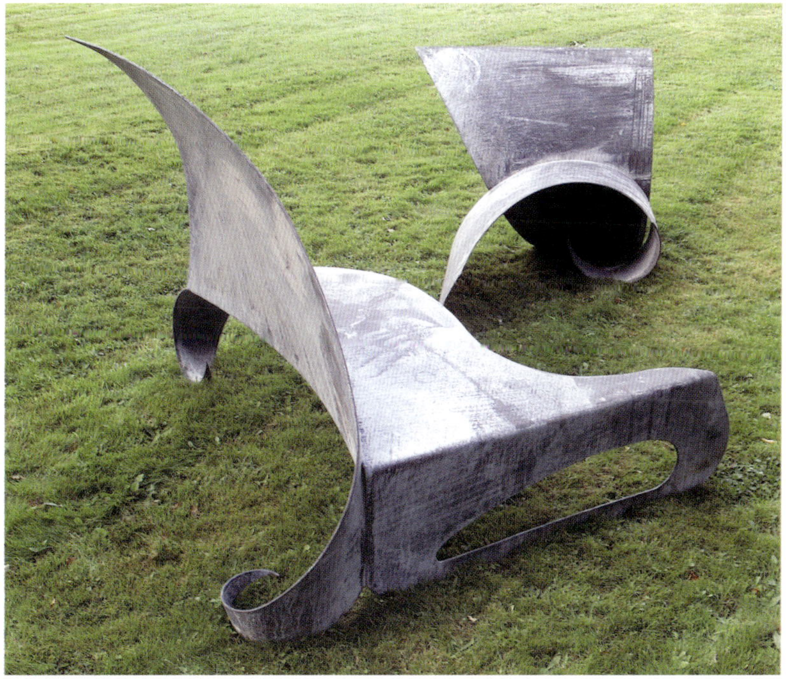

Paul Elliott. *Curly benches*. Mild steel acid etched. 48" high, 69" wide. *Photo, Jackie Phillips*

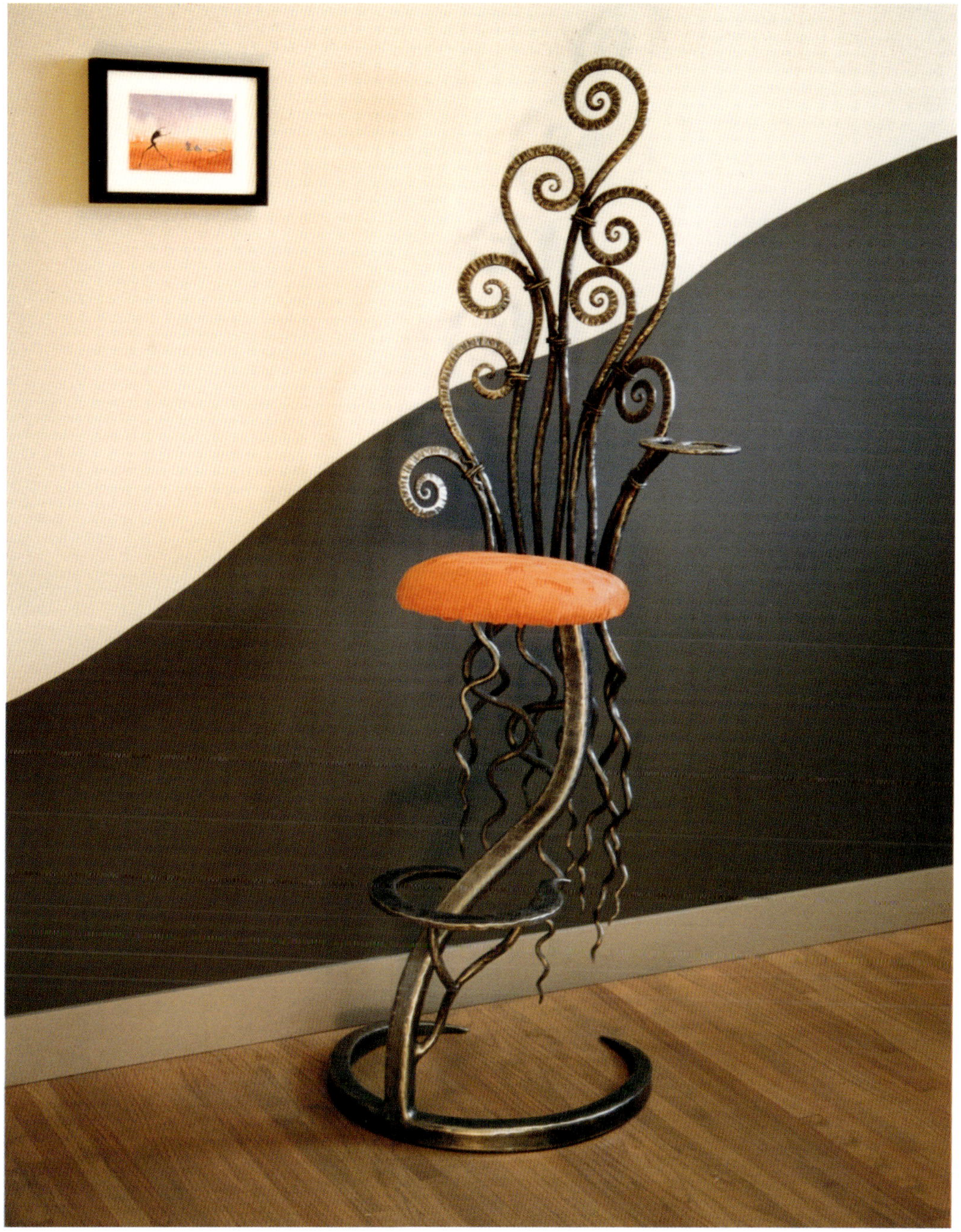

John Monteath and Brenda Field. Chair. Forged and fabricated mild steel, wax finished. 63" high, 23" wide, 18" deep. *Photo, artists*

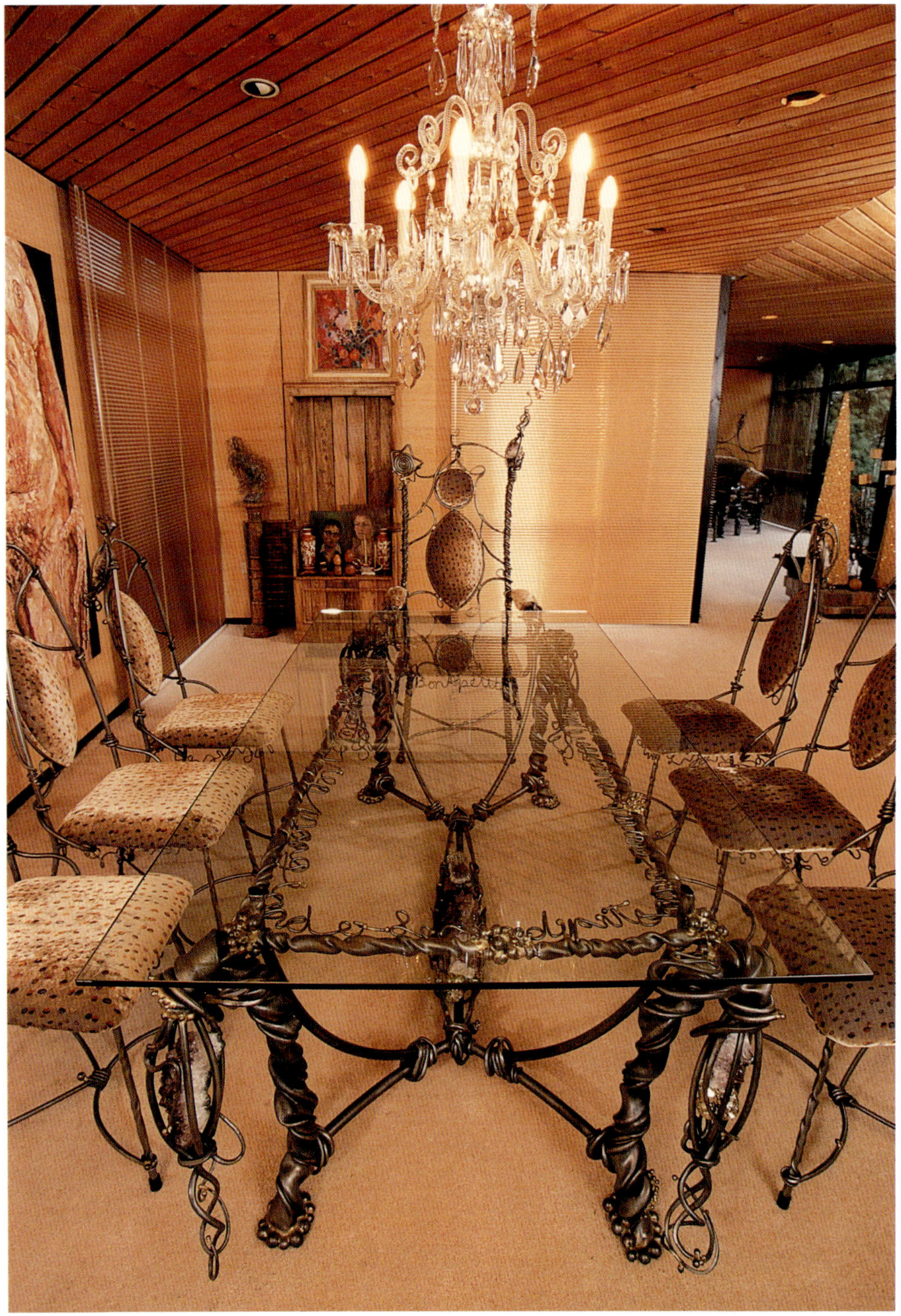

Shelley Thomas. Dining room set. Iron with upholstered seats. The sculpture table base shows beautifully through the glass tabletop. *Photo, Ian Macaulay*

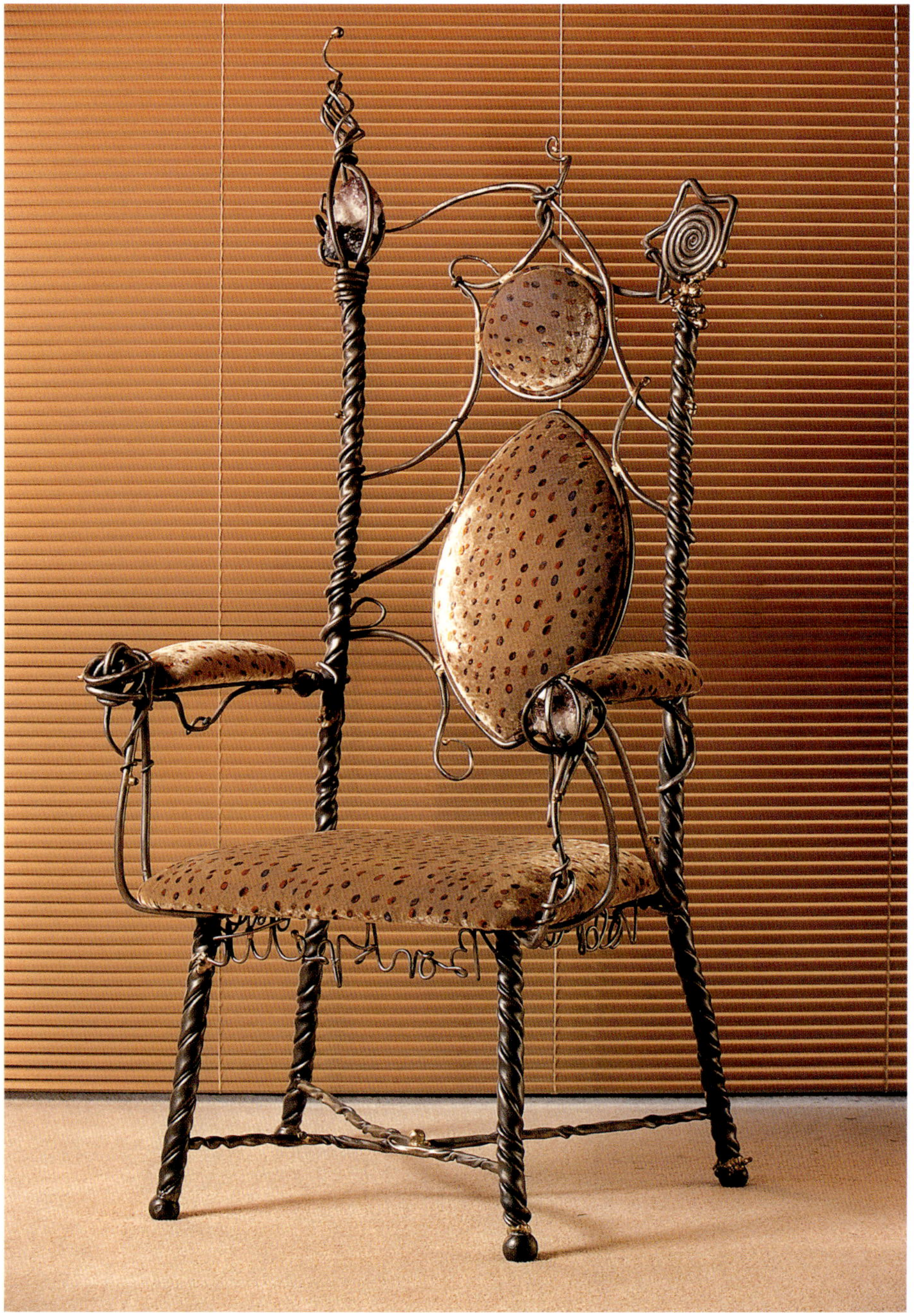

Shelley Thomas. Host Chair. Forged and fabricated steel with copper accents and velvet upholstery. *Photo, Ian Macaulay*

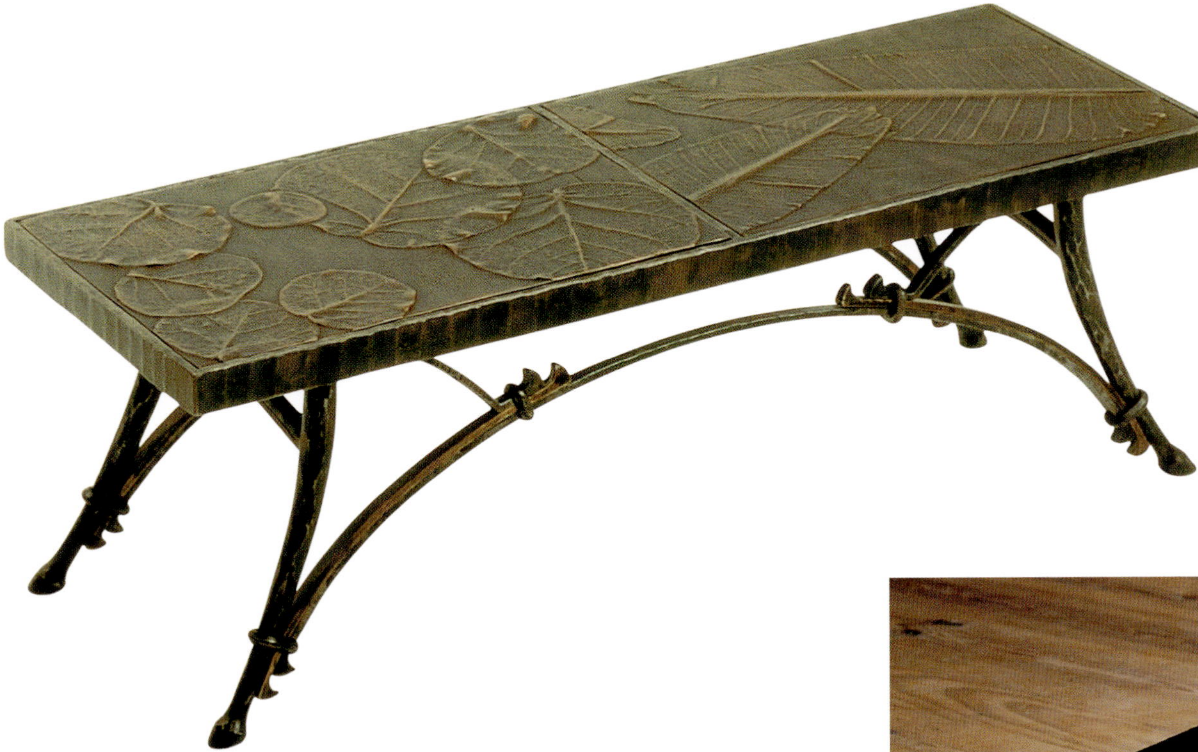

Tony Higdon and Erika Strecker. *Botanical Bench* (model). Forged steel, bronze, and cast bronze. *Photo, Leeann Greer*

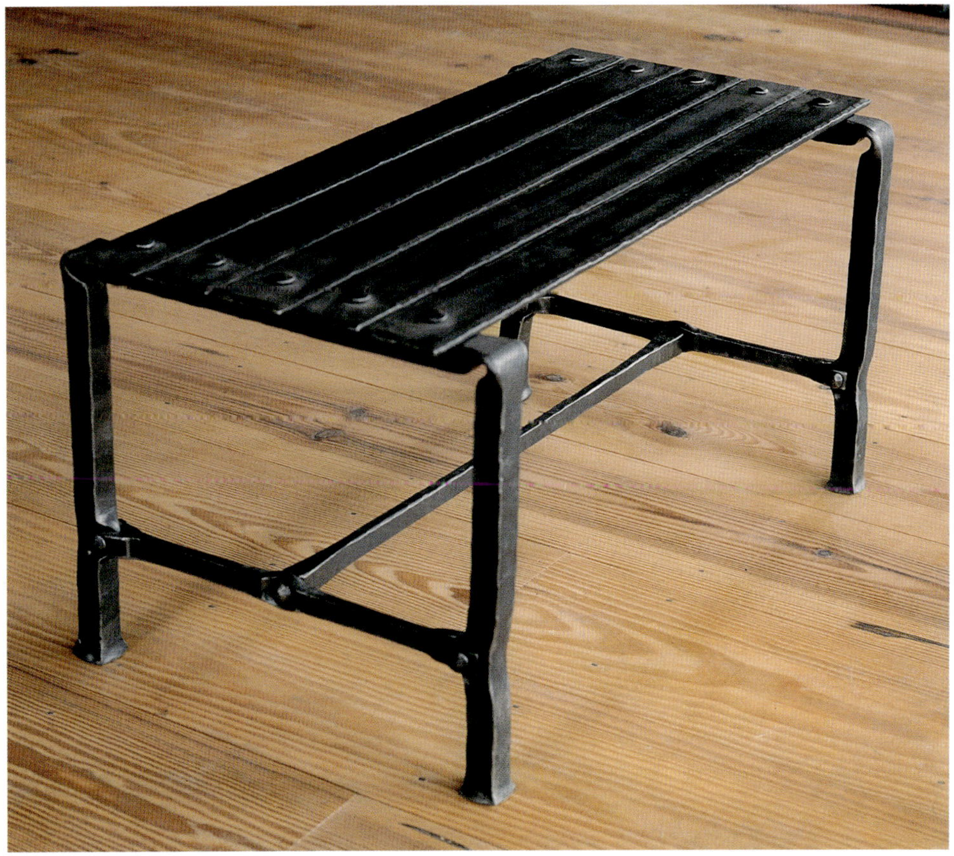

Morris L. Hallowell IV. Bench. Each of the pairs of legs is one continuous piece of steel, with upset feet. Five stretchers that make up the seat, are riveted to pinched flanges on the sides of the legs. 19" high, 38" wide, 20" deep. *Photo, artist*

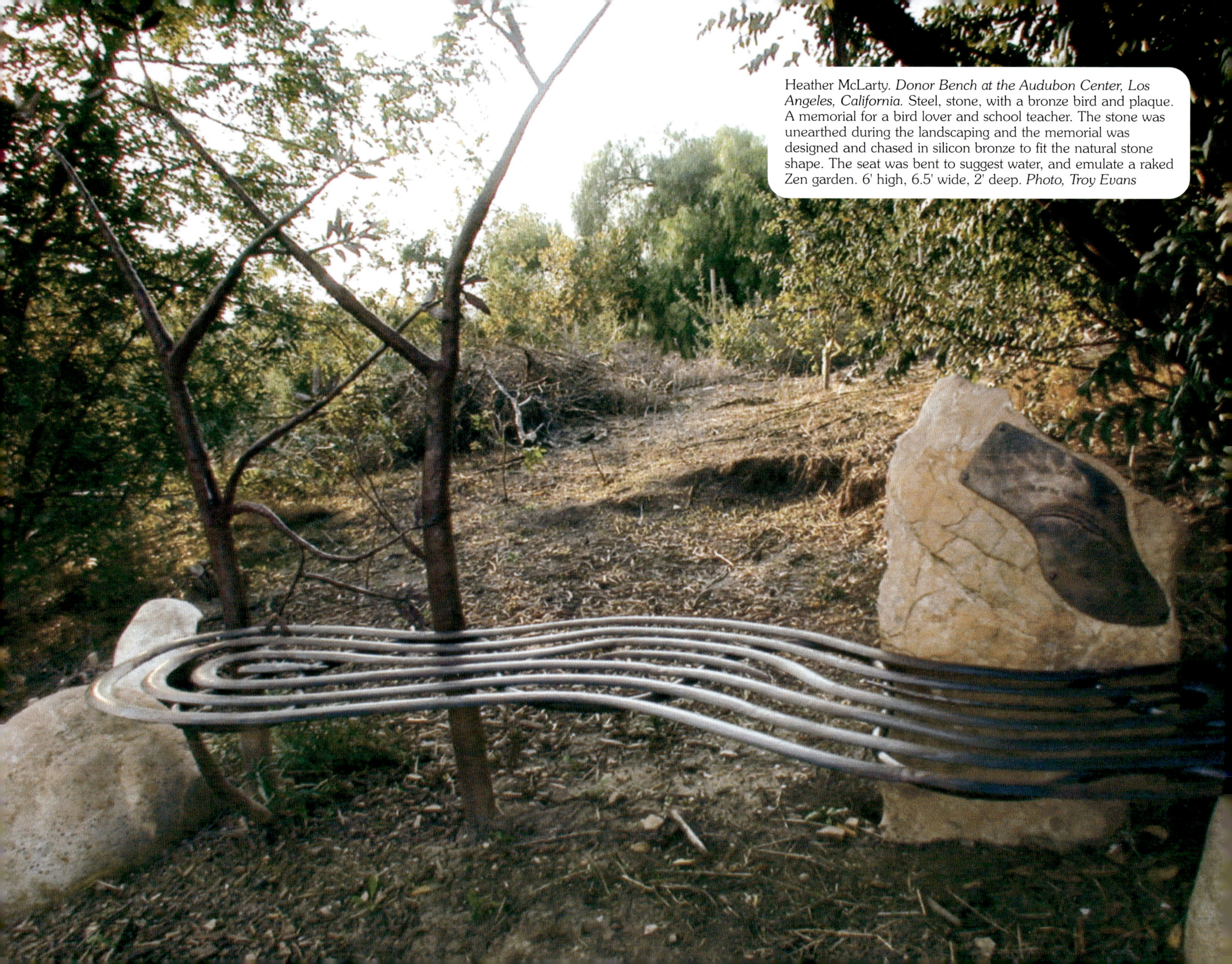

Heather McLarty. *Donor Bench at the Audubon Center, Los Angeles, California.* Steel, stone, with a bronze bird and plaque. A memorial for a bird lover and school teacher. The stone was unearthed during the landscaping and the memorial was designed and chased in silicon bronze to fit the natural stone shape. The seat was bent to suggest water, and emulate a raked Zen garden. 6' high, 6.5' wide, 2' deep. *Photo, Troy Evans*

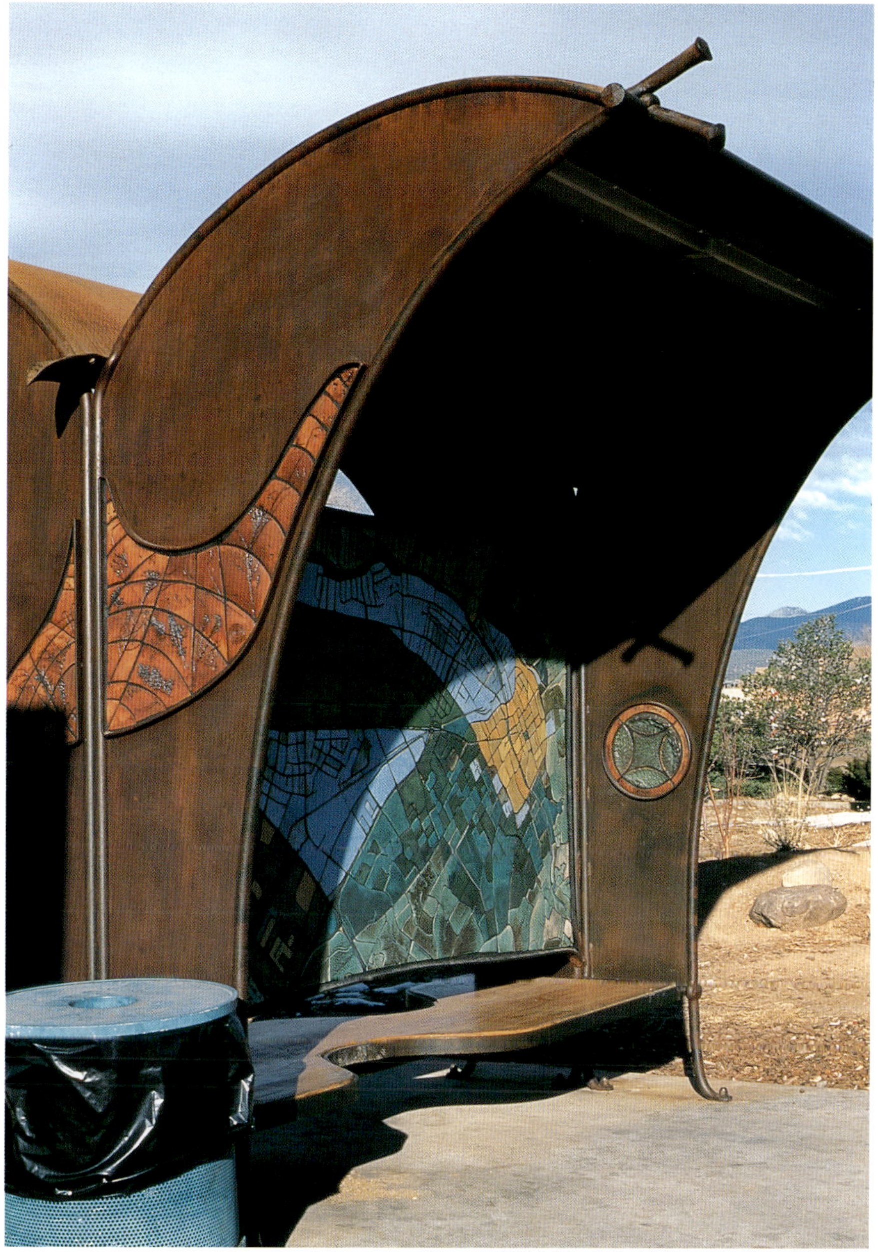

Helmut Hillenkamp. Tile work by Christy Hengst and Adam Frank. *Rail Yard Bus Stop Bench*. Iron, wood, and ceramics. The bench was part of a city development project that turned an old rail yard into studios, offices, performance spaces, etc. S-shape of the bench accommodates handicapped accessibility. Wood is a 2" solid maple butcher block. The main mosaic is a tile map of Santa Fe, New Mexico that is very precise but without words. Streets are the grout lines. *Photo, Helmet Hillenkamp*

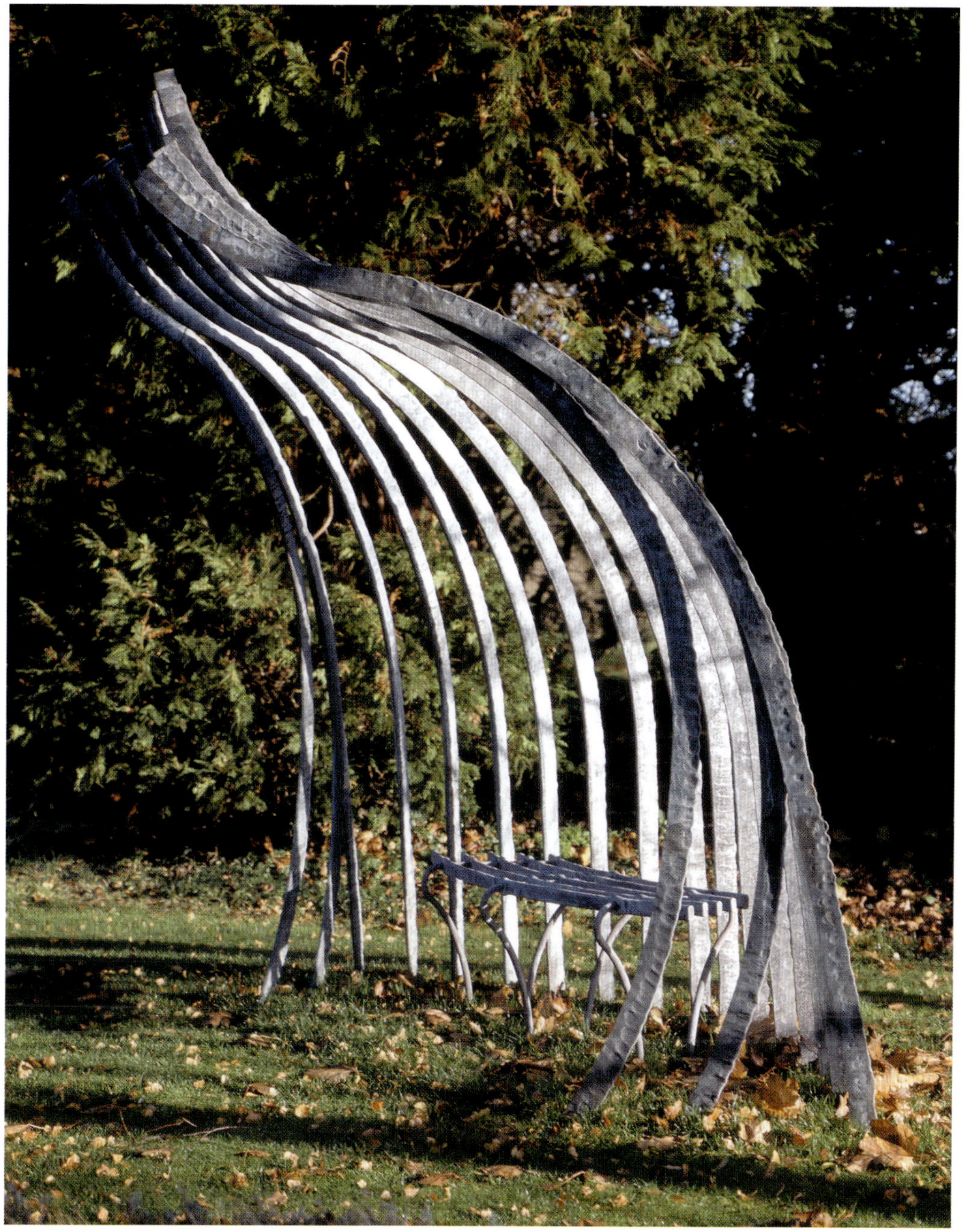

Paul Elliott. *Garden Onion Seat*. Heavy textured mild steel, with a galvanized and acid etched finish. The arbor seat was commissioned by a husband for his wife for their Ruby Wedding Anniversary. The cozy onion seat reflects their passion for vegetable gardening and for each other. 10.5' high, 3.4' wide. *Photo, Jackie Phillips*

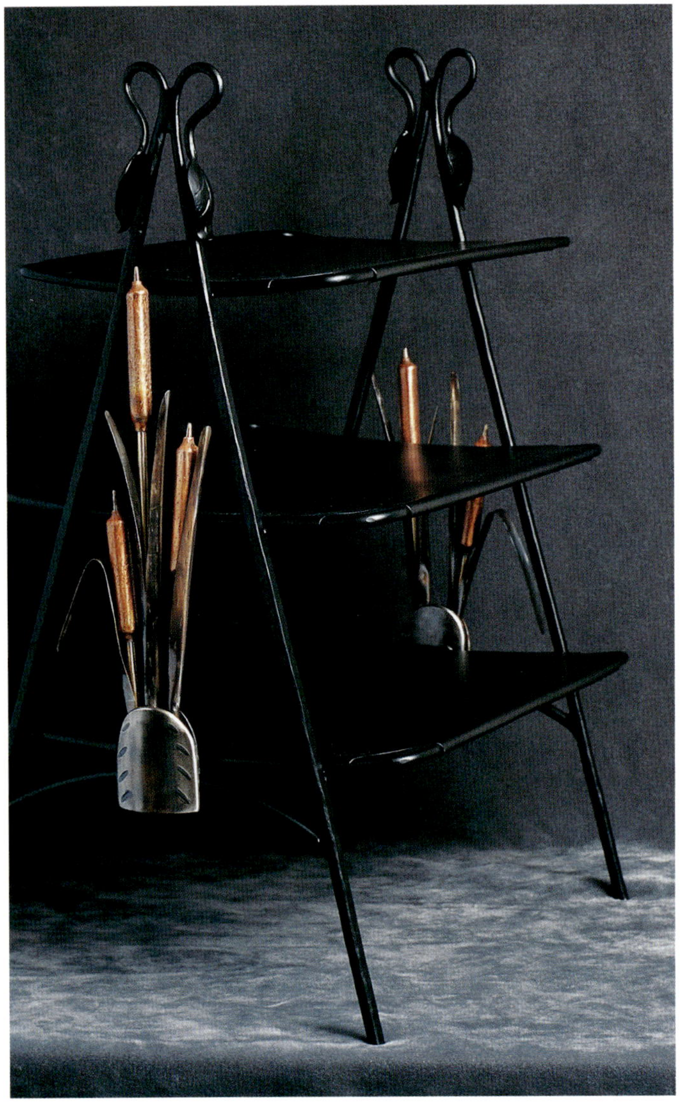

Keith A. Leavitt. Magazine Rack with Cattail Motif. The three-shelves are 16-gauge mild steel with 3/8" frame legs. The top has forged and incised leaf handles. Cattail pods are heat-patinated copper with brass stems and stainless steel fronds and medallions. 24" high, 17" wide, 15" deep. *Photo, Steven Dunn*

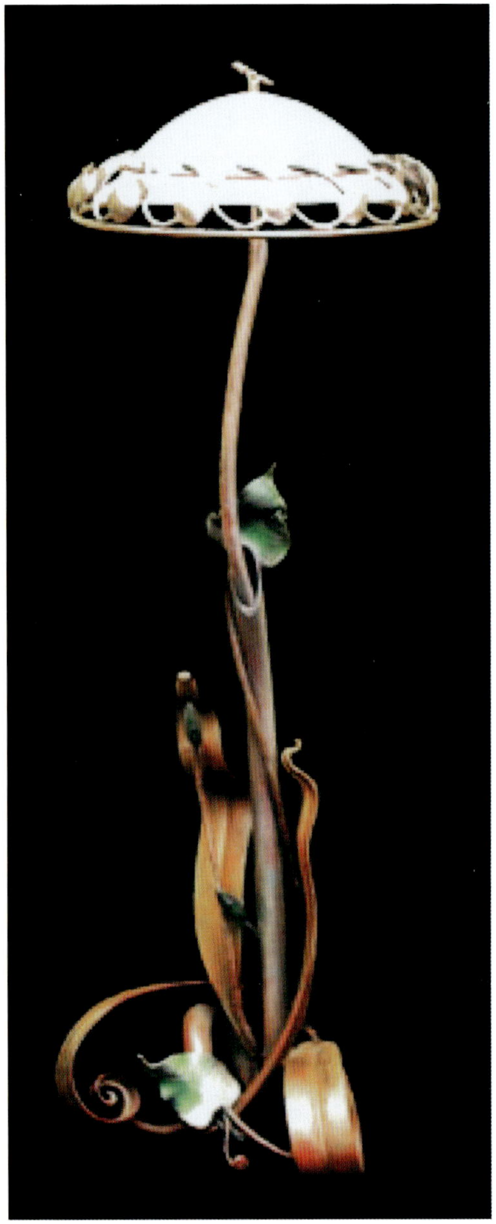

Jack Brubaker. *Brown Floor Lamp*. Iron with painted finish and glass shade. Hot bent pipe, angle iron leaves, forged leaves and seed pods. Spray painted by partially depressing the spray button so paint sputters in a fine mist that lets different colors overlap in a speckled pointillist manner. *Photo, artist*

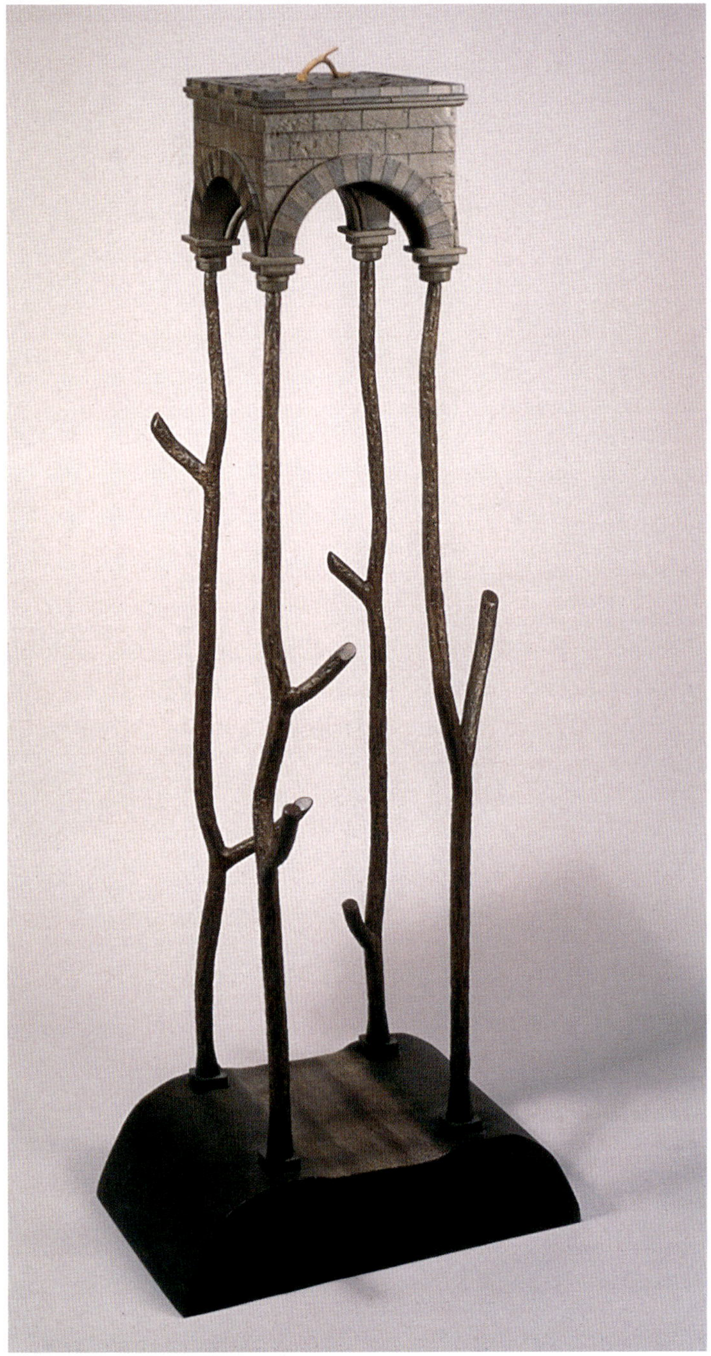

Eric Cuper. *Mississippi Flood Plain Reliquary*. Forged and fabricated steel. 50" high, 15" wide, 12" deep. *Photo, Jeffrey Bruce*

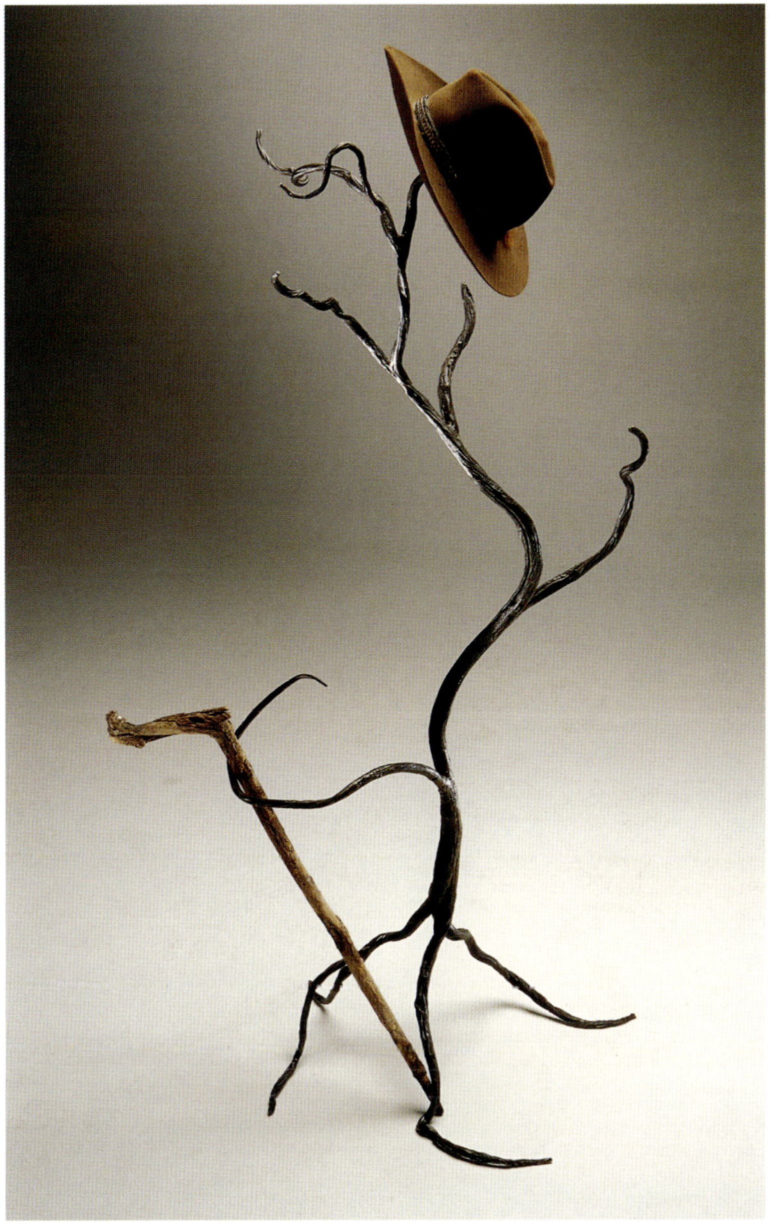

Ira Wiesenfeld. *Hall Tree*. Steel textured with a power hammer and finished with a sanded black oxide patina. Inspiration is the mesquite wood branches found in the Arizona desert where he lives; he dubs them "Ironwood". 68" high, 28" wide, 20" deep. *Photo, Balfour Walker*

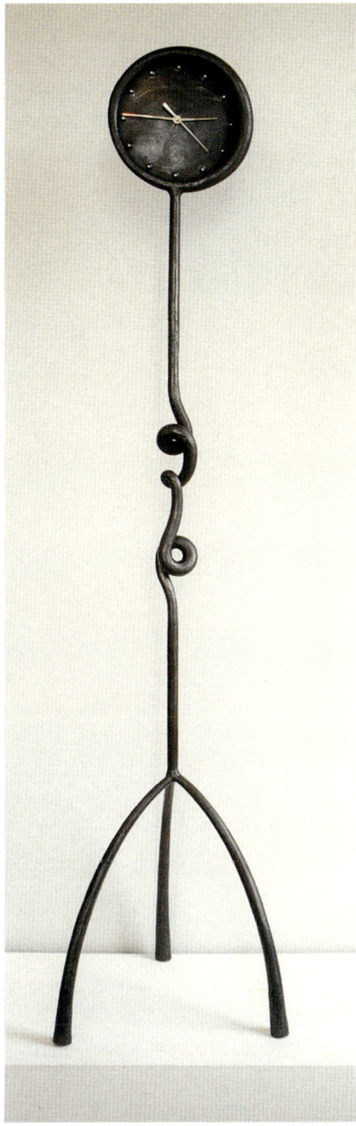

John Little. *Grandfather's Clock*. 52" high. *Photo, Gary Castle*

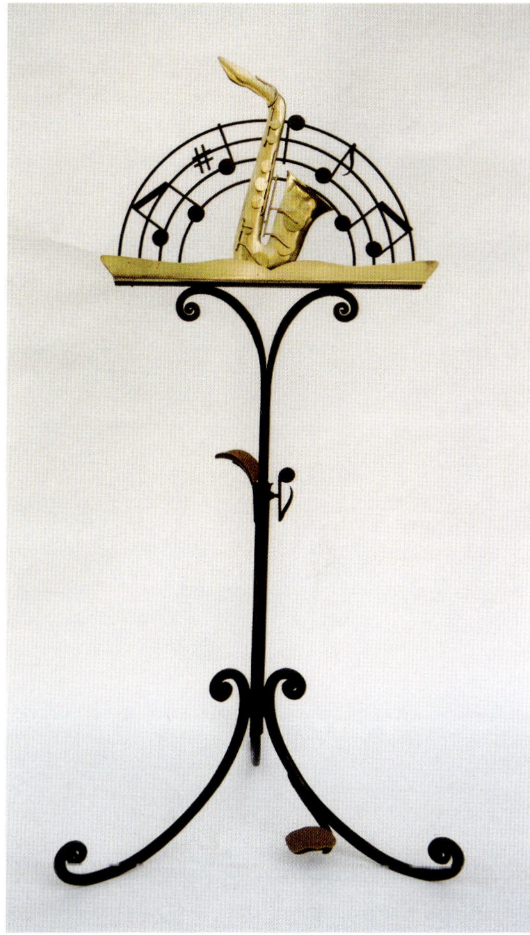

Peter Fishbein. *Music Stand for a Saxophonist*. Wrought steel and brass. When the instrument is not being played it rests on the leather-covered base and at a center holder. The "note" in the middle is the handle of a locking screw for adjusting the stand's height. *Photo, artist*

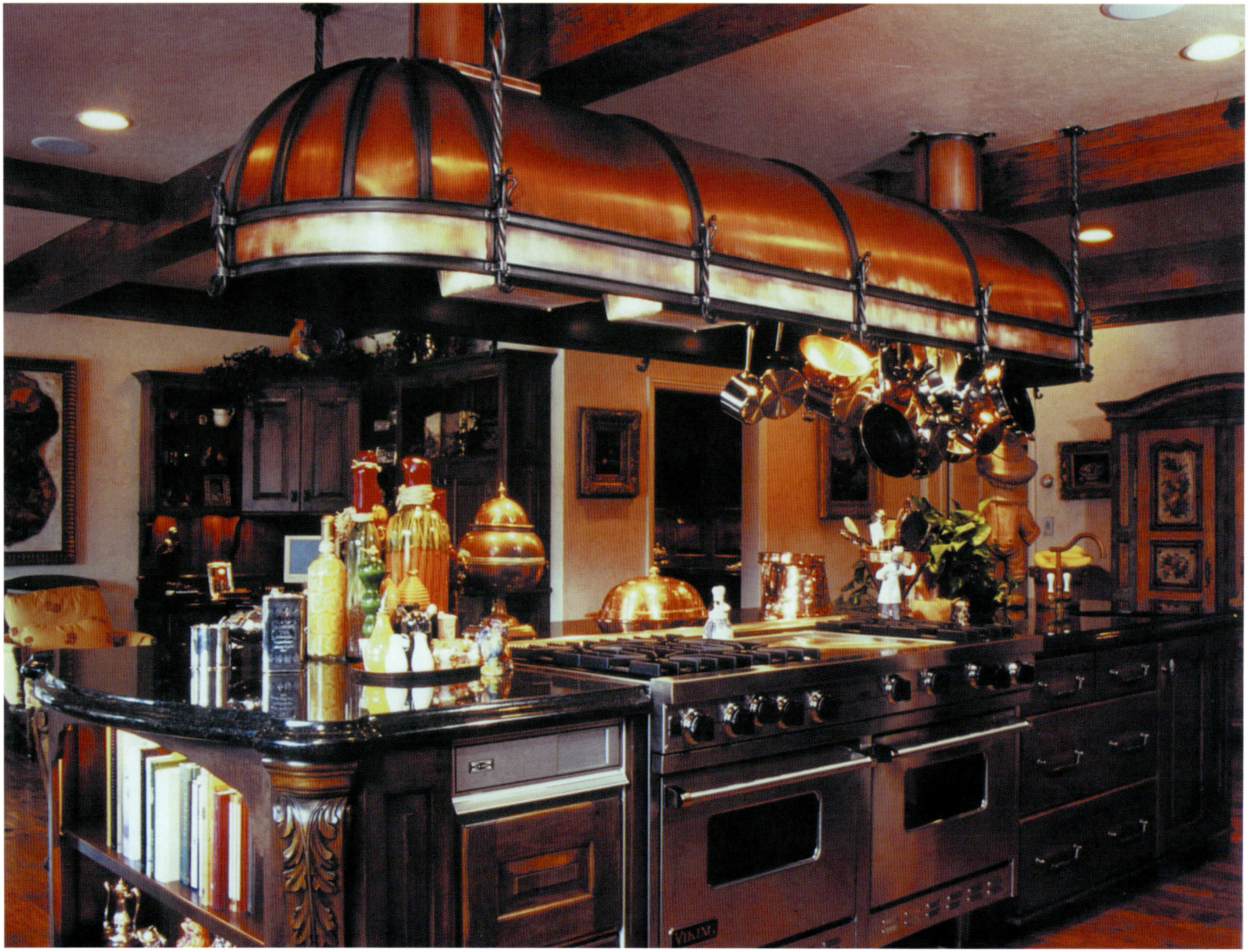

Wiemann Ironworks. *Pot Rack* in a private home in Wichita, Kansas. Copper and iron. The exposed iron is patinated and clear coated; the copper is stained, grained, patinated and clear coated. The inside is painted and has a pot rack with forged hooks. 3' high, 10' long. *Photo, courtesy Wiemann Ironworks*

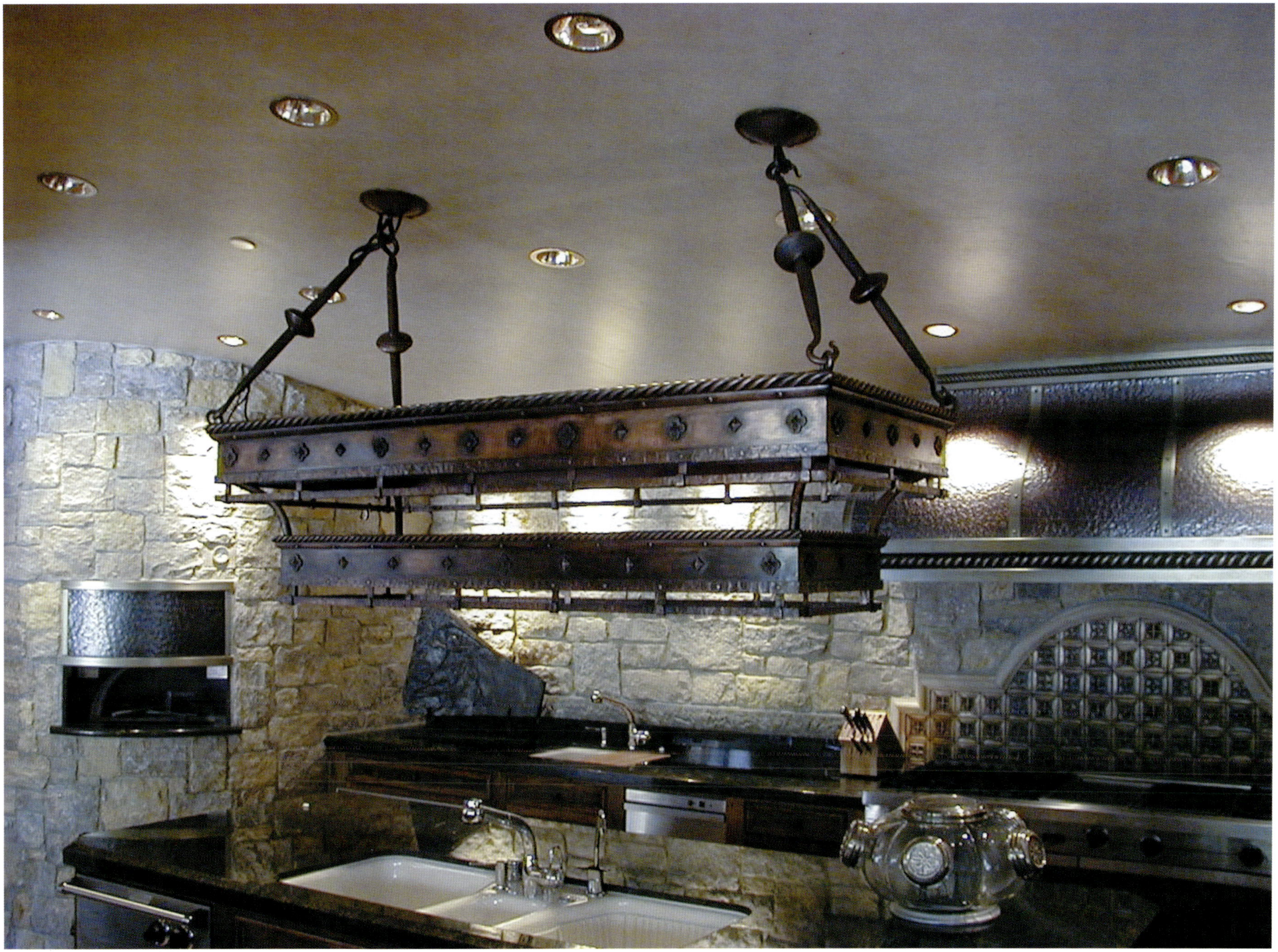

Greg Eng. *Pot Rack*. Mild steel with copper plating, a patina and colored wax finish. The only visible finished weld is at the corners where the rope design and half oval meet. 44" high, 72" long, 30" wide. *Photo, Brenda Eng.*

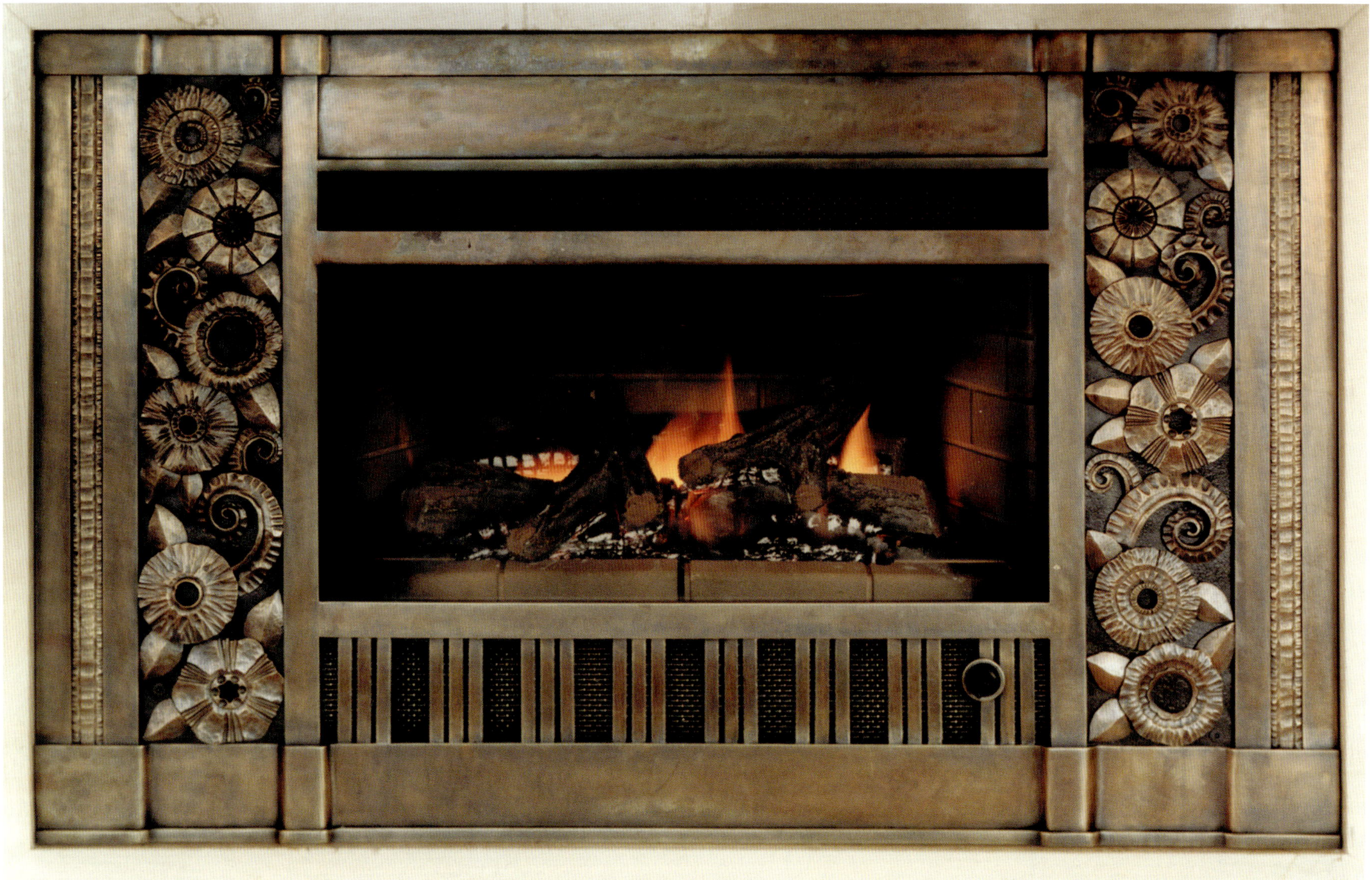

Maria Cristalli. Edward Brandt inspired fireplace surround. Steel brass plated with a patinated finish. *Photo, Todd Kalamar*

Chapter 7. Outfitting a Fireplace

A fireplace screen can represent much more than an object to cover a space and prevent embers from burning a rug. It can be a work of art just like a painting on a wall, a relief, or a three dimensional sculpture. People are recognizing the visual impact of a well-designed fireplace screen and tool set. They are thinking "art and utility" and commissioning screens that reflect their home's style and their special interests.

One can buy a ready-made mass produced screen at a home decorating store with traditional scrolls and bars, but they are ordinary. And the ordinary screen may not reflect the style of a house and its furnishings. Someone who builds a unique house, or furnishes a home in a specific style, needs fireplace accessories coordinated with the design elements.

Still others want the screen to capture their special interests. "Customized" is the norm for fireplaces by Glenn F. Gilmore who has risen to the demands, and fantasies, of clients who want their fireplace screen to represent their hobbies and life styles, from boating to mountain climbing, from sports to landscapes.

Keith Leavitt's client wanted a fireplace screen to "bring the outside in" for their lakeside home in central Maine. Leavitt chose different types of metals to achieve contrast and color differences. And he floated a duck on the water.

Rod Picket's peacock screen required research and materials beyond the ken of a blacksmith…a learn-as-you-need-it project. The commission requisite was for a screen that was light and airy, and did not block the fire. Picket had an idea of what the clients liked because he had worked with them before. His concept of the peacock's feathers spanning the opening was a brilliant solution. The peacock was laser cut and hammered into a three-dimensional sculptural form. Finding the right type of glass inserts was another research project.

Simulating the Arts & Crafts style of a historic home in San Diego required David Browne to use the geometry and textures that would echo early 1900s "craftsman" elements and still retain a customized, unique appearance.

You will find awesome examples of unusual one-of-a-kind screens and fire tools in this chapter. If you're a client the work will fire your imagination. If you're an artist-blacksmith you will have ideas to present to your clients and, possibly, another avenue for your talents and output.

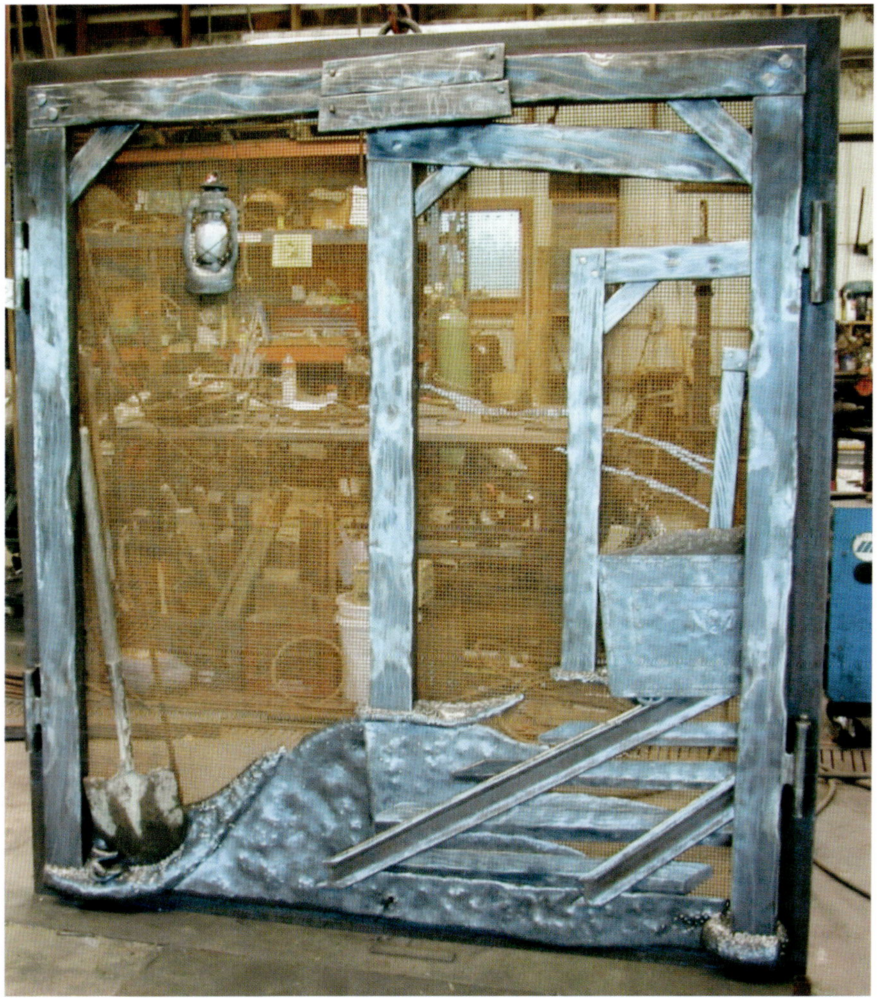

Kirk Sullens. Las Vegas fire door tells the story of early silver mines in Nevada and illustrates a mine entrance and other symbols. 6' high, 6' wide. Several narrative fire doors were created for the Bass Pro Shop Outdoor World chain of stores. *Photo, artist*

Kirk Sullens is a master at replicating animals from steel in scenes that are as carefully designed as a painter develops a landscape. His animals look incredibly realistic when he finishes wielding his hammers and chisels. Every hair on a fox's body and a bear's coat is chiseled in the metal. It's amazing to watch him work and see him raise a flat piece of metal to become the figure of a fox, a dog, a small rabbit, even a house and trees. He has created a series of scenic fireplaces and light fixtures for a chain of sporting goods stores…some are shown here along with the details.

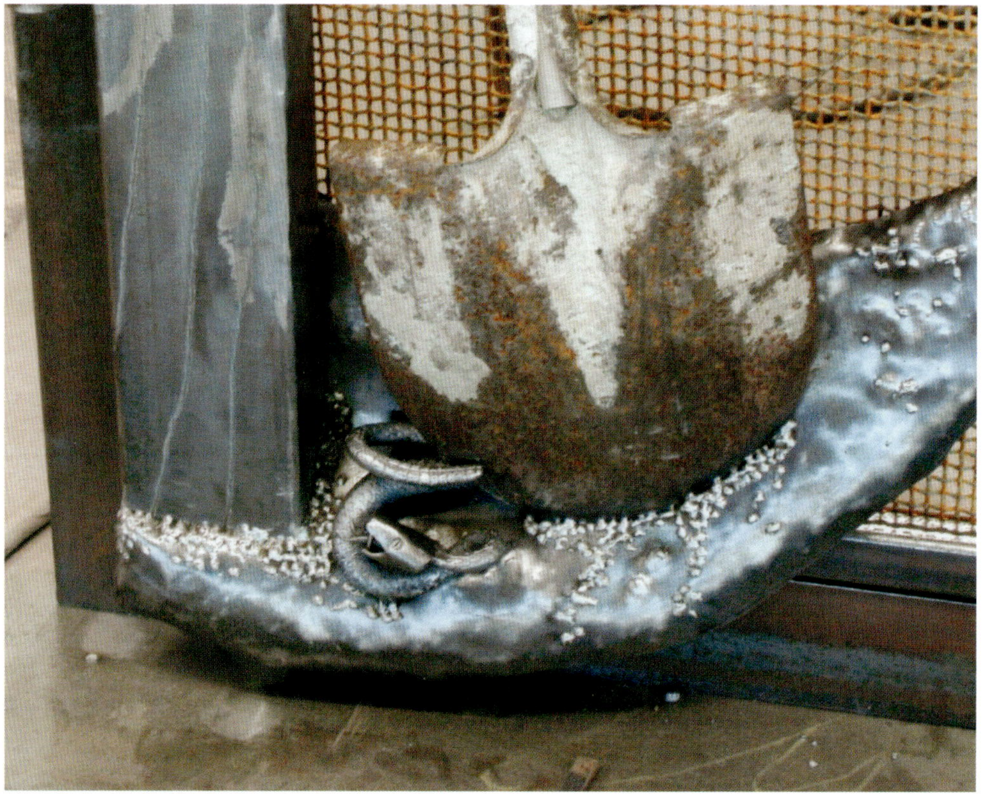

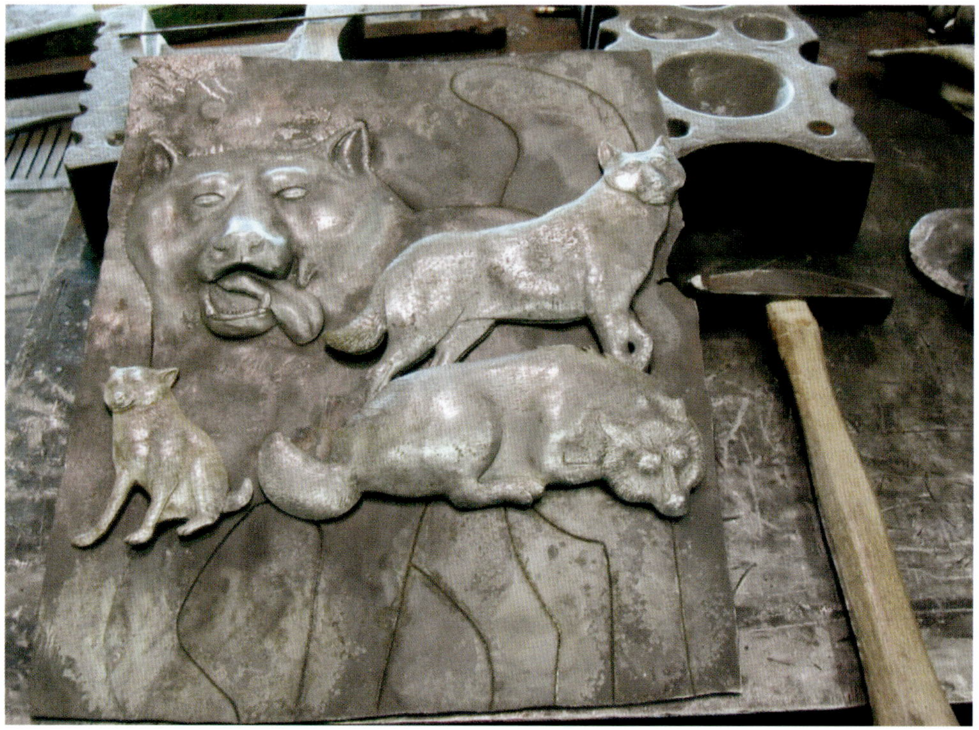

Above right:
Kirk Sullens. Detail from bottom left of the Las Vegas fire door, page 161, showing the shovel and rattlesnake that were always a part of silver mining in the old west. *Photo, artist*

Right:
Kirk Sullens. Details of sled dogs to be used in the *Toronto* screen, in progress, using repoussé techniques. *Photo, artist*

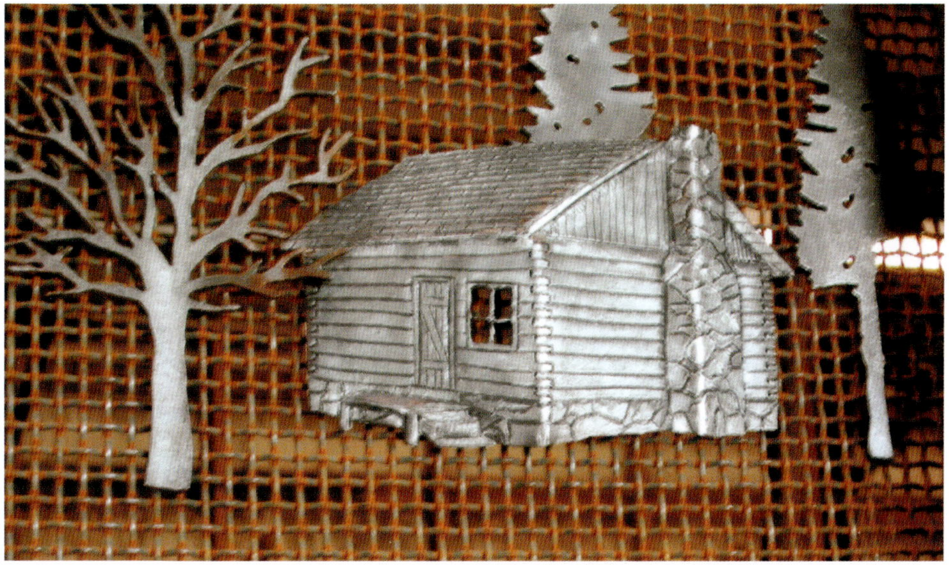

Kirk Sullens. Detail of a trapper's log cabin and trees from the *Toronto* fire screen. *Photo, artist*

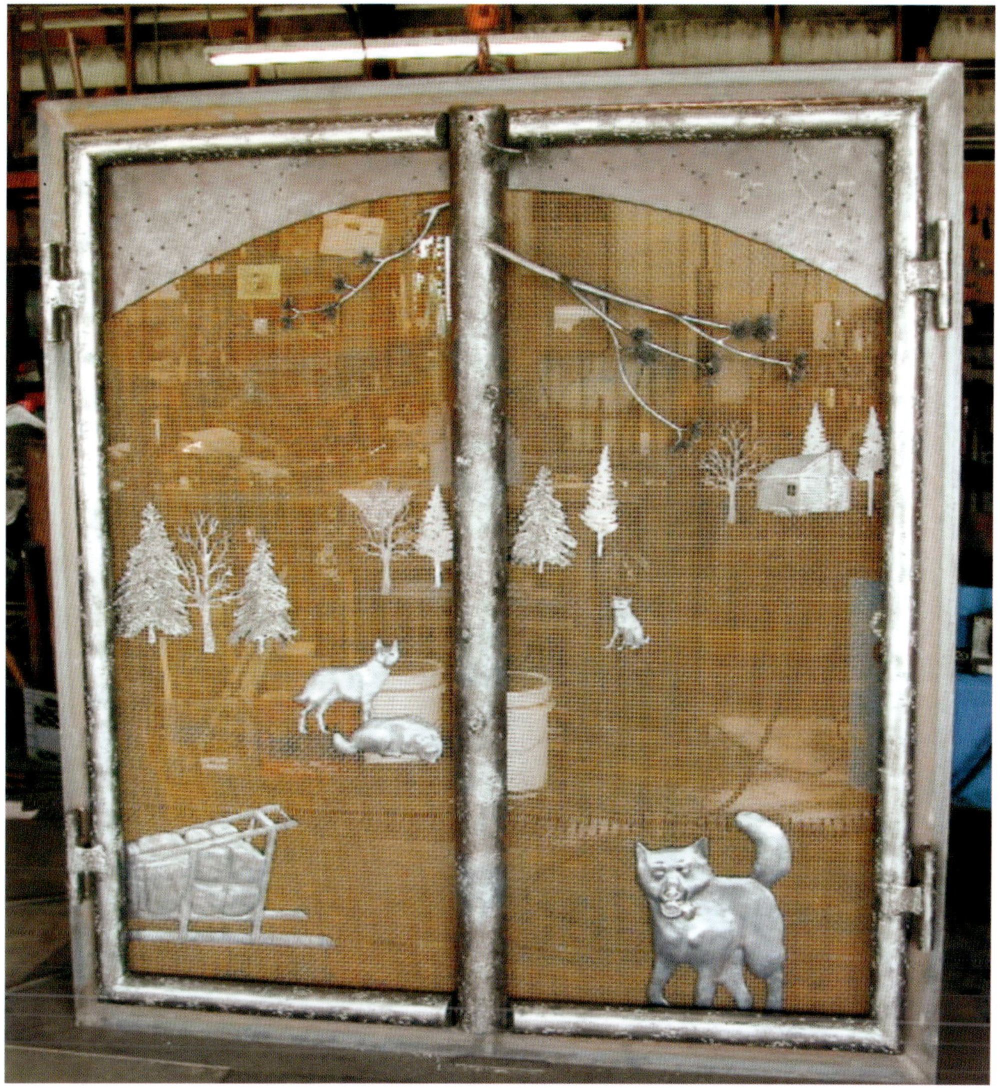

Kirk Sullens. *Toronto* fire screen ready for the final finish. *Photo, artist*

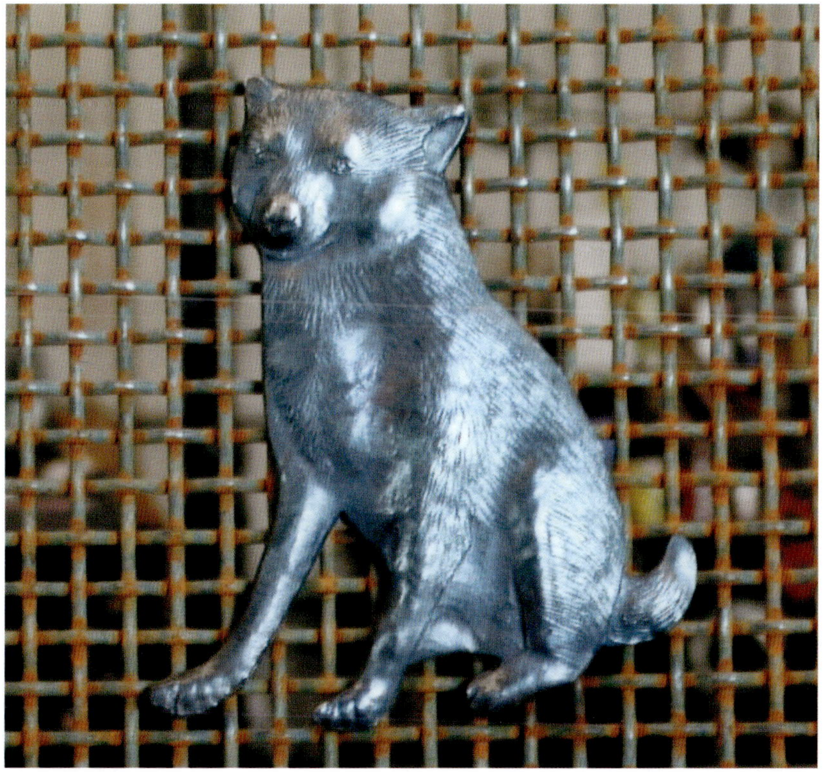

Kirk Sullens. Detail of a little dog complete with furry texture in the *Toronto* fire screen. *Photo, artist*

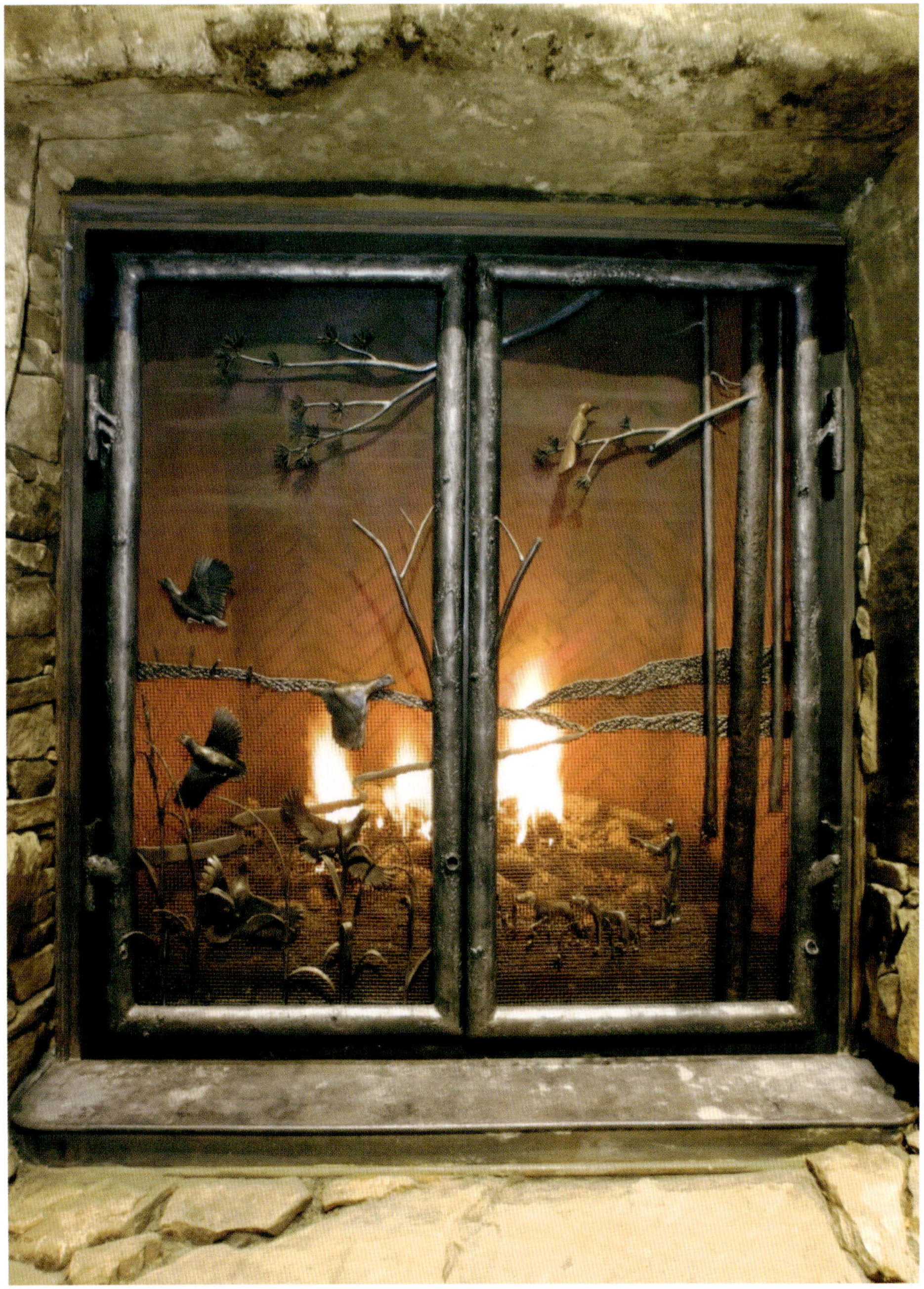

Kirk Sullens. *Atlanta fire doors.* At left, five quail are jumping up in the air, frightened by the hunter and his dog on the right side of the screen. A brown thrasher, the state bird of Georgia, is perched on the tree branch. Colored with a rust patina. 6' high, 6' wide. *Photo, courtesy Atlanta Bass Pro Shops Outdoor World.*

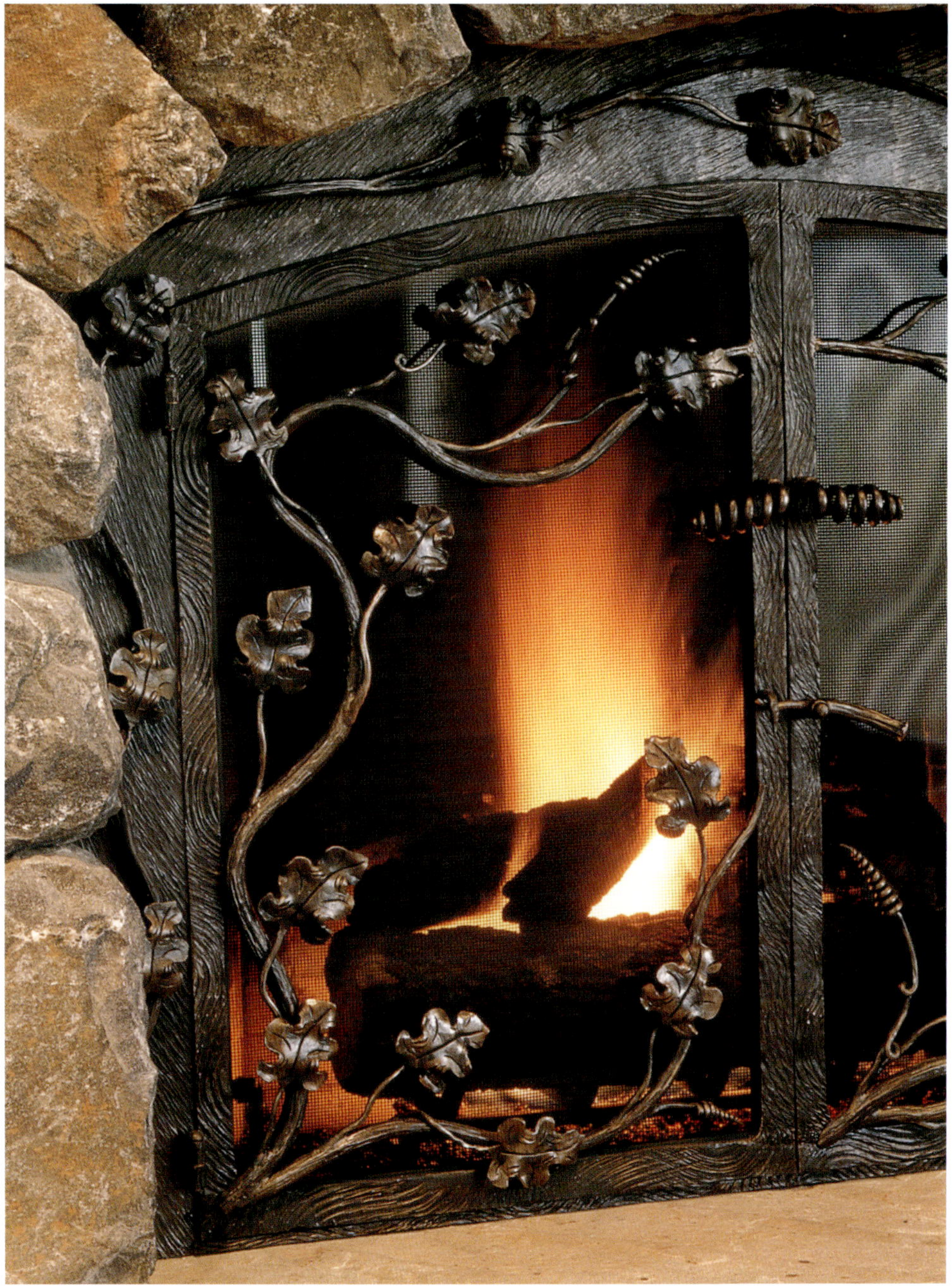

Glenn F. Gilmore. *Great Room Fireplace Doors.* (Detail.) One of four sets of doors in a Colorado residence. Gilmore's signature stylized grape leaf motif are in two sets of doors. A simplified design is used on two other sets of doors in smaller fireplaces. All doors feature PyroCeram heat tempered glass and woven mesh screening. They are carefully scribed to the stonework to appear as part of the original design and not as an after thought. *Photo, McNabb Studios*

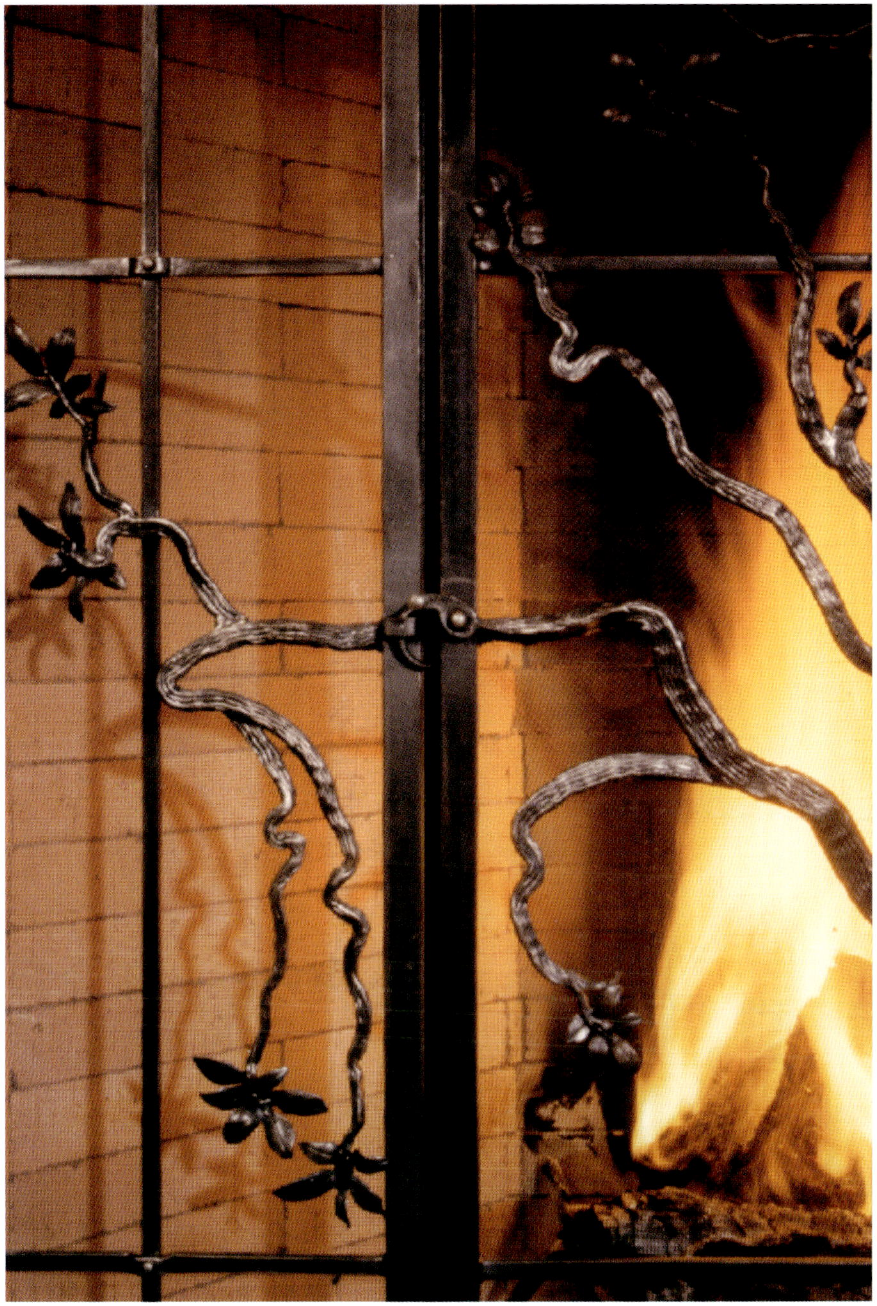

Lars Stanley. Detail.

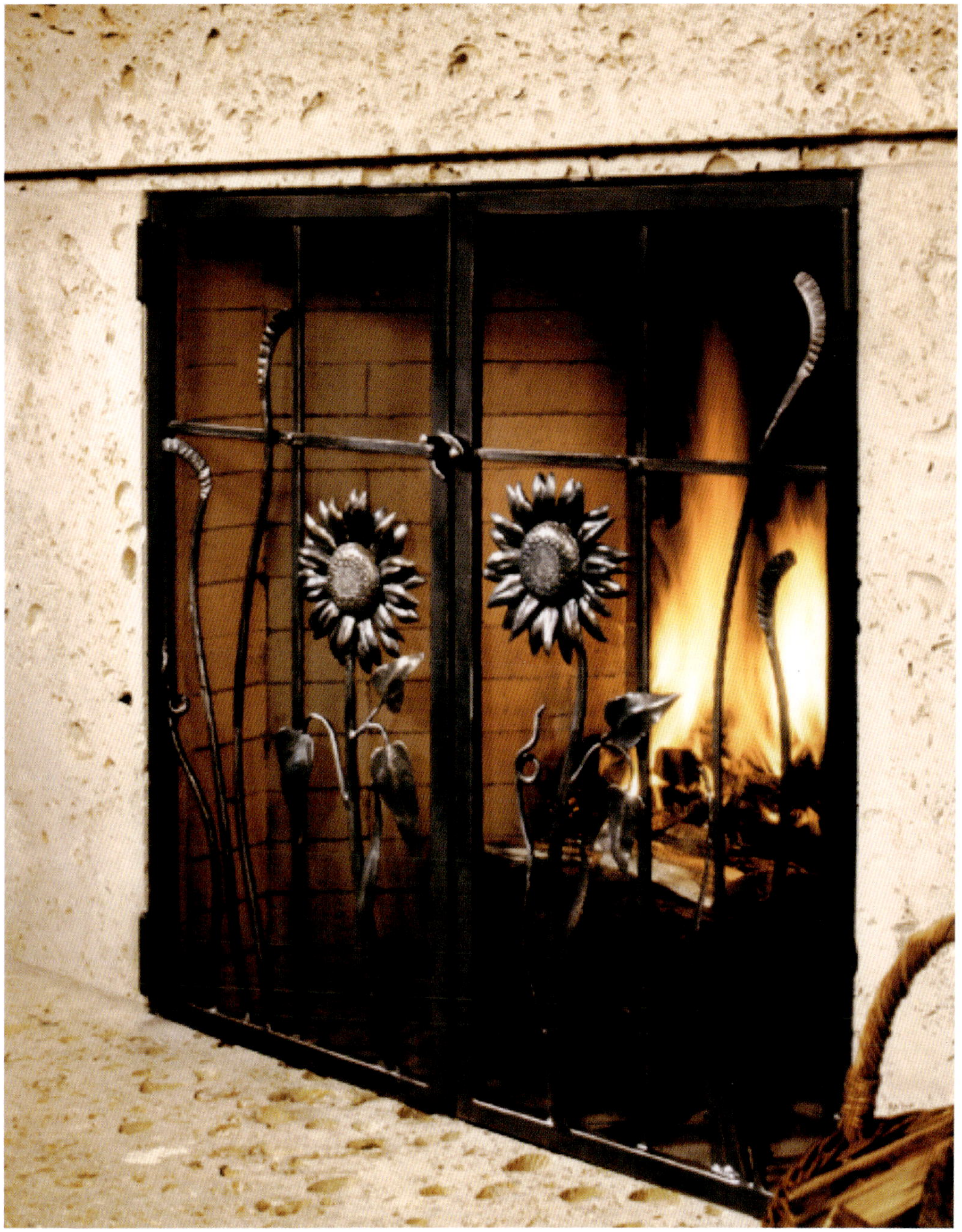

Lars Stanley, assisted by Suzanne Bass. *Sunflower Fireplace Screen.* The flowers were forged from steel plate, heat tempered for a slight patina, and a clear finish added. The clients loved sunflowers and wanted them incorporated into the screen that occupies a prominent position in their main dining room. 28" high, 28" wide. *Photos, Patrick Wong*

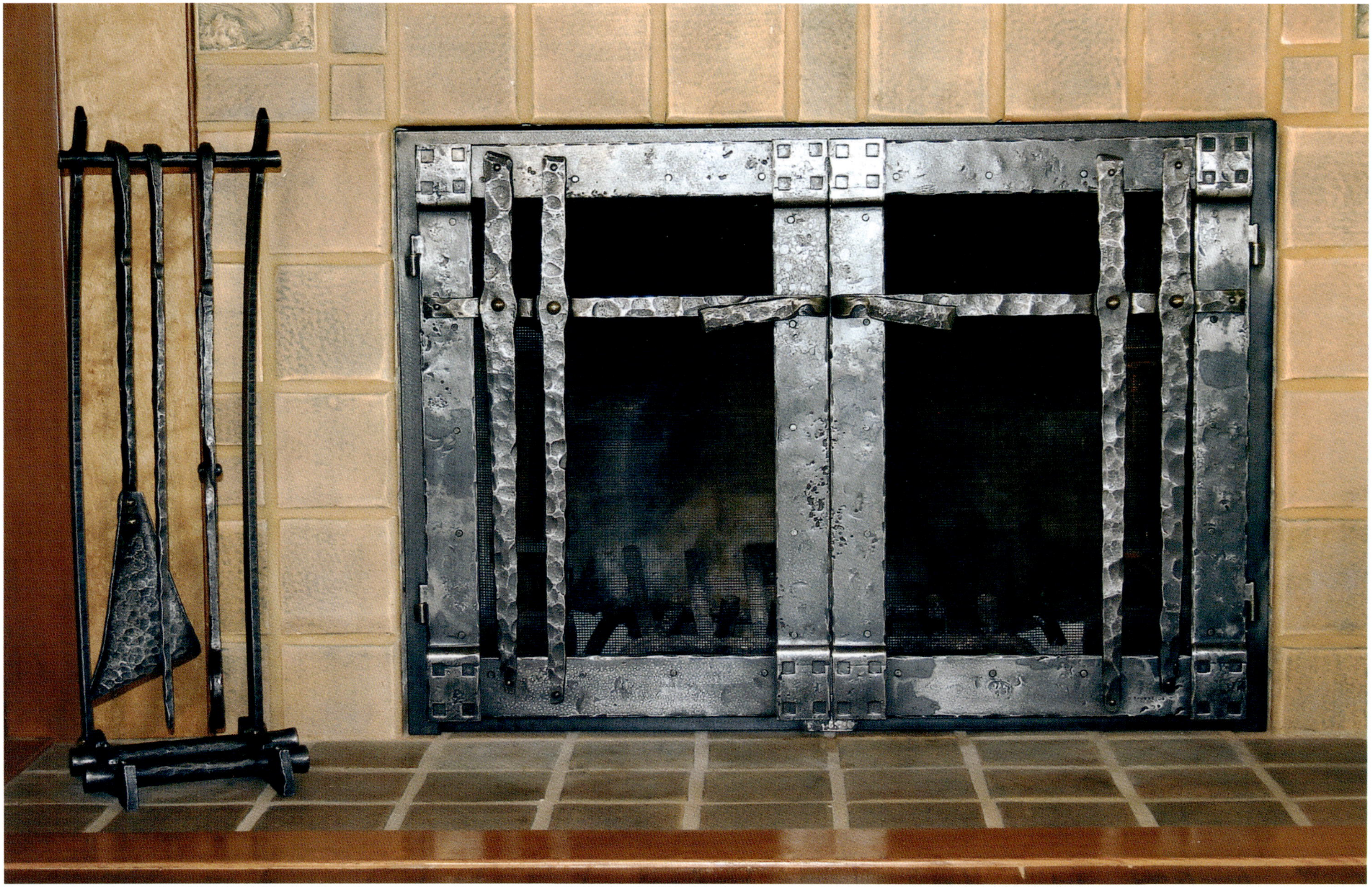

David Browne. *Arts & Crafts Style Fire Screen and Tools.* Forged and fabricated mild steel, wrought iron, with steel and brass rivets. Designed and constructed for a private residence in the historically designated neighborhood of Burlingame in San Diego, California. The Arts & Crafts style design features heavily textured hammer details and deep fullering on the screen handles and tools. 25" high, 34" wide. Tools for this set include a shovel, poker, log lifter, and broom (not pictured). 27" high, 10" wide. *Photo, Jo Anne Palasi*

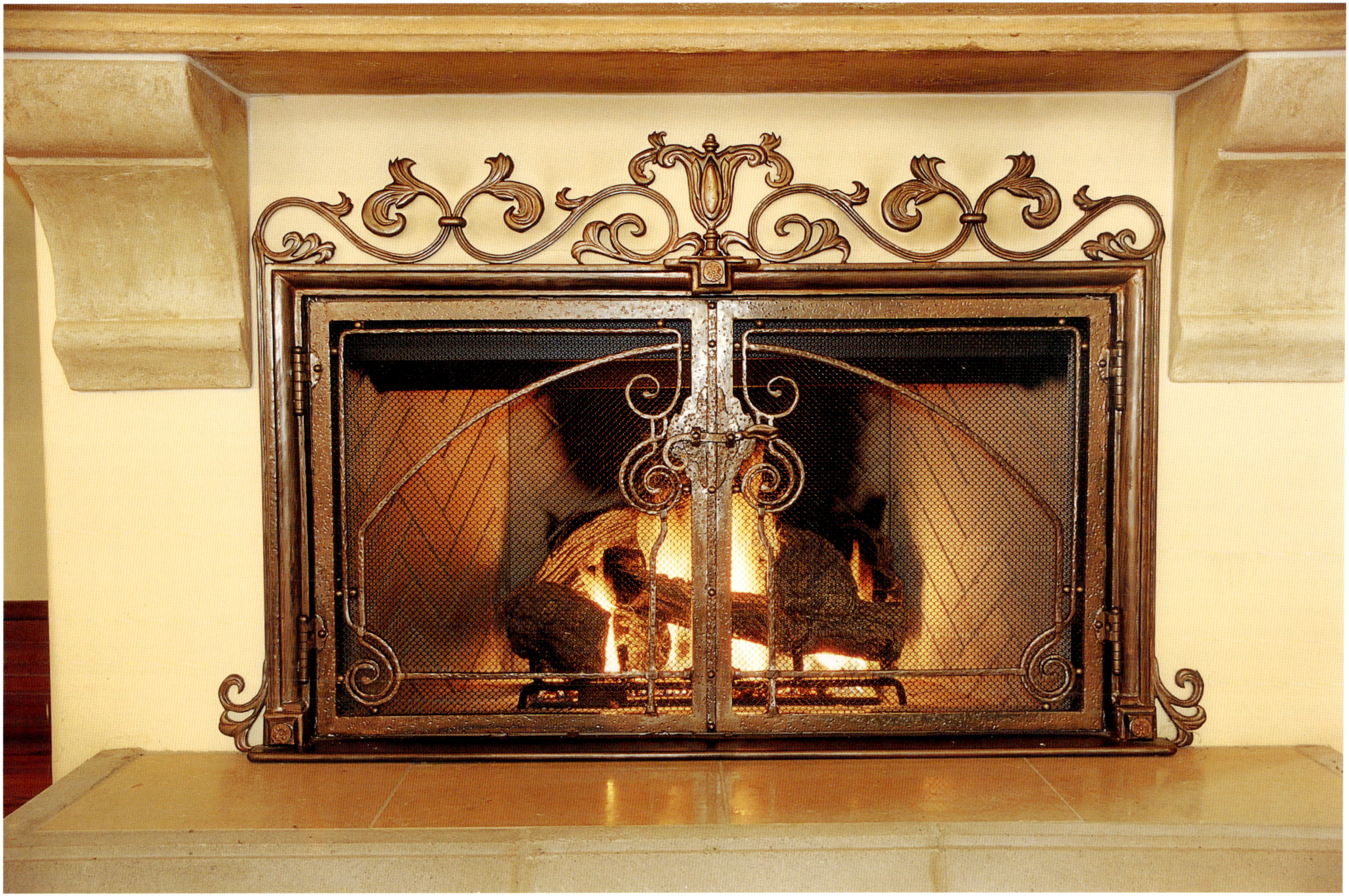

Robert C. Bentley. The Villa Toscana guest room fireplaces have additional scrollwork above the doors that incorporate the stylized tulip motif used throughout. Paso Robles, California. *Photo, Bruce Woodworth*

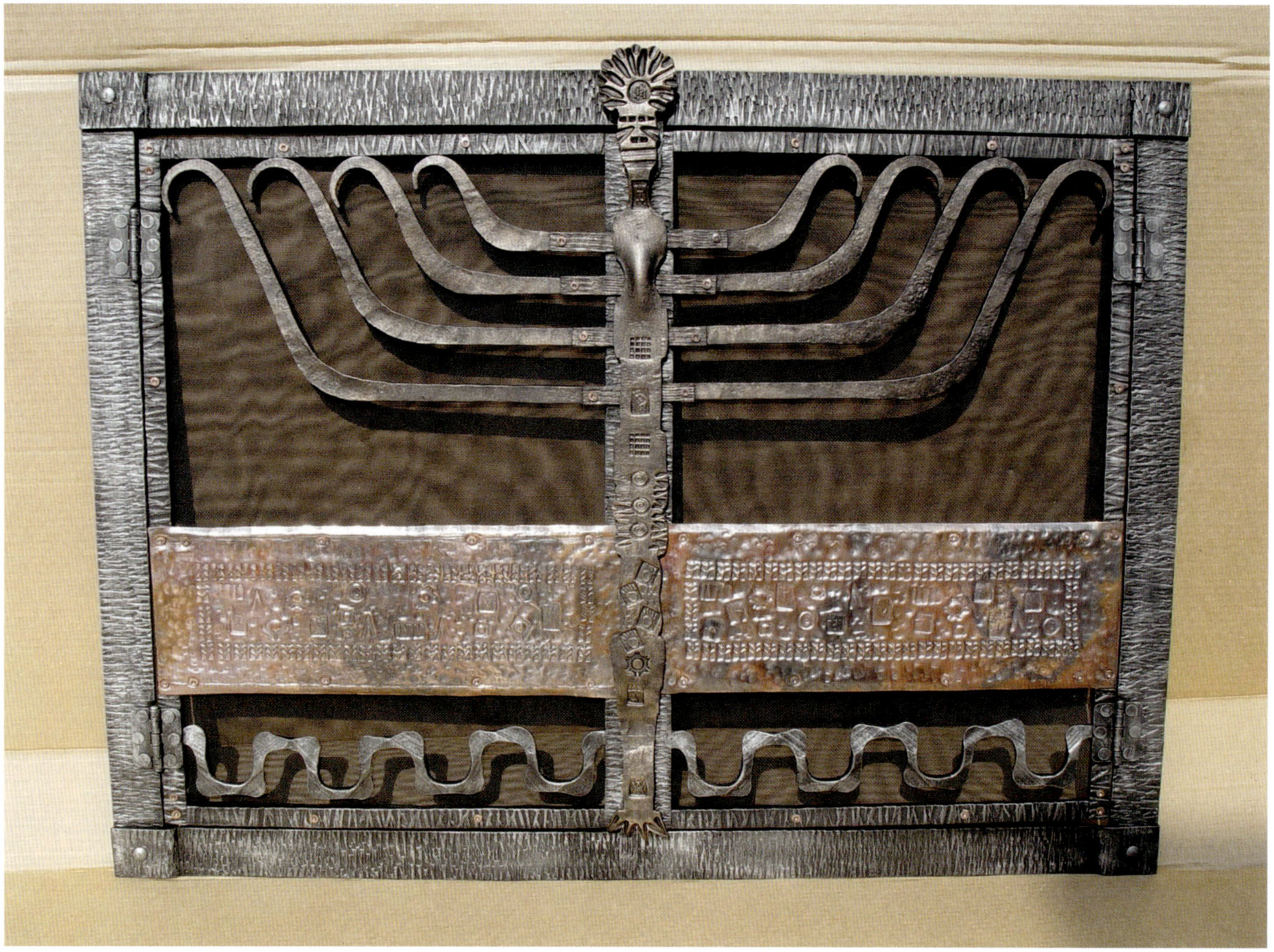

Vadim Filatov and Alexander Chumakov. Studio Gvozd. *Disarray Sense*. Forged iron fire screen. 30" high, 41" wide. *Photo, artists*

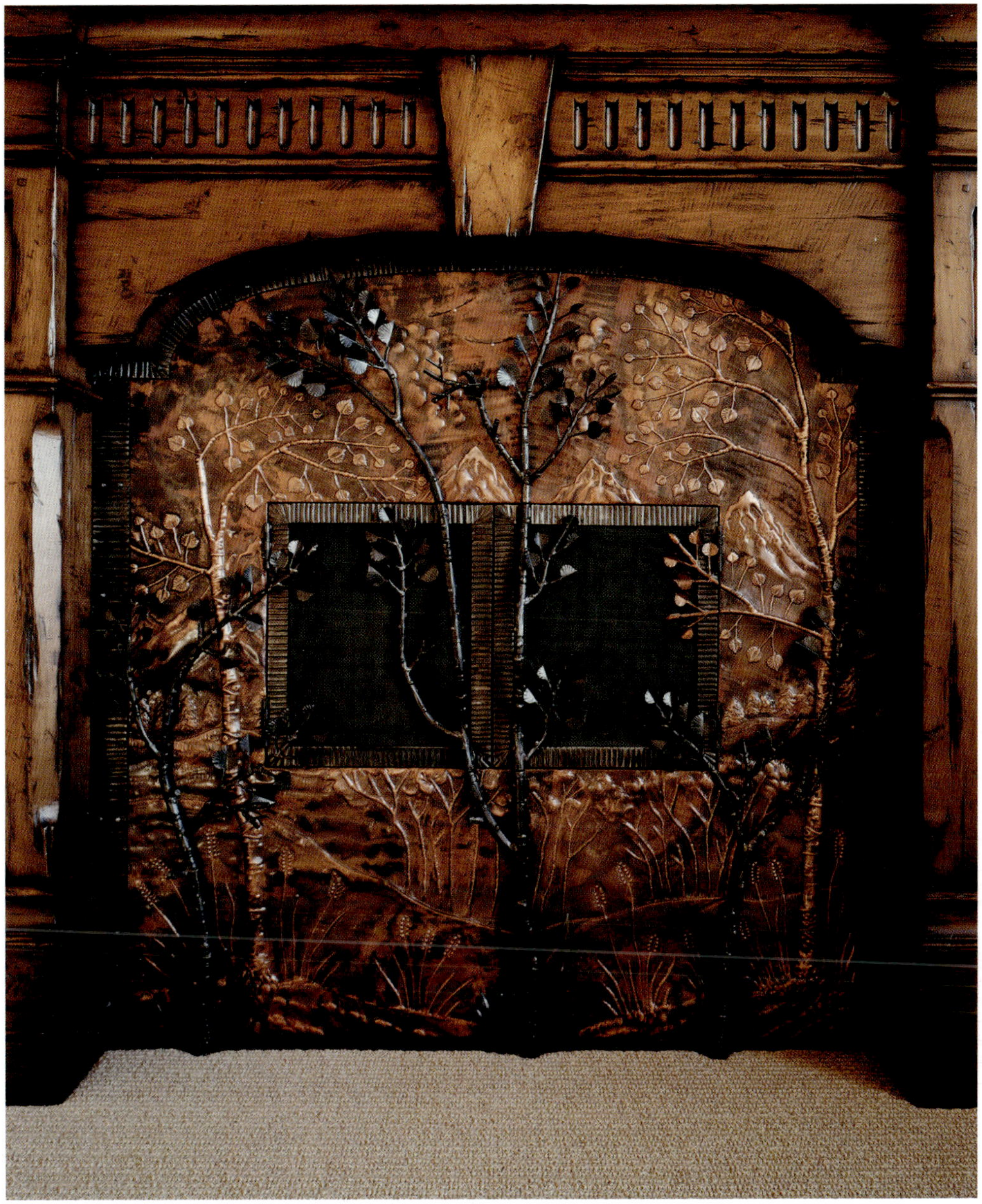

Hugh Culley. Fireplace surround with mountain scene. Forged and fabricated steel over copper repoussé. The scene includes forged and fabricated steel aspen trees and grasses that overlay the copper. The two central branches serve as the door handles. 5' high, 5' wide. *Photo, Richard Prehn*

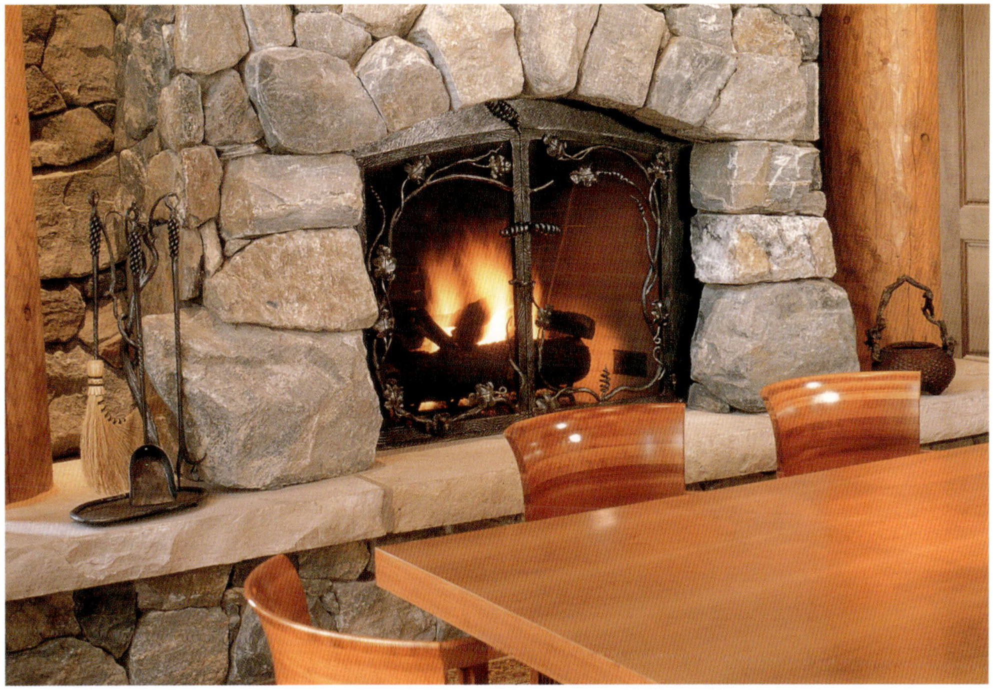

Glenn F. Gilmore. One of four fireplace doors and hardware made for a Colorado residence. In this dining room fireplace set, the doorframe is textured to simulate tree bark and it is surrounded with stylized grape leaves. PyroCeram glass and woven mesh screen are in the doors. The tools have woven style handles, hand tied brooms, and a textured branch for the tool stand. *Photo, McNabb Studio*

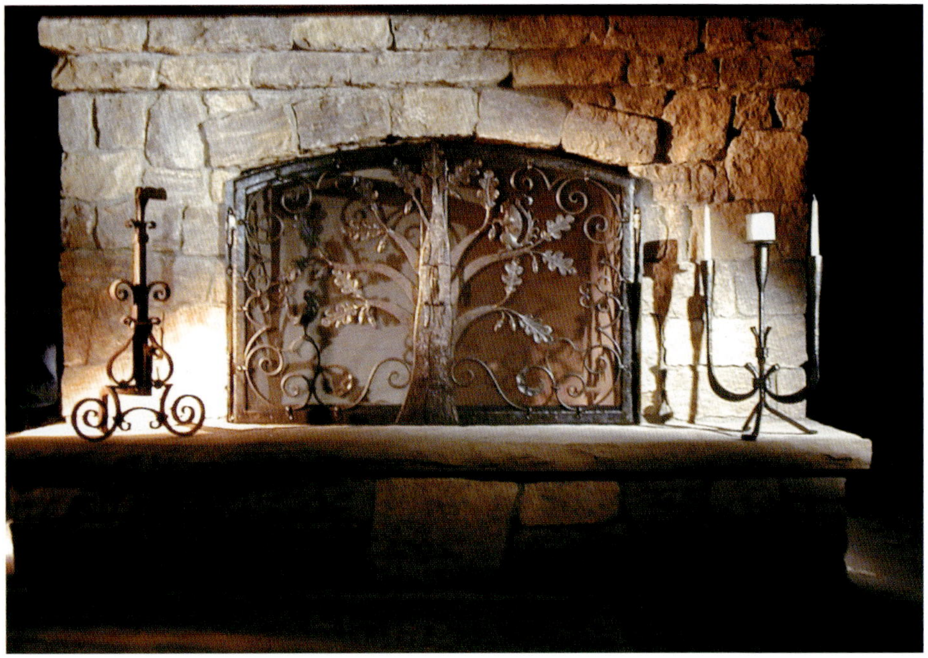

Greg Eng. Fireplace screen. Forged steel with a blackened oil finish. Special tooling had to be developed for creating the half profile acorns. Twigs and branches were developed with gas welding and texturing tools. Riveted half clips cover the welds. 37" high, 51" wide. *Photo, Brenda Eng*

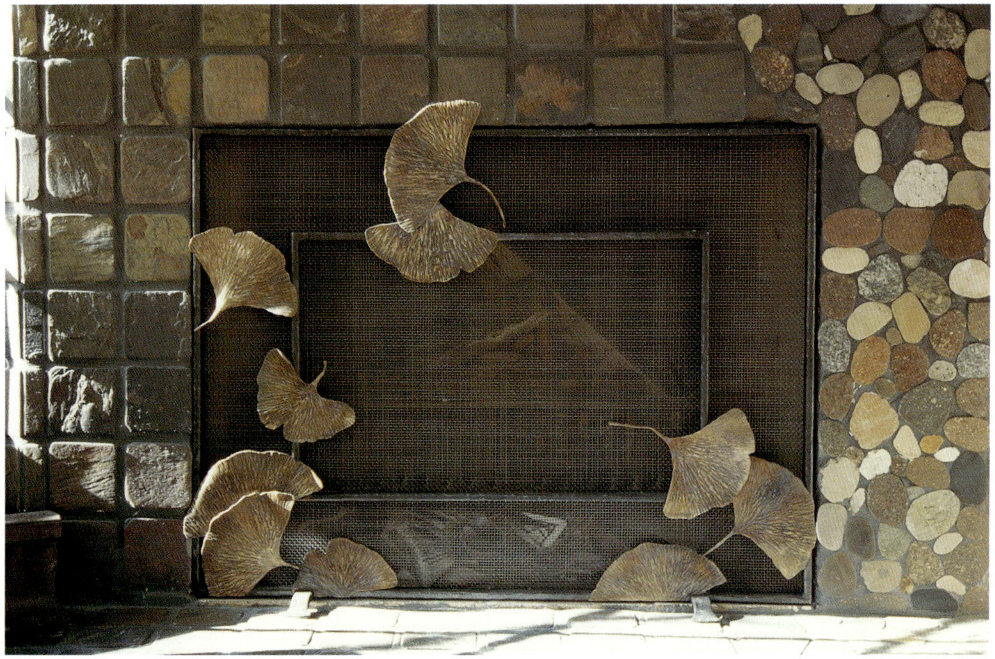

Erika Strecker. *Ginkgo* fire screen. Forged steel and bronze. The leaves continue beyond the screen and up the wall. 2.5' high, 3' wide, 3" deep. *Photo, Leeann Greer*

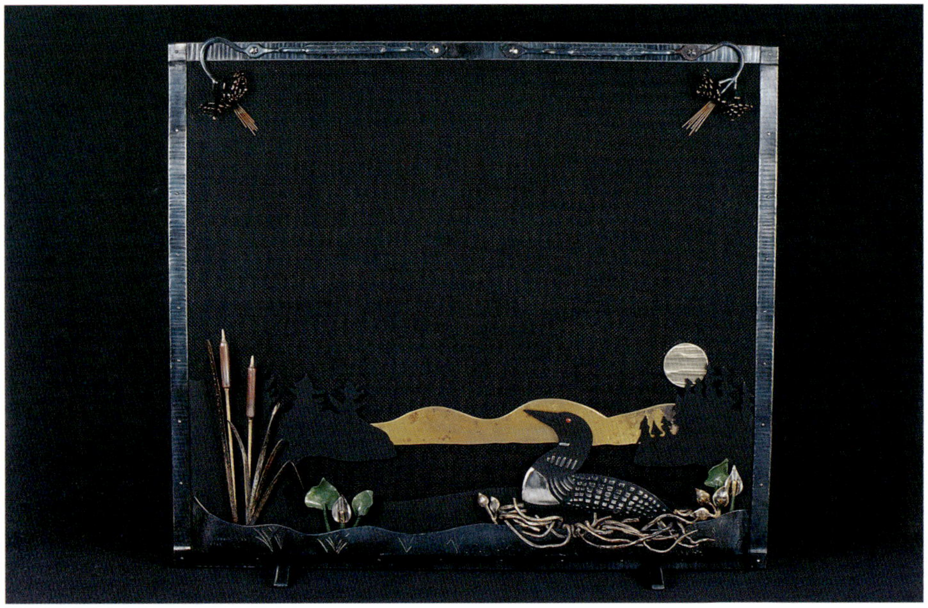

Keith A. Leavitt. *Alert!* Nesting loon free standing fire screen. Stainless steel loon and wild calla lilies, a bronze moon, copper nest, and hills, brass and stainless steel cattails, and mild steel pinecones for handles. 37" high, 42" wide 12" deep. *Photo, Steven Dunn*

Joel Haas. *Butterfly Screen*. Mild steel, scrap metal, and found objects. Inspired by an Alfonse Mucha poster. Found objects include an electric motor armature, an old lampshade ring, and ball bearings. Sand blasted and powder coat painted. The two folding side panels each measure 32" high, 10" wide. The central panel is 39" high, 34" wide. *Photo, artist*

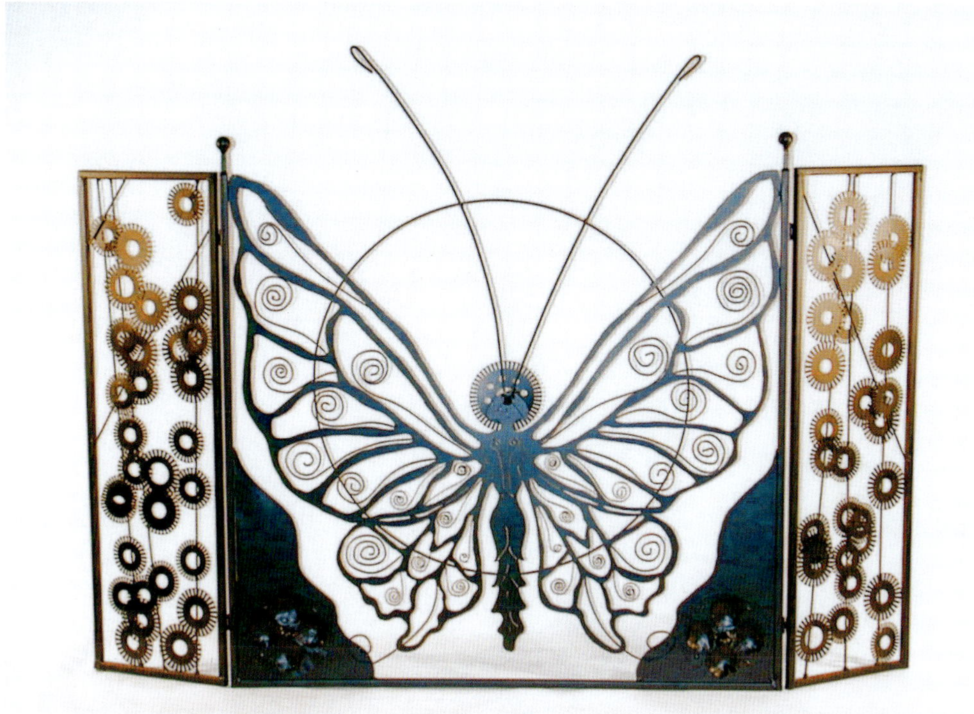

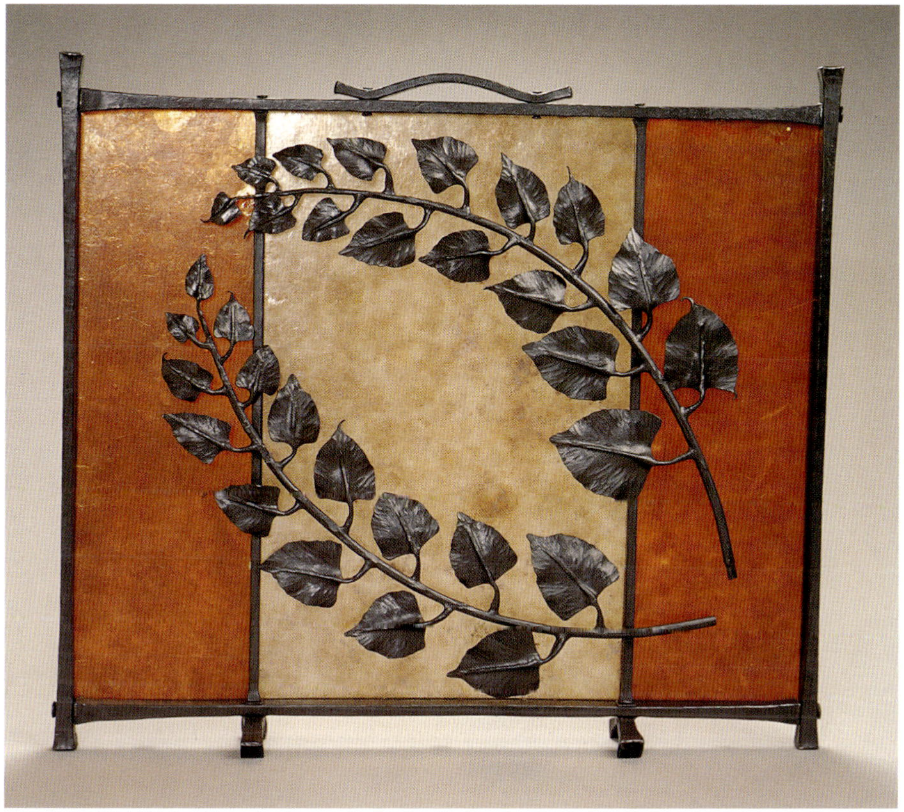

Susan Madacsi. Fire screen. Forged, fabricated steel with mica. 32" high, 36" wide. *Photo, R. J. Phil*

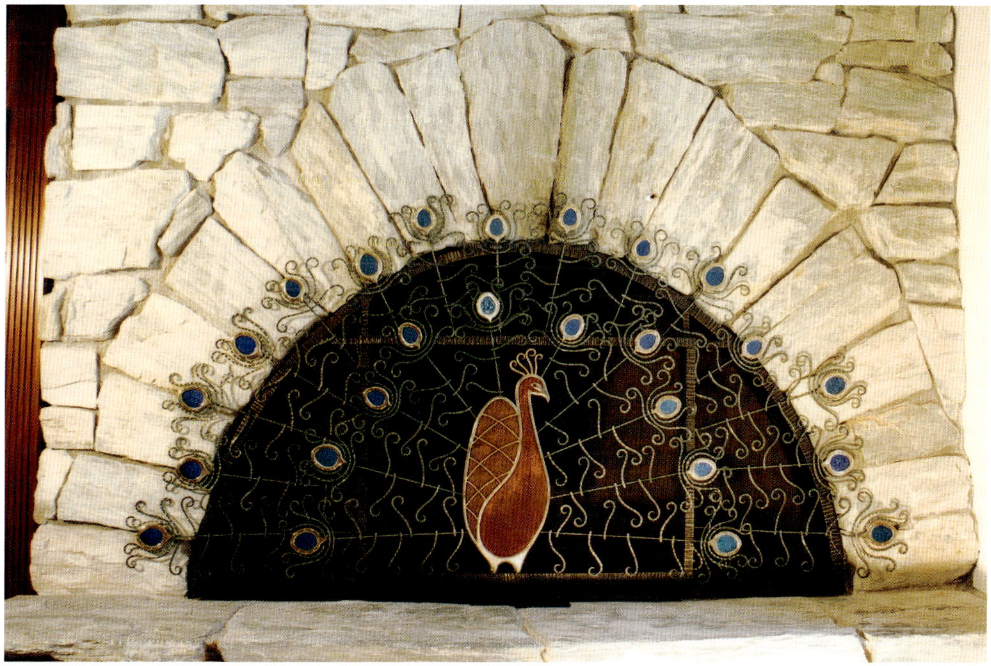

Rod and Lee Picket. *Peacock Screen.* Forged steel and dichroic glass. The peacock is glass over copper screen. To avoid hinges that would break up the look of the peacock, the door slides to the side for accessing the logs and fire. 25" high. *Photo, Julie Pickett*

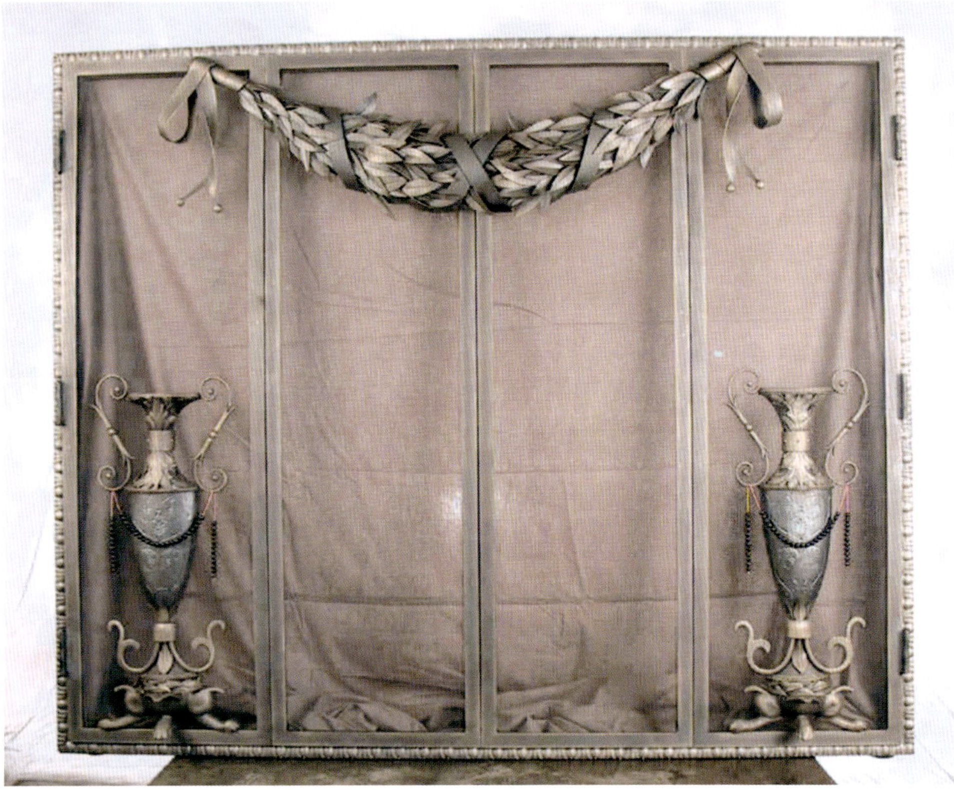

Steve Joslyn. *Roman Amphora* screen. Designed for a private residence. Each door weighs 60 lbs. *Photo, artist*

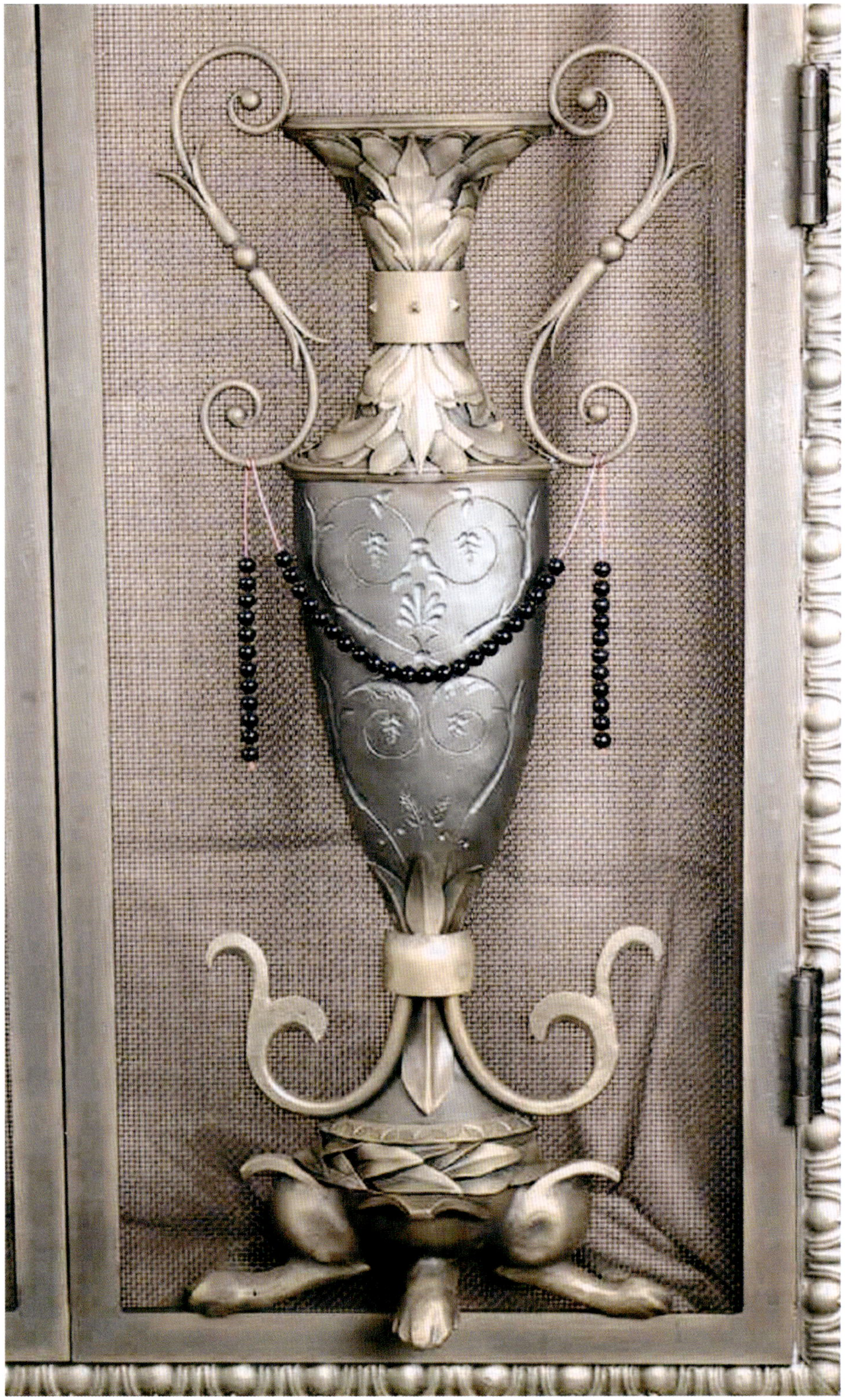

Steve Joslyn. *Roman Amphora.* (Detail.) Forged, fabricated steel finished in antique bronze. The urns, constructed of 65 individual forged pieces, include black jade beads. It fits into a Roman style white architectural surround. 60" high, 72" wide. *Photo, artist*

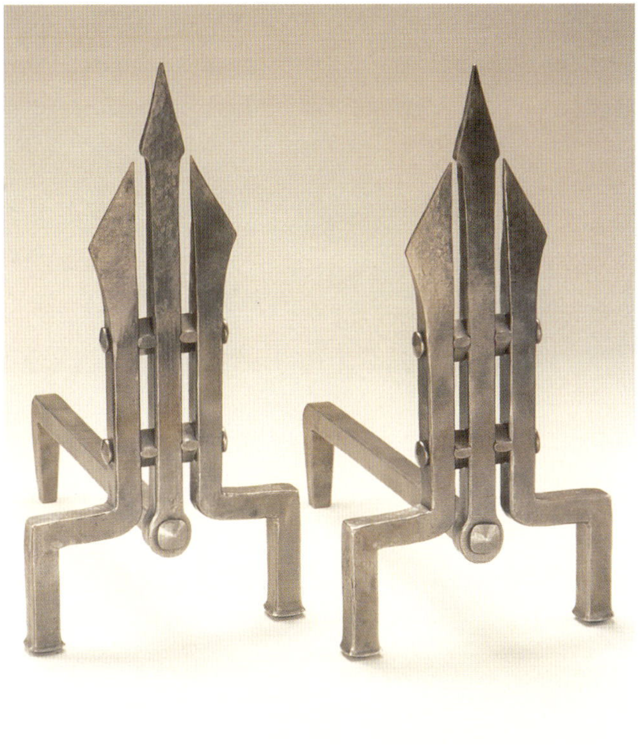

Zach Noble. Andirons. Mild steel. 18" high, 9" wide, 20" deep. *Photo, Tim Lee*

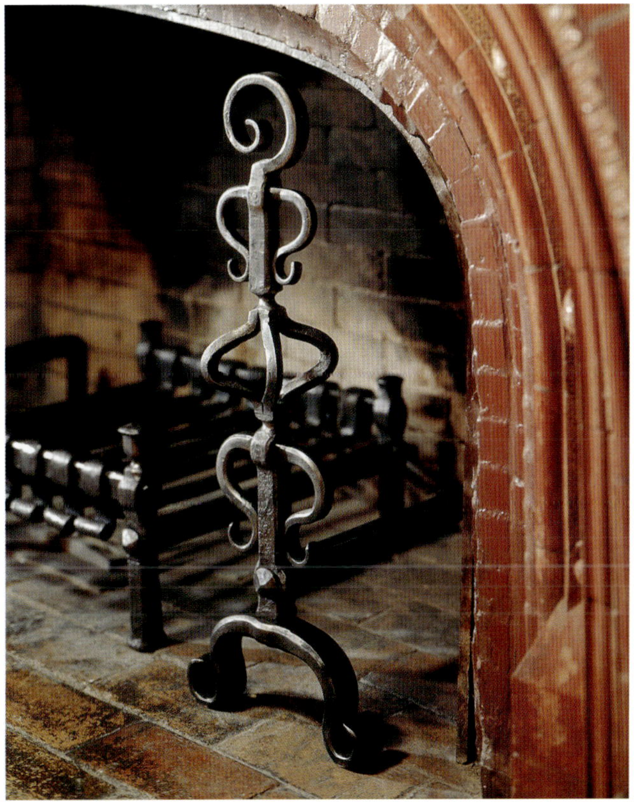

Christopher Thomson. Andirons (detail). Steel using traditional joinery. Installed in the lobby of the Montezuma Castle of the Armand Hammer United World College of The American West in Montezuma, New Mexico. *Photo, Peter Vitale*

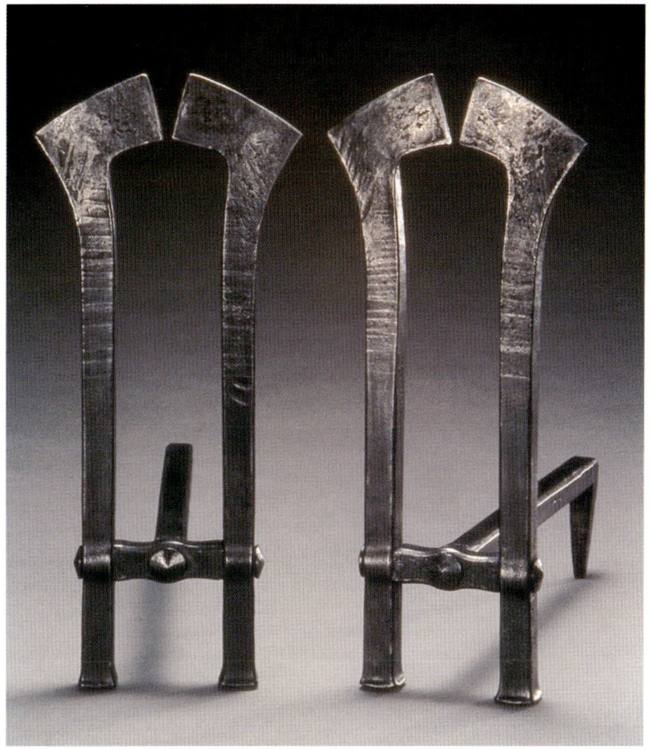

Zach Noble. Andirons. Mild steel. 18" high, 5.5" wide, 20" deep. *Photo, Tom Mills*

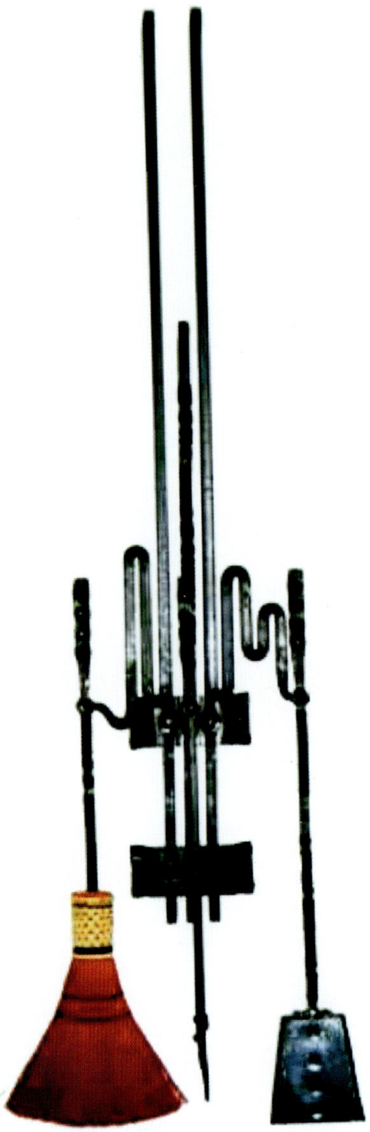

Stefan Duerst. Wall mounted fire tool set. The poker and shovel are each forged from one piece of steel. Based on an Arts & Crafts Style design combined with sculptural elements. 70" high, 20" wide, 8" deep. *Photo, artist*

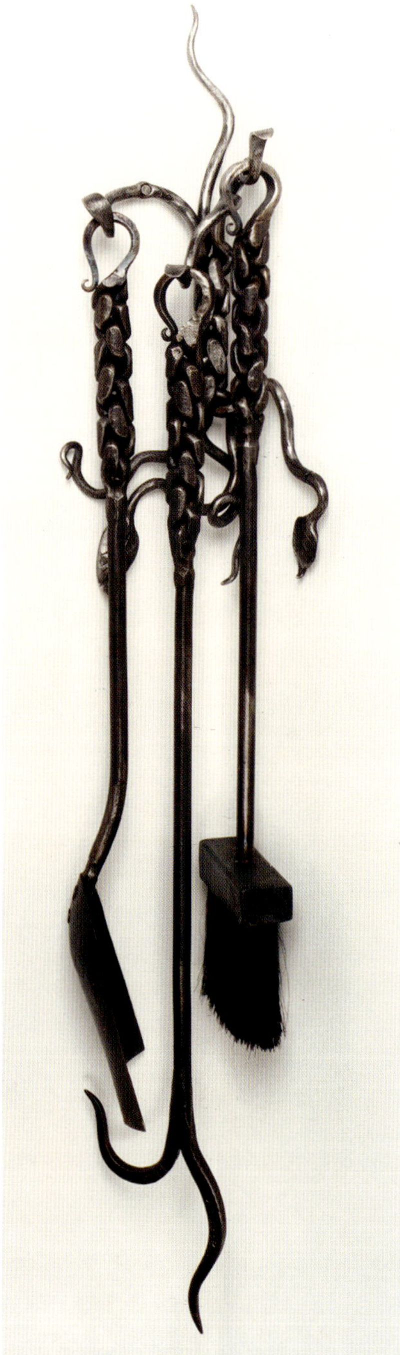

George Parker. Wall hung fire tool set. Forged steel with braided handle. 37" high. *Photo, Ansen Seale*

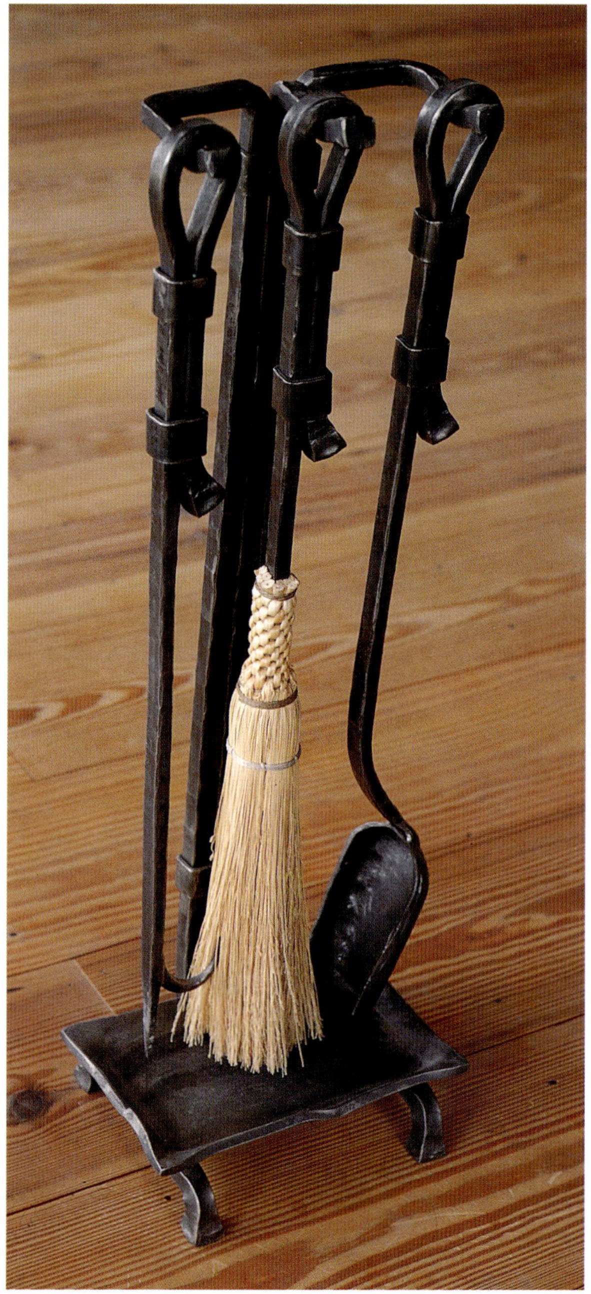

Morris L. Hallowell IV. Fireplace tool set with stand. The bottom tray is forged from 3/8" thick plate. 37" high. *Photo, artist*

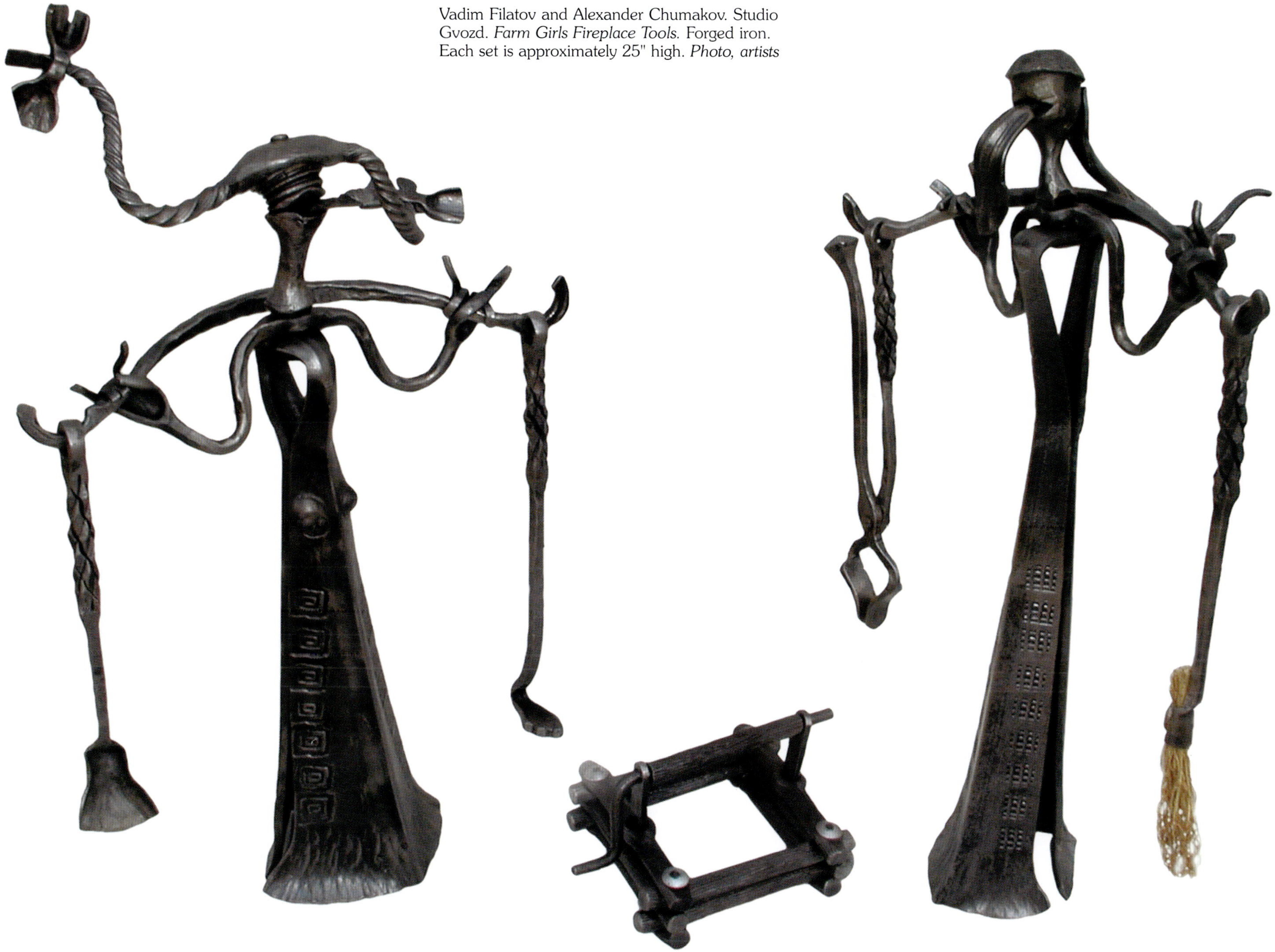

Vadim Filatov and Alexander Chumakov. Studio Gvozd. *Farm Girls Fireplace Tools.* Forged iron. Each set is approximately 25" high. *Photo, artists*

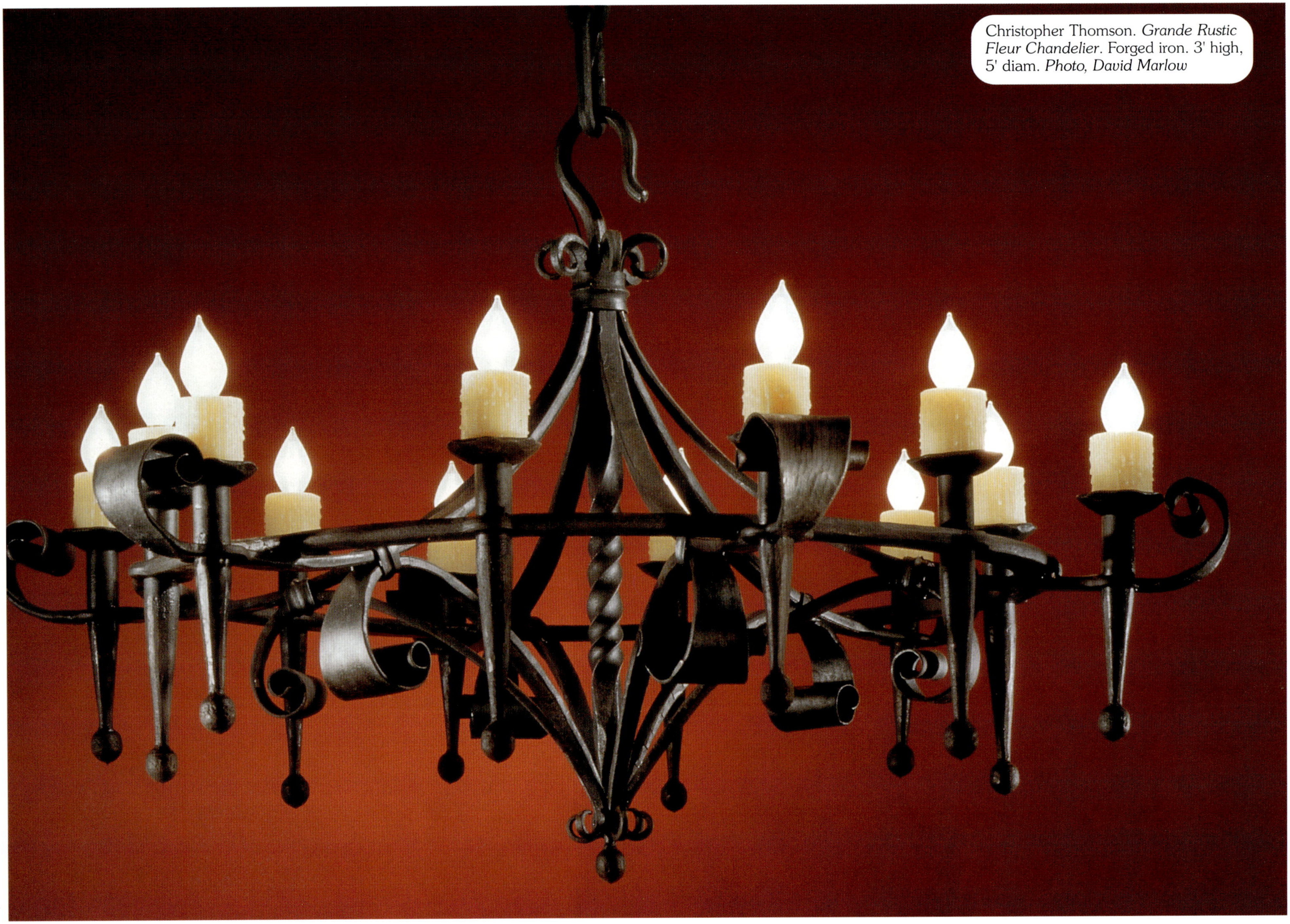

Christopher Thomson. *Grande Rustic Fleur Chandelier*. Forged iron. 3' high, 5' diam. *Photo, David Marlow*

Chapter 8. Lighting Fixtures & Candleholders

Metal candleholders date back to antiquity. Ornate ones used in churches and synagogues did not survive the Reformation. But one doesn't have to dig deep to appreciate how pervasive they have been since the sixteenth century. Paintings and etchings from medieval times often picture a single candleholder or a chandelier with candle lighting. In the painting, "The Wedding Portrait" by Jan Van Eyck, 1444, an ornate iron chandelier hangs directly between the two people portrayed. Art historians believe that the one candle burning in the left rear holder is a symbol of fertility.

The Dutch painter, Jan Vermeer, included an ironwork chandelier in his 1665 painting, "An Artist in his Studio." Daniel Kerem, writing in *The Anvils' Ring*, Spring 2005, notes that, "The chandelier's functional and decorative use has been in vogue for over 500 years and serves distinctively to this day in such celebrated interiors as the Spanish-Portuguese Synagogue in Amsterdam…"

Anyone who has traveled in Europe and Mexico, and been through religious buildings, castles, and palaces, will have no trouble spotting ironwork light fixtures from small wall sconces and single candleholders to grand circular multi-tiered units. Our American ancestors certainly lit their homes with candleholders made of iron and tin plate, and fashioned by local blacksmiths, often the same people who made and repaired farm tools.

The word "chandelier" meaning candleholder comes from 'chandelle', the French word for candle. Before electricity, candles were used in chandeliers that had elaborate pulley systems so they could be lowered for lighting the candles, and then raised. With the advent of electricity, bulbs replaced candles. Interestingly, many of today's ironwork fixtures imitate those of earlier eras and candle shaped bulbs are used. Some have small shades that reflect the light down, or camouflage the use of modern electricity to replace the wax candle.

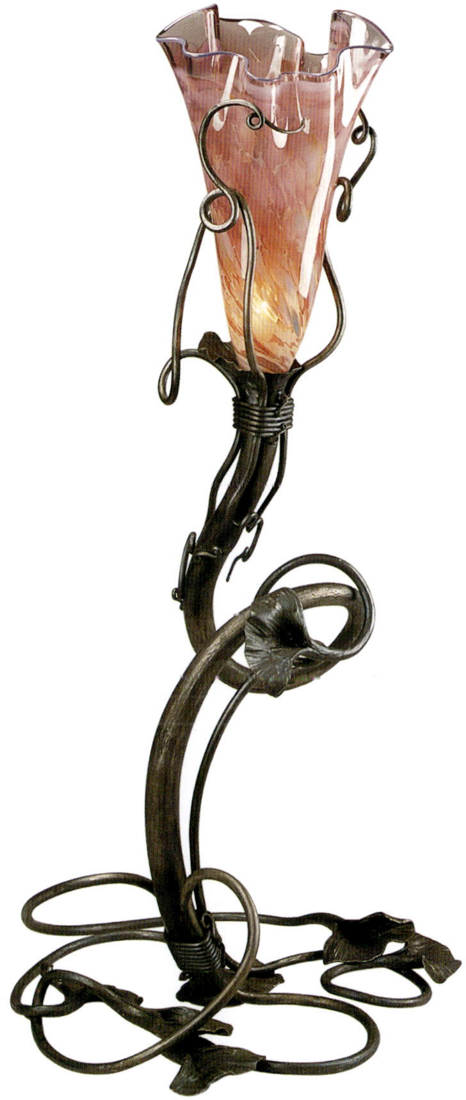

Roberta Elliott. Lamp of black mild steel pipe with a blown glass shade by Doug Becker. Inspired by calla lilies and ginkgo leaves. 36" high, 20" diam. *Photo, Jeff Bruce*

Lighting fixtures fall into different categories. There are chandeliers containing multiple tiers and arms or some with only a simple circle with lights around it. A pendant is a single droplight. Sconces are lights that are attached to a wall. There are freestanding reading lamps, night-lights, etc. Shades refer to globes attached to a ceiling, and there are myriad types of lights for outdoor use. Finally, there are candles in a variety of holders from single units to multiple units made for decorative, functional, and religious purposes.

Dan Nauman's recreation of Cyril Colnik's (1871-1957) light fixture illustrates the idea of replicating a design from an earlier craftsman. While the design is not contemporary, it represents the type of commission the contemporary blacksmith may tackle. Nauman has admired Colnik's work that appears in buildings in the Milwaukee, Wisconsin area. He was instrumental in creating a videotape of Colnik's ironwork and eventually having pieces installed in the permanent collection of the Milwaukee Art Museum, so that the legacy of Colnik's work would carry on.

Robert C. Bentley's ornate chandelier hearkens back to design elements of France at the turn of the century. Greg Eng recreated the look and feel of a Gothic chandelier for a private residence. Kirk Sullens embellishes fixtures with animals for stores that sell hunting equipment.

Contemporary ironwork light fixtures can be seen in the lighting departments of home decorating and furnishing stores and anywhere light fixtures are sold. Many are based on ornate historical designs but today's blacksmiths are creating new expressions in lighting. Steve Lopes and his group of blacksmiths customize chandeliers to the point where one has dangling sculptures inspired by long earrings worn by the client. Their fixtures are strictly modern and may represent the designs that blacksmiths will copy fifty years from now.

It seemed logical to show candleholders in a chapter on lighting. You'll find examples from liturgical candleholders to those that are strictly decorative and many that are unabashedly used to enhance romance.

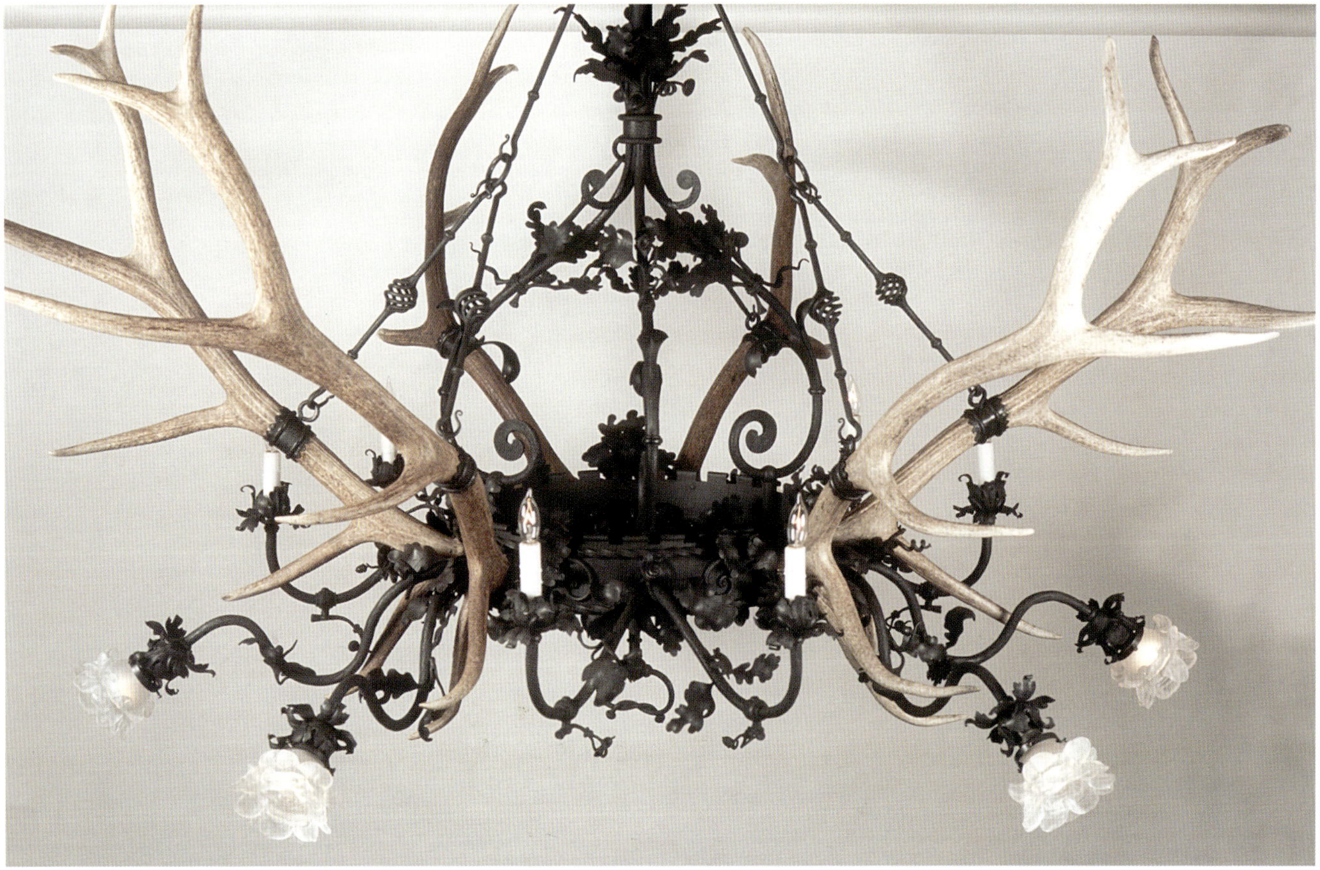

Dan Nauman. Reproduction of a lighting fixture complete with elk antlers does justice to the work of master blacksmith Cyril Colnik, whose work from the 1930s is peppered throughout Wisconsin. Nauman's trek through the re-creation of this fixture reads like an adventure story. The final fixture includes 133 oak leaves, 35 acorns, 6 basket twists, 6 water leaves, many tendrils, branches, an more totaling approximately 390 pieces not including rivets, nuts and bolts. There were about 830 actual working hours at the forge plus visits to study the originals, many drawings and test pieces, and finding the antlers. 57" high, 78" diam. *Photo, Lottermoser and Associates*

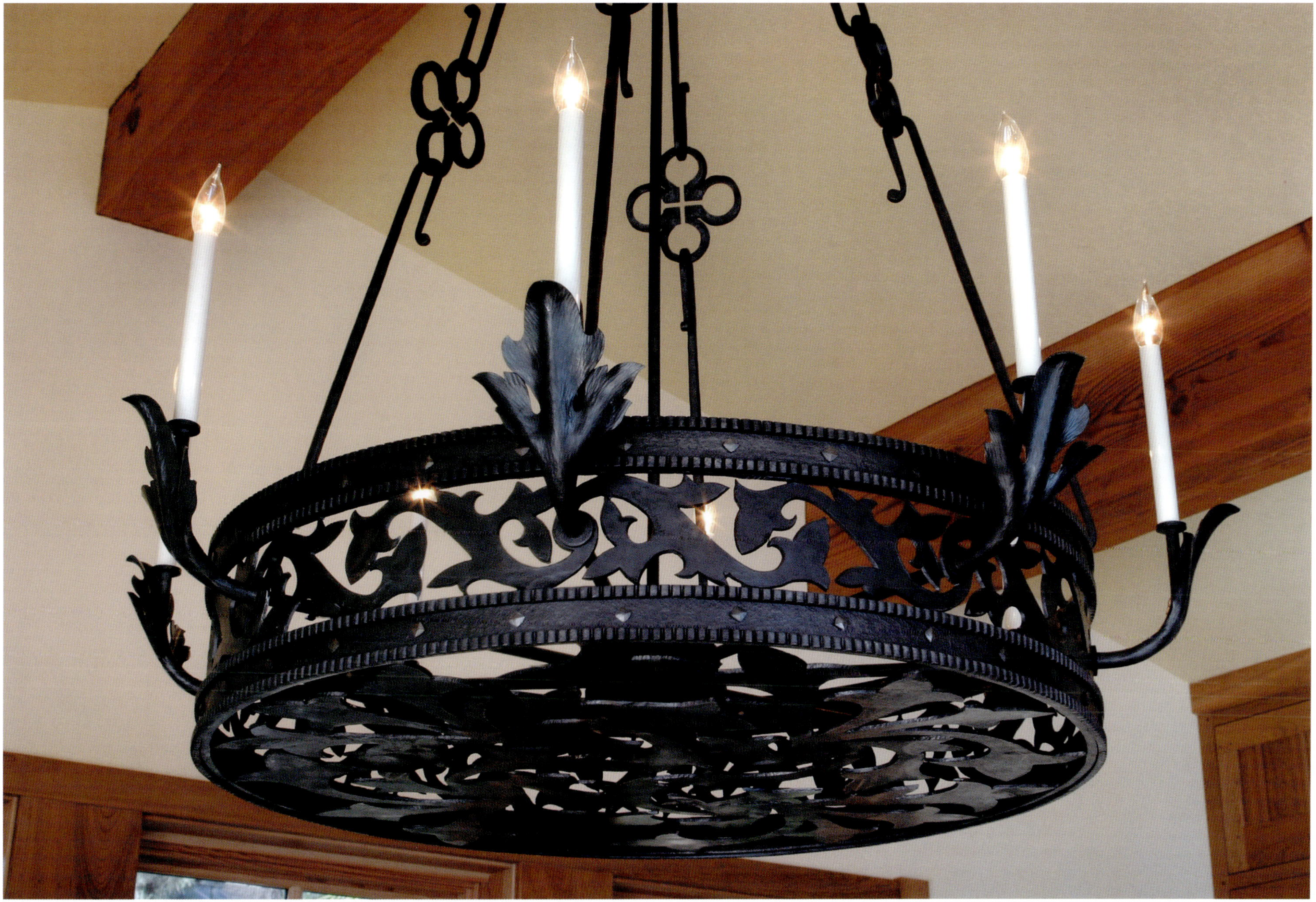

Russell Jaqua. Chandelier. Forged mild steel. A chandelier that hung in the sanctuary of an Episcopal Church and admired by the client inspired the gothic design. 36" diam. *Photo, David Conklin*

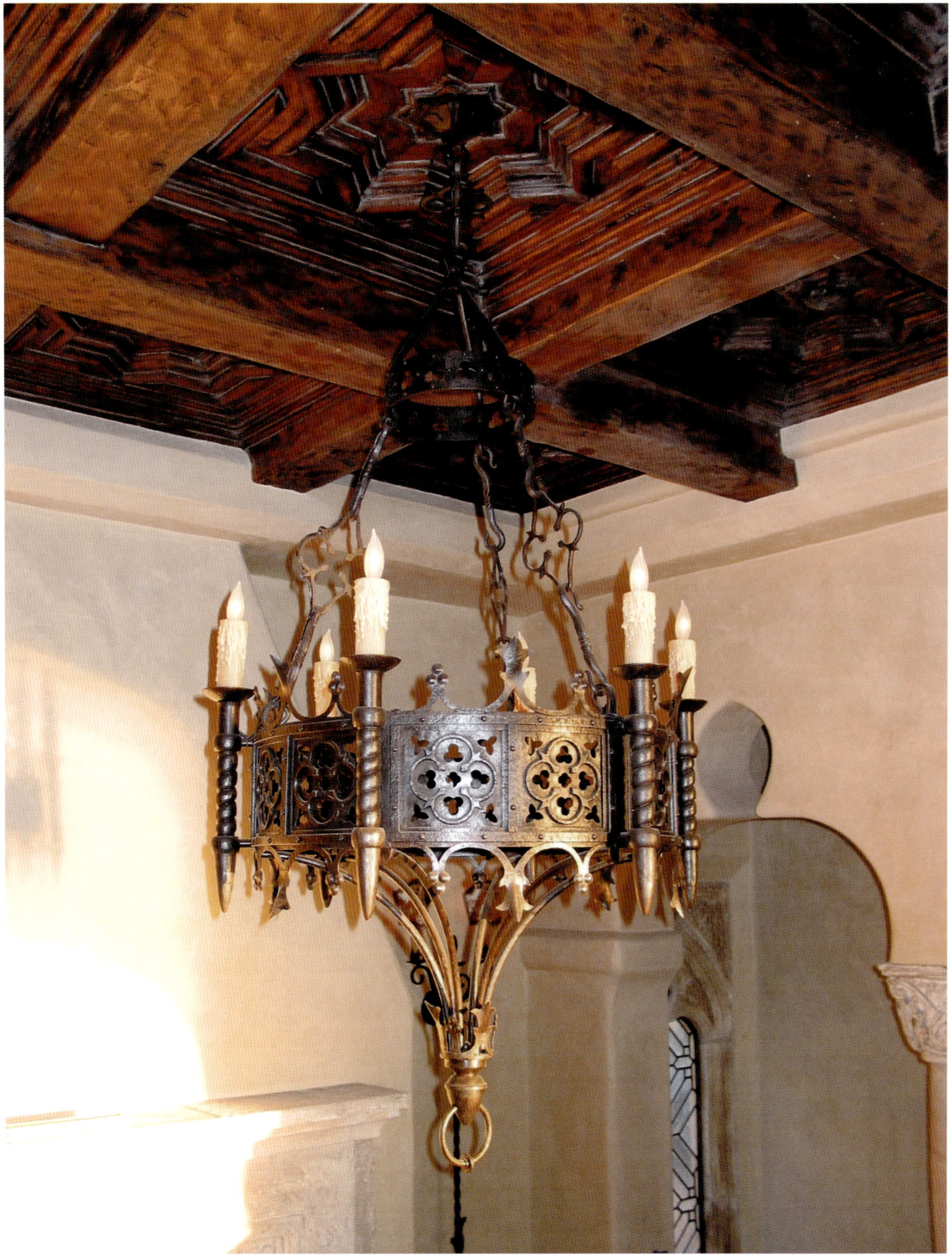

Greg Eng. *Gothic Chandelier*. Made from sheet steel, rods and pipe. All surfaces are hot forged over textured plate to give the metal a deep-pitted look. Sandblasted, blackened, rusted, wire brushed, oiled, and waxed. 65" tall and 125 lbs. *Photo, Brenda Eng*

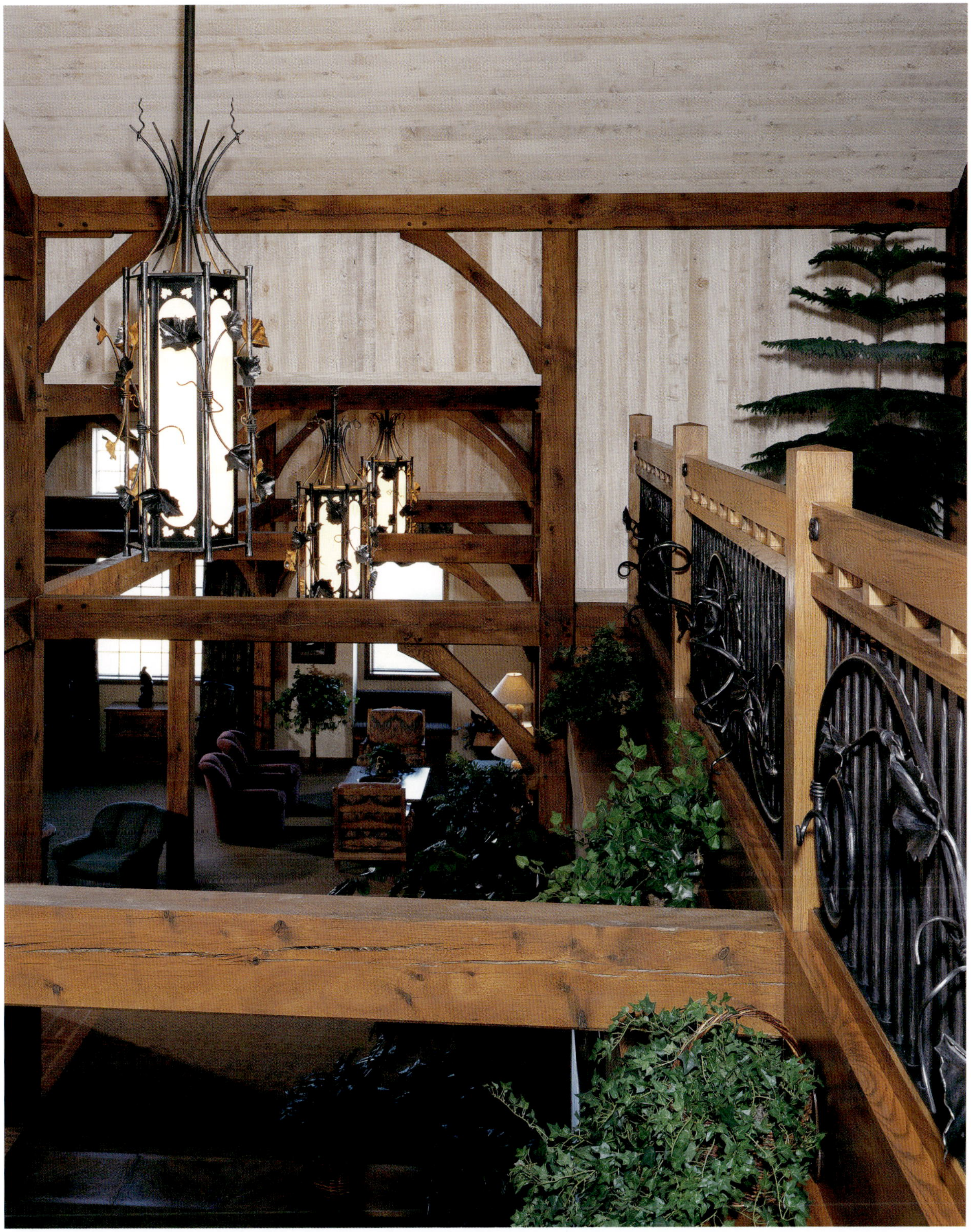

Michael Bendele. Lights and railing for The Heritage Inn, Archbold, Ohio. The final project included eleven lights, furnishings, and 518' of railing. *Photo, Jim King*

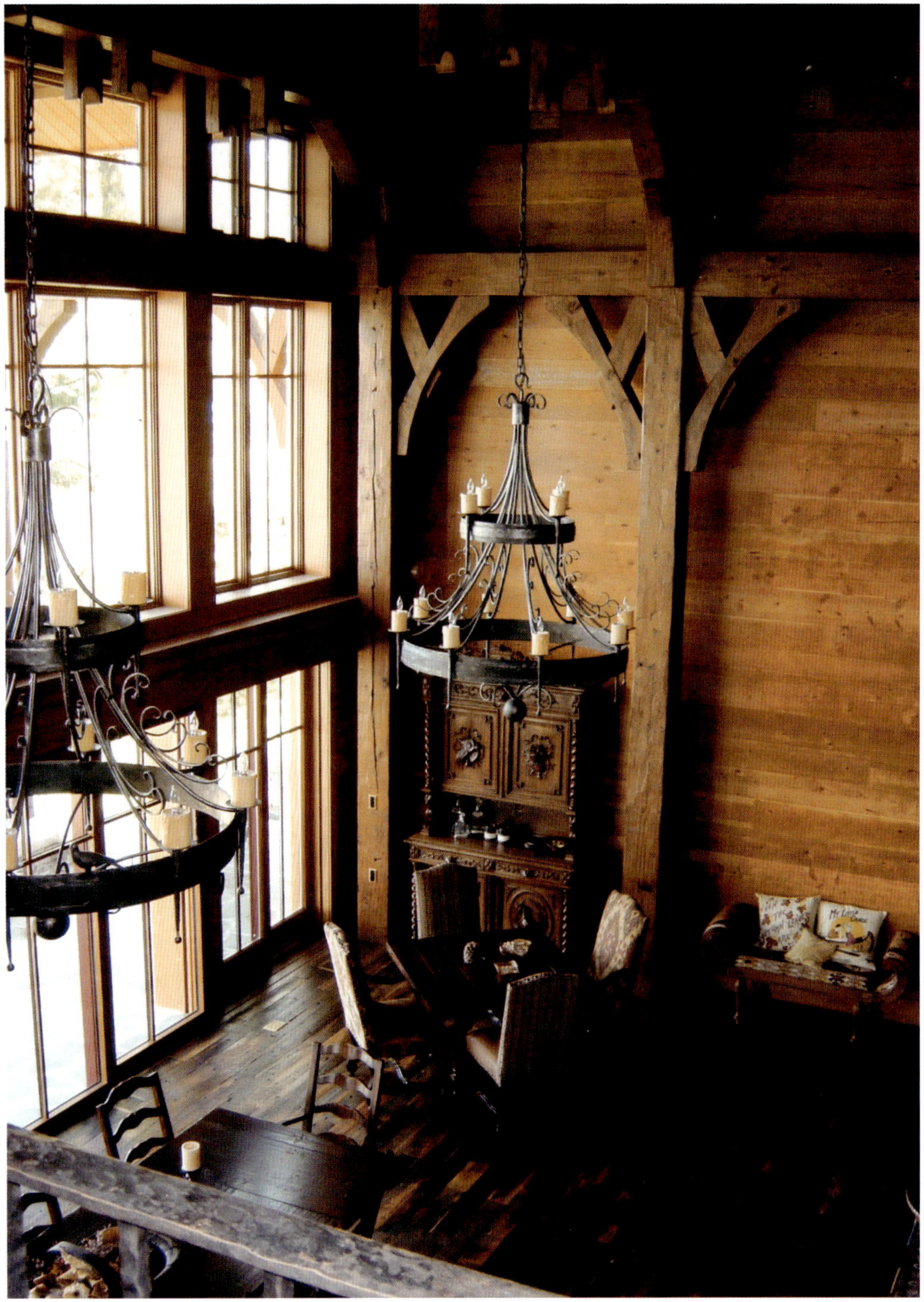

Lisa Elias. Chandeliers. One of three large chandeliers in this residence. The artist also made the 2nd floor railing incorporating plant fronds. *Photo, Locus Architecture*

Lisa Elias. Chandeliers in progress. When they are hung from a cathedral ceiling, the scale must be very large. *Photo, Andrea Rugg*

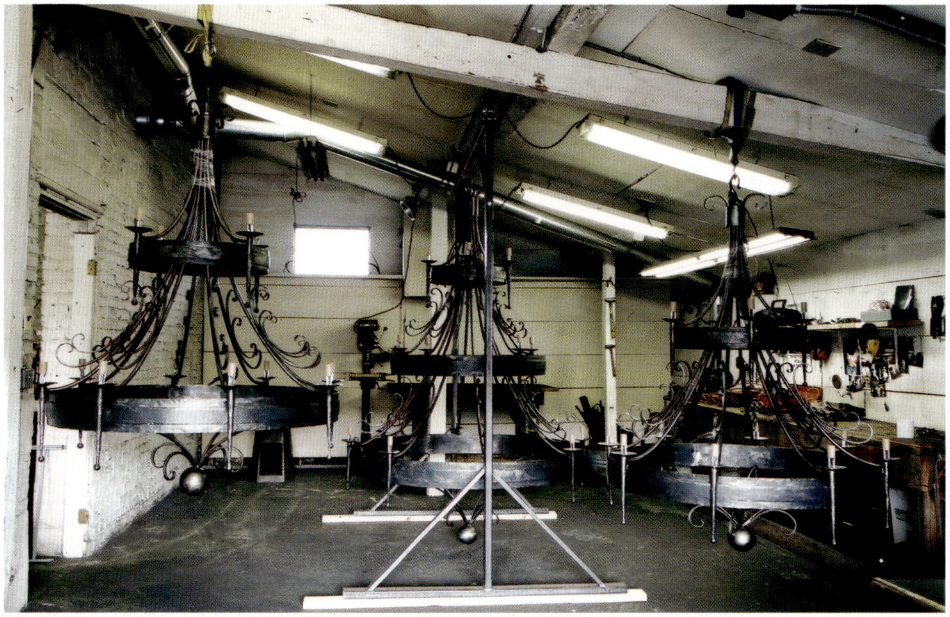

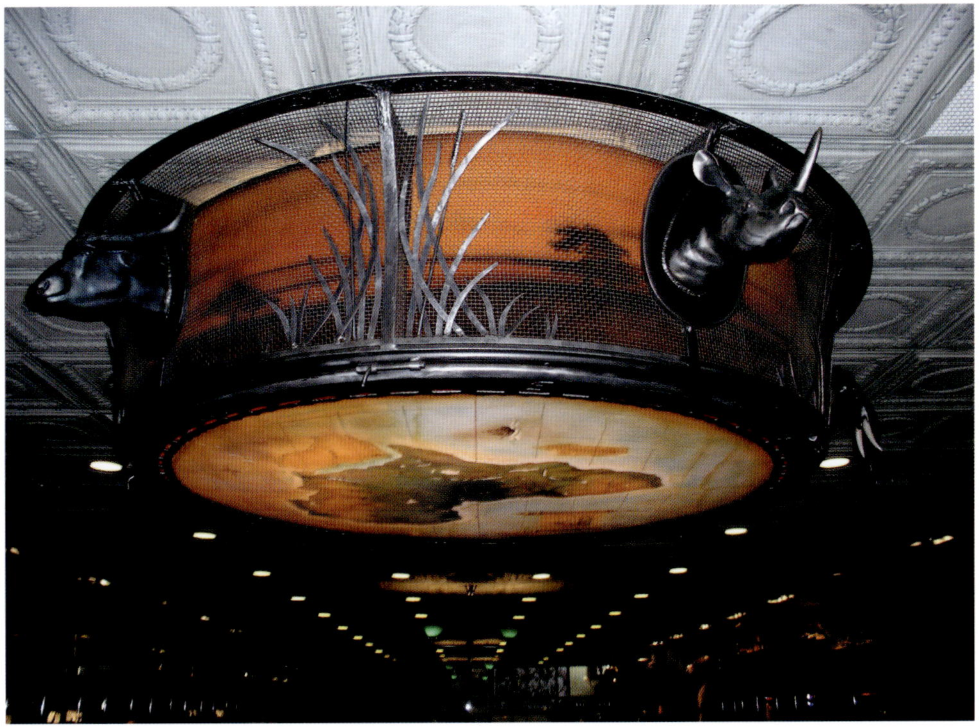

Kirk Sullens. Animal chandelier showing the heads of an elephant, and a rhinoceros. *Photo, artist*

Kirk Sullens. A jaguar head in progress. Sullens' rendition of animals on large and small scales is brilliant. He seems able to imbue them with life and personality although they are in steel. *Photo, artist*

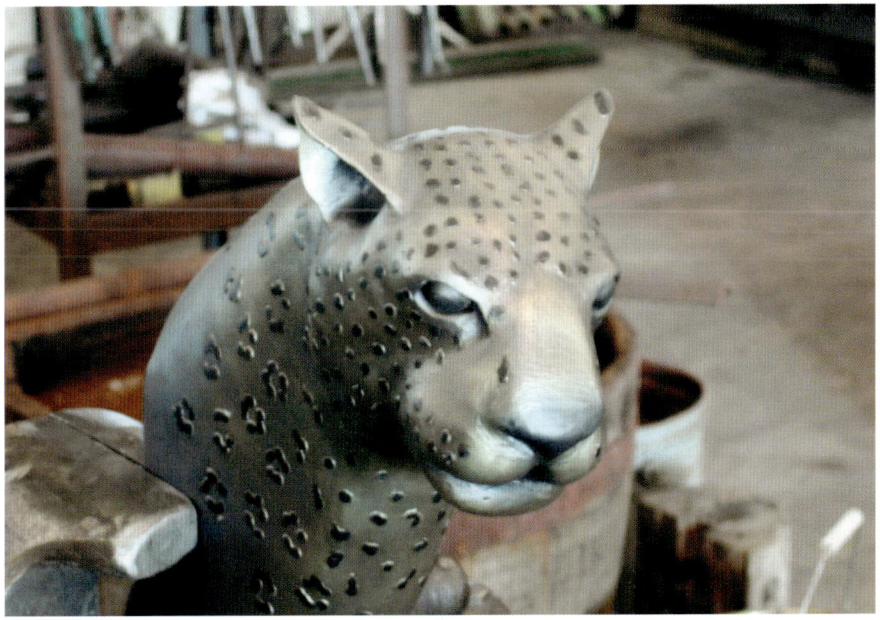

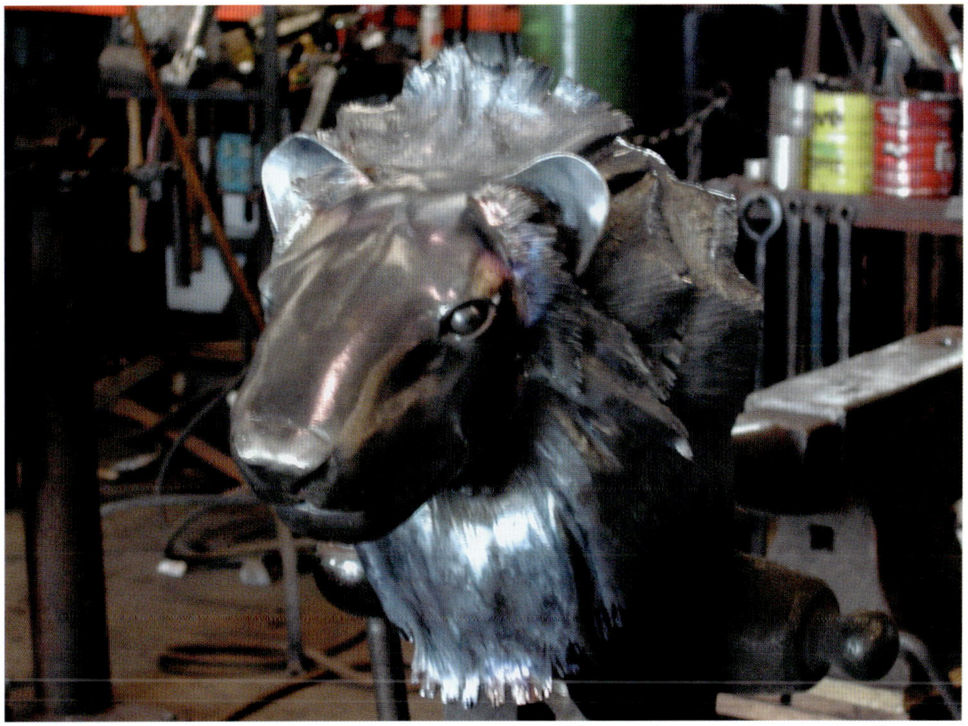

Kirk Sullens. A lion head in progress. Raising a flat sheet of metal to create a three dimensional animal complete with a hairy mane, requires specific expertise, experience, talent, and an in depth study of the animal. *Photo, artist*

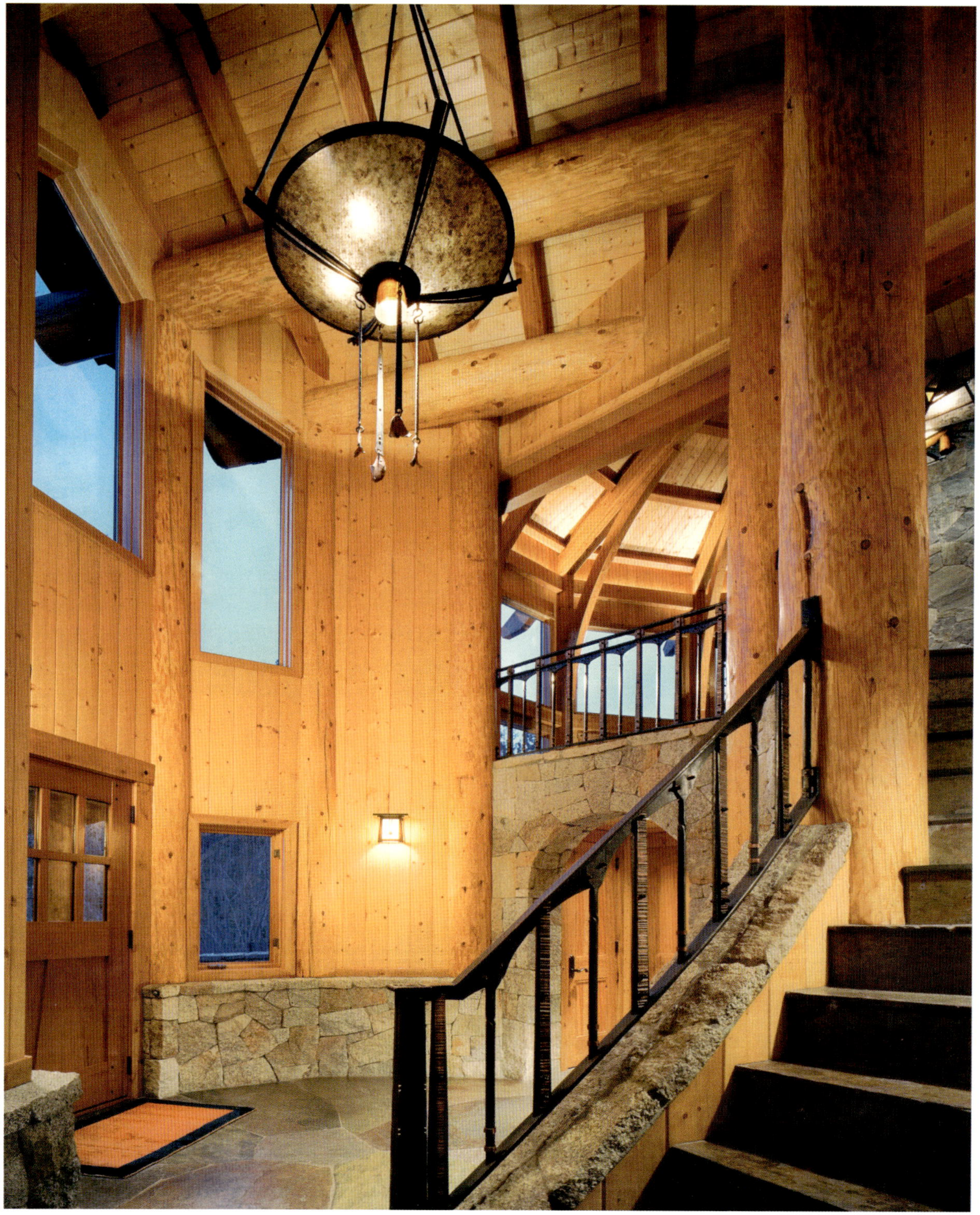

Steve Lopes, assisted by Dean Mook and Tri Ficker. Entry hall fixture. Copper, steel, and mica. Four dangling pieces are small sculptures inspired by the wife's dangling earrings. 5' high, 3' diam. *Photo, Vance Fox*

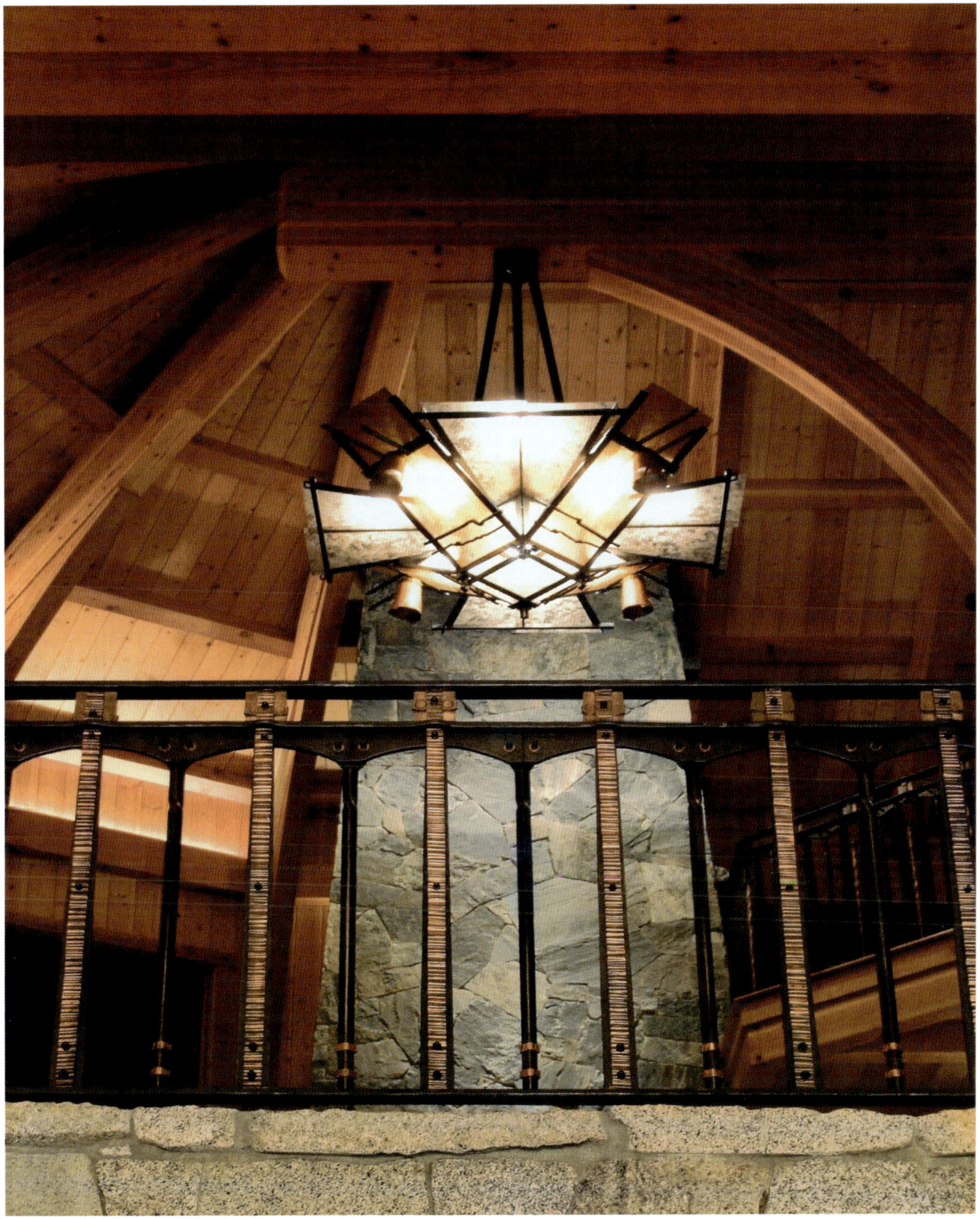

Steve Lopes and Josh Jones. Great Room Light. Copper, steel, and mica. Inspired by a toy being played with by a child. A drawing was made, a model produced, and the final fixture took shape. 5' high, 6' diam. *Photo, Vance Fox*

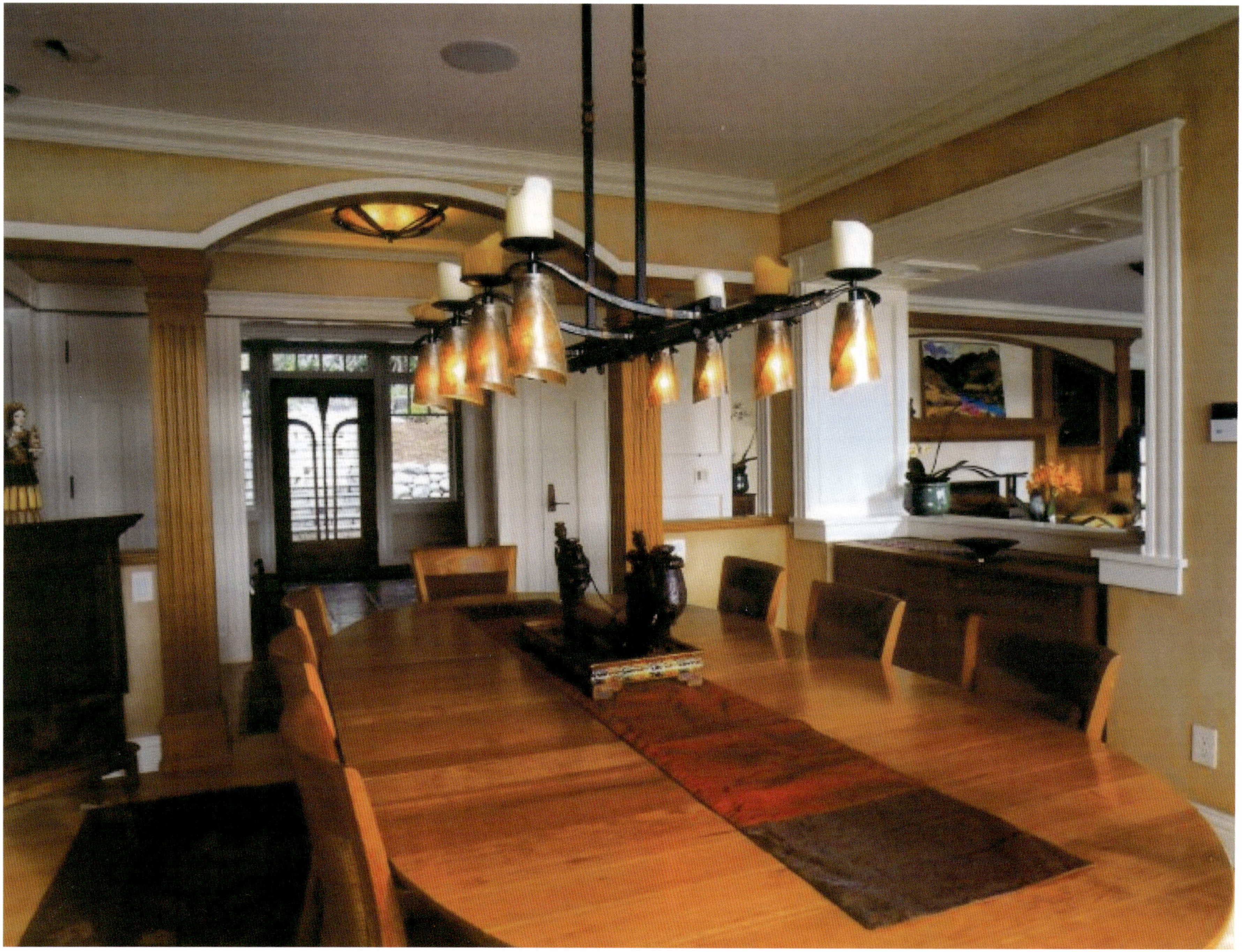

Steve Lopes, assisted by Tri Ficker. Dining room fixture. Candles are in the up lights and electric bulbs are in the down lights. 42" long, 21" wide. The coordinated hall ceiling light in the background is 3' diam. *Photo, Craig Wester*

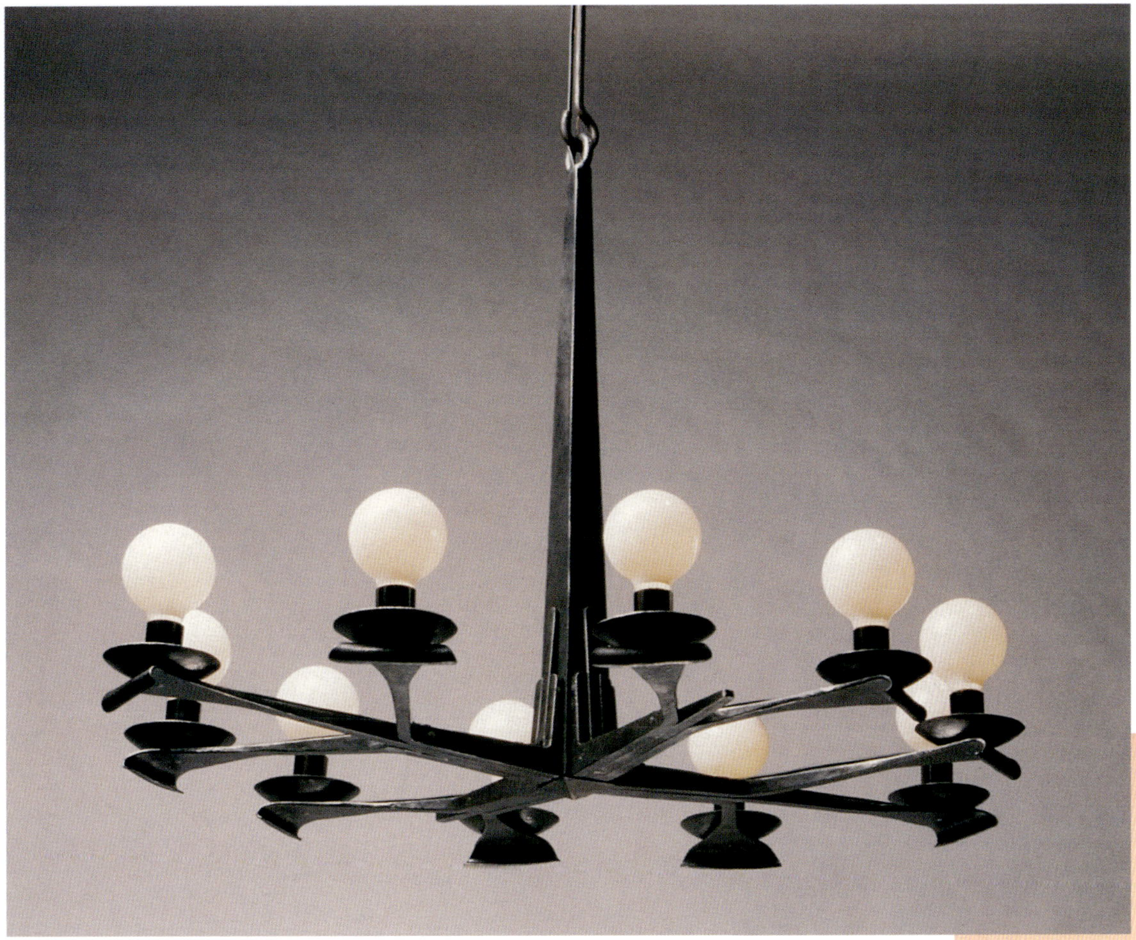

Glenn F. Gilmore. Dining room chandelier custom made to light up a long narrow table originally used in the client's grandfather's general store. 24" high, 36" wide, 24" deep. *Photo, McNabb Studio*

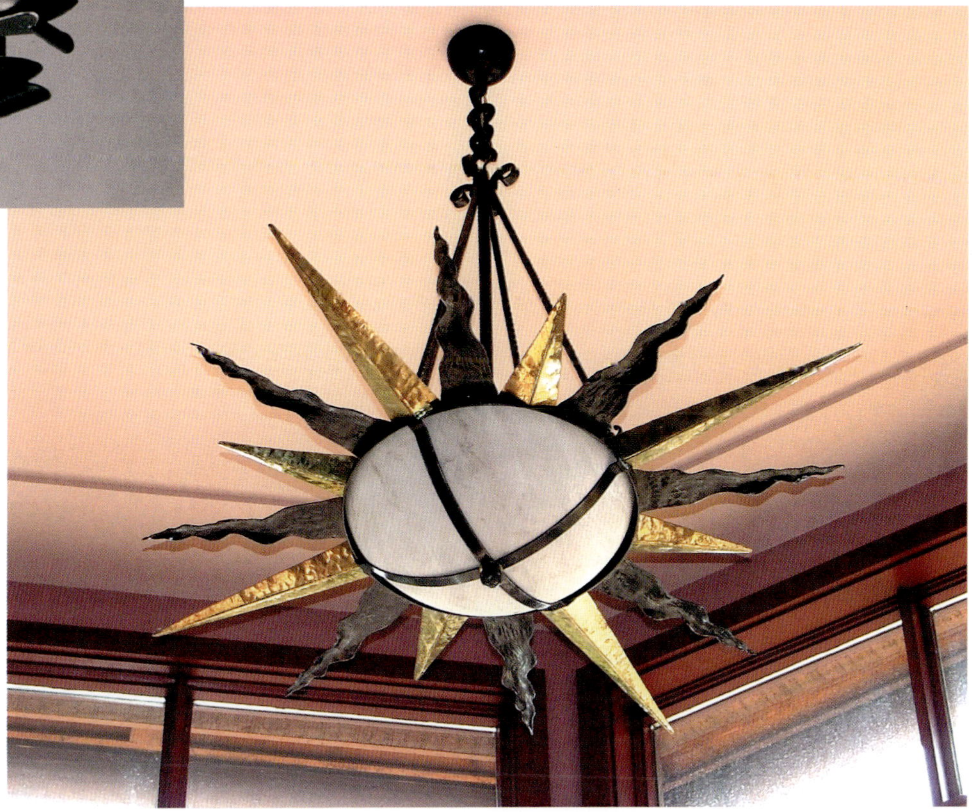

Frederic A. Crist and David W. Munn. *Sunburst chandelier* for the Black Friars Theater in Staunton, Virginia. Forged steel and brass with an alabaster bowl. *Photo, Frederic Crist*

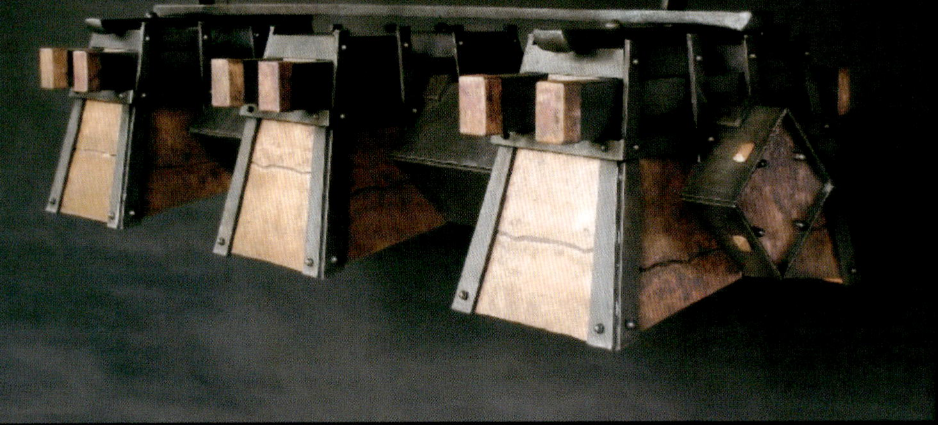

Steve Lopes assisted by Josh Jones and Tri Ficker. Pool table light. Copper and steel. The design imitates the exterior architecture of the house with the "beams" capped in copper. 16" high, 48" long, 21" deep. *Photo, Craig Wester*

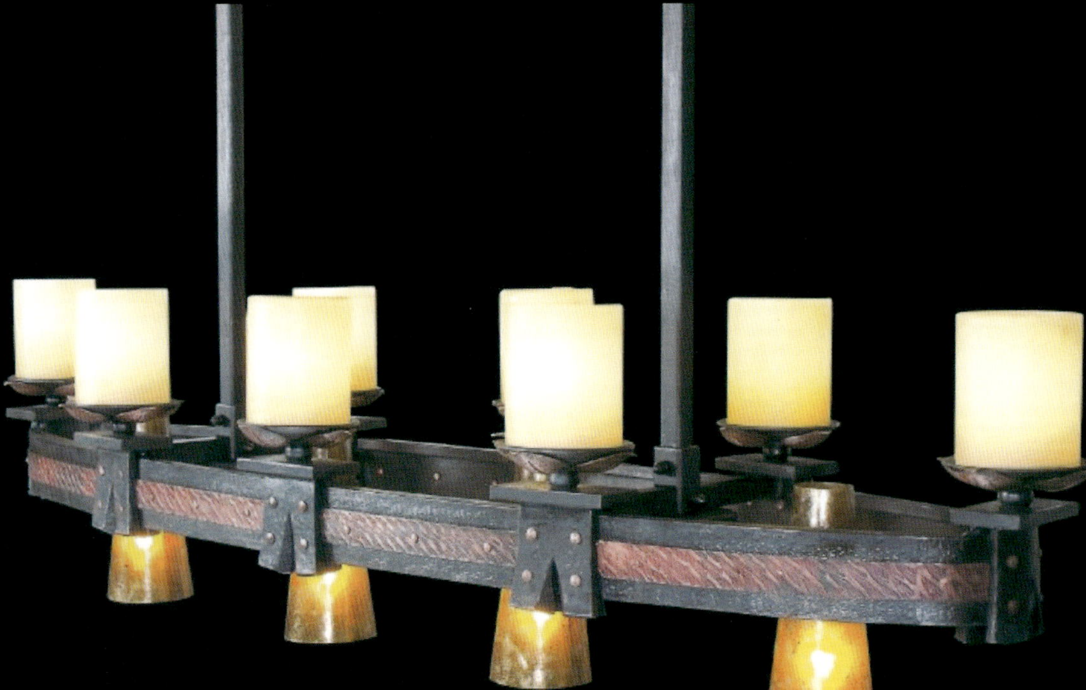

Steve Lopes, assisted by Josh Jones. Ellipse

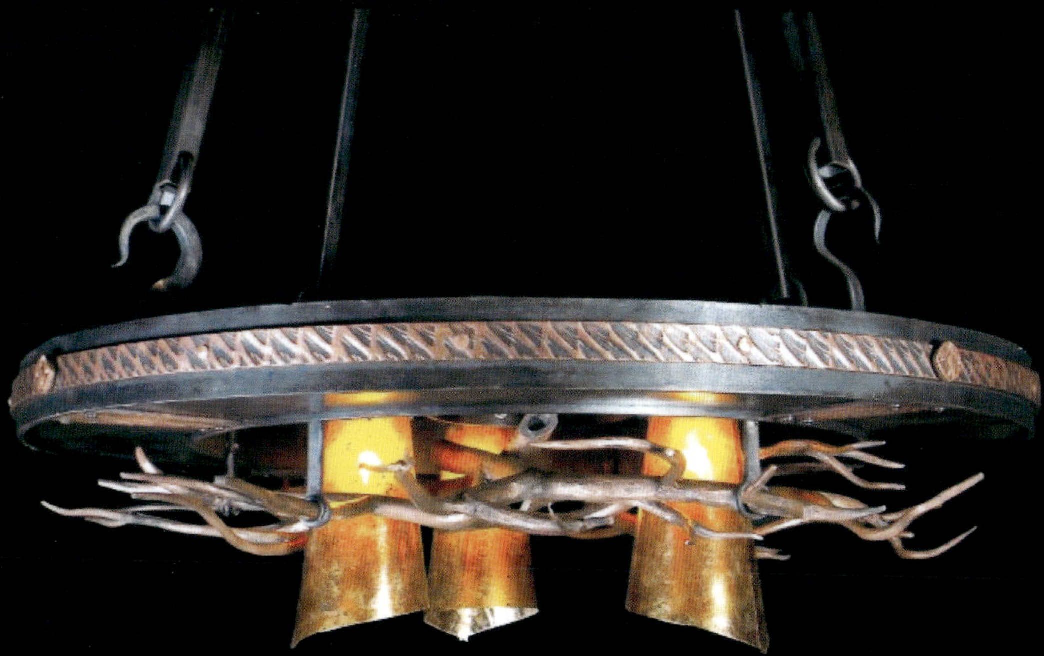

Steve Lopes, assisted by Dean Mook. Chandelier for a dining room. Forging steel to look like branches resulted in a feeling of "nature" desired by the clients. Copper, steel, and mica. 32" diam. *Photo, Craig Wester*

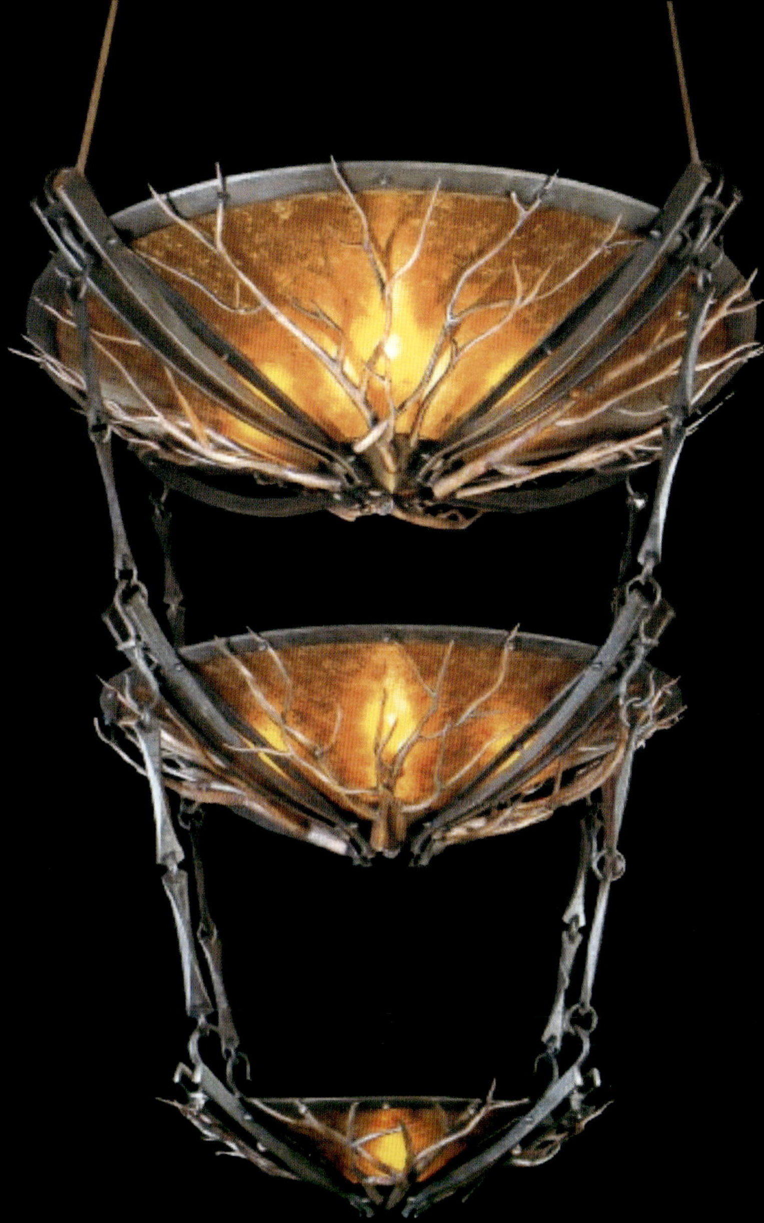

Steve Lopes, assisted by Dean Mook and Tri Ficker. Triple tier fixture. Copper and steel. 5' high, lights graduated in size: 4', 3', and 2' diam. *Photo, Craig Wester*

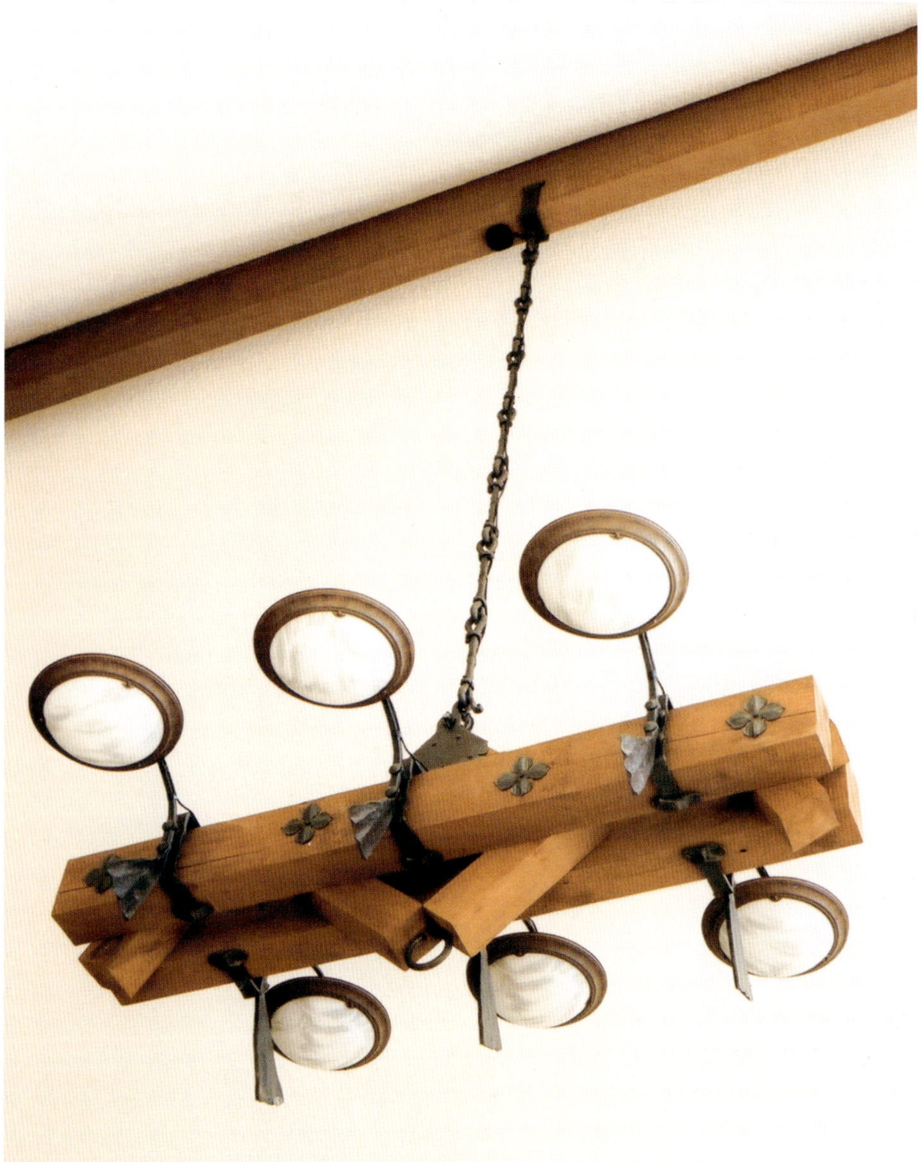

Bernhard Heer. Hanging light. Pine tree lumber with forged steel. 80" high, 60" wide. *Photo, artist*

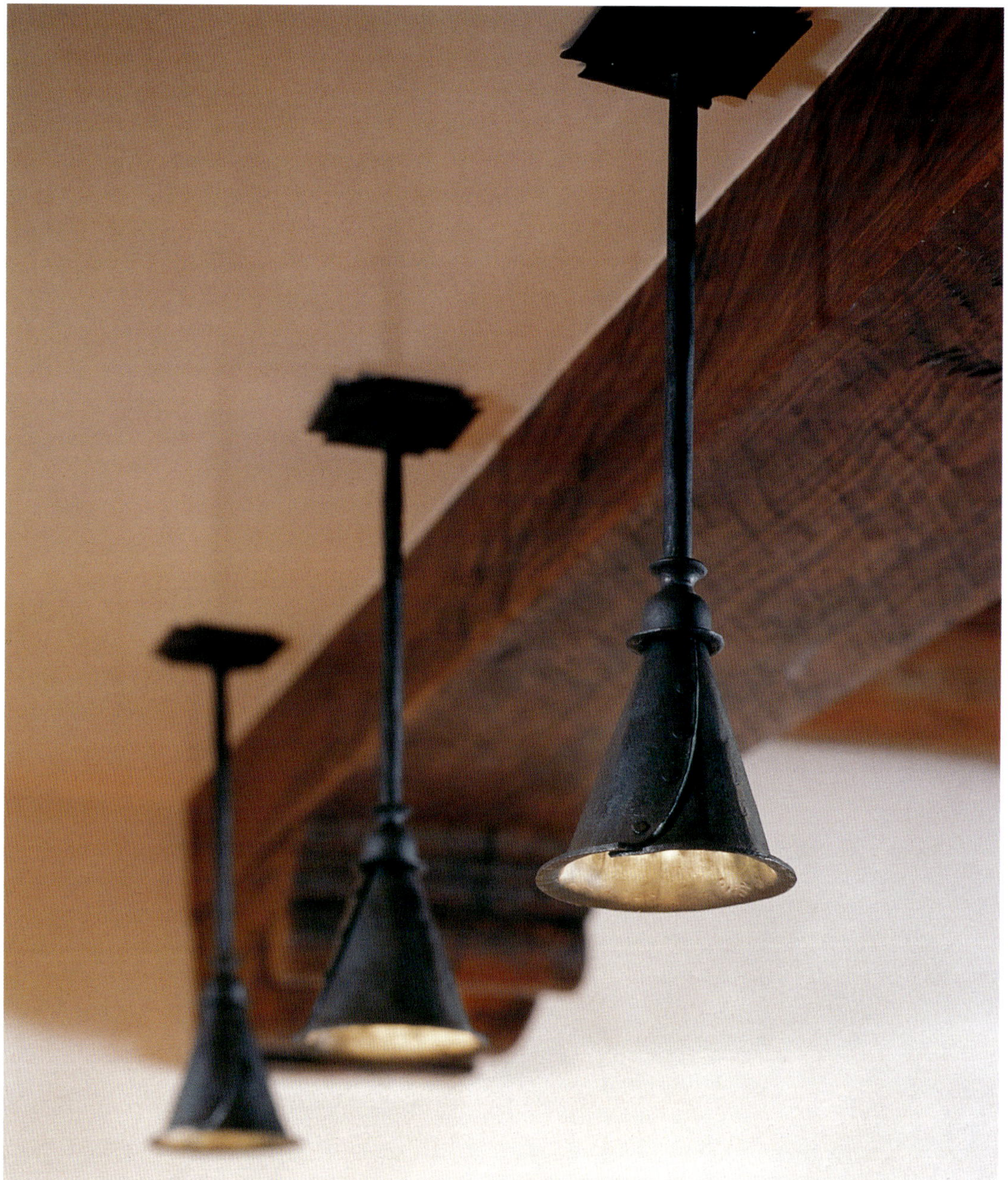

Christopher Thomson. Three ceiling pendants. Designed for over a kitchen island or sink. Each 20" high, 6.5" diam. *Photo, David Marlow*

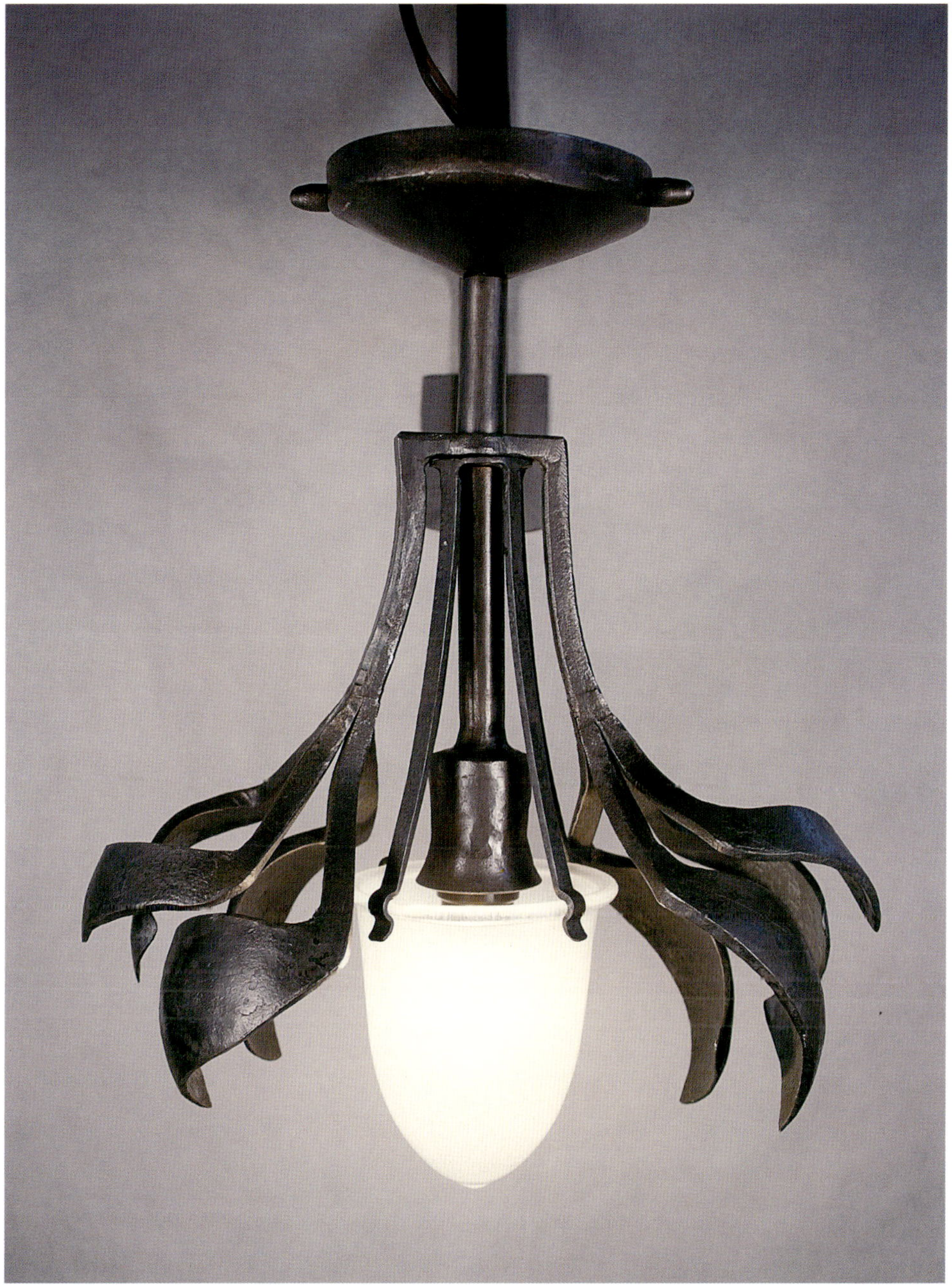

Daniel Smith. Ceiling lamp. Steel and glass. Spring steel "spiders" hold the glass. The entire piece can be dismantled for maintenance. 22" high, 18" wide, 10" deep. Glass globe by Helen Tegeler. *Photo, artist*

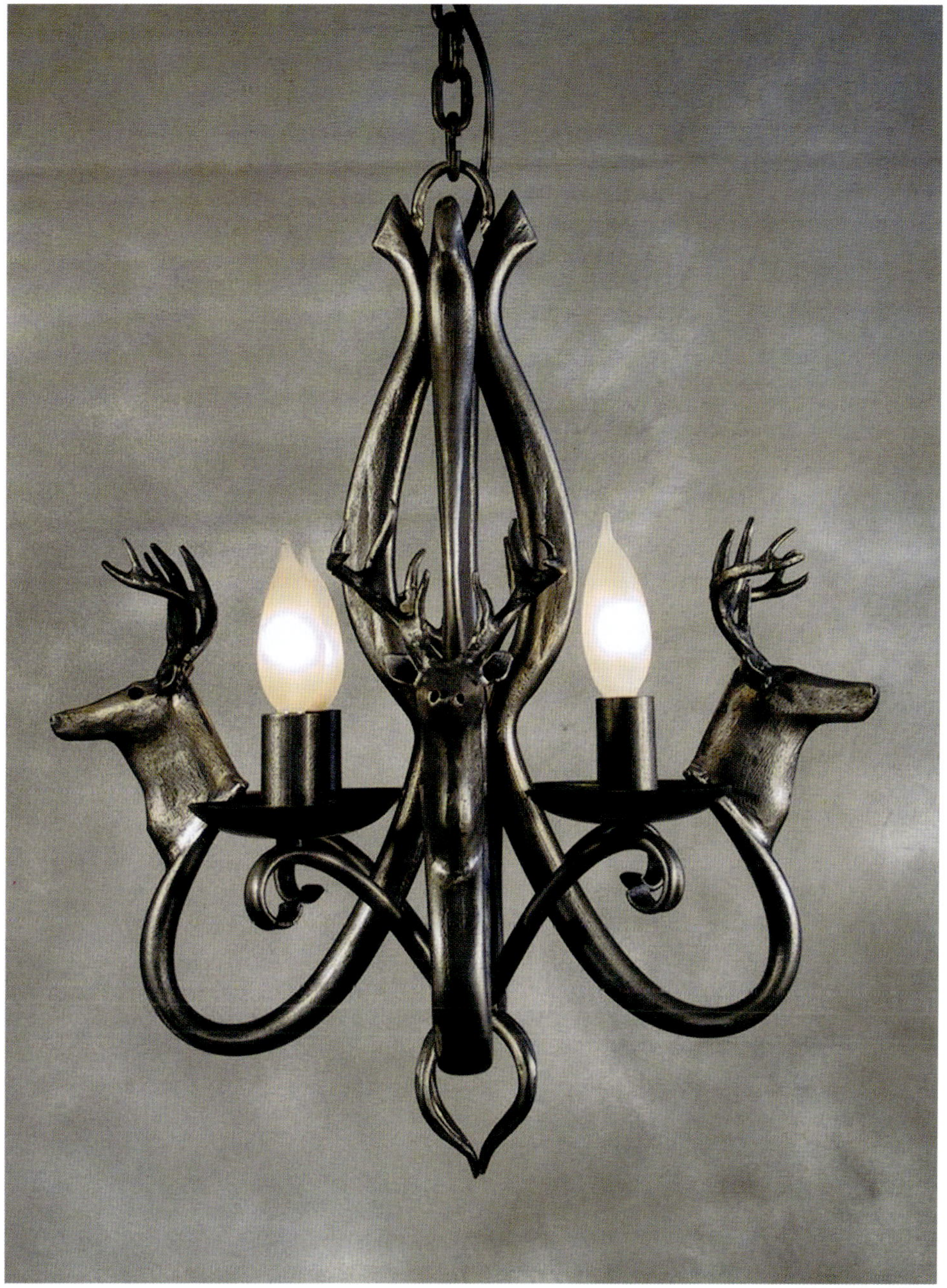

Steve Joslyn. Stag chandelier. Many of Joslyn's pieces incorporate animals, grasses, and flowers, always inspired by nature and the plants he sees growing around his studio in Smyrna, New York. *Photo, artist*

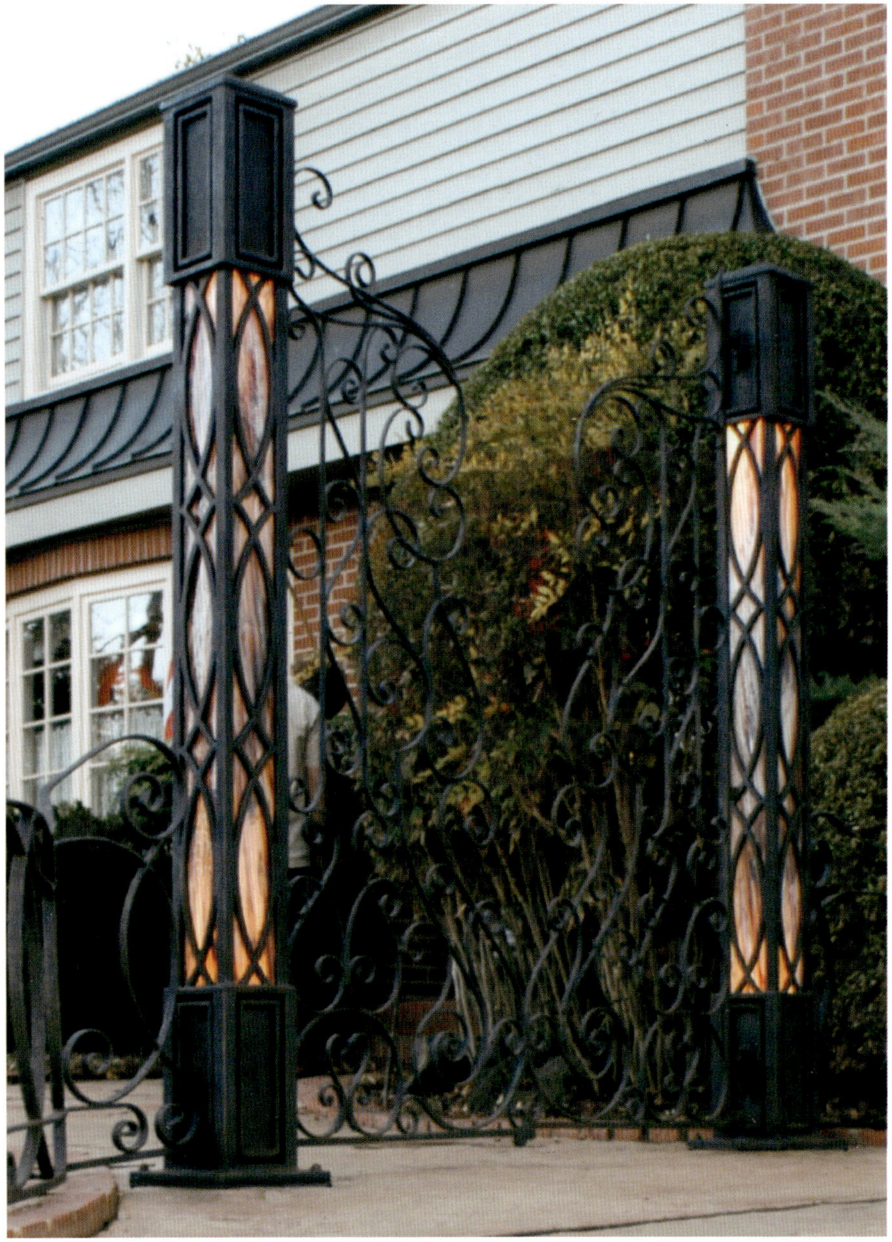

Arthur Taylor. Lampposts. Mild steel plate with plasma-cut designs. Fabricated using over 90 pieces of steel seamlessly welded and fit to form the top and bottom of each design. They can enhance a variety of different landscapes and walkways and may be used individually or in conjunction with a gate or railing. Texture and accents complement the art glass chosen for the lamp. 74" high, 7" wide and deep. *Photo, Jeff White*

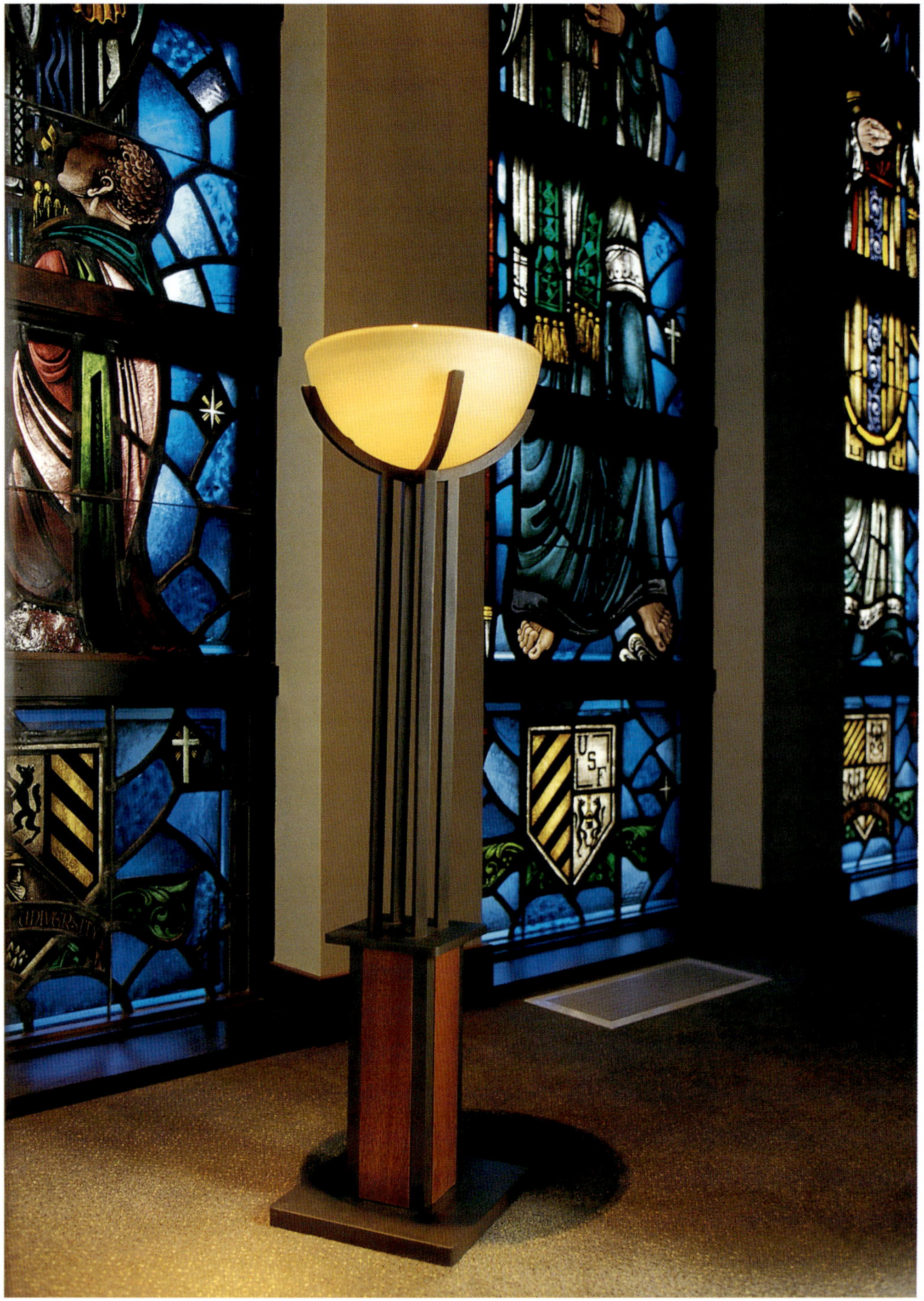

Stephen Marks. Holy water font with lighting. Steel, blown glass, and mahogany. Installed in the Seattle University chapel. 28" high, 10" wide, 10" deep. *Photo, William P. Wright*

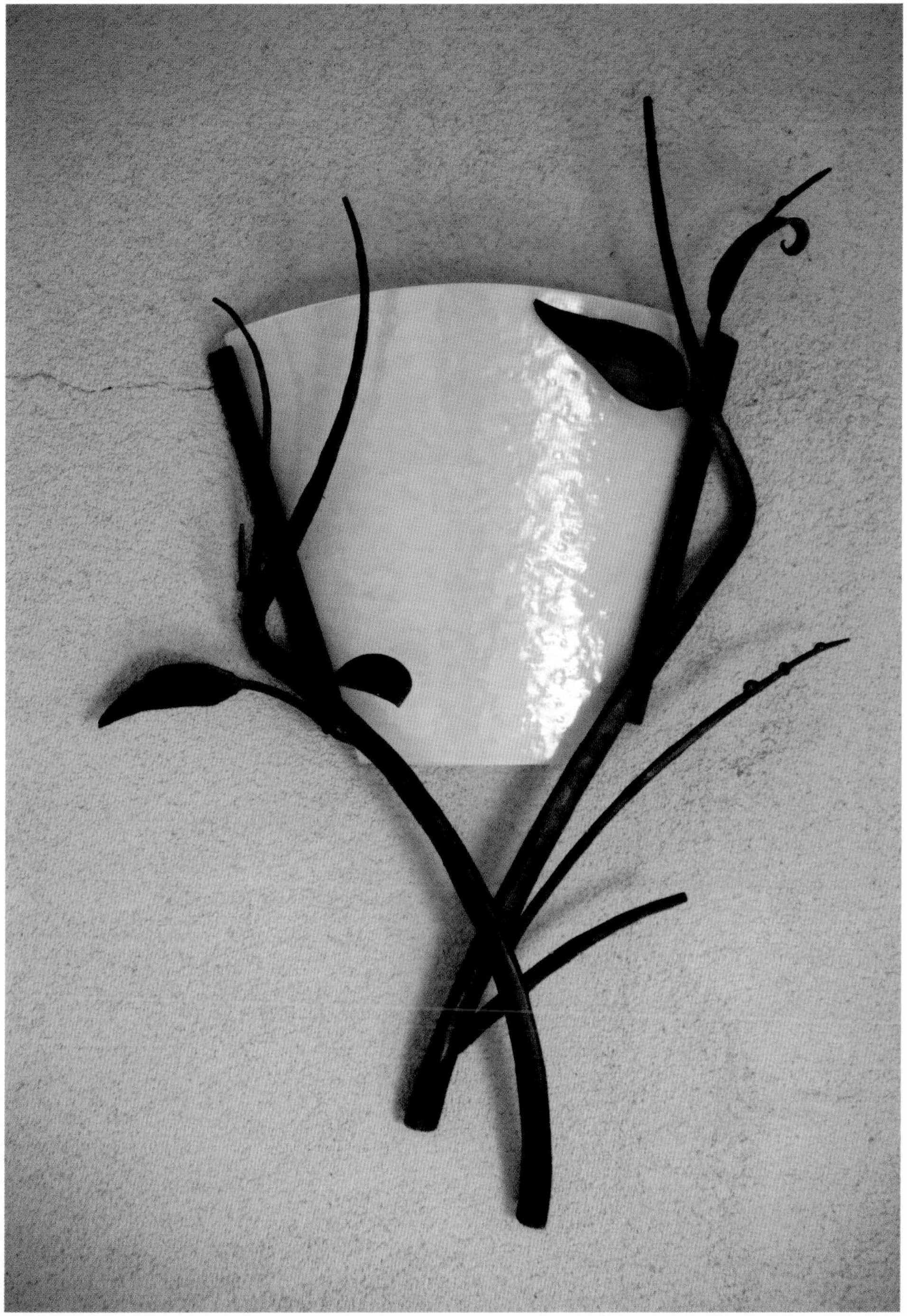

Julie Henry. *Spring Sconce.* Forged steel and slumped glass. 32" high, 12" wide, 3" deep. Each set of sconces at different doors represents a different season. Glass by Michelle Knox. *Photo, Chris Berggren*

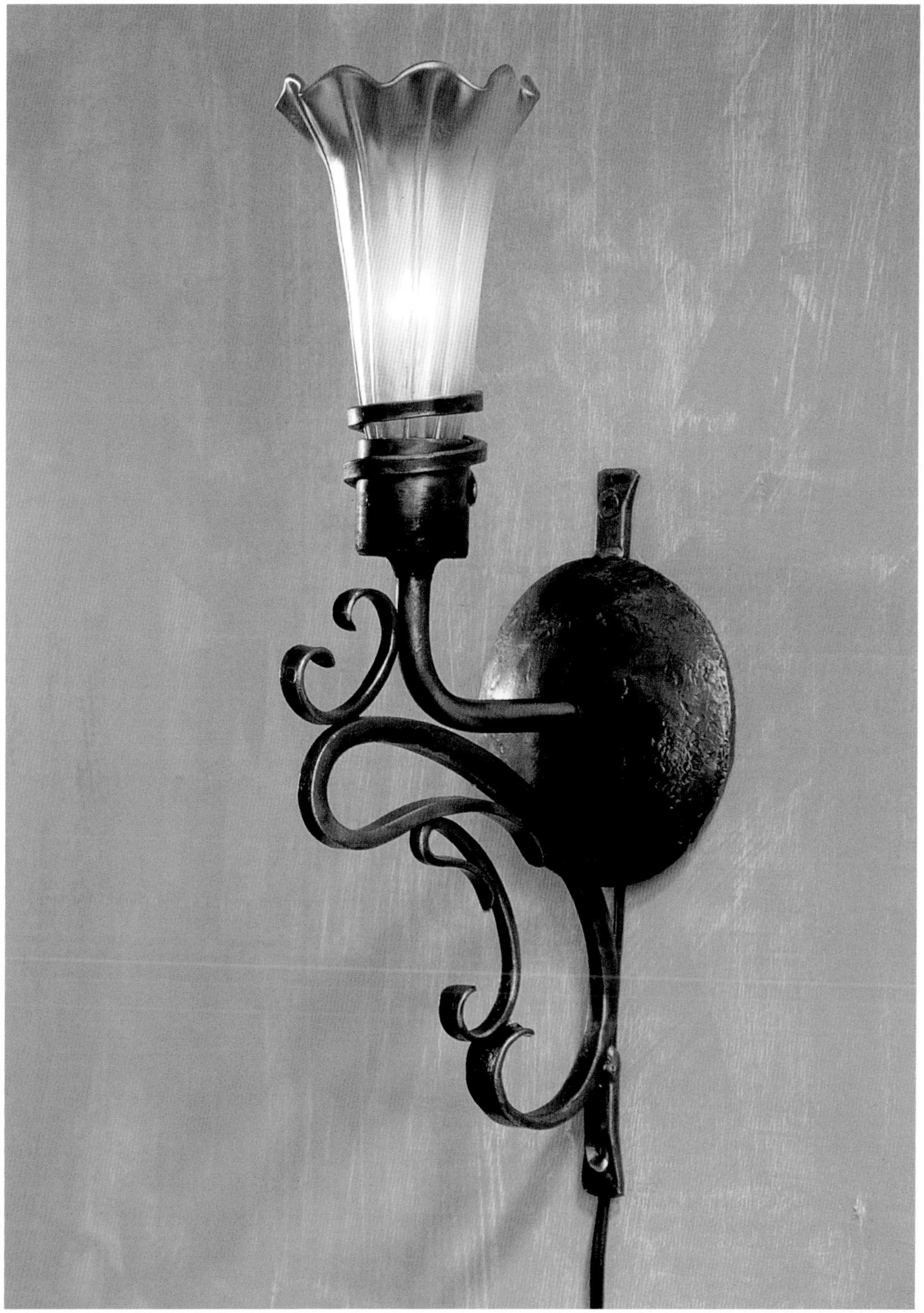

Lisa Elias. Wall sconce, steel with glass shade. *Photo, Andrea Rugg*

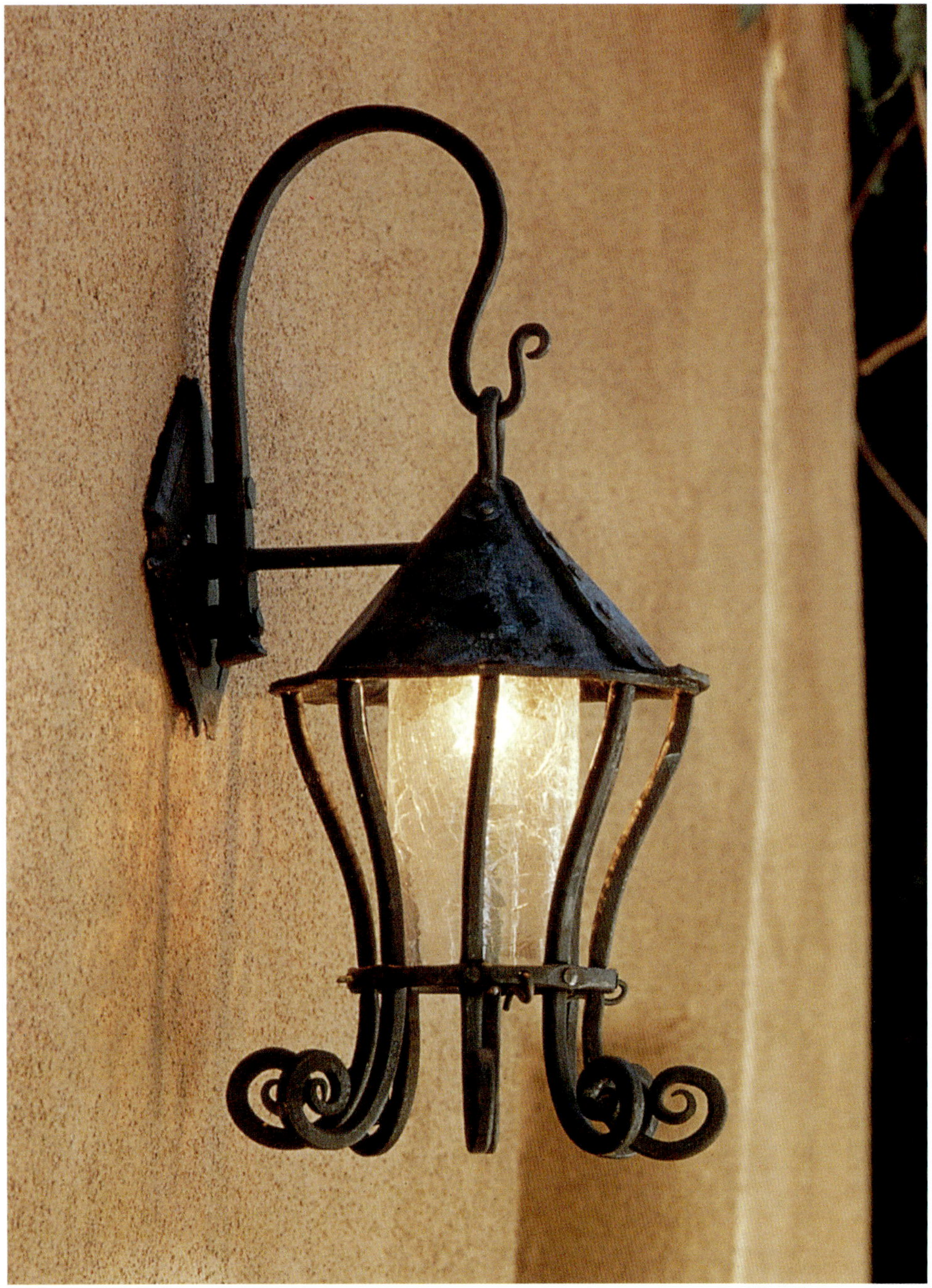

Christopher Thomson. Contemporary hanging lantern with blown glass. Lantern, 16" high. Overall 22" high, 13" deep. *Photo, David Marlow*

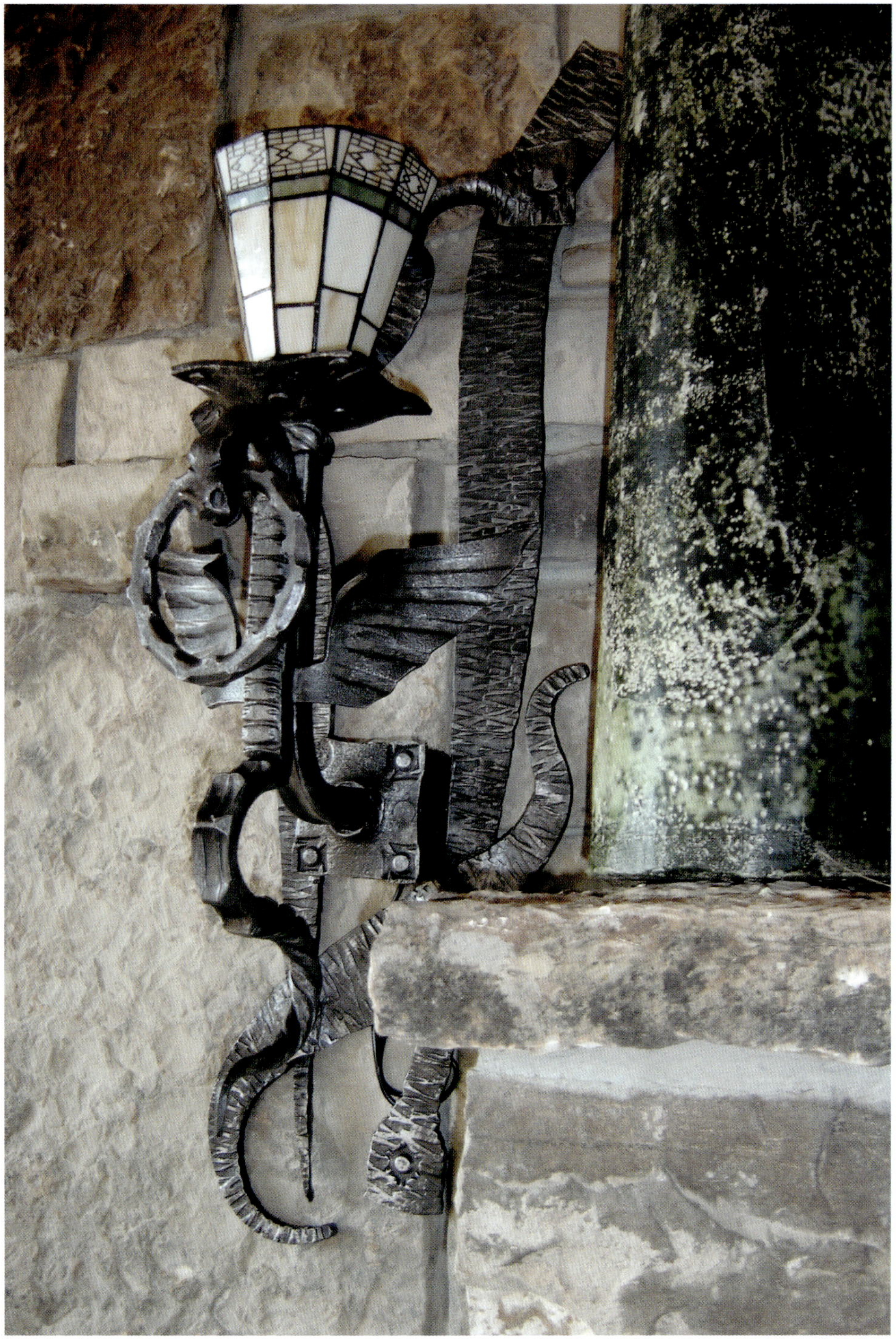

Vadim Filatov and Alexander Chumakov. Studio Gvozd. *Dragon sconce*. Forged iron and stained glass. 24" high, 15" wide. *Photo, courtesy, artists*

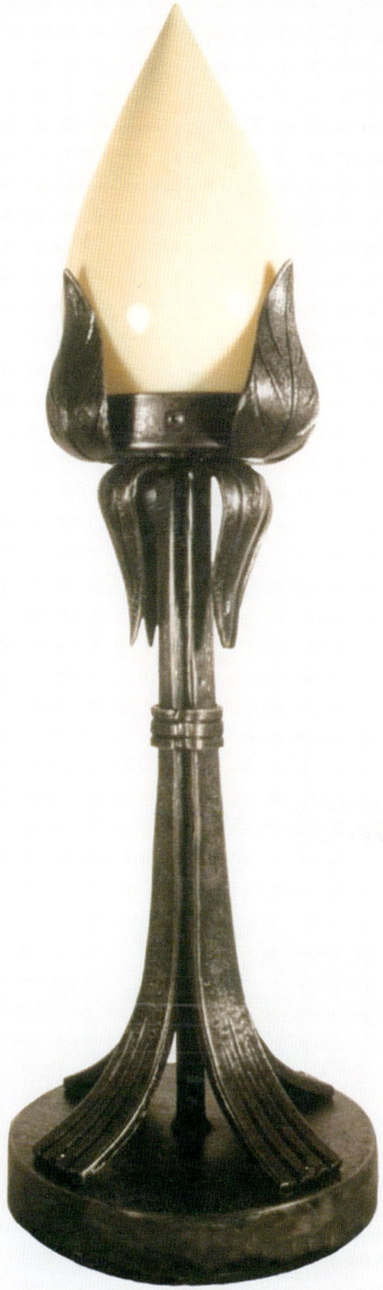

Frederic A. Crist and David W. Munn. *Torpedo Lamp*. Forged steel with antique glass globe. 26" high, 6" diam. *Photo, Fred Crist*

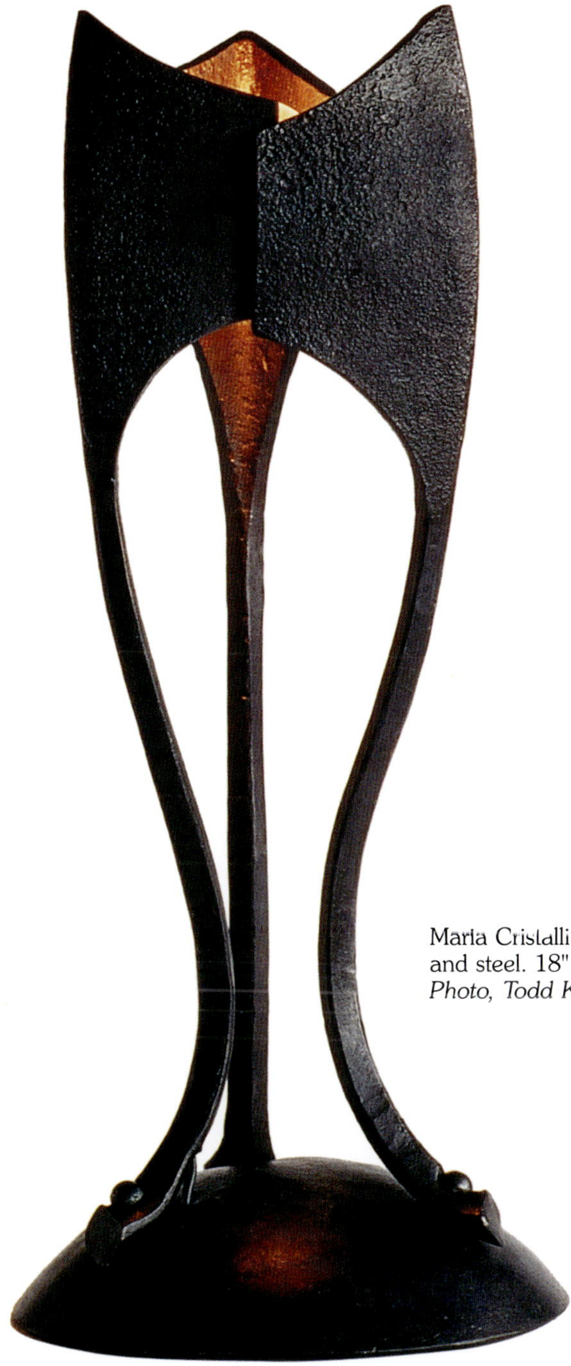

Maria Cristalli. Lamp. Angle iron and steel. 18" high, 8" diam. *Photo, Todd Kalamar*

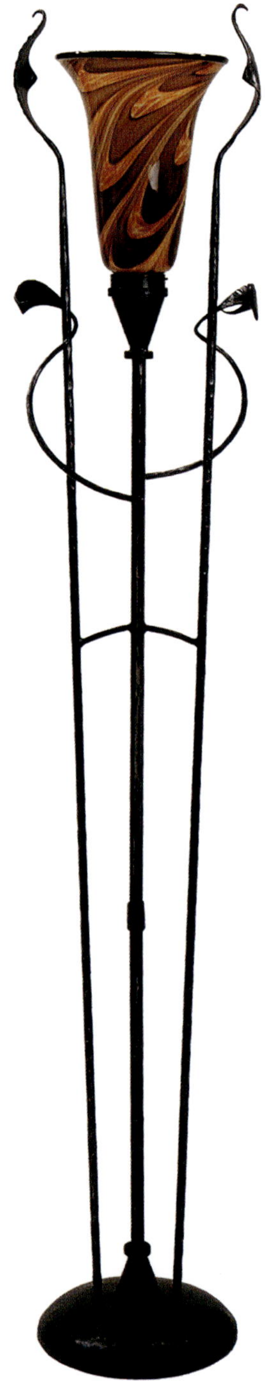

Erika Strecker. *Effervesce* floor lamp. Hand forged steel and hand blown glass. 12" high, 6" diam. *Photo, Leeann Greer*

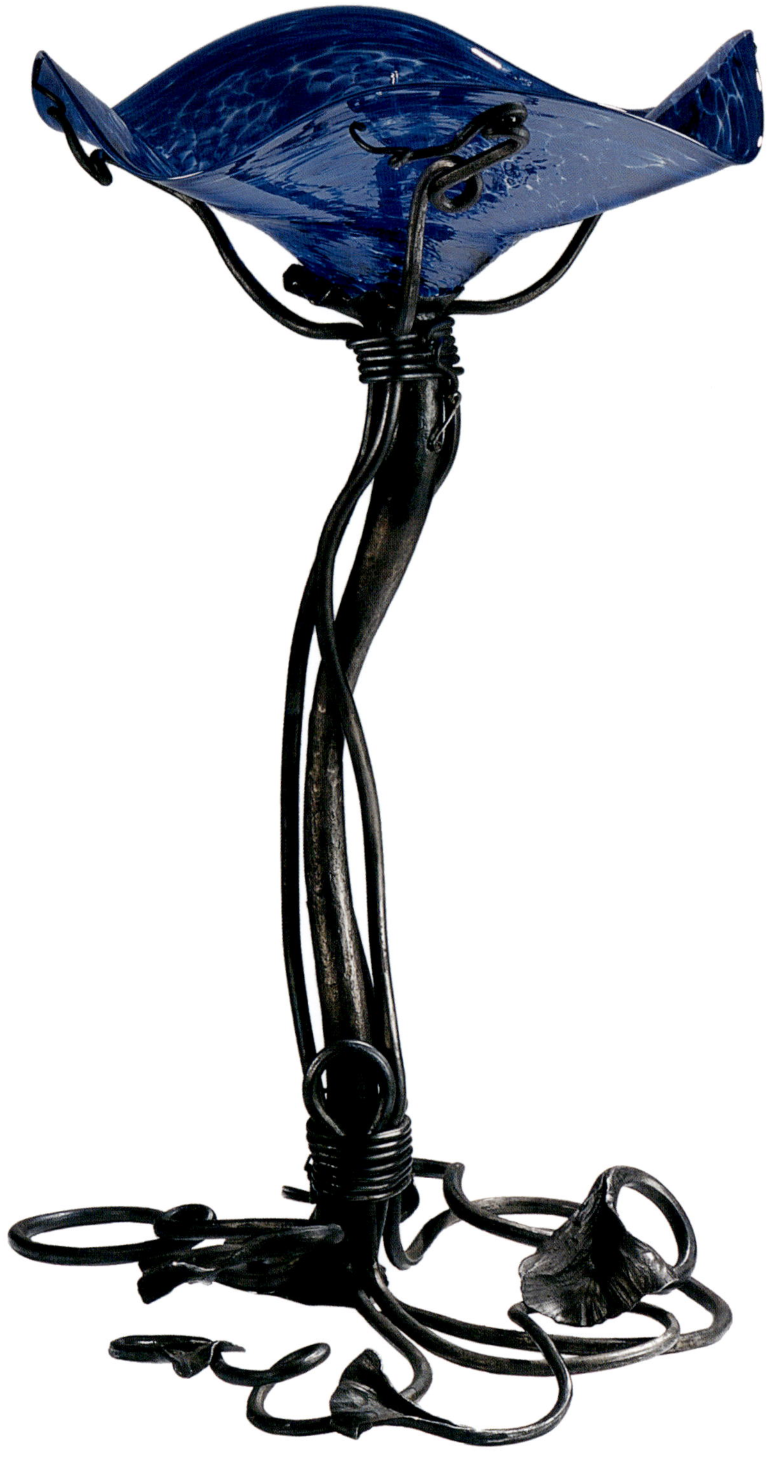

Roberta Elliott. Lamp. Mild steel black pipe with a blown glass shade by Marty Holmes. One of several in a lamp study series. 26" high, 18" diam. *Photo, Jeff Bruce*

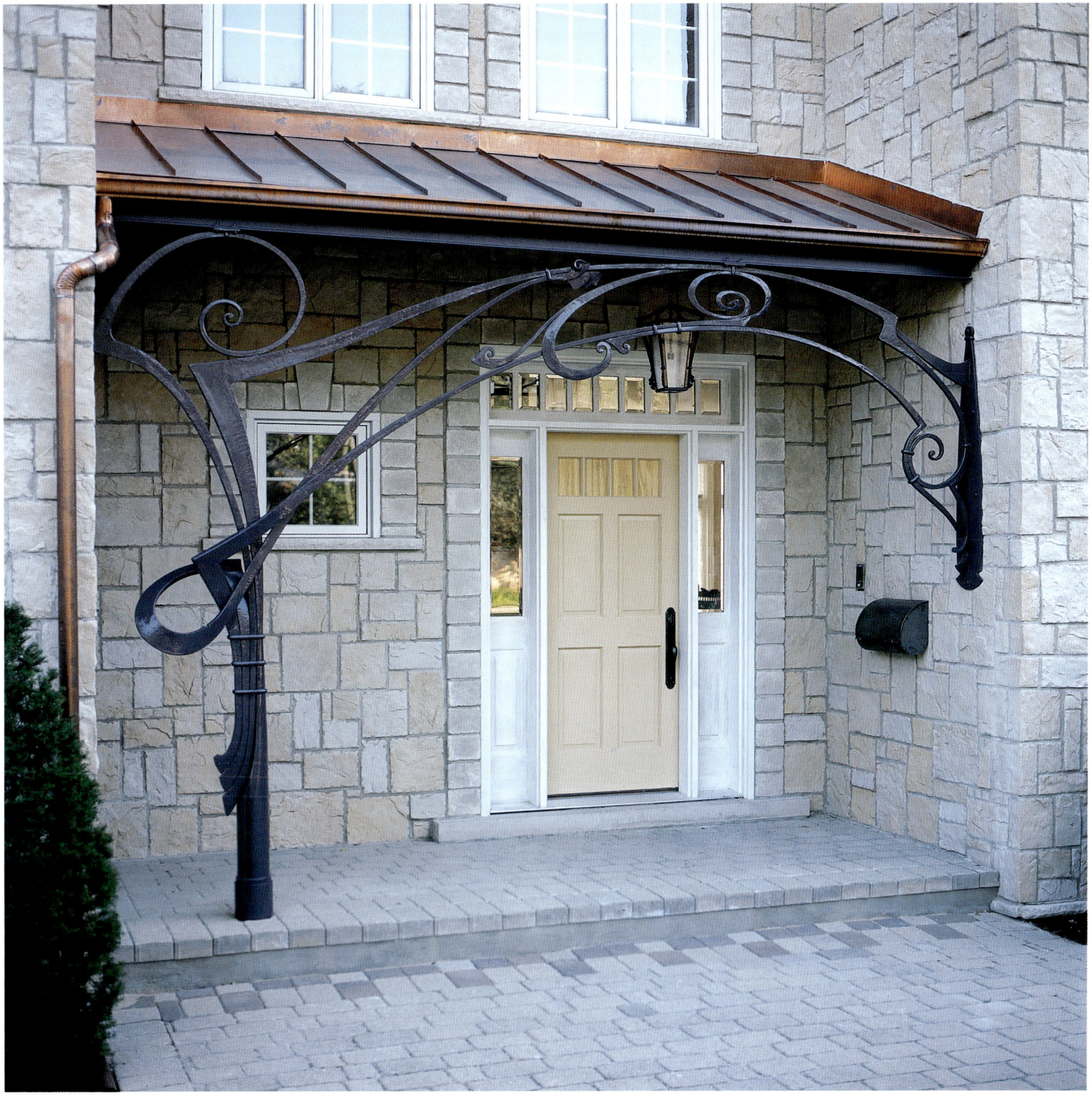

John Medwedeff. Gately Arch and light fixture. Forged and fabricated steel.14' high, 2' wide, 1.5' deep. *Photo, Jeff Bruce*

Candle Holders

With the growing popularity of ironwork chandeliers. it is logical that artist-blacksmiths would turn their hands to making smaller objects to hold one or more candles. Iron seems a natural material for candle holders, as evidenced by the many units sold in decorator shops, department stores, and lighting shops. But many of the chandeliers are designed to hold and burn candles, too, as people decorate their homes in historical styles, such as Victorian, Craftsman, and Early American. A 15th century crystal chandelier would have required 120 candles to equal a 100-watt electric bulb. Large rooms of old, lit by candles only, required chandeliers, sconces, and candle holders throughout. Thanks to Thomas Edison, our lighting fixtures now have bulbs, but people still like to use candles and artist-blacksmiths produce a variety of candle holders that are practical and decorative.

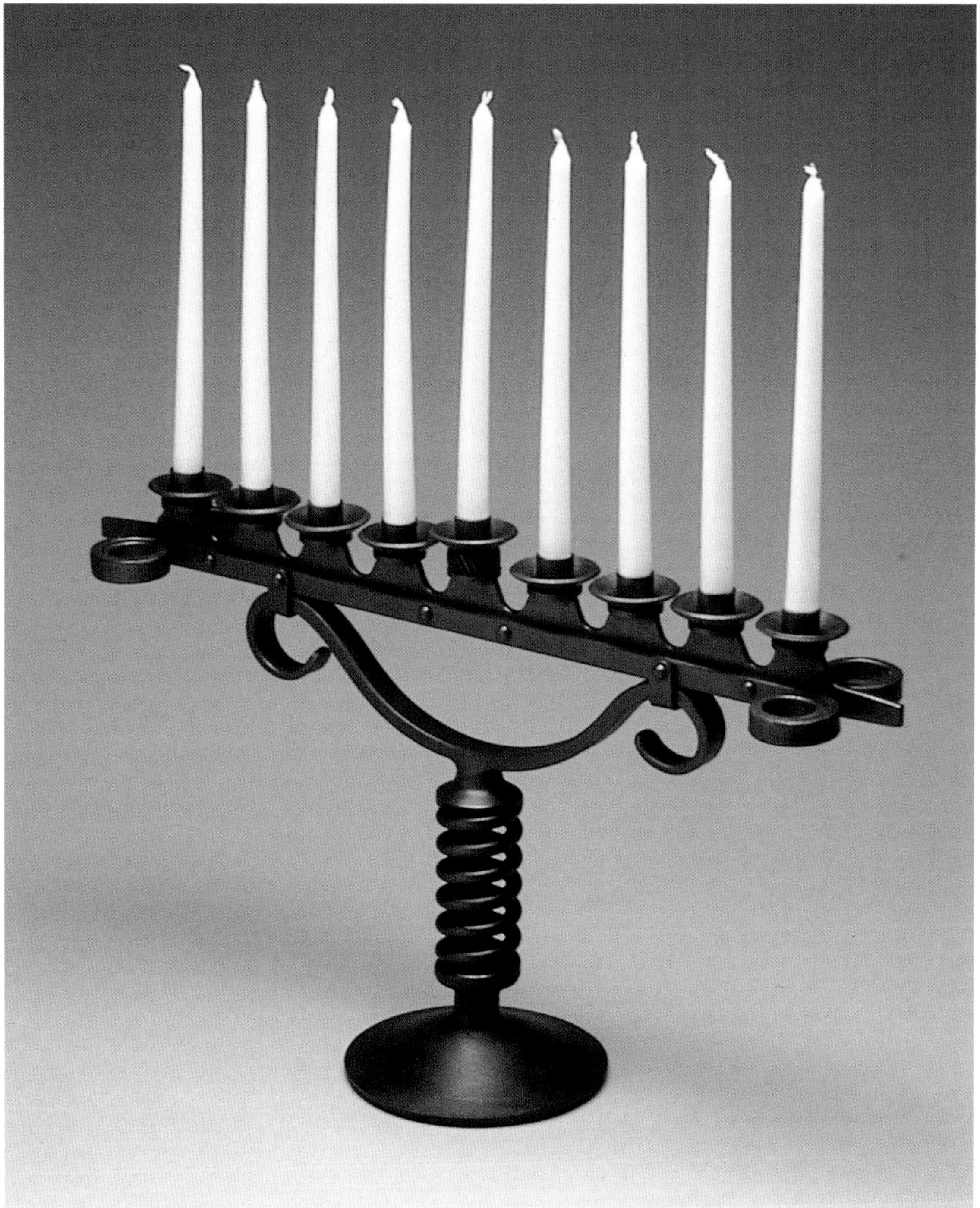

Tedd R. McDonah. Chanukah Menorah. Forged and fabricated mild steel and spring steel. 25" high, 20" wide, 8" deep. *Photo, Keith Meister*

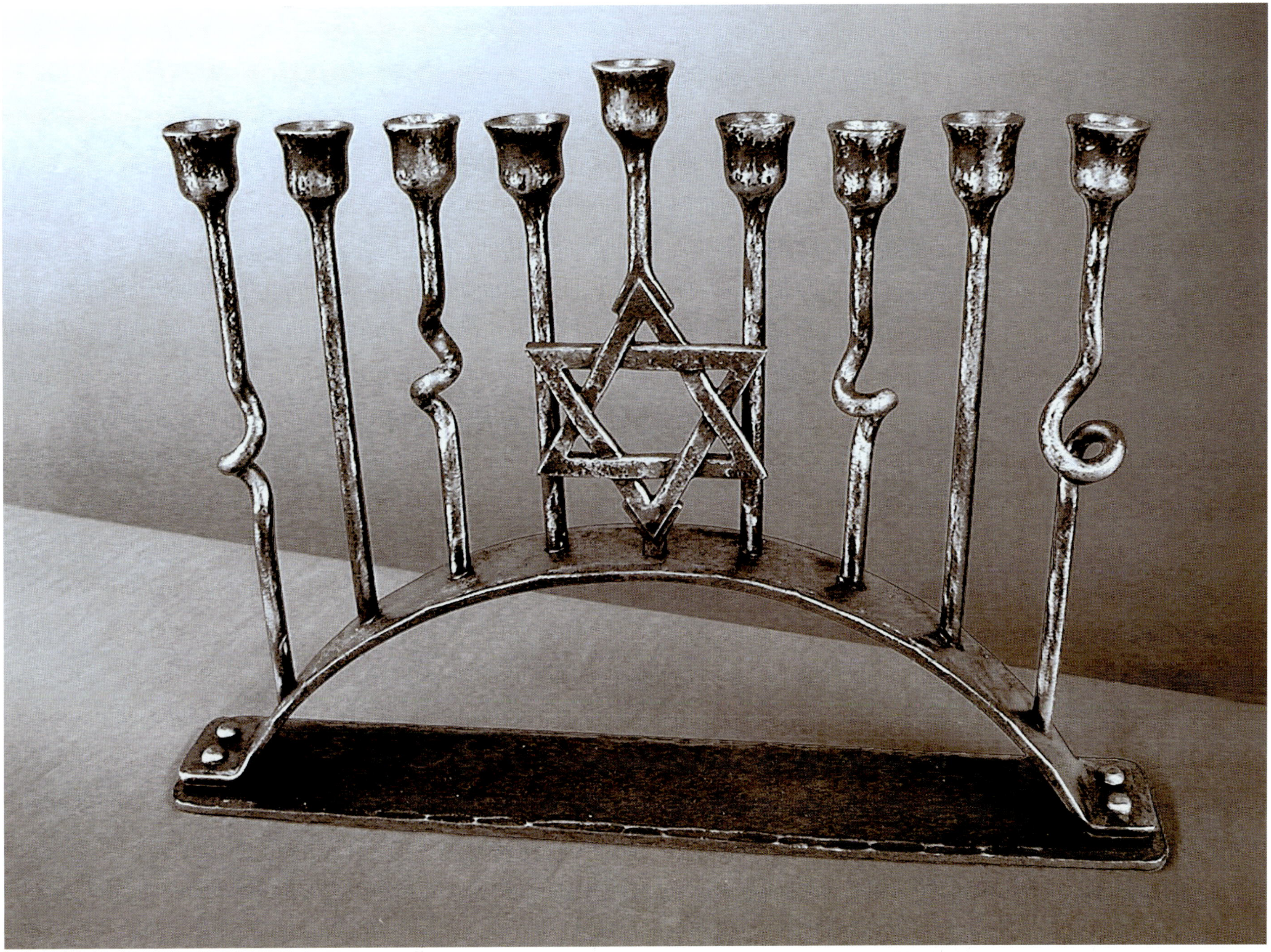

Steve Hackbarth. Menorah. *Photo, artist*

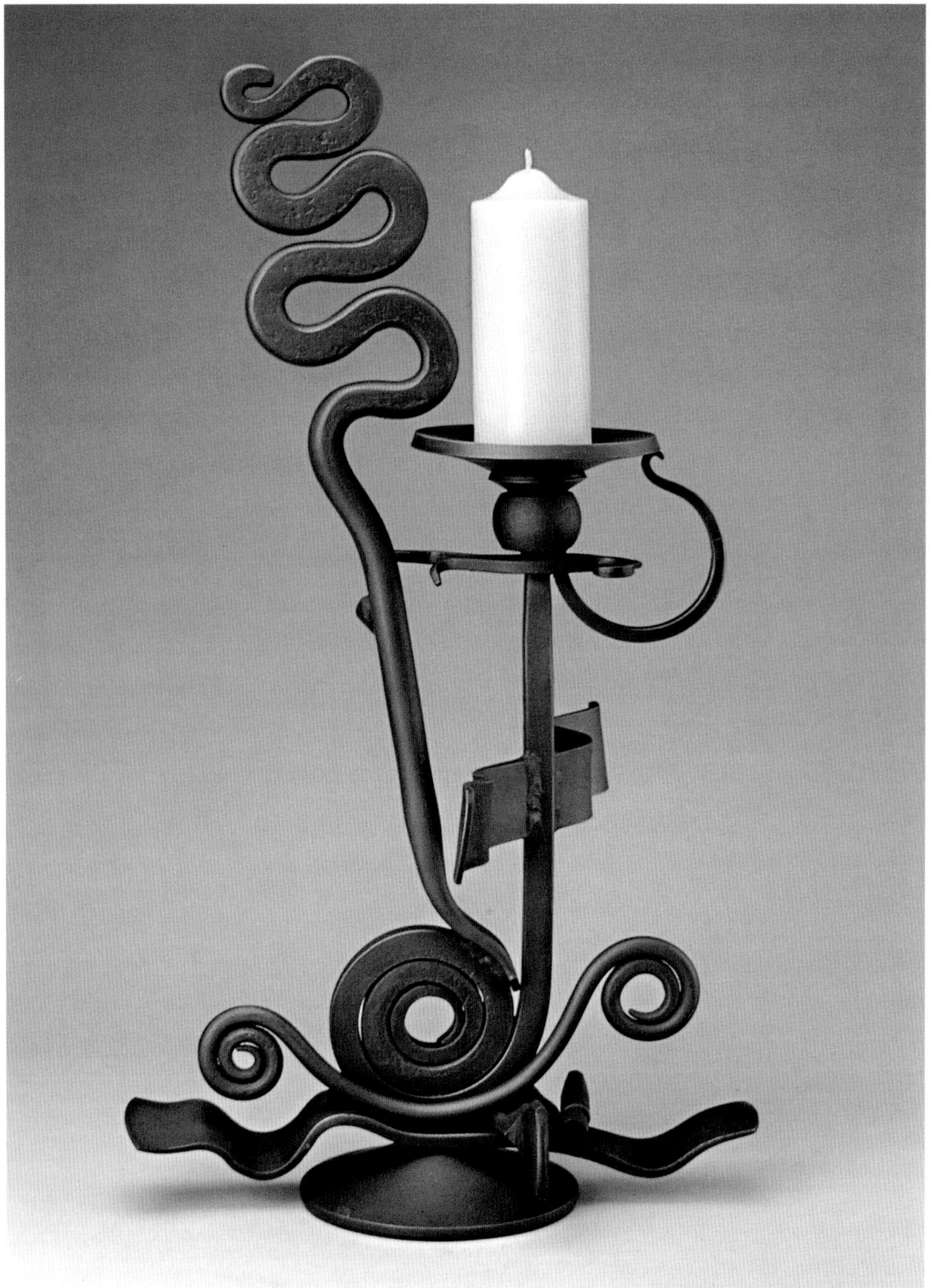

Tedd R. McDonah. Cockamamie Candleholder II. Forged and fabricated mild steel. 30" high, 18" wide, 24" deep. *Photo, Keith Meister*

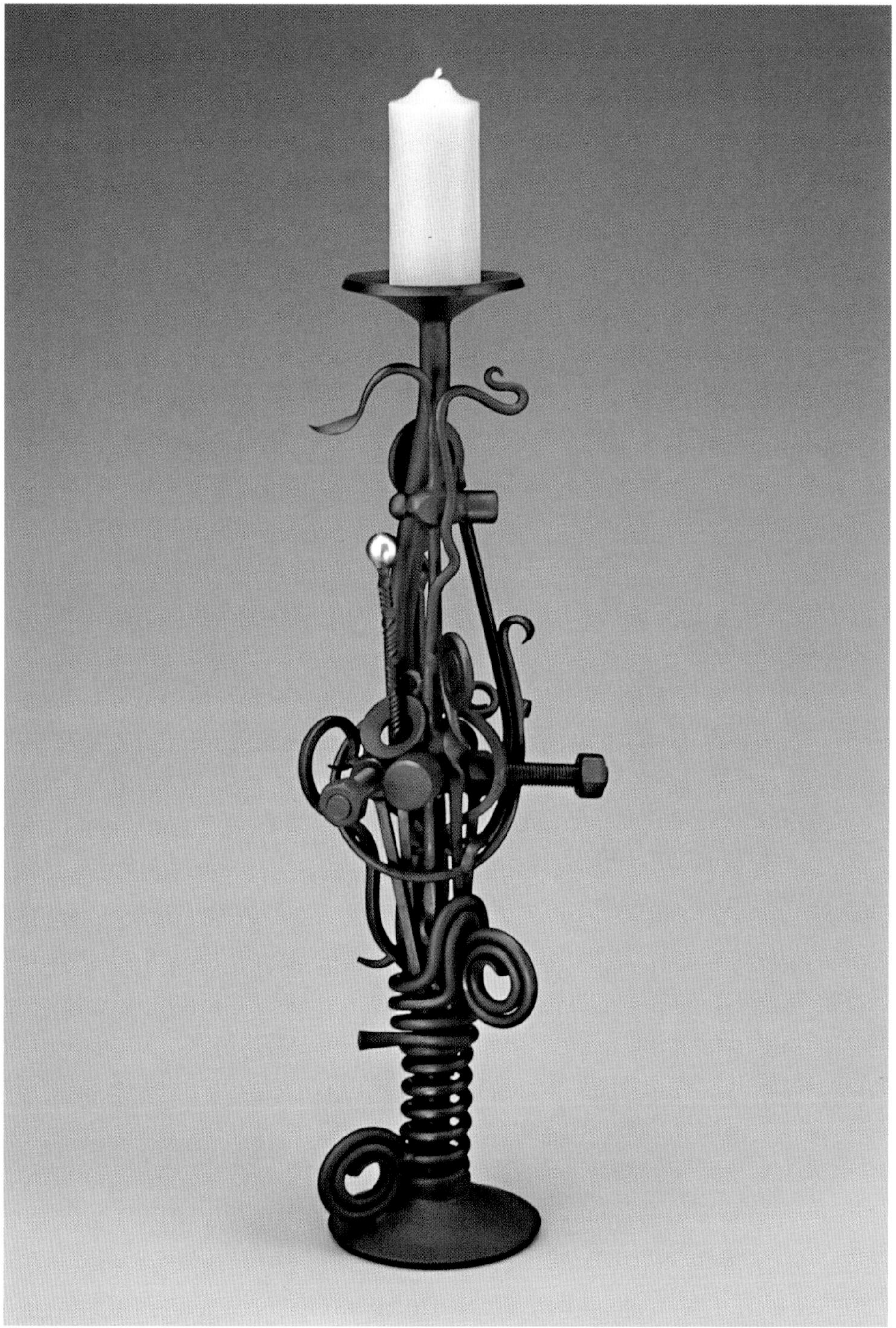

Tedd R. McDonah. Cockamamie Candleholder I. 36" high, 18" wide, 8" deep. *Photo, Keith Meister*

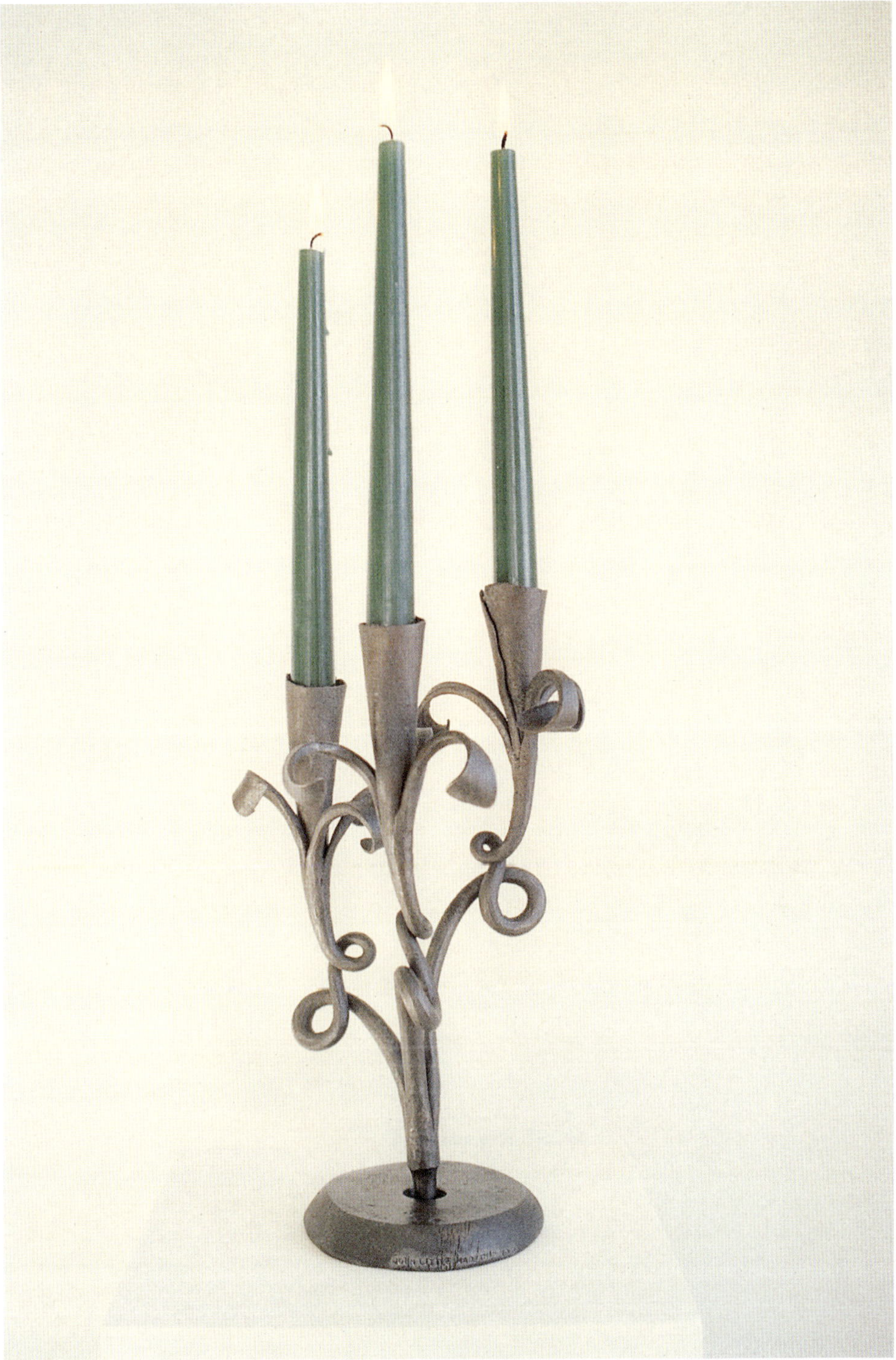

John Little. Candlestand. 26" tall with candles. *Photo, artist*

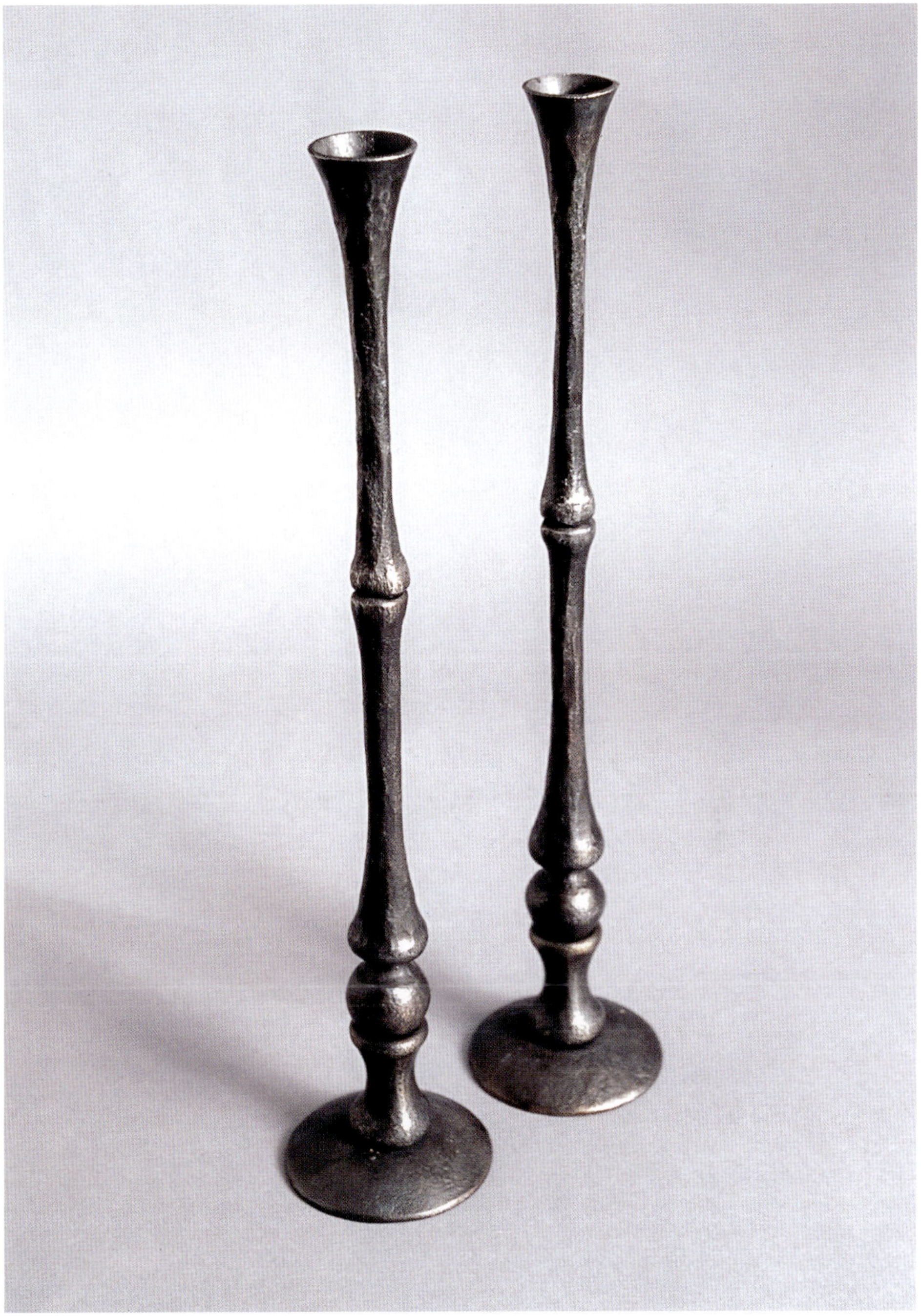

Maria Cristalli. Forged pipe candlesticks. 20" high, 4" base diam. *Photo, Stephanie Cristalli*

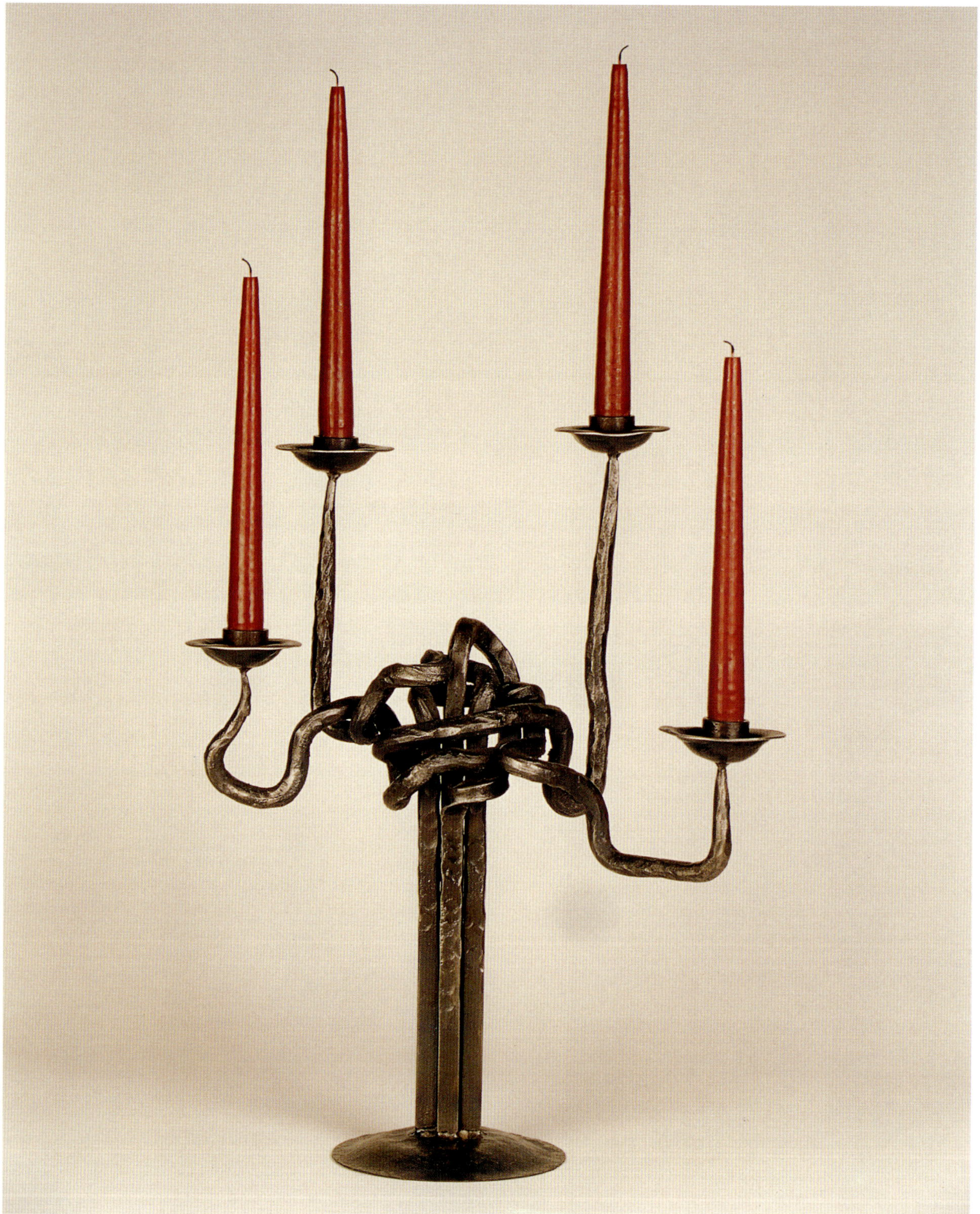

Stephen Marks. *Candelabra 2000*. Forged steel. 28" high with candles, 10" wide, 5" deep. *Photo, William P. Wright*

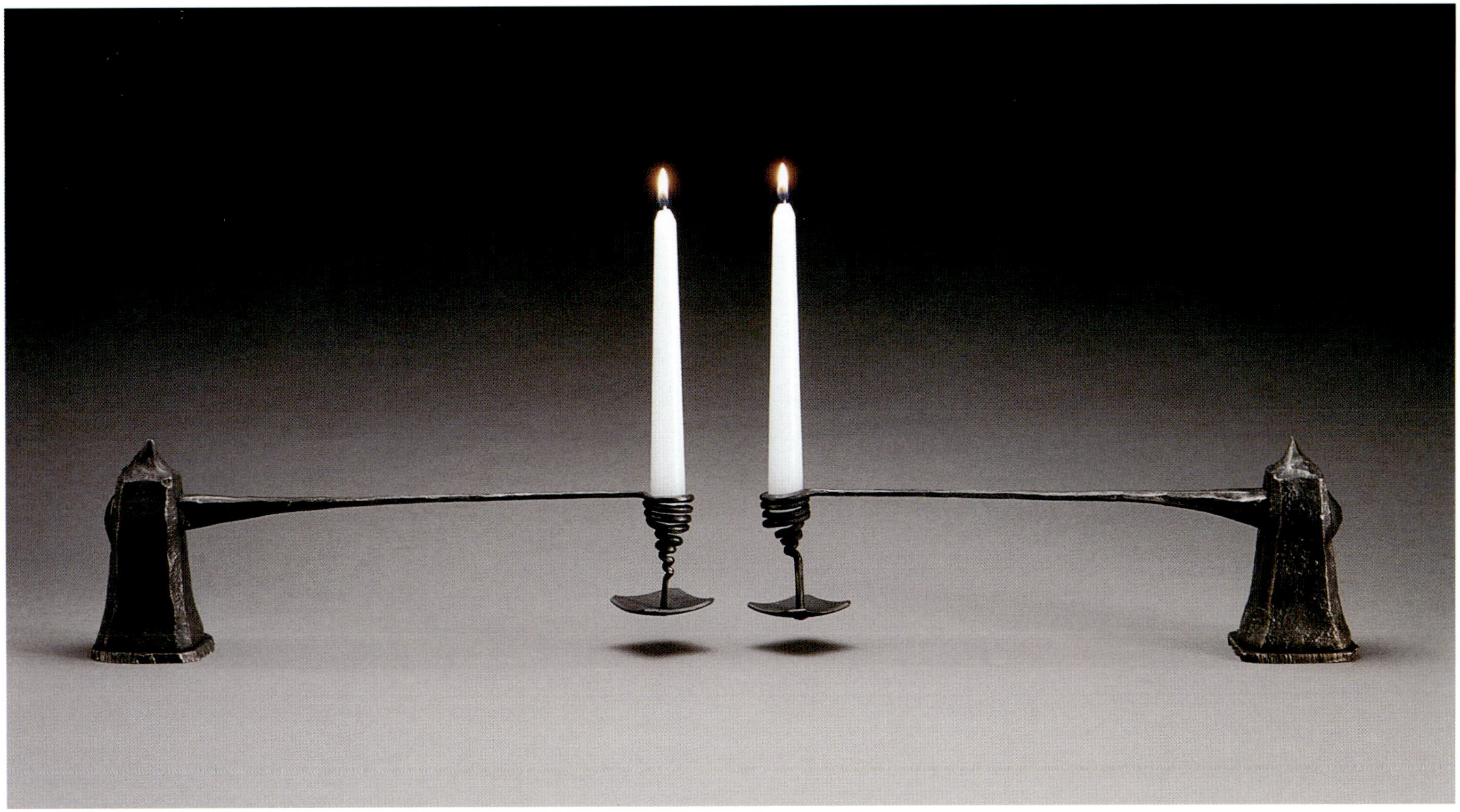

Jeff Wallin. *Sentinel Candlesticks*. Mild steel. 5" high, 12" wide, 2.5" deep. *Photo, Tom Mills*

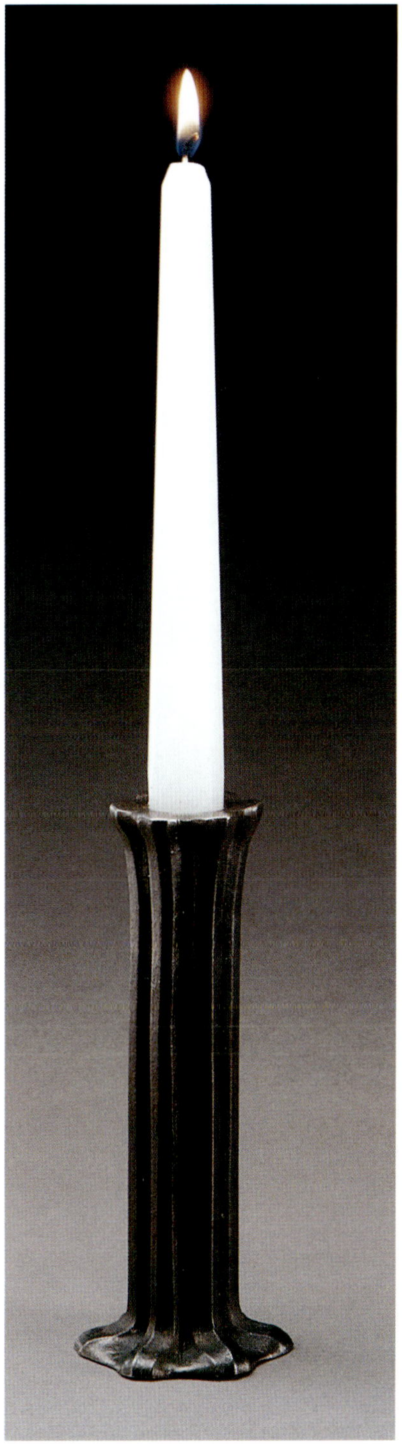

Jeff Wallin. Fluted candle staff. Mild steel. 6" high, 2" diam. *Photo, Tom Mills*

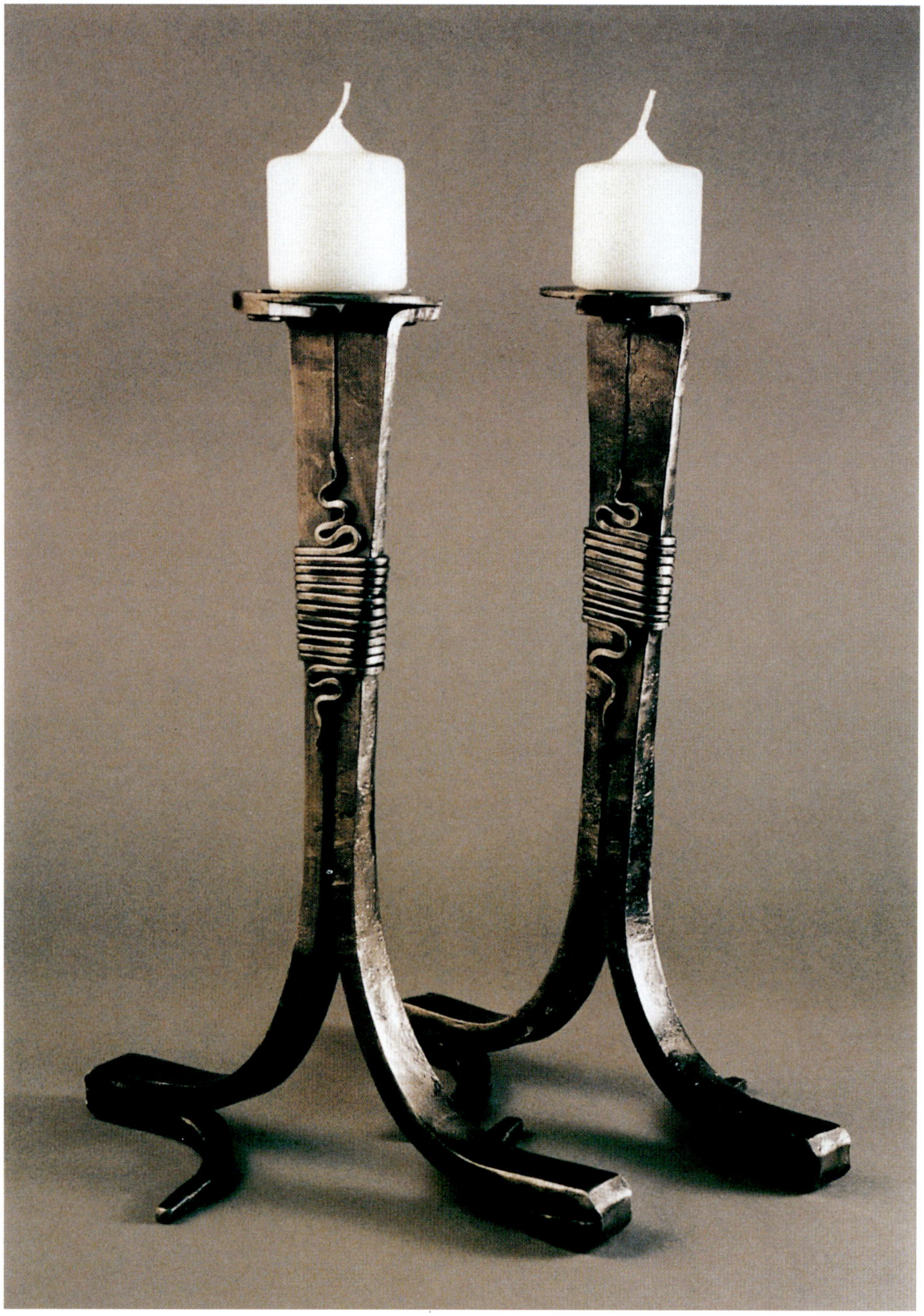

Lynda Metcalf. Wrap Candleholder. *Photo, John Lucas*

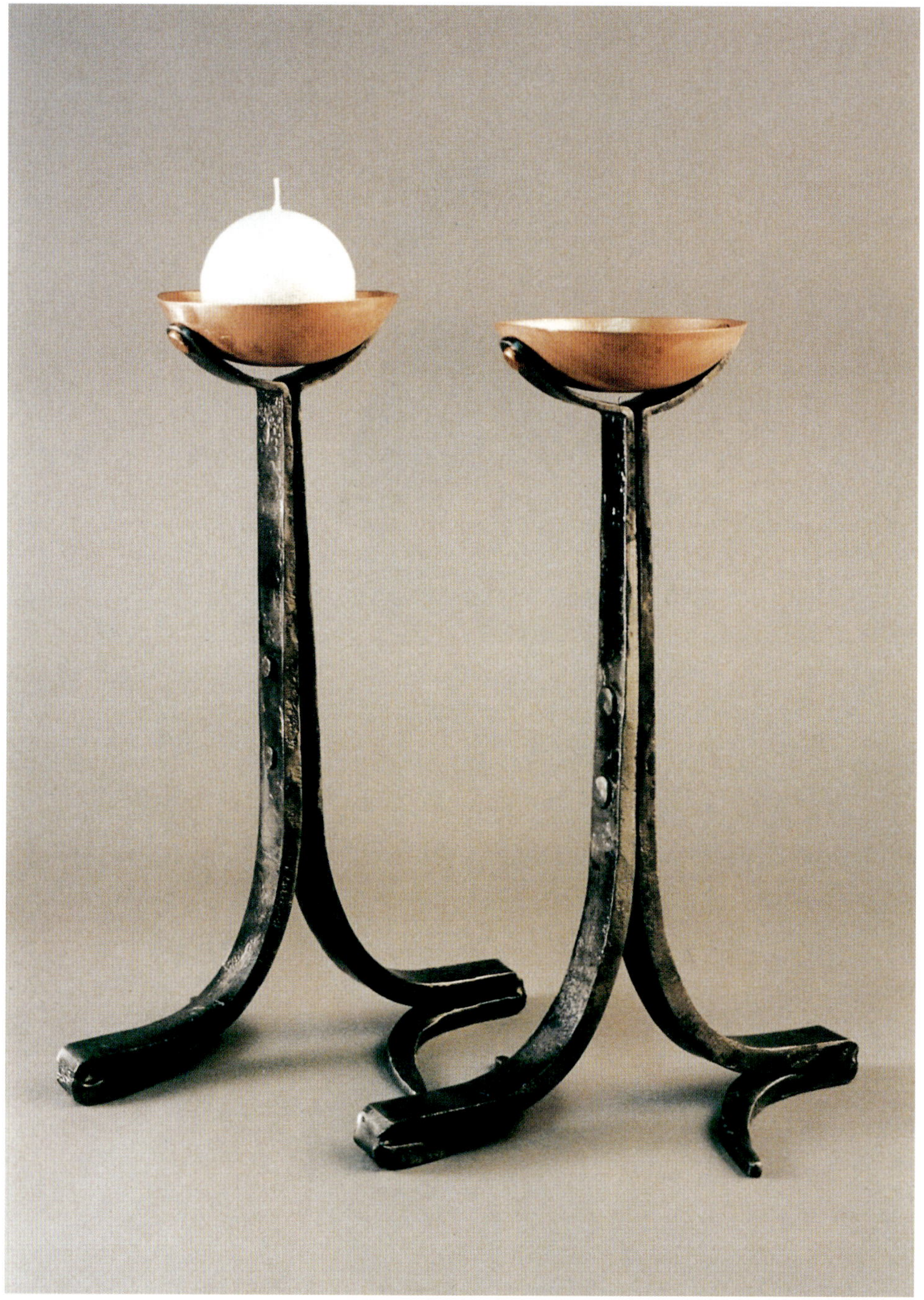

Lynda Metcalf. Copper bowl candleholder. *Photo, John Lucas*

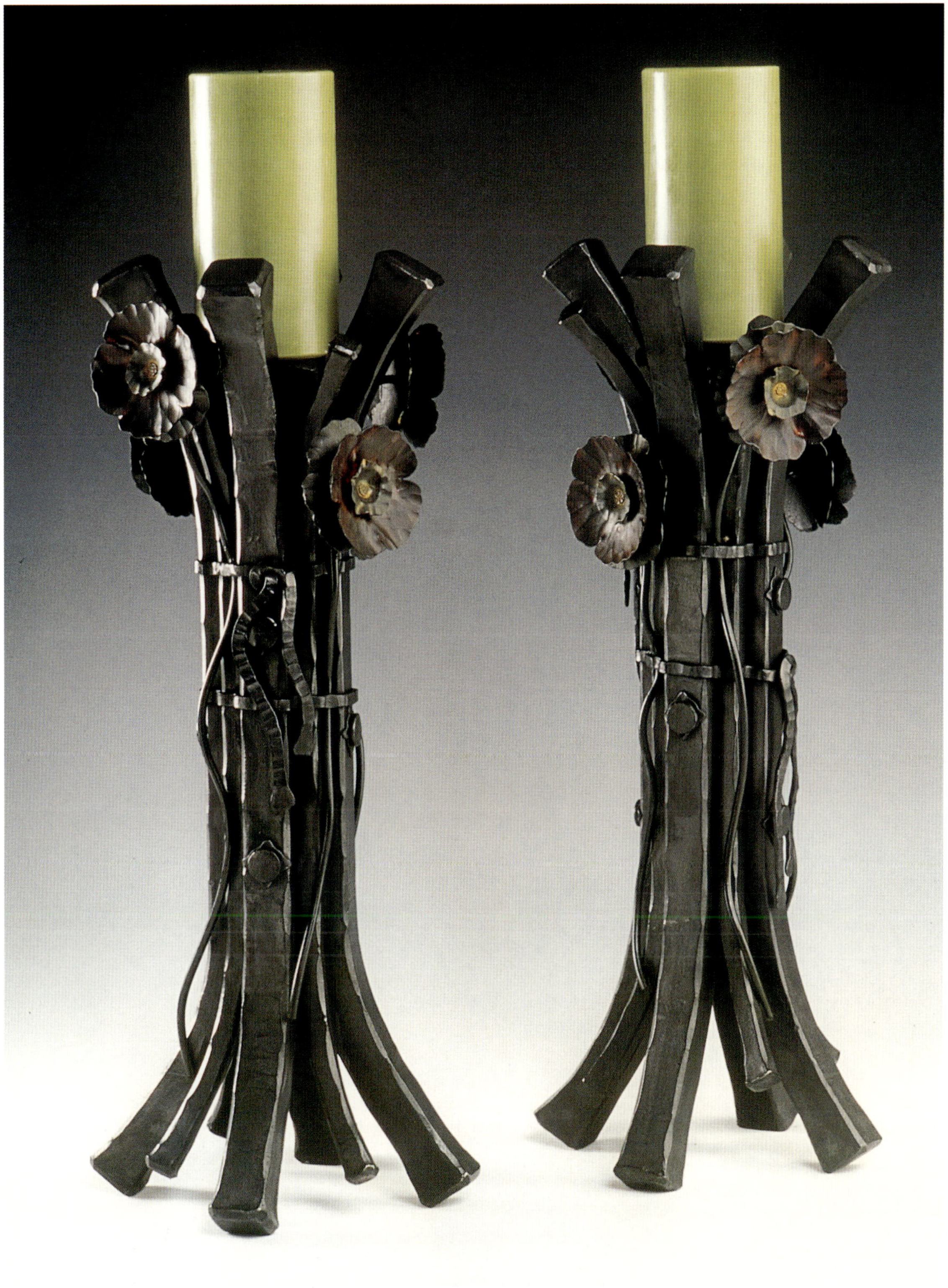

Susan Madacsi. Candleholders with poppies. Steel and artist's pigment. 22" high, 7" wide. *Photo, R. J. Phil*

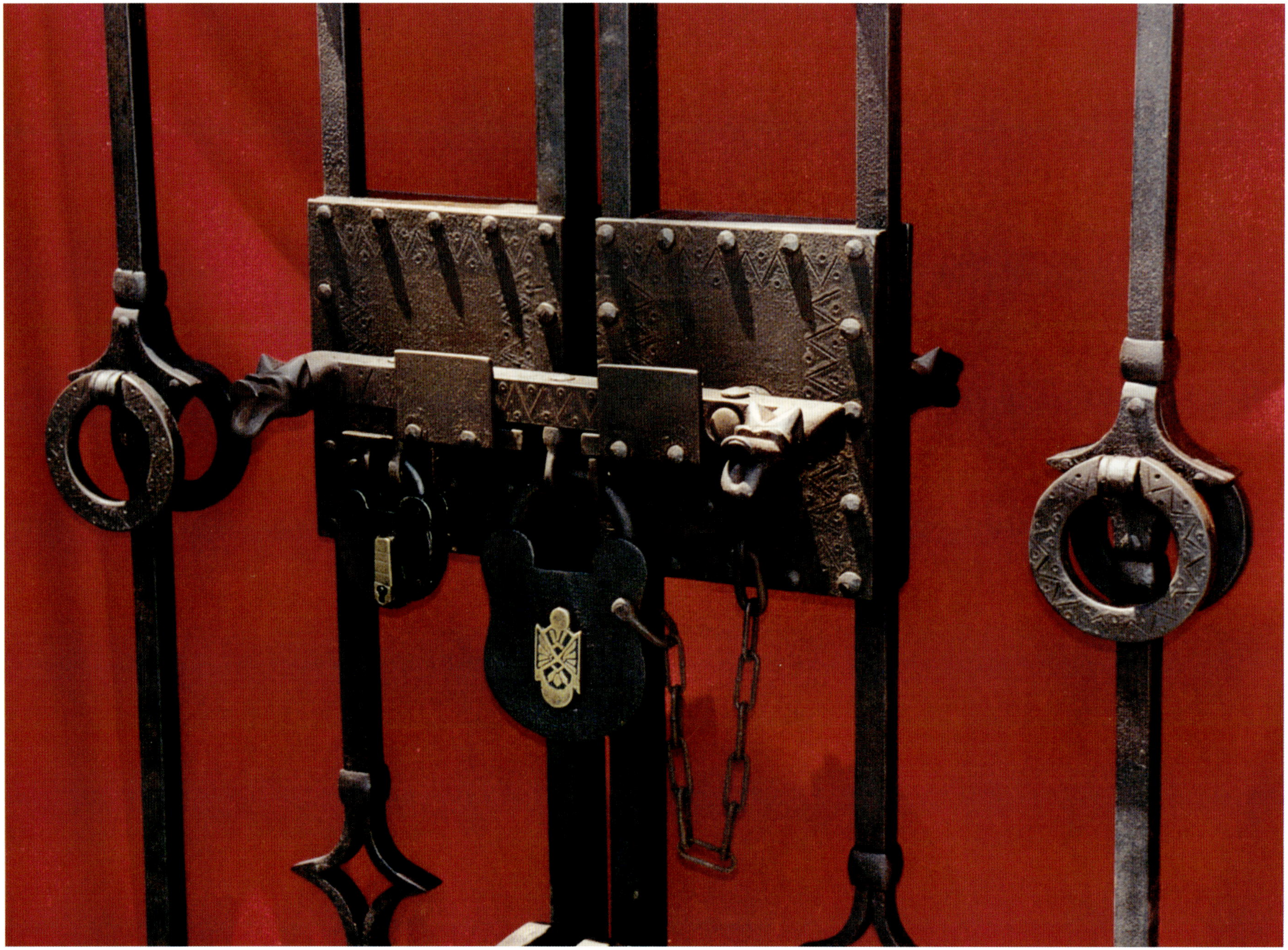

Michael J. Hart. Locking mechanism for the main gates at San Juan Capistrano Mission, San Juan Capistrano, California. The dogs' heads used as a motif in the locking mechanism were repeated on the gate stays. *Photo, Sue Hart*

Chapter 9. Decorate Doors Dynamically

Door hardware can be the open sesame to a lucrative activity for the artist-blacksmith. People who want unusual gates and doors also want unique hardware. It's pointless to have an artistic door and then outfit it with an inexpensive, mass-produced hardware store lock or handle. While many manufacturers today produce beautiful door hardware, still, there is nothing like one that is designed to integrate with the door design and carry out an artistic theme.

The doors and hardware by Robb Gunter are indicative of the type of coordinated hardware that will give a house a customized look. Gunter's knobs and handles are consistent throughout the house even if they vary in size.

Possibly the best known lock maker today is Tom Latané of Pepin, Wisconsin. He designs the lock and creates the mechanisms as well. Each lock works like a precision clock or a BMW motor. Latané's demos at blacksmithing meets are well attended, and his one-on-one training is sought by smiths who travel to work with him. Stephen Lee, of Estancia, New Mexico, has been traveling to Wisconsin for years learning how to make locks from Tom Latané.

Helmut Hillenkamp is so enamored of the locks made by his friend, Manuel Guerra, in Cuenca, Ecuador, that he prefers to have him make locks when he needs them.

Locks, door pulls, handles, and knobs are a staple of the objects that emanate from Steve Lopes' shop. Sometimes, he will cast some of the parts, then fabricate the locks to a client's specifications.

Other craftsmen will design door pulls, knobs, knockers, and handles that don't necessarily require locking mechanisms and they can be as beautiful and outrageous as the client demands. Good examples are door pulls in casinos in Las Vegas and elsewhere where the door pull represents the establishment. For example, the doors of the Hard Rock Café are in the shape of guitars. They are cast, but the original one had to be designed by someone who understood sculpture and metals.

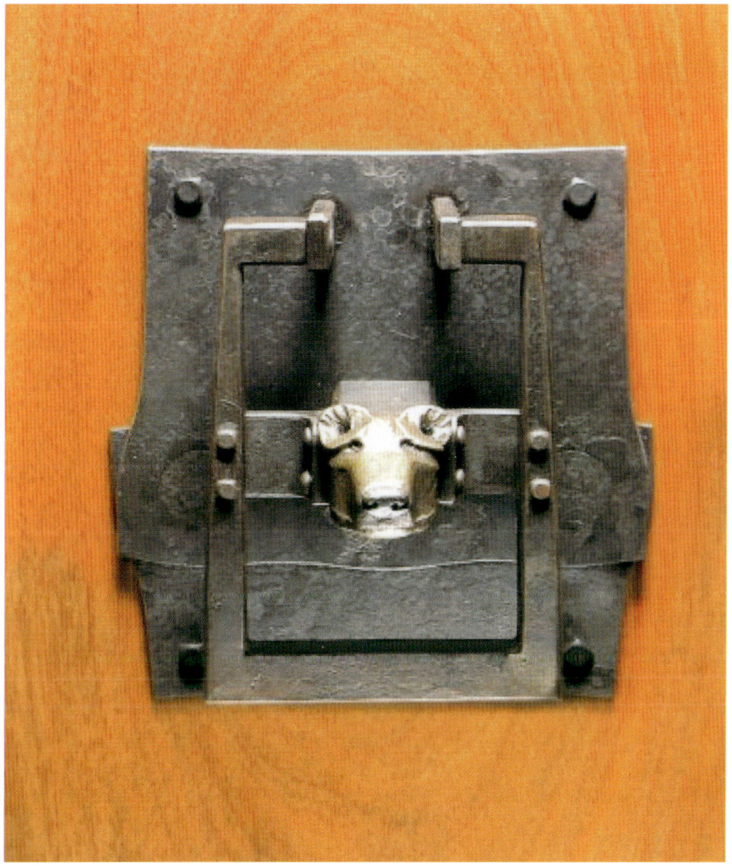

Tri Ficker from a design by Steve Lopes. Bear's head doorknocker. Repoussé with mild steel. 9" square. *Photo, Craig Wester*

What makes a person concentrate on creating door hardware? Benjamin Cowden says, "The concept of utility permeates my work. I am fascinated by mechanisms, secrecy, codes, and concealment." Cowden explains that he wants to create objects that people can touch, use, and keep for generations so that marks of use tell as much as the marks of creation. Iron has the ability to be rough and organic or sleek and polished and these characteristics can all come into play in door hardware.

After viewing the door hardware in this chapter, it is most likely that the next time you pull open a door at a hotel, a casino, a night club, anywhere that a theme exists, you'll observe the door hardware.

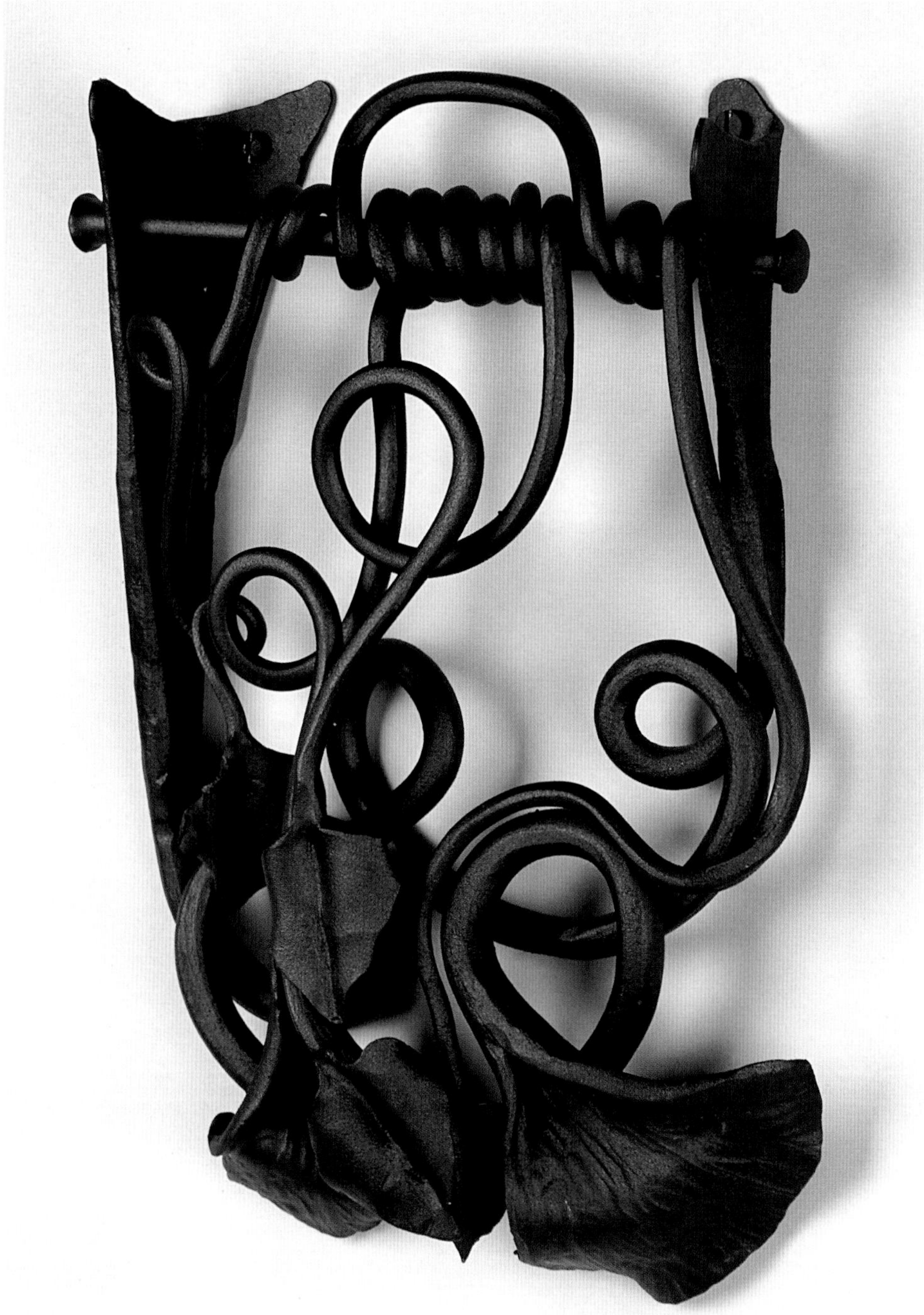

Roberta Elliott. Puzzle doorknocker. Mild steel. 10" high, 7" wide, 3" deep. *Photo, Jeff Bruce*

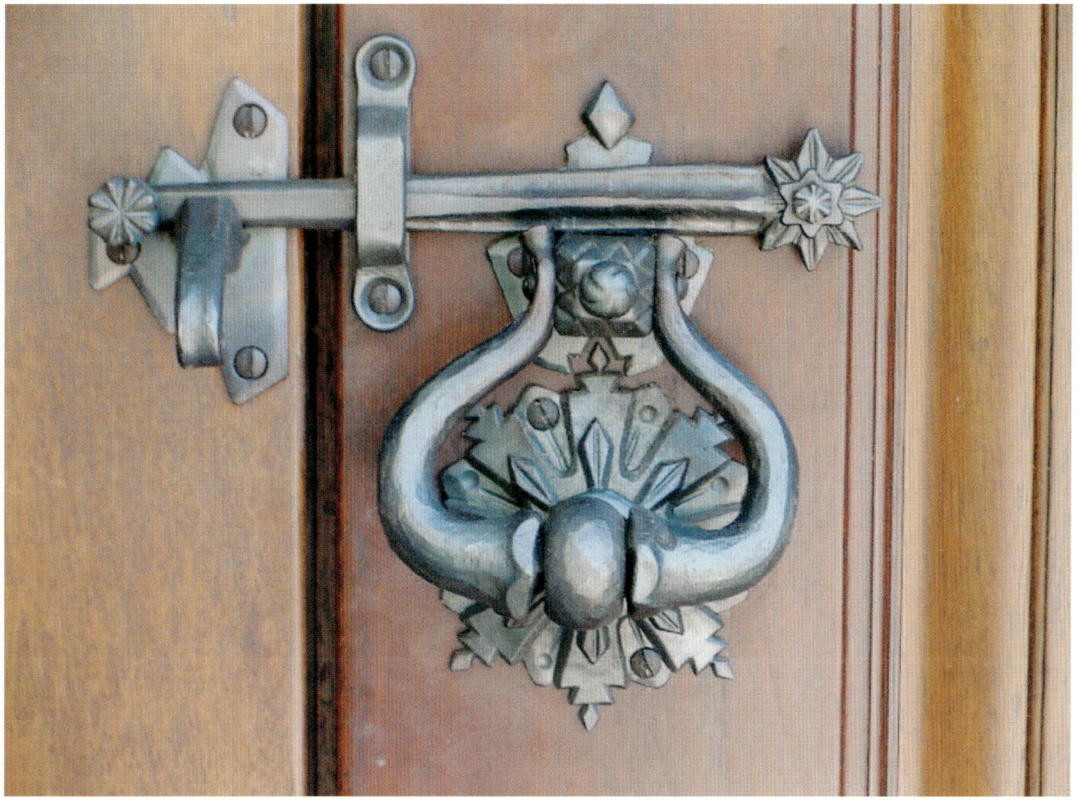

Robb Gunter. Doorknocker with a lifting bolt and lever mechanism. The back plate of the knocker became the theme design for the Robb Gunter project in Chapter 2. A light fixture picks up the same shape and overlapping of this plate. *Photo, artist*

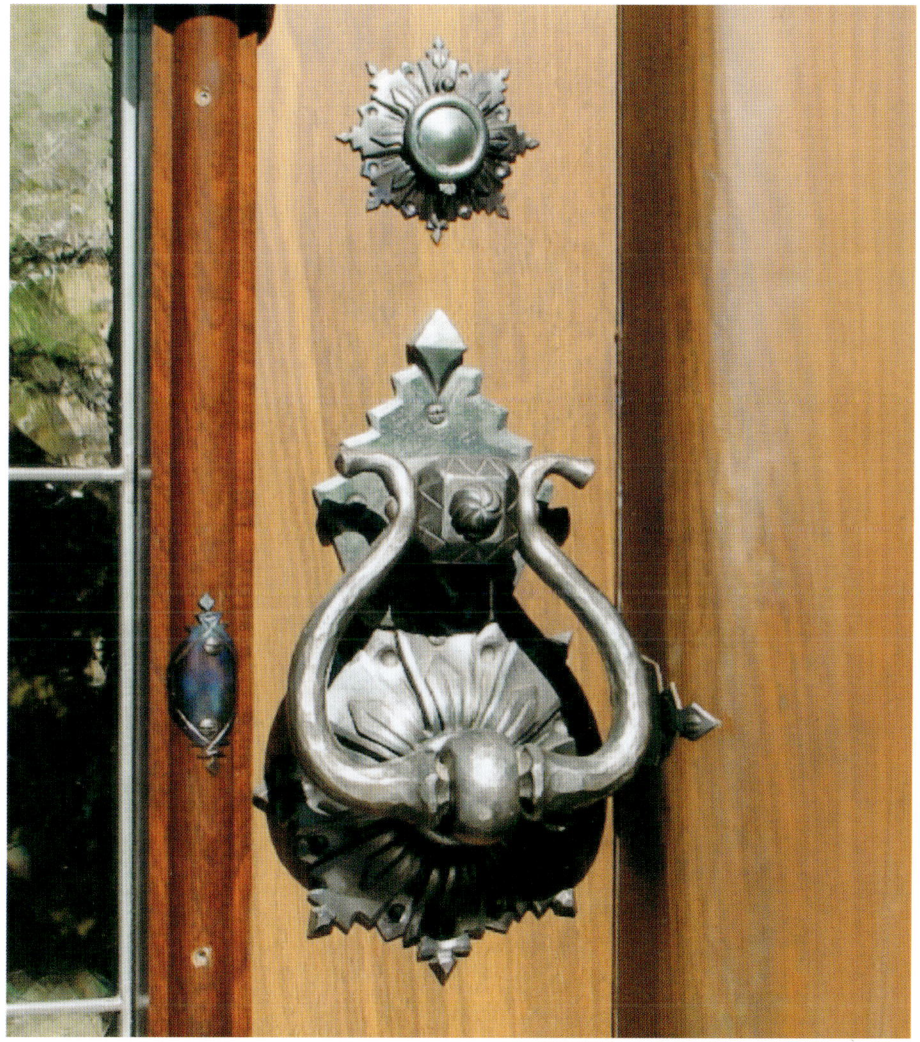

Robb Gunter. Doorknocker with a bell button above (in case the knocker isn't adequate). *Photo, artist*

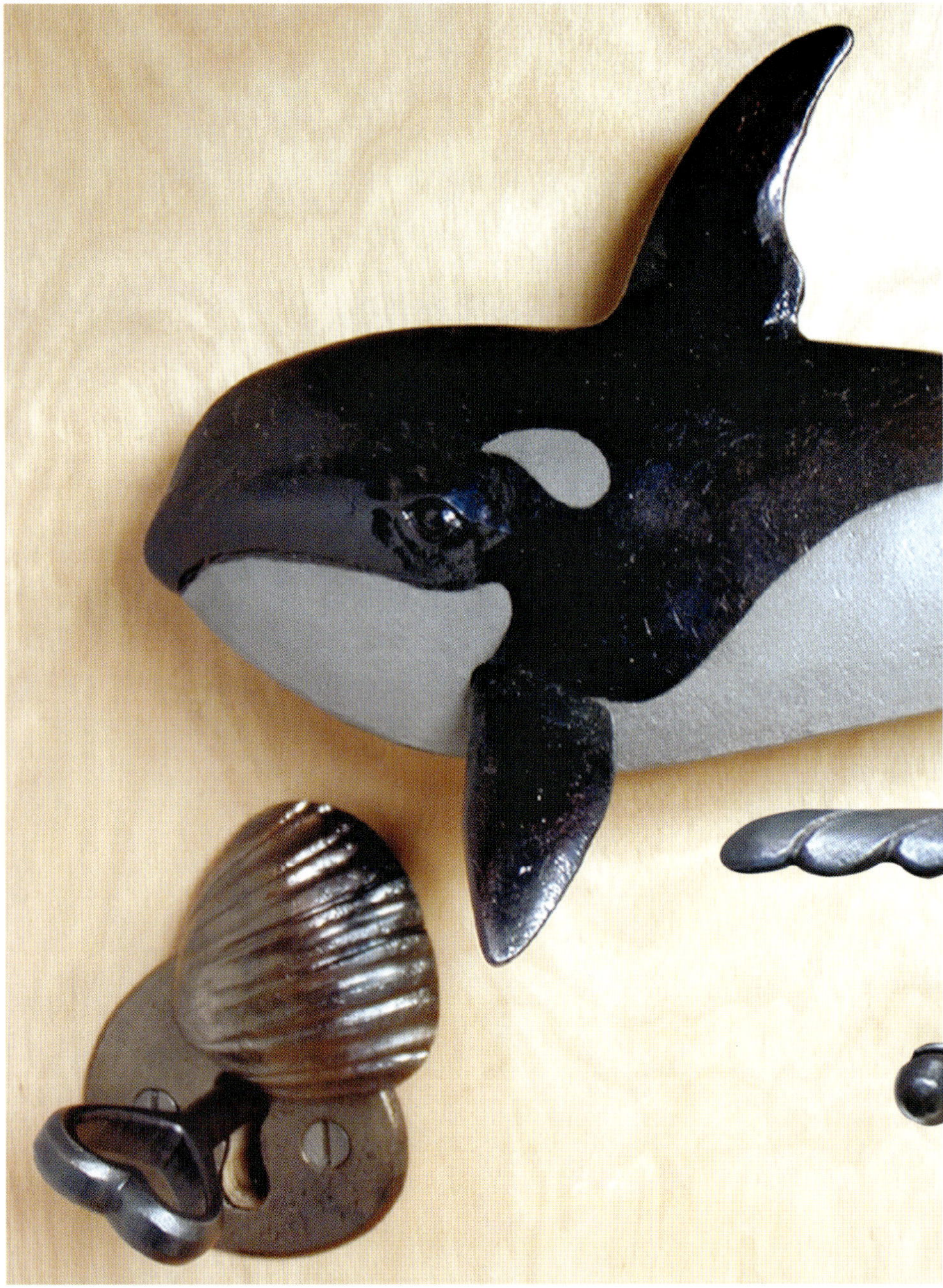

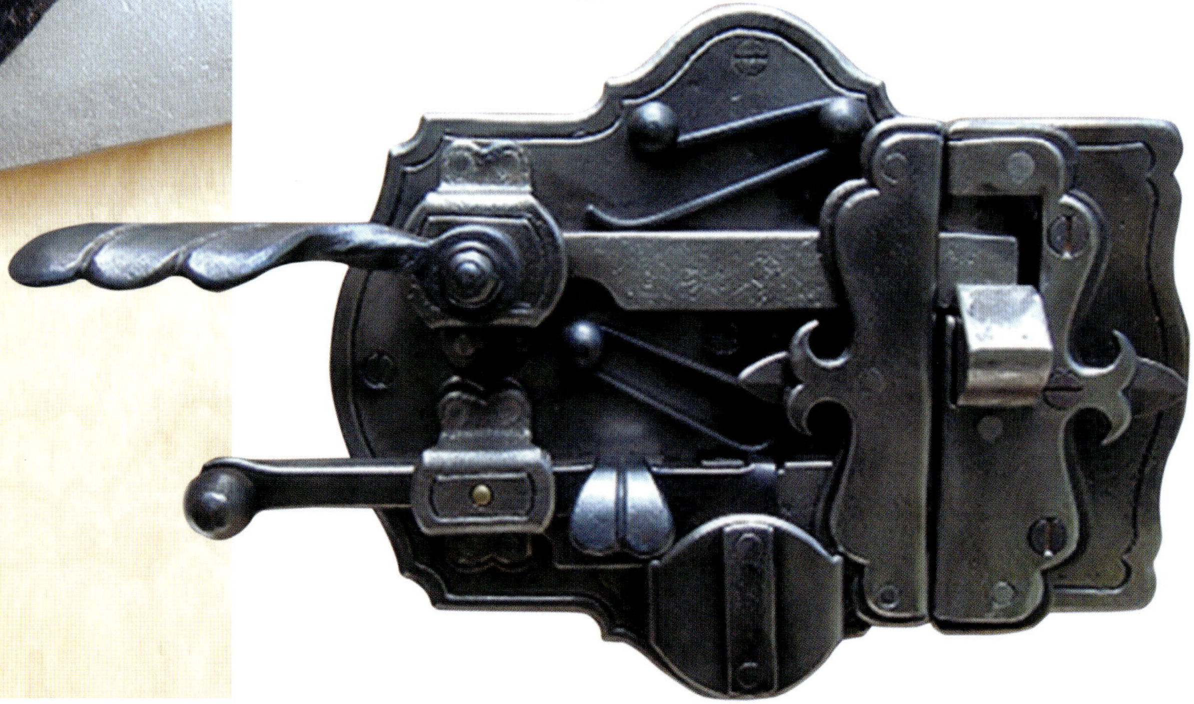

Jeff Holtby. The lock mechanism on the interior was based on a historical German lever latch with a lever tumbler slide bolt. Chevrolet coil springs pounded out to size and heat-treated became the lock's springs. 8" high, 9" long. *Photo, artist*

Jeff Holtby. *Orca Lock*. Exterior Orca whale lever handle and shell key cover. Whale was colored by taping dark areas and sandblasting the light areas. The eye was carved with chisels. Penetrol finish. *Photo, Don Wodjienski*

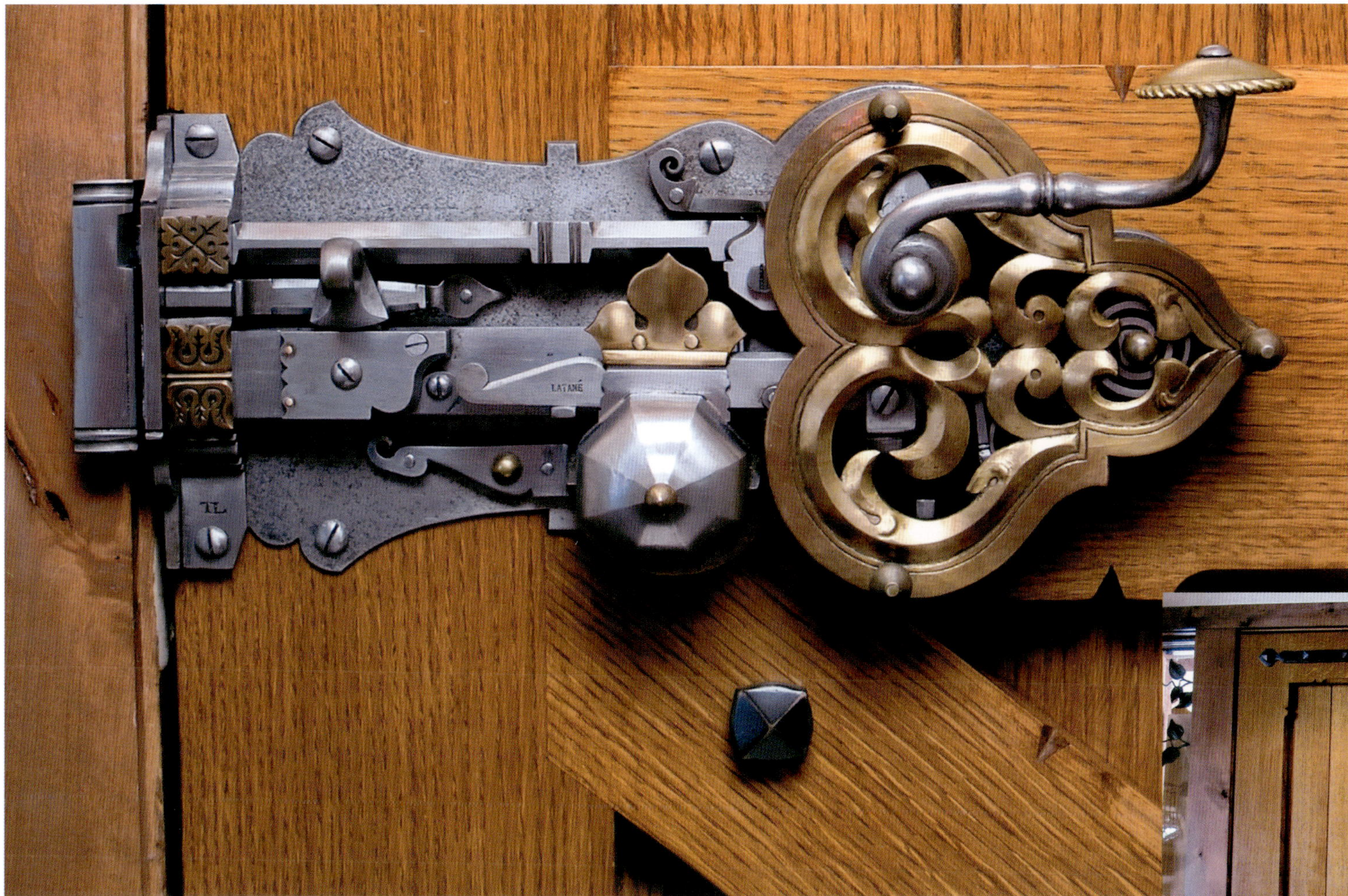

Tom Latané. Custom lock for a Renaissance style door. The flat coil springs keep the latch bolt and lever in place when the handle is at rest and they are mounted so they show beneath the pierced bronze plate. The lock, bolt, and tumbler are operated from the exterior. From the interior a lever can be pulled that raises the tumbler and draws the bolt in one motion. Spare keys were cast in bronze from a rubber mold made from the master key. *Photo, Bob Walsh*

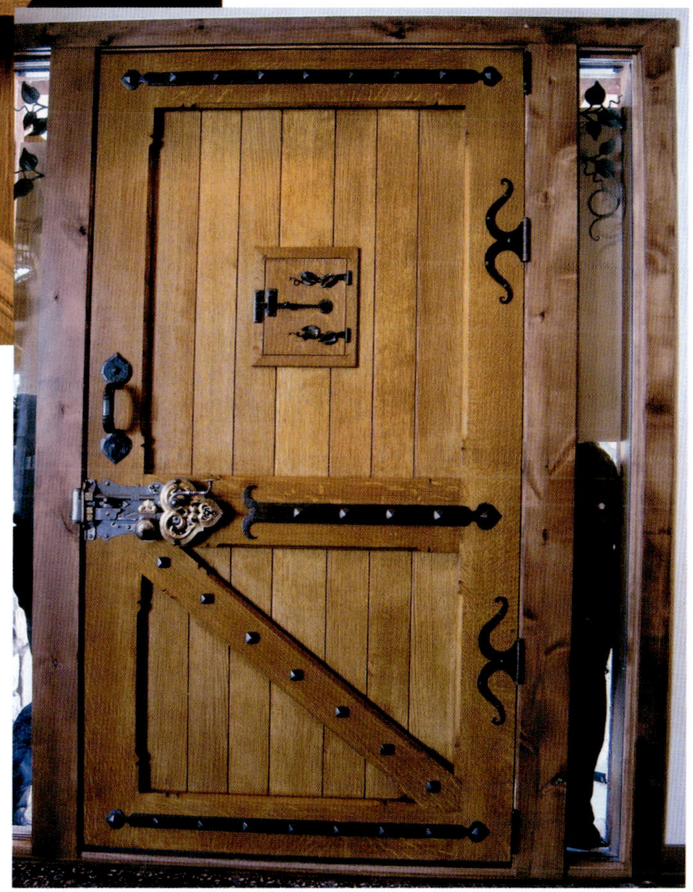

Tom Latané. Finished door (interior shown here, exterior on page 221) was a cooperative project. Bob Walsh designed the door to the client's specifications. John May constructed the wood door, Keith Johnson forged the leaves, window grille, door handles, hinges, and straps, and Tom Latané made the lock. *Photo, Bob Walsh*

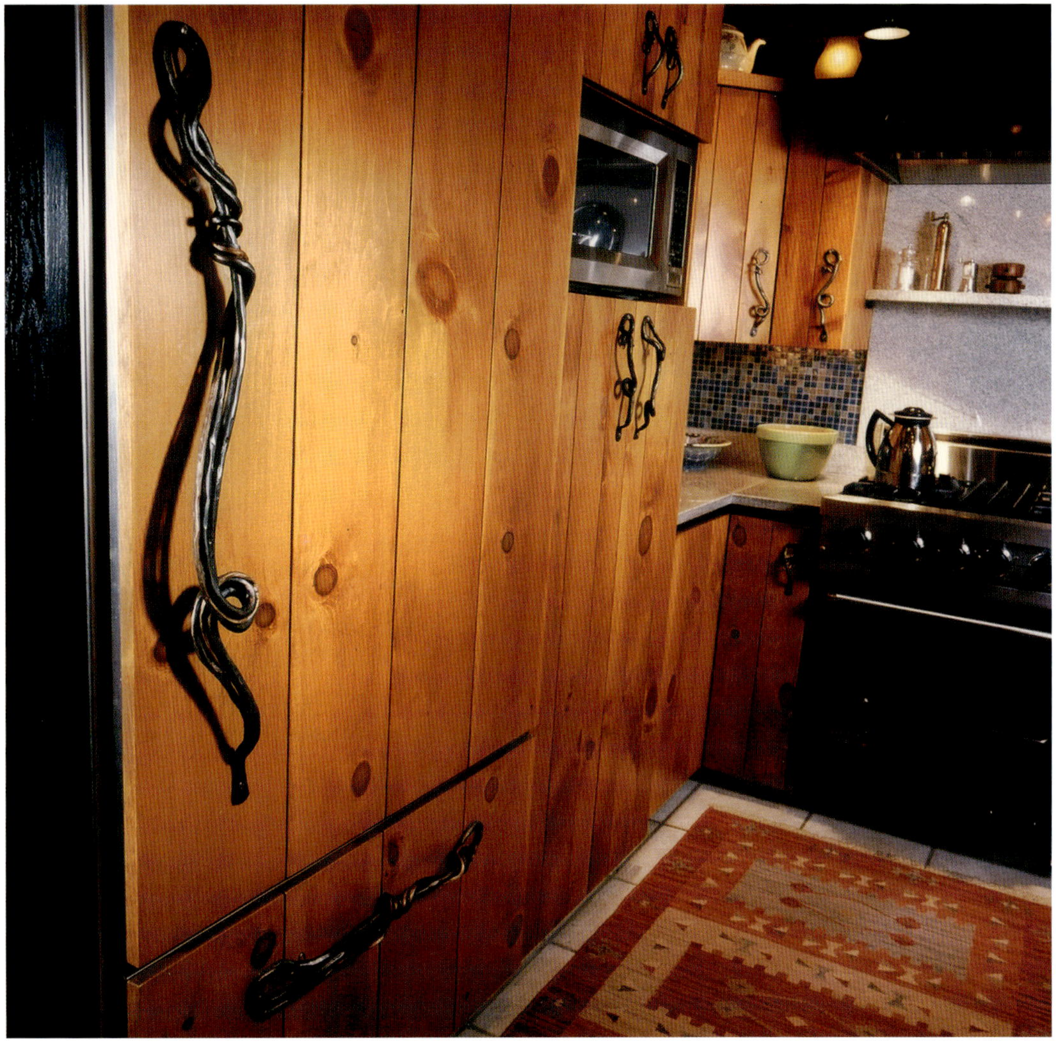

Lisa Elias. Customized hand made door and drawer handles add a unique decorating touch to a kitchen. *Photo, Andrea Rugg*

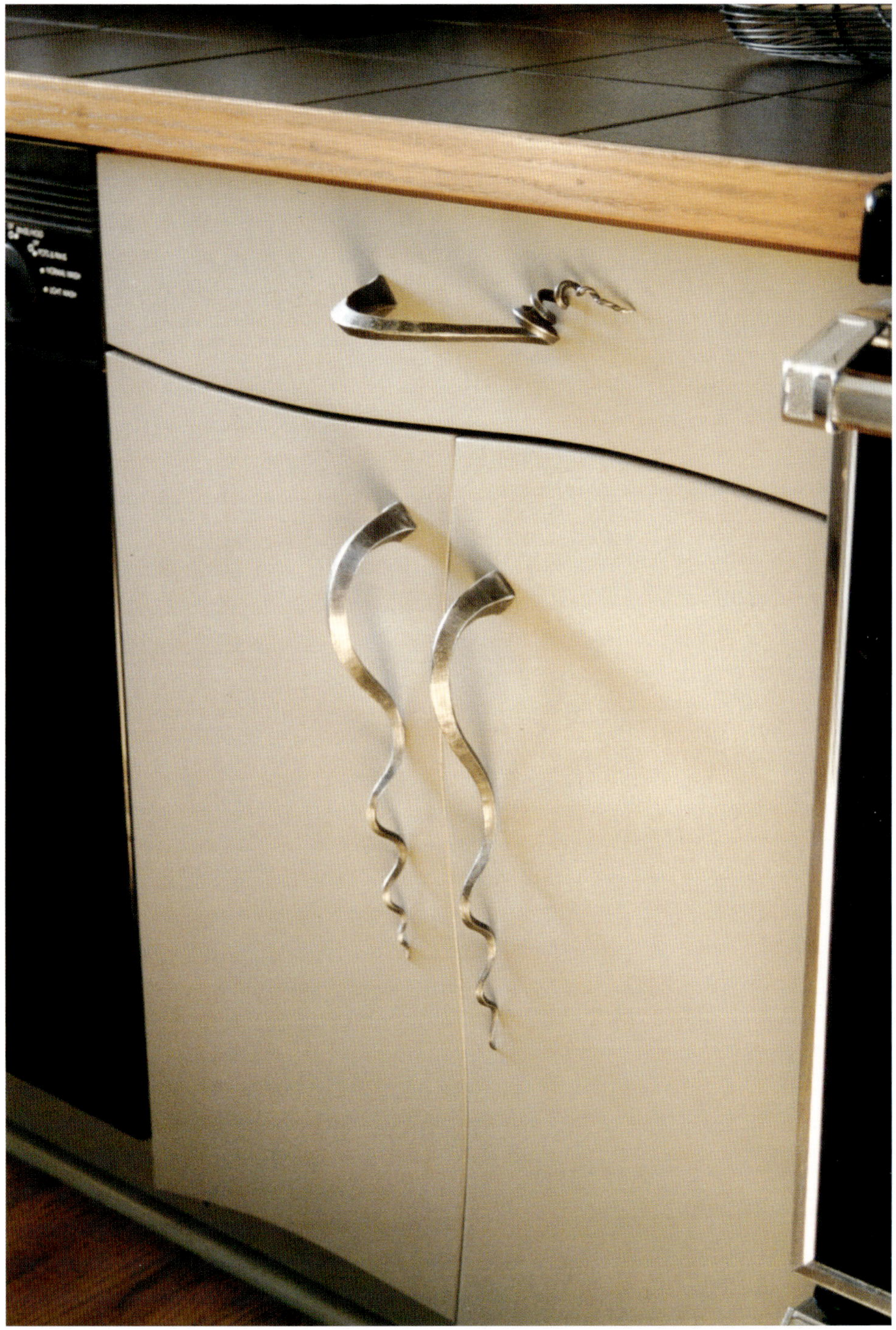

John Monteith and Brenda Field. Kitchen cupboard handles. Forged mild steel with a beeswax finish. *Photo, John Monteith*

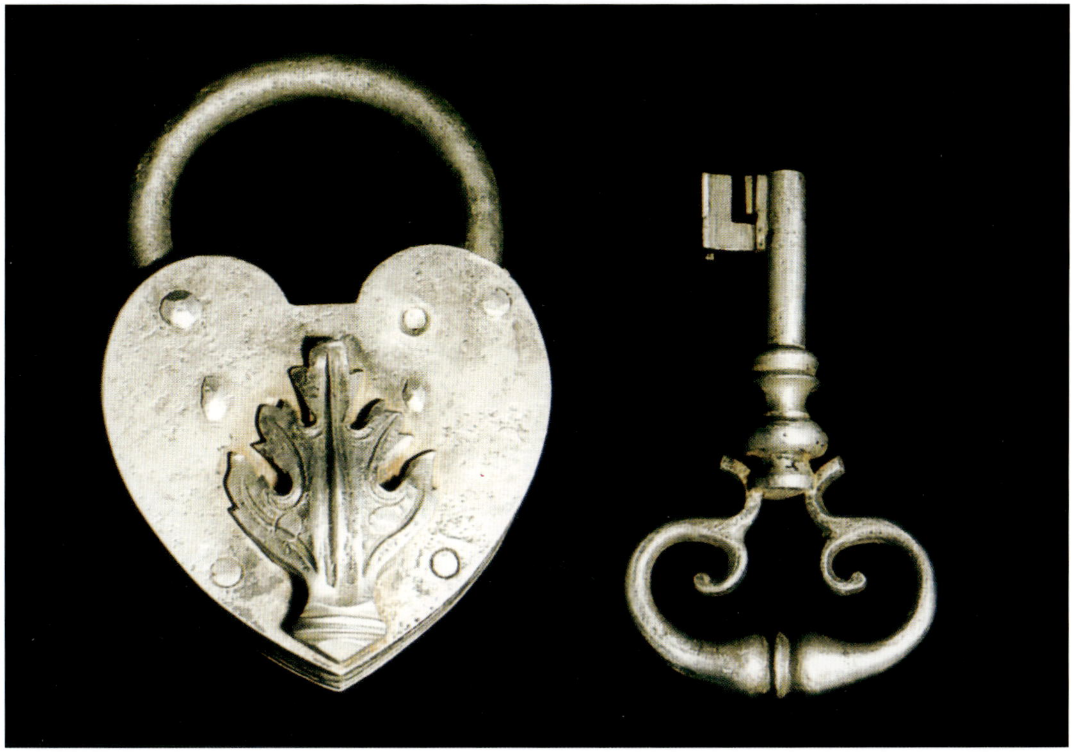

Stephen E. Lee and Tom Latané. Heart shaped padlock with leaf. *Photo, Kate Hoover*

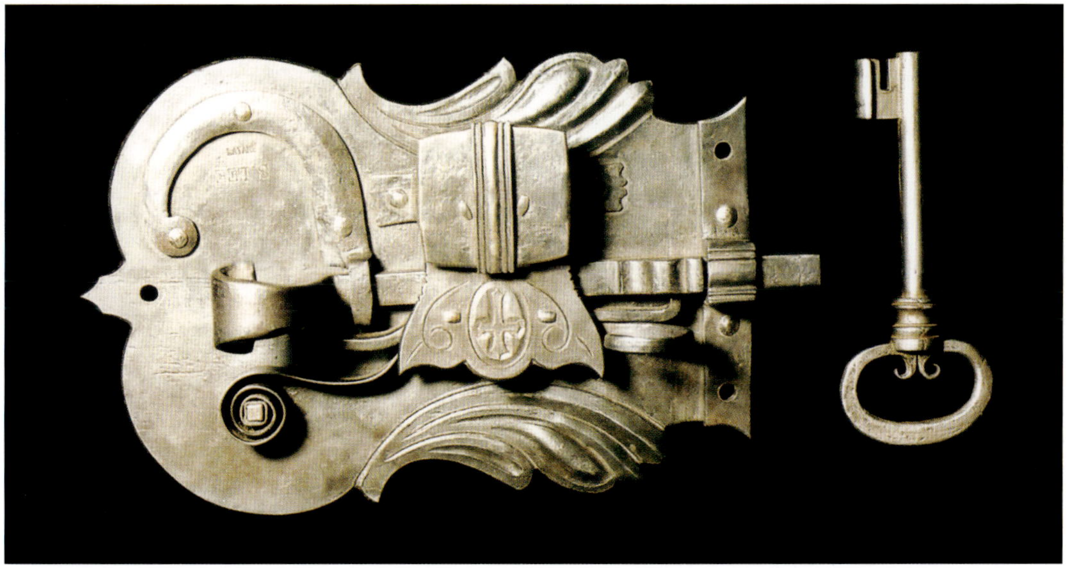

Stephen E. Lee. Door lock and master key. For several years, Stephan Lee traveled from his home in New Mexico to Pepin, Wisconsin to learn the intricacies of lock making from Tom Latané. *Photo, Kate Hoover*

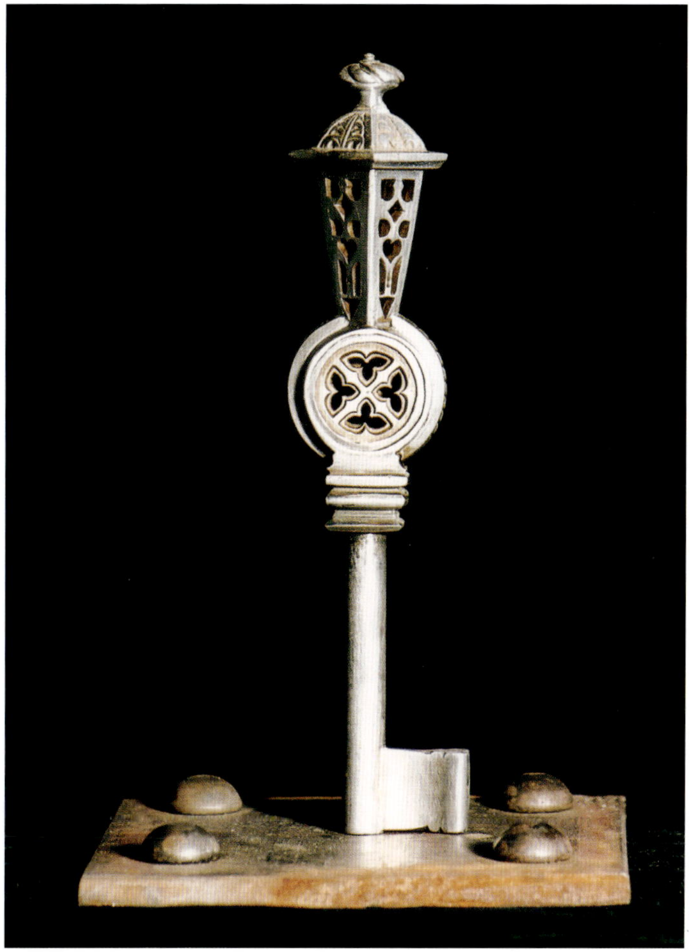

Stephen E. Lee and Tom Latané. Masterpiece key. *Photo, Kate Hoover*

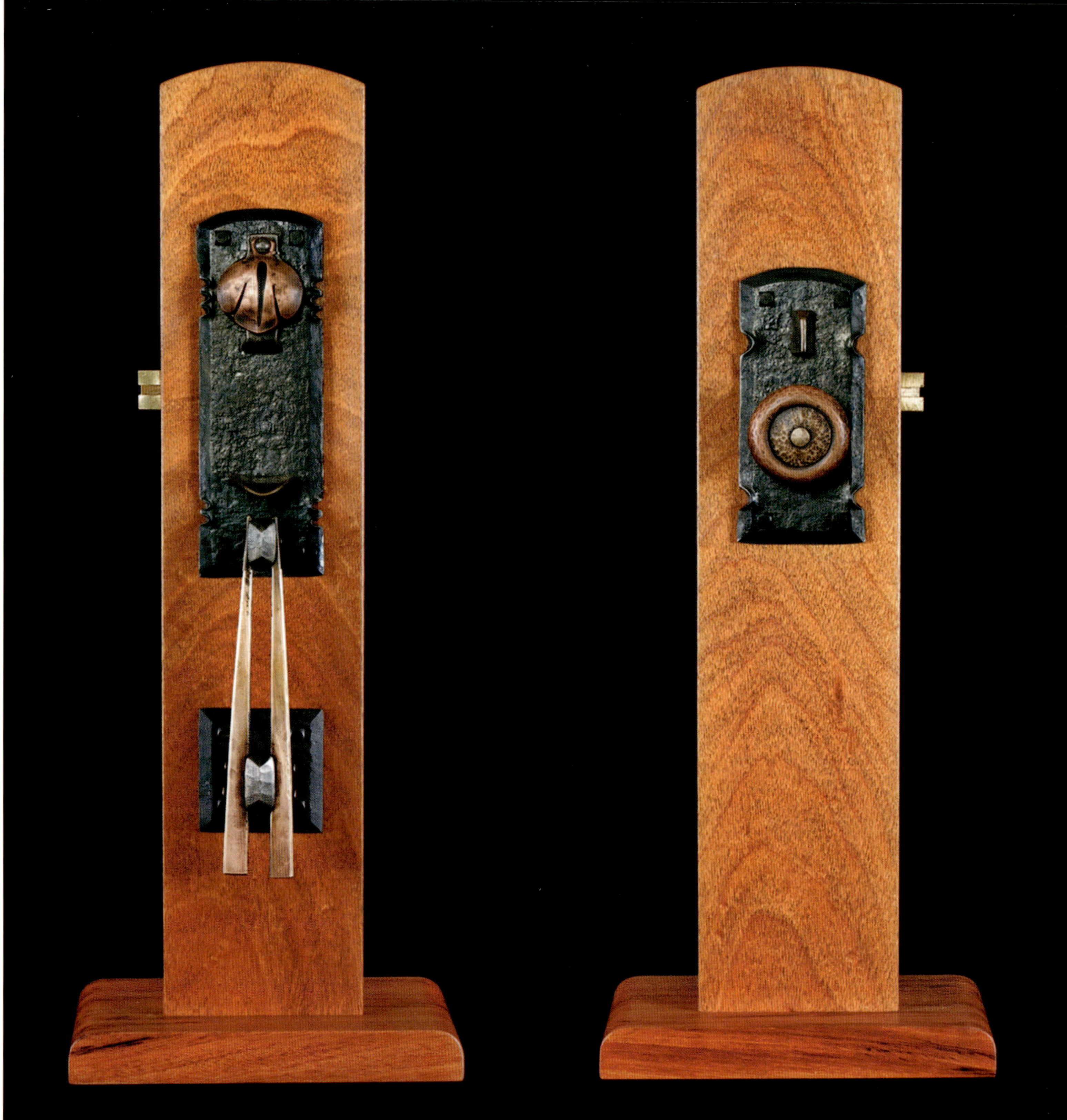

Steve Lopes. Thumb latch hardware, exterior, left. Right, interior, for back side of door. 16" high, 3" wide. *Photo, Craig Wester*

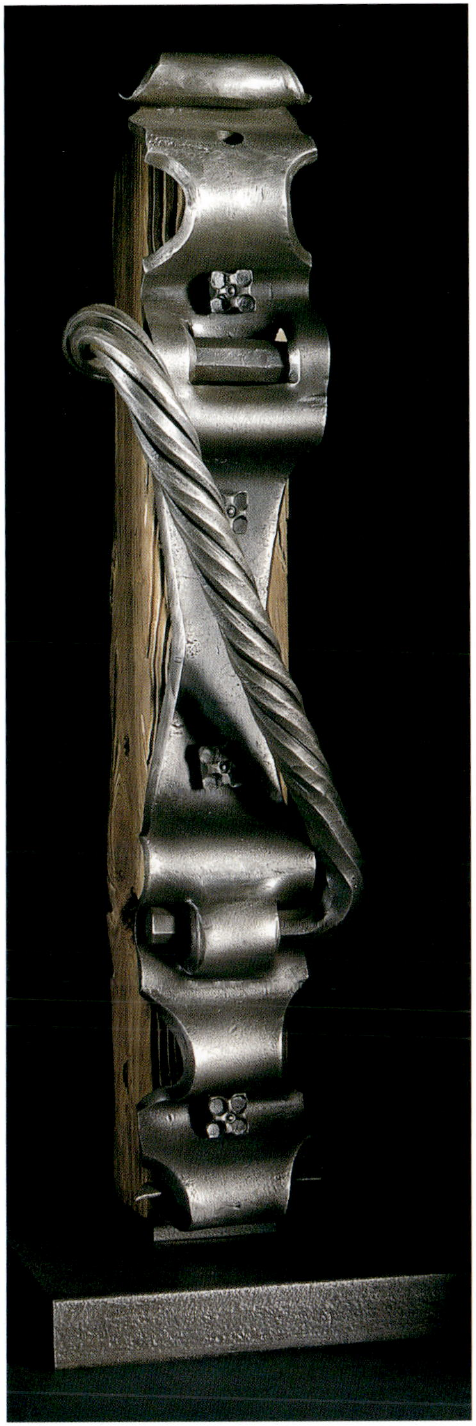

David Maurice. Baroque baronial door pull #1. 28" high, 8" wide. *Photo, Enrique Cubillo*

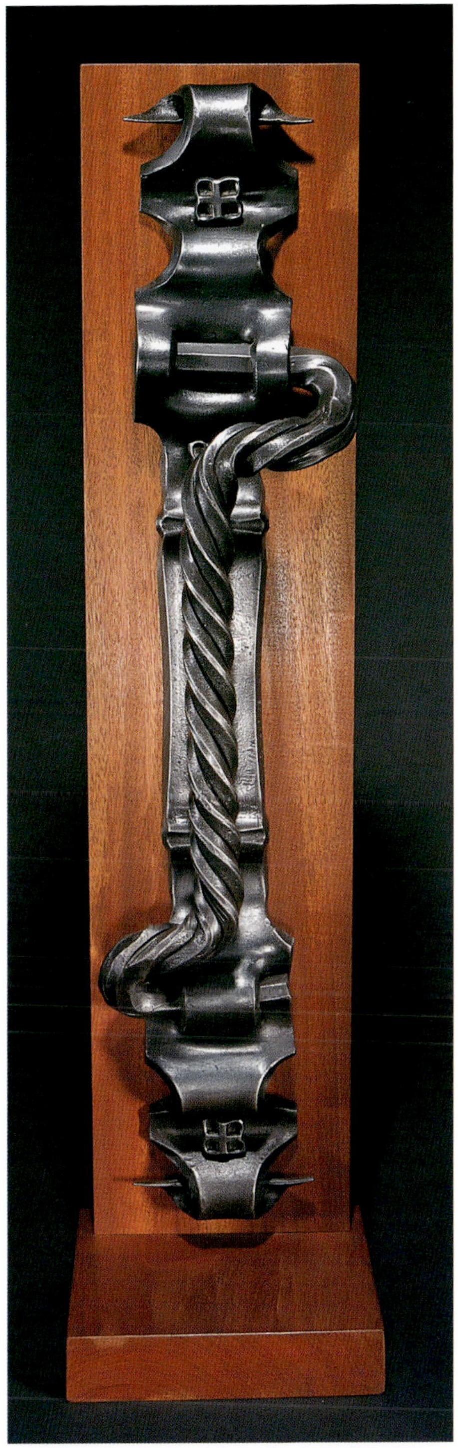

David Maurice. Baroque baronial door pull #2. 30" high 6" wide. *Photo, Enrique Cubillo*

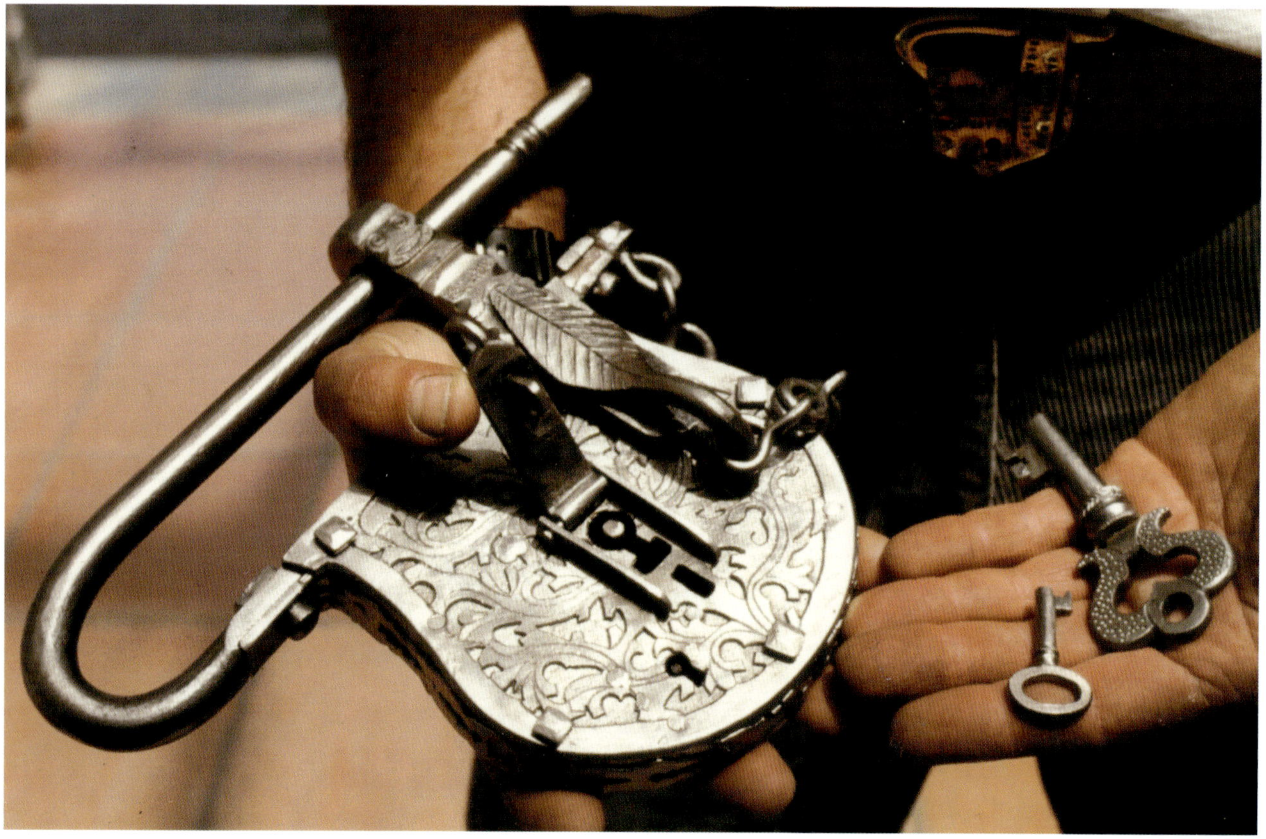

Manuel Guerra. A double locking padlock. The smaller key opens a door to put the big key into to open the lock. *Collection, Helmut Hillenkamp. Photo, Fausto Cardoso*

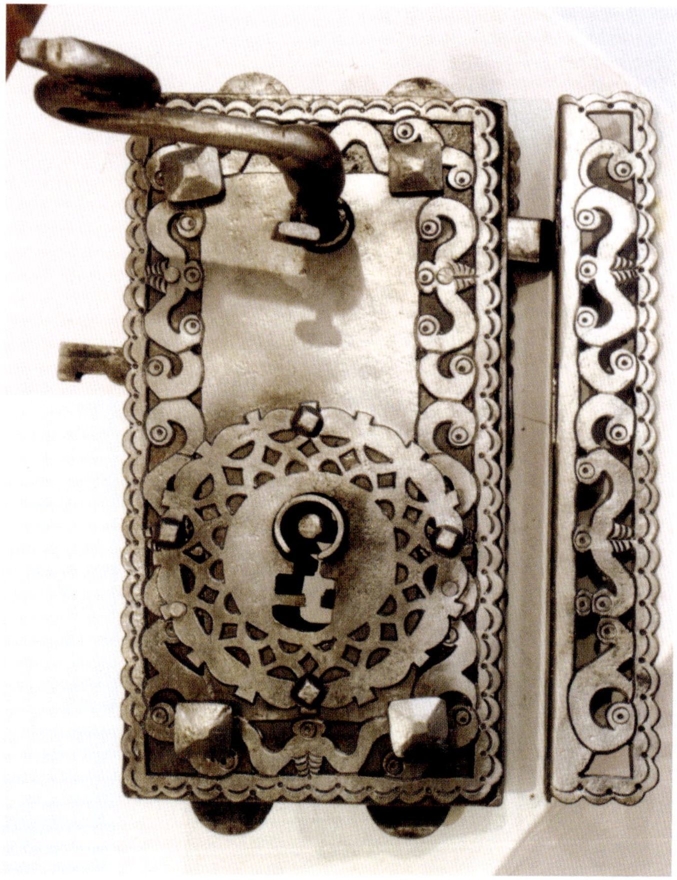

Manuel Guerra. Door lock with a goose handle and a night latch. *Collection, Helmut Hillenkamp. Photo, Fausto Cardoso*

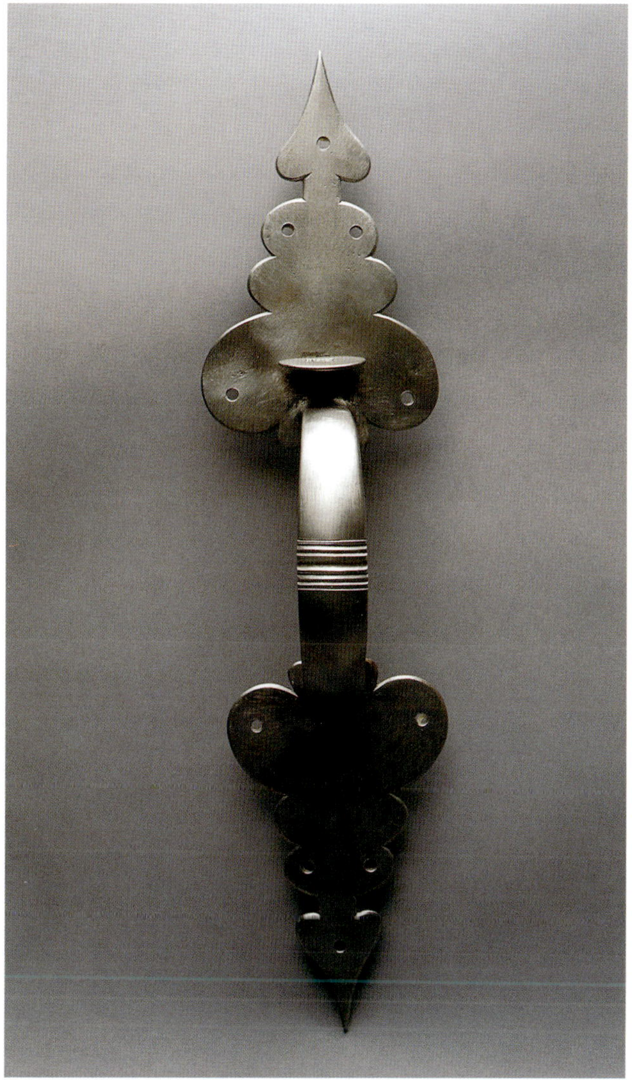

Michael J. Saari. *Suffolk Doorlatch #1*. Mild steel. 18" high, 4" wide, 6" deep.

Saari created a challenge for himself for these latches. He wanted to try free form forging using traditional techniques with designs based on 18th-19th century styles. He started with drawings he researched from books and museums, made tin patterns for the cusps, and used all hand tools. Techniques included traditional hand forging, forge welding, riveting, and filed finishes. The latches had to be precise, accurate, and functional. *Photo, artist*

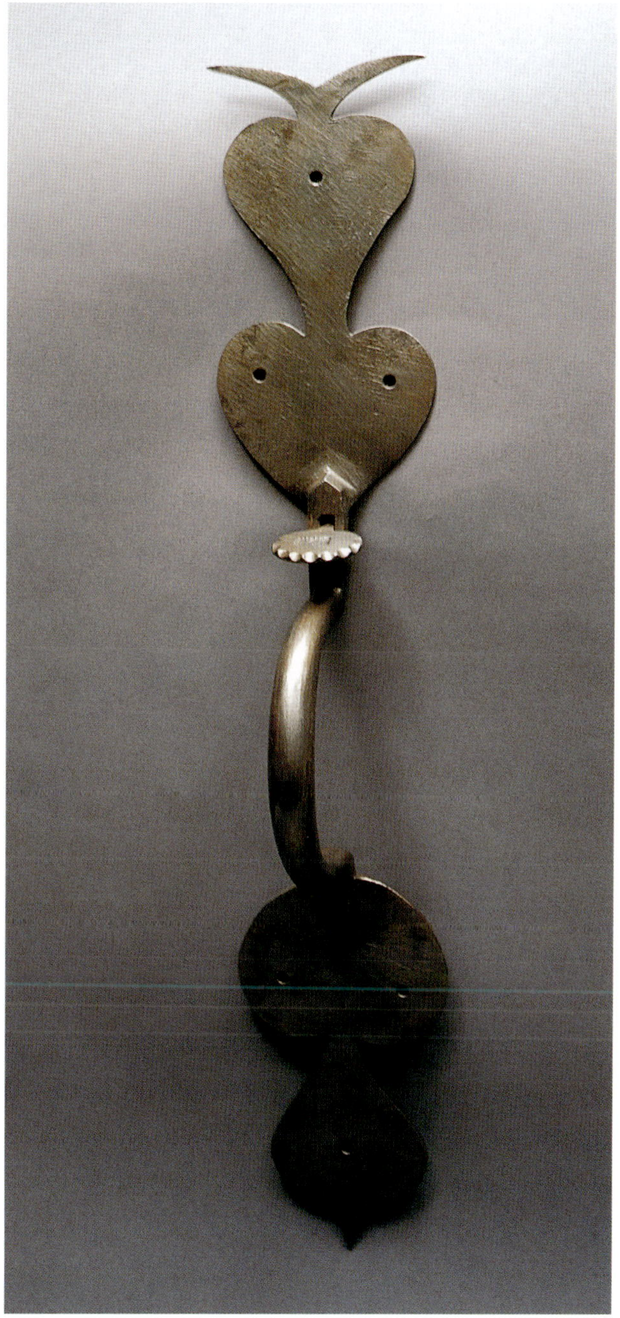

Michael J. Saari. *Suffolk Doorlatch #3*. Mild steel. 19" high, 3.75" wide, 3" deep. Mild steel. *Photo, artist*

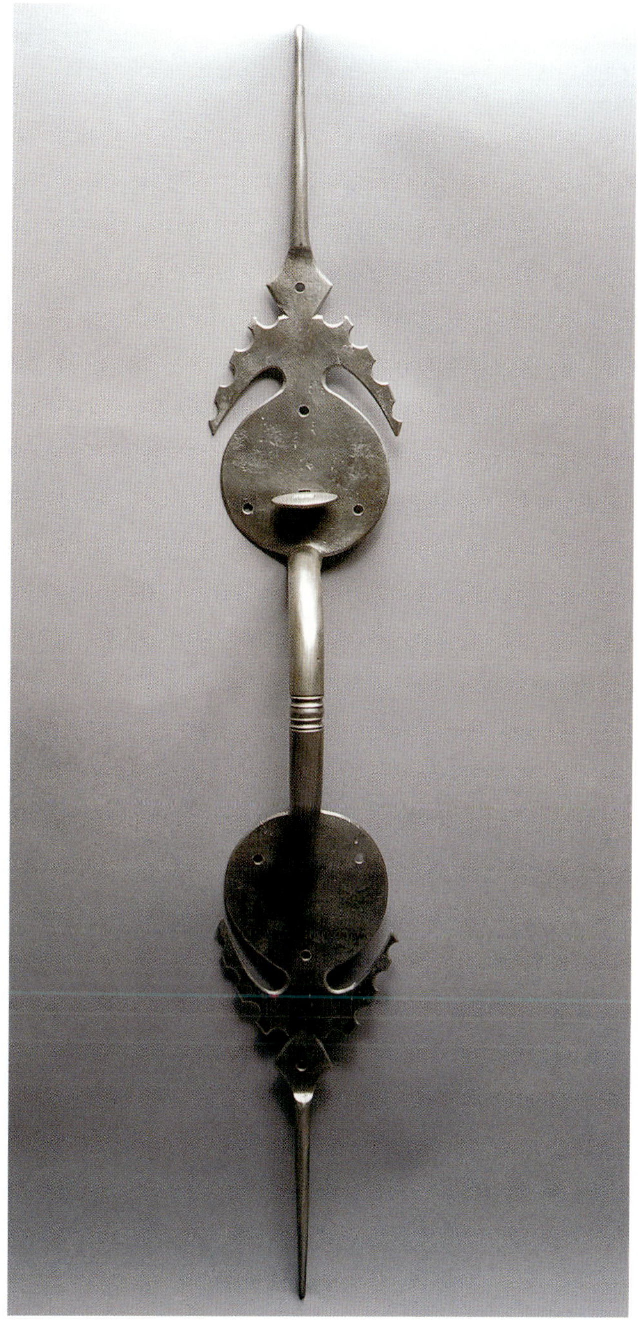

Michael J. Saari. *Suffolk Doorlatch #4*. 31" high, 5" wide, 4" deep. *Photo, artist*

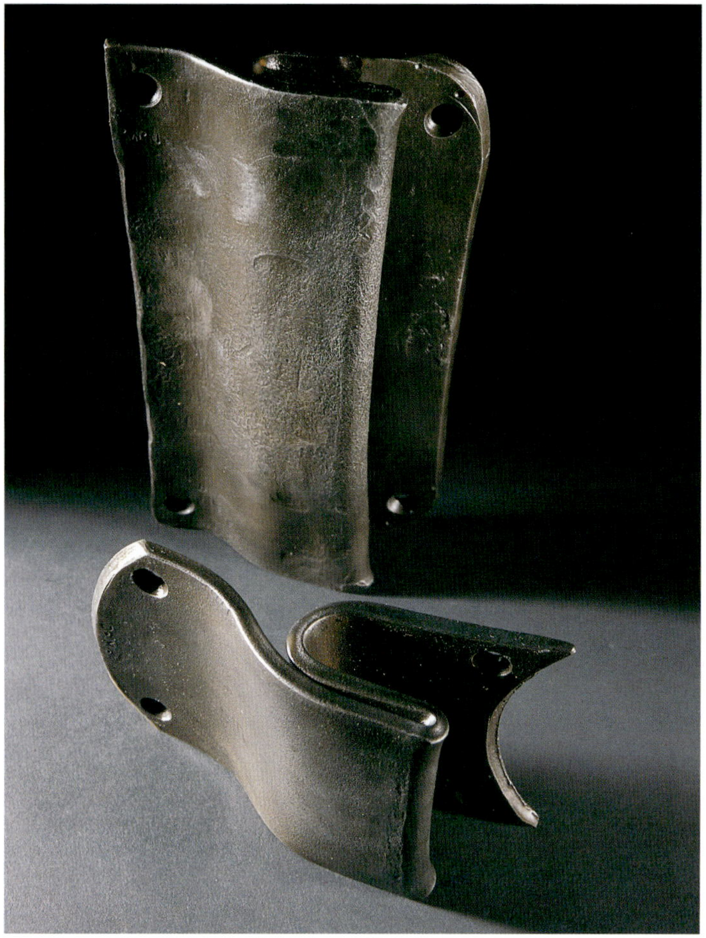

David Maurice. Folded door pulls. *Photo, Enrique Cubillo*

Jeff Wallin. Door pull. Mild steel and nickel steel. 10" high, 6" wide, 3" deep. *Photo, Tom Mills*

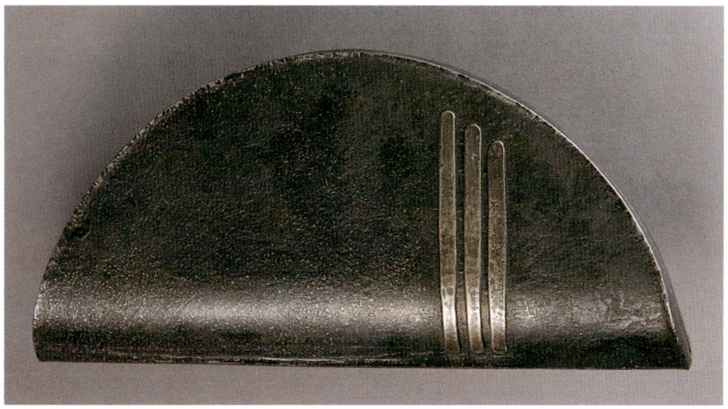

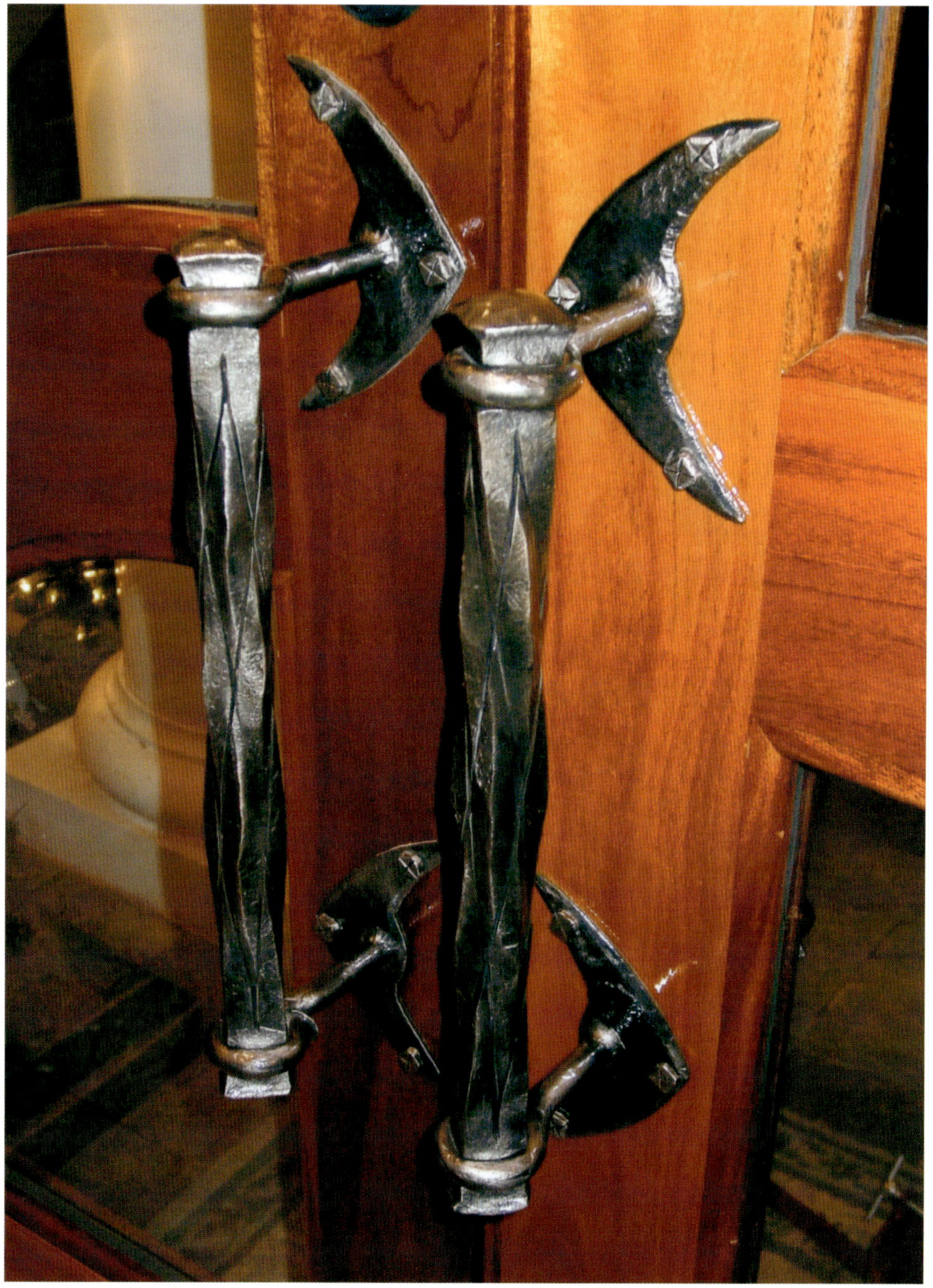

Andrew Chambers. Pineapple twist door handles. Forged steel, with a powder coat finish. 18" high, 5" deep. *Photo, Stacey Chambers*

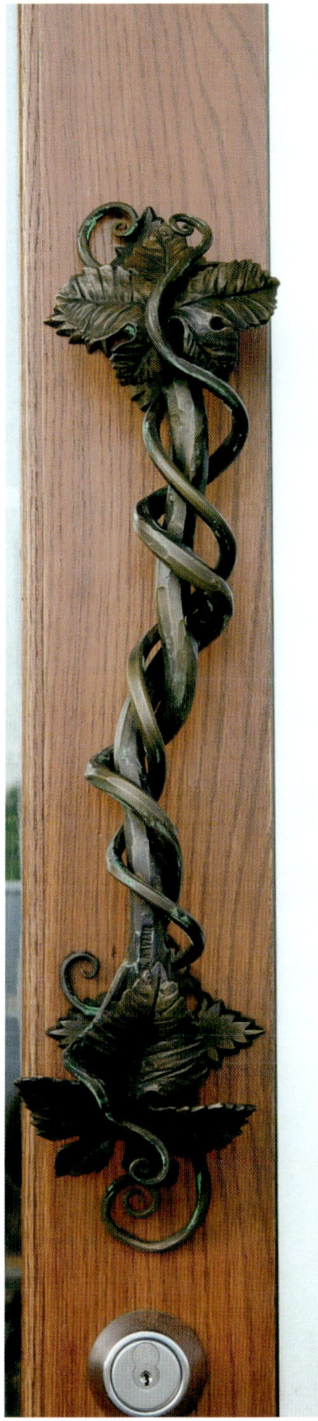

Craig Kaviar. Door handle for the wine shop of the Whole Foods market in Louisville, Kentucky. Appropriate imagery of a grape vine and leaves. 24" high. *Photo, artist*

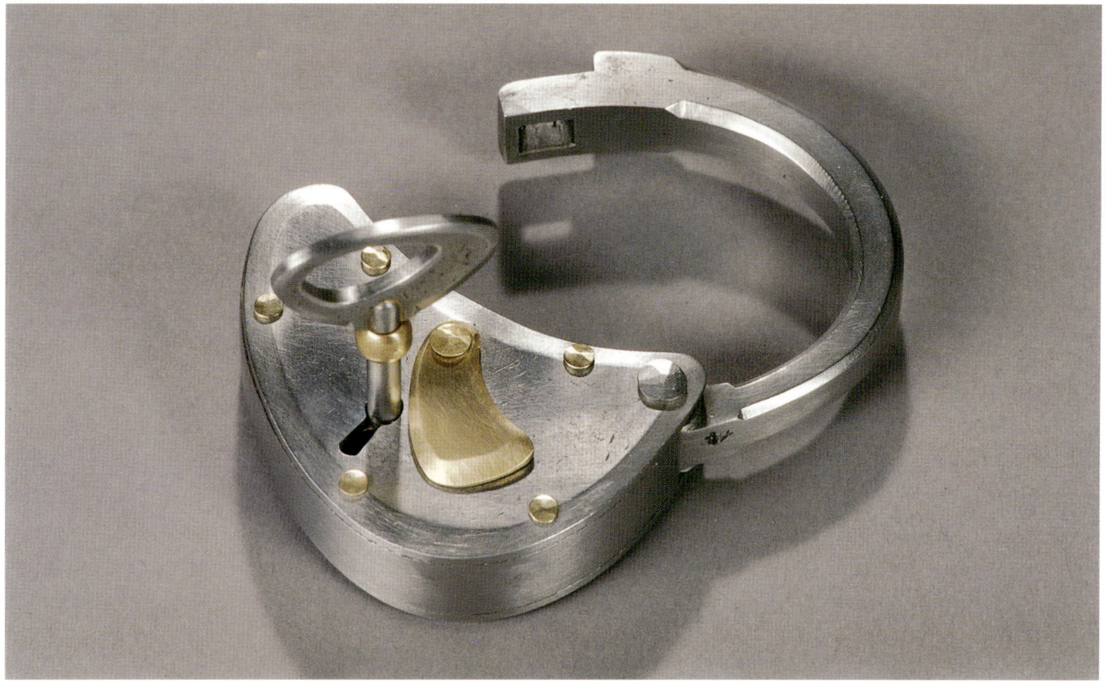

Benjamin O. Cowden. Oblong padlock. Mild and spring steel and brass. 3.5" high, 3" wide, 1" deep. *Photo, John Lucas*

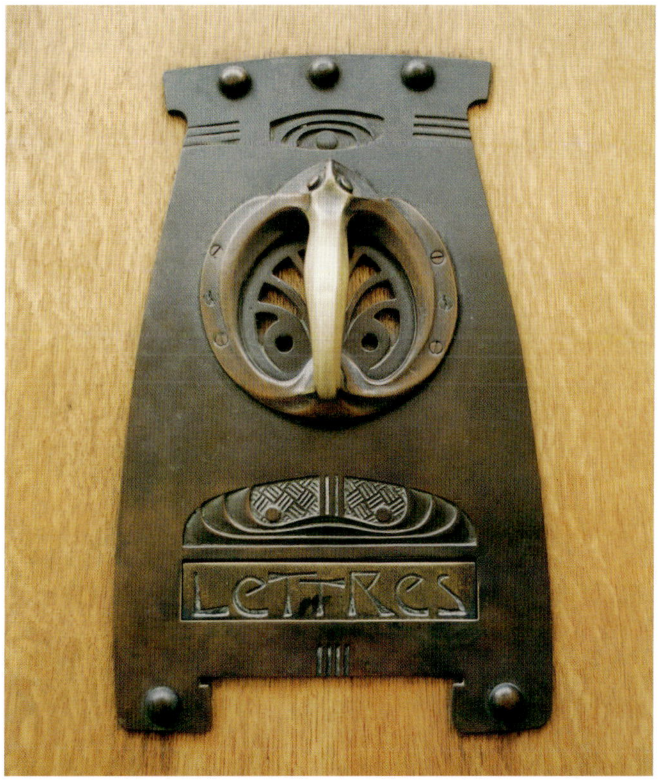

Paul Hamesse. Metal door handgrip combined with a mailbox, at an entry for a residential and laboratory building in Brussels, Belgium. An Art Nouveau design created in 1909. *Photo, Werner F. Bocqué*

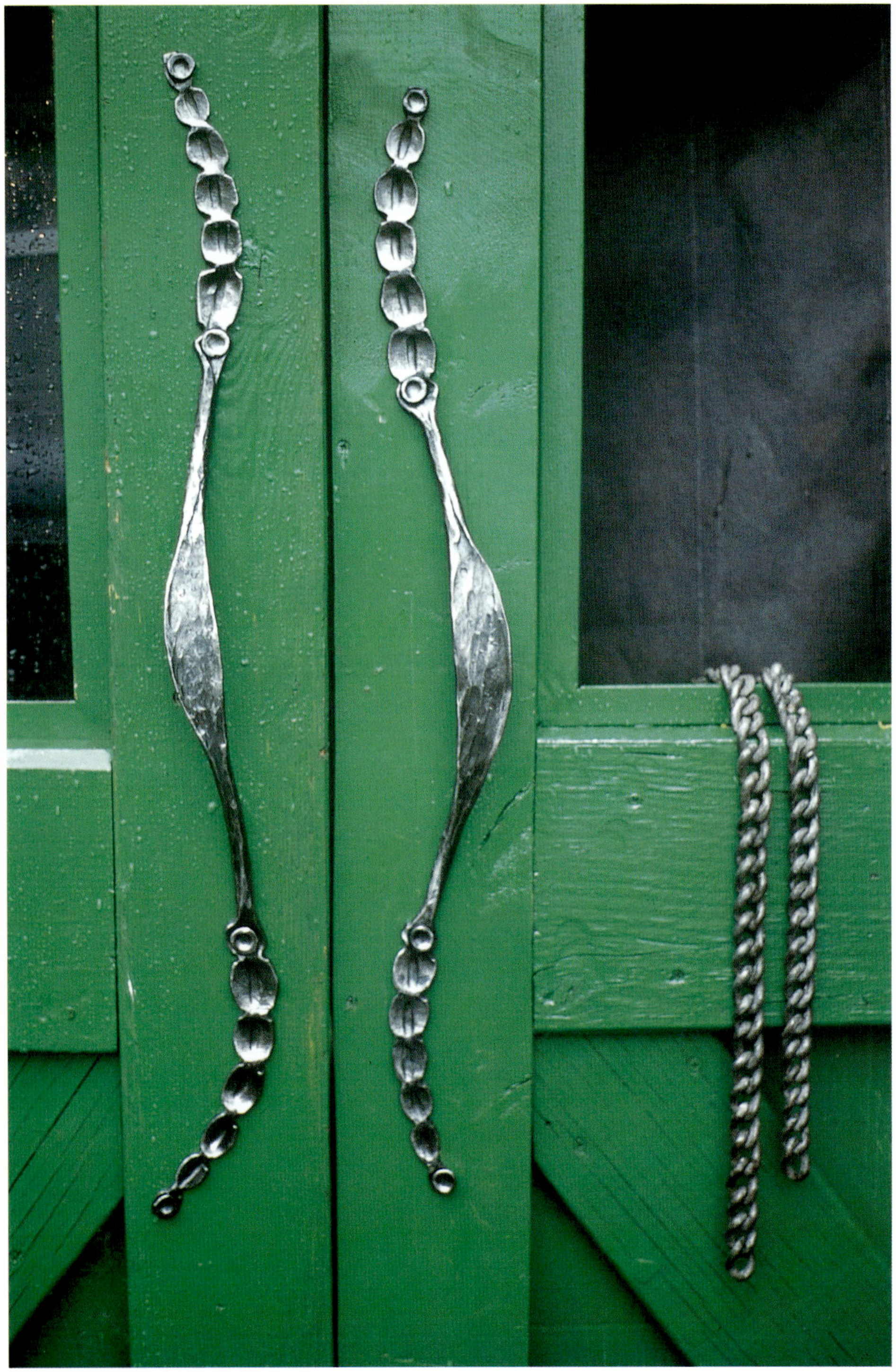

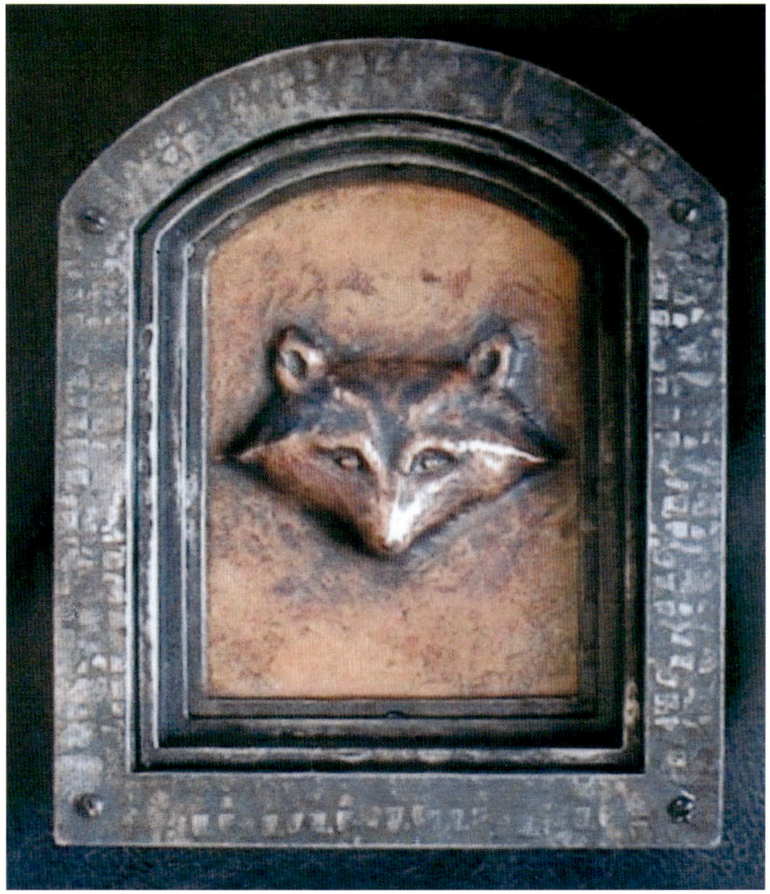

Josh Jones. Design by Steve Lopes. Fox peephole. 9" square. *Photo, Steve Lopes*

Susan Madacsi. Seaweed door pulls. Forged steel. 22" high, 1.5" wide. *Photo, R .J. Phil*

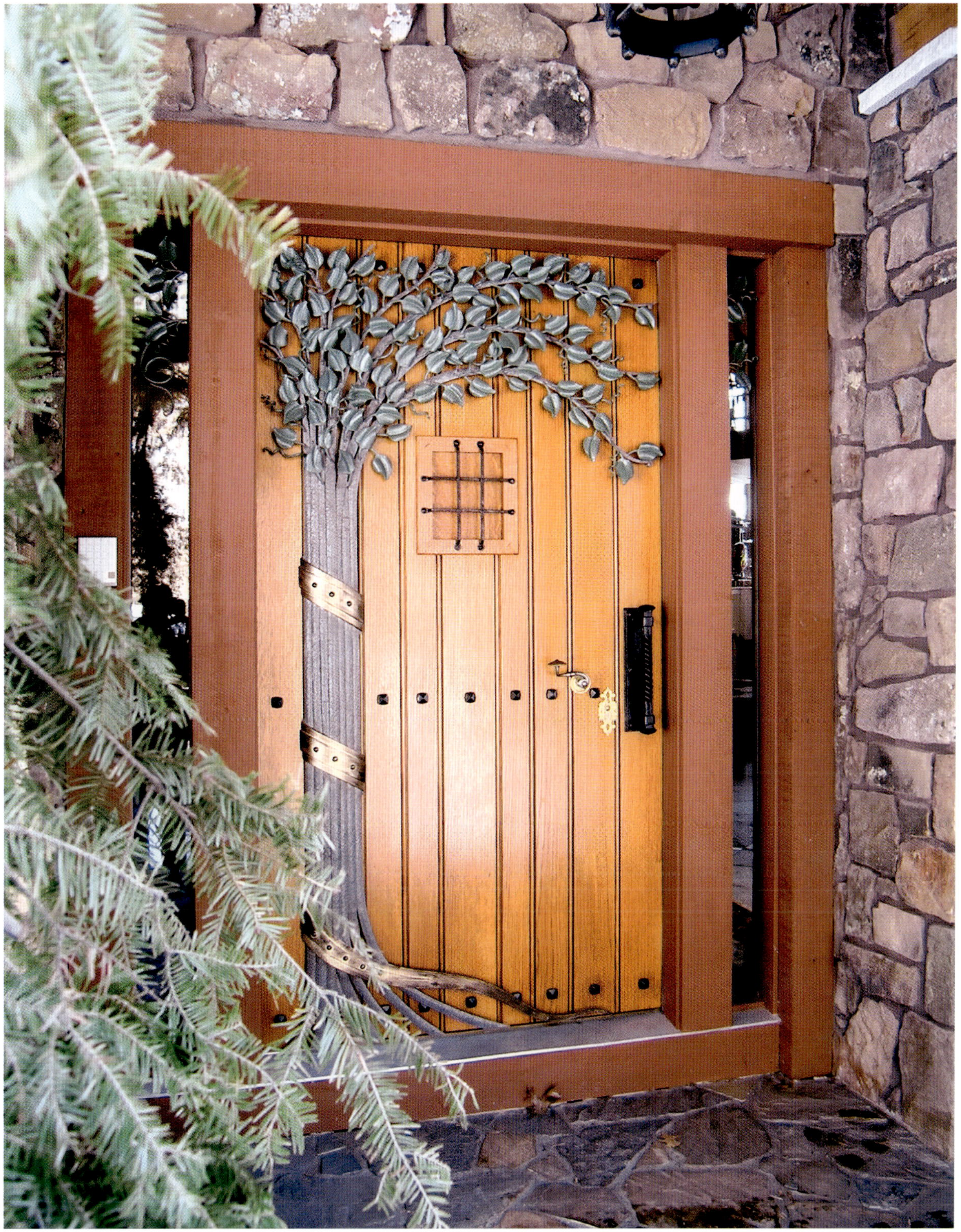

Tom Latané. Finished door (exterior shown here, interior on page 211) was a cooperative project. Bob Walsh designed the door to the client's specifications. John May constructed the wood door, Keith Johnson forged the tree, peep hole window grille, door handles, hinges, and straps. Tom Latané made the lock. *Photo, Bob Walsh*

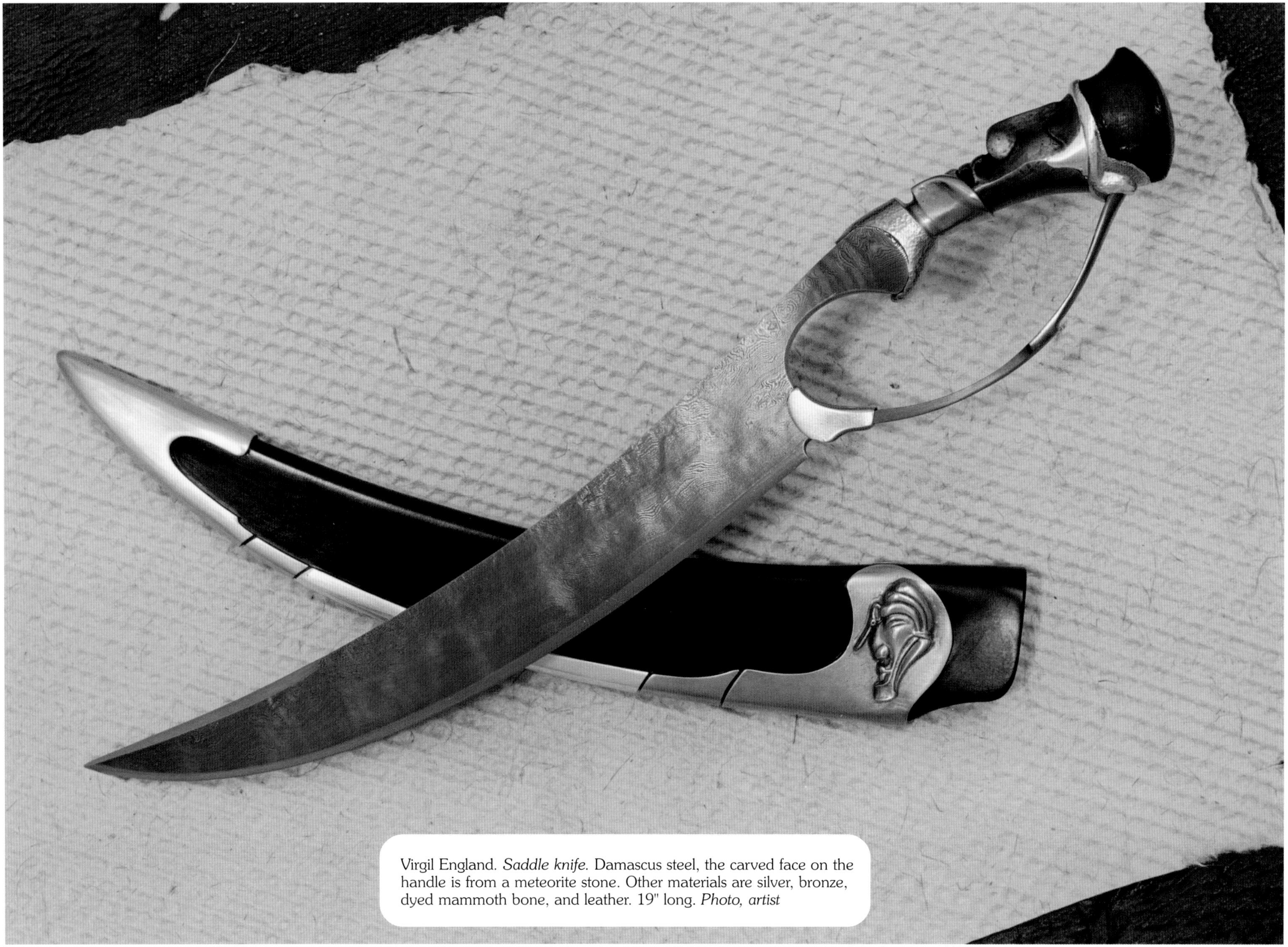

Virgil England. *Saddle knife.* Damascus steel, the carved face on the handle is from a meteorite stone. Other materials are silver, bronze, dyed mammoth bone, and leather. 19" long. *Photo, artist*

Chapter 10. And Still There Is More

After the ironworker creates public and pedestal art, gigantic spiders for a high ride, railings, staircases, fences, furniture, lighting fixtures, and more, what is there left for him to create?

Plenty.

The use of iron and the techniques involved are limited only by a person's imagination and skills. He, or she, doesn't have to create railroad cars, and huge motors, he can create small, utilitarian items. And he does. Here you will find a bounty of ideas you may not have thought about as the work of the artist-blacksmith.

Knives have been fashioned by blacksmiths since man was able to tame fire to melt and shape iron. Blacksmiths traveled with armies to make weaponry and horse gear throughout the ages. But today's artist who looks to knife-making often produces blades of such exquisite splendor that they are like jewels and command prices as high as diamonds and precious necklaces. They may require hundreds of hours to create. The Damascus knives by Virgil England, John Jenson, and Steven Schwartzer are a small sampling of the numbers and types of knives created. Additional examples can be seen at their web sites. Other's web sites can be found with a simple search for "knife makers." Knife-making societies and knife collectors are avid in their interests.

Containers of many shapes intrigue the ironworker who makes flasks, bottles, and boxes that are destined to become heirlooms of the future. They are sought by collectors, and may become museums acquisitions. Often they are not meant to be functional; instead they present something that must be made just as the mountain climber ascends a peak "because it's there." Forming the hot metal, finishing it with patinas, or other colorants represent a challenge because the potential is infinite.

In addition to the objects shown many other items in daily use are made of iron…such as signage, gardening tools, and serving utensils. Functional items that don't lend themselves readily to artistic treatments (or haven't here) are still objects to be made and contemplated as potential for art.

Helmut Hillenkamp's window treatment is a far cry from the mundane curtain rods that are now mass produced by casting and sold in every hard-

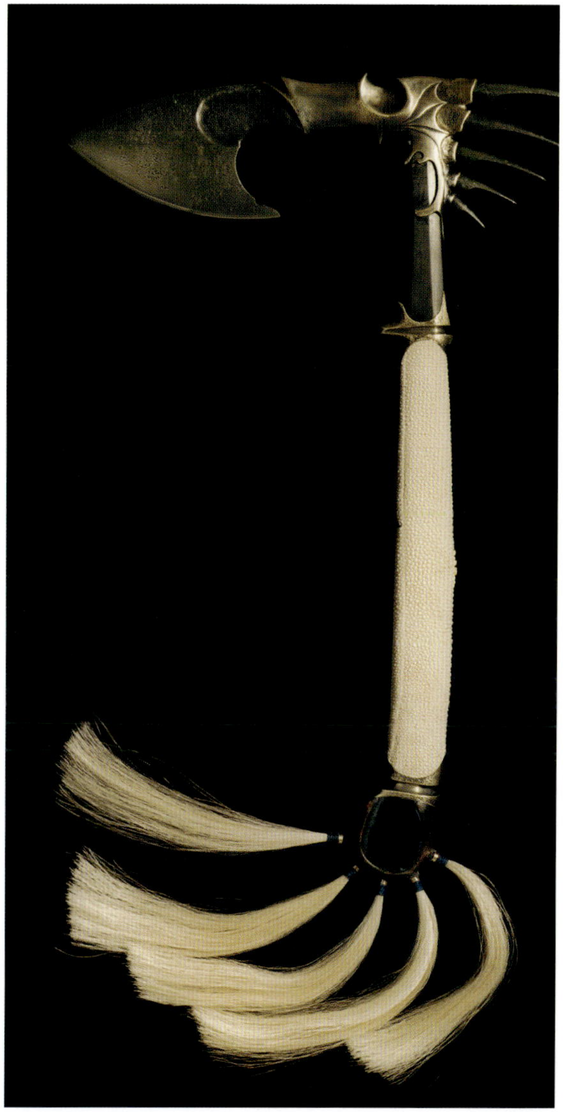

Virgil England. *Tidelands Banshee Axe*. Damascus steel, bronze, Madagascar ebony, stingray, leather, and horse hair. 32" long. *Photo, artist*

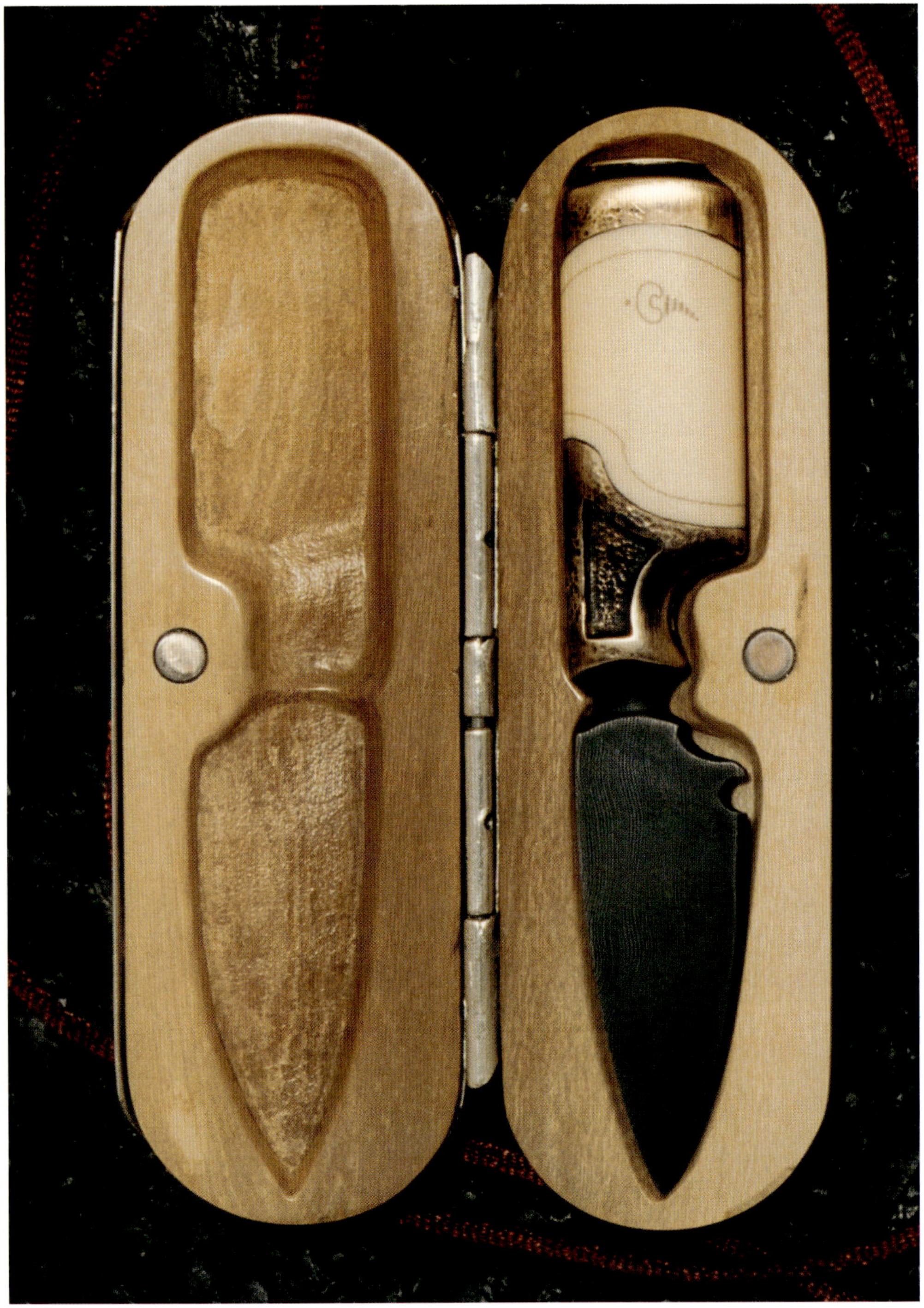

ware and house wares store. The same is true for pots and pans. Our ancestors who cooked over open fires used iron pots and kettles shaped by the blacksmith.

Then there is jewelry...an output not tackled by many because iron doesn't lend itself too readily to the kinds of forms that can better be served by silver or gold. Still the jeweler who works in precious metals uses the same techniques as does the blacksmith, only on a smaller scale. Albert Paley's career sets an example. He studied to be a jeweler but made the leap into iron and forging; today he is one of the most recognized metal sculptors in the world. Metals that are malleable may need to be heated; yet they have to be hammered and stretched by repoussé methods. They can be welded, or cast, and given finishes that will make them impervious to weather and wear.

Virgil England. *Cold Touch*. Cased pocketknife. Damascus steel, silver, bronze, Mammoth ivory. 3.8" high. *Photo, artist*

Opposite page:
John Lewis Jensen. *Stallion Talon*. Three layered, sandwich style, Damascus steel blade by Daryl Meyer. Titanium handle with sky blue, white, and orange fossil walrus ivory with precious stones set in 18k gold. 13.5" long. *Photo, artist*

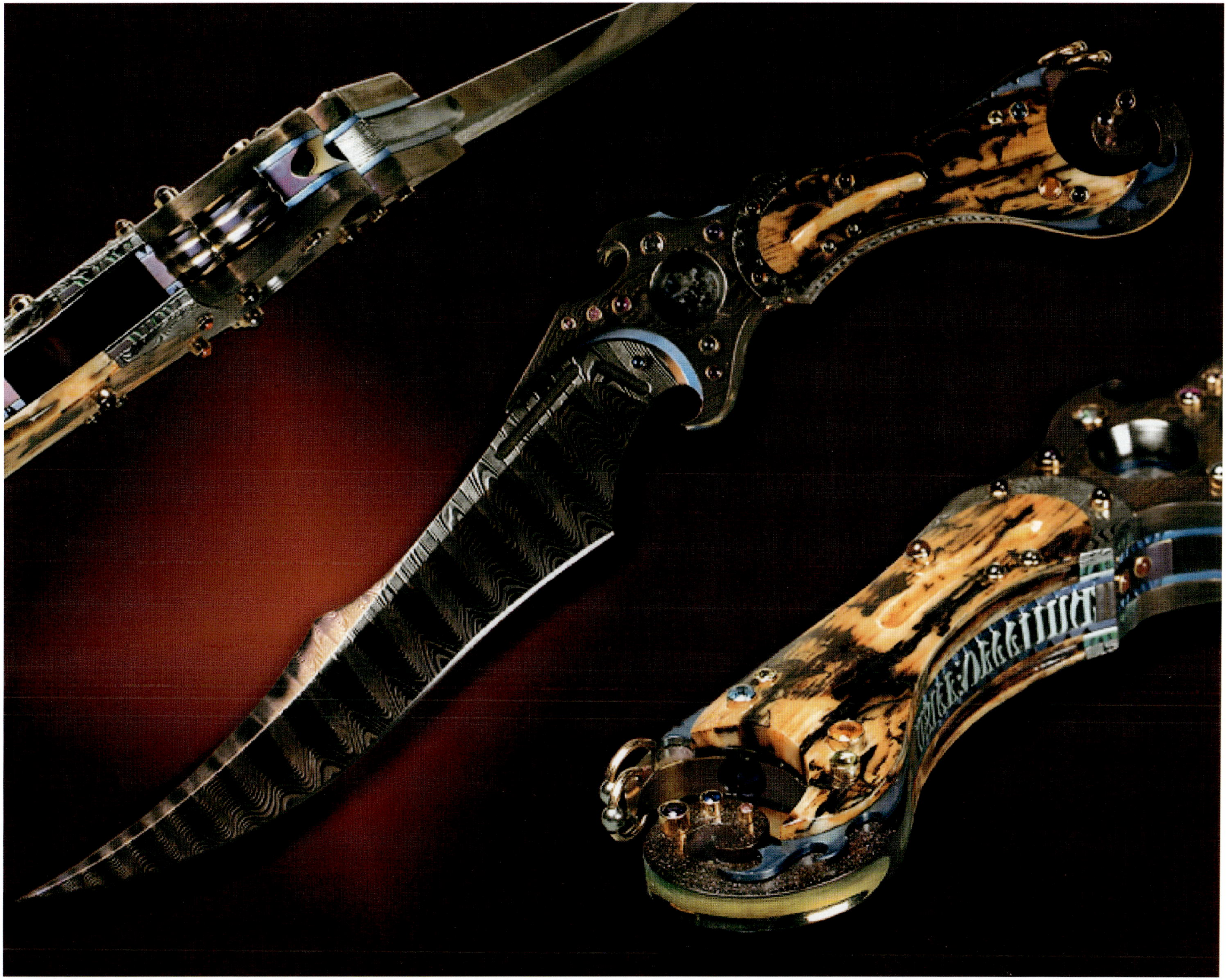

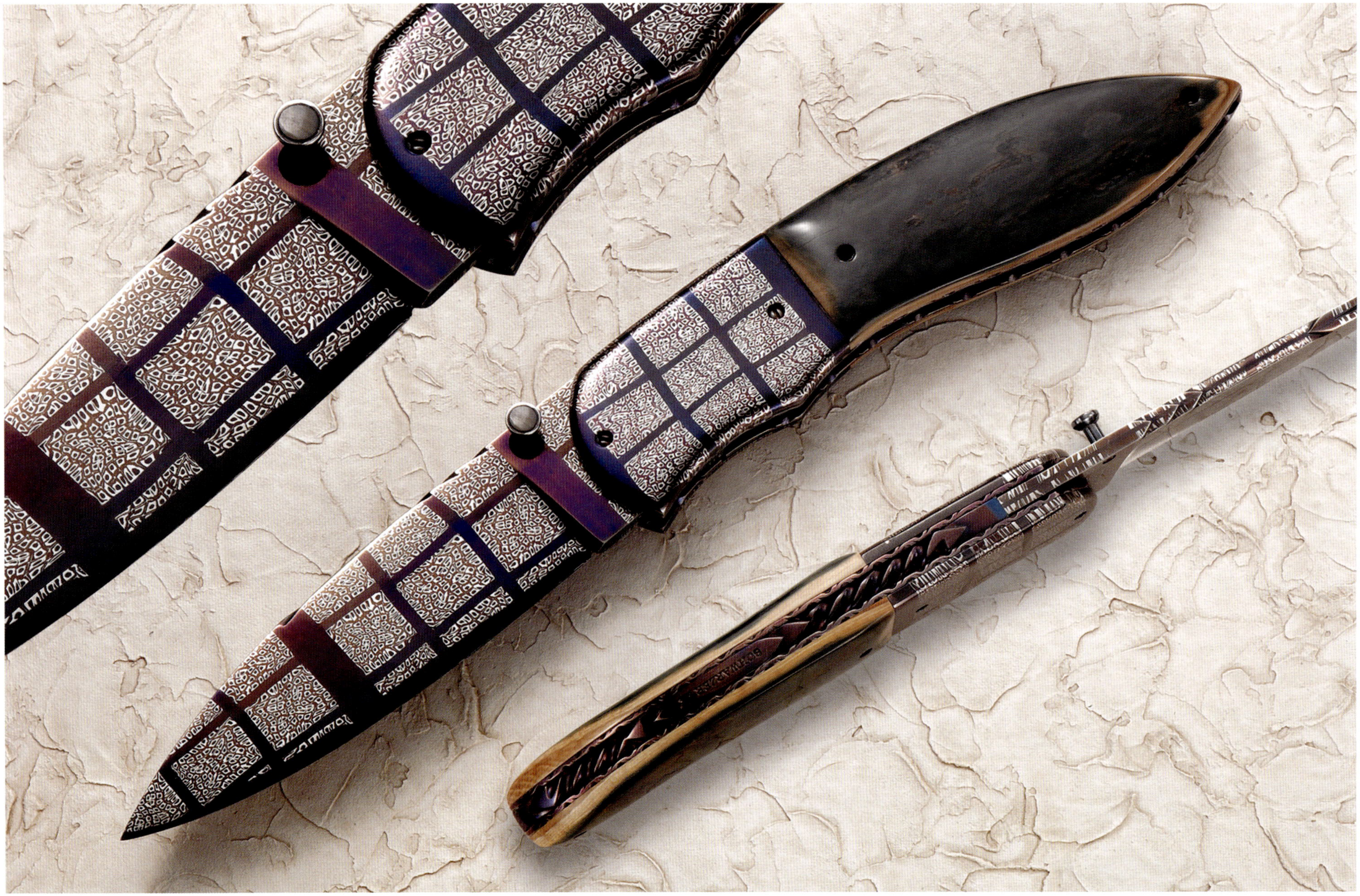

Steve Schwarzer. *Windows Folder Knife*. Damascus steel and mastodon ivory. A special mosaic pattern using square tubing, high carbon steel rods, and nickel powder in the blade and bolsters. These complicated patterns take days of labor to produce. There are seven different mosaic panels involved in just the blade. The handle is fossil ivory. The liners and back bar are carved inside and out. 8" long. *Photo, Point Seven Studios*

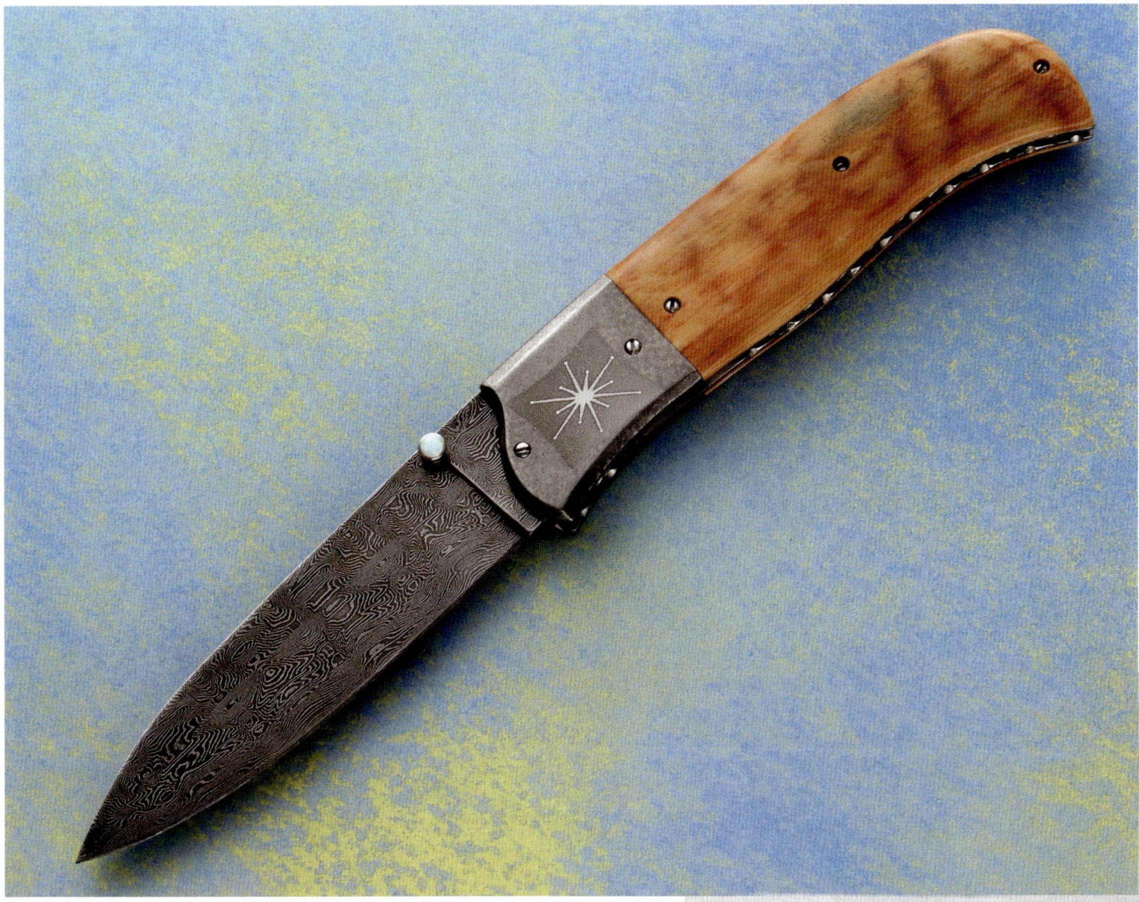

Steve Schwarzer. *Star Folding Knife*. Damascus steel, nickel, and mastodon fossil. The star image started out over 1.5" across and was reduced under a large air hammer to a ¾" bar containing the image. The border around the star is made from several hundred layers of parquet mosaic Damascus. The blade is a layered and laddered mosaic pattern. The handle is carved red fossil mastodon ivory. The back bar and liners are extensively carved. 8" long. *Photo, Point Seven Studios*

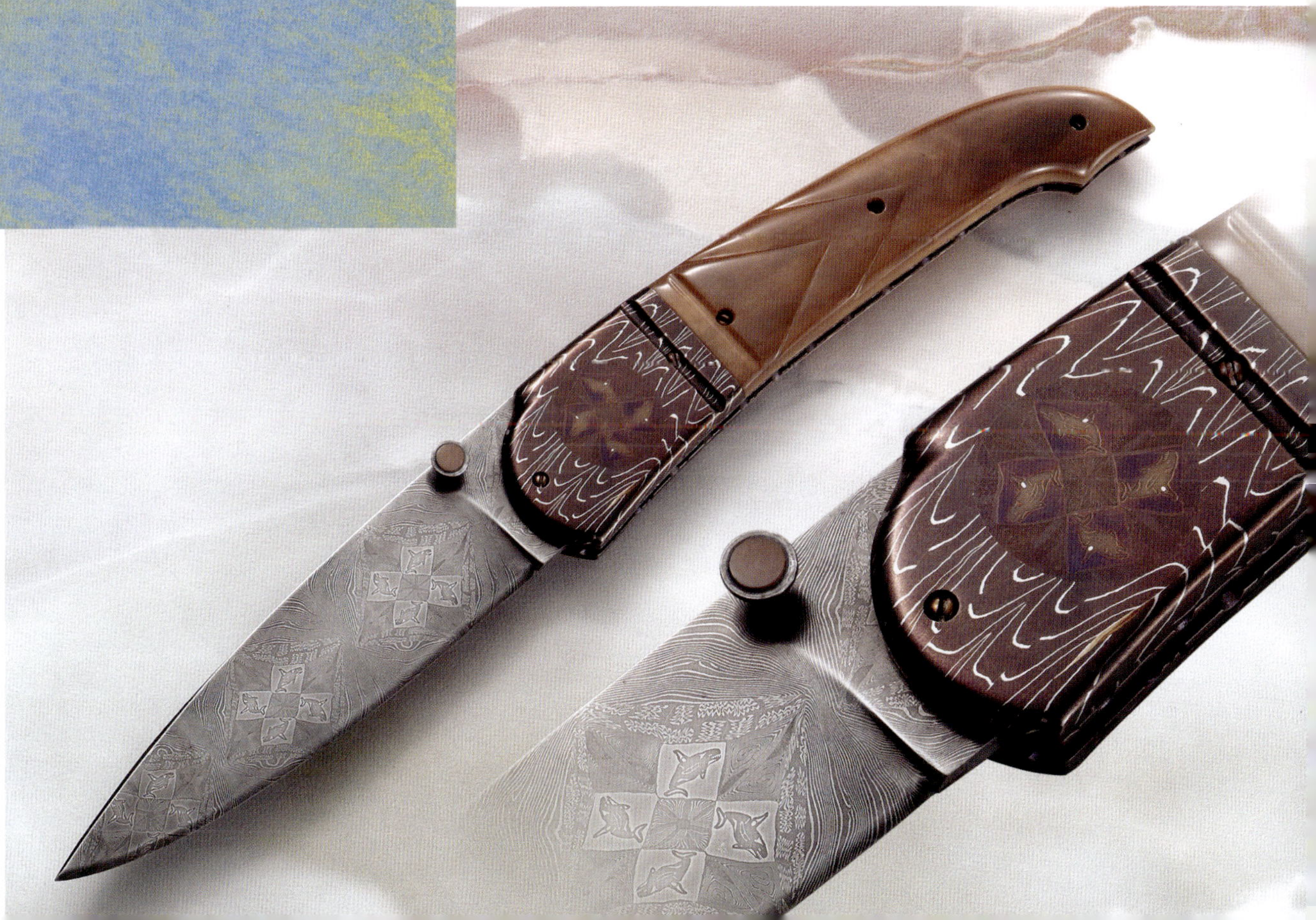

Steve Schwarzer. *Orca theme folder.* Whale images are laser cut from high carbon plate that are then stacked and tack welded together in a box shape. The box is forge welded into a solid bar containing the whale image which is reduced in size and incorporated in the mosaic pattern in the blade. Handle is carved fossil walrus ivory. These complex patterns take several hundred hours to complete. The bolster area also exhibits the killer whales and a hunter's circular star pattern. *Photo, Point Seven Studios*

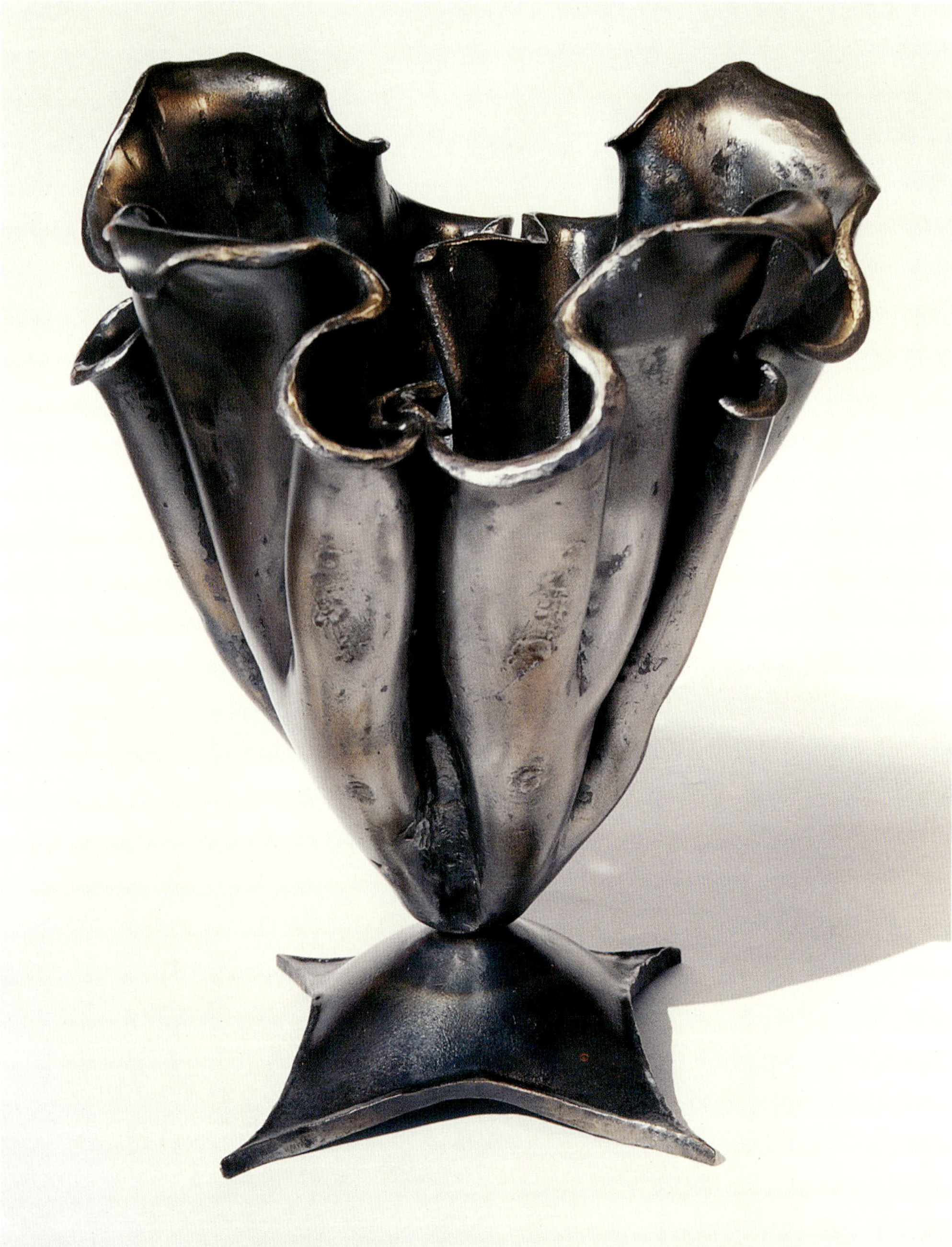

Nitzan Lilie. *Vase.* Forged and raised from steel pipe. 14" high, 12" diam. at top, 7" diam. at bottom. *Photo, Dona Meilach*

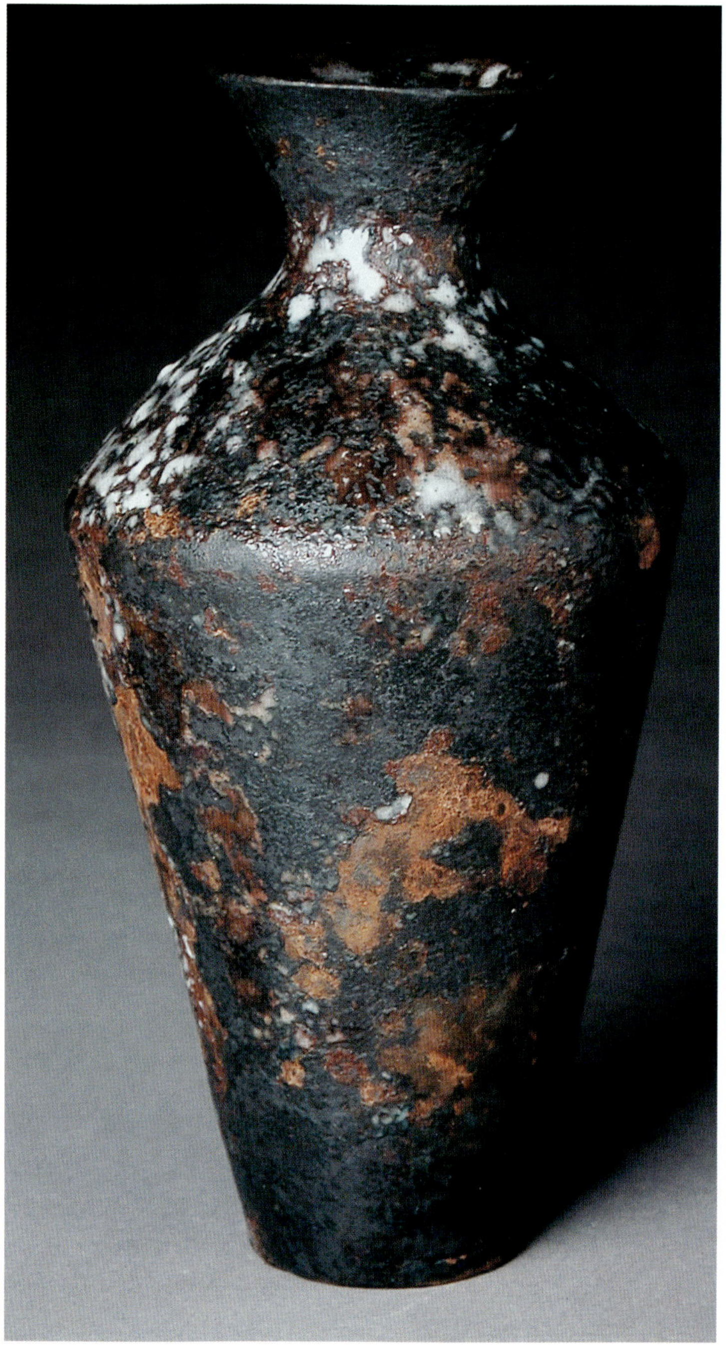

JoEleyn Trahan. *Deception*. Steel, copper and enamel. *Photo, artist*

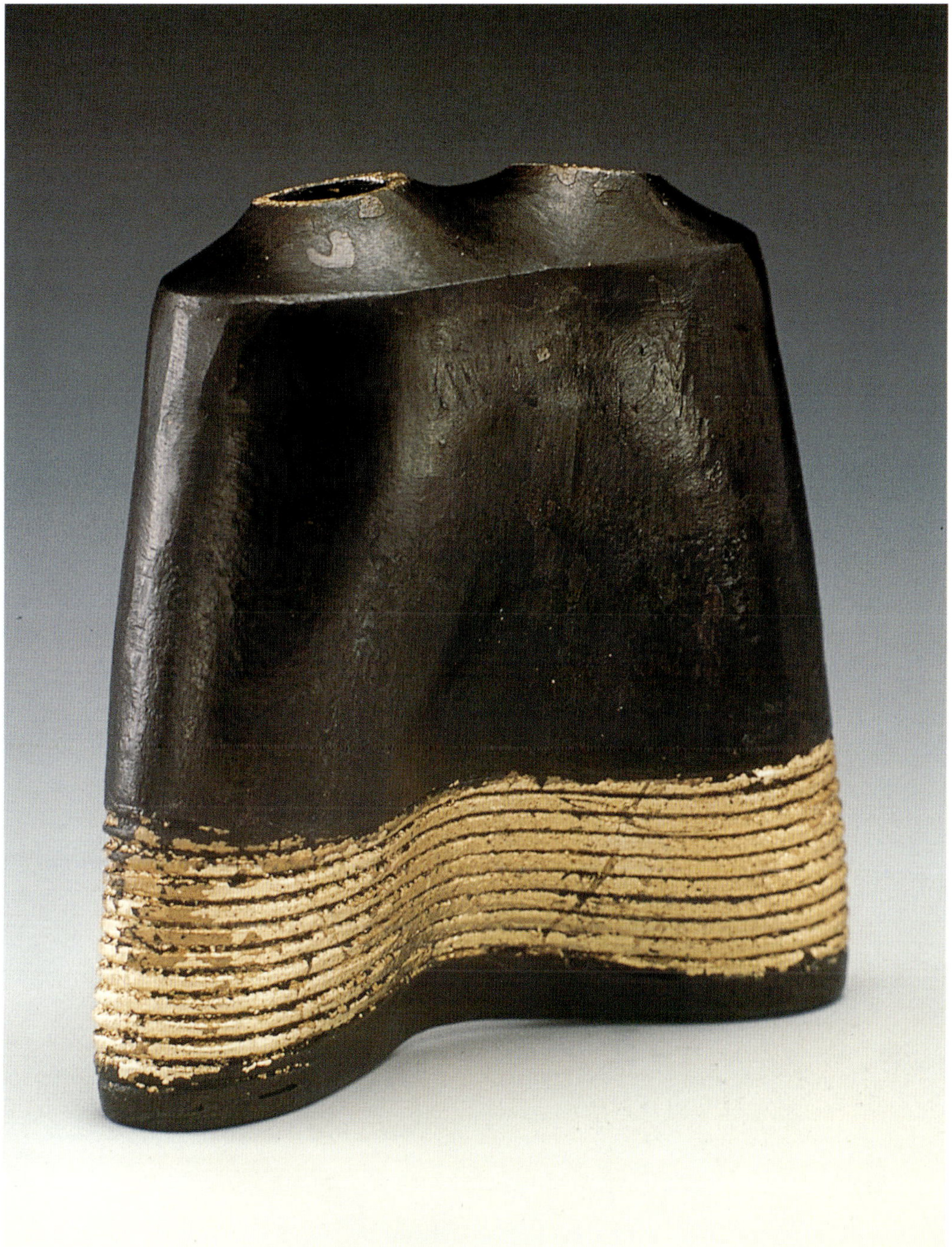

Susan Madacsi. *Flask*. Steel and gold leaf. 3.5" high 3.5" wide. *Photo, R. J. Phil*

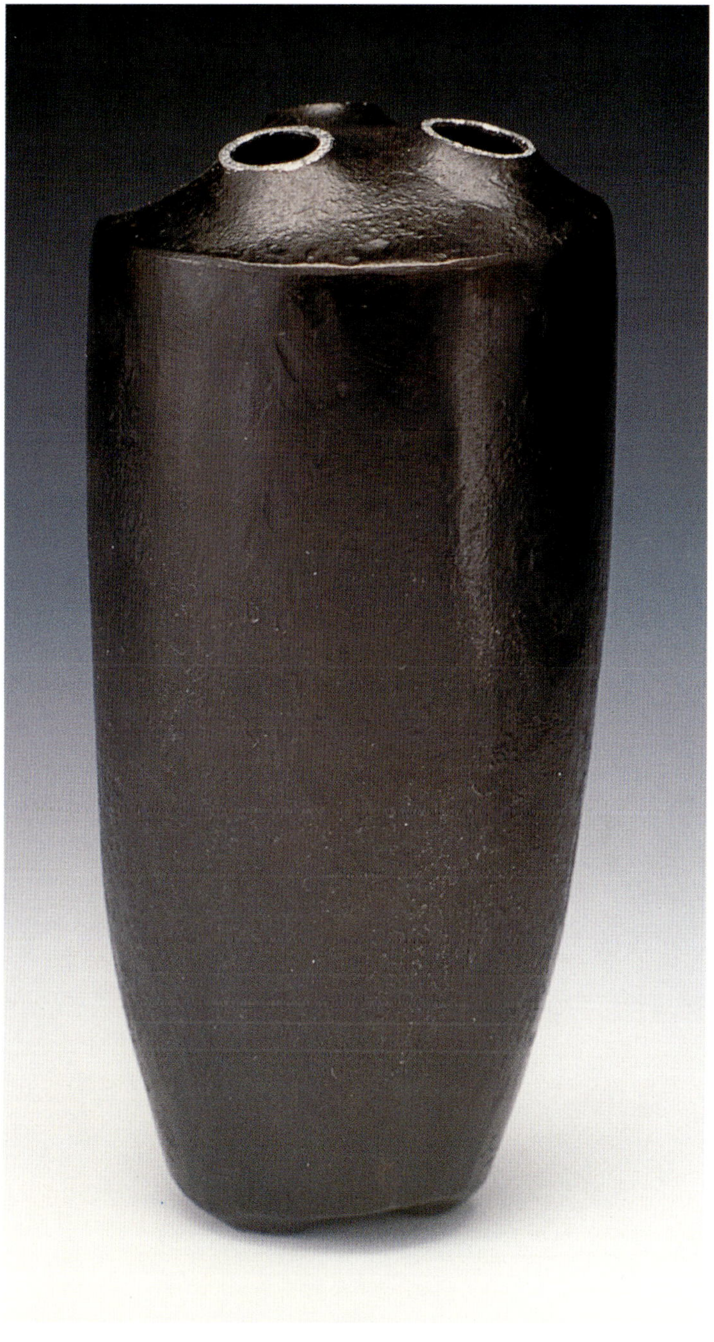

Susan Madacsi. *Chamber Vessel*. Steel and silver leaf. 7" high, 3" wide. *Photo, R. J. Phil*

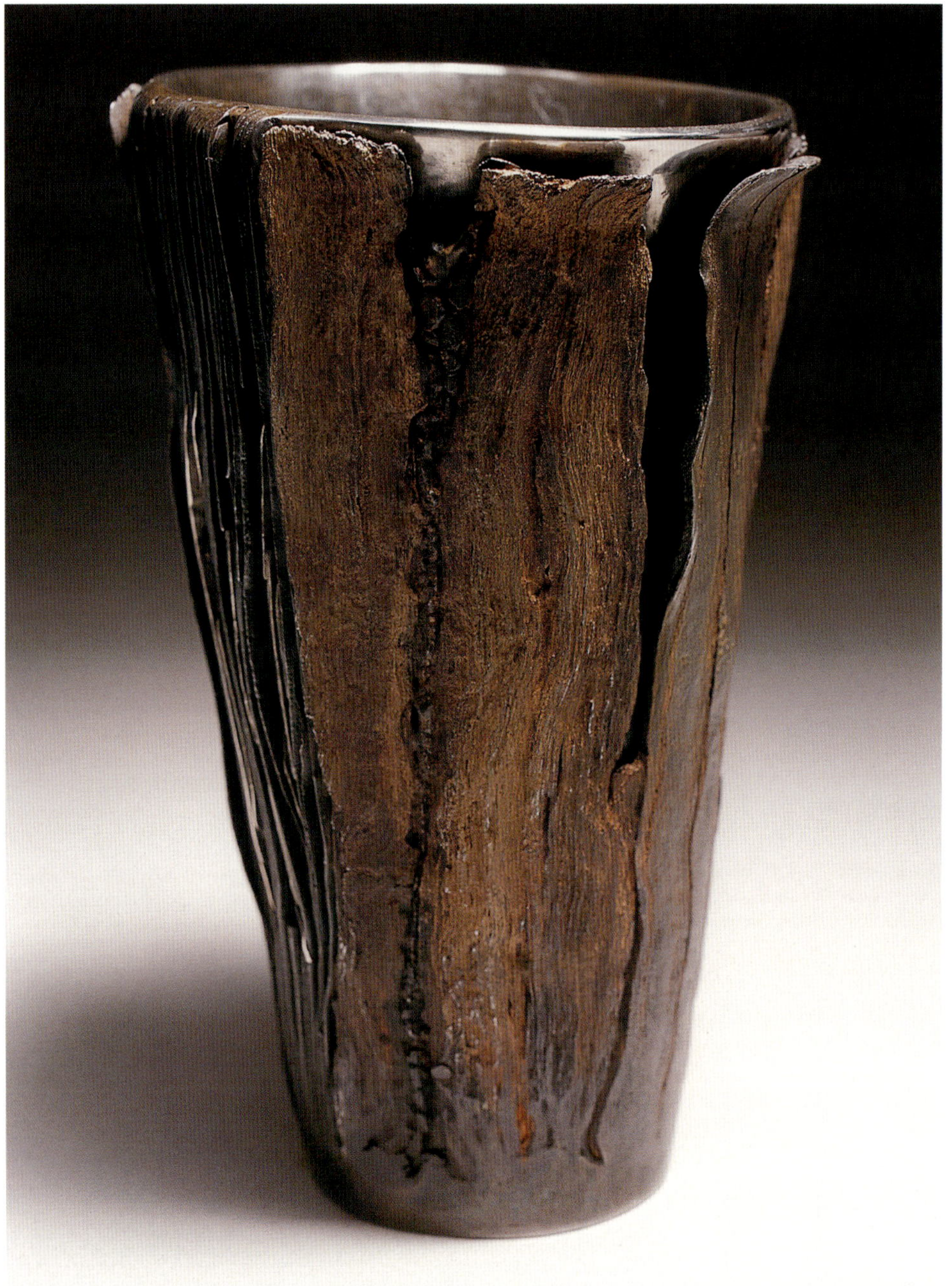

Nathan Blank. *Growth through Decay*. Wrought iron, mild steel, sterling silver, copper and springs. Forge welded, fabricated, and colored with patinas. 7.5" high, 3.5" wide, 4" deep. *Photo, artist*

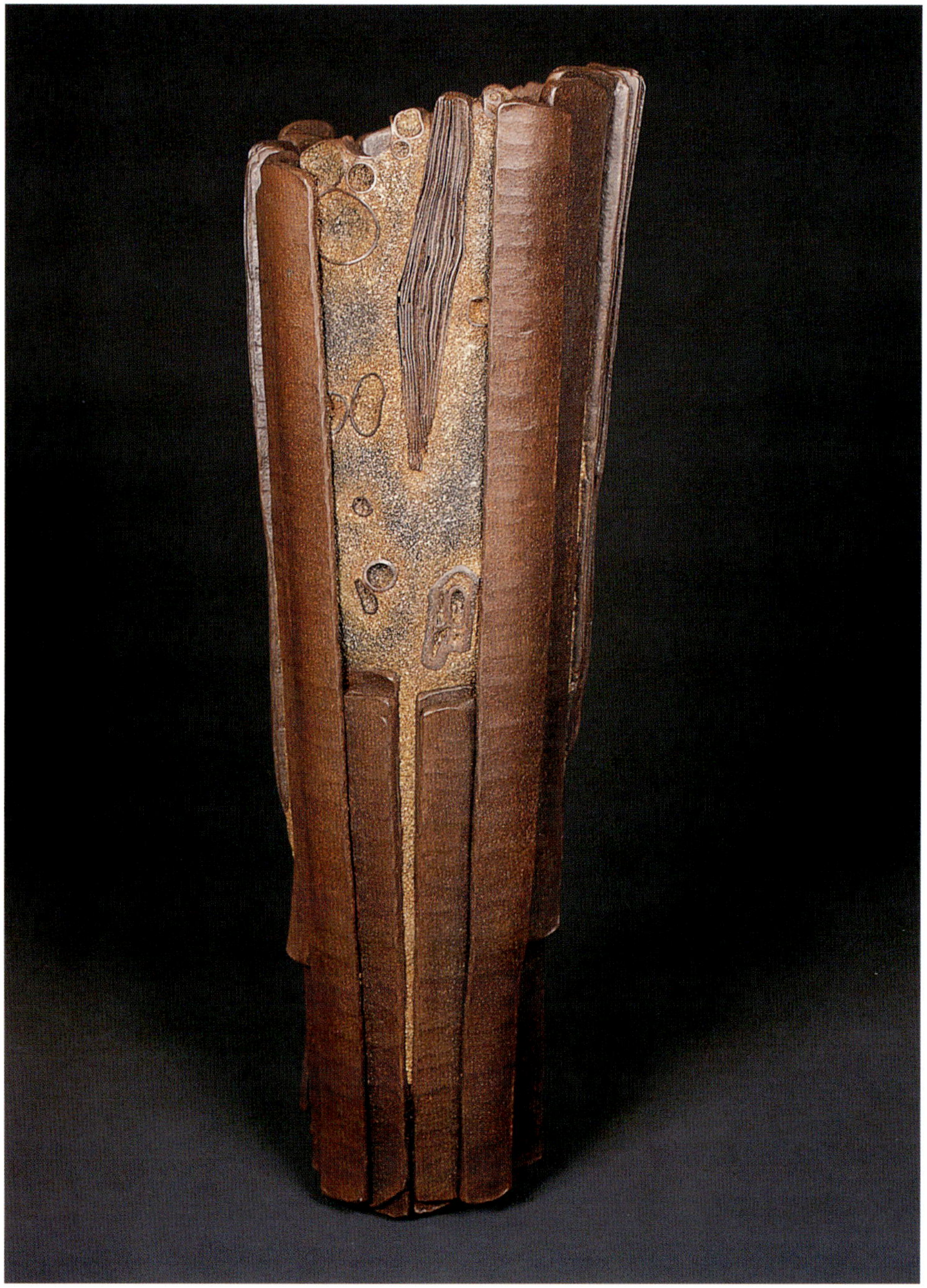

Nathan Blank. *Untitled Urn*. Mild steel and concrete. Forged and fabricated with forge welded details in the concrete, patinas. 30" high, 9" wide, 10" deep. *Photo, artist*

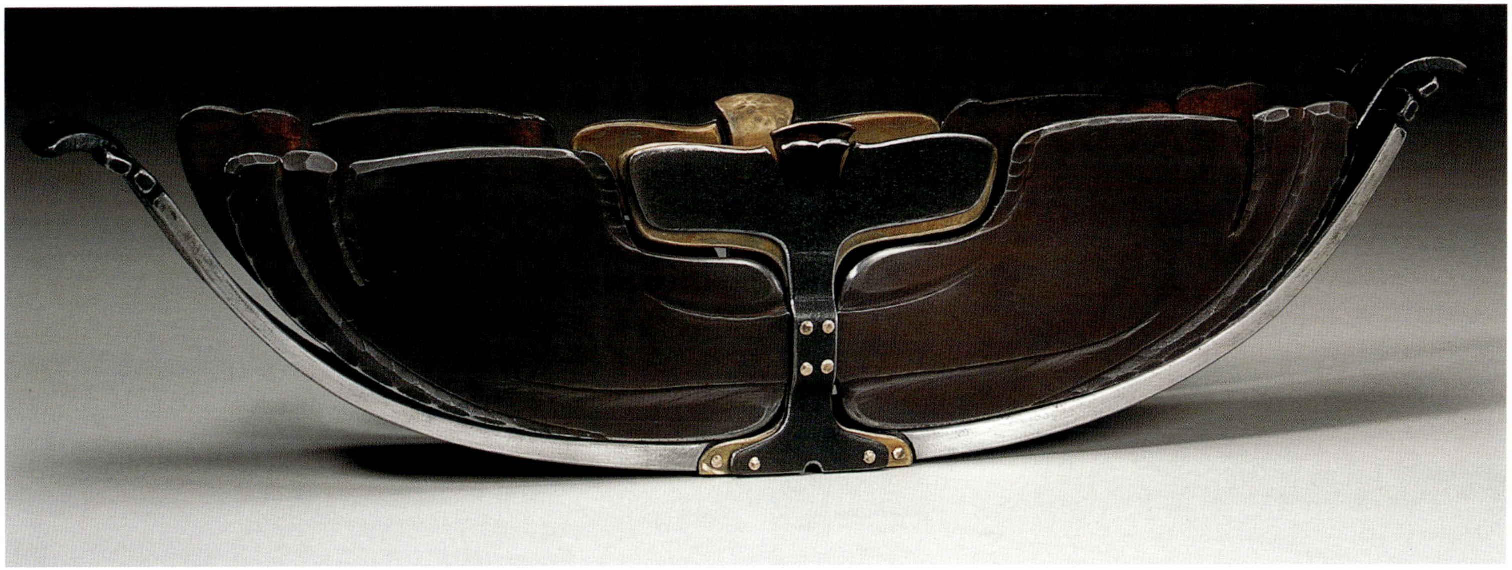

Matt Haugh. *Sky Vessel.* Iron and bronze. Suggestive flight form is symbolic of the sky. 5.5" high, 23" wide, 3.5" deep. *Photo, Jeffrey Bruce*

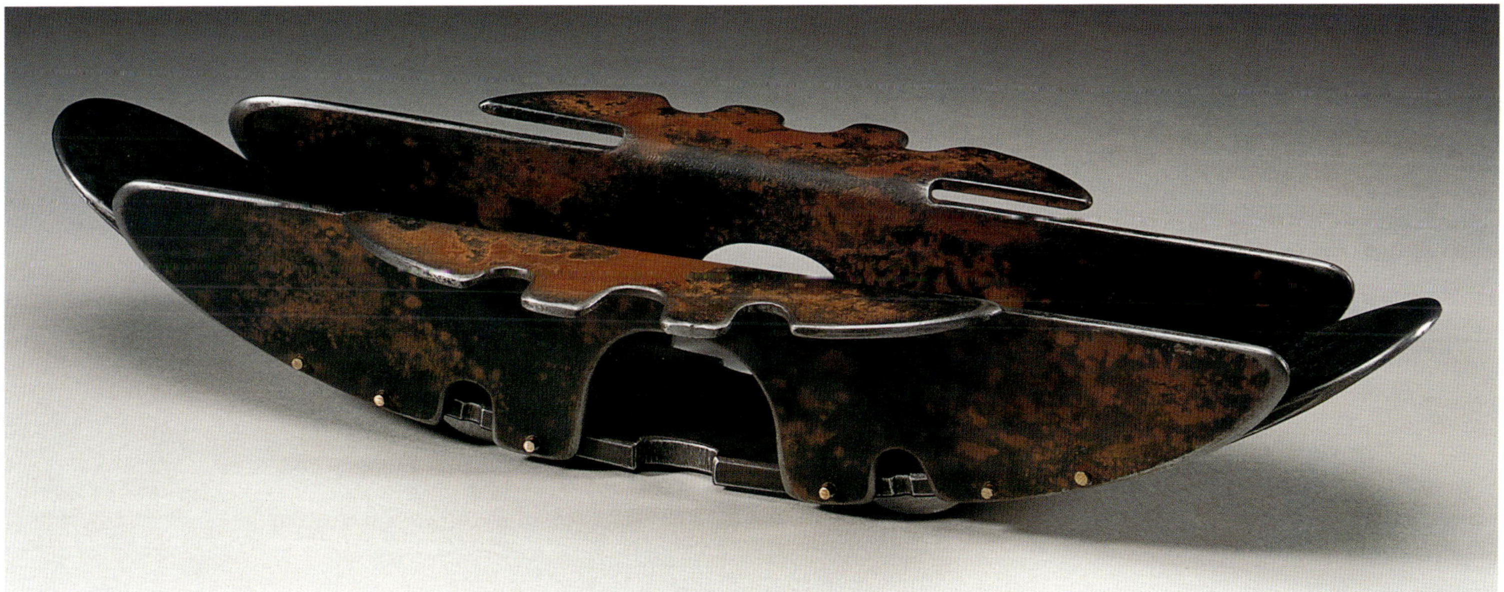

Matt Haugh. *Manus Vessel.* Iron and bronze. Manus is Latin for hand. The piece has an integrated handle built into the form. 3.5" high, 18" wide, 7" deep. *Collection, Richard Mawdsley. Photo, Jeffrey Bruce*

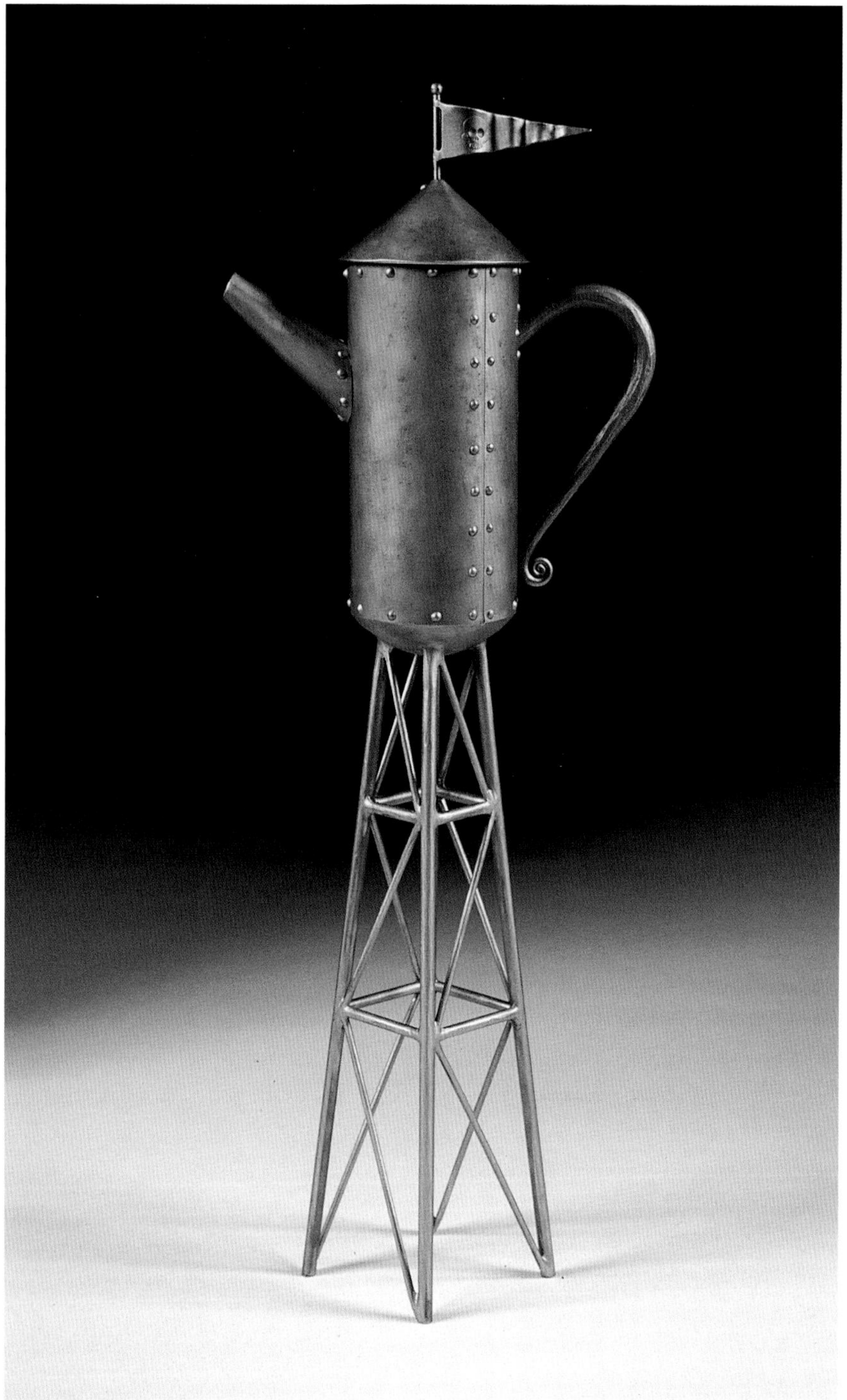

David Gignac. *Pirated Water Tower Teapot.* Forged and fabricated steel with a wax finish. 26" high, 9" wide, 5" deep. *Photo, artist*

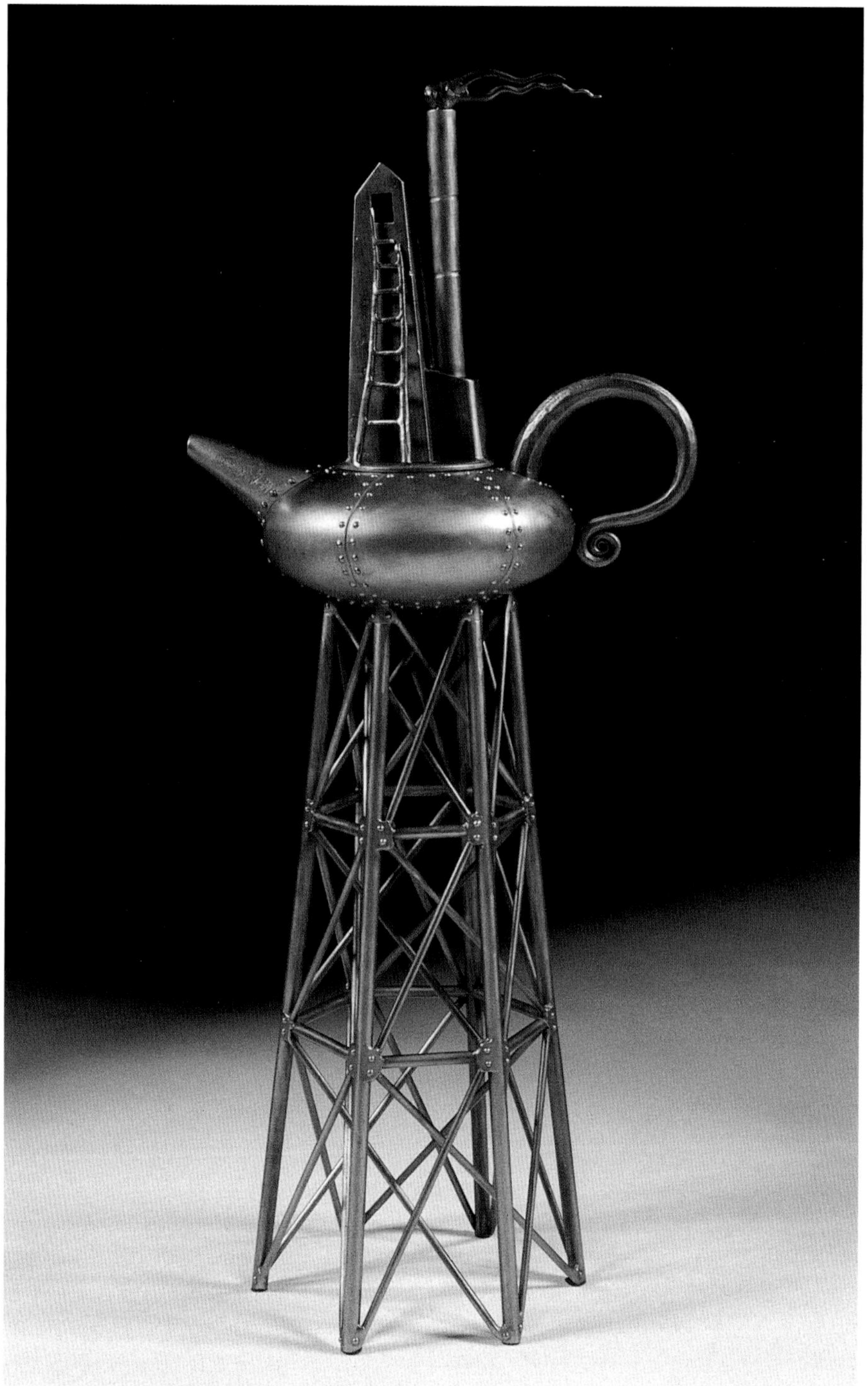

David Gignac. *Private Island Teapot.* Forged and fabricated steel with a wax finish. 36" high, 14" wide, 10" deep. *Photo, artist*

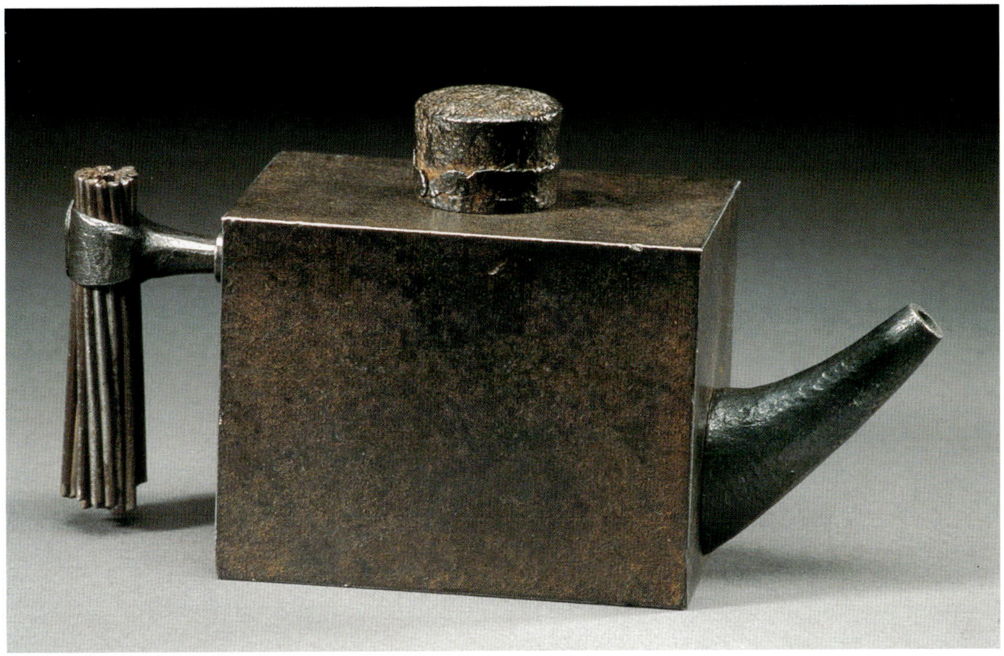

Stephen Yusko. *Mechanics of Solids: Teapot*. Steel. 4.5" high, 8" wide, 3" deep. *Photo, Jeff Bruce*

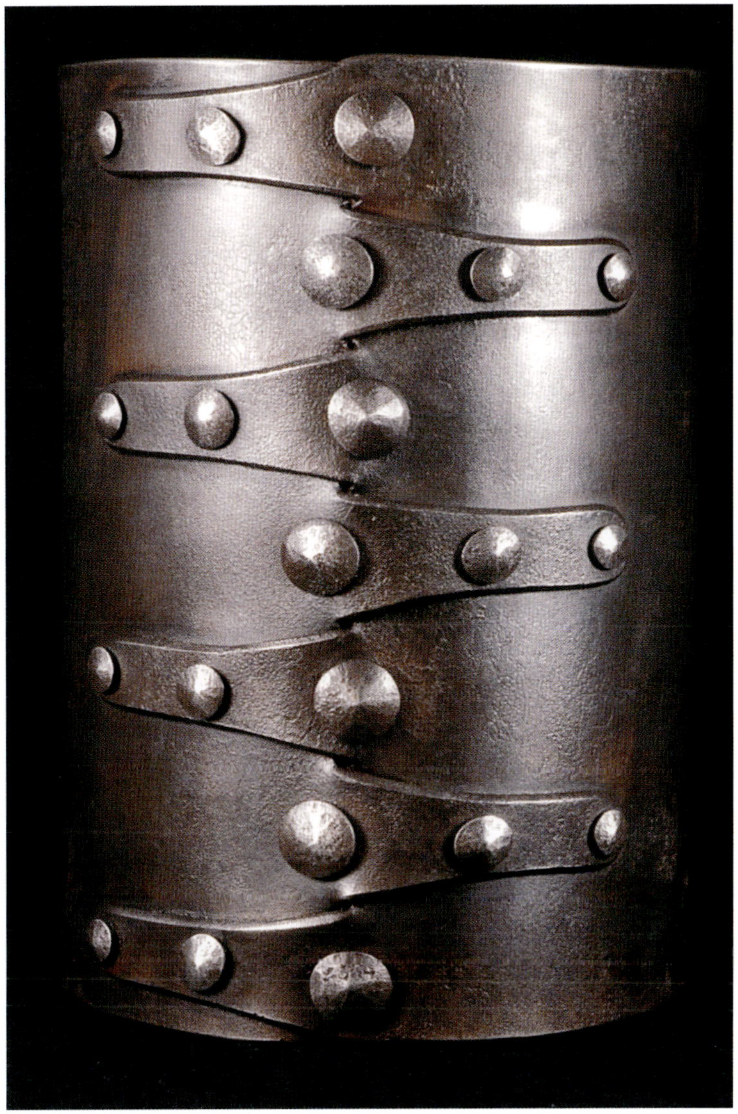

David Zatz. *Shaker Interlock.* Container. Forged, fire texture, sandblasted, browned steel with a waxed finish. 10" high. 6.75" diam. *Photo, artist*

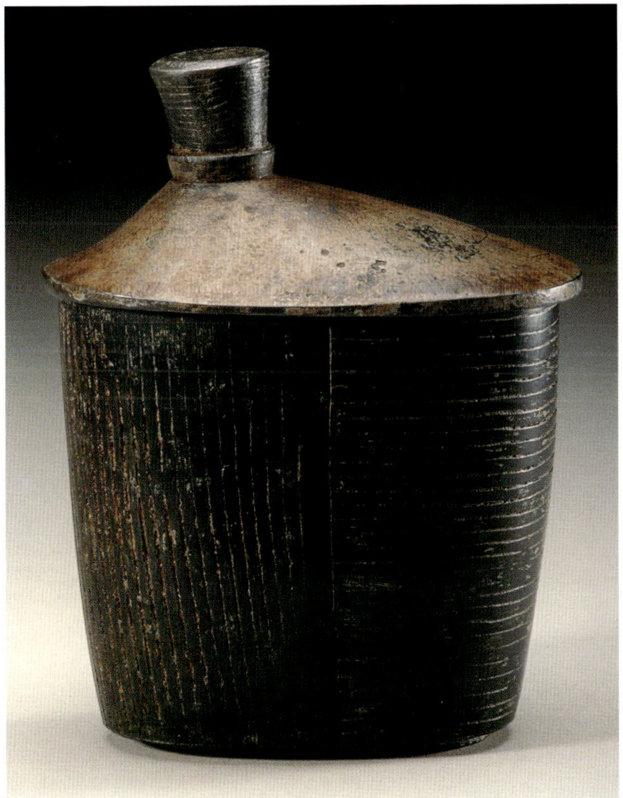

Stephen Yusko. *Cross Threaded Box*. Steel. 6" high, 5" wide, 3" deep. *Photo, Jeff Bruce*

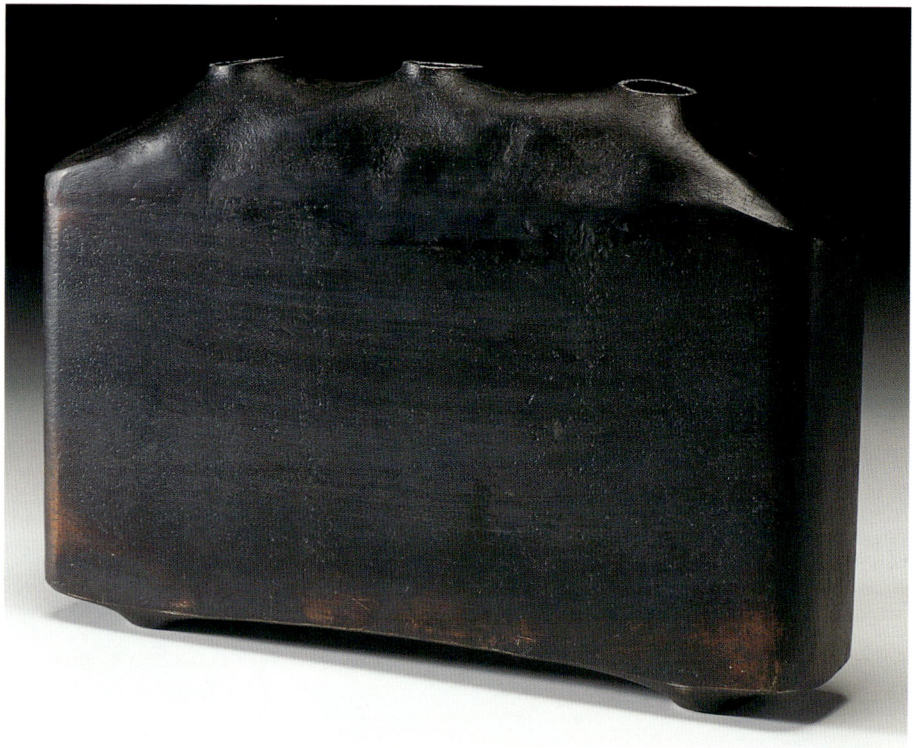

Susan Madacsi. *Mesa Vessel.* Steel and silver leaf. 7" high, 10" wide. *Photo, R. J. Phil*

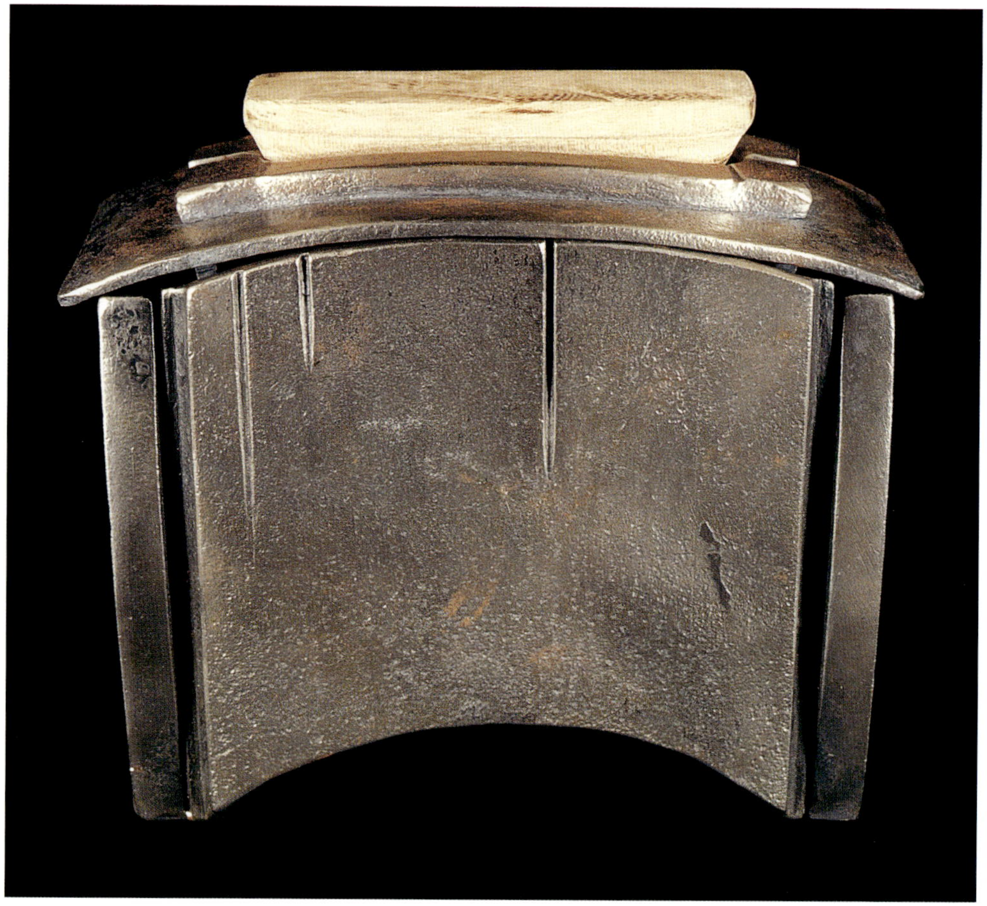

Amy Winkel. *Vessel.* Steel and wood. 5" high, 3" wide, 5" deep. *Photo, Cheryl Broadie*

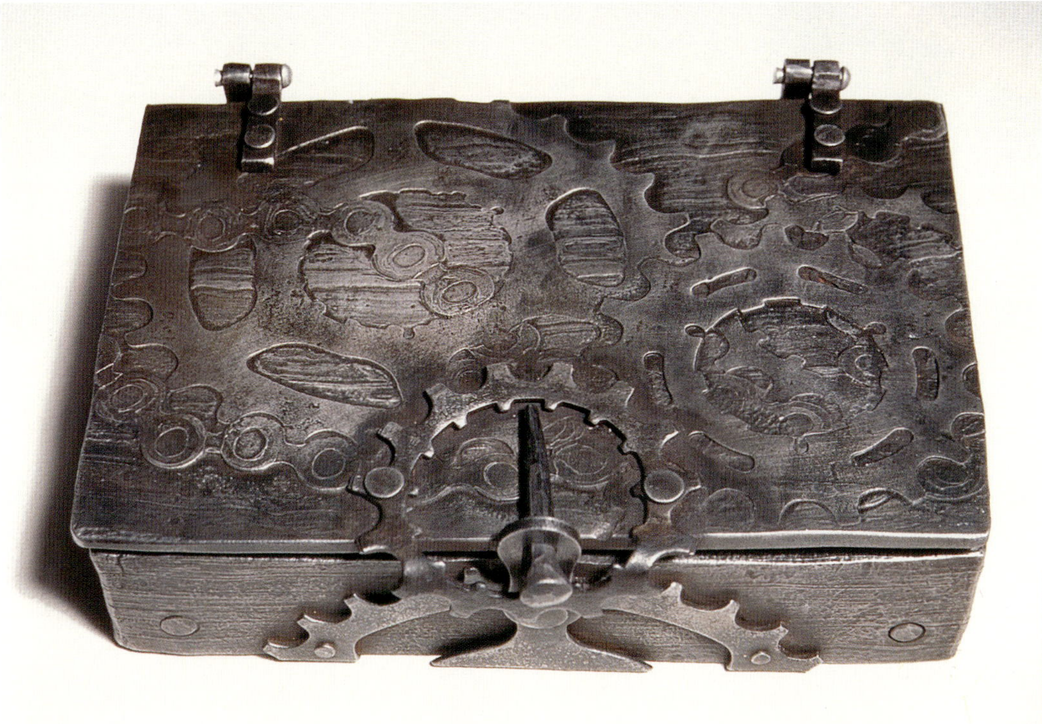

Maria Cristalli. *True.* Hinged box with wrought iron, bicycle chain, and sprockets. 7" high, 5" wide, 1.75" deep. *Photo, Stephanie Cristalli*

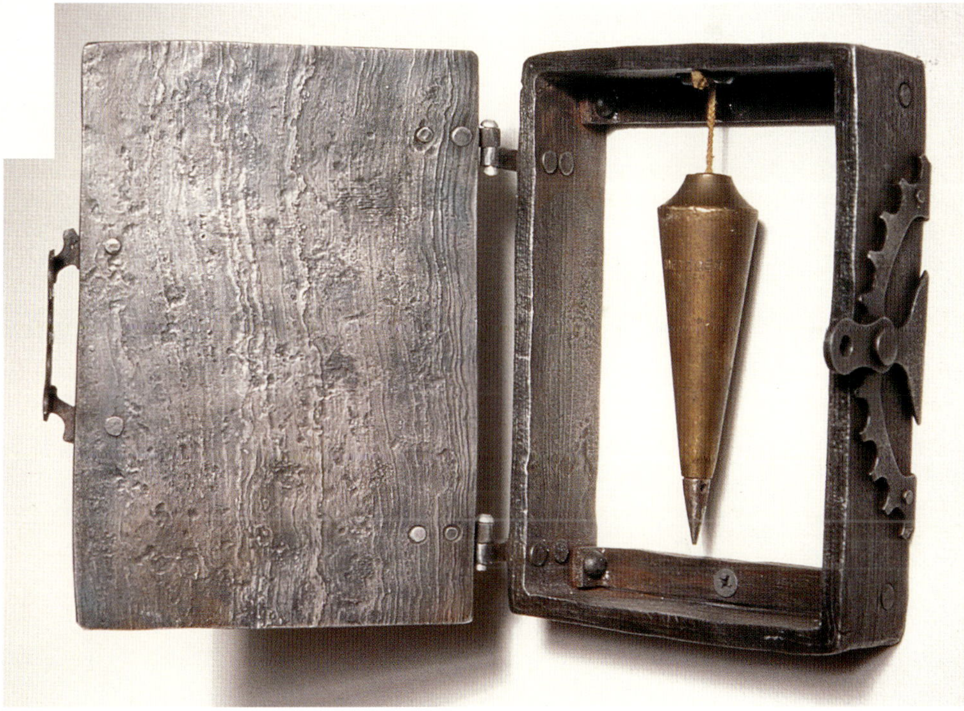

Maria Cristalli. Interior of *True. Photo, Stephanie Cristalli*

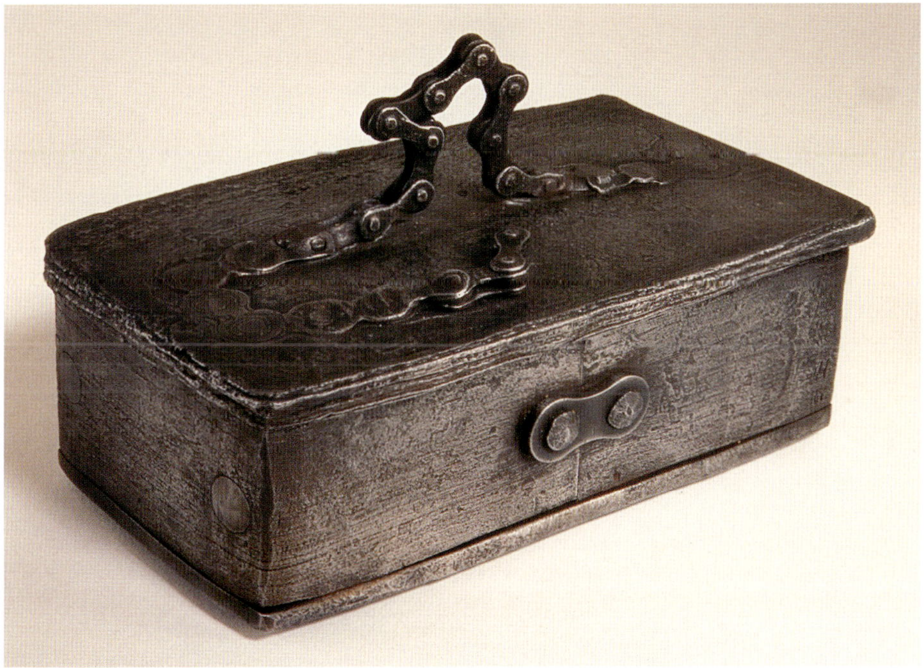

Maria Cristalli. *Bicycle Chain Box*. Wrought iron with bicycle chain. 3.5" high, 7" wide, 5" deep. *Photo, artist*

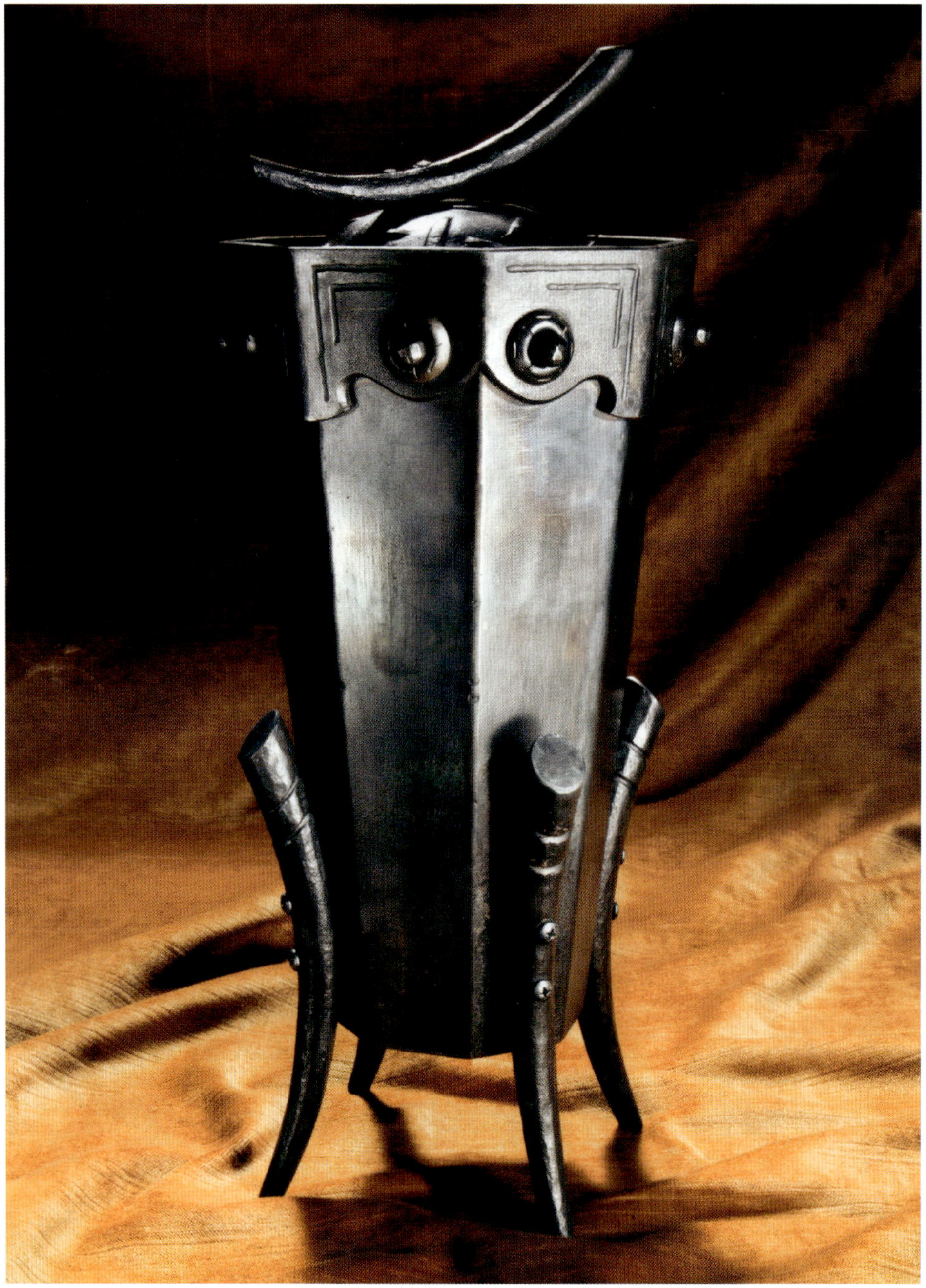

Jennifer Gilbert. *Prosperity.* Forged and fabricated steel. Cremation urn. 18" high, 7.5" diam. *Photo, artist*

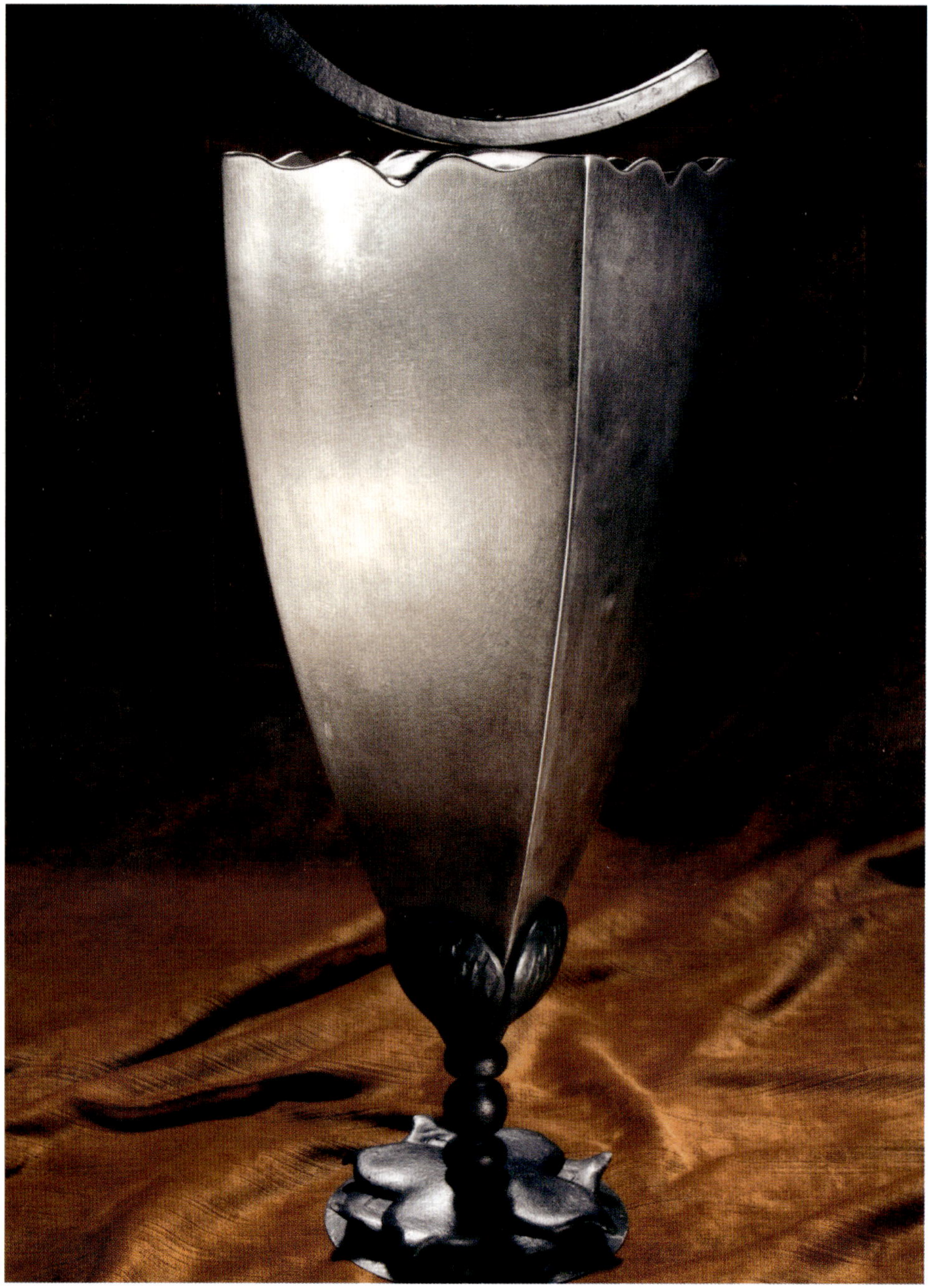

Jennifer Gilbert. *Blue Lotus*. Forged and fabricated steel and stainless steel. Cremation urn. 25" high, 7" square. *Photo, artist*

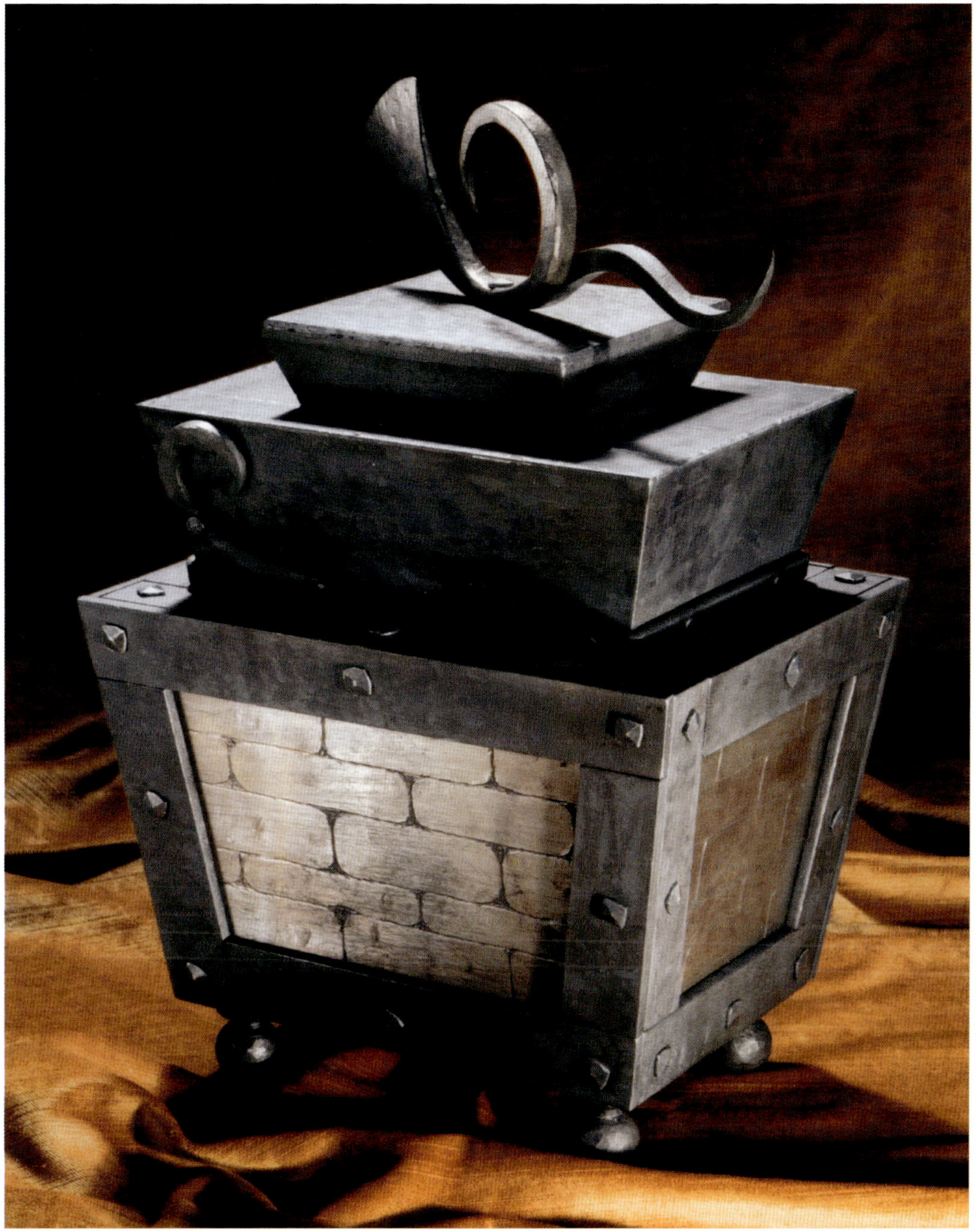

Jennifer Gilbert. *Still Temple.* Forged and fabricated steel and stainless steel. 19" high, 12" wide. 9.5" diam. *Photo, artist*

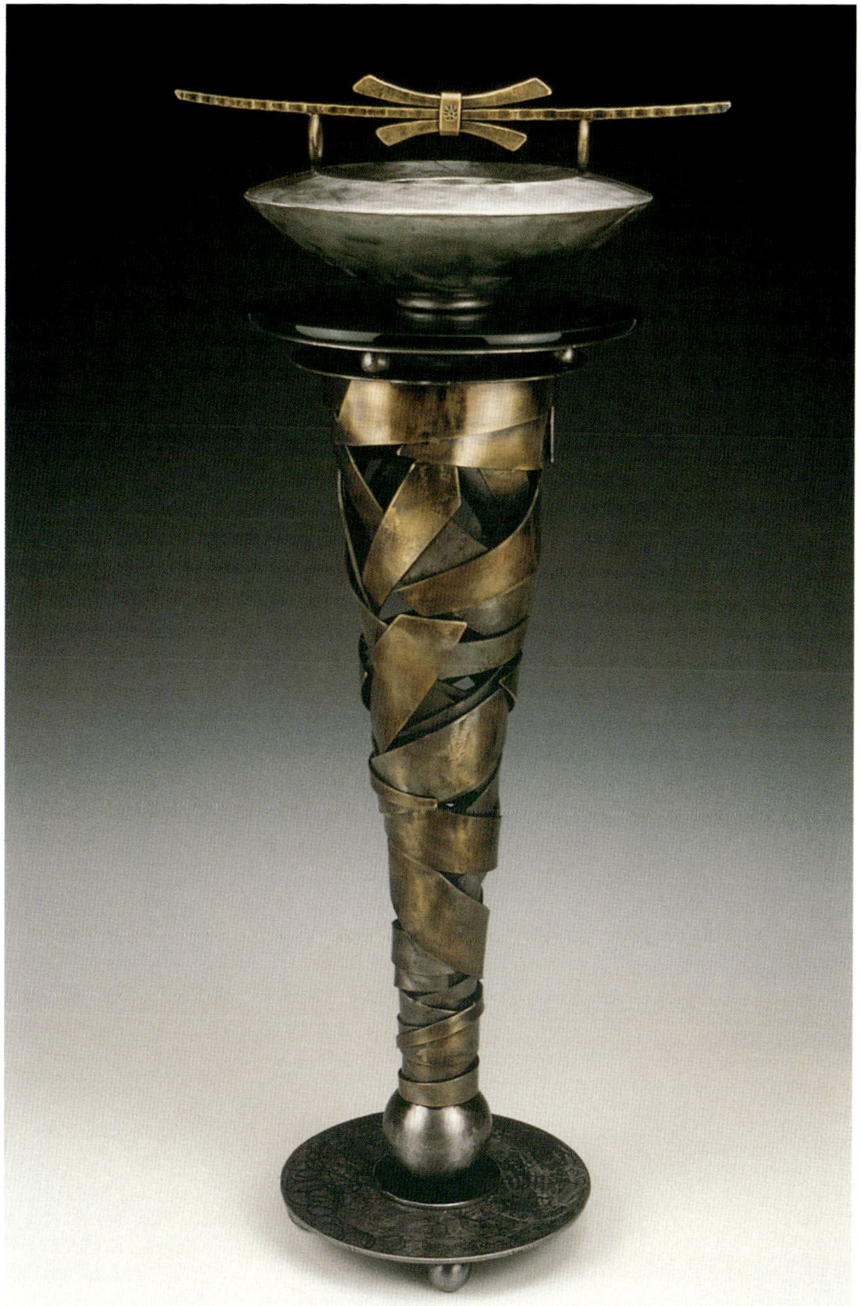

Robert L. Crecelius. *Tornado Table with steel vessel*. Forged and fabricated steel with bronze patinas. 42" high, 16" diam. *Photo, Jerry Anthony*

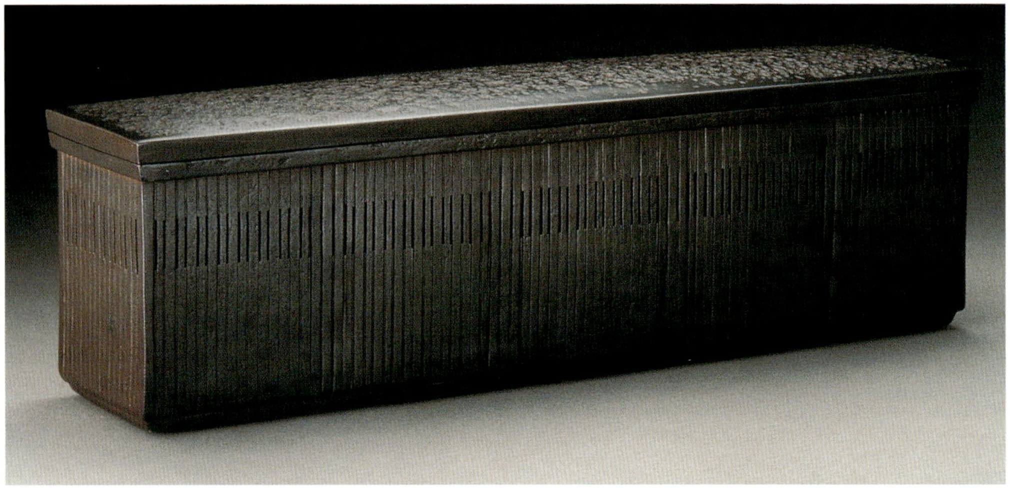

Rick Smith. *Container*. Forge welded mild steel. 24" high,10" wide, 10" deep. *Photo*

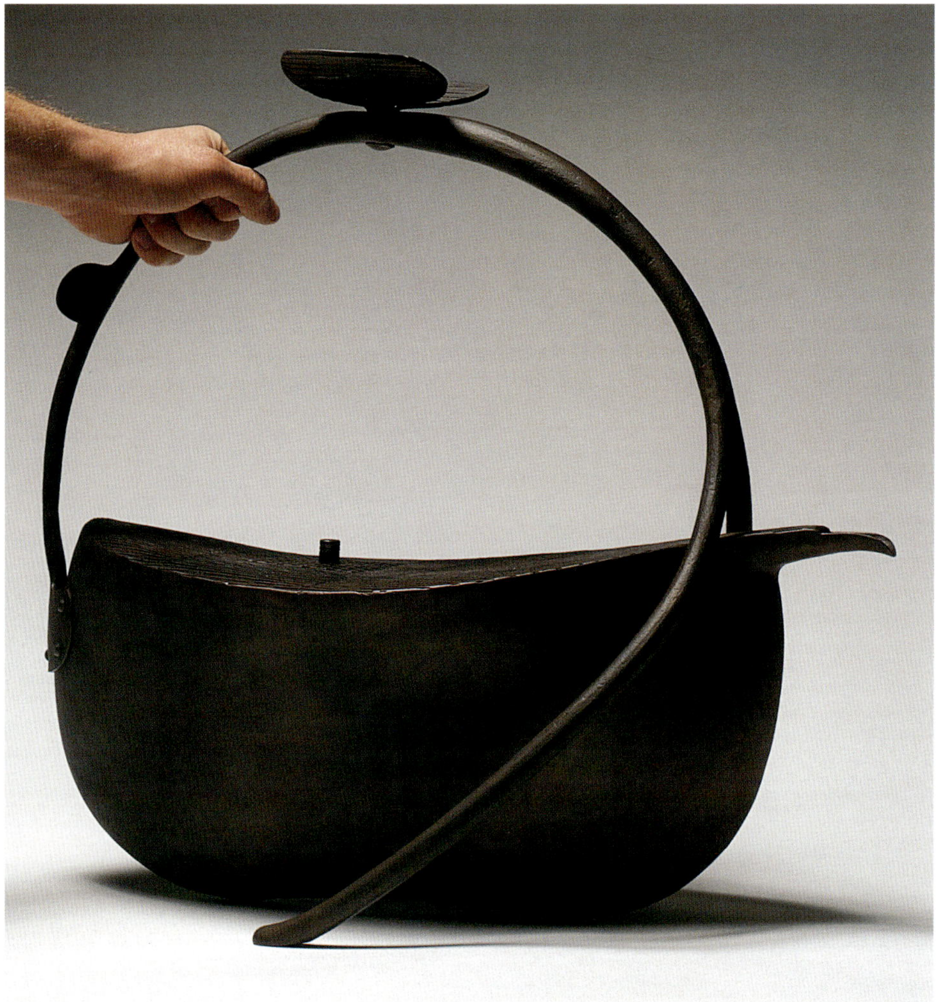

John Rais. *Swollen Chamber*. Hollow formed and forged steel with a patina. *Collection, Gloria and Sonny Kamm. Photo, D. James Dee*

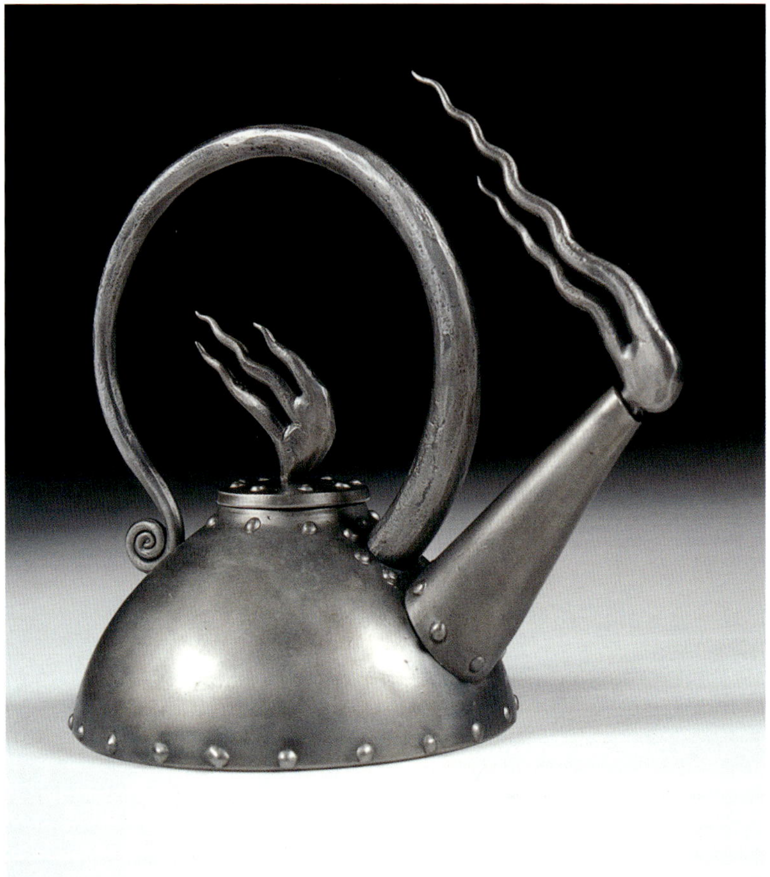

David Gignac. *Hot Pot*. Forged and fabricated steel with a wax finish. 14" high, 14" diam. *Photo, artist*

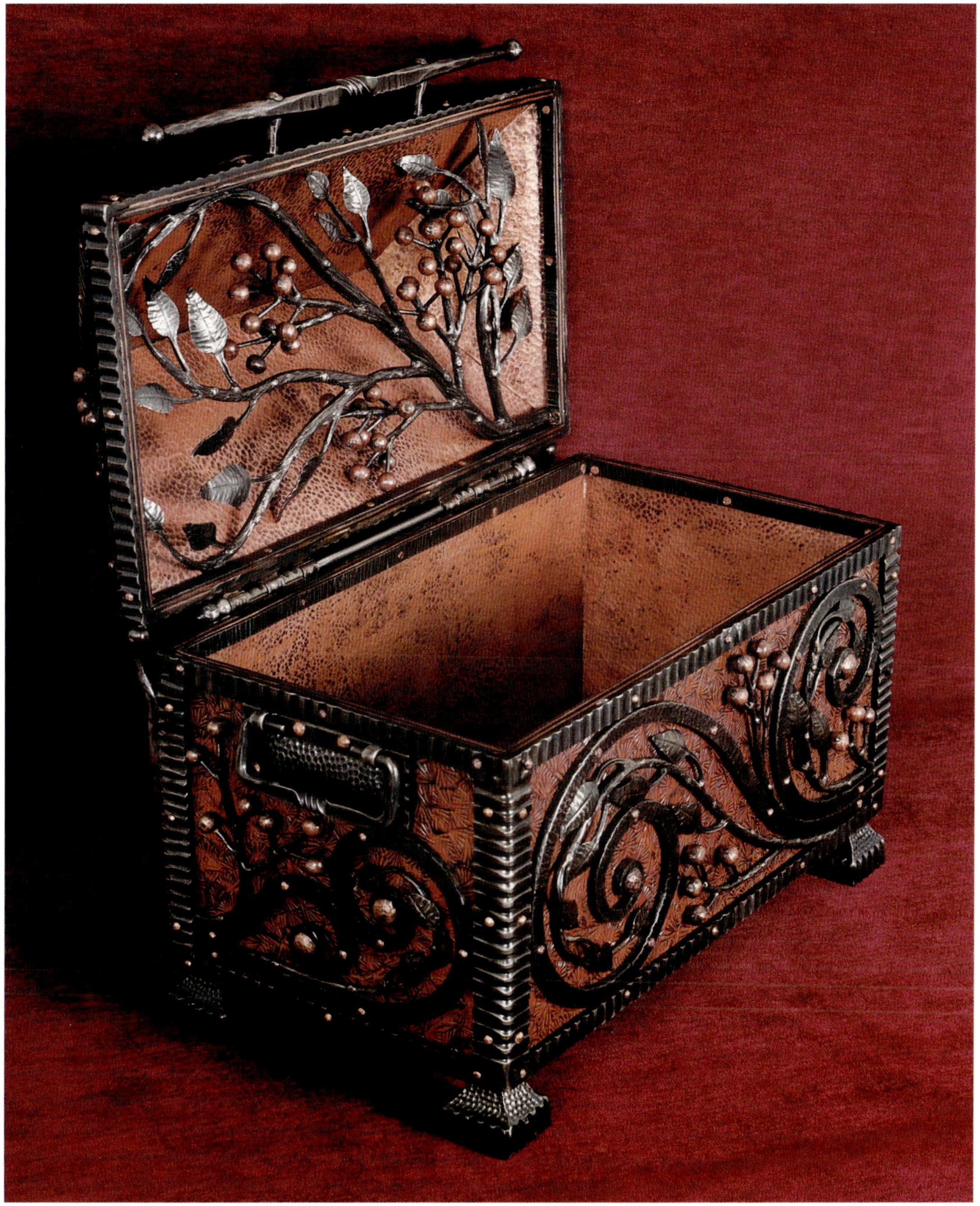

Hugh C. Culley. *Leaf and Berry chest.* Forged steel and hammered copper. An interest in antique locks and boxes inspired him to make a box ornamented with leaves and berries similar to those he made for fireplace screens. The branch inside the lid was based on those used in early locking caskets with sliding bolts concealed within the ornamentation. 15" high, 18" wide, 12" deep. *Photo, Richard Prehn*

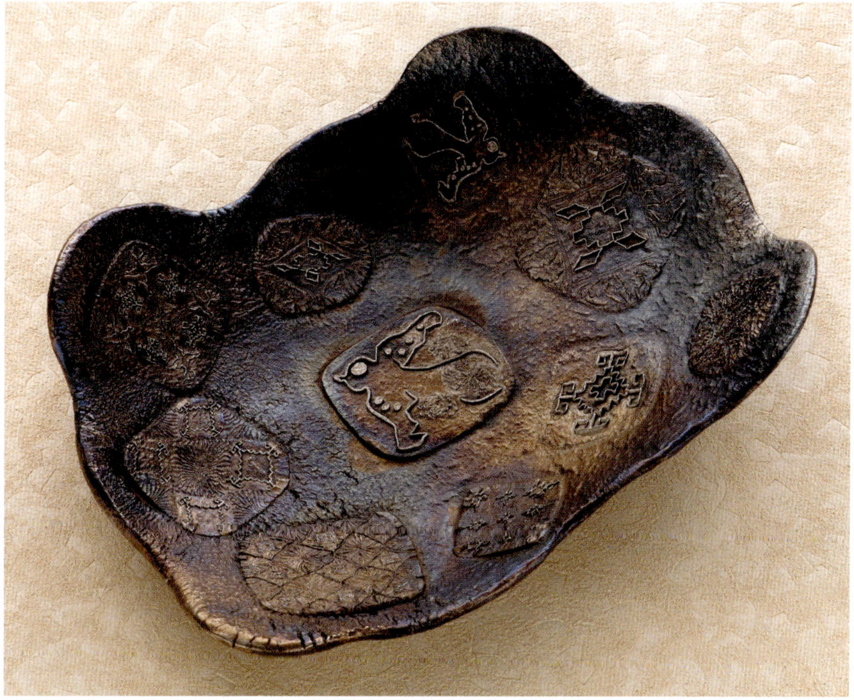

Gary L. House. *Zapotec Bowl.* Mosaic Damascus tiles are forge welded into a mild steel plate then forged to final shape by hand hammering. Fire etched and fire colored. Sealed with beeswax and linseed oil. 6" high, 8" wide. *Photo, Point 7 Studios*

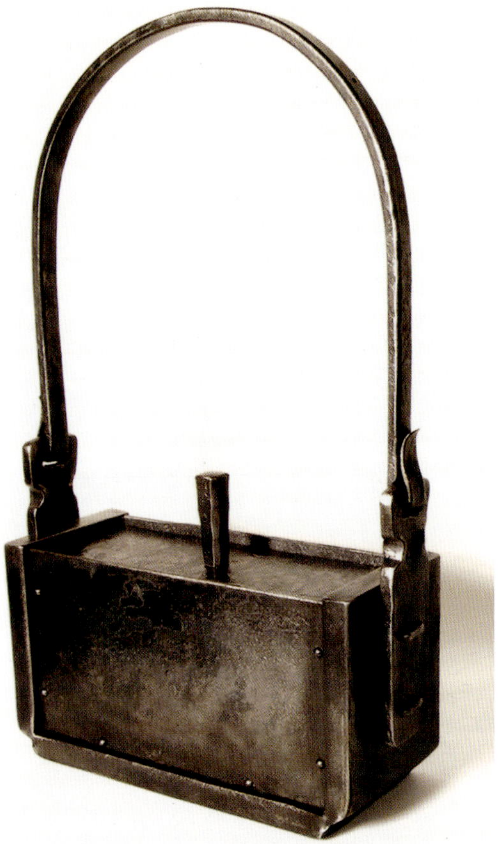

Maurice Hamburger. Box with bail and staples. Forged and fabricated steel. Obvious joinery is used as decorative elements. 13" high, 9" wide, 3" deep. *Photo, artist*

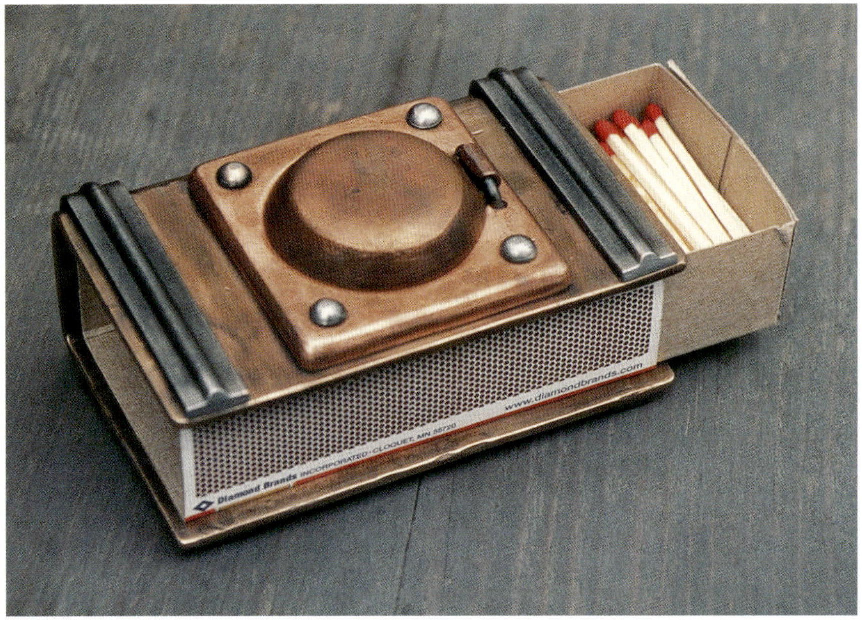

Helmut Hillenkamp. Commemorative matchbox, closed and open views. Copper, bronze, steel, leaf gold, wood, paper, beeswax, and matchbox. Drawing by Christy Hengst; metal assembly by Christen Boyd. *Photos, artist*

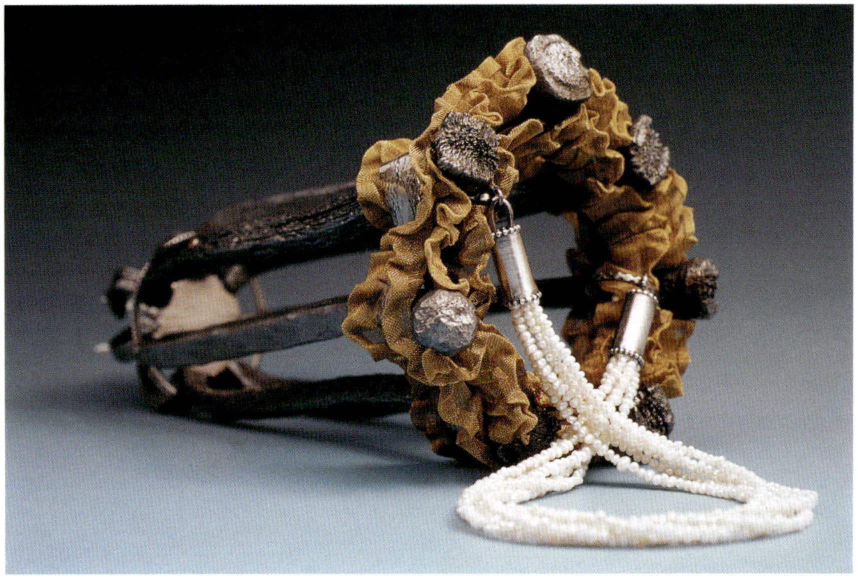

Jennifer Monroe. *Nailed handbag.* Wrought iron, silver, brass, 14k gold, ruby and seed pearls. *Photo, artist*

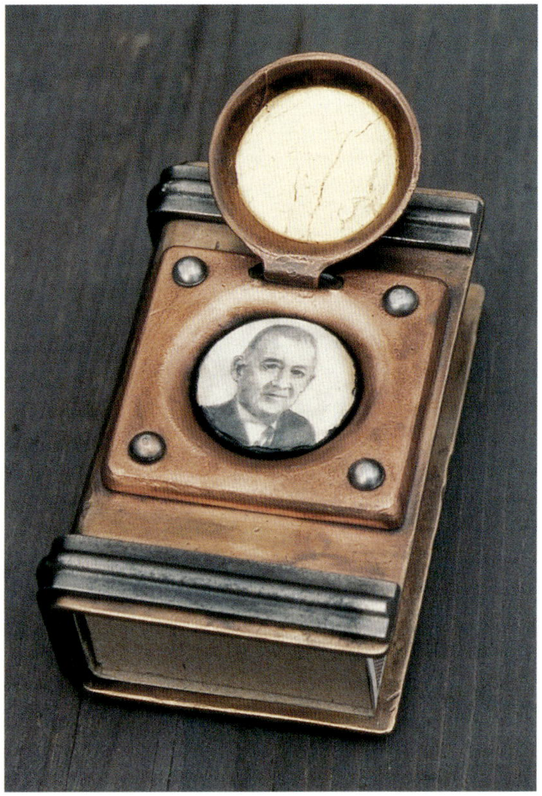

Helmut Hillenkamp. Open view.

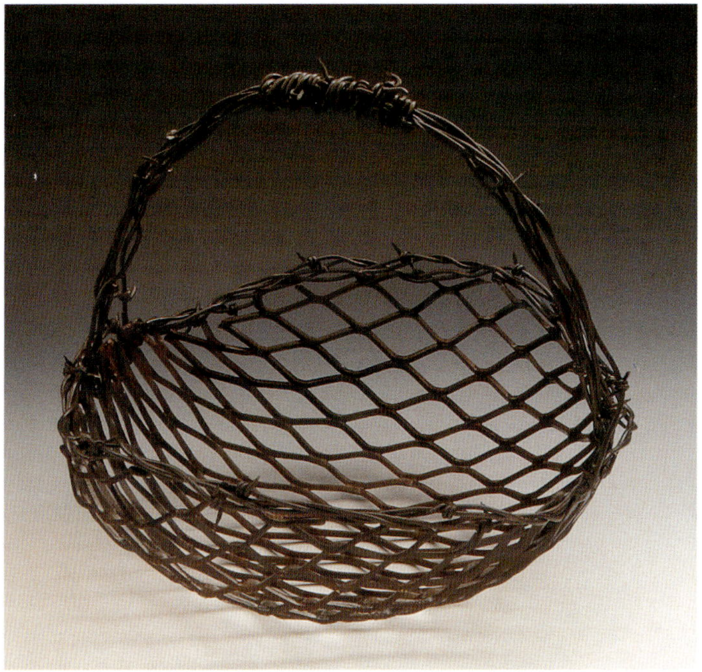

Eric A. Ryser. *Fruit Basket*. Mild steel and barbed wire. 12" high, 11" wide. *Photo, artist*

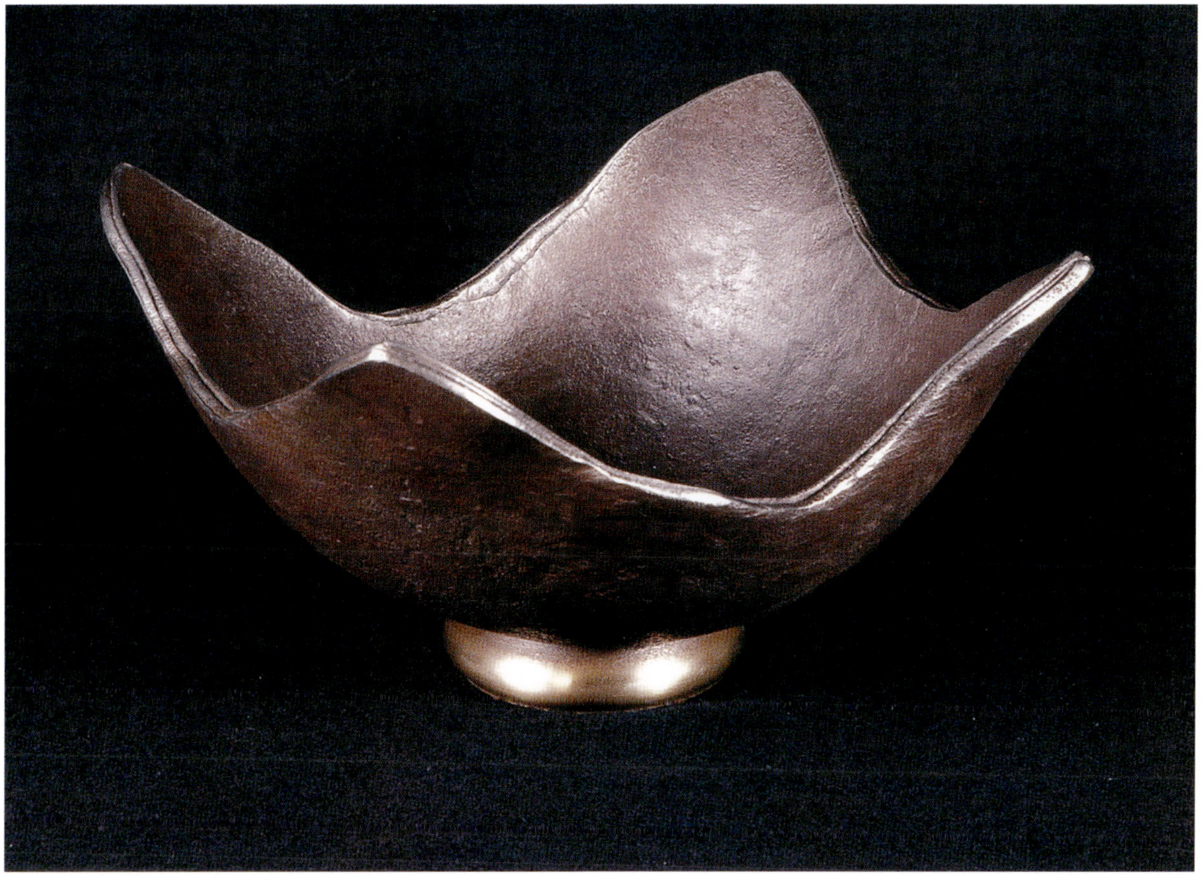

David Zatz. *Four-lobed Vessel*. Machine forged, sandblasted, patinated steel, and bronze with a waxed finish. 5" high, 7" diam. *Photo, artist*

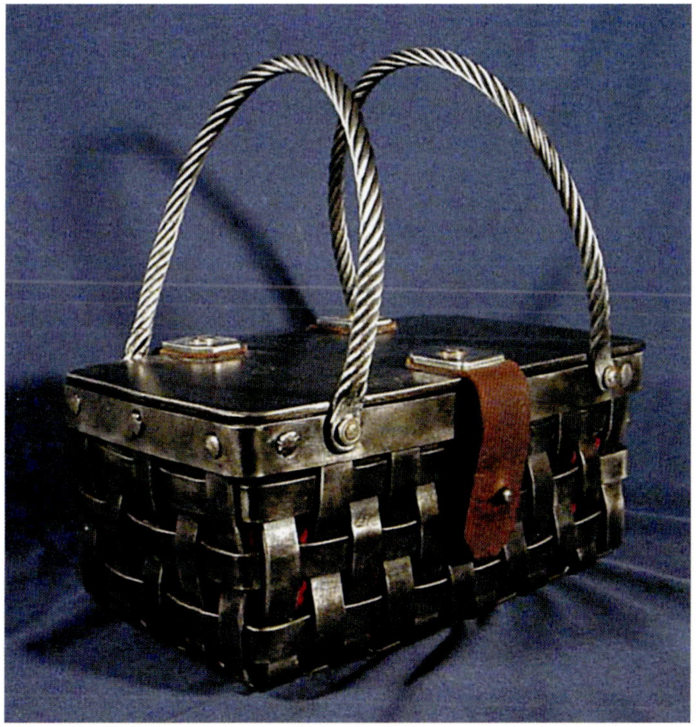

Ky Green. *Picnic Basket*. Forged and fabricated mild steel. The handles are forged welded wire rope. The hinges and hasp are leather with stainless steel accent pieces. Brass rivets with copper ferrules. 6" high, 12" wide, 8" deep. *Photo, artist*

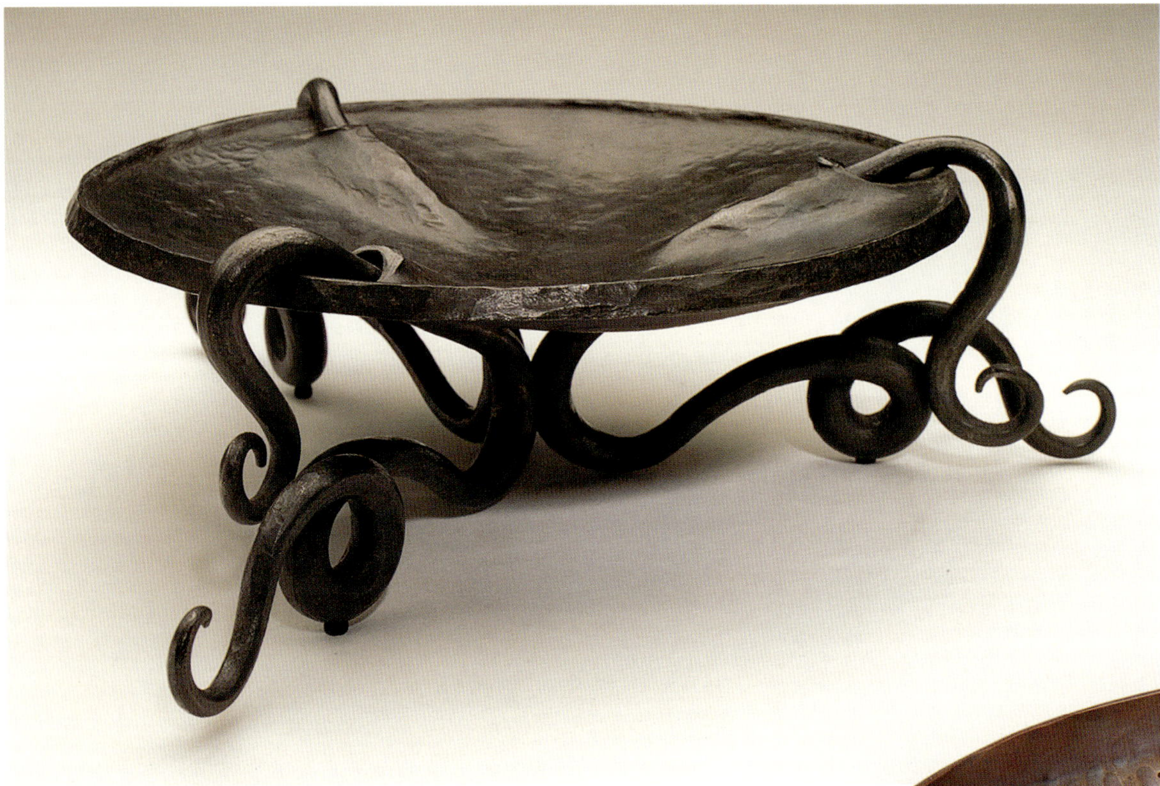

John Little. *Christina's Bowl.* Exploring the idea of the legs piercing the bowl's curvature. 14" diam. *Photo, Julian Beveridge*

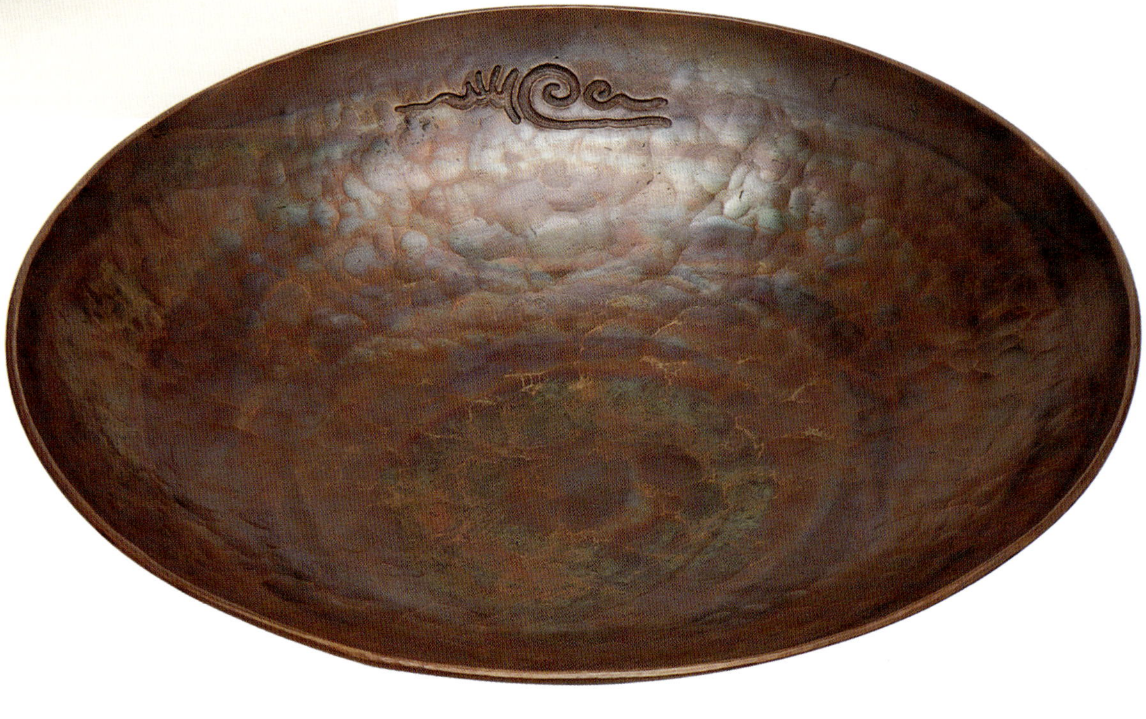

Michael Bendele. *Copper Bowl, Primac Chant Series.* The bowls start as 3" round bars and undergo such a transformation from the repeated hammering that the surface becomes a record of the process. The result is a surface that you can almost see into. 4" high, 15" diam. *Photo, Jim King*

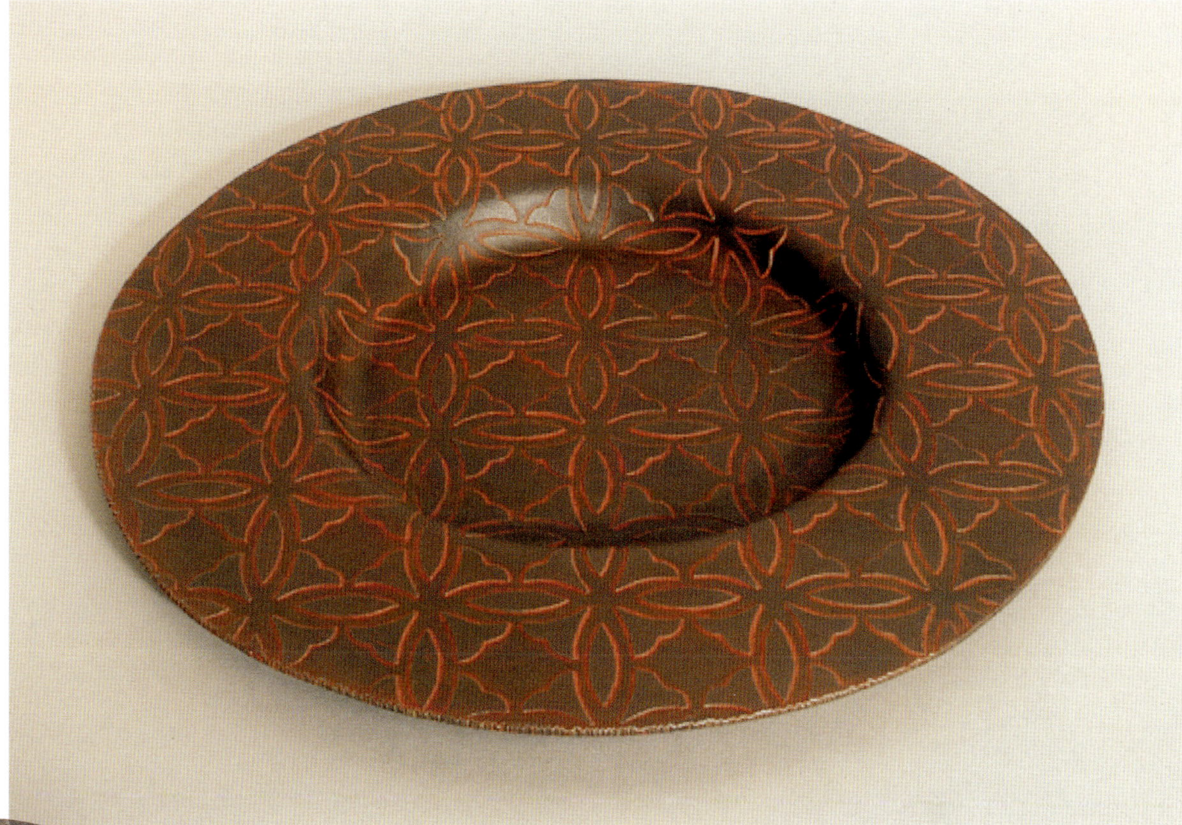

Eric A. Ryser. *Pattern Plate # 1*. Acid etched pattern on forged mild steel. 2" high, 15" diam. *Photo, artist*

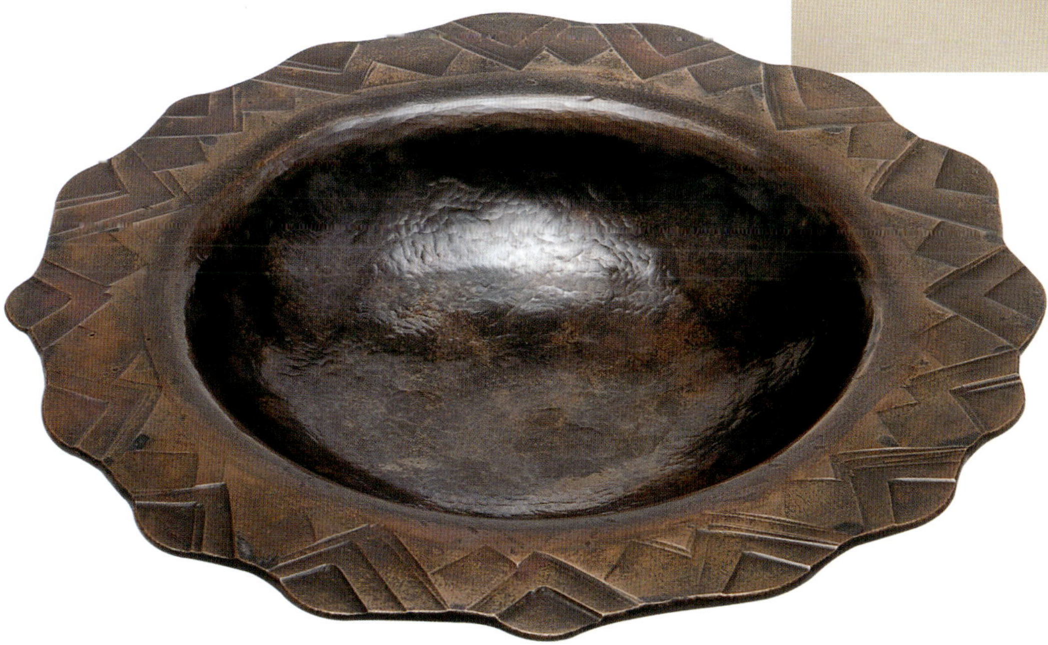

Michael Bendele. *Copper Bowl, Primac Chant Series. Photo, Jim King*

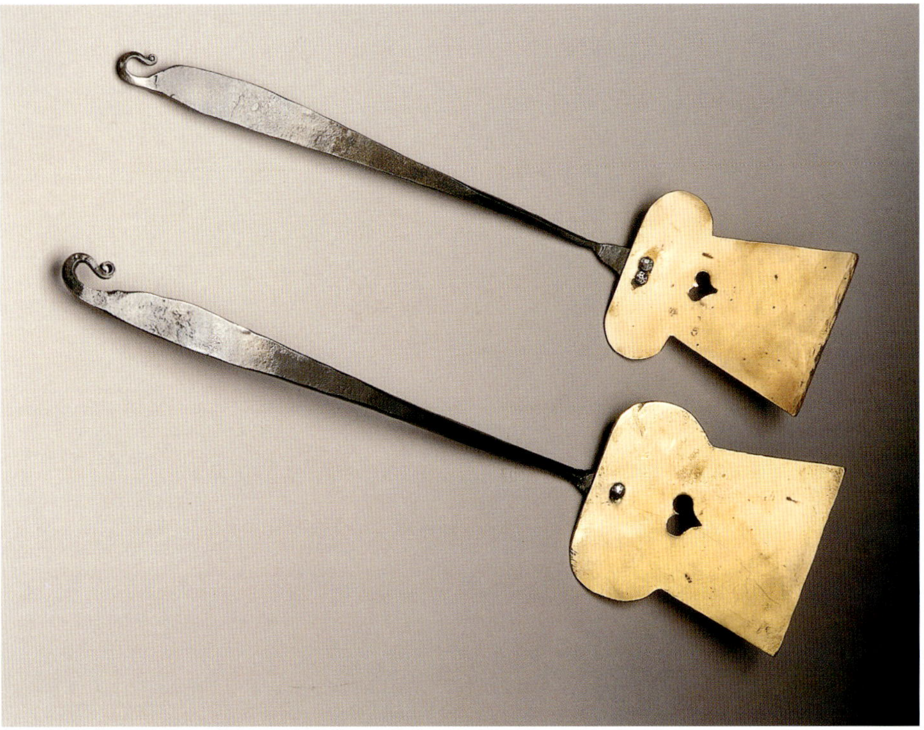

Brian Gilbert. Spatula and spoon. Forged steel. Each piece is 14" long, 3" wide. *Photo, Sandy Andrews*

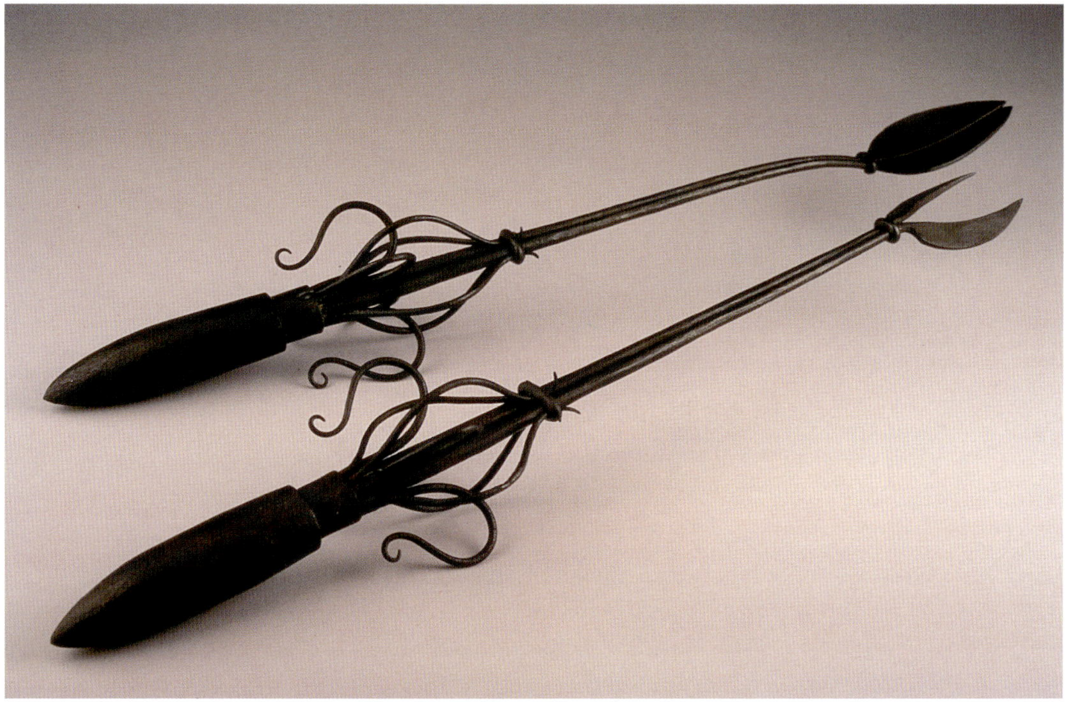

Eric Cuper. *Squid Serving Set*. Forged steel. Each piece is 20" long, 3" diam. *Photo, Jeffrey Bruce*

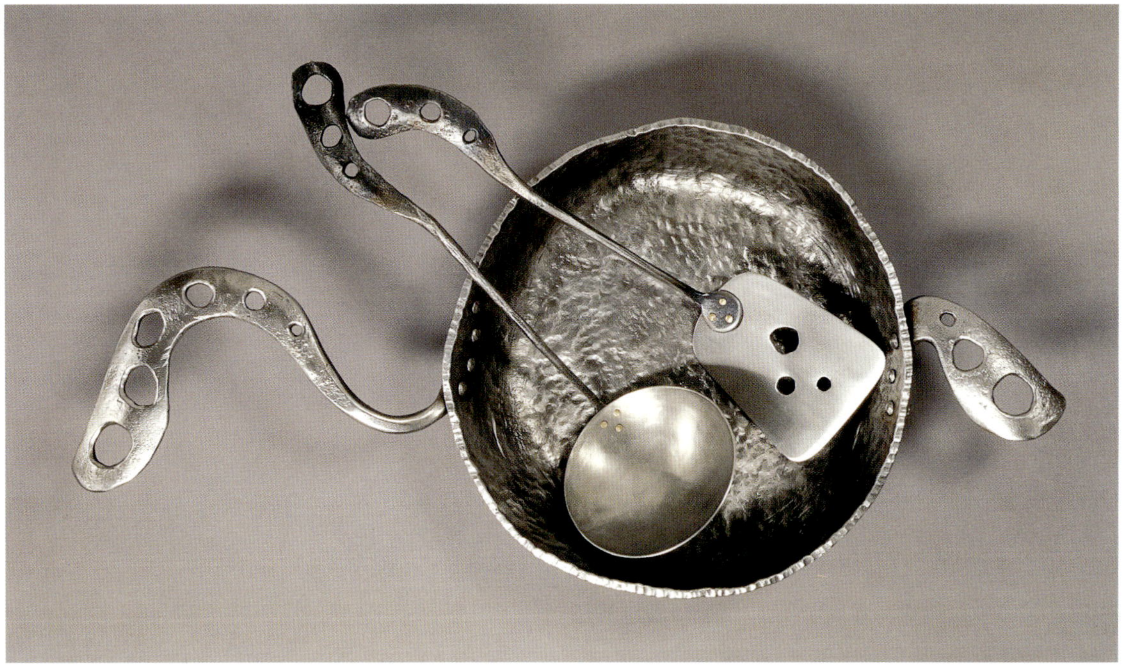

Benjamin O. Cowden. *Skillet and Utensils.* Mild steel, stainless steel, and brass. 14" high, 28" wide, 4" deep. *Photo, John Lucas*

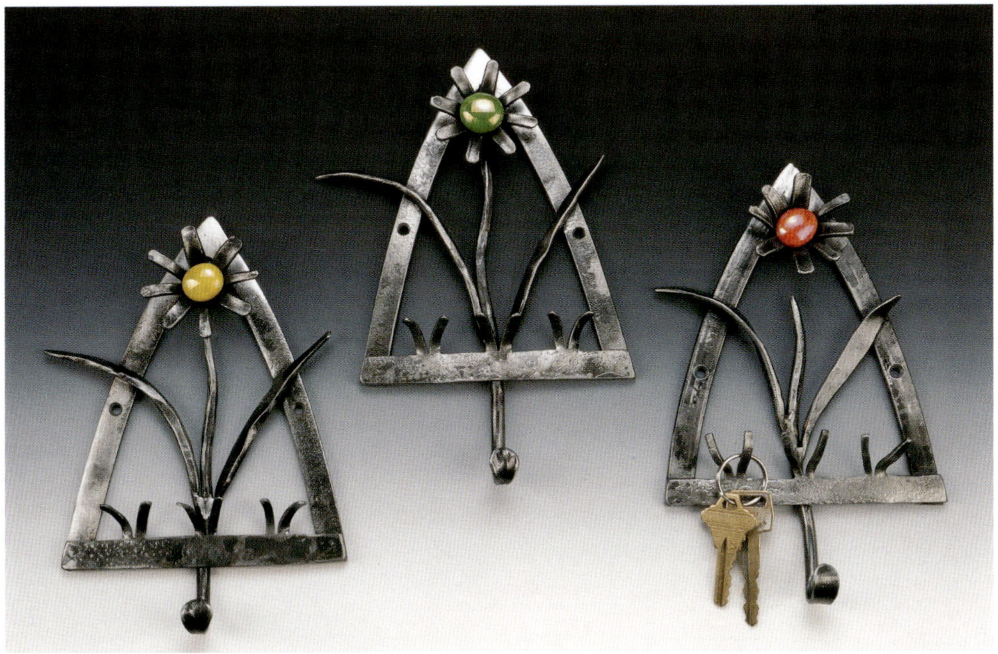

Jim Holahan and Erin Caruth. *Flower Key Holders*. Steel and glass. Each is 7" high, 5" wide. *Photo, Jerry Anthony*

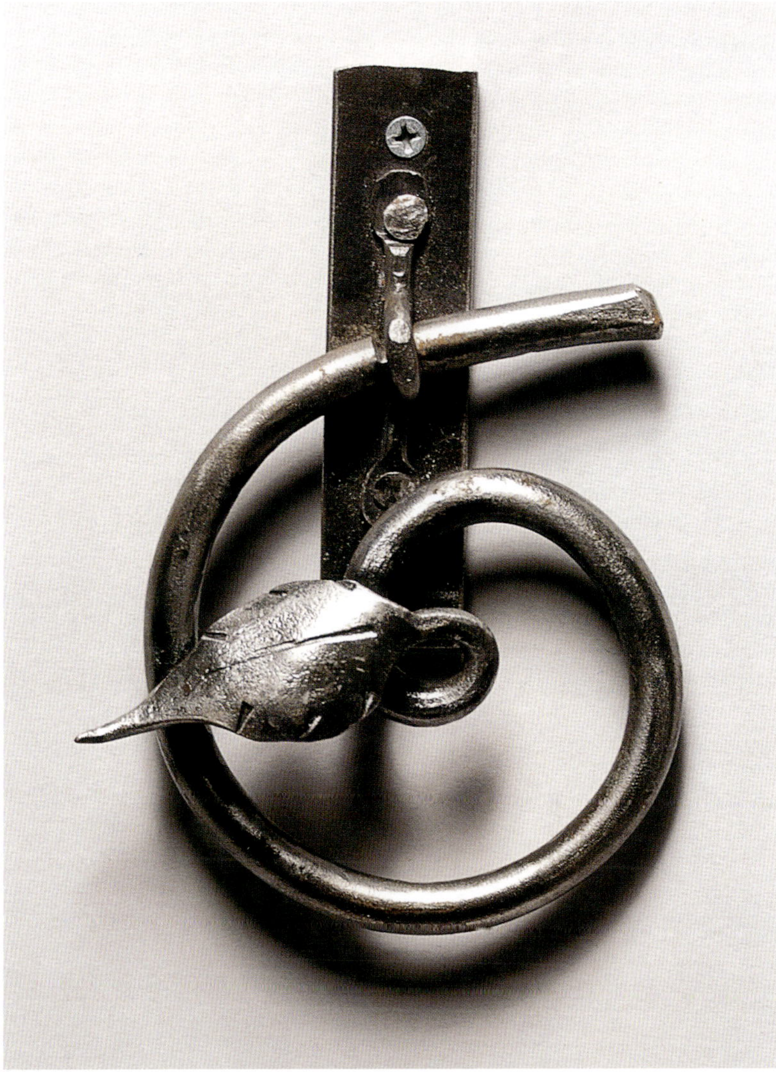

Jerry Veneziano. Towel ring/hanger. An example of the many types of accessories that can be made of steel. *Photo, Jeff Taylor*

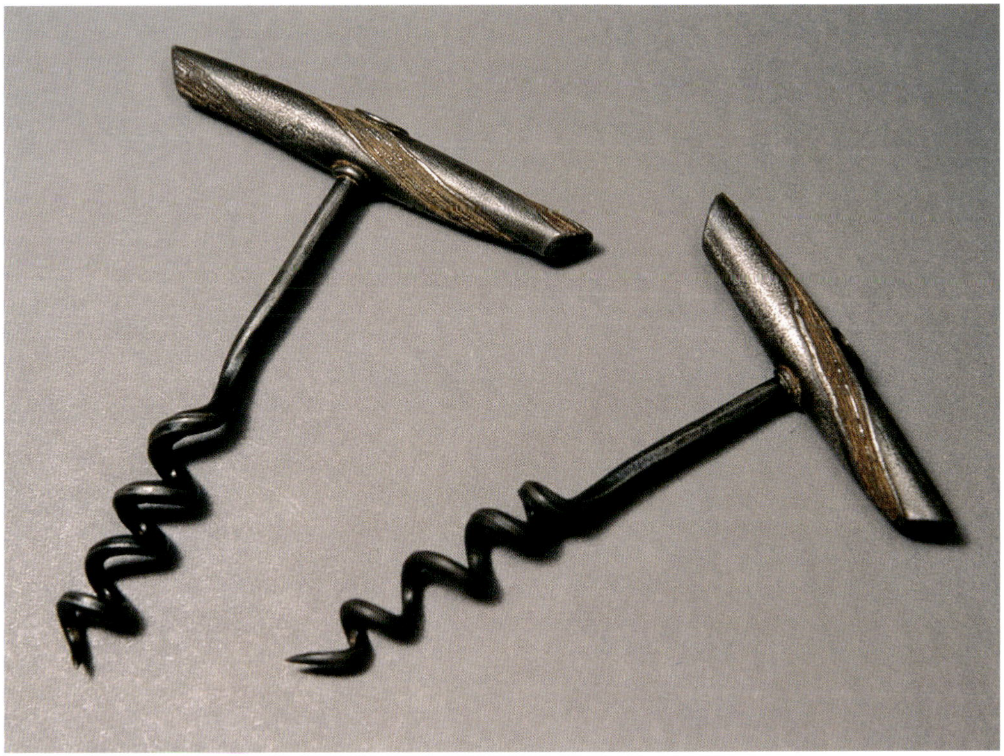

Nathan Blank. *Cork Screws*. Forge welded pattern of wrought iron and steel. Each: 3" high, 2.75" wide, .25" deep. *Photo, artist*

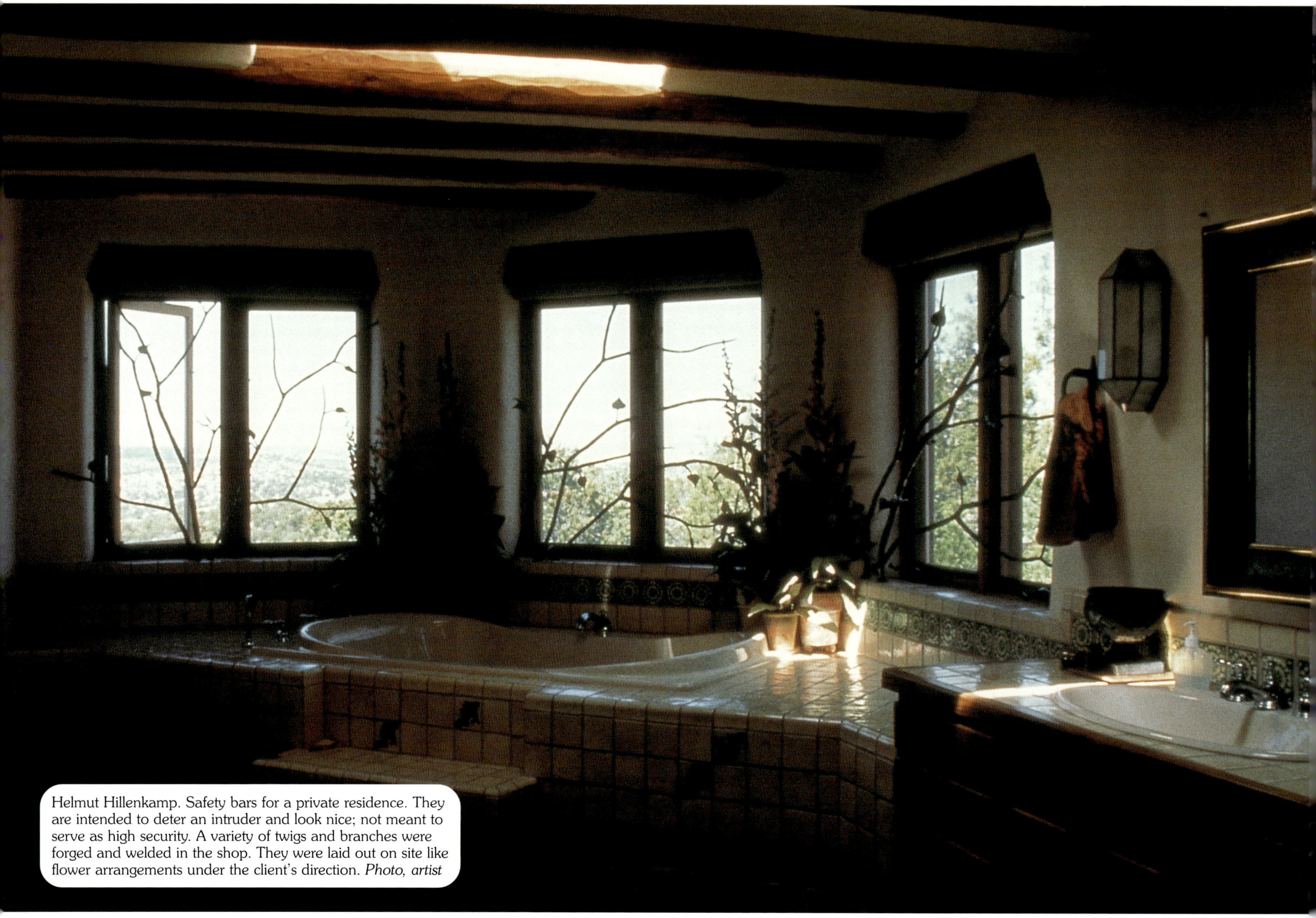

Helmut Hillenkamp. Safety bars for a private residence. They are intended to deter an intruder and look nice; not meant to serve as high security. A variety of twigs and branches were forged and welded in the shop. They were laid out on site like flower arrangements under the client's direction. *Photo, artist*

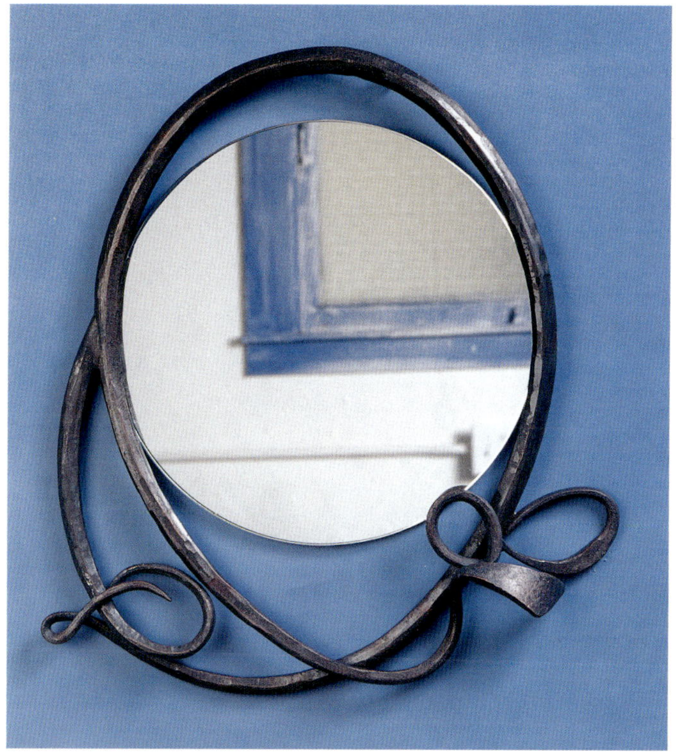

Julie Henry. *Capture.* Forged steel and mirror glass. 16" high, 10" wide, .75" deep. *Photo, artist*

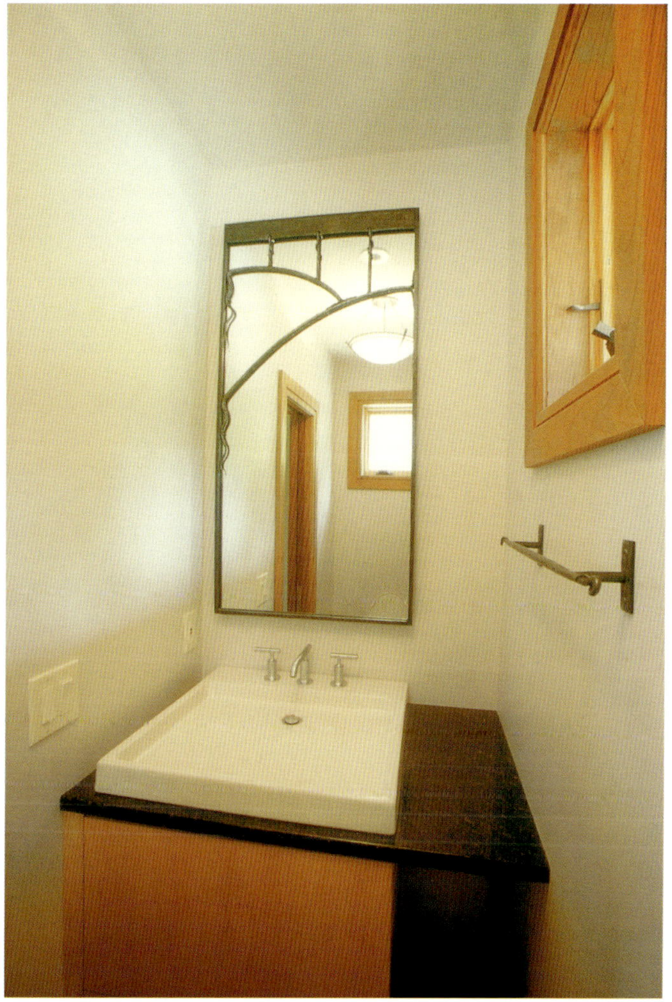

Erika Strecker. Mirror for Smith residence. Forged steel and mirror glass. 4' high, 2' wide. *Photo, Leeann Greer*

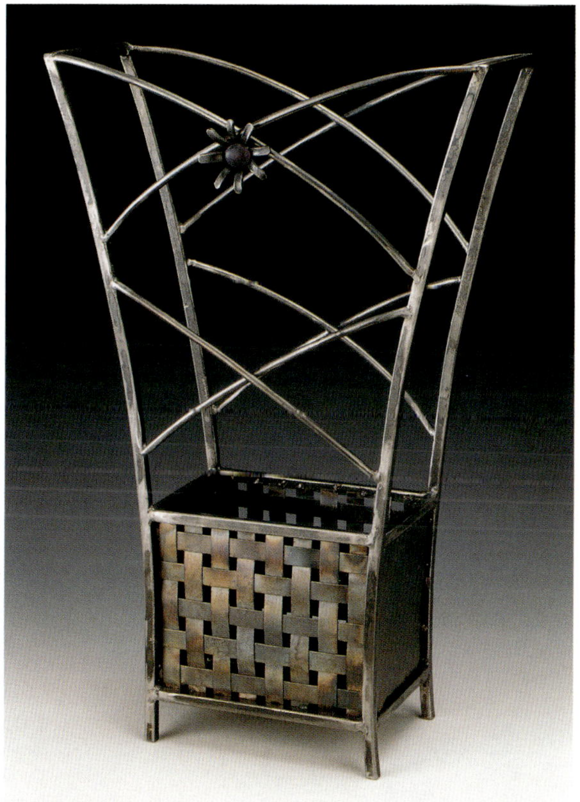

Jim Holahan and Erin Caruth. Umbrella stand. Forged, woven, and fabricated steel and glass flower center. 24" high, 14" wide, 7" deep. *Photo, Jerry Anthony*

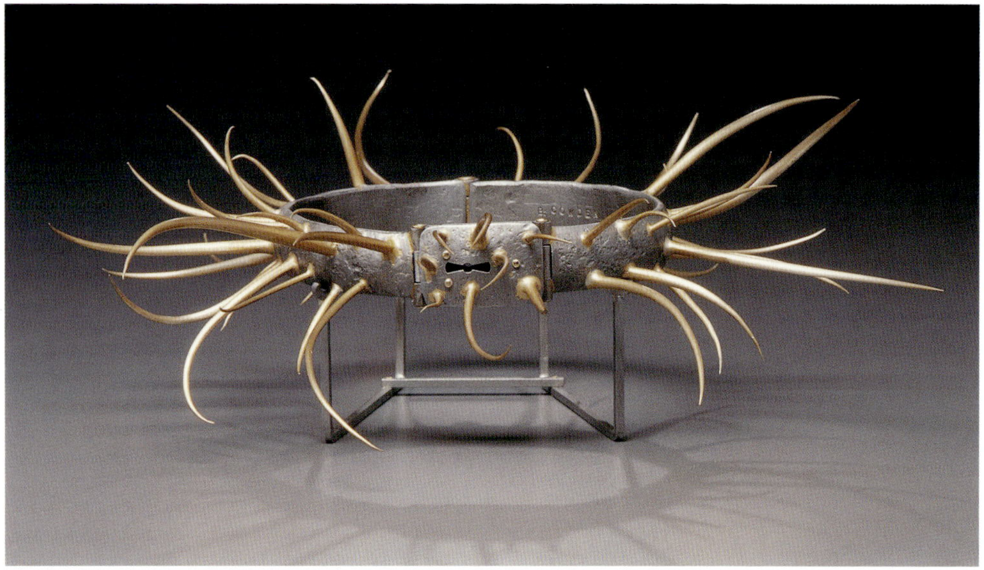

Benjamin O. Cowden. *Barbed Collar*. Mild and spring steel and brass. The design represents a stylized mother's head and arm wrapped around a bundled infant. 5" high, 15" diam. *Photo, John Lewis*

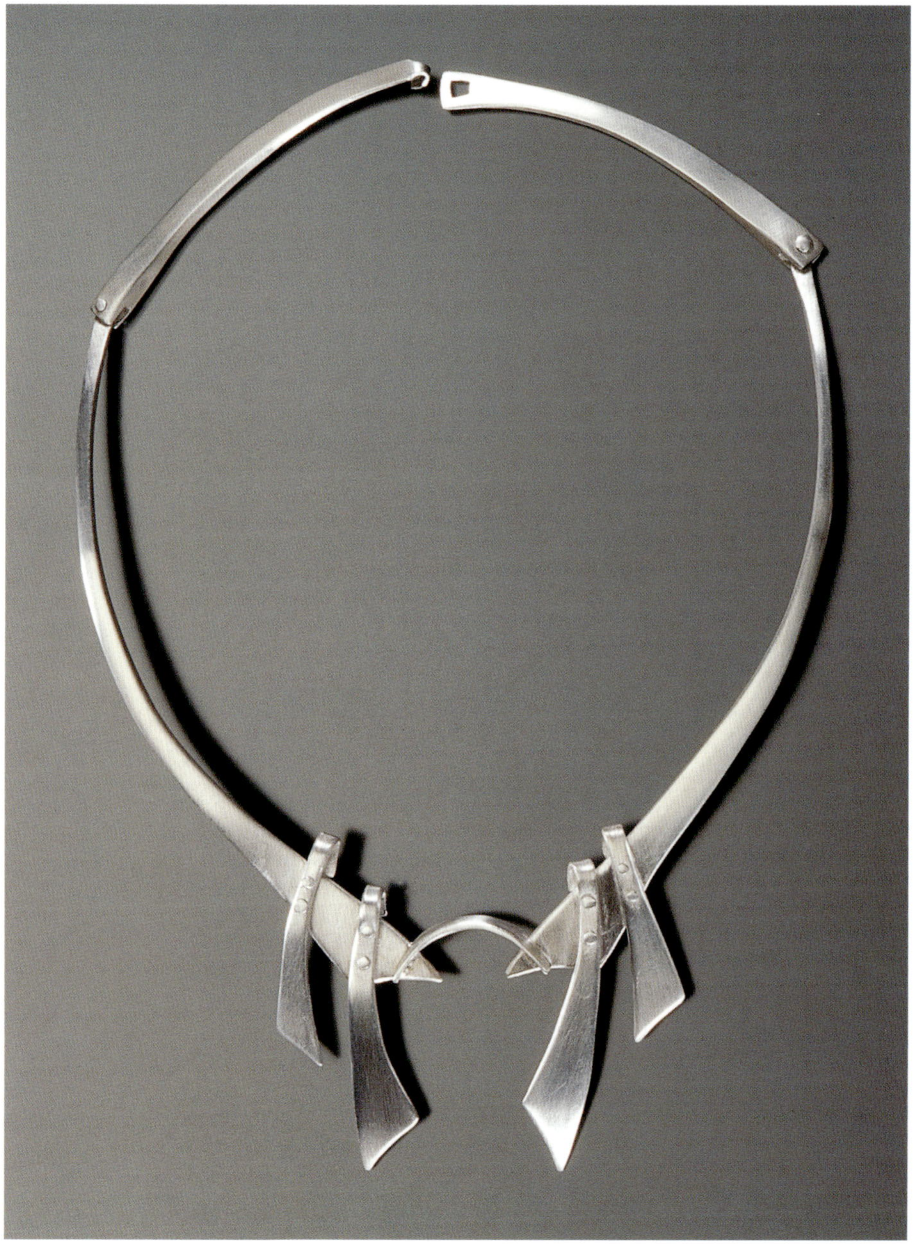

Julie Henry. *Bridal Necklace*. Forged silver and steel. 7" high, 6" wide, .2" deep. *Photo, Chris Berggren*

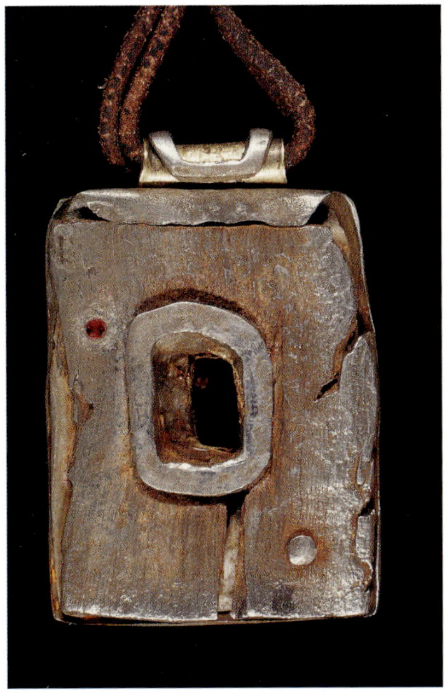

Amy Winkel. Untitled pendant. Wrought iron, steel, 18k gold, and a ruby. 1.5" high, 1.8" wide. *Photo, Cheryl Broadie*

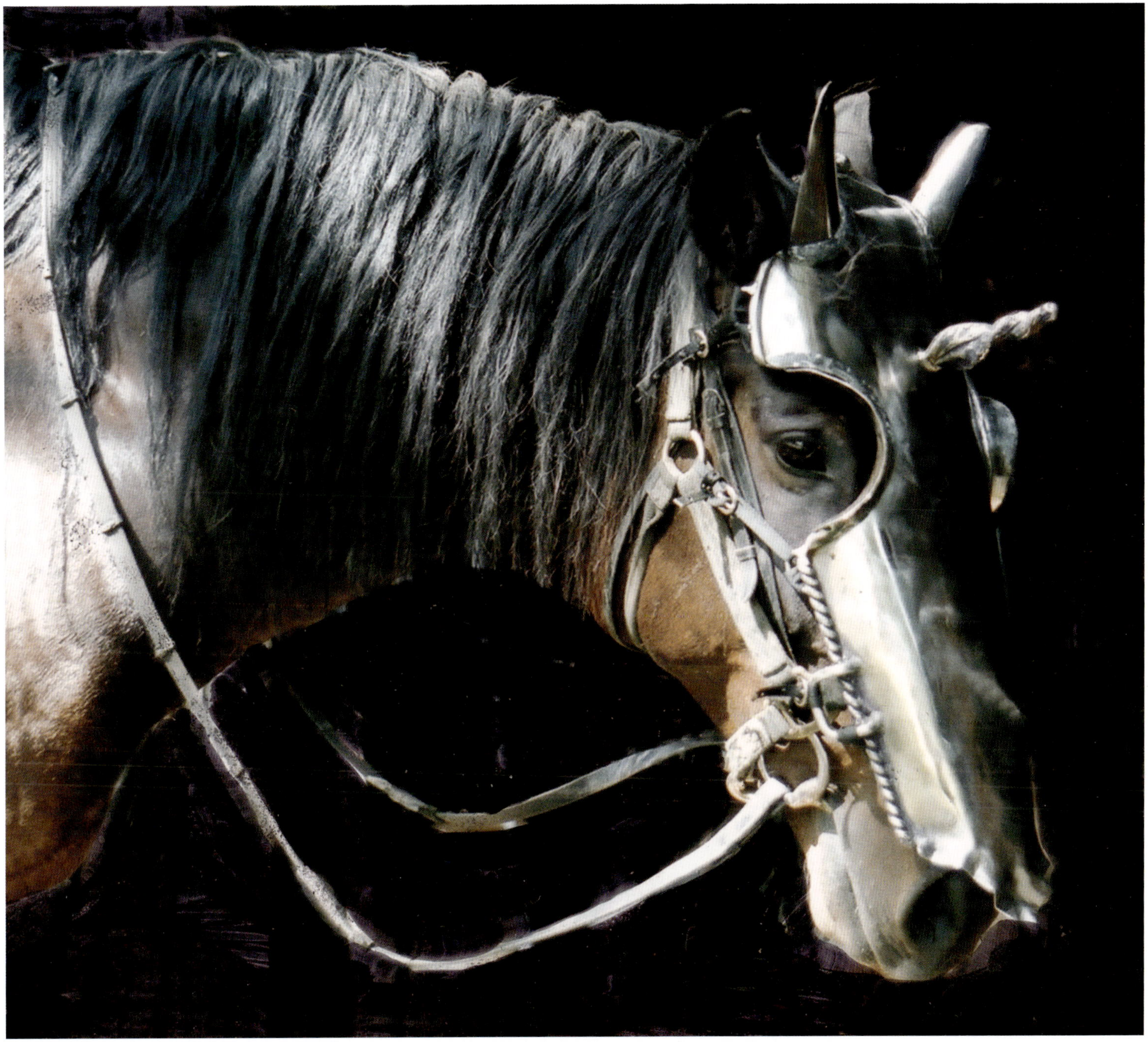

Frank Jackson. *Increase, the Warhorse, Arrayed in his Menacing Armor*. Jewelry for a horse. *Photo, artist*

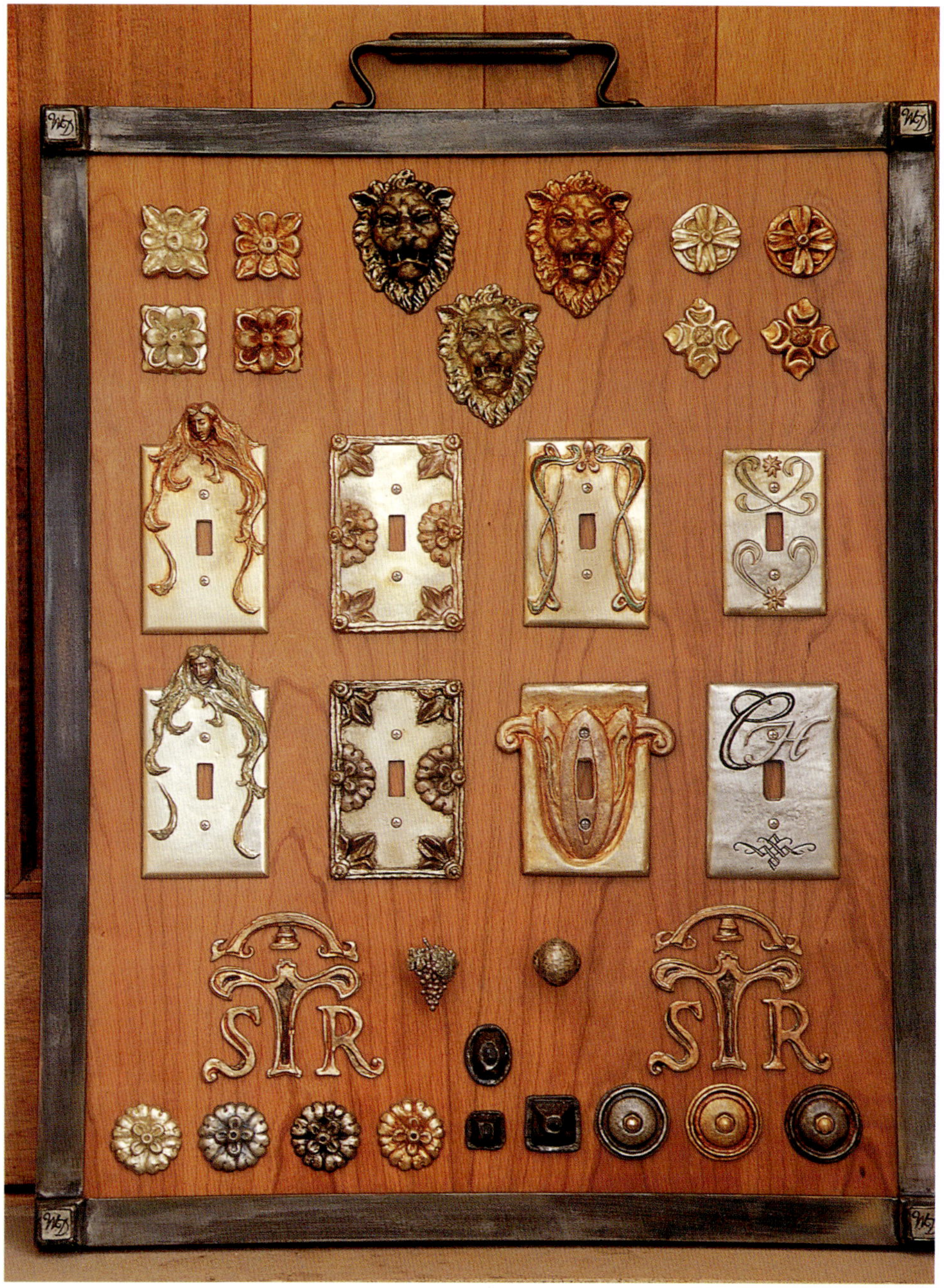

Robert C. Bentley. Customized light plates and other hardware used in The Villa Toscana and other properties throughout the Weyrich developments in Paso Robles, California. (See chapter 2) *Photo, Bruce Woodworth*

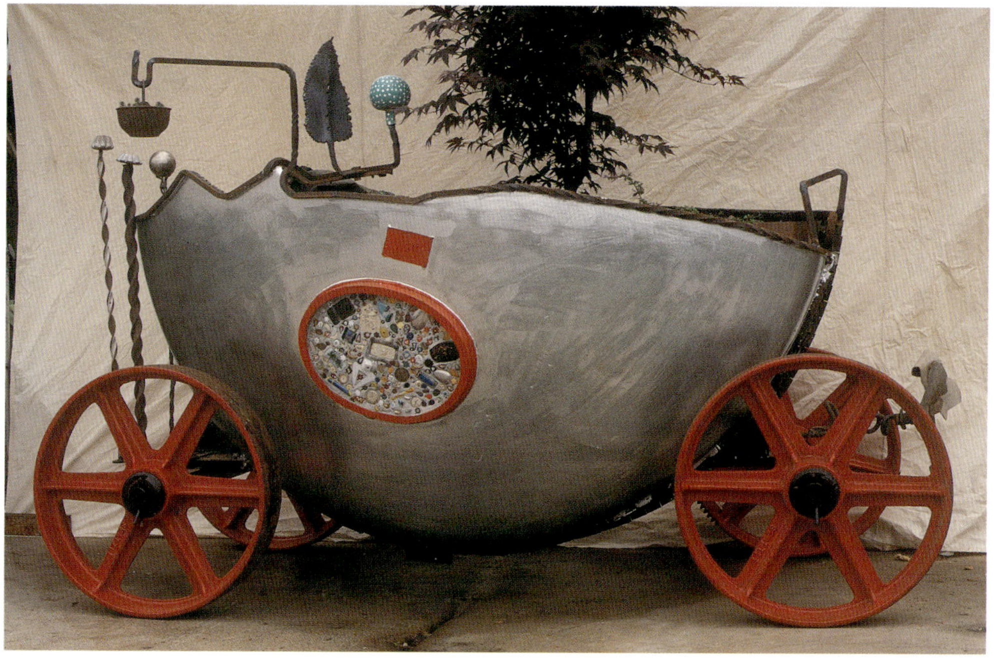

J. W. Adkins. Planter on wheels. Made from scrap metal and found objects. *Photo, Ron Dexter*

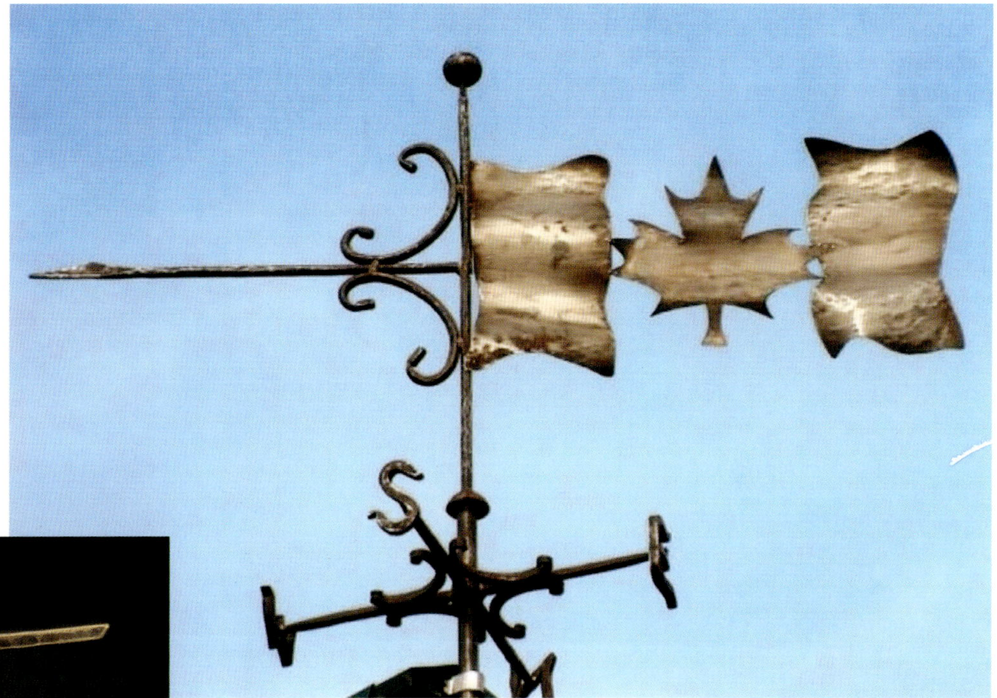

Mark Puigmarti. *Canadian Flag Weather Vane*. *Photo, artist*

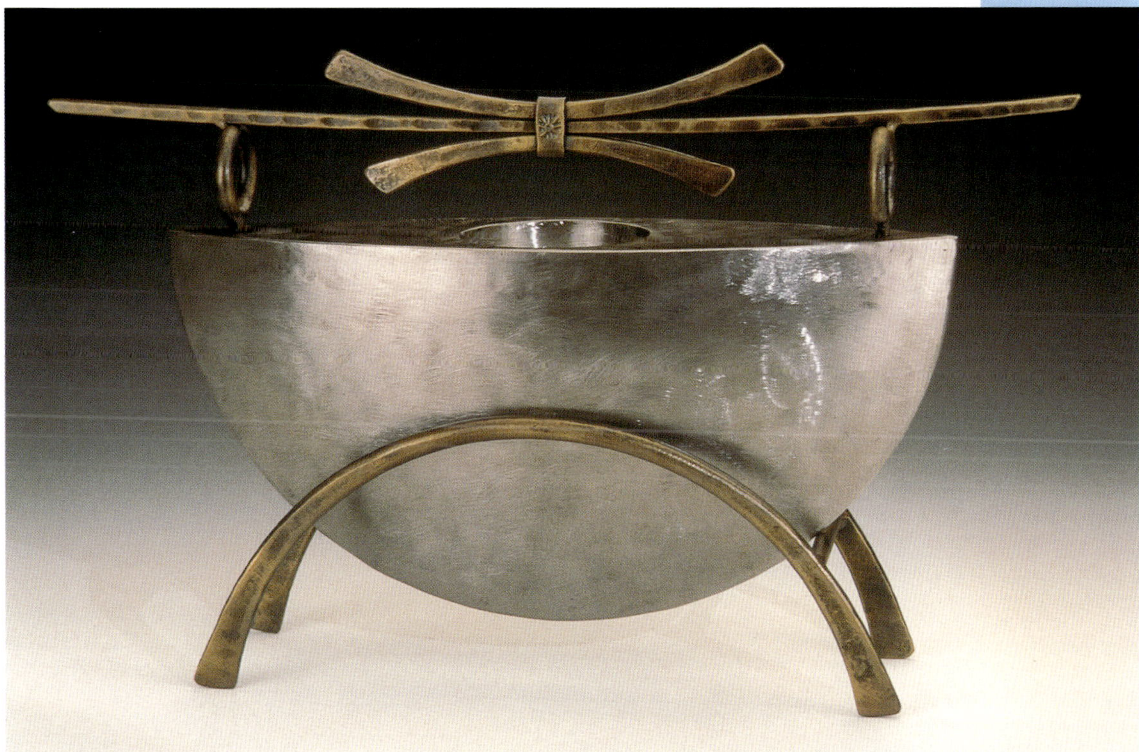

Robert L. Crecelius. *Ozark Plateau Ritual Vessel.* Forged and fabricated steel with bronze patinas. There is a remarkable contrast between contemporary styling and traditional techniques. 18" high, 20" wide, 7" deep. *Photo, Jerry Anthony*

Selected Bibliography

Andrews, Jack. *Edge of the Anvil.* Ocean City, Maryland: Skipjack Press, 1991.

Andrews, Jack. *Samuel Yellin, Metalworker.* Ocean City, Maryland: Skipjack Press, 1992.

Baur-Heinhold, Margarete. *Decorative Ironwork.* Atglen, Pennsylvania: Schiffer Publishing, Ltd., 1996.

Bennett, Malcolm. *The Bankside Gates at Shakespeare's Globe, a Guide.* London, England: Communication Dept., Shakespeare's Globe, 1999.

Campbell, Marion. *Decorative Ironwork.* New York, New York: Harry N. Abrams, Inc., 1997.

Chatwin, Amina. *Into the New Iron Age.* Cheltenham, Great Britain: Coach House Publishing, 1995.

Clouzot, Henri. *Art Déco Decorative Ironwork.* New York: Dover Publishing, 1997.

Elgass, Peter. *Alfred Habermann: Blacksmith and Designer.* Germany: Hephaistos, 2002.

Elgass, Peter. Metal Design Annuals. Germany: Hephaistos. 2204, 2005.

Fahr-Becker, Gabriele. *Art Nouveau.* Germany: Konemann Verlag, 1997.

Höver, Otto. *Style in Decorative Wrought-Iron Work, The Encyclopedia of Ironwork.* New York: Universe Books, 1962.

Geerlings, Gerald K., *Wrought Iron in Architecture.* New York: Dover Publications, 1983.

Joyce, Tom. *Life Force at the Anvil, The Blacksmith's Art from Africa.* Asheville, North Carolina: ABANA & University of North Carolina at Asheville, 1998.

Kahr, Joan. *Edgar Brandt. Master of Art Déco. Ironwork.* New York: Harry N. Abrams, 1992.

Meilach, Dona Z. *Architectural Ironwork.* Atglen, Pennsylvania: Schiffer Publishing Ltd., 2001.

Meilach, Dona Z. *Decorative & Sculptural Ironwork.* 2nd printing. Atglen, Pennsylvania: Schiffer Publishing Ltd., 1999.

Meilach, Dona Z. *The Contemporary Blacksmith.* Atglen, Pennsylvania: Schiffer Publishing Ltd., 2000.

Meilach, Dona Z. *Direct Metal Sculpture, Revised Edition.* Atglen, Pennsylvania: Schiffer Publishing Ltd., 2000.

Meilach, Dona Z. *Fireplace Accessories.* Atglen, Pennsylvania: Schiffer Publishing Ltd., 2002.

Permanyer, Louis. *Barcelona Art Nouveau.* New York, New York: Rizzoli, 1999.

Southern Highland Craft Guild. *Samuel Yellin Metalworkers; Three Generations.* (Exhibit Catalog). Asheville, North Carolina: Folk Art Center, 1998.

Southworth, Susan and Michael. *Ornamental Ironwork.* New York, New York: McGraw Hill, 1978, 1992.

Tijou, Jean. *Columbia Encyclopedia. Sixth Edition, 2000. Columbia* University Press, 2000.

Whitaker, Francis. *Beautiful Iron.* Carbondale, Colorado: Whitaker Foundation, 1997.

Zerbst, Rainer, and Francoise Rene Roland (photographers). Gaudi. Taschen America, 1999.

A search for architecture, Art Nouveau, Baroque, Art Deco, and other art styles will bring up a wonderful list of resources with links to others. Other words to use in a search are "blacksmithing," "ironwork," and specific objects such as "ironwork furniture." Many blacksmiths have personal sites and a search under the artist's name will yield their Internet address, site, and links to additional sites.

Resources

Organizations

ABANA - Artist-Blacksmith's Association of North America
Washington, MO 63090
http://www.abana.org

American Craft Council (ACC) Information Center
New York, NY 10012
www.craftcouncil.org

BABA - British Artist Blacksmith Association
http://www.baba.org.uk

Crafts Council of Great Britain
http://www.craftscouncil.org.uk.

NOMMA-National Ornamental & Miscellaneous Metals Association
Forest Park, GA 30297
http://www.nomma.com

Internet Resources

A search for architecture, Art Nouveau, Baroque, Art Deco, and other art styles will bring up a wonderful list of resources with links to others Other words to use in a search are "blacksmithing," "ironwork," and specific objects, such as "ironwork funiture." Many blacksmiths have personal sites and a search under the artist's name will yield their Internet address and site.

These sites often provide links to a variety of other related sites, host chat and discussion groups, current events, photos of work, artist listings, book lists, and more. Additional resources are in the Bibliography.

Amazon Books: Search using the words: blacksmith, blacksmithing, ornamental ironwork, http://www.amazon.com

Anvil Fire
Probably your best source with links to many other sources.
http://www.anvilfire.com

Architecture
http://www.greatbuildings.com/architects.html

ArtMetal Village
http://www.artmetal.com

Metal Web News
http://www.mindspring.com/~wgray1

Touchmark Registration

Artist-blacksmiths can now sign their work and have their imprint registered.

anvilfire! Touchmark Registry
1684 Mitchell Mill Rd.
Gladys, VA 24554-2938
www.anvilfire.com

Museums and Places to See Ironwork

The only United States museum devoted solely to ironwork as an art form and medium is:

The National Ornamental Metal Museum
374 Metal Museum Drive
Memphis, TN 38106-1539
901-774-6380
http://www.metalmuseum.org

Other museums and historical sites will have some ironwork. You'll find a comprehensive list of the museums, their holdings, and the ability to search by type of objects at:

WWW. Virtual Library: Museums Around the USA
http://vlib.org

Here are a few ideas for ironwork sources. Often a walk around a city's old towns and centers will reveal a wealth of historical ironwork. New buildings may have more modern examples. Look for public art, fences, gates, door hardware and decoration, balcony railings, building enhancements. "Pioneer" museums are often in the historical area of many cities. Also find cathedrals, banks, contemporary buildings, and residences.

20th Century Museum of History and Technology, San Bernardino, CA

Art Institute of Chicago, Chicago, Illinois (Especially the arms and armor collection)

Barcelona, Spain

Biltmore House, Asheville, North Carolina

Folk Art Museum, Asheville, North Carolina

New Orleans, Louisiana

Shelburne Museum, Shelburne, Vermont

Victoria and Albert Museum, London, England

San Francisco, California

Education Opportunities

ABANA Journeyman Program (See ABANA above)

California Blacksmiths Association
www.calsmith.org

John C. Campbell Folk School
Brasstown, N.C.
http://www.folkschool.com

Forgery School of Blacksmithing
Robb Gunter
Tijeras, NM 87039
505-286-3513
forgery@earthlink.net

Heritage Blacksmith Association
Victoria, B.C. Canada
blacksmith@pacificcoast.net

NOMMA
Forest Park, GA 30050
nonmainfor@aol.com

Northwest Blacksmiths Association (*Hot Iron News Quarterly*)
Spokane, WA 99203
www.blacksmith.org

Ozark School of Blacksmithing
Potosi, MO
www.ozarkschool.com

Penland School of Crafts
Penland, NC
www.penland.org

Peters Valley Craft Education Center
Layton, NJ
http://pvcrafts.org

Pratt Fine Arts Center
Seattle, WA
www.pratt.org

Touchstone Center for Crafts
Farmington, PA
www.touchstonecrafts.com

Turley Forge Blacksmithing School
Santa Fe. NM
www.turleyforge.com

Uri Hofi Blacksmithing School
Kibbutzin Ein Schmer. Israel
hofi@ein-shemer.org.il

The Wareham Forge
Proton Station, Ontario, Canada
Wareham.Forge@Headwaters.com

Yucaipa Valley Forge
Yucaipa, CA
www.yucaipaforge.com

Publications

The Anvils Ring published by ABANA (see organizations, above)

Hammer's Blow published by ABANA (see organizations, above)
also regional and state ABANA newsletters

Anvil Magazine
Georgetown, CA 95634
www.anvilmag.com

ARCHI-TECH Magazine
Portland, ME 04104
http://architechmag.com

Blacksmith's Gazette
Camano Island, WA 98292
Fholder@sos.net

Blacksmith's Journal
Washington, MO
http://www.blacksmithsjournal.com

Fabricator Magazine
National Ornamental & Miscellaneous Metals Association
Forest Park, GA
http://www.nomma.com

The Fabricator.com
An on-line magazine
www.thefabricator.com

Traditional Building Magazine
Brooklyn, New York 11217
http://www.traditional-buiding.com

Index

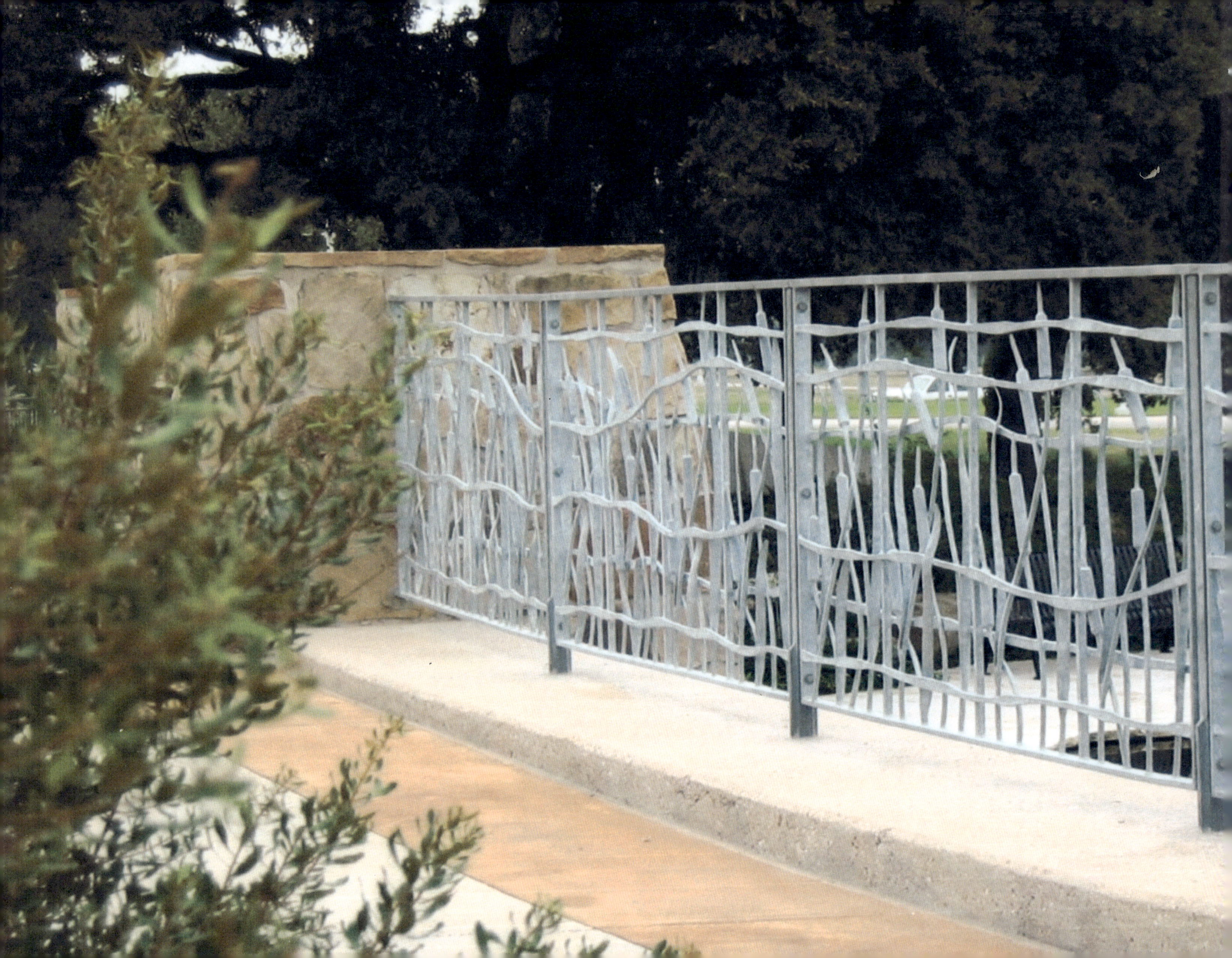